STARTING RUSSIAN

STARTING

RUSSIAN

PARTS ONE AND TWO

by

DENNIS WARD

Part one is based on the scripts for broadcasting
by Dr Kyra Ericsson

BRITISH BROADCASTING

CORPORATION

1962

STARTING RUSSIAN

A Series of 41 Lessons

To be broadcast on SUNDAYS at 3.40 P.M.
and repeated on TUESDAYS at 6.40 P.M.
from 25 November 1962

Scripts for broadcasting by
Dr Kyra Ericsson,
edited by Ariadne Nicolaeff

Professor B. O. Unbegaun of the University of Oxford read both the scripts and the text of this book to verify the accuracy of the grammatical statements. We are very grateful to him for his invaluable help as consultant.

Scenes from Russian Life were specially written and recorded by Professor A. Efimov, Moscow University, and Mrs N. Efimov.

The Russian–English and English–Russian vocabularies compiled by Noel Owen.

Handwritten alphabet and words by A. Nikolsky.

I Love You, Life reprinted with permission from *Russian Song-Book*, Vol. 1, edited by C. V. James, Pergamon Press 1962. Acknowledgment is due to Sidgwick and Jackson Ltd for permission to reproduce pronunciation diagrams, based on diagrams in *Manual of Russian Pronunciation* by S. C. Boyanus.

Published by the British Broadcasting Corporation
35 Marylebone High Street, London W.1

Printed in England by Stephen Austin and Sons, Limited, Hertford
No. 4973

Contents

ABBREVIATIONS

acc.	accusative	*instr.*	instrumental
act.	active	*intrans.*	intransitive
ca.	circa *or* about	*lit.*	literally
conjug.	conjugation	*masc. (m.)*	masculine
dat.	dative	*neut. (n.)*	neuter
det.	determinate	*nom.*	nominative
dim.	diminutive	*pass.*	passive
fem. (f.)	feminine	*pers.*	person
fut.	future	*pfv.*	perfective
gen.	genitive	*pl.*	plural
imper.	imperative	*p.p.p.*	past passive participle
impfv.	imperfective	*prep.*	prepositional
inc.	including	*pres.*	present
indet.	indeterminate	*sing.*	singular
infin.	infinitive	*trans.*	transitive

NB Where two accents showing two stresses are given above a word, either stress is correct.

Foreword

Learning a foreign language is not without difficulties. There is first of all the pronunciation, for to acquire a new habit of articulating sounds is apt to be difficult in any foreign language. To some extent this applies also to the study of the vocabulary. Other difficulties, however, are distributed differently in various languages. The Russian student of English, for example, is puzzled by the often unpredictable English spelling, but agreeably surprised at the relative simplicity of the grammar, especially when it comes to handling nouns and adjectives. From the very beginning he is able to embark upon fairly simple conversation. Only much later does he come to realize that for the simplicity of the grammar he must pay a high price by having to assimilate the idiomatic stock of the language and to struggle through the capricious tyranny of its usage. If he becomes disheartened, it is usually at this final stage of his study of the English language.

By contrast, the English student of Russian observes with pleasure that the spelling is simple and that Russian words are, with certain regular deviations, usually pronounced as they are written. But he may be alarmed at the wealth of forms any particular word can take, and especially at the number of cases he must learn in both singular and plural for nouns, adjectives and pronouns, before he can venture on a simple conversation. In addition he has to face the peculiar pattern of the Russian verb. If he feels discouraged, it is frequently at the initial stage of his study of Russian. If he succeeds in overcoming this early despondency, he may be sure that it will not recur and that as he progresses he will not be plagued by the same kind of idiomatic pitfalls which he only too often encounters in English.

This is why it is so important for a student of Russian to be given a correct approach to his subject and an encouraging start. The present course, in my opinion, offers such a start. Dr Kyra Ericsson, Lecturer in Russian at the School of Slavonic and East European Studies in the University of London, composed the lessons for broadcasting on which Part I of the book is based. She has skilfully graded the initial difficulties and incorporated them into lively, amusing and every day pieces of conversation; she has happily avoided the abstract phrases which so often encumber less original textbooks. Her explanations are as simple as the Russian language allows.

Mr Dennis Ward, Head of the Department of Russian in the University of Edinburgh, has drawn on his ample experience as a scholar and a teacher in providing the course with a convenient book. Part I is closely related to the broadcast course but by no means identical with it. The book is fuller in fact and Part II provides a basic reference grammar.

The producer, Miss Ariadne Nicolaeff, has secured the collaboration of several distinguished Russians, namely Professor Chukovsky, Professor Efimov and Mrs Efimov, whose recorded readings are incorporated in the course.

Listeners with some experience in learning foreign languages by means of broadcasts will have no difficulty in discovering the method of using the course which suits them best. Others may perhaps find the following hints helpful.

The lessons should be studied thoroughly before each broadcast – and after – and the broadcast should be regarded mainly as sound practice in the earlier lessons and later as an opportunity to hear Russian as it is spoken. The reading passages should be read aloud – slowly at first, then more rapidly, as greater proficiency is achieved. They should also be repeated aloud simultaneously with the broadcasts. The exercises in translation into Russian will not occur in the broadcasts, but they are essential if students are to obtain an active as well as passive knowledge of the language. The summaries at the end of each lesson are not detailed: they are meant to act as 'reminders', or as a framework which students should try to fill in with the help of what they have learned from the appropriate lesson. There is a detailed grammatical Index at the end to help students to find their way about in the book.

I wish this course a well-deserved success.

B. O. UNBEGAUN

Professor of Comparative
Slavonic Philology in the
University of Oxford

Lesson 1

К	к	$\mathcal{K}\ \varkappa$	=	k
Т	т	$\mathcal{T}\ m\ (\tau)$	=	t
М	м	$\mathcal{M}\ \mathcal{M}$	=	m
А	а	$\mathcal{A}\ a$	=	a
У	у	$\mathcal{Y}\ y$	=	oo
И	и	$\mathcal{U}\ u$	=	ee
О	о	$\mathcal{O}\ o$	=	aw
Н	н	$\mathcal{H}\ \mathcal{H}$	=	n
Р	р	$\mathcal{P}\ \rho\ \rho$	=	r
Я	я	$\mathcal{Я}\ \mathcal{я}$	=	ya
Б	б	$\mathcal{B}\ \delta$	=	b
Ы	ы	$-\ \mathcal{b}\iota$	=	'y'

PRONUNCIATION

With very few exceptions Russian words have only one accent or stress.
Stressed vowels are pronounced clearly and with much more *volume* than
unstressed vowels.

A difference in stress may convey a difference in meaning

му́ка torment   мука́ flour

In unstressed syllables **a** and **o** sound alike – approximately like *u* in *cup*
when immediately in front of the stress and like *a* in *china* in other unstressed
positions.

Some consonants, both in Russian and in English, are *voiced*, i.e. the vocal
chords vibrate when you pronounce them. Others are *voiceless*, i.e. there is

only breath issuing through the mouth. Here, in English letters, are pairs of voiced and voiceless consonants:

voiced		*voiceless*	
	B		P
	D		T
	G		K
	V		F
	Z		S
	'zh' (as in *leisure*)		'sh'

In Russian the voiced sounds are replaced by their voiceless counterparts at the end of a word or before another voiceless sound, but the spelling does not change. Hence the second **б** in **боб** sounds like English *p* and so do the **б**s in **трубка, коробка, робко**.

1. **К к** *К к*   **Т т** *Т т (т)*   **М м** *М м*   **А а** *А а*

как *how*		так *so, thus*
как так *how so, why?*		так как *because, as*
мак *poppy(-seed)*		мама *mama, mummy*
	там *there*	

как там мама

The initial hook of *м* must always be written, no matter what precedes it. The vertical stroke of *к* does not rise above the upper line of the letters.

2. THREE GRAMMAR POINTS

a There is no article, i.e. no word for *a* and *the* in Russian.

мак = *a poppy* or *the poppy*

b The present tense of the verb *to be* (*am, is, are*) is not expressed as a rule. *The poppy is there* is simply **Мак там**, literally *Poppy there*.

c In a simple question the same word-order as in a statement is generally used. In speaking, the intonation shows whether a question or a statement is intended. *Is the poppy there?* is **Мак там?**

Мак там.	Мама там.	Как мама?
Там мак.	Там мама.	Мама как?
Как так?	Мама там?	Мама там, так как там мак.

3. **У у** *У у*

sounds like English *oo* but is shorter. There are no long and short vowels in Russian.

тут *here*	утка *duck*
мука *torment*	мука *flour*

2

Утка тут.   Утка там.

Как так? Утка там?

Утка там, так как там мука́.

Утка там, так как там мука́

4. И и *И и*

sounds like *ee* in *seen* but is shorter than the English sound.

кит *whale*   ита́к *and so*

On its own, **и** means *and*. It also means *as well, also, too*. When it is repeated it means *both . . . and . . .* as in:

и тут и там *both here and there.*

The letter **а** on its own is also a word. It implies a slight contrast and is sometimes translated *but*, sometimes *while* or *whereas* and sometimes *and*.

Тут мак и мука́.   Тут ма́ма и у́тка.

Тут и ма́ма.   *Mama too is here.*

Тут и мак и мука́.   Тут ма́ма, а мука́ там.

Тут у́тка, а там кит.   Тут кит и у́тка.

И у́тка тут? – И у́тка тут, так как тут мука́.

5. О о *О о*

sounds like the vowel in *all* but is said with a slight pursing of the lips at the beginning so that it is *almost* like *wa* in *wall*. It is pronounced like this *only in a stressed position*. When it is immediately in front of the stress the letter **о** sounds like **а**, or like *u* in English *cup*. When it is after the stress it has an *obscure*, indeterminate sound, like the *a* in *china*. The letter **а** also has this sound after the stress.

кот *tomcat*   ток *current (electric)*

том *volume*   като́к *skating-rink*

ком *lump, clod*   ко́мик *comic, comedian*

тома́т *tomato*   комо́к *small lump, bundle*

а́том *atom*   кто́-то *somebody*

като́к   ко́мик   комо́к

6. Н н *Н н*

sounds like English *n*.

А́нна *Ann(e)*   но́та *note (musical)*

тон *tone*   кана́т *rope*

тума́н *fog*   ко́мната *room*

мину́та *minute*   нау́ка *science*

ну! *well!*   ну́-ка *well then! get on with it*

ну как? *well, how are things?*

окно́ *window*   конта́кт *contact*

он *he*   она́ *she*   оно́ *it*

ми-ну-та   мину́та

3

7. GENDERS

Russian is an *inflected* language – the endings of certain words change according to their role in the sentence. Nouns, i.e. words for persons, animals, objects, concepts etc., fall into three large classes according to the kind of endings they have. These classes are called *genders*. Most pronouns, words representing or standing in the place of nouns, do the same thing. Nouns and pronouns ending in a *consonant* belong to a class called the *masculine gender*. They are *masculine*, grammatically speaking, though they may denote objects.

кот *tomcat*	он *he*	
контáкт *contact*	он *it*	
том *volume*	он *it*	

Nouns and pronouns ending in **a** belong to the *feminine gender*. They are *feminine*.

кóмната *room*	онá *it*	
ýтка *duck*	онá *it*	
мáма *mummy*	онá *she*	

Nouns and pronouns ending in **o** belong to the *neuter gender*. They are *neuter*.

окнó *window*	онó *it*

8. PRONOUN 'THAT'

The word *that* is a pronoun in Russian, i.e. it can stand for a noun.

masculine	*feminine*	*neuter*
тот	та	то
тот кот – он тут	та мукá – онá там	то окнó – онó там
тот тумáн – он там	та нóта – онá там	

9. PRONOUN 'WHO'

The pronoun *who* кто does not end in a consonant but, as will be seen later, it behaves in other respects like a masculine pronoun, though it can refer to persons of either sex.

Кто он? *Who is he?*	Том. *Tom.*
Кто онá? *Who is she?*	Мáма. *Mummy.*

10. ADVERBS

The ending **o** is also characteristic of many adverbs – words describing the manner, time or place of an action, which in English mostly end in -*ly*.

4

умно́ *cleverly*

как умно́! *how clever!* (i.e. how *cleverly* it is done)

то́нко *subtly*

как то́нко! *how subtle!*

In Russian an adverb is often used where an adjective is used in English. Adjectives are words which describe nouns.

11. Р р *Р р*

is a trilled *r*. Many Scots pronounce their *r* as Russians do.

Арара́т, Арара́т (Mount) *Ararat*

Марк Mark   *Арту́р, Арту́р* Arthur

ра́ма *frame*	рак *crayfish*
рот *mouth*	ром *rum*
конто́ра *office*	ка́рта *map*
ма́рка *postage-stamp*	март *March (month)*
кома́р *mosquito*	рука́ *hand*
у́тро *morning*	у́тром *in the morning*

Adverbs with the letter **р**:

мо́кро *wet(ly)*   кру́то *steep(ly)*

ра́но *early*; on its own it may mean *too early*.

Тут мо́кро. Там кру́то, так кру́то!

    Как там кру́то!

Ра́но у́тром! Как ра́но! Как так ра́но?

Ра́но! Ра́но! Ра́но у́тром тут так мо́кро.

Как? Тут мо́кро и кру́то?

Тут мо́кро, а там кру́то.

12. Я я *Я я - ꝑ ꝑ ꝑ ꝑ ꝑ я*

Stressed **я** at the beginning of a word or after another vowel has a two-fold sound – English *y* followed by the Russian **a** sound. When **я** comes *after* the stress its vowel sound is like *a* in *china*.

я *I (the pronoun)*	Мари́я *Mary*
я́ма *pit, hole*	я́рко *bright(ly)*
мая́к *lighthouse*	я́рмарка *fair, market*

я-ма я́ма   *яр-ко я́рко*

Notice that the initial hook of *я* must always be written.

13. Б б *Бб*

sounds like *b* in English.

бóмба *bomb*	банк *bank*
банкúр *banker*	табáк *tobacco*
борт *ship's side*	на бортý *on board*
бок *side*	бóком *sideways*
брат *brother*	барáн *ram (sheep)*
рабóта *work*	бáба *peasant-woman*
кабáк *'pub'*	трубá *chimney*
кýбок *(presentation) cup*	
барабáн *drum*	оборóна *defence*

ра-бо-та   работа   о-бо-ро-на   оборóна

But in these words **б** sounds like English *p*:

боб *bean*
трýбка *pipe*   See *Pronunciation* at the
корóбка *box*   beginning of this lesson.
рóбко *timidly*

14. Ы ы

If you say the *oo* of *book* and smile, you will produce a sound very like Russian **ы**. It is an *i* sound (as in *bit*) but with the middle of the tongue raised instead of the front.

ты   мы   ры́ба

ты,   ты   мы   рыба

15. EXERCISE

1 Copy out all the nouns in this lesson and put the appropriate pronouns with them, e.g. **тот кóмик – он.**

2 Make up ten simple sentences saying where who and what is, e.g. **трýбка там.**

SUMMARY

1 There is no article in Russian (§ 2a).
2 There is no present tense of the verb *to be* (§ 2b).
3 Questions may be expressed with the same word-order as statements (§ 2c).
4 There are three genders –
  masculine, ending in a consonant,
  feminine, ending in **a**,
  neuter, ending in **o** (§ 7).
5 Many adverbs end in **o** (§ 10).

6

Lesson 2

Ы ы – *ы* = 'y'

Е е *Ɛ е* = yeh

Д д *Ɗ g д* = d

PRONUNCIATION

When it does not have a consonant in front of it, stressed **e** is pronounced like the first two letters of English *yet*.

Unstressed **e** is more like the *i* in *bit*. **Я** has this sound in front of the stress but after the stress it represents a vowel like the *a* in *china*.

When **я** or **e** is preceded by a consonant the *y* element is absorbed by the consonant, which is said to be *softened*. With some consonants the effect is much more obvious than others. The vowel **и** has the same *softening* effect, though it does not have the initial *y* element when not preceded by a consonant.

The word **не** *not* is usually pronounced as if it were combined with the following word as an unstressed syllable. In this word therefore **e** usually has the *i* sound.

Д is one of the sounds that at the end of a word or before a voiceless consonant is replaced in pronunciation by its voiceless counterpart, i.e. **т** (see Lesson 1, Pronunciation).

SPELLING

There are seven letters which cannot be followed by **ы**. They are followed instead by **и**. One of these letters is **к**.

КИ КИ КИ *ки ки ки*

Words with **ы**

ты *you* ты, *ты*	бык *bull* *бык*
мы *we* *мы*	рынок *market* ры-нок *рынок*
рыба *fish* *рыба*	быт *way of life* *быт*

I. NOMINATIVE PLURAL I – MASCULINE AND FEMININE

When a word denotes a person or thing performing an action it is said to be the *subject*, i.e. the subject of the verb (the word denoting the performing of the action). Thus in *dogs swim* the word *dogs* is a noun and it is the subject

7

of the verb *swim*. Words which denote the subject in Russian are in the *nominative case*.

If a word denotes one person or thing, it is in the *singular*, whereas a word which denotes more than one person or thing is in the *plural*. The words *singular* and *plural* denote the grammatical *number* of nouns and also of adjectives, pronouns and verbs.

The nominative plural therefore is the grammatical form of a word telling us that more than one person or thing perform an action.

Masculine nouns which end in a consonant letter in the nominative singular add **ы** to form the nominative plural:

nom. sing.	*nom. pl.*
томáт *tomato*	томáты
áтом *atom*	áтомы
канáт *rope*	канáты
тумáн *mist*	тумáны
кармáн *pocket*	кармáны
барабáн *drum*	барабáны

Some masculine nouns shift the stress in the nominative plural:

nom. sing.	*nom. pl.*
комáр *gnat*	комары́
кот *tomcat*	коты́

Feminine nouns which end in **a** in the nominative singular replace this by **ы** in the nominative plural:

nom. sing.	*nom. pl.*
бóмба *bomb*	бóмбы
бáба *peasant-woman*	бáбы
кáрта *map*	кáрты
кóмната *room*	кóмнаты

2. NOMINATIVE PLURAL SPELLING AFTER **к**

Since **к** is followed by **и** not **ы** (see *Spelling* above), nouns which end in **к** or **ка** in the nominative singular form the nominative plural in **ки**:

nom. sing.	*nom. pl.*
банк *bank*	бáнки
брак *marriage*	брáки
кабáк *'pub'*	кабаки́[1]
мáрка *stamp*	мáрки
мýка *torment*	мýки
корóбка *box*	корóбки
трýбка *pipe*	трýбки

1 Note the stress-shift in this word.

8

3. NOMINATIVE PLURAL II – NEUTER

Neuter nouns which end in **o** in the nominative singular replace this by **a** in the nominative plural:

nom. sing.	*nom. pl.*
окно́ *window*	о́кна

Note the stress-shift, which is usual with neuter nouns of two syllables and with some others.

4. MOBILE VOWEL

Some masculine nouns contain the vowel **o** in the nominative singular but drop it in the nominative plural (and, as will be seen, in all other cases too):

nom. sing.	*nom. pl.*
рот *mouth*	рты

A vowel that drops out in this way is called the *mobile vowel* in this book.[1] It is impossible to forecast which nouns have a mobile vowel (**кот,** for instance, does not), so those which do, have to be learnt. However, the ending **ок,** which usually means *a small . . .,* drops the **o** in the majority of words in which it occurs.

nom. sing.	*nom. pl.*
като́к *skating-rink*	катки́
комо́к *small lump*	комки́
ку́бок *(presentation) cup*	ку́бки

5. NOMINATIVE PLURAL III – PRONOUNS

We have seen that the 'plural' of **я** *I* is **мы** *we*. Many pronouns form the plural with **и** (not **ы**):

он *he, it* **она́** *she, it* **оно́** *it* have a common plural **они́** *they.*

6. DIALOGUE

Dialogue in Russian is usually shown by introducing the speaker's words with a dash (cf. French). See if you can understand the following dialogue:

– Кто там?
– Мы тут; я тут, брат Марк и Мари́я.
– Ну как?
– Как тут? Тут му́ка – тут комары́.
– Тут комары́, так как тума́н, тут мо́кро, но тут каба́к.

---

1 Two other terms often used are *fill-vowel* and *fugitive vowel.*

И sounds like *ee* in seen but is shorter and sharper. When it is unstressed **и** sounds more like *i* in *bit*. **И** softens preceding consonants (see Part II – Pronunciation).

крик *a shout*

ру́ки *hands*

кит *whale*

Рим *Rome*

каби́на *cabin* – каби́ны *cabins*

битко́м наби́то *crowded out, full up*

мину́та *minute* – мину́ты *minutes*

микро́б *microbe* – микро́бы *microbes*

мир *peace; world* – миры́ *worlds*

ками́н *fireplace* – ками́ны *fireplaces*

Ни́на *Nina*

Ни ни! *No, no! Don't you dare!*

никто́ *nobody*

ни́тка *thread* – ни́тки *threads*

Я when stressed represents Russian **a** preceded by *y*, if it is initial or has another vowel in front of it. When a consonant precedes it the *y* element is *absorbed* by the consonant, which is said to be *softened*. When **я** follows the stress it sounds like the *a* in *china*, preceded by *y*, or a soft consonant, if it is preceded by a consonant letter. Here are some words with **я**:

я́ма *pit*	мая́к *lighthouse*
мя́та *mint (plant)*	и́мя *name*
ня́ня *Nanny*	ба́ня *bath house*
А́ня (А́нна) *Anya (Ann)*	Ма́ня (Мари́я) *Manya (Mary)*
Та́ня *Tanya (Tatiana)*	
они́ ку́рят *they smoke*	он/она́ ку́рит *he/she smokes*
они́ ко́рмят *they feed*	он/она́ ко́рмит *he/she feeds*

Е behaves like **я**; it sounds like '*yeh*' when it does not have a consonant in front of it but when it is preceded by a consonant the *y* is absorbed into the preceding consonant, which is then soft. When it is unstressed, **е** sounds rather like *i* in *bit*.

я ем *I eat*	Ерма́к *Yermak* (a famous Cossack)
буке́т *bouquet*	буке́ты *bouquets*
коме́та *comet*	коме́ты *comets*
ме́ра *measure*	ме́ры *measures*
метр *metre*	ме́тры *metres*
нет *no; there is not*	не *not*

ремо́нт *repair*	метро́ *underground*
река́ *river*	ре́ки *rivers*
я беру́ *I take*	они́ беру́т *they take*
он ката́ет *he rolls*	не́бо *sky*

8. NEGATIVES

Нет means *no*, as in answer to a question, or *there is not*, *there are not* (this usage will be dealt with later). **Не** is the word used for negating a sentence or a verb and corresponds to *not*.

$$\textbf{нет} = no$$
$$\textbf{не} = not$$

Here are examples of the use of **не**:

Я не ем. Он не тут. Она́/Оно́/Они́ не тут.

Буке́ты не тут, а там. Коме́та не там, а тут. Не так.

Он не ката́ет. Мы не ката́ем. *We do not roll.*

Она́ не ку́рит. Мы не ку́рим. Они́ не ку́рят. *They do not smoke.*

THE LETTER Д д *Ꭰ g ∂* PRONOUNCED AS *d*

Ꭰa, ga, or *∂a yes*

дом *house*	до́ма *at home*
да́ма *lady*	дра́ма *drama*
до́ктор *doctor*	еда́ *food*
я дам *I shall give*	они́ даду́т *they will give*
дым *smoke*	дуб *oak*
оби́да *offence*	оби́дно *offensively*
беда́ *misfortune*	бе́дно *poorly*
труд *labour*	тру́дно *difficult*

---

9. 'AT HOME'

До́ма *at home*, though connected in meaning with **дом** *house*, is not a form of this word: it is independent.

Брат до́ма. Банки́р до́ма.

Да́ма до́ма. Ма́ма до́ма.

Да, да́ма до́ма, ма́ма до́ма, брат и банки́р до́ма, и кот до́ма!

До́ктор не до́ма. Она́ не до́ма.

Они́ не до́ма. А́ня не до́ма.

IO. NOMINATIVE PLURAL IV—MASCULINE IN **a**

There are some masculine nouns which form the nominative plural in stressed **a**:

nom. sing.	nom. pl.
до́ктор *doctor*	доктора́
дом *house*	дома́
бок *side*	бока́
но́мер *number, room*	номера́
(*in a hotel*)	

THE LETTER **д** pronounced as *t*

In the following words **д** sounds like *t* because it is either in the final position or it is followed by a voiceless consonant (see *Pronunciation* above):

наро́д *people* (cf. наро́ды *peoples*)
обе́д *dinner* (cf. обе́ды *dinners*)
труд *work, labour* (cf. труды́ *works*)
ряд *row* (cf. ря́дом *beside*)
бу́дка *booth*   бу́дки *booths*
ка́дка *tub*   ка́дки *tubs*

II. DATIVE CASE I – PRONOUNS

To express *to me*, *to him*, *to the doctor* etc., Russians use a special form of the appropriate word. This special form is known as the *dative case*. With nouns, adjectives and most pronouns the dative is obtained by adding something to the word or changing its ending. With the personal pronouns (*I*, *you*, *he*, *we*, *they* etc.), however, quite different forms are used.

nom.	dat.
я	мне
мы	нам
он	ему́
они́	им

The dative case is often used in what are known as *impersonal* expressions. This has nothing to do with the attitude of the persons concerned! It is simply a grammatical term for an expression in which either there is no logical subject or the logical subject is expressed in the dative and the action is expressed by an adverb or some other word.

12

Мне трудно *I find it difficult*, lit. (It is) difficult to (i.e. for) me.
Нам обидно *We feel hurt*, lit. (It is) offensive to us.
Им трудно и им обидно *They find it difficult and they feel hurt* (offended).

Брат дома, тут работа и ему трудно.
А мне обидно, так как ему трудно. Да, трудно!

12. EXERCISE

Read these sentences and see if you can understand them:

a Я не ем.   Он не тут.   Трубы не тут, а там.
  Букет не там, а тут.   Не так! – Не так? А как? – Так!
  Дом не тут? – Дом не тут, а там.
  Доктора дадут? – Нет, доктора не дадут, а я дам.
  Кто катает? Она катает? – Нет, он, брат, катает.
  Кто курит? – Она курит, а брат не курит.
  Они курят.   Мы не курим.

b Брат дома.   Банкир дома.   Дама дома.   Мама дома.
  Да, дама дома, мама дома, брат и банкир дома, и кот дома!
  Тут дома – Как?   Тут дома? Как так? – Тут дома, так как тут река.
  Дама дома? – Да, она дома.   Дамы дома? – Да, они дома.
  Кто он? – Он доктор. – Ты доктор? – Нет, я не доктор, а брат –
  доктор.[1]

1 In a sentence of this type where two nouns are linked – *A is B* – it is customary to
indicate *is* by a dash.

SUMMARY

1 *Singular* forms express one person or thing.
  Plural forms express more than one person or thing.
  Ы is the nominative plural ending of feminine nouns ending in **a** and the
  usual nominative plural ending of masculine nouns ending in a consonant
  (§ 1). Since one cannot write **ы** after **к**, but must write **и** instead, nouns
  ending in **к** or **ка** have the nominative plural in **ки** (§ 2).
2 Neuter nouns ending in **o** form the nominative plural in **a** (§ 3).
3 Some masculine nouns with **o** in the nominative singular lose the **o** in
  forming the plural (and in other forms too) (§ 4).
4 The nominative plural of **он, она, оно** is **они** *they* (§ 5).
5 Verbs are negated by means of the word **не** *not* (§ 8).
6 Some masculine nouns form their plural in stressed **a** (§ 10).
7 To express *to me, to him* etc. the dative case is used (§ 11)
8 The dative is used in *impersonal expressions* (§ 11).

13

Lesson 3

C c *C c* = s

B в *B b* = v

Words with the letter c

как-тус   ка́ктус cactus

бас *bass*	ма́сса *mass*
кио́ск *kiosk*	матро́с *sailor*
мост *bridge*	на мосту́ *on the bridge*
ме́сто *place*	страна́ *country*
суд, суды́ *court(s) of law*	су́дно, суда́ *vessel(s), ship(s)*
(NB stress-shift in plural)	(NB no н in plural)
я́сно *clear(ly)*	сад *garden*
стук *knock*	соба́ка *dog*
нос, носы́ *nose(s)*	сон, сны *dream(s), sleep*
сыр, сыры́ *cheese(s)*	сын *son*
доска́, до́ски *board(s)*	оса́, о́сы *wasp(s)*
сам *himself*	сама́ *herself*
само́ *itself*	са́ми *themselves*
ско́ро *soon*	бы́стро *quickly*
сы́ро *damply*	стра́нно *strangely*
стака́н *glass*	а́дрес *address*
ма́ска *mask*	и́скра *spark*
кра́ска *paint*	крест *cross*
восто́к *east*	на восто́к *to the east*

Соба́ка сама́   *ско́ро сы́ро*

I. VERB FORMS I

Remember there is no present tense of the verb *to be* – it is 'understood'.
There is, however, a future tense of this verb:

я бу́ду *I shall be* (1st pers. sing.)

они́ бу́дут *they will be* (3rd pers. pl.)

These endings **-у** and **-ут** are typical of the first pers. sing. and third pers. pl. of many verbs in *the present tense* (such verbs end in **-ет** in the third pers. sing. and have a consonant before the **-ет** ending):

> я иду́ *I am going (on foot)*
> они́ иду́т *they are going (on foot)*
> я е́ду *I am going (in a vehicle)*
> они́ е́дут *they are going (in a vehicle)*
> я расту́ *I grow/am growing*
> они́ расту́т *they grow/are growing*
> я несу́ *I am carrying*
> они́ несу́т *they are carrying*

Verbs with these endings are among those which are said to be of the *first conjugation*. Other verbs are of the *second conjugation*. These terms simply mean that the vowel before the last consonant of the ending is different in the two conjugations.

2. EXERCISE

Я бу́ду там. Там я бу́ду ра́но у́тром. Я не бу́ду до́ма у́тром. Они́ бу́дут у́тром до́ма. Ра́но у́тром они́ до́ма.

DIALOGUE – Куда́[1] они́ иду́т? Туда́?[2]
  – Они́ не иду́т туда́, но[3] я иду́ туда́.
  – Как так, они́ не иду́т?
  – Они́ не иду́т туда́.
  – Но как так – они́ туда́ не иду́т?
  – Да[4] так, – туда́ они́ не иду́т. Они́ до́ма, они́ ку́рят.

  – Куда́ они́ е́дут?
  – Они́ е́дут туда́, и я е́ду туда́.

Суда́ иду́т[5] туда́. Стук-стук! – Кто там? – Мы! Я! Мы тут! Они́ бу́дут там, но не ско́ро.
Как стра́нно! Так ско́ро тут сы́ро! Да тут тума́ны.

3. VERB FORMS II

There are two verbs which have quite exceptional conjugations: the first

---

1 **Куда́** *whither, to where, where*. Always implies *motion towards*, never *location* or *place where*.

2 **Туда́** *thither, to there, there*. Always implies *motion towards*, never *location* or *place where* (cf. **тут** *here*, location).

3 **Но** *but*.

4 **Да** when standing alone or followed by a comma means *yes*; when not followed by a comma means *well*; *and*. Translate **да так** *well*, (*it just is*) *so*.

5 With ships, trains etc., you use **иду́т**, since they go by their own steam.

15

pers. sing. is unique in ending in **м** and the third pers. sing. in having the consonant **с** before the ending **т**:

я ем *I eat*   он ест *he eats*

я дам *I shall give* (NB future!)   он даст *he will give*

они дадут *they will give*

– Он нам[1] даст?

– Да, он даст, но она мне даром[2] не даст.

– Нет, нет, и[3] она даст. Он даст и она даст. Они нам дадут даром.

Words with the letter **В в**[4] *Ꞵ ℓ*

Иван Иван *Ivan*	*Москва* Москва *Moscow*
Виктор Виктор[5] *Victor*	*вера* вера[5] *faith*
верно *right*	неверно *wrong*
наверно *probably*	уверенно *confidently*
вода *water*	водка *vodka*
водород *hydrogen*	время *time*
два *two*	вот *here (is)*
вино *wine*	вина *fault, guilt*
корова *cow*	остановка *(bus) stop*
Титов *Titov*	Иванов[6] *Ivanov*

---

4. VERB FORMS III

Verbs which end in **-ит** in the third pers. sing. end in **-ят** (or **-ат**) in the third pers. pl. Their first pers. pl. (*we* do such-and-such) ends in **-им**. These are second conjugation verbs:

он стоит *he stands*	он строит *he builds*	он верит *he believes*
мы стоим *we stand*	мы строим *we build*	мы верим *we believe*
они стоят *they stand*	они строят *they build*	они верят *they believe*

5. GENITIVE CASE I

To express *of* or 'apostrophe s' in Russian a letter or letters are added or changed at the end of a word. The resulting new form is called the *genitive case*.

1 See Lesson 2, § 11, and Lesson 5, § 4.   2 *Gratis, for nothing.*   3 *Too, also.*

4 **В** represents the sound *f* at the end of a word or before a voiceless consonant.

5 **Е** and **и** soften the preceding consonant, so in some of the examples **в** is soft.

6 Stressed on the second *or* on the third syllable.

a Feminine nouns ending in **a** change the **a** to **ы,** as in the nominative plural, which also ends in **ы:**

nom. sing.	gen. sing.	nom. pl.
ко́мната *room*	ко́мнаты	ко́мнаты
оби́да *offence*	оби́ды	оби́ды

Sometimes there is a difference in stress between genitive singular and nominative plural:

nom. sing.	gen. sing.	nom. pl.
труба́ *chimney*	трубы́	тру́бы
оса́ *wasp*	осы́	о́сы
страна́ *country*	страны́	стра́ны

After **к** of course we write not **ы** but **и** (see Lesson 2):

nom. sing.	gen. sing.	nom. pl.
рука́ *hand*	руки́	ру́ки
река́ *river*	реки́	ре́ки
доска́ *board*	доски́	до́ски

b To masculine nouns ending in a consonant the letter **a** is added:

брат – бра́та,   кот – кота́,   сын – сы́на

Here are some masculine nouns with genitive singular and nominative plural:

nom. sing.	gen. sing.	nom. pl.
конта́кт *contact*	конта́кта	конта́кты
банк *bank*	ба́нка	ба́нки
обе́д *dinner*	обе́да	обе́ды
кот *tomcat*	кота́	коты́
труд *work, labour*	труда́	труды́
стари́к *old man*	старика́	старики́
сад *garden*	са́да	сады́
дуб *oak*	ду́ба	дубы́
бас *bass*	ба́са	басы́

Here are three nouns which lose the **о** of the *nominative singular* (see Lesson 2):

nom. sing.	gen. sing.	nom. pl.
носо́к *sock*	носка́	носки́
рот *mouth*	рта	рты
сон *dream*	сна	сны

Those nouns which form the nominative plural in stressed **a** form the genitive singular in unstressed **a**:

nom. sing.	gen. sing.	nom. pl.
дом *house*	до́ма[1]	дома́
до́ктор *doctor*	до́ктора	доктора́
но́мер *number*, (hotel) room	но́мера	номера́
тон *tone*	то́на	тона́

1 Identical with the word **до́ма** *at home.*

C

c Neuter nouns ending in **o** change this to **a** to form the genitive singular, which is often distinguished from the nominative plural by a difference in stress:

nom. sing.	gen. sing.	nom. pl.
окно́ *window*	окна́	о́кна
ме́сто *place*	ме́ста	места́
у́тро *morning*	у́тра	у́тра
су́дно *vessel*	су́дна	суда́ (NB по **н**)
сукно́ *cloth*	сукна́	су́кна
ядро́ *nucleus, kernel*	ядра́	я́дра

6. EXERCISE

Тут сад А́нны.   Тут стои́т дом банки́ра Сми́та.

Там стои́т дом старика́ Бра́уна, и ря́дом дом до́ктора.

О́кна до́ма тут.   Тут окно́ бу́дки, а там окно́ кио́ска.

А тут носки́ бра́та Ма́рка. – Нет, тут носки́ не бра́та,[1] а сы́на.

Сын матро́с.   Он сам на борту́ су́дна, а носки́ тут.

Носки́ бра́та Ма́рка там.   Да, да, – там они́.

7. GENITIVE CASE II

The genitive also expresses absence or non-existence of something or somebody and is therefore obligatory with **нет,** which, you remember, apart from meaning *no*, also means *there is/are no* (Lesson 2). You might think of the genitive here as expressing *negative quantity – none of*:

моста́ нет	*or*	нет моста́ *there is no bridge*
окна́ нет	*or*	нет окна́ *there is no window*
реки́ нет	*or*	нет реки́ *there is no river*

Note the difference between **до́ктор не до́ма** *the doctor is not at home* (implying that he is somewhere else, e.g. **а на борту́ су́дна** *but is on board the ship*) and **до́ктора нет до́ма** which simply says *the doctor is not at home/is out*, without any further implications.

8. EXERCISE

Тут нет кабака́ и нет табака́.   Ни[2] кабака́, ни табака́!

Тут нет моста́, так как нет реки́.   Ни моста́, ни реки́.

Тут окно́?   Да, окно́ тут, а ра́мы окна́ нет.

Тут нет ни соба́ки, ни кота́.   Тут ры́ба.

А там соба́ка и кот, а ры́бы нет.

Кот и соба́ка не тут, а там.

1 **Носки́ не бра́та** etc. *not the brother's (but the son's socks).*
2 **Ни... ни...** *neither . . . nor . . .*

18

Доктор дома? – Доктор не дома, а на борту судна.

Нет, доктора нет дома.

Тут места нет. – А место там? – Нет, и там нет места.

Они стоят там, а мы стоим тут.

Кто стоит там? – Доктора стоят там.

И брата доктора нет дома.   Брат доктора стоит тут.

Иван тут? – Нет, Ивана тут нет.   Тут Виктор и я.

Неверно! – Тут и Иван и Виктор.

9. TRANSLATION

Translate the following sentences into Russian, omitting the words in brackets:

Is the doctor's garden here?

No, the doctor's garden is there, but (my) brother's garden is here.

The tobacco is here, not (over) there.

There is no tobacco here!

Who is standing (over) there?

The sailors are standing over there, but the directors are standing here.

Wrong! The sailors are here. Ivan and Victor are (over) there.

There is no dog here, but the tomcat is probably here.

The window of the room is here.

No, no, the windows are (over) there.

They are going there,[1] but I am not going.

The doctors are going there (by car).

Is there a place here? No, there is no place here.

Is there a pub here? No, there is no pub here.

The wine is here, the vodka and the water are standing (over) there.

1 **Туда,** since motion is meant, not location.

SUMMARY

1 Many verbs having third pers. sing. ending in **-ет** have first pers. sing. in **-у** and third pers. pl. in **-ут** (§§ 1 and 4).

2 Verbs which have third pers. sing. ending in **-ит** have third pers. pl. in **-ят** or **-ат** (§ 4).

3 Feminine nouns with nom. sing. in **a** change this to **ы** to form the gen. sing. (§ 5a).

4 Masculine nouns with nom. sing. ending in a consonant add **a** to form the gen. sing. (§ 5b).

5 Neuter nouns with nom. sing. ending in **o** change this to **a** to form the gen. sing. (§ 5c).

6 The genitive expresses *possession* and *absence of* (§§ 5 and 7).

Lesson 4

Г	г	*Γ г*	= g
Ю	ю	*Ю ю*	= you
Й	й	*Й й*	= y

PRONUNCIATION

Г sounds like *g* in *gallows*, except at the end of a word, when it sounds like *k*.

At the beginning of a word or after a vowel **ю** has a double value and sounds similar to the English word *you*. Otherwise the *y* element is absorbed by the preceding consonant, which is softened. Like **y, ю** does not represent a long drawn out vowel, like *oo* in English *moon*.

The letter **й** has two functions:

a After a vowel the value of **й** is not unlike that of *y* in *boy*, *toy*, but there is quite a big difference between the pronunciation of **бой** (*battle*) and *boy*, **конвой** (*convoy*) and *convoy* since **й** is rather like the Russian **и** while *y* in *boy* is rather like the *i* in *bit*. After **ы** and **и**, **й** is hardly audible.

b Between two vowels **й** sounds like *y* in *yield*: **район** *region*, **майор** *major*, as it does on the few occasions when **й** is at the beginning of a word.

SPELLING

Г like **к** cannot be followed by **ы**. Write: *ги   ги   ги   ки   ки   ки*

Words with **Г г** *Γ г*

Га-га-рин   Гагарин Gagarin

год *year*	в году *in the year*
город[1] *town*	град *hail, hailstones*
гром *thunder*	громко *loudly*
игра *game*	гора *mountain*
бумага *paper*	дорога *road*

1 In many place-names the form **-град** (not to be confused with **град** *hail, hailstones*) is used, as in Leningrad, Volgograd (Stalingrad) etc.

друг *friend*
нога́ *foot, leg*

кругóм *around*
мнóго *much, many*
губа́ *lip*
вагóн *railway carriage, wagon*
ГУМ² *State Stores*

кни́га *book*
госуда́рство¹ *state, i.e. the organization of a nation*

круг *circle*
готóво *ready*
я́года *berry*
сигарéта *cigarette*
МГУ³ *Moscow State University*

Two common verbs with the letter **г** *are*:

to be able
я могу́ *I can*
они́ мóгут *they can*

to speak, to say
он говори́т *he says/speaks*
мы говори́м *we say/speak*
они́ говоря́т *they say/speak*

Они́ говоря́т грóмко и мнóго.

I. GENITIVE CASE I

We saw in Lesson 3 that masculine nouns form the genitive singular in **a** and that *some* of them have nominative plural in stressed **a**; that feminine nouns form the genitive singular in **ы**, identical with the nominative plural but sometimes distinguished from it by a difference in stress. Since **и** not **ы** is written after **г**, as well as **к**, the genitive singular and nominative plural of some nouns given above ends in **и**.

masculine noun with nominative plural in **a**:

nom. sing.	gen. sing.	nom. pl.
гóрод *town*	гóрода	города́

masculine nouns with *normal* nominative plural:

год *year*	гóда	гóды
гром *(peal of) thunder*	грóма	грóмы
круг *circle*	кру́га	круги́ (stress-shift)

feminine nouns *with* change in the stress:

игра́ *game*	игры́	и́гры
гора́ *mountain*	горы́	гóры
нога́ *foot, leg*	ноги́	нóги
губа́ *lip*	губы́	гу́бы

---

1 Take it slowly! **го-су-да́р-ство.**
2 An initial word which is pronounced as spelt, i.e. 'Goom'.
3 An initial word which is pronounced as initials, i.e. 'Em-gay-oo'.

feminine nouns with no change in the stress:

nom. sing.	gen. sing.	nom. pl.
бума́га *paper*	бума́ги	бума́ги
доро́га *road*	доро́ги	доро́ги
кни́га *book*	кни́ги	кни́ги

2. IDIOMS I

The use of the common prepositions by no means always corresponds with the English use of 'equivalent' prepositions. Note the following expressions, with the preposition **в**:

в году́ *in the year* . . .
игра́ в кри́кет *a game of cricket*
игра́ в те́ннис *a game of tennis*

3. GENITIVE CASE AFTER **мно́го**

The word **мно́го** followed by the genitive plural means *many*, and by the genitive singular means *much*:

Тут мно́го ды́ма и мно́го воды́. *There's a lot of smoke and water here.*
До́ма мно́го сы́ра и мно́го икры́ (икра́ *caviar*).
Там мно́го бума́ги.

On its own or with a verb **мно́го** is simply an adverb meaning *much* or *a lot*.

4. TEXT

Тут сад. В саду́ стоя́т дубы́. У́тром сы́ро в саду́. Так как тут сы́ро и мо́кро, то[1] тут тума́ны. Тума́ны как бы[2] расту́т, они́ расту́т как дубы́ – но дубы́ расту́т не бы́стро, а тума́ны бы́стро расту́т. Тума́ны и тут и там. Нет, у́тром я туда́ не иду́. У́тром я до́ма, я туда́ не иду́. В саду́ ра́но у́тром сы́ро и мо́кро, там стоя́т дубы́ и стоя́т тума́ны.

Words with **Ю ю**   *Ю ю*

Юг   на юг   на ю́ге

юг (sounds like юк!) *south*   ю́мор *humour*
ю́бка *skirt*   брю́ки *trousers*
каю́та *cabin*   рю́мка *wine-glass*

каю́та, каю́та   ю́бка   брю́ки

---

1 *Then, so* (may often be omitted in translation).
2 *As if, sort of* (translate **как бы расту́т** *seem to grow*).

5. IDIOMS II

Compass direction and location are expressed by means of the preposition **на**:

на юг *south(wards)*   на ю́ге[1] *in the south*
на се́вер *north(wards)*   на се́вере[1] *in the north*
на восто́к *east(wards)*   на восто́ке[1] *in the east*

Суда́ иду́т на юг. Я е́ду на юг.
На ю́ге нет тума́на. – Нет, неве́рно, и на ю́ге мно́го тума́на.
Они́ е́дут на восто́к. И на восто́ке мно́го тума́на.

6. VERB FORMS AND VERB TABLE I

Verbs which in the third pers. sing. end in **-ет** preceded by a vowel have the first pers. sing. ending in **-ю** and the third pers. pl. ending in **-ют**:

3rd pers. sing.	1st pers. sing.	3rd pers. pl.
VOWEL + **ет**	VOWEL + **ю**	VOWEL + **ют**
он, она́, оно́ ката́ет *rolls*	я ката́ю	они́ ката́ют
ду́мает *thinks*	ду́маю	ду́мают
игра́ет *plays*	игра́ю	игра́ют
обе́дает *dines*	обе́даю	обе́дают
бе́гает *runs*	бе́гаю	бе́гают
тро́гает *touches*	тро́гаю	тро́гают
открыва́ет *opens*	открыва́ю	открыва́ют
кида́ет *throws*	кида́ю	кида́ют
отнима́ет *takes away*	отнима́ю	отнима́ют
нанима́ет *hires (takes on)*	нанима́ю	нанима́ют
гре́ет *heats*	гре́ю	гре́ют
ду́ет *blows*	ду́ю	ду́ют

7. VERB FORMS AND VERB TABLE II

Verbs which in the third pers. sing. end in **-ет** preceded by a consonant have the first pers. sing. ending in **-у** and the third pers. pl. ending in **-ут.**

3rd pers. sing.	1st pers. sing.	3rd pers. pl.
CONSONANT + **ет**	CONSONANT + **у**	CONSONANT + **ут**
он, она́, оно́ бу́дет *will be*	я бу́ду	они́ бу́дут
——	могу́[2] *I can*	мо́гут
е́дет *goes (by vehicle)*	е́ду	е́дут
идёт[3] *goes (on foot)*	иду́	иду́т
ведёт *leads*	веду́	веду́т

1 These are in the *prepositional* case, which will be dealt with later. For the time being simply learn the idioms and the sentences in which they appear.
2 The third pers. sing. of *to be able* has been omitted for the time being since a consonant change is involved.
3 In some of the verbs in which **-ет** is preceded by a consonant, **е** turns into **ё**, a letter which will be dealt with later. For the time being simply learn the look of the third pers. sing.

3rd pers. sing.	1st pers. sing.	3rd pers. pl.
несёт *carries*	несу́	несу́т
украдёт *will steal*	украду́	украду́т
растёт *grows*	расту́	расту́т
берёт *takes*	беру́	беру́т

Verbs shown in Tables I and II all belong to the first conjugation. They have the letter **e** in all forms of the conjugation except for the first pers. sing. and the third pers. pl. The first pers. sing. and the third pers. sing. give you the clue to the conjugation of all except one or two verbs.

8. SECOND CONJUGATION

In Lesson 3 you were told that verbs with the third pers. sing. in **-ит** have the third pers. pl. in **-ят** or **-ат**. Such verbs belong to the second conjugation. They have the letter **и** in all forms of the conjugation, except the first pers. sing. and third pers. pl.

Он гро́мко говори́т, стои́т и ку́рит.

Они́ гро́мко говоря́т, стоя́т и ку́рят.

9. SENTENCES

Я мно́го ду́маю. Они́ мно́го говоря́т, а ду́мают[1] они́ не мно́го. А он и не ду́мает и не говори́т.[2]
Я бы́стро бе́гаю и мно́го игра́ю. Он не игра́ет, не бе́гает, а стои́т. Они́ не стоя́т, они́ бе́гают, но бе́гают не так бы́стро, как я.
Они́ е́дут на юг. Они́ обе́дают на борту́ су́дна. Я никуда́ не е́ду и не иду́. Я обе́даю до́ма в саду́.

10. ACCUSATIVE CASE AND EXERCISE

In the sentence *I am renting a house* the word house is said to be the *object*, more precisely the *direct object* of the action of the verb. In Russian the direct object is in the *accusative case*. This is identical with the nominative for certain nouns.

subject (nominative)	object (accusative)
Дом стои́т там	Я нанима́ю дом
The house stands there	*I am renting the house*

Read the following sentences and decide whether the objects of the verbs are animate or inanimate, whether they are masculine, feminine or neuter,

---

1 The verb **ду́мают** is brought forward to give it emphasis and to contrast it with **говоря́т**.
2 Lit. 'both does not think and does not talk', i.e. *neither thinks nor talks*.

singular or plural, and whether their endings are like the nominative or the genitive cases.

Я нанимаю дом.   Доктора нанимают дома.

Иван открывает рот и ест томат.   Дамы берут томаты.

Я курю табак.

Я несу стакан воды, а матросы несут стаканы водки.

Я дам адрес, она даст номер дома.

Я открываю окно.   Они открывают окна.

Они строят судно.   Государство строит суда.

Банкир даст вино.   Они несут стаканы вина.

Words with **Й й** *Й й*

май May	*край* edge
рай *paradise, heaven*	бой *battle*
строй *system*	конвой *convoy, escort*
домой *homewards*	тайна *secret*
район *region*	майор *major*
район	*майор*

II. GENITIVE SINGULAR OF FEMININE PRONOUNS

The genitive singular of feminine pronouns (except the pronoun **она** *she*) and feminine adjectives ends in **ой** or **ей**:

nom. sing.	gen. sing.
та *that*	той
сама *herself, itself*	самой

Той доски тут нет. *That (black)board is not here.*

Там нет той рюмки. *That wine-glass is not there.*

Дамы самой нет дома. *The lady herself is not at home.*

12. TRANSLATION

'The doctors stand and talk and talk, while[1] the banker stands there and smokes cigarettes. He feels bad[2] early in the morning.'

'Ivan doesn't talk but he thinks a lot . . .'

'Are the glasses here?'

'The glasses are here but there's no wine.'

'What?[3] There is no wine?'

'The State Stores stands over there and (there is) plenty of wine there.'

1 **В то время как.**   2 **Ему дурно.**   3 **Как?**

'(There's) a lot of mist here. Yes, (there's) a lot of mist here because the river is here.'

'(There's) a lot of water here. Yes, a lot of water – but (there's) no wine.'

'Where are they going? I am going south.'

'They are going home because they are dining at home.'

'The doctor, they say,[1] is dining on board ship.'

'Ah![2] There is the wine! Ivanov is warming the wine.'

'What? I am going home. Goodbye!'[3]

1 **Говоря́т** (NB without **они́** when it means *people say*).   2 **А!**   3 **До свида́ния!**

SUMMARY

1 The gen. sing. of feminine nouns ending in **a** is formed by replacing **a** by **ы** or **и**. A stress difference sometimes distinguishes gen. sing. and nom. pl. (§ 1).

2 The gen. sing. is used with **мно́го** *much* (§ 3).

3 First conjugation verbs have first pers. sing. ending in **-у** or **-ю**, third pers. sing. in **-ет** and third pers. pl. in **-ут** or **-ют** (§§ 6 and 7).

4 Second conjugation verbs have third pers. sing. ending in **-ит** and third pers. pl. in **-ят** or **-ат** (§ 8).

5 The direct object in a sentence goes into the *accusative case* (§ 10).

6 The gen. sing. of feminine pronouns ends in **ой** or **ей** (§ 11).

Lesson 5

Ч ч *Ч ч* = ch

Х х *Х х* = kh

PRONUNCIATION

In the words **что** *what, that* and **конéчно** *of course*, **ч** is pronounced *sh*, not *ch*.

In the adjective and pronoun endings gen. sing. masc. and neut. **ого** and **его** (see below), the **г** is pronounced *v*, i.e. these endings are pronounced as though spelt **ово/ево**. This also applies to **его** in **сегóдня** *today*.

SPELLING

Ч and **х** are two more letters which will not tolerate **ы**. Only **чи! чи! чи!** and **хи! хи! хи!**

Don't forget: **ки, ги, чи, хи; ки, ги, чи, хи.**

Most words derived from English words beginning with *w* have initial **в** in Russian as in **ватт** *watt*. Proper names have **у** and sometimes **в** as in **Уéстминстер, Вéстминстер** *Westminster*; **Уóрдсуорс** *Wordsworth*.

Ч ч *Ч ч*

usually sounds like English *ch*

Сейчáс ҁас   ҁас сейчáс

чай *tea*	час *hour, one o'clock*
сейчáс *now*	четы́ре *four*
чáсто *often*	так чáсто *so often*
тóчно *precisely*	так тóчно *just so*
начáло *beginning*	сначáла *from the beginning*
нарóчно *deliberately, on purpose*	чи́сто *clean(ly)*
ученúк *pupil*	дáча *country house*
рýчка *little hand, pen(holder)*	рýчка двéри *door-handle*
дóчка *daughter*	внýчка *grand-daughter*
вéчер *evening*	вéчером *in the evening*

27

тóчка *full stop, dot*   чемодáн *trunk, suitcase*
вчерá *yesterday*   свéчка *candle*
рéчка *stream*   чертá *trait, line*

but in **что** *what, that* and **конéчно** *of course* **ч** is pronounced like *sh*.

Да, конéчно так   Да, конéчно так

The following verbs with **ч** are verbs of the first conjugation; they conjugate like **дýмаю** (Lesson 4):

я читáю *I read*	он читáет	мы читáем	они читáют
я кончáю *I finish*	он кончáет	мы кончáем	они кончáют
я качáю *I rock*	он качáет	мы качáем	они качáют

I. SOME SIMPLE EXPRESSIONS OF TIME

котóрый час? *what time is it?* or *what is the time?*
час *one o'clock; it's one o'clock*
два часá *two o'clock; two hours*
три часá *three o'clock; three hours*
четы́ре часá *four o'clock; four hours*

2. SENTENCES

Тут чи́сто? Нет, тут не чи́сто.
Тут всегдá (*always*) чи́сто.   Конéчно тут чи́сто.
Вы ученики́.   Да, вы ученики́.   Ученики́ читáют урóк.
Дáча на ю́ге.
Дóчка сейчáс дóма, дóчка обéдает дóма.
Дóчка и внýчка éдут домóй.   Дóчка и внýчка вéчером éдут домóй.
Сейчáс качáет.[1]   На сýдне качáет[1] и нам дýрно.
Как так качáет? – Качáет, так как дýет[1] с[2] востóка (*from the east*).
Нет, дýет с сéвера (*from the north*).
Кто там? – Там сам банки́р.   Я дýмаю, он читáет.
Что там?   Там конвóй, а вот там вагóны.
Что вы!   Что вы!   *How can you!* or *Well, really!*

DIALOGUE
– Что тут?
– Тут рекá и стои́т мост, ря́дом Вéстминстер.

1 **Качáет** lit. 'it rocks', and **дýет** lit. 'it blows', are used here as *impersonal verbs*. This means that they have no subject. **На сýдне качáет** lit. 'on the ship it is rocking'. You would say in English *the ship is rocking* or *pitching*, making *ship* the subject. **Дýет с востóка** lit. 'it is blowing from the east' would be, idiomatically, *there's an east wind blowing*.
2 **С** + genitive means *from, off* as in **с востóка** *from the east*.

28

– Не Вéстминстер, а Уéстминстер.

– Нет, Вéстминстер. Тут стоúт бýква (*letter*) в – вот онá – итáк Вéстминстер. Конéчно Вéстминстер.

– Что вы! Что вы! Уéстминстер. Уéстминстер банк.

– Вéстминстер банк и мост и аббáтство (*abbey*).

– Уéстминстер и банк, и мост, и аббáтство.

– Невéрно! Невéрно!

– Ну! Ну! Мы говорúм грóмко!

3. GENITIVE SINGULAR OF MASCULINE AND NEUTER PRONOUNS

The genitive singular of masculine and neuter pronouns and adjectives ends in **ого** or **его,** where **г** is pronounced as *v* (see Pronunciation above).

nom. sing.	*gen. sing.*
кто *who,* used for people	когó
что *what, that,* used for animals, birds, insects, and things	чегó
тот, то *that*	тогó
сам, самó *himself, itself*	самогó

Except in the nominative case, masculine and neuter pronouns have the same case endings in the singular.

Nobody and *nothing* frequently occur in the genitive case, since they are always negative:

никтó – никогó *nobody*
ничтó – ничегó *nothing*

Ничегó on its own means *never mind, it doesn't matter.*
The form **когó** is *not* used when asking, for instance, *whose is that.*

Когó тут нет? *Who is not here?*
Самóй Нúны нет, тут Мáня. *Nina herself is not here. Manya is here.*
Самогó Ивáна тут нет, но друг тут.
Чегó тут нет? Тут нет той бумáги, нет той кнúги.
Тут нет тогó рýнка, нет тогó товáра.
Тут нет никогó. Тут нет ничегó, ничегó тут нет.
Что там? – Да[1] ничегó там нет. – Ну вот,[2] ничегó нет! Как так – ничегó нет?
Да так – нет и нет,[3] ничегó там нет – ни винá, ни табакá, так обúдно!

---

1 **Да** on its own or separated by a comma from what follows means *yes.* When it is not separated by a comma it is a different word, having the function of adding a slight emphasis. Translate *well* or omit. In this function **да** is unstressed – pronounce it like the second syllable of *soda.* Sometimes **да** means *and.*

2 **Ну вот** *well then.*

3 Emphatic negative *there just isn't (anything).*

Ну ничего, ничего – вот я иду домой, дома и табак и вино, и книги и бумаги. Вам обидно, что[1] нет табака, но я вам дам, и я вам дам стакан вина.[2]

4. THE DIRECT OBJECT AND THE ACCUSATIVE CASE

In **я вам дам стакан вина** *I shall give you a glass of wine*, **стакан** is the thing which will be given, the direct object on which the action of the verb is performed. In the exercise in Lesson 4, § 10 we asked you to decide whether the direct objects in the sentences were:

    a animate or inanimate
    b masculine, feminine or neuter
    c singular or plural
    d like the nominative or genitive in their grammatical form.

The direct objects were things and so inanimate in every case; their gender was either masculine or neuter; their number was either singular or plural and their grammatical forms were like the nominative.

    Hence *the accusative case* of masculine nouns which are inanimate, and neuter nouns, both in the singular and the plural, is identical with the nominative case.

5. THE INDIRECT OBJECT AND THE DATIVE CASE

In **я вам дам стакан вина** the person to whom the glass will be given, in this case *you*, is the *indirect object*. As you see, the indirect object in Russian is expressed by the dative case, **вам** *to you* being dative of **вы**. The dative of **мы** *we* is **нам** *to us*.

    Я вам дам тот стакан.
    Я вам дам то место.
    Брат даст вам то вино.
    Вера даст нам тот самовар.

X x $\mathcal{X}\,x$

sounds like *ch* in the Scots pronunciation of *loch*, though there is not so much friction in the Russian sound.

X is soft before **е** and **и**.

хата *hut*	хор *choir*
старуха/хи *old woman/women*	смех *laughter* (no pl.)

1 *That* (conjunction) always preceded by a comma, e.g.: **он думает, что я читаю** *he thinks that I am reading*.
2 *I shall give you a glass of wine* (see below).

страх/хи *fear, fears*　　　　　духи́ *perfume* (no sing.)
дух *spirit, ghost*　　　　　　ду́хи *spirits, ghosts*

Ха-та ста-ру-хи　　　　　　*Ха́та стару́хи*

---

6. TRANSLATION

(It is) two o'clock now. I am going home because I dine at three o'clock.
And today I am dining at home. (My) grand-daughter always dines at home.
Yes, today I am going home early.

There is an east wind blowing (*it is blowing from the east*).

Is she an old woman? No, she is not an old woman. The doctor is an old
man and there he is! I think that he will be at home this evening.

Does (your) brother read a lot? – Yes, (my) brother reads a lot, but there is
no book here. There is nothing here – neither book nor paper.

What will he give us? Will he give us (his) address? – Yes, he will give
you (his) address. – No, I do not think that he will give us the address of
(his) home. I think that he will give the address of (his) office.

SUMMARY

1 **C** + gen. means *from* (from the direction of), *off* (§ 2²).
2 The gen. of masculine pronouns and adjectives ends in **oro** or **ero** (§ 3).
3 Neuter pronouns have the same endings as masculine pronouns in the
sing. except in the nom. (§ 3).
4 The accusative case of masculine and neuter nouns denoting inanimate
things is the same as the nom. case in both sing. and pl. (§ 4).
5 The indirect object is in the dative case (§ 5).

Lesson 6

Ф	ф	*Ф* *ф*	= f
Ё	ё	*Ё* *ё*	= yaw
Ь	ь	– *ь*	= soft sign

PRONUNCIATION

In Lesson 2 the feature known as *softening* was introduced (Lesson 2, Pronunciation 5). Of the vowels we have had so far the following produce the softening effect:

и я е ю

So does the letter **ё.**

Ё has a double value: *y + aw*, when it is at the beginning of a word or has a vowel in front of it. When it has a consonant in front of it the *y* is absorbed by the consonant and it softens the consonant. A few consonants are unaffected by **ё,** which has the value of **o** when it follows them.

Some consonants *let through* the softening effect of **е, и, я, ю, ё** to the preceding consonant.

Д lets the softening through to the preceding **н** in **индю́к** *turkey*, for example.

В lets the softening through to the preceding **д** or **т** in **дви́гаю** *I move*, **две** *two* (fem.), **твёрдо** *firmly*, for example.

The soft sign **ь** simply shows that the preceding consonant is soft, so it is most often used when there is no following soft vowel letter. It has no sound itself.

SPELLING

Stress-marks are used regularly only in grammars, elementary readers and dictionaries, and occasionally elsewhere to avoid ambiguity.

Ё is always stressed and so it does not need a stress-mark. It is printed **ё** in grammars, elementary readers and dictionaries, and occasionally elsewhere to avoid ambiguity. Otherwise the two dots are omitted and it looks the same as **e.**

32

1. SECOND PERSON PLURAL

The second pers. pl. of the verb, the form which means *you do such-and-such*, ends in **-те,** with a soft **т.** Those verbs that have **-ет** in the third pers. sing. have **-ете** in the second pers. pl.

The verbs of this type (first conjugation) which we have seen so far all have a vowel in front of the **e.**

3rd pers. sing. (he, she, it)	*2nd pers. pl. (you)*
vowel + **ет**	*vowel* + **ете**
он нанима́ет *he hires*	вы нанима́ете
он ду́мает *he thinks*	вы ду́маете
он надева́ет *he puts on* (garments)	вы надева́ете
он начина́ет *he begins*	вы начина́ете
он конча́ет *he finishes*	вы конча́ете
он гре́ет *he heats*	вы гре́ете
он ду́ет *he blows*	вы ду́ете

Those verbs which have **-ит** in the third pers. sing. (second conjugation) have **-ите** in the second pers. pl.

3rd pers. sing.	*2nd pers. pl.*
-ит	**-ите**
он стои́т *he stands*	вы стои́те
он стро́ит *he builds*	вы стро́ите
он говори́т *he speaks*	вы говори́те
он ку́рит *he smokes*	вы ку́рите
он ве́рит *he believes*	вы ве́рите
он твори́т *he creates, makes*	вы твори́те

2. INFINITIVE I

We have seen that some verbs have a consonant before the ending **-ет.** A number of these verbs have the infinitive ending **-ти.** This infinitive ending, which is always stressed, is much less frequent than the one given in the next paragraph but several very common verbs have it. Here are some of them, together with the first pers. sing. of the present tense:

infin. in **-ти**	*1st pers. sing.*
вести́ *to lead*	веду́
нести́ *to carry*	несу́
расти́ *to grow*	расту́
идти́ *to go*	иду́

3. INFINITIVE II

The commonest ending of the infinitive is **-ть.** Here are some such infinitives, preceded by the third pers. sing.:

а он ду́мает *he thinks*	ду́мать
он конча́ет *he finishes*	конча́ть

он начина́ет *he begins*	начина́ть
он игра́ет *he plays*	игра́ть
он бе́гает *he runs*	бе́гать
он надева́ет *he puts on*	надева́ть
он гре́ет *he heats*	греть
он ду́ет *he blows*	дуть
он дви́гает *he moves*	дви́гать
он е́дет *he goes* (in a vehicle)	е́хать (NB! exceptional infinitive)
b он стро́ит *he builds*	стро́ить
он говори́т *he speaks*	говори́ть
он ку́рит *he smokes*	кури́ть
он ве́рит *he believes*	ве́рить
он твори́т *he creates, makes*	твори́ть

c The infinitive of **бу́ду** *I shall be* is **быть** *to be*.

4. NOMINATIVE PLURAL те

The nominative plural of **тот, та, то** *that* is **те** *those*.

Куда́ веду́т те доро́ги?	*Where do those roads lead?*
Те доро́ги веду́т в Рим.	*Those roads lead to Rome.*
Те тома́ты расту́т в саду́.	*Those tomatoes grow in the garden.*
Я вам дам те тома́ты.	*I shall give you those tomatoes.*

5. GENITIVE PLURAL OF PRONOUNS

The genitive plural of pronouns and adjectives ends in **х**.

nom. pl.	*gen. pl.*
те *those*	тех
они́ са́ми *they themselves*	их сами́х
они́ са́ми тут	их сами́х тут нет
они́ са́ми иду́т туда́	их сами́х нет до́ма

6. GENITIVE PLURAL OF FEMININE AND NEUTER NOUNS

Nouns ending in the nominative singular in **a** and **o** form the genitive plural by dropping the **a** or **o**.

nom. sing.	*gen. pl.*
соба́ка *dog*	соба́к
ко́мната *room*	ко́мнат
страна́ *country*	стран
бума́га *paper*	бума́г
дра́ка *scuffle*	драк
ме́сто *place*	мест

Most nouns of this type which have two consonants before the **a** or **o** insert a vowel between the two consonants in the genitive plural. For many nouns this *mobile vowel* is **o**:

nom. sing.	gen. pl.
окно́ *window*	о́кон
бу́дка *booth*	бу́док
коро́бка *box*	коро́бок
кра́ска *paint*	кра́сок
ни́тка *thread*	ни́ток
тру́бка *pipe*	тру́бок
откры́тка *post-card*	откры́ток

For others the mobile vowel is **e**:

то́чка *full stop, dot*	то́чек
све́чка *candle*	све́чек
ре́чка *stream*	ре́чек

We have now had the following cases of feminine and neuter nouns: nominative and genitive singular and nominative and genitive plural.

nom. sing.	gen. sing.	nom. pl.	gen. pl.
ко́мната	ко́мнаты	ко́мнаты	ко́мнат
страна́	страны́	стра́ны	стран
откры́тка	откры́тки	откры́тки	откры́ток
ме́сто	ме́ста	места́	мест
окно́	окна́	о́кна	о́кон

The stress-shift between singular and plural, as in **страна́, ме́сто** and **окно́** is quite common in feminine and regular in neuter nouns of two syllables.

7. GENITIVE PLURAL OF MASCULINE NOUNS

a Most masculine nouns ending in a consonant in the nominative singular form the genitive plural by adding **ов**:

двор *yard*	дворо́в
сад *garden*	садо́в
банк *bank*	ба́нков
конве́рт *envelope*	конве́ртов

Here are four cases of some masculine nouns:

nom. sing.	gen. sing.	nom. pl.	gen. pl.
двор *yard*	двора́	дворы́	дворо́в
сад *garden*	са́да	сады́	садо́в
мост *bridge*	моста́	мосты́	мосто́в
дуб *oak*	ду́ба	дубы́	дубо́в
до́ктор *doctor*	до́ктора	доктора́	докторо́в
дом *house*	до́ма	дома́	домо́в
го́род *town*	го́рода	города́	городо́в

The neuter noun **су́дно** *ship* has a genitive plural of this type and loses the **н** in the plural:

nom. sing.	gen. sing.	nom. pl.	gen. pl.
су́дно	су́дна	суда́	судо́в

b The mobile vowel found in the genitive plural of many feminine and neuter nouns is also found *in the nominative singular only* of some masculine nouns.

Mobile vowels **о, е** or **ё**:

nom. sing.	gen. sing.	nom. pl.	gen. pl.
комо́к *lump*	комка́	комки́	комко́в
рот *mouth*	рта	рты	ртов
сон *dream, sleep*	сна	сны	снов
ковёр *carpet*	ковра́	ковры́	ковро́в

8. GENITIVE AFTER PREPOSITIONS

Apart from its use in negative sentences with **нет** and to indicate possession, the genitive singular and plural is also used after certain prepositions, including:

до *to*   **от** *from*   **у** *at, next to, by*

The preposition must come before the noun or pronoun to which it applies.

От Москвы́ до Ки́ева.	*From Moscow to Kiev.*
От Ри́ма до Москвы́.	*From Rome to Moscow.*
От того́ до́ма до того́ моста́.	От тех гор до той реки́.
У того́ до́ма стои́т дуб.	*By that house stands an oak.*
У тех домо́в стоя́т дубы́.	*By those houses stand (some) oaks.*
У того́ ду́ба стои́т дом.	У тех дубо́в стоя́т дома́.
У той реки́ гора́.	У тех рек го́ры.
У той горы́ река́.	У тех гор ре́ки.
Го́род стои́т у реки́.	Города́ стоя́т у горы́.
Банк стои́т у моста́.	Мост стои́т у ба́нка.

У того́ до́ма река́, а моста́ там нет.

By that house there is a river, but there is no bridge there.

Дом там, дом у реки́, а не у горы́.

The house is there, the house is by the river, and not by the mountain.

9. TEXT

Тури́сты стоя́т у воро́т. Они́ гото́вы. Они́ нанима́ют авто́бус. Они́ бы́стро е́дут до го́рода. Мно́го тури́стов, мно́го чемода́нов, мно́го су́мок, мно́го книг, мно́го бума́г. Но чемода́ны тури́стов, их су́мки, их кни́ги, их бума́ги до́ма. Они́ ничего́ не несу́т. Им на́до в банк. От ба́нка они́ иду́т в рестора́н. Там они́ обе́дают и я обе́даю там. Мы кончáем обéдать. От ресторáна турúсты идýт до мостá. У мостá рынок. Там онú стоя́т, говоря́т, кýрят. Там им интерéсно. А вéчером онú все идýт в кинó и оттýда éдут домóй. И я идý в кинó и оттýда éду домóй. Я чáсто так отдыхáю.

10. 'TO HAVE'

There is a verb *to have* in Russian but by far the commoner way of expressing possession is the idiomatic construction: **у** + genitive.

In this construction the possessor is in the genitive while the thing possessed becomes the grammatical subject of the sentence.

У турúстов чемодáны.	*The tourists have suitcases.*
	(lit. 'At/by the tourists are suitcases')
У Ивáна сын.	*Ivan has a son.*
У сы́на дóчка.	*The son has a daughter.*
У чемодáна рýчка.	*The suitcase has a handle.*
У кóмнаты óкна.	*The room has windows.*
У тех домóв сады́.	*Those houses have gardens.*
У тогó кармáна дырá.	*That pocket has a hole.*

Ф ф *Ѳ ѳ   Ф Ф Ф Ф Ф Ф*

sounds like English *f*.

Фёдор   факт   кóфе

факт *fact*	фактúчески *in fact*
фáктор *factor*	фáбрика *factory*
фéрма *farm*	фонтáн *fountain*
кóфе *coffee*	Фёдор *Theodore*
рóстбиф *roast-beef*	Мáрфа *Martha*
грáфик *graph*	графúчески *graphically*
фотóграф *photographer*	тиф *typhus*

Тут мнóго домóв и ферм, но

фактúчески тут не гóрод

Remember that **ф** is softened by following **и, я, ю, е** and **ё**.

Words with soft **д** i.e. followed by **и, е, я, ю, ё**

одúн *one*	дирéктор *director*
рáдио *radio*	Úндия *India*
индю́к *turkey*	бандúт *bandit*
дúво *marvel*	дúвно *marvellous*

дико *wild, absurd*   сердито *angrily*
дед *grandfather*   две *two* (fem.)
дети *children*   десять *ten*

---

11. 'WHERE'

There are two words for *where* in Russian. **Где** is used when a person or thing is stationary and you are asking about his or its location.

Где вы будете сегодня вечером? *Where will you be this evening?*

(lit. 'today in the evening').

Я буду дома сегодня вечером. *I shall be at home this evening.*

Куда is used when asking where a person or thing is moving to (English *whither*).

Куда мы едем? *Where are we going?*

Мы едем в кино. *We're going to the cinema.*

> **Где** = location where
> **Куда** = motion where to

12. VERB CONJUGATIONS I

In the following verbs there are examples of soft **д** and hard or ordinary **д**:

я ем *I eat*   я дам *I shall give*
он ест *he eats*   он даст *he will give*
мы едим *we eat*   мы дадим *we shall give*
вы едите *you eat*   вы дадите *you will give*
они едят *they eat*   они дадут *they will give*

Normally verbs with **-им** in the first pers. pl. have **-ят** in the third pers. pl. The pattern **дадим – дадут** is unique.

я буду *I shall be*   я еду *I go (not on foot)*
он будет   он едет
мы будем   мы едем
вы будете   вы едете
они будут   они едут

In the following verb the softening effect can be transmitted through the **в** to the **д,** which may be pronounced hard or soft:

я двигаю *I move*
он двигает
мы двигаем
вы двигаете
они двигают

38

13. NUMBERS

a **Один** *one* is the only number that has three different gender forms:

masc.	*fem.*	*neut.*
один год	одна́ мину́та	одно́ ме́сто
один час	одна́ секу́нда	одно́ су́дно
один ве́чер	одна́ дра́ма	одно́ окно́

Higher numbers ending in **один** etc., also agree in gender with the noun, *which remains in the singular.*

Notice that **и** is found only in the nominative singular masculine. **Один** is also used where English has *alone.*

Я один до́ма. *I am at home alone.*
Она́ одна́ там. *She is there alone.*

There is a *plural* **одни** common to all genders, meaning *some* or *alone*:

Мы одни́ тут. *We are alone here.*

b **Два** *two* is used with masculine and neuter nouns, **две** with feminine nouns.

Три *three*, **четы́ре** *four* and other numbers have no gender distinction.

With **два/две, три** and **четы́ре** (and all higher numbers ending in these words, as for instance 22, 23, 24 and 32, 33, 34 etc.) the noun is in the *genitive singular*:

два часа́ *two hours*	два ме́ста *two places*
две соба́ки *two dogs*	две ко́мнаты *two rooms*
три часа́	четы́ре го́рода
три соба́ки	четы́ре ко́мнаты
три-четы́ре (*three to four*) ме́ста	

c Higher numbers and **мно́го** *many* are followed by the genitive plural.

один внук	*grandson*	два вну́ка	мно́го вну́ков
одна́ ры́ба	*fish*	две ры́бы	мно́го рыб
одно́ окно́	*window*	два окна́	мно́го о́кон
одна́ да́ча	*country-house*	две да́чи	мно́го дач
одно́ су́дно	*ship*	четы́ре су́дна	мно́го судо́в
одна́ страна́	*country*	две страны́	мно́го стран

14. VERB CONJUGATIONS II

When **e** in verb-endings is stressed, it becomes **ё**. Here are three common verbs with **ё** in some of the endings:

идти́ *to go*	**вести́** *to lead*	**брать** *to take*
я иду́	я веду́	я беру́
он идёт	он ведёт	он берёт

мы идём	мы ведём	мы берём
вы идёте	вы ведёте	вы берёте
они́ иду́т	они́ веду́т	они́ беру́т

Он берёт ковёр

More words with ё

In the following list **ё** is a *mobile vowel* in the two masculine nouns in the nominative singular. In the two neuter nouns **e** (not **ё**) is the *mobile vowel* in the genitive plural.

nom. sing.	*gen. sing.*	*nom. pl.*	*gen. pl.*
ковёр *carpet*	ковра́	ковры́	ковро́в
овёс *oats*	овса́	(*no plural*)	
ведро́ *bucket*	ведра́	вёдра	вёдер
бедро́ *hip*	бедра́	бёдра	бёдер

SUMMARY

1 The second pers. pl. of the verb ends in **-те** (§ 1).
2 The infinitive ends in **-ть** and also, less commonly, in **-ти** (§§ 3 and 2).
3 The nom. pl. of **тот** etc. is **те** (§ 4).
4 The gen. pl. of pronouns and adjectives ends in **x** (§ 5).
5 The gen. pl. of fem. and neut. nouns ending in **a** or **o** in the nom. sing. is formed by dropping the **a** or **o** (§ 6).
6 The gen. pl. of masc. nouns ending in a consonant in the nom. sing. is formed by adding **ов** (§ 7a).
7 The prepositions **до, от, y** control the gen. (§ 8).
8 The preposition **y** + gen. is the common way of expressing *to have* (§ 10).
9 The number 1 **оди́н,** as well as 21, 31, 41 etc., agrees with its noun, i.e. it goes into the same gender and case, the noun remaining in the singular (§ 13a).
10 The numbers 2 **два/две,** 3 **три** and 4 **четы́ре** as well as 22, 23, 24, 32, 33, 34 etc., control the gen. sing. (§ 13b).
11 Higher numbers and **мно́го** control the gen. pl. (§ 13c).

Lesson 7

Ж ж *Жж* = zh

Ц ц *Цц* = ts

Цц
цирк цифра цыган

ж ж ж ж ж
жук жужжит уже жара

PRONUNCIATION

Ж sounds like *s* in *leisure, pleasure,* except at the end of a word when it sounds like *sh* in *shawl*. It also has this value before a voiceless consonant, e.g. before к, as in но́жка *foot, leg*.

After ж and ц the letter и is pronounced ы.

SPELLING

Ж is one of the six letters that are never follówed by ы. Write жи! жи! жи! But pronounce as if spelt with ы!

Ц is followed by ы in case endings and the suffix ын:

птица *bird/s* птицы; сестрицын *sister's;*

also in a few words of which the commonest is цыга́н *gypsy*. Otherwise ц is followed by и: цинк *zinc*, цифра *cipher, number*.

Words and sentences with ж

жук *beetle* Жук жужжи́т. *The beetle buzzes.*

жара́ *hot weather* Сего́дня тут сто́ит жара́. *Today it's hot here.*

Сего́дня нет той жары́ как вчера́. *Today there isn't the same heat as yesterday.*

уже́ *already* Вот уже́ ве́чер.[1] *It's already evening.*

уже́ нет *no more* Вот уже́ нет жары́.[1] *There's no more heat.*

жа́рко *hot(ly)* Сейча́с (*now*) не так жа́рко. Уже́ ве́чер. Вот уже́ не так жа́рко.[1]

---

[1] In these sentences **вот** introduces or stresses the following statement: *Well, here we are – it's already evening* etc.

муж *husband*   жена́ *wife*   Муж идёт рабо́тать ра́но у́тром. (*My*)
   husband goes to work early in the morning.

До́ма как жук жужжи́т жена́. *At home (my) wife buzzes like a beetle.*

нога́ *leg, foot*   но́жка *small leg, foot; leg (of furniture)*

У дива́на четы́ре но́жки. *The divan has four legs.*

бума́га *paper*   бума́жка *small piece of paper*

кни́га *book*   кни́жка *small book, booklet*

доро́га *road*   доро́жка *path; carpet-strip, runner*

нож *knife*   ножа́ (*gen.*)   ножи́ (*nom. pl.*)   Тут нож? – Тут нет ножа́.

гара́ж *garage*   гаража́ (*gen.*)   гаражи́ (*nom. pl.*)

Гара́ж у до́ма.   Мост у гаража́.

бага́ж *luggage*   багажа́ (*gen.*)   Бага́ж до́ма? – Нет, до́ма нет багажа́.

жир *lard, fat*   Тут нет жи́ра.

жи́рно *greasy, greasily*

граждани́н *citizen*   гражда́нка *citizeness*   гра́ждане *citizens*

I. GENITIVE PLURAL

Masculine nouns ending in **ж** in the nominative singular form the genitive
plural by adding **ей**:

> нож – ноже́й; мно́го ноже́й
> гара́ж – гараже́й; мно́го гараже́й

Тут нет ноже́й. *There are no knives here.*

Там нет гараже́й. *There are no garages there.*

2. VERB FORMS I

Жить *to live*, with **е** in the present tense, i.e. a first conjugation verb.
Notice the form of the root in the present tense **жив-** (cf. **жи́во**
lively; as a command *look lively, come on!*).

Мочь *to be able.* First conjugation, a verb with the third and rarest kind
of infinitive ending **-чь.** In the infinitive the **г** of this verb's root
мог- is absorbed by the infinitive ending. In the present tense the **г**
changes to **ж** before the letter **е.** This interchange of **г** and **ж**
is found in other roots. It is one of a limited number of consonant
changes.

Ждать *to wait (for)*, first conjugation verb with a consonant before **е.**

жить	я живу́	мочь	могу́	ждать	жду
	он живёт		мо́жет		ждёт
	мы живём		мо́жем		ждём
	вы живёте		мо́жете		ждёте
	они́ живу́т		мо́гут		ждут

3. SENTENCES

a – Вы тут мо́жете жить?
– Вы мо́жете так жить, а я не могу́. Я живу́ ина́че.[1]
– Мы живём у моста́. Круго́м[2] авто́бусы.
– Муж живёт о́чень ти́хо. Он мно́го рабо́тает, ему́ на́до[3] отдыха́ть до́ма. Вы живёте ина́че, а он так жить не мо́жет.
– Мы живём как мо́жем. И они́ живу́т как мо́гут.

b – Тут мо́жно[4] кури́ть? – Нет, тут не на́до[5] кури́ть.
– Тут мо́жно говори́ть? – Да, мо́жно, мо́жно.

4. VERB FORMS II

Most second conjugation verbs have **-ю** in the first pers. sing. and **-ят** in the third pers. pl.

говори́ть *to speak*	я говорю́	он говори́т	они́ говоря́т
кури́ть *to smoke*	я курю́	он ку́рит	они́ ку́рят
стро́ить *to build*	я стро́ю	он стро́ит	они́ стро́ят
стоя́ть *to stand*	я стою́	он стои́т	они́ стоя́т

Certain consonants, including **ч** and **ж,** cannot be followed by **ю** and **я.** They are followed instead by **y** and **a:**

учи́ть *to teach*	я учу́	он у́чит	они́ у́чат
дружи́ть *to be friends with*	я дружу́	он дру́жит	они́ дружа́т

5. SUMMARY OF VERB FORMS

It is evident from preceding lessons that first conjugation verbs fall into two large groups: those with a vowel before **e,** such as **ду́мает** *he thinks,* and those with a consonant before **e,** such as **е́дет** *he goes* (not on foot). The verbs with infinitive in **ти** belong to the second group: **нести́ – несёт, вести́ – ведёт** etc., and so do some with infinitive in **-ать,** but the great majority of verbs in **-ать** belong to the first group of the first conjugation.

The majority of verbs of the second conjugation, i.e. those with **и** running through most of the conjugation, have their infinitive in **-ить:**

говори́т – говори́ть, ку́рит – кури́ть, стро́ит – стро́ить.

But there are some second conjungation verbs with infinitive ending in **еть:**

смотре́ть *to look*	горе́ть *to burn*
я смотрю́	я горю́
он смо́трит	он гори́т
мы смо́трим	мы гори́м
вы смо́трите	вы гори́те
они́ смо́трят	они́ горя́т

---

1 *Otherwise, in a different way.*   2 *(All) around.*   3 **Ему́ на́до** *he must* (see below, § 9).
4 **Мо́жно** *it is permitted, one may.*   5 *One must not* (see below, § 9).

There are also some second conjugation verbs with infinitive ending in **-ать** or **-ять:**

кричáть *to shout*	держáть *to hold*	стоя́ть *to stand*
я кричý	я держý	я стою́
он кричи́т	он дéржит	он стои́т
мы кричи́м	мы дéржим	мы стои́м
вы кричи́те	вы дéржите	вы стои́те
они́ кричáт	они́ дéржат	они́ стоя́т

The number of verbs of this kind, i.e. second conjugation with infinitive in **-еть** or **-ать/-ять** is much smaller than that of *normal* first and second conjugation verbs but as the examples above show some of these verbs are very common.

6. EXERCISE I

a Read and try to understand the following passage:

Дом гори́т. Домá горя́т, нарóд стои́т и смóтрит.
Он стои́т в садý и кричи́т. Они́ стоя́т в садý и кричáт.
Не кричи́те так грóмко. Не кричи́те![1]
Женá стои́т ря́дом. Онá дéржит и бумáги и чемодáн.
Они́ дéржат и бумáги и чемодáны.

b Write down the infinitives of all the verbs used in this passage.

7. EXERCISE II

In the following sentences every verb except **идёт** is followed by a direct object, which is therefore in the accusative case. Check the gender of each direct object and decide whether the word denotes an animate being or an inanimate thing. Decide which other case these accusatives are identical with. We shall return to this in the next lesson.

Ры́бы едя́т комарóв.   Дед ест рáков.   Кот дéржит рáка.
Я держý сы́на, а дед ведёт внýка.   Он несёт котá.
Мы идём домóй и ведём и дéда, и внýков, и брáта, и дрýга.
Женá ведёт мýжа.   Он несёт индюкá.   Они́ ведýт тури́стов и матрóсов домóй.

8. THE GENITIVE AND DATIVE OF PERSONAL PRONOUNS AND THE INTERROGATIVE PRONOUNS **КТО** AND **ЧТО**

	nom.	*gen.*	*dat.*
1st pers. sing.	я *I*	меня́	мне
2nd pers. sing.	ты[2] *thou, you*	тебя́	тебé

1 **Кричи́те** is the imperative of **кричáть**, i.e. it is the command *shout!*
2 The *familiar* form of address, used in addressing relatives, close friends, children and animals. It is also used in addressing God or a saint in prayer. Cf. French *tu*, German *du*.

	nom.	gen.	dat.
3rd pers. sing., masc.	он *he, it*	его[1]	ему́
3rd pers. sing., fem.	она́ *she, it*	её	ей
3rd pers. sing., neut.	оно́ *it*	его[1]	ему́
1st pers. pl.	мы *we*	нас	нам
2nd pers. pl.	вы *you*	вас	вам
3rd pers. pl.	они́ *they*	их	им
Interrogative	кто *who*	кого́	кому́
Interrogative	что *what*	чего́	чему́

9. OBLIGATION WITH на́до

The word **на́до** (*it is*) *necessary*, (*one*) *must* is used to express obligation.

> на́до чита́ть *one must read*
> на́до дать *one must give*
> на́до рабо́тать *one must work*

If it is obvious that the obligation refers to some specific person, then such phrases as these can mean *we must read, you must read* etc. To specify on whom the obligation rests, you use the dative case:

> Мне на́до обе́дать. *I must dine.*
> Тебе́ на́до чита́ть. *You must read.*
> Ему́ на́до быть тут. *He has to be here.*

The negative **не на́до** means *must not, has not to, need not*:

> Тебе́ не на́до чита́ть. *You don't need to read.*

On its own, or with an infinitive, but no pronoun, **не на́до** can be used as the equivalent of the English *don't* in the sense of prohibition:

> Не на́до кури́ть. *Don't smoke.*
> Не на́до! Не на́до! *Don't (do that)! or Stop it!*

10. SENTENCES

Мне на́до е́хать.   Ве́чером мне ча́сто на́до рабо́тать.
Тебе́ на́до чита́ть.   Не на́до тебе́ идти́ в кино́ сего́дня.
У́тром ему́ на́до быть тут. Не на́до ему́ е́хать в Москву́. Отдыха́ть ему́ на́до.
Ей там на́до быть ра́но у́тром. Не на́до ей сейча́с идти́ в теа́тр. Никуда́[2] ей не на́до идти́.
Сего́дня нам на́до игра́ть в те́ннис. Нам не на́до обе́дать до́ма. Сейча́с уже́[3] нам на́до идти́.

---

1 Remember **г** has the value of **в** in the genitive ending **ого/его**.
2 **Никуда́... не на́до** – notice the double negative, lit. 'nowhere . . . need not'.
3 **Уже́** *already* is often added to expressions of time where English does not usually have *already*.

Вам на́до игра́ть и вам на́до бе́гать.   Вам на́до мно́го есть и отдыха́ть.
Им на́до нести́ ко́фе домо́й.   Им не на́до брать мя́со.   Им на́до нести́
ко́фе и чай домо́й.

Кому́ на́до идти́ домо́й?   Кому́ на́до е́хать?

II. REFLEXIVE PRONOUN

The word **себя́** means *oneself* and refers to whoever is the subject of the
sentence. So it will be the equivalent, according to the context, of English
myself, yourself, himself, herself, itself, ourselves, yourselves or *themselves*.
The form **себя́** is accusative or genitive. There *are* other cases but there is
no nominative since *oneself* is always the object of a verb or is governed by
a preposition.

Preposition + **себя́:** Он у себя́ до́ма. *He is at his own home.*

Here **у себя́** means at *one's own place* rather like French *chez soi.* **Он у
меня́ до́ма** means *He is at my home;* where he might feel himself quite
at home: **Тут он как у себя́ до́ма,** lit. 'Here he is as (if) at his own home'.

Verb + **себя́** is used in expressions where the subject performs the action
on himself; the action is *reflected* on to himself, so **себя́** is known as the
reflexive pronoun.

> Вести́ себя́ *to behave,* lit. 'to lead oneself'
> Он ведёт себя́ как учени́к. *He behaves like a pupil.*

12. REFLEXIVE VERBS

An older form of the reflexive pronoun **ся/сь** has become attached to many
verbs to form *reflexive verbs,* i.e. verbs which denote that the action is
performed on the subject; *it reflects back* on to the subject:

греть *to warm*	гре́ться *to warm oneself*
дви́гать *to move* (*something*)	дви́гаться *to move* (*oneself*), *to move about*
ката́ть *to roll*	ката́ться *to go for a ride* or *a drive*
ката́ться верхо́м *to go for a ride on horseback*	

Ся/сь is called the *reflexive particle* and is attached after all other verb
endings – **ся** after consonants, **сь** after vowels.

я гре́юсь	дви́гаюсь
он гре́ется	дви́гается
мы гре́емся	дви́гаемся
вы гре́етесь	дви́гаетесь
они́ гре́ются	дви́гаются

Reflexive verbs are very common in Russian. Sometimes they are used to
express the passive. Some reflexive verbs have lost all their original reflexive
meaning. We shall meet such verbs later.

Вéчером камúн грéет. Я грéюсь у камúна. Две собáки грéются у камúна. Я могý идтú в кинó, но мне не нáдо двúгаться. Кот всё двúгается кругóм, емý жáрко. Чáсто ýтром я берý сýна и мы катáемся верхóм.

И совсéм не дýрно сейчáс вéчером тúхо грéться у камúна.

Words with **ц** $\mathcal{U}$ *ц*

цирк *circus*	цúфра *number, cipher*
цыгáн *gypsy*	отéц *father*
торгóвец *trader*	кýрица *hen*
цех *department, shop* (in a factory)	центр *centre*

ица is a suffix used to form feminine from masculine nouns:

рабóчий, рабóтник *worker*	рабóтница
газéтчик *paper-seller*	газéтчица
лётчик *pilot*	лётчица

---

13. DECLENSION OF NOUNS ENDING IN **ц**

Masculine nouns ending in **ц** form the genitive plural in **ов** if the stress is on the ending, otherwise in **ев**:

близнéц *twin* близнецóв; мéсяц *month* мéсяцев

The suffix **ец** is common in masculine nouns and in nearly all instances the **е** is *mobile*, i.e. it disappears after the nominative case.[1]

	gen. sing.	nom. pl.	gen. pl.
отéц *father*	отцá	отцы́	отцóв
торгóвец *trader*	торгóвца	торгóвцы	торгóвцев

14. TRANSLATION

Round and round we go! Всё кругóм идём!

'It was hot here yesterday but today there isn't the same heat.'
'No, it's already evening and in the evening it is not so hot.'
'Where's the luggage?'
'Over there by the garage.'
'By the garage? But there are lots of garages over there. I can't live like this – you don't know where the luggage is.'

---

1 It is prevented from doing so in e.g. **близнецóв** simply by the difficulty of pronunciation which would otherwise arise.

'We live as (best) we can. There's no need to get angry (серди́ться).'
'We live differently. We live quietly.'
'It's quiet here too.'
'What?! (Как?!) There are buses and garages all around!'
'Now you are shouting. There's no need to shout.'
'I am not shouting! My wife is standing over there, she's holding a suitcase and waiting.'
'Why?' (Как так?)
'She has to live quietly. She has to rest.'
'She can rest here.'
'No, we must go.'
'There is no need to go anywhere. You can sit by the fire (у ками́на) and warm yourselves and read quietly. In the morning you can go for a ride on horseback.'
'No, I must go to Moscow.'
'To Moscow? But it's not quiet there!'
'We must go. Where is the luggage?'
'Over there, by the garage . . .'

15. EXERCISE

a Write down the infinitives of the following verbs:

ку́рит	ду́мают	стои́т	говори́т
крича́т	несёт	де́ржит	смо́трит

b Write down the first pers. sing., third pers. sing. and third pers. pl. of the following verbs:

крича́ть	горе́ть	чита́ть	вести́
держа́ть	стро́ить	стоя́ть	учи́ть

SUMMARY

1 Masculine nouns ending in **ж** form the gen. pl. in **ей** (§ 1).
2 The alternative first pers. sing. ending **-у** and third pers. pl. ending **-ат** are used in second conjugation verbs when the root ends in **ч** or **ж** (and certain other consonants) (§ 4).
3 Some second conjugation verbs have infinitives in **-еть** and some in **-ать/-ять** (§ 5).
4 Obligation is expressed by means of **на́до** used in an impersonal construction (§ 9).
5 The reflexive pronoun **себя́** refers to whoever is the subject of the sentence (§ 11).
6 Reflexive verb forms end in the reflexive particle **-ся/-сь** (§ 12).
7 Masculine nouns ending in **ц** form the gen. pl. in **ов** or **ев** depending on the stress (§ 13).

Lesson 8

$$\text{П} \quad \text{п} \quad \mathcal{P} \; \mathit{n} \qquad = \text{p}$$
$$\text{З} \quad \text{з} \quad \mathcal{Z} \; \mathit{z} \qquad = \text{z}$$

PRONUNCIATION

З is one of the letters which changes its value at the end of a word and before voiceless consonants. It then has the same value as **с,** as in:

газ *gas*   блу́зка *blouse*

I. GENITIVE OF THE THIRD PERSON PRONOUN AFTER A PREPOSITION

When the third person pronouns are controlled by a preposition they acquire an initial **н**. Hence the genitives **его́, её, их** become **него́, неё, них**.

у него́ *he has*   у неё *she has*   у них *they have*

– У кого́ дом? – У него́ дом, а у неё кварти́ра, у неё две ко́мнаты.

– А у них что? – У них и дом, и сад; а у вас?

– У нас дом, но са́да нет. У вас кварти́ра? – Да, у меня́ три ко́мнаты.

2. REVISION OF DEMONSTRATIVE AND EMPHATIC PRONOUNS

nom. sing.	*gen. sing.*	*nom. pl.*	*gen. pl.*
тот *that* (masc.)	того́		
та *that* (fem.)	той	те *those*	тех
то *that* (neut.)	того́		
сам *self* (masc.)	самого́		
сама́ *self* (fem.)	само́й	са́ми *selves*	сами́х
само́ *self* (neut.)	самого́		

У того́ до́ма нет окна́.   У тех домо́в нет о́кон.

У самого́ окна́ нет ра́мы.   У сами́х о́кон нет рам.

У той да́мы нет кварти́ры.   У тех дам нет кварти́р.

У меня́ само́й нет той бума́ги до́ма.   У нас сами́х нет тех бума́г до́ма.

3. 'ALONE'

Alone in such phrases as *I alone, you alone* etc. is expressed by **оди́н** in the appropriate gender and case, i.e. it agrees with I, you etc.:

я оди́н, ты (fem.) **одна́** etc.

I alone have **у меня́ одного́**   *I* (fem.) *alone have* **у меня́ одно́й.**

E

The word-order makes very little difference: **у одного́ меня́, у одно́й меня́** may add a slight emphasis to *I*.

у тебя́ одного́/у одного́ тебя́ ⎫
у тебя́ одно́й/у одно́й тебя́ ⎬ *you alone have*

у вас одни́х/у одни́х вас *you alone have*
у нас одни́х/у одни́х нас *we alone have*
Ма́рки у нас одни́х. *We alone have stamps.*
У вас одни́х нет книг. *You alone have no books.*
У одного́ тебя́ нет уро́ков. *You alone have no lessons.*

With the emphatic negative particle **ни – ни оди́н, ни одна́** etc. means *not a single*. The noun for the thing lacking is in the singular, and **оди́н** agrees with the noun:

У нас нет ни одно́й ма́рки. *We haven't a single stamp.*
У вас нет ни одно́й кни́ги. *You haven't a single book.*

With the noun in the plural and no negative particle **ни** the translation is somewhat different:

У нас нет одни́х ма́рок. *All we haven't got is stamps.*
У меня́ нет одни́х книг. *All I haven't got is books.*

Again **одни́** agrees with the noun for what is lacking.

The converse of this is:

У нас одни́ ма́рки. *All I have is stamps* (lit. 'I have
stamps alone').

See if you can now understand the following sentences:

У меня́ одни́ кни́ги, а сами́х уро́ков нет.
Ма́рки у них одни́х, а у него́ конве́рты, но ма́рок нет.
У сами́х сестёр[1] да́чи нет, у них одна́ кварти́ра.
У неё само́й нет рабо́ты.

4. 'ALL'

Весь may be translated as *all* or *the whole*, according to English usage. **Весь** has a mobile vowel in the nominative singular masculine only:

nom.	весь дом (*m.*)	вся кварти́ра (*f.*)	всё ме́сто (*n.*)
gen.	всего́ до́ма	всей кварти́ры	всего́ ме́ста
dat.	всему́ (*masc. and neut.*, cf. ему́)	всей (*fem.*, cf. ей)	
nom. pl.	все дома́	все кварти́ры	все места́
gen. pl.	всех домо́в	всех кварти́р	всех мест
dat. pl.	всем им		

1 Gen. pl. of **сестра́.**

50

The neuter **всё** on its own means *everything*, while the plural **все** on its own means *everybody*. **Всё** is one of the few words in which **ё** is regularly written in everyday printed matter – to distinguish it from **все,** of course.

Весь го́род наби́т битко́м. *The whole town is full up.*

Вся да́ча наби́та битко́м. *The whole villa is full up.*

Всё ме́сто наби́то битко́м. *The whole place is full up.*

Тут ка́рта райо́на (*region*), но всего́ го́рода тут нет.

Тут нет книг, все кни́ги до́ма.

Мы все до́ма ве́чером.

У́тром нас всех до́ма не бу́дет,[1] оди́н Ива́н бу́дет до́ма.

Вас всех до́ма не бу́дет у́тром,[1] одни́ де́ти бу́дут до́ма.

Всех их до́ма нет, одна́ Ни́на до́ма.

У нас всех де́ти.   У вас всех мно́го рабо́ты.

У них всех вну́чки.   Нам всем тру́дно. *It is hard for us all.*

Вам всем жа́рко. *We are all hot,* lit. 'it is hot for us all.'

Им всем ра́но. *It is too early for them all.*

Words and sentences with **п**   * Π n*

   Па́па Papa   *па́ра* pair

У па́пы нет па́ры носко́в (gen. pl.). *Papa hasn't got a pair of socks.*

сапо́г *boot*, сапога́ (gen. sing.), сапоги́ (nom. pl.), сапо́г (gen. pl., irregular)

Тут нет той па́ры сапо́г. *That pair of boots isn't here.*

пра́вда *truth; that's true*   У меня́ нет того́ но́мера «Пра́вды». *I haven't got that number of 'Pravda'.*

пра́во *right*   права́ наро́да *the people's rights*

          У тебя́ нет того́ пра́ва. *You do not have that right.*

          У нас нет всех прав. *We do not have all the rights.*

напра́во *to the right*   Вам на́до идти́ напра́во. *You have to go to the right.*

па́спорт *passport* (pl. паспорта́)   У них всех паспорта́. *They all have passports.*

пра́ктика *practice* (no. pl.)   У них мно́го пра́ктики. *They have a lot of practice.*

пре́сса *press*   пар *steam*

парохо́д (*steam*)*ship*   Сего́дня нет парохо́да. *There's no ship today.*

          Все парохо́ды иду́т на восто́к. *All the ships go east.*

          Как мно́го парохо́дов! *What a lot of ships!*

1 **Не бу́дет** *there will not be* future of **нет** *there is not*, hence the genitives **нас всех** and **вас всех.**

по́чта *post*	По́чты пока́ нет. *There's no post yet.*
перро́н *platform*	перча́тка *glove*
письмо́ *letter*	перо́ *feather, pen*
перепи́ска *correspondence*	паке́т *parcel*
поря́док (gen. . . . дка) *order*	беспоря́док (gen. . . . дка) *disorder*
пока́ *yet, for the time being*	подно́с *tray*

Тут нет той па́ры сапо́г   *Все парохо́ды иду́т на восто́к*

---

5. VERB FORMS I

The following verbs conjugate like **ду́мать**:

понима́ть *to understand*   покупа́ть *to buy*   пу́тать *to confuse, to muddle*

Я понима́ю	Он ничего́ не понима́ет.
Я покупа́ю	Она́ не то[1] покупа́ет.
Я пу́таю	Вы что-то[2] пу́таете.

– Почему́[3] вы всё пу́таете?   – Я пу́таю, потому́ что[4] не понима́ю.

6. VERB FORMS II

In these three verbs of the first conjugation the vowel in the root is **-o-**, but in the infinitive it changes to **-ы-**:

мыть *to wash*	крыть *to cover*	рыть *to dig*
я мо́ю	я кро́ю	я ро́ю
он мо́ет	он кро́ет	он ро́ет
мы мо́ем	мы кро́ем	мы ро́ем
вы мо́ете	вы кро́ете	вы ро́ете
они́ мо́ют	они́ кро́ют	они́ ро́ют

Мы́ться *to wash (oneself)* is a reflexive verb.

я мо́юсь, он мо́ется, мы мо́емся, вы мо́етесь, они́ мо́ются

Only two other verbs have this correlation of **o** in the conjugation with **ы** in the infinitive: **ныть: но́ю, но́ет** etc. *to whimper, to mope; to ache;* **выть: во́ю, во́ет** etc. *to howl.*

7. THE GENITIVE-ACCUSATIVE CASE

In Lesson 7, § 7, you were asked to decide the gender of the direct objects and whether they denoted animate beings or inanimate things. You should have come to the following conclusion: all the examples were masculine and

1 *The wrong thing*, lit. 'not that one (that she should)'.   2 *Something.*   3 *Why.*
4 *Because.*

52

denoted animate beings. You should also have noticed that they were all apparently in the genitive case. Yet they were the direct objects of non-negated verbs. In the singular, masculine nouns which denote animate beings have an accusative identical with the genitive. This accusative is known as the genitive-accusative.

	nom. sing.	*gen.-acc. sing.*
	до́ктор	до́ктора
	сын	сы́на

Pronouns and adjectives referring to 'masculine animates' also have a genitive-accusative.

In the plural, whatever the gender, nouns which denote animate beings have their accusative identical with the genitive:

	nom. pl.	*gen.-acc. pl.*
masc.	тури́ст *tourist*	тури́стов
fem.	домрабо́тница *domestic help*	домрабо́тниц

Pronouns and adjectives referring to animate beings also have a genitive-accusative plural.

Examples with the genitive-accusative:

Дя́дя (*uncle*) понима́ет тех дам.   Да, тех дам понима́ет дя́дя.[1]

Те да́мы понима́ют тех де́вочек.   Тех де́вочек понима́ют те да́мы.[1]

Те де́вочки понима́ют тех дам.   Тех дам понима́ют те де́вочки.[1]

8. THE NOMINATIVE-ACCUSATIVE CASE

You remember that the accusative of the inanimate direct object of the verb, whether the word for it is masculine or neuter, singular or plural, is the same as the nominative. This also applies to the direct object if it is a feminine word in the plural.

Мы чита́ем те кни́ги.   Те кни́ги мы чита́ем.

Те де́вочки чита́ют те кни́ги.   Те кни́ги чита́ют те де́вочки.[1]

Те сёстры нанима́ют те ко́мнаты.   Те ко́мнаты нанима́ют те сёстры.[1]

9. THE ACCUSATIVE SINGULAR OF FEMININE NOUNS AND PRONOUNS

a Feminine nouns in **a** form their accusative singular in **y**:

nom. sing.	*acc. sing.*
ко́мната *room*	ко́мнату
де́вочка *girl*	де́вочку
ма́ма *Mama*	ма́му
карти́на *picture*	карти́ну
сестра́ *sister*	сестру́
коро́бка *box*	коро́бку
до́чка *daughter*	до́чку
па́па *Papa*	па́пу (NB fem. decl.)

---

1 The form *or* the meaning of the words tells you which is subject and which is object in these sentences.

b Feminine pronouns have their accusative singular in **y** or **ю**:

nom. sing.	одна́	сама́	та	вся
acc. sing.	одну́	саму́	ту	всю

EXAMPLES

Я чита́ю всю кни́гу. Я веду́ одну́ да́му домо́й.
Сестра́ даёт мне ту коро́бку. Ту коро́бку даёт мне сестра́.
Кот ест всю ры́бу. Всю ры́бу ест кот.
Жена́ говори́т пра́вду. Муж у́чит до́чку.

Words and sentences with **з** *З з*

Заво́д и фа́брика *Не́бо и звёзды*

звезда́ *star* не́бо и звёзды *sky and stars*
заво́д *factory, works* заво́д и фа́брика *works and factory*
зуб *tooth* рот и зу́бы *mouth and teeth*
зима́ *winter* зима́ и весна́ *winter and spring*
  зимо́й и весно́й *in winter and spring*
ра́зум *reason* разу́мно *reasonably, sensibly*
Он говори́т разу́мно. неразу́мно *unwisely*
раз *time, once* оди́н раз *once*
  два ра́за, три ра́за, четы́ре ра́за, пять раз (NB gen. pl. irregular)
знать *to know* Я всё зна́ю. *I know everything.*
Ты ду́маешь, что ты всё зна́ешь. *You think (that) you know everything.*
  Он то́же ничего́ не зна́ет. *He too knows nothing.*
Он то́же ду́мает, что всё зна́ет. *He also thinks (that) he knows everything.*
забо́р *fence* зо́нтик *umbrella*
знак *sign, symbol* звоно́к (gen. звонка́) *bell*
зерно́ *grain, seed* за́втрак *breakfast*

---

10. EXERCISE

Put the words in brackets into the appropriate form of the accusative:

Она́ чита́ет (письмо́). Я чита́ю (откры́тка).
Та́ня понима́ет (та де́вочка). Сын понима́ет (те доктора́).

54

Де́вочка мо́ет (кот).

Сего́дня я жду (до́ктор).

Я дам ему́ (коро́бки).

Вы ждёте (Ни́на)?

Кто несёт (дива́ны) сюда́?

(Сын) я жду до́ма.

Вну́чка всегда́ говори́т (вся пра́вда).

Я сама́ мо́ю (до́чка).

Они́ мо́ют (ру́ки).

До́ктор даст мне (коро́бка).

Он ку́рит (папиро́са).

Нет, я жду (па́па).

До́ктор ведёт (те да́мы) туда́.

Мы зна́ем (те де́вочки).

Друг чита́ет (все пи́сьма).

Жена́ мо́ет (до́чки).

SUMMARY

1 When controlled by a preposition the third pers. pronoun has an initial **н** (§ 1).

2 *Alone* is expressed by **оди́н** in the appropriate gender and case. **Ни оди́н** means *not a single* (§ 3).

3 *All* or *the whole* is expressed by **весь** in the appropriate gender and case (§ 4).

4 A small group of five verbs has **o** in the conjugation but **ы** in the infinitive (§ 6).

5 Feminine nouns in **a** and feminine pronouns in **a/я** have the acc. sing. in **y** and **y/ю.** Otherwise the acc. is identical with nom. or gen. (§ 7, 8, 9).

The following table sums up the accusative case:

	sing.		*pl.*
masc. inanimates and neut.	}	nom. acc. {	all inanimates
masc. animates	}	gen.-acc. {	all animates

nom. sing.	*acc. sing.*
а/я	у/ю

Lesson 9

Ш ш *Ш ш* = sh

Щ щ *Щ щ* = shch

You may write **ш** with a bar underneath so that it is not confused with other letters:

ш *шипит*

Do not forget to bring the last stroke of **ш** down to the line

ш ш *шум кошка*

PRONUNCIATION

Ш represents a sound like English *sh* but in forming **ш** the tip of the tongue is curled up and touches the roof of the mouth, the body of the tongue being hollowed. **Ш** always represents a hard consonant, whatever follows it; even if the soft sign follows, it is still hard.

Щ always represents a soft sound. It is one letter but it represents a double or long consonant either like *shch* in *fish cheap* or like a long English *sh* (*not* Russian **ш**) as in *wish sheep*. The letters **сч** as in **считать** *to count* and **жч** as in **мужчина** *man* represent the same sound as **щ**.

SPELLING

Ш is one of the seven letters that cannot be followed by **ы**. Write **ши**! But keep the **ш** hard and pronounce **и** as if it were **ы**. So **шина** *tyre* sounds as though it were spelt with **ы**.

Щ too can never be followed by **ы**. Always **щи** – and here **и** retains its normal sound value. You now know the seven letters which cannot be followed by **ы** – **к, г, х, ч, ж, ш, щ**. Write only:

ки ги хи чи жи ши щи

Words with **ш** *Ш ш*

шум *noise*   шумно *noisy*

тишина *silence, quiet*   шуметь *to make a noise*

он шумит мы шумим   вы шумите они шумят

шуба *fur-coat*   кошка *cat*

Миша *Misha, Mike, short for Michael*

56

Cáша *Sasha, Sandy,* short for *Alexander*
Máша *Masha,* short for Мари́я *Mary*
меша́ть (+ dat.) *to disturb, to interfere;* (+ acc.) *to mix*
хорошо́ *good, all right, O.K.*   нехорошо́ *bad*
ши́на *tyre*   маши́на *machine; car*
машини́ст *engine-driver*   машини́стка *typist*
кры́ша *roof* (cf. крыть *to cover*)

---

1. EXERCISE

a Тут так мно́го шу́ма.   Тут так шу́мно.
Нет, тут не шу́мно, тут ти́хо[1] – тут уро́к.
Тут нет шу́ма, тут ти́хо – стои́т тишина́,[2] да, тишина́.
А сейча́с у вас до́ма шум? У вас шу́мно? У вас[3] де́ти игра́ют и шумя́т?
Да, де́ти игра́ют и шумя́т, нам тру́дно.
Не на́до шуме́ть.   Éсли они́ шумя́т, коне́чно вам тру́дно.
Я и говорю́,[4] что мне о́чень тру́дно.   Они́ всё вре́мя шумя́т.

b – У вас шу́ба? – Нет, у меня́ нет шу́бы, а одна́ да́ма, вот та да́ма,[5] покупа́ет шу́бу. Она́ сего́дня покупа́ет шу́бу, а я не покупа́ю.

c – Ми́ша, Cáша, Máша, пора́ идти́.[6] Ну, ребя́та, идём домо́й.[7]
– Нам не на́до меша́ть, меша́ть нехорошо́.
– Я вам меша́ю?
– Нет, вы мне не меша́ете, а вот[8] де́ти меша́ют. До́ма всё шум, всегда́[9] шум; они́ всё вре́мя шумя́т. Да, мне де́ти всегда́ меша́ют рабо́тать.
– Де́ти всегда́ кому́-то[10] меша́ют. Почему́ де́ти всегда́ меша́ют кому́-то?
– Де́ти всегда́ меша́ют, потому́ что они́ всё вре́мя шумя́т. Где де́ти – там шум.

d – Тут ши́на маши́ны. Маши́на не идёт.[11] Вот ши́на маши́ны, но где меха́ник? Меха́ника нет. Где он? Почему́ его́ тут нет? Где шофёр?
– Меха́ник идёт сейча́с.
– У него́ папиро́са. Тут не на́до кури́ть, а он ку́рит. Тут не ку́рят.

2. NUMBERS

The numbers one to ten are: **оди́н/одна́/одно́, два/две, три, четы́ре, пять, шесть, семь, во́семь, де́вять, де́сять.**
2, 3, 4, control the genitive singular, 5 to 10 control the genitive plural:
одна́ ко́шка, две/три/четы́ре ко́шки, пять/шесть ко́шек etc.

1 *Quiet.*   2 Lit. 'stands silence'; trans. *there is silence.*   3 Trans. *your.*   4 **И** here is emphatic particle; trans. *that's what I'm saying.*   5 *That lady over there.*   6 *It's time to go;* **пора́** *it's time.*   7 *Well, chaps, let's go home* (**домо́й**).   8 Omit or trans. *but the children here.*   9 *Always.*   10 Dat. of **кто́-то** *somebody.*   11 Trans. *won't go.*

3. 'YOUNGSTERS'

The names of young animals end in **ёнок**, the **o** being a mobile vowel, so that the genitive ends in **ёнка.**

котёнок *kitten*   котёнка   Кóшка несёт котёнка.

These nouns are masculine in the singular but have a neuter declension in the plural; the ending **ёнок** is changed to **ята.**

nom. sing.	*nom. pl.*
котёнок	котя́та

After **ш, ж, ч** these endings are written **óнок** and **а́та.**

nom. sing.	*gen. sing.*	*nom. pl.*	*gen. pl.*
котёнок *kitten*	котёнка	котя́та	котя́т
ребёнок *child*	ребёнка	ребя́та	ребя́т
поросёнок *piglet*	поросёнка	порося́та	порося́т
медвежóнок *bear-cub*	медвежóнка	медвежáта	медвежáт

The word **ребёнок** *child* has **дéти** as its plural. The plural **ребя́та** means *chaps, folks, kids, lads* and need not necessarily apply to children.

мнóго котя́т	мнóго ребя́т	мнóго порося́т
нет котя́т	нет ребя́т	нет порося́т
два котёнка	два ребёнка	два поросёнка

два, три, четы́ре котёнка

пять, шесть котя́т	пять, шесть ребя́т	пять, шесть порося́т

Там ма́ма, и па́па, и там ребя́та.

Все дéти, все ребя́та шумя́т.

Дéти читáют кни́гу.

Дéти счита́ют оди́н, два, три. *The children are counting one, two, three.*

4. VERB FORMS I

The second pers. sing. of the present and future conjugation ends in **шь,** the soft sign having no effect on the pronunciation of **ш.**

First Conjugation

ты дýмаешь *you think*	ты бéгаешь *you run about*
ты мóешь *you wash*	ты крóешь *you cover*
ты меша́ешь *you disturb*	ты покупа́ешь *you buy*
ты понима́ешь *you understand*	ты пу́таешь *you confuse*
ты грéешь *you warm*	ты бу́дешь *you will be*
ты идёшь *you go, come*	ты éдешь *you go*
ты берёшь *you take*	ты живёшь *you live*

Second Conjugation

ты говори́шь *you say*	ты вéришь *you believe*
ты стои́шь *you stand*	ты стрóишь *you build*
ты шуми́шь *you make a noise*	ты кýришь *you smoke*

Like **ты,** the second pers. sing. is used only when addressing intimates, children or animals.

5. VERB FORMS II – IRREGULAR VERBS

Here are the complete conjugations of three common, irregular verbs. You have already noticed the exceptional first pers. sing. and third pers. sing. of *to eat* and *to give*, as well as the д which occurs in the plural of these verbs. Notice that *to want* is first conjugation in the singular but second conjugation in the plural. Moreover, in the singular the т of the root changes to ч. This is another of the possible consonant changes (we have already met the change of г into ж in Lesson 7, § 2).

хотéть *to want*	есть *to eat*	дать *to give*
я хочý *I want*	я ем *I eat*	я дам *I shall give*
ты хóчешь	ты ешь	ты дашь
он хóчет	он ест	он даст
мы хотúм	мы едúм	мы дадúм
вы хотúте	вы едúте	вы дадúте
онú хотя́т	онú едя́т	онú дадýт (NB у!)

6. EXERCISE

– Ты идёшь домóй?

– Нет, не идý; мне нáдо рабóтать. Ты мне мешáешь. Ты всё[1] кýришь и говорúшь и шумúшь тут; как ты не понимáешь, что ты мне прóсто[2] мешáешь. Я всё пýтаю.

– Почемý ты так говорúшь? Что ты хóчешь есть?

– Я совсéм не хочý есть. Ну, что тебé нáдо?[3]

– Ты хóчешь, я тебé дам...

– Я ничегó не хочý!

– А папирóсы ты не хóчешь?

– Ну да, папирóсы.... Ты мне мóжешь дать две–три[4] папирóсы?

– Вот[5] я тебé дам пáчку (*packet*).

– Спасúбо! Спасúбо! Но я тебé говорю́, что ты мне мешáешь. Ты всё[6] тут стоúшь.

– Хорошó! Хорошó! Я идý.

Words with **щ** *Щ, щ*

Никúта Хрущёв *Nikita Khrushchov*
ищú *seek! look for it!* щи *cabbage-soup*
борщ *beetroot-soup* пúща *food*
жéнщина *woman* товáрищ *comrade*
жéнщина *товáрищ*

---

1 *Always, all the time.*   2 *Simply.*   3 *What do you need/want?*   4 *Two or three.*
5 *Here you are.*   6 *Still.*

59

Verbs with the infinitive ending in **-ять** preceded by **e** belong to the first conjugation:

смея́ться *to laugh*	се́ять *to sow*	ве́ять *to blow, to winnow*
я смею́сь	я се́ю	я ве́ю
ты смеёшься	ты се́ешь	ты ве́ешь
он смеётся	он се́ет	он ве́ет
мы смеёмся	мы се́ем	мы ве́ем
вы смеётесь	вы се́ете	вы ве́ете
они́ смею́тся	они́ се́ют	они́ ве́ют

Смея́ться is a *formally reflexive* verb, i.e. it is reflexive in form but not in meaning. It does not mean *to laugh at oneself* but simply *to laugh.*

Же́нщина смеётся. *The woman is laughing.*
Това́рищи смею́тся. *The friends are laughing.*
Ве́тер ве́ет. *The wind is blowing.*
Ве́тры ве́ют. *The winds are blowing.*
Он се́ет зерно́. *He is sowing grain.*
Они́ се́ют зерно́. *They are sowing grain.*

8. EXERCISE

Read the following passages for comprehension. Then study the pronouns in the passage and decide which nouns they refer to. Decide too which of the pronouns are the object of the sentence and what case they remind you of.

a Домрабо́тнина идёт на ры́нок покупа́ть ры́бу. Мы зна́ем, что она́ сама́ ест её ве́чером. Мы еди́м ку́рицу¹ – нам на́до её конча́ть сего́дня. Они́ едя́т ку́рицу. Да, они́ её едя́т на обе́д.²

b Мы нанима́ем рабо́тника. Мы его́ нанима́ем ра́но у́тром, но нам ча́сто его́ на́до ждать. Он у нас начина́ет ремо́нт.³ Он его́ всё начина́ет. Рабо́та уже́ идёт ме́сяц. Он её начина́ет, но ничего́ не конча́ет. То⁴ у него́ нет кра́ски,⁵ то⁴ у него́ нет изве́стки.⁵ – Вы зна́ете, что вам на́до рабо́тать системати́чески, мы ему́ говори́м. – Да, да, на́до, на́до, я зна́ю! Коне́чно на́до! Он говори́т ти́хо и ведёт себя́ скро́мно,⁶ но рабо́та не конча́ется. Нам так жить неудо́бно.⁷ Невозмо́жно! – Да, да, зна́ю, зна́ю, я понима́ю, коне́чно я вас понима́ю! и я сего́дня рабо́таю системати́чески и бы́стро, говори́т он, но ему́ всё равно́.⁸

c У нас живёт и брат му́жа. Потому́ что у нас хао́с до́ма, мы ведём его́ в конто́ру. Он берёт рома́н и его́ чита́ет весь день. Он мо́жет чита́ть весь день одну́ кни́гу. Он конча́ет чита́ть её ве́чером до́ма.

---

1 *Chicken.*   2 *For dinner.*   3 *Repairs, redecoration.*   4 **То... то** *now ... now or first ... then.*   5 *Gen. of* **кра́ска** *paint and* **изве́стка** *lime.*   6 *Modestly, quietly, nicely.*   7 *Inconvenient, uncomfortable.*   8 *It's all the same to him, he doesn't care.*

Так он читáет мнóго книг. Он их начинáет и кончáет их все. Не все книги ромáны. Ромáны он кончáет бы́стро. Он их бы́стро читáет.

9. TRANSLATION

Use **ты** and second pers. sing.

A Quiet Little Corner[1]

HUSBAND	Noise, noise, noise all the time. It disturbs me. How can I work?
WIFE	Children, you're making a noise!
HUSBAND	I can't work. It is so noisy here.
WIFE	Of course, it's difficult for you when they make a noise.
HUSBAND	I keep saying[2] it's difficult for me.
WIFE	Still, they aren't making a noise all the time.
	(*A noise.*)
WIFE	What's that?
HUSBAND	Cars. When the children aren't making a noise, it's the cars.[3]
WIFE	Yes, but not all the time. There are no cars passing now.[4]
HUSBAND	No, but that engine-driver – he lives next door[5] – comes home and shouts.
WIFE	(It's) a typist (who) lives next door, I think, not an engine-driver.
HUSBAND	Yes, that's right. She comes home early and starts to work. She works in the evening too.[6]
WIFE	Where are you going? Don't you want to eat?
HUSBAND	No, I don't want anything. Perhaps you'll give me two or three cigarettes?
WIFE	Here you are.[7] I'll give you the whole packet. But where are you going?
HUSBAND	Thanks. Where am I going? I'm going to the park. It's quiet there.
WIFE	But the children play there.
HUSBAND	Yes, but they don't disturb me. Goodbye.
WIFE	Goodbye.

1 **Тихий уголóк.** 2 **Я и говорю́.** 3 Say *the cars make a noise.* 4 Say *now cars are not going past.* 5 **Ря́дом.** 6 Put **и** in front of *in the evening* to express *too.* 7 **Вот.**

SUMMARY

1 Sing. and pl. declensions of nouns ending in **ёнок** (§ 3).
2 The second pers. sing. of the verb ends in **-шь** (§ 4).
3 **Хотéть** like **дать** and **есть** has an irregular conjugation (§ 5).
4 Verbs with infinitive in **-ять** preceded by **е** are first conjugation (§ 7).

LESSON 10 REVISION

Lesson 11

Л л *Л л* = L l

Л is written rather like an English copperplate capital A - *A* - without the cross-bar. The initial hook is an essential part of this letter and must always be written, whatever comes in front:

Луна́ луна́ стул стол па́лка

PRONUNCIATION

This diagram shows the position of the tongue in relation to upper teeth and palate when pronouncing hard **л**.

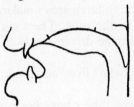

Words with **л** *Л л*

стол *table*	пол *floor; sex; half*
на_пол *on to the floor*	на полу́ *on the floor*
вол *ox*	у́гол (gen. угла́) *corner, angle*
в у́гол *into the corner*	в углу́ *in the corner*
стул *chair*	гул *dull, humming noise*
волк *wolf*	полк *regiment*
ло́дка *boat*	па́лка *stick*
бу́лка *roll*	иго́лка *needle*
хо́лод *cold*	хо́лодно *cold* (adj. and adv.)
го́лод *hunger*	го́лодно *hungry* (adj. and adv.)
холостя́к *batchelor*	челове́к *man, person*

чуло́к *stocking* gen. sing. чулка́ nom. pl. чулки́
gen. pl. чуло́к (irregular).

ла́мпа *lamp*	светло́ *bright, light* (adv.)
ма́ло *few, little*	пло́хо *bad(ly)*
полно́ *full*	тепло́ *warm(ly)*
буты́лка *bottle*	кре́сло *arm-chair*
ве́село *gaily*	де́ло *business, affair, thing*

Practice saying: У вас не ло́дка, а во́дка.

I. EXERCISE

A conversation between Peter and Vera:

– У вас тут хао́с – вы холостяки́, у вас тут беспоря́док и хо́лодно.

– Непра́вда, у нас тут совсе́м не хао́с. Никако́го[1] хао́са, никако́го беспоря́дка у нас нет. У нас поря́док, всё о́чень хорошо́ и аккура́тно.[2] Да, аккура́тно.

– Совсе́м не аккура́тно, вот тут стоя́т и сапоги́, и сыр, и вот тут бума́ги и носки́, а тут, да, тут па́ра чуло́к. Пе́тя, отку́да они́? Почему́ у холостяка́ па́ра чуло́к?

– Тут, тут – ничего́...

– Как так ничего́?[3]

– Ничего́ тут нет, совсе́м нет чуло́к; тут бума́га, а не чулки́... Вот беда́![4] Вот всё сюда́[5] в у́гол и на_пол, и всё сейча́с бу́дет аккура́тно – вот сапоги́ сюда́, и носки́ сюда́, а чулки́ – чулки́ сестры́ вот сюда́.

– А тепе́рь ты говори́шь, что[6] то не бума́га, а чулки́?

– Да, да, чулки́ сестры́ Ни́ны – чулки́ сюда́.[5] Ве́ра, ты мне не ве́ришь?

– Как я могу́ тебе́ ве́рить? Как я могу́ тебе́ не ве́рить? У тебя́ просто́ хао́с, и мне хо́лодно.[7] Я иду́ домо́й.

– Как так хо́лодно? У меня́ ками́н[8] хорошо́ гре́ет. Не на́до идти́ домо́й. Вот кре́сло. Тут тепло́, совсе́м не хо́лодно.[9]

– Кре́сло полно́ книг.

– И кни́ги сюда́ в у́гол и на_пол.

– Всё у тебя́ в углу́ и на полу́. Всю́ду[10] беспоря́док. У холостяко́в всегда́ хао́с.

– Непра́вда, у холостяко́в поря́док. У же́нщин хао́с, да, вот[11] у же́нщин хао́с. У меня́ тут о́чень хорошо́, тепло́. Вот и ла́мпа гори́т.[12] У меня́ две буты́лки вина́ и две буты́лки пи́ва. Четы́ре буты́лки хва́тит.[13] Вот буты́лка вина́. Я тебе́ сейча́с дам рю́мку вина́. Ми́ша и Ни́на ско́ро тут бу́дут. Ско́ро бу́дет обе́д. Вот как хорошо́ вино́ гре́ет.[14] Вот[15] ви́дишь, как тут хорошо́.

– Да, тепе́рь мне не хо́лодно. Пра́вда, что ками́н гре́ет хорошо́. Мне совсе́м не хо́лодно, мне тепло́.

Further illustrations of **л**

сло́во *word*   nom. pl. слова́   gen. pl. слов.

луна́ *moon*

Вот луна́, и светло́ и ве́село. *Here's the moon, it's bright and gay.*

1 **Никако́й** *not any, no.*   2 *Neat, tidy.*   3 *What do you mean – nothing?*
4 *What a calamity!*   5 English would need a verb here: *Let's put* or *I'll put.*
6 As a conjunction **что** = *that.*   7 Impersonal expression. Words like **хо́лодно, тепло́** with the dative mean, e.g. *I am cold, I am warm.*
8 *My fire;* **ками́н** *fire-place, (open) fire.*   9 *It's not cold at all;* **совсе́м** *quite, at all.*
10 *Everywhere.*   11 *That's it!*   12 *And now the lamp/light is lit.*
13 **Хва́тит** *will be enough.*   14 *See how well the wine warms (you up).*   15 *There.*

ла́вка *small shop, stall*   шко́ла *school*

Где ла́вка? Ла́вка у шко́лы, там на углу́. *The shop is by the school, there on the corner.*

мы́ло *soap*   во́лос *a hair* nom. pl. во́лосы

Где мы́ло? Мне на́до мыть во́лосы.

го́лос *voice* nom. pl. голоса́   слы́шать *to hear*

Тут шко́ла и я слы́шу голоса́ ребя́т.

посы́лка *parcel (post)*   посыла́ть *to send*

кана́л *canal*   Кана́л где? Вот там кана́л, а тут река́ Во́лга.

сканда́л *scandal, row*   У них сканда́л! Вот пло́хо! *They're having a row! That's bad!*

бал *ball*   У нас бал – вот ве́село. *We're having a ball. What fun!*

баскетбо́л *basketball*   Они́ хорошо́ игра́ют в баскетбо́л.

гол *goal*   У них два го́ла – нет, три го́ла. Ма́ло!

У нас мно́го голо́в – у нас пять голо́в, а тепе́рь шесть голо́в (. . . and now we have six goals).

голки́пер *goalkeeper*   Голки́пер пло́хо игра́ет сего́дня.

мно́го голо́в *many goals* or *many heads*

голова́ *head*   nom. pl. го́ловы   gen. pl. голо́в

Голки́пер пло́хо игра́ет сего́дня

---

2. PAST TENSE I

In Russian the past tense is not conjugated. It changes its ending according to the gender and number of the subject.

л is the sign of the past tense.

For the great majority of verbs the infinitive ending **-ть** is removed and **-л** is added to form the past tense masculine, **-ла** the past tense feminine and **-ло** the past tense neuter.

Infinitive	Past tense masc.	fem.	neut.
ду́ма – ть *to think*	ду́ма – л	ду́ма – ла	ду́ма – ло
мы – ть *to wash*	мы – л	мы́ – ла	мы́ – ло
е́ха – ть *to travel*	е́ха – л	е́ха – ла	е́ха – ло
стоя́ – ть *to stand*	стоя́ – л	стоя́ – ла	стоя́ – ло
бра – ть *to take*	бра – л	бра – ла́	бра́ – ло

We shall deal with the plural ending later. It is important to remember that there is only one past tense in Russian.

3. EXERCISE WITH THE PAST TENSE

a Я стоя́л, я брал мы́ло и мыл ру́ки и ду́мал.

Да, ты стоя́л, ты брал мы́ло и мыл ру́ки и ду́мал.

Он стоя́л, он брал мы́ло и мыл ру́ки и ду́мал.
Мы́ло мы́ло, оно́ мы́ло хорошо́. *The soap washed, it washed well.*

b быть *to be*   игра́ть *to play*   говори́ть *to speak/say*
слу́шать *to listen*   де́лать *to do*

У́тром я была́ до́ма. Я слу́шала ра́дио. Ра́дио что́-то игра́ло.
Па́па совсе́м не говори́л. Я говори́ла ма́ло и де́лала уро́ки.
У́тром ты была́ до́ма. Ты слу́шала ра́дио. Ра́дио что́-то игра́ло.
Па́па совсе́м не говори́л. Ты говори́ла ма́ло и де́лала уро́ки.
У́тром она́ была́ до́ма. Она́ слу́шала ра́дио. Она́ говори́ла ма́ло
и де́лала уро́ки.

c   стро́ить *to build*   рабо́тать *to work*
           кури́ть *to smoke*   смотре́ть *to look*

Дя́дя стро́ил до́мик в саду́. Но он ма́ло рабо́тал – он стоя́л, он смотре́л
и мно́го кури́л.
Дя́дя, когда́ ты стро́ил до́мик в саду́, ты ма́ло рабо́тал, ты стоя́л,
смотре́л и мно́го кури́л.

4. PAST TENSE II

Идти́ *to go* forms its past tense from a different root:

masc.	fem.	neut.
я шёл	я шла	—
ты шёл	ты шла	—
он шёл	она́ шла	оно́ шло

Notice the mobile vowel **ё,** which occurs only in the masculine form.

Я (masc.) бы́стро шёл домо́й.
Я (fem.) бы́стро шла в конто́ру.
Су́дно шло на юг.
Куда́ ты (fem.) шла так ра́но у́тром?
Я (fem.) шла в конто́ру, а ты (masc.) шёл домо́й.

5. PAST TENSE III

In general, verbs with infinitive in **-ти** or in **-ть** preceded by a consonant
do not entirely follow the simple rule given for forming the past tense of
verbs with infinitive in **-ть** preceded by a vowel.

a **Нести́** *to carry* has **с** in the infinitive and in the present tense, **я несу́**
etc. The **с** remains in the past tense but in the past tense masculine there
is no **л** since **сл** and **зл** never occur at the end of verb forms:

он нёс   она́ несла́   оно́ несло́

Он нёс муку́ (*flour*) и буты́лку вина́, а я несла́ помидо́ры (*tomatoes*) и
мя́со (*meat*).

b **Вести́** *to lead* has **с** in the infinitive only, but in the present tense it has **д:**
я веду́ etc. Verbs with infinitive in **-сти** or **-сть** and **д** or **т** in the present

F   65 or future tense drop the last three letters of the infinitive in forming the past tense.

он вёл   она́ вела́   оно́ вело́

Ты вёл сестру́ домо́й, когда́ я вела́ ма́му и шла в конто́ру.

Он ведёт до́ктора домо́й.   Он вёл до́ктора домо́й.

Муж шёл домо́й и нёс мно́го паке́тов.   Жена́ шла домо́й и вела́ сы́на.

Он никого́ не вёл.   Она́ ничего́ не несла́, кро́ме су́мки (*apart from her handbag*).   Всё шло хорошо́.   До́ма их ждал (*waited for*) тури́ст.   У него́ бы́ло мно́го чемода́нов (*suitcases*).   Он сам нёс чемода́ны, но шёл бы́стро.

The rules given above determine the past tense of the following verbs:

infin.	*fut.*	*past*
укра́сть *to steal*	я украду́ ты украдёшь	укра́л, укра́ла, укра́ло

Я не укра́л чемода́н.   Она́ не укра́ла кни́ги.

упа́сть *to fall down*	я упаду́ ты упадёшь	упа́л, упа́ла, упа́ло

Чемода́н упа́л на_пол.   Кни́га упа́ла на_пол.

сесть *to sit down*	я ся́ду (NB vowel change) ты ся́дешь	сел, се́ла, се́ло

Я сел на дива́н.   Сестра́ се́ла на дива́н.

6. ASPECTS OF VERBS

You have noticed that with some verbs the conjugation has a present meaning:

я беру́ *I take*   я ем *I eat*   я стою́ *I stand*   я творю́ *I create*

with others it has a future meaning:

я дам *I shall give*   я украду́ *I shall steal*   я растворю́ *I shall dissolve*

All Russian verbs have built into them a comment on or a particular view of the action performed. This view or way of regarding the action is called *aspect*. With a handful of exceptions, all Russian verbs have two aspects.

If you want to draw attention to or emphasize the fact that the action is completed you use what is called the *perfective* aspect.

If you do not want to emphasize completion or if you are thinking of the action as going on, in process of being performed, you use the *imperfective* aspect.

Those verbs which, when conjugated, have a future meaning (**я дам, я украду́** etc.) are perfective and their conjugation is in the *future perfective*. This means that though the action is not yet performed you are thinking

66

of it as a completed action in the future. As you will see later, there is also a future imperfective, used when you are thinking of the action going on in the future or as consisting of a whole series of acts in the future.

The present tense has only one aspect, imperfective, because the action is going on as you speak of it or it consists of a whole series of acts that are performed time after time, as in: **Я ча́сто чита́ю рома́ны** *I often read novels.*

The same aspect difference applies to the past tense too:

perfective = completed action, very often a single act
imperfective = action going on, or a series of acts being
performed time after time in the past.

Он стоя́л на углу́ и дал мне паке́т. *He was standing on the corner and gave me a parcel.*

Стоя́л is imperfective because the action is not one which you want to emphasize the completion of: *he went on standing, he kept standing there.*

Дал is perfective because he completed the act of giving: *he gave me the packet* and that was that.

Я получи́л паке́т. *I received the parcel.*

Получи́л is perfective, because the act of receiving was completed: *I took the packet* and that was that. But

he was still standing on the corner но он всё стоя́л на углу́.

The infinitive is also modified by the aspect system, so nearly every verb has two sets of forms.

The *imperfective* has an infinitive
a present tense conjugation
a past tense
a compound future tense

The *perfective* has an infinitive
a past tense
a future tense conjugation

The conjugation and the past tense are formed according to the same rules in both aspects.

7. TRANSLATION: EXERCISE ON PAST TENSE

Who[1] was doing what and who was going where?

'The woman was standing over there but (my) brother was standing here.'
'No, Peter was standing over there.'
'Peter was at home in the morning, I thought.'
'I don't know – but his sister was at home in the evening.'

1 With **кто** introducing a question always use the *masculine singular* form of the past tense, even if you are thinking of a woman or more than one person.

'Yes, she was washing her hair.'

'No, I was listening to the radio but father was talking all the time.'

'That's not true – he said very little. Nina was talking all the time.'

'And Alexander was washing his hands and making a lot of noise.'

'Yes, I had been building[1] a hut[2] in the garden.'

'You were building a hut? When Tanya saw you, you were standing and smoking.'

'Who? Me?[3] I don't smoke. Irina smokes a lot – she smoked[4] all the cigarettes yesterday. She smoked a lot of cigarettes.'

'She works hard.'[5]

'Perhaps.[6] She was going home early, when I saw her.'

'She wasn't going home. She was going to the office.'

'In the evening? I saw her in the morning too and she wasn't going to the office.'

'Father was going to the park[7] and had the dog on the lead.'[8]

'Vera was going to the office, you were saying?'

'No, Masha was going to the office.'

'Did you see Sonya? Was she bringing[8] (our) son home?'

'I didn't see her. I saw Tanya. She was carrying an umbrella and your son was there too. He was carrying her handbag.'[9]

'But father was waiting for them at home!'

'Who[10] was he waiting for?'

'Well,[11] I don't know. . . . You've confused[12] me.'

---

1 **Стро́ил** since completion is not indicated.   2 **До́мик.**   3 Nominative case in Russian: **Я.**   4 **Вы́курила** a perfective of **кури́ла** meaning *smoked (them) up.*
5 **Мно́го.**   6 **Мо́жет быть.**   7 **В парк.**   8 Say 'was leading', using the past of **вести́.**   9 *Handbag* **су́мка.**   10 NB accusative case: **кого́.**   11 **Ну.**
12 The perfective infinitive of **пу́тать** is **спу́тать**; form the past tense in the usual way.

SUMMARY

1 The past tense changes according to gender and number: **-л** is masculine, **-ла** feminine and **-ло** neuter (§ 2).

2 **Идти́** has a past tense formed from a different root: **шёл, шла, шло** (§ 4).

3 Some verbs do not have **л** in the past tense masculine (§ 5).

4 Verbs with infinitive in **-сти** or **-сть** and having a root ending in **д** or **т** omit the last three letters of the infinitive in forming the past tense (§ 5).

5 The tenses (and the infinitive) are modified in meaning by the aspects, the perfective emphasizing *completion* of an action, the imperfective not doing so (§ 6).

Lesson 12

$$Э \quad э \quad \mathcal{Э} \quad э = e$$

Э is called **э оборо́тное** *backwards* **Э**

э́тот   э́та   э́то   э́ти

PRONUNCIATION

When **л** is followed by **е, ё, и, ю, я** or **ь** it represents soft **л**. The two diagrams below show the position of the tongue in relation to teeth and palate in pronouncing soft **л**.

Э has the same vowel value as **e** but lacks the initial *y* element or the softening effect.

I. VERBS, FIRST CONJUGATION

We have so far met several groups of verbs of the first conjugation, having **e** with a preceding vowel in most forms of the present tense. The largest group is that typified by **ду́мать: я ду́маю, ты ду́маешь, он ду́мает** etc.

There is a small group with **o** before the **e** and with infinitive in **-ыть: мыть: я мо́ю, ты мо́ешь, он мо́ет** etc. (Lesson 8, § 6), and a somewhat larger group with infinitive in **-ять** preceded by a vowel: **се́ять: я се́ю, ты се́ешь, он се́ет** etc. (Lesson 9, § 7).

There are three groups of verbs of the first conjugation with the infinitive ending in **-ава́ть** which drop the **-ва-** element in the conjugation. The commonest verbs of these three groups are **дава́ть** *to give*, **встава́ть** *to get up, to stand up*, **узнава́ть** *to recognize*. **Встава́ть** and **узнава́ть** are compound verbs. They consist of a root-verb, **-става́ть** and **-знава́ть** respectively, with a prefix (**в-** and **у-**). These root-verbs never occur without a prefix and they form other compounds with other prefixes. **Дава́ть** may also form compounds but it frequently occurs without a prefix. All these are *imperfective* (Lesson 11, § 6). You have already met the perfective that forms a pair with the imperfective **дава́ть**, namely **дать: я дам** *I shall give*, **ты дашь** *you will give*, **он даст** *he will give* etc.

Here are the *present* tenses of these three verbs, which have the same form of conjugation:

давáть	вставáть	узнавáть
я даю́	встаю́	узнаю́
ты даёшь	встаёшь	узнаёшь
он даёт	встаёт	узнаёт
мы даём	встаём	узнаём
вы даёте	встаёте	узнаёте
они́ даю́т	встаю́т	узнаю́т

NB the final stress. The verb **плáвать** *to swim, to sail* as you see is not an **-авáть** verb. It and its compounds have a normal **дýмать** type conjugation: **я плáваю, ты плáваешь** etc.

2. VERBS, FIRST CONJUGATION (CONTINUED)

There is a very large group of verbs with the infinitive ending in **-овать** in which **-ова-** changes to **-у-** in the conjugation:

торговáть *to trade*	совéтовать *to advise*
я торгу́ю	совéтую
ты торгу́ешь	совéтуешь
он торгу́ет	совéтует
мы торгу́ем	совéтуем
вы торгу́ете	совéтуете
они́ торгу́ют	совéтуют

This large group of verbs in modern Russian contains many verbs based on roots from other languages. Sometimes the **-овать** is preceded by another element **-ир-** or **-из-** or the two elements together **-изир-**, producing **-ировать, -изовать** and **-изировать.** In these verbs too the **-ова-** changes to **-у-** but the **-ир-, -из-** and **-изир-** remain unaltered. Many technical and scientific verbs are formed in this way.

You should be able to guess the meaning of the following verbs. Practice conjugating some of them.

адресовáть	телефони́ровать	телеграфи́ровать
иронизи́ровать	организовáть	атаковáть
абстраги́ровать	публиковáть	национализовáть

3. EXERCISE

Verbs of the types described in the preceding two sections form the past tense according to the rules given in Lesson 11, § 2.

Он мне даёт кóфе и идёт на слýжбу (*to the office, to work*).

Он мне давáл кóфе и шёл на слýжбу.

Мне не нáдо давáть кóфе ýтром. *There's no need to give* or *Don't give me* etc.

Онá встаёт рáно ýтром.   Онá вставáла рáно ýтром.

Ей на́до встава́ть ра́но у́тром. *She has to* etc.

Он нас узнаёт? Он нас узнава́л?

Ему́ тру́дно узнава́ть всех сосе́дей.[1] *It's difficult for him to recognize all his neighbours.*

Он торгу́ет на углу́. *He carries on his trade on the corner.*

Он торгова́л на углу́. Ему́ тру́дно торгова́ть на том углу́. *It's hard for him* etc.

Я тебе́ сове́тую[2] идти́ домо́й. Я тебе́ сове́товала идти́ домо́й.

Мне не на́до тебе́ сове́товать. (*There's no need for me* etc.)

Words with soft л

Еле́на *Helen*. Pet forms of this name are:

Ле́на, Ле́нушка, Ле́ночка, Лёля, Ля́ля

лес *forest*	лесни́к *forester*
лист *a leaf* or *a piece of paper*	
Елизаве́та *Elizabeth* pet forms Ли́за, Ли́зочка	
коро́ль *king*	короле́ва *queen*
Короле́ва Елизаве́та Пе́рвая *Queen Elizabeth I*	
Короле́ва Елизаве́та Втора́я *Queen Elizabeth II*	
неде́ля *week*	ле́то *summer*
земля́ *earth, land*	лю́ди *people*

---

4. PAST TENSE PLURAL

The plural of the past tense, for all genders, ends in **-ли** with soft **л**. Here are some sentences in which nearly all the verbs are in the past tense plural:

Они́ мне дава́ли ко́фе и шли на слу́жбу. Они́ встава́ли ра́но у́тром и сове́товали мне встава́ть ра́но.

Они́ там до́лго жи́ли. Они́ говори́ли, что сосе́ди не узнава́ли их.

Муж и жена́ е́хали вме́сте на ры́нок. Они́ там торгова́ли. Ры́нок был у моста́. Лю́ди там стоя́ли, гро́мко говори́ли, смея́лись и мно́го всего́[3] покупа́ли. Де́ти бе́гали, игра́ли и крича́ли. Бы́ло ве́село.[4]

5. DAYS OF THE WEEK

понеде́льник	*Monday*
вто́рник	*Tuesday* (cf. второ́й, втора́я, второ́е *second*)
среда́	*Wednesday* (cf. середи́на *middle*)

1 **Сосе́д** *neighbour* is exceptional in that it has soft endings in the plural and, as will be seen later, many nouns with soft endings form the genitive plural in **ей.**

2 **Сове́товать** has the *dative* of the person to whom advice is given.

3 *All sorts of things.* 4 *It was jolly.*

четве́рг	*Thursday* (cf. четвёртый, четвёртая, четвёртое *fourth*)
пя́тница	*Friday* (cf. пя́тый, пя́тая, пя́тое *fifth*)
суббо́та	*Saturday*
воскресе́нье	*Sunday*

6. ACCUSATIVE CASE AFTER **в** I – MOTION

The accusative is used, as you have seen, to express the direct object of a verb. It is also used after certain prepositions.

The preposition **в** with the accusative case means *into*, i.e. motion is implied:

> Я иду́ в го́род. *I go into town.*
> Мы идём в сад. *We go into the garden.*   Они́ иду́т в лес.
> Она́ идёт в конто́ру. (*to the office*).   Он идёт в ко́мнату.

В + accusative is used to express *into town* and also *to a specified town*. Russian assumes that you will actually go into the town.

> Мы идём в го́род.   Мы е́дем в Рим.
> Вы е́дете в Ло́ндон, а они́ е́дут в Эдинбу́рг.
> Мы е́дем в Пари́ж (*Paris*).
> Они́ е́хали в Москву́ (*Moscow*), а мы е́хали в Варша́ву (*Warsaw*).

Moscow and *Warsaw* are feminine nouns ending in **a: Москва́, Варша́ва,** and therefore have accusative in **y.**

В + accusative is also used to express *to a particular continent or country:*

> Дя́дя (*uncle*) е́дет в Аме́рику.   Они́ е́дут в А́фрику.
> Он е́дет в Евро́пу.   Я е́ду в Кана́ду.

7. ACCUSATIVE CASE AFTER **в** II – IDIOMS

No two languages behave in quite the same way in their use of prepositions. This is particularly so in expressions of time; compare English *at one o'clock*, German *um zwei Uhr*, Russian **в час.** English has *on* a certain day of the week, whereas Russian has **в** + accusative. This is purely idiomatic usage and has nothing to do with motion.

> В понеде́льник я иду́ в ла́вку (ла́вка *shop*).
> Во вто́рник[1] вы идёте в рестора́н.
> В сре́ду вы идёте в шко́лу (шко́ла *school*).
> В четве́рг мы е́дем в го́род.
> В пя́тницу он е́дет в Ленингра́д, а в суббо́ту в Оде́ссу.

8. ACCUSATIVE CASE AFTER **на** – MOTION

a **На** followed by the accusative expresses motion *on to*. The verb *to put*,

---

1 **Во** is a form of **в** which occurs before many words beginning with two consonants, especially when the first consonant is **в** or **ф.**

to place **класть: я кладу́, ты кладёшь** etc. is often used with the accusative.

> Я кладу́ кни́гу на стол.
> Ты кладёшь тру́бку (*pipe*) на таре́лку (*plate*).
> Сосе́д кладёт одея́ло (*blanket*) на дива́н.
> Мы кладём чемода́ны на_пол.
> Вы кладёте ю́бку на край (*edge*) стола́.
> Они́ кладу́т бума́ги на по́лку.
> Я кладу́ шля́пу на шкаф. *I put the hat on the cupboard.*
> Я кладу́ шля́пу в шкаф. *I put the hat in the cupboard.*

b **На** + accusative is used to express *to a place* when the place is an open space, such as a street or a yard:

> Де́ти иду́т на у́лицу (*street*).
> Я иду́ на двор (*yard*).

c **На** + accusative is also used when the noun denotes the activity that occurs at a certain place and is not actually the name of the place:

> Я иду́ на рабо́ту. *I am going to work.*
> Я иду́ на слу́жбу. *I am going to work* (of a non-manual kind).
> but Я иду́ на рабо́ту в конто́ру. *I am going to the office to work.*
> Я иду́ на ми́тинг. *I am going to a meeting.*
> but Я иду́ в зал на ми́тинг. *I am going to the hall to a meeting.*
> Я иду́ в теа́тр на конце́рт. *I am going to the theatre to a concert.*
> Я иду́ в шко́лу на уро́к. *I am going to school to a lesson.*

d **На** + accusative is also used to express motion to most places of work:

> Мы идём на заво́д (*the works*).
> Мы идём на фа́брику (*factory*).
> Они́ е́дут на вокза́л (*station*).
> Она́ идёт на ры́нок (*market*).
> Вы идёте на по́чту (*post-office*)?

In **они́ иду́т на перро́н/платфо́рму** the use of **на** is to be expected – they are going *on to* an open space.

e **На** + accusative is used to express motion in a particular compass direction (Lesson 4, § 5).

> По́езд идёт на се́вер.   Они́ все е́дут на юг.
> Парохо́д идёт на восто́к.   Маши́ны иду́т на за́пад.

9. THE DEMONSTRATIVE PRONOUN 'THIS'

The letter **э** appears mostly in words of foreign origin:

> э́хо *echo*   этА́ж *floor, storey*
> электри́чество *electricity*   эне́ргия *energy*

The only important native word in which **э** appears is the demonstrative pronoun *this*:

э́тот   э́та   э́то   э́ти

Э́тот дом, а не тот.   Э́та карти́на, а не та.   Э́то мы́ло, а не то.
Э́тот полко́вник (*colonel*) тут, тот полко́вник там.
Э́та ла́вка тут, та ла́вка там.
Э́то окно́ тут, то окно́ там.

In the singular **э́тот** declines like **тот** (also losing the **-от** after the nominative singular masculine) but in the plural it declines not like **те** but like **са́ми**.

Э́тих столо́в тут ма́ло, тех столо́в там мно́го.
Э́тих по́лок ма́ло. *There are (too) few of these shelves.*
Тех по́лок мно́го. *There are (too) many of those shelves.*

Э́то is used where English has *it is, this/that is:*

Э́то хорошо́. *It's good/That's good.*
Э́то не хорошо́, э́то пло́хо (*bad*).
Э́то ма́ло. *It's not much* or (*too) little.*
Э́то мно́го. *It's a lot.*
Э́то всегда́ так, да, э́то так всегда́. *It's always like that.*
    Yes, it's always so.
Кто э́то? *Who is it?* Э́то ма́ма. *This is mother.* Э́то сестра́. *This*
    is my sister.
Э́то брат.   Э́то ребёнок.   Э́то де́ти. *They are children.*
Э́то жёны матро́сов (матро́с *sailor*).   Э́то ребя́та.
Э́то что?/Что э́то? *What is this?*
Что э́то?   Э́то беспоря́док, э́то хао́с.
Э́то ла́мпа. Э́то ла́мпы. Э́то мы́ло. Э́то шко́ла. Э́то шко́лы.
Э́то стол. Э́то столы́.

As you see, **э́то** *this is, it is* remaining in the neuter singular when referring to *these* is also used with plural nouns, where English would have *they/these are lamps* etc.

Э́тот etc. is often used where English has *that*. In Russian **тот** etc. is only used to draw attention to the fact that it is *that over there*, or in such phrases as: **в том смы́сле** *in that sense* (**смысл** *sense*).

When you say *this* or *that* person or thing, then **э́тот** must, of course, agree in case, gender and number:

Э́тот полк тут, а тот полк вот там у (*by*) го́рода.

But: Э́то полк. *This/It is a regiment.*

Similarly: Те шко́лы там, а э́ти ла́вки тут. But: Э́то шко́лы, а не ла́вки.

74

10. EXERCISE

– Что это? – Это пакеты.

– Ну, конечно, это пакеты! Это пакеты! Я сам вижу,[1] что это пакеты! Ты много покупаешь.

– Это всё на[2] обед. У нас будут и Ваня, и Саша, и Миша, и Маша. Утром я бегала на рынок, много покупала, много несла. Тебя не_было утром, и мне тоже надо было вести[3] собаку.

– Ну, хорошо! Хорошо! Я же[4] работал. А что на обед? Эта банка[5] на обед?

– Это суп.

– Этот суп на обед?

– А что,[6] это плохо?

– Нет, почему плохо? Это совсем не плохо, это даже[7] хорошо. А это что?

– Это рыба.

– Это рыба? А это не мясо?

– Конечно это не мясо. Утром я долго покупала[8] рыбу – вот эту рыбу.[9]

– Ты думаешь, что это рыба – что это не мясо?

– Что ты там всё говоришь[10] – это мясо – это не мясо, это рыба – это не рыба! Я несла рыбу, вот эту рыбу. И вечером ты будешь есть[11] эту рыбу.

– Но это не рыба. Надо смотреть, что[12] ты несёшь!

– Я ничего не понимаю! Утром я покупала рыбу и несла рыбу! Где этот пакет? Это не тот пакет![13]

– Вот тебе на![14]

11. TRANSLATION

They are giving us a chair.

I advise you not to go on Monday.

He has to get up early because he is going to work.

He is going to the station because he is organizing a trip[15] to London.

1 *I can see (for) myself.*   2 **На** here means *for.*   3 Transl. *to take.*
4 **Же** is an *emphatic particle*; it emphasizes the word it follows.
5 *Can, jar.*   6 *So what? So?*   7 *Even.* Transl. *in fact it's good.*
8 Lit. *I was a long time buying,* i.e. *I spent a long time buying.*   9 *This fish here.*
10 *What are you on about? What do you keep on about?* **Там** here is used in an idiomatic way: it adds a slight sense of disparagement.
11 *You will be eating,* future imperfective.
12 **Что** here is not the conjunction *that* but – *what.* It is written with a stress-mark to distinguish it from **что** = *that,* when there is a possibility of misunderstanding.
13 *It's the wrong packet/parcel.* **Не тот** – in the appropriate case – is the usual way of expressing *the wrong* . . .
14 Idiom – *Well, I don't know! Well, it just shows you! Well there you are!*
15 **Поездка.**

The doctor did not recognize me.

Sasha is putting his books and papers on the shelf.

The ship went[1] east. They were going to Europe.

This is (my) wife and these are (my) children. They are going to a concert.

Tanya gave me these books – this is 'Anna Karenina' and this is 'The Three Sisters'.

There aren't many of those books here but there are plenty of these newspapers.

1 Use the past tense of идти́.

SUMMARY

1 Verbs of the type дава́ть drop the -ва- in the conjugation: даю́, даёшь etc. (§ 1).

2 Verbs of the type торгова́ть change -ова- to -у- in the conjugation: торгу́ю, торгу́ешь etc. (§ 2).

3 Accusative after в and на means motion (§§ 6 and 8).

4 В + acc. is used in some expressions of time, corresponding to English on (§ 7).

Lesson 13

I. VERB FORMS OF THE SECOND CONJUGATION

In previous lessons you have had several verbs of the second conjugation, i.e. of the и type, with various infinitive endings:

-ить:	говори́ть	я говорю́	он говори́т	они́ говоря́т
-ить:	ве́рить	я ве́рю	он ве́рит	они́ ве́рят
-еть:	смотре́ть	я смотрю́	он смо́трит	они́ смо́трят
-еть:	горе́ть	я горю́	он гори́т	они́ горя́т
-ать:	крича́ть	я кричу́	он кричи́т	они́ крича́т
-ять:	стоя́ть	я стою́	он стои́т	они́ стоя́т

With these verbs all you had to do was to learn that they belong to the second conjugation and to apply the second conjugation endings, taking into account the spelling conventions, e.g. **смо́трят** but **крича́т**. There are many verbs of this kind but there are also many verbs in which there is another feature.

Take the following two verbs:

буди́ть *to wake, to rouse*   суди́ть *to judge*

Both have **д** in the infinitive but the first pers. sing. is:

я бужу́ *I rouse*   я сужу́ *I judge*

As you see, **д** changes into **ж,** but only in the first pers. sing. The complete conjugation is:

буди́ть	суди́ть
я бужу́	сужу́
ты бу́дишь	су́дишь
он бу́дит	су́дит
мы бу́дим	су́дим
вы бу́дите	су́дите
они́ бу́дят	су́дят

This change of **д** into **ж** in the first pers. sing. happens in all second conjugation verbs with **д** before the infinitive ending:

ви́деть *to see*	оби́деть (pfv.) *to offend*	сиде́ть *to be sitting*
я ви́жу *I see*	оби́жу *I shall offend*	сижу́ *I sit*
ты ви́дишь	оби́дишь	сиди́шь
он ви́дит	оби́дит	сиди́т
они́ ви́дят	оби́дят	сидя́т

There are other consonants which change in the first pers. sing. but the number of such consonants is small.

77

З, for example, like **д,** changes into **ж:**

грузи́ть *to load*		грози́ть *to threaten*	
я гружу́ *I load*		грожу́ *I threaten*	
ты гру́зишь		грози́шь	
они́ гру́зят		грозя́т	

Both **з** and **ж** are voiced consonants. Their voiceless counterparts are **с** and **ш.** It is not surprising therefore to find that **с** changes to **ш** in the first pers. sing.:

бро́сить (pfv.) *to throw*	кра́сить *to paint*
я бро́шу *I shall throw*	кра́шу *I paint*
ты бро́сишь	кра́сишь
они́ бро́сят	кра́сят

The consonant **т** changes into **ч** in some verbs and **щ** in other verbs:

плати́ть *to pay*	верте́ть *to turn, spin*
я плачу́ *I pay*	верчу́ *I turn*
ты пла́тишь	ве́ртишь
они́ пла́тят	ве́ртят

but   запрети́ть (pfv.) *to forbid*
                я запрещу́ *I shall forbid*
                ты запрети́шь
                они́ запретя́т

The two consonants **ст** always change to **щ:**

                пусти́ть (pfv.) *to allow*
                я пущу́ *I shall allow*
                ты пу́стишь
                они́ пу́стят

2. CONSONANT CHANGES

You have just seen that **т** can change into **ч** or **щ.** As you accumulate more imperfective-perfective pairs you will find that there is a clue in the imperfective and perfective of the pair to the difference in the consonants. The consonant which occurs in the first pers. sing. only of the perfective is found *throughout* the imperfective, including the infinitive.

	pfv.		impfv.
оби́деть	я оби́жу	обижа́ть	я обижа́ю
	ты оби́дишь		ты обижа́ешь
запрети́ть	я запрещу́	запреща́ть	я запреща́ю
	ты запрети́шь		ты запреща́ешь
вообрази́ть	я вообража́у	вообража́ть	я вообража́ю
to imagine	ты вообрази́шь		ты вообража́ешь
вы́разить	я вы́ражу	выража́ть	я выража́ю
to express	ты вы́разишь		ты выража́ешь

	pfv.		*impfv.*
нагрузи́ть	я нагружу́	нагружа́ть	я нагружа́ю
to load	ты нагру́зишь		ты нагружа́ешь
вы́грузить	я вы́гружу	выгружа́ть	я выгружа́ю
to unload	ты вы́грузишь		ты выгружа́ешь
прости́ть	я прощу́	проща́ть	я проща́ю
to forgive	ты прости́шь		ты проща́ешь

The verb **бро́сить** *to throw*, perfective, without a prefix, is irregular and does not show the change of **с** to **ш** in the imperfective:

бро́сить	я бро́шу	броса́ть	я броса́ю
	ты бро́сишь		ты броса́ешь

3. SECOND CONJUGATION IN -ать

In Lesson 7 you were given some verbs which are second conjugation verbs but have infinitives ending in **-ать, -ять** or **-еть**. There are twenty-five verbs with the infinitive ending in **-ать** which are second conjugation and in all of them the **-ать** is preceded by **ж, ш, ч** or **щ**. The group includes some common verbs, such as the following:

-жать: держа́ть *to hold*   лежа́ть *to be lying*
         я держу́   лежу́
         ты де́ржишь   лежи́шь
         он де́ржит   лежи́т
         они́ де́ржат   лежа́т

-шать: слы́шать *to hear*   дыша́ть *to breathe*
         я слы́шу   дышу́
         ты слы́шишь   ды́шишь
         он слы́шит   ды́шит
         они́ слы́шат   ды́шат

-чать: крича́ть *to shout*   молча́ть *to be silent*
         я кричу́   молчу́
         ты кричи́шь   молчи́шь
         он кричи́т   молчи́т
         они́ крича́т   молча́т

-щать: треща́ть *to rattle, crackle*   пища́ть *to squeak*
         я трещу́   пищу́
         ты трещи́шь   пищи́шь
         он трещи́т   пищи́т
         они́ треща́т   пища́т

Other common verbs in this group are:

         дрожа́ть *to tremble*   жужжа́ть *to buzz*
         стуча́ть *to knock*   ворча́ть *to grumble*
         мыча́ть *to moo*   рыча́ть *to roar*
         звуча́ть *to sound*

4. EXERCISE I

Take all the second conjugation verbs in the passage below and write out their infinitive, first pers. sing., third pers. sing. and third pers. pl., e.g.:

буди́ть бужу́ бу́дит бу́дят

Verbs of this conjugation with a consonant formed with the lips (**б, п, в, ф, м**) before **и** have a different change in the first pers. sing., which will be dealt with later. Do not then write out the first pers. sing. of any such verbs in the passage.

You may assume that any verbs not covered by this remark and the remarks in preceding paragraphs have *no* consonant change in the first pers. sing., which will end in **-ю**, except after those consonants which cannot be followed by **ю**, e.g. **звоню́**, but **трещу́**.

The past tense of the verbs in this passage is formed in the normal way from the infinitive and will thus give you a clue to the infinitive.

Прошу́ has infinitive **проси́ть, молю́ – моли́ть. Гнать** *to drive, to chase* has an extra syllable in the conjugation: **гоню́, го́нишь** etc. All the forms which you need to consider for your answer are printed in italics.

Ýтром ра́но на́до *буди́ть* бра́та. Он ча́сто встаёт о́чень по́здно и вот на́до его́ *буди́ть*. Буди́льник *звони́т* в семь часо́в, *звони́т* так гро́мко, что все круго́м *слы́шат*, все – но то́лько не брат. Он коне́чно не *слы́шит*. Буди́льник *звони́т*, *трещи́т*, ко́шка с испу́га на шкаф, *сиди́т* и *смо́трит* и *бои́тся*,[1] а брат хоть бы что, *спит* и *храпи́т*.

Вот я иду́ в его́ ко́мнату: «Встава́ть пора́, лентя́й, чего́ ты *спишь?* Вот бу́дет тебе́, что всегда́ опа́здываешь.» А он ни сло́ва, повора́чивается на бок и *спит*. Я продолжа́ю *буди́ть*: «Встава́ть пора́, всё на́до *гнать* тебя́ в конто́ру. Ра́зве ты не *слы́шишь?* Пото́м бу́дет по́здно, буди́льник уже́ *звони́л*, *звони́л* – *звони́л*, *трещи́л* – *трещи́л*, ра́зве ты мне не *ве́ришь?* Уже́ по́здно.» *Молчи́т* и *спит*, нет, повора́чивается, начина́ет зева́ть, *ворча́ть* – зева́ет, *ворчи́т*. «Да по́лно тебе́ *ворча́ть*, встава́ть на́до, а ты всё *лежи́шь*, *храпи́шь*.»

Иду́ в ку́хню за́втрак *гото́вить*, *стою́ – стою́* – нет его́. Иду́ в его́ ко́мнату, *смотрю́*, он всё ещё *лежи́т*, и ко́шка тут же *лежи́т* и *спит*. «Как тебе́ не сты́дно, ты э́то что, наро́чно?» Он опя́ть *ворчи́т*, я опя́ть его́ *бужу́*: «И тебе́ не сты́дно так до́лго *спать*, ты совсе́м не *стыди́шься*, что всегда́ опа́здываешь?» А он мне в отве́т: «Совсе́м не *стыжу́сь*, а тебе́ что?» Вот тебе́ на, *груби́ть* начина́ет, я начина́ю *серди́ться*, *сержу́сь*, *кричу́*: «Ты дура́к, ты про́сто дура́к!» Тепе́рь и ко́шка зева́ет, и да́же встаёт, ко́шка встаёт, а он всё *лежи́т*.

Я иду́ вниз. Во́семь часо́в – нет бра́та. Иду́ наве́рх: «Да ты бу́дешь

---

1 **Боя́ться** *to be afraid, to fear* (+ gen.), is a *formally* reflexive verb *and is second conjugation*: **бою́сь, бои́шься, бои́тся, бои́мся, бои́тесь, боя́тся.**

вставáть, дурáк?» А он нахáл мне в отвéт: «Ты самá дýра, самá ты *лю́бишь* дóлго *спать*, самá ты пóздно встаёшь, *спишь* до десятú, а мне *спать* не даёшь.» «А тебé всё *спóрить*. Я прóсто *боюсь*, что ты всё опáздываешь, *говорю́* тебé, *прошý* тебя́, *молю́* тебя́, а тебé ничегó. Вставáть нáдо, а ты *спóришь*.» «А тебé что? Самá ты *лю́бишь спóрить*, *спóрить* и *ссóриться*.» «Э́то ты *ссóришься*, а не я, я тóлько тебя́ *бужý*». «Не хочý вставáть, и не бýду. Вот тебé!» «Ну, éсли ты хóчешь, так мóжешь *спать* весь день. И *будúть* тебя́ ýтром рáно я не бýду, не хочý и не бýду!»

И вот так у нас всегдá – я *бужý, бужý*, он *спит* и *спит*, он *грубúт*, я *сержýсь*, а кóшка всё *сидúт* и *смóтрит* на нас.

5. FIRST CONJUGATION IN -жать, -шать, -чать AND -щать

After reading § 3 you realize that most verbs with infinitive ending in **-ать** preceded by **ж, ш, ч** or **щ** are first conjugation verbs, i.e. they conjugate like **дýмать**. Among them are such common verbs as:

воображáть *to imagine*	кончáть *to finish*
обижáть *to offend*	встречáть *to meet*
решáть *to decide*	прощáть *to forgive*
мешáть *to interfere; to stir*	запрещáть *to forbid*

6. FUTURE PERFECTIVE

All the examples given at the end of the preceding paragraph are imperfective verbs. Their conjugation has a present tense meaning: **я обижáю** *I offend, I am offending* etc. Earlier in this lesson you met **обúдеть** *to offend* – the *perfective* to **обижáть**.

THE CONJUGATION OF PERFECTIVE VERBS HAS THE MEANING OF FUTURE TENSE

To be more accurate, it has the meaning of future perfective, i.e. the action will take place in the future and is thought of as a completed action, not an action that will be going on or repeated. Hence:

я обúжу *I shall offend* он обúдит *he will offend* онú обúдят *they will offend*

7. EXERCISE II

In the following exercise, to be read for comprehension, each set of sentences is headed by the verb used, the perfective being given first, the imperfective second:

обúдеть – обижáть *to offend, to hurt somebody's feelings*
Я не обúжу вас.   Мы вас не обúдим.
Онú всегдá обижáют брáта, и сын сосéда тóже егó обижáет.

G

реши́ть – реша́ть *to decide*

Эту зада́чу мы реши́м за́втра.

Мы ча́сто реша́ем э́ти зада́чи, но не всегда́ мы их реша́ем пра́вильно.

ко́нчить – конча́ть *to finish*

Эту рабо́ту мы так ско́ро не ко́нчим, мы её ко́нчим за́втра.

Вот мы всегда́ рабо́таем, рабо́таем, конча́ем, конча́ем, но всё не мо́жем ко́нчить (i.e. *we keep finishing but still we cannot come to an end*).

запрети́ть – запреща́ть *to forbid, to prohibit* (+ dative of person forbidden)

Тут тепе́рь опа́сно игра́ть, я им запрещу́ тут игра́ть.

Я всегда́ им запреща́ю крича́ть, но я не запреща́ю говори́ть гро́мко.

дать – дава́ть (see Lesson 12, § 1) *to give*

Я вам за́втра дам э́ту кни́гу.

Я им всегда́ даю́ биле́ты.

8. PREPOSITIONAL CASE

To express *place where* or location you use the prepositional case after **в** *in* or **на** *on*. Nearly all the nouns you have met so far, have the ending **е** for the prepositional case. Masculine nouns ending in a consonant add the **е** to the nominative singular, feminine nouns ending in **а/я** (but not **ия**) and neuter nouns ending in **о/е** (but not **ие**) replace these letters by **е**:

| стол – на столе́ *on the table* | по́лка – на по́лке *on the shelf* | кре́сло – в кре́сле *in the armchair* |

In the plural the ending of the prepositional case is **ах** or, after a soft consonant other than **ч** or **щ, ях.**

на стола́х *on the tables* на по́лках *on the shelves* в кре́слах *in the armchairs*

Я сижу́ на дива́не.	Мы сиди́м на дива́нах.
Кни́га лежи́т на столе́.	Кни́ги лежа́т на стола́х.
Матро́с (*sailor*) стои́т на су́дне.	Матро́сы стоя́т на суда́х.
Де́ти игра́ют на дворе́ (*outside*, lit. 'on/in the yard').	
На дворе́ хо́лодно.	*It's cold outside.*
На у́лице тепло́.	*It's warm outside.*
В ко́мнате жа́рко (*hot*).	В кварти́ре тепло́.
В шко́ле мно́го дете́й (genitive plural of де́ти *children*).	
В коро́бке пау́к.	*There is a spider in the box* (коро́бка).
В ла́вках нет хле́ба.	*There is no bread in the shops* (ла́вка).
Бума́ги лежа́т в столе́.	*The papers are lying in the desk.*
В го́роде на у́лицах мно́го маши́н, (маши́на *car*) мно́го авто́бусов.	
В до́ме не на́до шуме́ть.	

The prepositional case is always used with a preposition, hence its name. Three more prepositions govern the prepositional case and of these the commonest is **о** meaning *about, concerning*. Before words beginning with a vowel, **o** takes the form **об,** while before a few words beginning with two consonants it takes the form **обо.**

Я ду́маю о вну́ке.   Я ду́маю о вну́ках   (внук *grandson*).
Она́ говори́т о сестре́.   Она́ говори́т о сёстрах.
Я ду́маю о са́де.   Я говорю́ о мосте́.   Я чита́ю о ле́се.

9. LOCATIVE CASE

In earlier lessons you were given such phrases as **на мосту́** *on the bridge,* **на борту́** *on board,* **в саду́** *in the garden,* **в лесу́** *in the forest.* These are in fact examples of a special kind of prepositional case which occurs with only *some masculine nouns.* This form of the prepositional case is always stressed on the **у** and occurs only after **в** *in* and **на** *on* denoting location. To distinguish it from the prepositional case it is known as the locative case.[1]

Nouns which have the locative case also have the normal form of the prepositional case with the other prepositions which govern the prepositional case.

Here are some more nouns with the locative case:

на берегу́ *on shore*   в году́ *in the year*
в кругу́ *in the circle*   на балу́ *at the ball*
в Крыму́ *in the Crimea*   на лугу́ *in the meadow*
на носу́ *on the nose*   на полу́ *on the floor*
в тылу́ *in the rear*   в углу́ *in the corner*

For nouns ending in a soft consonant or **й** and having a locative case the ending is **ю:**

край – на краю́ *on the edge*   бой – в бою́ *in battle*

Notice that it does not matter which of the two prepositions, **в** or **на** governs these nouns:

в углу́ *in the corner*   на углу́ *on the corner*

10. PREPOSITIONAL CASE ILLUSTRATED

In the following lines of verse illustrating the prepositional case notice the use of **кто.** When repeated, **кто** can have the meaning *some . . . some . . . others. . . .* The verb with **кто** is in the singular.

Кто тряс́сь от[2] стра́ха   *Some trembling with fear*
Спря́тался в чула́не,   *Hid themselves in the boxroom,*
Кто в соба́чьей бу́дке,   *Some in the dog-kennel,*
Кто на[3] чердаке́.   *Some in the attic.*
Па́па схорони́лся   *Papa hid himself*

1 In some grammars the prepositional case in general is called the locative case.
2 NB Russian has **от** *from,* English has *with* here.
3 NB Russian **на** *on,* English *in* the attic.

В ста́ром[1] чемода́не,
Тётя под дива́ном,[2]
Дя́дя в сундуке́.

In an old suitcase,
Auntie under the divan,
Uncle in a trunk.

II. TRANSLATION

(Omit the words in brackets.)

Telephone Conversation[3]

I am sitting in the room and looking through the window.[4] It is warm outside and the children are playing in the garden. . . . John? – No, I can't see[5] John but I can hear[6] him. He just stands and shouts. . . . I don't let them[7] shout in the house. . . . Papa is working in the wood. He is loading wood[8] on to a barrow.[9] He'll throw the wood in the corner of the yard but I shall forgive him. The wood crackles so merrily in the fireplace when[10] it is cold outside and the lamp is burning on the table and we are all sitting in (our) armchairs and reading. . . . Now the children are knocking on[11] the door. They are asking me to play outside. I have to go, otherwise[12] I shall hurt their feelings.[13] . . . We'll finish (our) conversation tomorrow. We were talking about (my) sister. We keep trying to settle[14] the problem – perhaps[15] we'll settle it tomorrow.

1 Prepositional case masculine singular of the adjective, to be dealt with later.
2 This is the instrumental case, which will be dealt with later.
3 **Разгово́р по телефо́ну.**　4 **В окно́.**　5 Say *I do not see.*　6 Say *I hear.*
7 Say *I forbid them* (dat.).　8 **Дрова́** (neuter pl.).　9 **Та́чка.**　10 **Когда́.**
11 **В + accusative, в дверь.**　12 **А то.**　13 Say *I shall offend them.*　14 Say *we settle and settle* and put **всё** *always* before the verb.　15 **Мо́жет быть.**

SUMMARY

1 Many second conjugation verbs have a consonant change in the first pers. sing. (§§ 1 and 2).

2 Twenty-five verbs with infinitive ending in **-жать, -шать, -чать** or **-щать** are second conjugation (§ 3).

3 The conjugation of perfective verbs has the meaning of future perfective (§ 6).

4 The prepositional case ends in **e** for most nouns in the singular, and in **ax/ях** in the plural. Five prepositions govern the prepositional case, of which the commonest are **в** *in*, **на** *on*, **o** *about* (§ 8).

5 Some masculine nouns have a special form of the prepositional case ending in **ý** or **ю́** and expressing location – the *locative case* (§ 9).

Lesson 14

I. REVISION OF VERB FORMS

Much of this lesson is devoted to revision of the conjugations and the use of the aspects. Some new verbs, belonging to one or other of the types you have studied, are introduced.

Points to remember are: nearly every verb has imperfective and perfective forms. Imperfective forms mean that the action is repeated or is thought of as going on. Perfective forms mean that the action is thought of as completed. Past and future have imperfective and perfective forms while the present has only the imperfective form.

	pfv.		*impfv.*
	дать *to give*		дава́ть
future	я дам	*present*	даю́
tense	ты дашь	*tense*	даёшь
	он даст		даёт
	мы дади́м		даём
	вы дади́те		даёте
	они́ даду́т		даю́т
past	я, ты, он дал		дава́л
tense	я, ты, она́ дала́		дава́ла
	оно́ дало́		дава́ло
	мы, вы, они́ да́ли		дава́ли

– Он дал мне паке́т.   *pfv.* single, completed act.
– Он мне ча́сто дава́л биле́ты на конце́рт. ⎫
– Он всегда́ мне даёт биле́ты на конце́рт. ⎬ *impfv.*, repeated act
– Он мне не́ дал биле́та, он и вам не даст.   *pfv.*, single, completed acts

	откры́ть *to open* (conjug. like мыть)		открыва́ть (conjug. like ду́мать)
fut.	я откро́ю	*pres.*	я открыва́ю
	он откро́ет		он открыва́ет
	они́ откро́ют		они́ открыва́ют
past	я, ты, он откры́л		открыва́л
	я, ты, она́ откры́ла		открыва́ла
	оно́ откры́ло		открыва́ло
	мы, вы, они́ откры́ли		открыва́ли

За́втра они́ откро́ют ла́вку.   *fut. pfv.*, single, completed act
Я открыва́ю ла́вку о́чень по́здно.   present tense
Сего́дня у́тром я о́чень ра́но откры́ла окно́. *This morning I opened the window very early.*   *past pfv.*, single, completed act

Ле́том я всегда́ открыва́ла все о́кна о́чень ра́но. *past impfv.*, repeated acts.
In summer I always used to open all the windows very early.

закры́ть *pfv.*, **закрыва́ть** *impfv.*, to close, conjugates in the same way as **откры́ть, открыва́ть.**

Она́ закры́ла окно́ по́здно, тут тепе́рь хо́лодно.
She closed the window (too) late, now it's cold here.

Она́ зимо́й и ле́том закрыва́ла о́кна о́чень ра́но.
Winter and summer she used to close the windows very early.

оби́деть *pfv.*, **обижа́ть** *impfv.*, to hurt somebody's feelings, to offend
Э́тот челове́к меня́ никогда́ не обижа́л, а вчера́ я сама́ его́ оби́дела.
This man has never offended me, but yesterday I myself offended him.

> In the first half of this sentence the imperfective is used because it is not that a single complete act did not take place but the action in general has never taken place.

реши́ть *pfv.*, **реша́ть** *impfv.*, to decide, to solve
Э́ту зада́чу мы все вме́сте реша́ли весь ве́чер.   Реша́ли... Реша́ли...
We were trying to solve this problem together all evening. We kept trying and trying.

> Here the imperfective is used because the action was going on for some time and success, i.e. completion is not implied. Hence the imperfective often corresponds to English *kept doing such-and-such* or *tried to and did not succeed.*

И что́ же, реши́ли? Вы реши́ли зада́чу?   *pfv.*, single, completed act
Well, did you solve it? You've solved the problem?

Ничего́ не реши́ли.   *pfv.*, a single, complete act which was not
We solved nothing.   achieved

Реша́ли, но не реши́ли. Уж о́чень тру́дно.   *impfv.*, attempt going on,
We tried (to solve it) but didn't manage it.   *pfv.*, single act not achieved.
It's really very difficult.

ко́нчить *pfv.*, **конча́ть** *impfv.*, to finish
Говоря́т, ко́нчили стро́ить э́тот дом.
Ко́нчили стро́ить!? Ничего́ они́ не ко́нчили! Стро́или, стро́или – конча́ли стро́ить весь год, конча́ли, конча́ли – ничего́ не ко́нчили! Всё еще стро́ят, всё еще конча́ют!

> Here again the imperfective past **конча́ли** can be translated *they've been trying to finish* or *they've been finishing*, whereas the perfective past implies actual, successful completion.

86

запрети́ть *pfv.*, **запреща́ть** *impfv.*, *to prohibit, forbid*
обрати́ть внима́ние *pfv.*, **обраща́ть внима́ние** *impfv.*, *to pay attention*

Да мы им ча́сто запреща́ли тут игра́ть, запреща́ли мно́го раз, но они́ не обраща́ют внима́ния. *past impfv.* запреща́ли repeated acts

Не обраща́ют внима́ния? А вот когда́ я им запрещу́, то они́ обратя́т внима́ние!

fut. pfv. запрещу́ and обратя́т single acts to be completed in the future.

Ну что, он запрети́л им игра́ть? – Да, запрети́л.

past pfv., a single completed act

И они́ обрати́ли внима́ние, что он запрети́л тут игра́ть?

past pfv. single, completed acts.

Нет, не обрати́ли внима́ния. Он да́же мно́го раз запреща́л, а они́ всё же игра́ют, про́сто не обраща́ют внима́ния на него́.

past pfv. обрати́ли, a single act which was not realized; *past impfv.* запреща́л, repeated acts.

нагрузи́ть *pfv.*, **нагружа́ть** *impfv.*, *to load*
вы́грузить *pfv.*, **выгружа́ть** *impfv.*, *to unload*

Ну что же, грузови́к там стоя́л у них весь день и весь день нагружа́ли
Well then, the lorry was standing at their house all day and all day they were
грузови́к. Всё что у них бы́ло, всё на грузови́к;
loading the lorry. Everything (which) they had, everything on to the lorry;
нагружа́ли, нагружа́ли, и вот наконе́ц нагрузи́ли маши́ну!
they kept loading and then at last they had loaded up the vehicle!
И что же? Сли́шком мно́го нагрузи́ли – маши́на ни с ме́ста!
And then what? They had loaded too much – the vehicle would not move!
Мото́р не рабо́тает. Вот и нагрузи́ли. А пото́м тут у
The engine won't work. That's how they had loaded (it) up. And then there
нас выгружа́ли, выгружа́ли, до́лго выгружа́ли, полови́ну полома́ли;
they were unloading, unloading, for ages and ages; half (the stuff) they broke;
наконе́ц всё вы́грузили, и вот тут они́ тепе́рь и живу́т!
at last they had unloaded everything and now they're living here!

In this passage the past imperfectives стоя́л, нагружа́ли and выгружа́ли denote actions going on for some time, while the past perfectives нагрузи́ли, полома́ли (impfv. лома́ли) and вы́грузили denote the completion of the acts.

2. 'TO BE SITTING,' 'TO SIT DOWN'

You have had the imperfective verb *to sit*:

сиде́ть: я сижу́   он сиди́т   они́ сидя́т

It means *to be sitting* in the place where you have sat down, and the place where you are sitting is often expressed by **в** or **на** with the prepositional case.

Я сижу́ на сту́ле.   Я сиде́л на сту́ле.
Она́ сиди́т на полу́.   Она́ сиде́ла на полу́.
Они́ сидя́т в ко́мнате.   Они́ сиде́ли в ко́мнате.

To sit down, to seat oneself, impfv., is **сади́ться**.

Since it means motion towards the place where you sit down, the verb is followed by the prepositions **в** and **на** with the accusative case.

Сади́ться на что? во что?

Я сажу́сь на дива́н.   Мы сади́мся в маши́ну
Ты сади́шься на стул.   Вы сади́тесь в кре́сло.
Он сади́тся в авто́бус.   Они́ садя́тся на ме́сто.

The past: *he used to sit himself down, was in the process of sitting himself down* etc., is:

сади́лся   сади́лась   сади́лось   сади́лись

The following examples illustrate the difference between **сади́ться** and **сиде́ть,** both imperfective verbs, but denoting different actions.

Я сажу́сь на дива́н.   Я сижу́ на дива́не.
I sit down on the divan.   *I am sitting on the divan.*

Он всегда́ сади́тся на стол, когда́ отца́ нет до́ма.
He always sits (down) on the table, when father is not at home.

Он сиди́т на столе́, так как отца́ нет до́ма.
He is sitting on the table, since father is not at home.

Он всегда́ сади́лся на стол, когда́ отца́ не́_было до́ма.
He always used to sit (down) on the table, when father was not at home.

Он сиде́л на столе́, так как отца́ не́_было до́ма.
He was sitting on the table, since father was not at home.

The perfective of **сади́ться** *to sit down* is **сесть**.

As you see, the perfective is *not* reflexive. It has an unusual conjugation. The vowel **е** of **сесть,** in the infinitive, changes to **я** in the conjugation and the **д** of **сиде́ть** and **сади́ться** appears here too.

Я ся́ду на дива́н.
Ты ся́дешь на стул.
Он ся́дет в авто́бус.
Мы ся́дем в маши́ну.
Вы ся́дете в кре́сло.
Они́ ся́дут на ме́сто.

The past tense of **сесть** is **сел, се́ла, се́ло, се́ли.**

Он сел и там сиди́т. *He sat down, and remains sitting there.*
Она́ се́ла и там она́ сиде́ла до́лго. *She sat down and there she sat for a long time.*

Вы се́ли на то ме́сто, где я вчера́ сиде́ла. *You sat down in the place where I sat yesterday.*

The following sequence may help you to memorize these *sitting* verbs:

я сади́лась   *I was sitting down*, impfv., the process going on
я се́ла   *I sat down*, pfv., completion of the process
я сиде́ла   *I was sitting*, impfv., the state you were in after carrying out
           the act

Кот до́лго сади́лся, наконе́ц сел и вот он сиди́т тут.
The cat took a long time sitting down, finally he sat down and so here he sits.

3. EXERCISE

И вот я е́ду домо́й...

Я е́ду домо́й, уже́ по́здно, сажу́сь в авто́бус, там то́лько одно́ ме́сто свобо́дно, я бы́стро сажу́сь, – се́ла, – сижу́, – е́дем, е́дем о́чень до́лго, и вдруг сосе́д, мужчи́на ря́дом, говори́т:

– Прости́те,[1] но вы се́ли на шля́пу.

– Как так, я се́ла на шля́пу? Кака́я тут шля́па?[2]

– Да так вот,[3] тут шля́па, вы се́ли на шля́пу и сиди́те на шля́пе.

Я бы́стро встаю́ – да, в са́мом де́ле,[4] тут его́ шля́па, я се́ла на его́ шля́пу и всё вре́мя, всю доро́гу[5] сиде́ла на его́ шля́пе.

– Да, сади́ться на шля́пы не на́до.

Как я зна́ла, что[6] сажу́сь на его́ шля́пу; и он мог[7] сра́зу же[8] обрати́ть внима́ние[9] на то, что[10] я сажу́сь на его́ шля́пу, а он молчи́т; я се́ла на его́ шля́пу, сижу́ на его́ шля́пе всю доро́гу, а он молчи́т.

– Так на́до смотре́ть, куда́ сади́шься,[11] вот и всё. Если не смотре́ть куда́ сади́шься, то мо́жно сесть и на ежа́![12]

Не сове́туем сади́ться на ежа́, уж лу́чше[13] сесть на шля́пу.

4. READING PASSAGE

The following passage is given for practice in reading aloud. Practice phrases repeatedly until you can read them smoothly and then increase the length of the phrases. A line-by-line translation is given, together with grammatical notes where necessary.

1 *Excuse me.*   2 *What hat are you talking about?*
3 *Well, just here.*   4 *Indeed, in fact.*   5 *The whole way.*
6 Remember that words such as **что** *what, that,* **где** *where,* **когда́** *when* etc., must be preceded by a comma when they are not at the beginning of a sentence.
7 *He could* past tense: **мог, могла́, могло́, могли́.** Present tense: **я могу́, ты мо́жешь, он мо́жет, мы мо́жем, вы мо́жете, они́ мо́гут.**
8 *At once.*   9 Here *call my attention.*   10 *To the fact that.*
11 *One must look where one is sitting down.* The second pers. sing. is often used where English has *one* or *you.*
12 **Ёж** *hedgehog.*   13 *It's better* or *you might as well (in that case).*

Метéль
A Snowstorm | feminine noun ending in **ь**

Сильнá метéль на Ю́жном Урáле.
Strong is the snowstorm in the Southern Urals. | сильнá short form feminine of the adjective
NB *на* Урáле

Начинáется онá внезáпно.
It begins suddenly. | начинáть *to begin something*
начинáться *to begin to take place*

Сначáла идёт мéлкий снег,
First, fine snow falls; | *rain* дождь and *snow* снег are said to *come* идти́ in Russian

он сменя́ется крýпным.
it is replaced by heavier (snow). | крýпный *large, coarse (in size)*
крýпным is instrumental sing. masc.

Вéтер нарастáет
The wind grows in strength | нарастáть first conj., дýмать type

и перехóдит в вихрь,
and develops into a whirlwind, | перехóдит в lit. *'goes over into';*
переходи́ть: перехожý, перехóдишь; вихрь, masc. noun ending in ь

вóет, свисти́т, крýжит,
howls, whistles, whirls, | выть: вóю, вóешь (cf. мыть)
свистéть second conj. – свищý, свисти́шь etc.; кружи́ть: second conj. кружý, крýжишь

поднимáет огрóмные столбы́
raises huge columns
снéга с земли́.
of snow from the ground. | поднимáть first conj. дýмать type; столб *column*
земля́ *earth, land, ground*

Станóвится темнó.
It becomes dark. | становáться impfv., *to become*

В снéжном мрáке ничегó не ви́дно.
In the snowy darkness nothing can be seen. | снéжный adj. from снег
снéжном prep. sing. masc. of the adj.
ви́дно *visible.* NB in a negative sentence everything that can be negated *is* negated.

Н. Ефи́мова
N. Efimova

5. PREPOSITIONAL CASE OF PRONOUNS

a Masculine and neuter pronouns have the same case endings except in the nominative – accusative singular.

	nom. sing.		prep. sing.
	masc.	neut.	
this	э́тот	э́то	э́том
that	тот	то	том

	nom. sing.		prep. sing.
	masc.	neut.	
one	оди́н	одно́	одно́м
self	сам	само́	само́м
all	весь	всё	всём
who	кто	—	ком
what	—	что	чём

О ком говоря́т?	*Who are they talking about?*
О чём говоря́т?	*What are they talking about?*
Говоря́т об э́том парохо́де.	*They are talking about this ship.*
Говоря́т об э́том де́ле.	*They are talking about this business.*
В э́том мра́ке ничего́ не ви́дно.	*You cannot see anything in this gloom.*
Говоря́т об одно́м ученике́.	*They are talking about a certain (lit. one) pupil.*
На само́м су́дне нет никого́, они́ все на берегу́.	*There is nobody on the ship itself – they are all on shore.*
На том де́реве сиди́т воро́на.	*There is a crow sitting on that tree.*
Во всём ми́ре нет ми́ра.	*There is no peace throughout the world* (мир *world; peace*).

b Feminine pronouns take the ending **ой** or **ей:**

nom. sing.	prep. sing.
э́та	э́той
та	той
одна́	одно́й
сама́	само́й
вся	всей

На э́той кни́ге лежа́т бума́ги.	*There are papers lying on this book.*
В одно́й коро́бке пау́к.	*There is a spider in one box* (коро́бка *box*).
О само́й куха́рке мы не говори́м.	*We are not talking about the cook herself.*
На той ла́мпе му́ха.	*There is a fly on that lamp.*
Во всей кварти́ре нет све́та.	*The whole flat is in darkness* (lit. 'there is no light in the whole flat').

c As usual, plural forms do not show any difference of gender, so there is only one form of the prepositional plural for each pronoun and it is the same as the genitive plural:

nom. pl.	prep. pl.
э́ти	э́тих
те	тех
одни́	одни́х
са́ми	сами́х
все	всех

Note that the prepositional plural, like the genitive plural, ends in **x**, preceded by the vowel that is found in the nominative plural. The same vowel is found in the other plural cases of these pronouns.

На тех ла́мпах сидя́т му́хи.

Говоря́т об э́тих дела́х.

Говори́м об одни́х ученика́х. (*About the pupils alone* . . . and not about anybody else).

На сами́х суда́х нет никого́.

6. EXERCISE

Make up twenty short sentences using the prepositional case of the pronouns given above – ten in the singular and ten in the plural.

SUMMARY

1 Revision of the forms and use of imperfective and perfective (§ 1).

2 The verbs **сиде́ть** *to be sitting* and **сади́ться, сесть** *to sit down* (§ 2).

3 The prepositional of the pronouns ends in **ом/ём** in the masc. and neut. sing., **ой/ей** in the fem. sing. and **их/ех** in the plural (§ 5).

Lesson 15

I. ASPECTS – PREFIXED VERBS

You have now had a few dozen verbs presented as imperfective-perfective pairs. The imperfective and the perfective in these pairs were distinguished from each other by differences in the last consonant of the root or the last syllable of the infinitive and by differences in conjugation, such as:

perfective		*imperfective*	
запрети́ть:	запрещу́	запреща́ть:	запреща́ю
	запрети́шь		запреща́ешь
нагрузи́ть:	нагружу́	нагружа́ть:	нагружа́ю
	нагру́зишь		нагружа́ешь
дать:	дам, дашь, даст	дава́ть:	даю́, даёшь, даёт

There are many verbs which show the difference between the two aspects by the presence or absence of a prefix. With few exceptions simple verbs (ones without prefixes) are imperfective. When a prefix is added to a simple verb, again with few exceptions, it becomes perfective. In this way you make an imperfective-perfective pair: simple verb = imperfective, prefixed verb = perfective. The conjugation remains the same and the only difference between the present and the future perfective is that the latter has a prefix.

In the examples below the imperfective is given first, then the prefixed perfective.

Prefix **с-**

	imperfective		*perfective*
	уме́ть *to know how, to be able*		суме́ть
pres.	я уме́ю	*fut.*	суме́ю
	он уме́ет		суме́ет
past	уме́л, уме́ла, уме́ли		суме́л, суме́ла, суме́ли
	де́лать *to do, to make*		сде́лать
pres.	я де́лаю	*fut.*	сде́лаю
past	он де́лал		сде́лал

Prefix **у-**

	ви́деть *to see*		уви́деть *to catch sight of*
pres.	я ви́жу	*fut.*	уви́жу
	он ви́дит		уви́дит
past	он ви́дел		уви́дел

	imperfective		*perfective*
	слы́шать *to hear*		услы́шать *to catch the sound of*
pres.	я слы́шу	*fut.*	услы́шу
	он слы́шит		услы́шит
past	слы́шал		услы́шал

Prefix **по-**

	imperfective		*perfective*
	стро́ить *to build*		постро́ить
pres.	я стро́ю	*fut.*	постро́ю
	он стро́ит		постро́ит
past	он стро́ил		постро́ил

	imperfective		*perfective*
	теря́ть *to lose*		потеря́ть
pres.	я теря́ю	*fut.*	потеря́ю
	он теря́ет		потеря́ет
past	он теря́л		потеря́л

In these examples the three prefixes **с-**, **у-** and **по-** have no meaning of their own. They do not alter the basic meaning of the action, they only turn an imperfective verb into a perfective verb. Without the prefixes the conjugation has a present tense meaning, with the prefixes a future tense meaning. Such prefixes may be called *empty* prefixes, to distinguish them from those which *do* add something to the meaning of the simple verb. The two commonest empty prefixes are **по-** and **с-**.

Сего́дня мы стро́им наве́с, за́втра мы постро́им забо́р.
Today we are building a shed, tomorrow we shall build a fence.

Э́тот дом стро́или три го́да.
It took them three years to build this house. Lit. 'They were building this house for three years'.

Тут в го́роде э́та фи́рма постро́ила больни́цу, две шко́лы и вокза́л.
This firm has built here in the town a hospital, two schools and a station.

Я всегда́ теря́ю перча́тки. *I always lose my gloves.*

Е́сли ты нам дашь биле́ты, мы их потеря́ем.
If you give us the tickets we shall lose them.

Notice particularly the use of the future after **е́сли** *if.* When a clause with **е́сли** refers to the future the verb *must* be in the future. In Russian you say 'If you will give us' etc., whereas English does not use the future in these circumstances.

Е́сли я вам дам биле́ты, вы их потеря́ете.
If I give you (lit. 'shall give') *the tickets* etc.

Он ча́сто теря́л терпе́ние до́ма. *He often lost his patience at home.*
Они́ говори́ли весь ве́чер и вдруг он потеря́л терпе́ние.
They were talking the whole evening and suddenly he lost his temper.

2. PERFECTIVE PREFIX по- (*contd.*)

Here are some more common verbs which form the perfective by adding
по- to the simple imperfective.

	imperfective		*perfective*	
	звать *to call*		позва́ть	
pres.	я зову́	*fut.*	позову́	NB **o** appears in the
	он зовёт		позовёт	conjugation but not
	они́ зову́т		позову́т	in the infinitive and
past	звал, звала́, зва́ло		позва́л	past tense.

Я зову́ соба́ку уже́ полчаса́, её нигде́ нет. *I've been calling the dog for half-
an-hour (already), it's nowhere (to be found).*

> Notice that Russian has the present tense here, because the action
> has been going on for half-an-hour and is *still going on* up to the
> moment of speaking.

Я сейча́с позову́ дете́й на обе́д. *I'll call the children (in) to dinner at once.*
Он звал дете́й. *He called/was calling the children* (i.e. for some time).
Я позва́л дете́й домо́й. *I called the children home* (called once and they
probably came).

	imperfective		*perfective*
	ве́рить *to believe*		пове́рить
pres.	я ве́рю	*fut.*	пове́рю
	он ве́рит		пове́рит
past	ве́рил		пове́рил

Дед-моро́з in the following sentences is the Russian equivalent of *Father
Christmas*, lit. 'Grandad-Frost'. Notice that both parts decline.

Э́ти де́ти не ве́рят в[1] де́да-моро́за, они́ вам[1] не пове́рят, что вы дед-
моро́з. Ра́ньше[2] они́ ве́рили в де́да-моро́за, они́ пове́рили бра́ту,[3] что он
дед-моро́з, но э́то бы́ло два го́да тому́ наза́д.[4]

1 *To believe in* is **ве́рить в** + accusative but *to believe somebody* or *something*, i.e. to
  put trust in the veracity or trustworthiness of somebody or something is **ве́рить**
  + dative.
2 *Earlier.*
3 Perfective because they 'came to believe', on a specific occasion. The perfective not
  infrequently has the meaning of entering into the state expressed by the root verb.
  Translate here *They took my brother for Father Christmas.*
4 **Тому́ наза́д** *ago.*

imperfective	perfective
проси́ть *to ask, to beg*	попроси́ть
pres. я прошу́	*fut.* попрошу́
он про́сит	попро́сит
past проси́л	попроси́л

Бедня́к про́сит, про́сит – не даю́т.	The poor man begs and begs, but they don't give (*him anything*).
Бога́ч попро́сит – всё даду́т.	(*If*) *a rich man asks* (cf. § 1), *they'll give* (*him*) *everything.*
Бедня́к проси́л, проси́л – не дава́ли.	. . . *but they did not give* (*him anything*) – imperfective because it is a statement of something which in general, not just on one occasion, did not happen.
Бога́ч то́лько раз попроси́л – всё ему́ да́ли.	The rich man asked only once – they gave him everything.

imperfective	perfective
тре́бовать *to demand*	потре́бовать
pres. я тре́бую	*fut.* потре́бую
он тре́бует	потре́бует
past тре́бовал	потре́бовал

NB This verb governs the genitive case. It is an **-овать** verb and conjugates like **торгова́ть** (Lesson 12).

Э́та зада́ча тре́бует мно́го труда́.

Дире́ктор ско́ро потре́бует отчёта, а у нас ничего́ не гото́во (отчёт *report*, гото́во *ready*).

Чле́ны парла́мента тре́бовали отве́та от прави́тельства, а ли́дер оппози́ции вчера́ потре́бовал отчёта от самого́ премьёр-мини́стра (член *member*, прави́тельство *government*, вчера́ *yesterday*).

imperfective	perfective
туши́ть *to put out, to extinguish*	потуши́ть
pres. я тушу́	*fut.* потушу́
он ту́шит	поту́шит
past туши́л	потуши́л

туши́ть, потуши́ть свет *to put out the light.*

У нас был пожа́р. Туши́ли пожа́р о́чень до́лго и наконе́ц потуши́ли (пожа́р *fire*, i.e. a building on fire).

imperfective	perfective
кра́сить *to paint, to decorate*	покра́сить
pres. я кра́шу	*fut.* покра́шу
он кра́сит	покра́сит
past кра́сил	покра́сил

Что ты кра́сишь забо́р? На́до дом покра́сить, а не забо́р (что here *why*, забо́р *fence*).

Дом кра́сили уже́ мно́го раз, год тому́ наза́д покра́сили дом, а забо́р никто́ никогда́ не кра́сил, и вот я реши́л – я покра́шу забо́р, и тепе́рь я кра́шу забо́р, а не дом, (никогда́ *never*, see next paragraph).

3. NEGATION

If a verb is negated then everything else *that can be negated* in the same sentence must be negated. Hence pronouns and adverbs which have negative forms must be used in a negative sentence. In the middle of the last example above, we have **никто́ никогда́ не кра́сил,** lit. 'nobody never not painted,' i.e. *nobody ever painted.* In English one negative word is enough to make the sentence negative and two negatives will cancel each other out, but in Russian the sentence remains negative no matter how many negative words are used:

Никто́ нигде́ никогда́ ничего́ ника́к не кра́сит. *Nobody anywhere ever paints anything anyhow.*

You have seen already (Lesson 3) that **нет** *there is/are not*, **не́_было** *there was/were not*, require the genitive case. After negated verbs the object may also be in the genitive case but usage is not as rigid as with **нет.** On the average the genitive case is used in about 70 per cent and the accusative in about 30 per cent of negative sentences.

The following remarks are no more than a rough guide to the notions behind the use of genitive and accusative with negated verbs.

If you are thinking of the negative particle **не** and the verb as forming a unit, i.e. as a negated action, controlling an object, then the object goes into the genitive case:

Я [не кра́шу] забо́ра. *I'm not painting the fence.*
Он [не ви́дел] Со́ни. *He hasn't seen Sonya.*

If, however, you are thinking of the verb and its object together, as a unit, which is then negated, then the object goes into the accusative case:

Я не [понима́ю Со́ню]. *I can't understand Sonya.*
Она́ не [узна́ла ба́бушку]. *She didn't recognize her grandmother.*

It is for this reason that in the preceding paragraph we have **я кра́шу забо́р, а не дом.** This is equivalent to two sentences: **я кра́шу забо́р, я не кра́шу дом,** which, in our interpretation would be:

я [кра́шу забо́р], я не [кра́шу дом]

The same choice between genitive and accusative is present when the object is controlled by an infinitive which is itself controlled by a negated verb:

In **я [не хочу́ кра́сить] до́ма,** *I don't want to paint the house* the negation 'reaches over' the infinitive and causes *house* to be in the genitive.

In **я [не хочу́] [кра́сить дом]** the negated verb controls the infinitive + object, taken together as a unit.

The choice between accusative and genitive sometimes serves to distinguish between 'definite' and 'indefinite' as in:

> Я не [купи́л велосипе́д]. *I did not buy the bicycle.*
> Я [не купи́л] велосипе́да. *I did not buy a bicycle.*

Verbs which govern a case other than the accusative retain the same case when negated. The genitive after a negative concerns only the direct object.

4. MORE PERFECTIVES WITH THE PREFIX **по-**

	imperfective		*perfective*	
	брить *to shave (somebody)*		побри́ть	
pres.	я бре́ю	*fut.*	побре́ю	NB First conjugation,
	он бре́ет		побре́ет	with **e** in conjugation
	они́ бре́ют		побре́ют	but **и** in infinitive and
past	брил		побри́л	past tense.

бри́ться *to shave (oneself)* is a reflexive verb:

> я бре́юсь   ты бре́ешься   он бре́ется

Он мы́лся и бри́лся всё у́тро.
Он бы́стро помы́лся, побри́лся и на́чал рабо́тать (нача́ть perfective of начина́ть *to begin*).

обе́дать *to dine* **пообе́дать**   } all first conjuga-
за́втракать *to lunch* or *to breakfast* **поза́втракать** } tion, **ду́мать**
у́жинать *to sup* **поу́жинать**   } type

Они́ до́лго обе́дали. *They took a long time over dinner.*
Они́ хорошо́ пообе́дали. *They had a good dinner.*
Они́ всегда́ за́втракали ра́но. Сего́дня они́ поза́втракали по́здно (*late*) и по́здно на́чали рабо́ту.
Они́ ча́сто у́жинали в рестора́не, и вчера́ они́ поу́жинали в рестора́не.

смотре́ть *to look* **посмотре́ть**

A second conjugation verb (Lesson 7, § 5): **я смотрю́, он смо́трит; я посмотрю́, он посмо́трит** etc.

Я смотрю́ и смотрю́ – никого́ нет.

Я посмотрю́ ещё раз, там ведь кто́-то идёт (ещё раз *once more*, ведь *why,
   you know*, кто́-то *somebody*).
Станови́лось уже́ темно́, а он всё ещё смотре́л на у́лицу (всё ещё *still*).
Он посмотре́л на у́лицу, но там никого́ не_́было.

5. По- 'FOR A LITTLE WHILE'

With some verbs **по-** is not quite an *empty* prefix. It adds the meaning of
doing something for a little while or doing a little of something. **Посмотре́ть**
at the end of the preceding paragraph is such a verb and can be translated
as *to glance, take a look*.

Он посмотре́л на меня́ и пото́м не обраща́л на меня́ внима́ния.

It is not always necessary to add 'for a little (while)' in translating these verbs.

imperfective	perfective
ду́мать *to think*	поду́мать
стоя́ть *to stand*	постоя́ть

Вот я поду́маю немно́го и тогда́ решу́, что де́лать (немно́го *a little*).
Он постоя́л, поду́мал мину́ту и́ли две, но так и не_́дал отве́та (но так и
   but still, отве́т *reply*).

слу́шать *to listen* **послу́шать** first conjugation **ду́мать** type.
Мы до́лго слу́шали, что там говори́ли, но бы́ло о́чень ску́чно (ску́чно
   boring).
Ну, я послу́шаю, что они́ там говоря́т.
Послу́шала, постоя́ла немно́го, но говори́ли они́ одну́ ерунду́ (ерунда́
   rubbish).
Он сиде́л на дива́не и смотре́л на у́лицу – и вдруг уви́дел нас.
Она́ слу́шала меня́ внима́тельно, но ничего́ не понима́ла; бы́ло я́сно,
что она́ хотя́ и слу́шала, но ничего́ не слы́шала, ничего́ не понима́ла
(внима́тельно *attentively*, я́сно *clear*, хотя́ (и) *although*).
Они́ слу́шали ра́дио и вдруг услы́шали го́лос отца́ на у́лице.

The following verbs when prefixed with **по-** also have the meaning 'a little'
or 'for a little while':

игра́ть, поигра́ть	рабо́тать, порабо́тать
кури́ть, покури́ть	говори́ть, поговори́ть
чита́ть, почита́ть	

Дя́дя постоя́л, посмотре́л, и покури́л. Он порабо́тал, но о́чень ма́ло
(ма́ло *little*). (Cf. Lesson 11, § 3: Дя́дя ма́ло рабо́тал, он стоя́л, он
смотре́л и мно́го кури́л.)
Ты сиде́ла и слу́шала ра́дио и ма́ло говори́ла с на́ми (с на́ми *with us*).
Ты посиде́ла и послу́шала ра́дио и поговори́ла с на́ми, но о́чень ма́ло.

The perfectives of *to sit*, *to lie* and *to hold* also have this built-in meaning
of short duration.

Он полежа́л на дива́не, а пото́м посиде́л в кре́сле, подержа́л вну́ка на рука́х, почита́л газе́ту.

The other second conjugation verbs ending in **-жать, -шать** etc. (Lesson 13, § 3) can also have perfectives with **по-** meaning 'a little'.

6. EXERCISE FOR COMPREHENSION

– Тут так хо́лодно, э́то нехорошо́, вот когда́ нача́льник[1] ся́дет тут…

– Ну, так что? Нача́льник поворчи́т, вот и всё.

– Он не то́лько поворчи́т, но и покричи́т и кулако́м[2] по_столу[3] постучи́т.

– Ну так что же?[4] Он кулако́м по_столу стучи́т, а вы уже́ бои́тесь и дрожи́те.

– Вот когда́ ты услы́шишь, как он кричи́т[5]…

– Он кричи́т! Поду́маешь![6] Вы и дыша́ть бои́тесь, когда́ он про́сто[7] молчи́т. А вот у нас[8] нача́льник и ворчи́т, и рычи́т и кричи́т, не то́лько кулако́м по_столу стучи́т, но и нога́ми[9] стучи́т – то́пает[10] нога́ми – и крик[11] и шум, я никогда́ не бою́сь, никогда́ не дрожу́, и сама́ покричу́ и кулако́м постучу́. Вот![12]

– А ты зна́ешь что, ты лу́чше помолчи́,[13] ты помолчи́ немно́го!

7. READING EXERCISE

Мете́ль (*contd.*)

Места́ обши́рные.	
The areas are vast.	
Селе́ния нахо́дятся	находи́ть *to find*, находи́ться
The villages are (*situated*)	*to be found, to be situated*
на расстоя́нии	prepositional case of расстоя́ние
at a distance	neuter
пяти́ киломе́тров и бо́лее.	пяти́ is genitive of пять *five*
of five kilometres and more.	
Жи́тели прокла́дывают	жи́тель *inhabitant*
The inhabitants lay down	
зи́мние коро́ткие доро́ги	
short winter roads	
че́рез боло́та и ре́чки,	че́рез + accusative *across*
across the marshes and streams,	боло́то *marsh, swamp, bog*
	ре́чка *stream*

---

1 *Boss.*   2 *With his fist.*   3 *On the table/desk.*

4 **Же** is an emphatic particle: it emphasizes the preceding word *so what?*

5 Note this construction. To hear, to see, to watch, to listen to somebody doing something are expressed by saying 'to hear etc., how he does such-and-such.'

6 Idiom: *Just fancy! Fancy that!*   7 *Simply, just.*   8 Translate *our.*

9 *With his feet.*   10 **То́пать** *to stamp.*   11 *Shouting.*   12 *So there!*

13 This is an imperative, to be dealt with in the next lesson. Translate *You'd better keep quiet* (*for a bit*).

кото́рые замерза́ют в ноябре́ ме́сяце	ноя́брь *November*
which freeze up in the month of November	ме́сяц *month*
	NB both are in the same case
и покрыва́ются сне́гом.	
and are covered with snow.	сне́гом instrumental case of снег
Ве́село быть в гостя́х,	гость *guest* быть в гостя́х
It is fun to be visiting,	(prepositional plural) *to be visiting*
но пора́ и домо́й.	
but it's time (to go) home.	пора́ *it is time*
Ло́шади бы́стро прое́хали	ло́шадь *horse*
The horses have swiftly passed through	
небольшо́й берёзовый лесо́к.	берёза *birchtree*
a small birch copse.	
Но что́-то хму́рится не́бо,	что́-то *something*; as adverb
But the sky is rather lowering,	*somewhat, somehow, for some reason*
	хму́риться *to frown, to glower*
нависа́ют ни́зкие облака́,	о́блако *cloud*
low clouds hang over(head),	
они́ бы́стро сгуща́ются в ту́чи,	ту́ча *storm-cloud*
they quickly thicken into storm-clouds,	
поду́л ве́тер.	поду́ть (perfective of дуть *to blow) to start to blow*
a wind has got up.	

8. TRANSLATION

They are building a house. – They were building it when I was here two years ago. – Yes, they've been building[1] it (for) three years. This firm has also built two hospitals.

Will you lose these gloves if I give them to you? – I always lose (my) gloves, in the theatre, in the bus, in the street.

Have you called the children home yet?[2] Mother was calling them (for) half-an-hour.

Do you believe in Father Christmas? Mary used to believe in Father Christmas but now[3] she doesn't.

John believed the doctor, though usually[4] he never believed him at all.[5]

---

1 See § 2 above. 2 **Уже́** before the verb. 3 **Бо́льше не** *no longer*, before the verb.
4 **Обы́чно.** 5 **Совсе́м не** *not at all*, before the verb.

Have they put the fire out yet? – No, they've been putting it out for two hours but they haven't put it out yet.

The doctor looked and looked but he couldn't see[1] the ticket. He glanced on the desk but the ticket wasn't on the desk.

Father stood for a while in the garden, then sat on a chair. He sat there for a while[2] and smoked his pipe.

The boss will shout and bang on the desk a little but the secretaries are not afraid of him.

1 Say 'didn't see'.   2 **Посиде́л.**

SUMMARY

1 Many imperfective-perfective pairs consist of the simple verb (imperfective) and the 'same' verb prefixed (perfective) (§ 1).

2 A prefix which simply makes a verb perfective is an 'empty' prefix and the two commonest are **по-** and **с-** (§ 1).

3 After **е́сли** *if* Russian has the future tense if the clause refers to the future (§ 1).

4 Russian expresses 'has/have been doing' by the *present tense* when the period of time is mentioned (§ 2).

5 Pronouns and adverbs must be in the negative form in a negated sentence (§ 3).

6 A negated verb may govern the genitive case (§ 3).

7 With some verbs the prefix **по-** means *for a little (while)* (§ 5).

Lesson 16

I. IMPERATIVE I

The imperative is the form of the verb which expresses a command.

To form the imperative of verbs of the first conjugation, i.e. those of the **дýмать** group, having **-ет** in the third pers. sing. with a vowel in front of this ending, you lop off the ending **-ет** and add **-й**. This gives you the imperative singular, the form that, like the pronoun **ты** and the second pers. sing. of the verb, is used when addressing relations, close friends, animals etc.

дýмать *to think*	он дýмает	дýмай *think!*
мыть *to wash*	он мóет	мой *wash!*
сéять *to sow*	он сéет	сей *sow!*
торговáть *to trade*	он торгýет	торгýй *trade!*

The few second conjugation verbs with a vowel before the third pers. sing. ending form the imperative in the same way:

стрóить *to build*	он стрóит	строй *build!*
стоя́ть *to stand*	он стоúт	стой *stop!*
боя́ться *to be afraid*	он боúтся	не бóйся *don't be afraid*

The last imperative here is given in the negative form, since it is unlikely that you will want to say *be afraid!*

Notice that **-й** is treated as a consonant: it is followed by the reflexive particle in its form **-ся**, which follows consonants.

The plural of the imperative, i.e. the form you use when addressing more than one person or when addressing a single person in the polite fashion, is formed simply by adding **-те** (cf. second pers. pl. of the conjugation) to the imperative singular:

дýмай	дýмайте
мой	мóйте
сей	сéйте
торгýй	торгýйте
строй	стрóйте
стой	стóйте
не бóйся	не бóйтесь

The reflexive verb *to laugh* смея́ться goes like **сéять:**

он смеётся	смéйся	смéйтесь
	не смéйся	не смéйтесь

Do not confuse the reflexive verb **смея́ться** with the verb *to dare* **сметь,** conjugated like **дýмать:**

103

он смéет	смей	смéйте

И он смéет смея́ться! Не смей смея́ться! Не смéйте смея́ться!

Here are some more verbs with their imperative:

to sing

петь *impfv.*	пою́, поёшь, поёт	пой, пóйте
спеть *pfv.*	спою́, споёшь, споёт	спой, спóйте

to soothe

успокáивать *impfv.*	успокáиваю	успокáивай, успокáивайте
успокóить *pfv.*	успокóю	успокóй, успокóйте

These verbs occur in the following quotation from a song:

Лáсточка	*The Swallow*
Пой, лáсточка, пой!	*Sing, swallow, sing!*
Сéрдце мне успокóй!	*Quieten my heart!*

The perfective-imperfective pair *to give* **дать, давáть,** which has a special conjugation, has imperative:

дать	он даст	дай, дáйте
давáть	он даёт	давáй, давáйте

Notice that **дать** behaves almost normally. Before adding the imperative ending it removes the third pers. sing. ending, which in this case consists of **-ст. Давáть** is unusual in that it forms the imperative from the stem of the infinitive. The other verbs in **-авáть** which conjugate in **-аю́, -аёшь** etc., form their imperative in the same way:

вставáть *to get up*	он встаёт	не вставáй, вставáйте
признавáть *to admit*	он признаёт	не признавáй, признавáйте

The imperative **давáй, давáйте** is very common in idiomatic usage and means *let's*. In this usage it combines either with the first pers. pl. future perfective of a verb or with the imperfective infinitive.

a **Давáй, давáйте** + first pers. pl. future perfective:

Давáйте поигрáем. *Let's play a bit.*

Давáйте почитáем. *Let's read a bit.*

Давáйте посиди́м у окнá. *Let's sit by the window.*

Давáй посмóтрим телеви́зор. *Let's watch television.*

Давáй послу́шаем рáдио. *Let's listen to the radio.*

Давáй поу́жинаем. *Let's have supper.*

Давáй пообéдаем. *Let's have dinner.*

Давáй позáвтракаем. *Let's have breakfast/lunch.*

А потóм, давáй поку́рим и поговори́м. *And then let's have a smoke and a chat.*

b **Дава́й, дава́йте** + imperfective infinitive:

Дава́йте у́жинать. *Let's have supper.*

Дава́й игра́ть в ша́хматы. *Let's play chess.*

Дава́йте чита́ть вме́сте. *Let's read together.*

A colloquial use of **дава́й** is in the sense of *get on with it*. Here **дава́й** is often repeated for emphasis:

Дава́й! дава́й! *Come on, get a move on/get on with it!*

If you ask someone to do something, the perfective form is somewhat politer. If you ask people not to do something, that is if you prohibit, you use: **не** + imperfective of the imperative.

Ты ду́маешь о бра́те. Не ду́май о нём.

Вы не ду́маете о бра́те. Поду́майте о нём.

Ты мо́ешься без мы́ла (мы́ло *soap*). Не мо́йся без мы́ла.

Вы не мо́ете ру́ки? – Нет мы́ла. – Помо́йте ру́ки, мы́ло на по́лке.

Вы се́ете о́чень ра́но. Не се́йте зимо́й. – Когда́ же? – Дава́йте посе́ем весно́й.

Ты даёшь ему́ чересчу́р (*too*) мно́го де́нег на (*for*) обе́д. Не дава́й ему́ сто́лько (*so much*). Дай ему́ полови́ну. Бо́льше не на́до.

Дава́йте, ребя́та, постро́им бу́дку на дворе́ (бу́дка *hut*).

Да нет, не стро́йте бу́дку, заче́м она́ вам? (*What use is it to you?*). Е́сли хоти́те, лу́чше постро́йте забо́р (лу́чше *better*).

If you want to order somebody to keep on doing something or to keep repeating an action you will of course use the imperfective imperative:

Мо́йте ру́ки пе́ред едо́й. *Wash your hands before a meal.*

Принима́йте лека́рство по́сле обе́да. *Take the medicine after dinner.*

Игра́йте в гольф, е́сли не хоти́те толсте́ть. *Play golf, if you don't want to get fat.*

2. Бить, пить, лить, шить, вить

Five monosyllabic verbs in **ить** (and their compounds) are first conjugation verbs which change the **и** of the infinitive to **ь** in the conjugation.

бить *to strike*	пить *to drink*	лить *to pour*	шить *to sew*
я бью	пью	лью	шью
ты бьёшь	пьёшь	льёшь	шьёшь
он бьёт	пьёт	льёт	шьёт
мы бьём	пьём	льём	шьём
вы бьёте	пьёте	льёте	шьёте
они́ бьют	пьют	льют	шьют

Тепе́рь я пью вино́, ра́ньше я пила́ во́дку. *Now I drink wine, formerly I drank vodka.*

Ве́тер бьёт в лицо́. *The wind strikes (you) in the face.*

Он бил соба́ку. *He beat his dog.*
Он льёт во́ду на_пол. *He is pouring the water onto the floor.*
Она́ шьёт мне руба́шку. *She is making (sewing) me a shirt.*

The perfectives of these verbs are as follows:

бить, поби́ть		пить, вы́пить *to drink up*	
лить, нали́ть		шить, сшить[1]	
поли́ть *to pour a little*			

In the imperative of these verbs the **ь** turns into **е**:

бей	пей	лей	шей
бе́йте	пе́йте	ле́йте	ше́йте

Не бей соба́ку, не на́до бить соба́ку.
Не пе́йте так мно́го, не хорошо́! Не на́до пить во́дку!
Не ле́йте мне на_ноги, поле́йте мне на_руки.
Не ше́йте сейча́с воротни́к, сше́йте его́ по́сле (*later*).

Вить, pfv. **свить,** *to twine, to weave* forms its parts in exactly the same way as the verbs illustrated.

3. IMPERATIVE II

Verbs of the first conjugation with a consonant before stressed endings, such as **идти́: иду́, идёшь** etc., **нести́: несу́, несёшь** etc., and verbs of the second conjugation of the type listed below, form the imperative in **-й** (sing.), **-йте** (pl.) if the first pers. sing. is stressed on the ending. Remove the ending of the third pers. sing. and add **-й/-йте:**

идти́ *to go*	иду́, идёт	иди́	иди́те
нести́ *to carry*	несу́, несёт	неси́	неси́те
звать *to call*	зову́, зовёт (NB **о**)	зови́	зови́те
брать *to take*	беру́, берёт (NB **е**)	бери́	бери́те
жить *to live*	живу́, живёт (NB **в**)	живи́	живи́те
говори́ть *to say, to speak*	говорю́, говори́т	говори́	говори́те
смотре́ть *to look*	смотрю́, смо́трит	смотри́	смотри́те
молча́ть *to keep silent*	молчу́, молчи́т	молчи́	молчи́те
буди́ть *to wake (somebody)*	бужу́, бу́дит	буди́	буди́те

Verbs with infinitive in **-чь** also form the imperative in stressed **-й/-йте** but this replaces the ending of the *first* pers. sing.:

помо́чь *to help*	помогу́, помо́жешь	помоги́, помоги́те
печь *to bake*	пеку́, печёшь	пеки́, пеки́те

1 Do not try to pronounce **с** as **с** in this word. When **с** is followed by **ш** it takes on the value of **ш**, so **сшить** is pronounced as if spelt with a double **ш**. See Part II – Pronunciation.

Verbs of either conjugation having two or more consonants before **-ет** or **-ит** and which are stressed on the stem throughout and not on the endings form the imperative in unstressed **-и/-ите**:

кри́кнуть *to cry out*	он кри́кнет	кри́кни	кри́кните
умо́лкнуть *to fall silent*	он умо́лкнет	умо́лкни	умо́лкните
ко́нчить *to finish*	он ко́нчит	ко́нчи	ко́нчите

Verbs of either conjugation having only one consonant before **-ет** or **-ит** and which are stressed on the stem throughout form the imperative in **-ь/-ьте,** which replaces the **-ет** or **-ит** of the third pers. sing.:

быть *to be*	он бу́дет	будь	бу́дьте
сесть *to sit down*	он ся́дет	сядь	ся́дьте
встать *to stand up*	он вста́нет	встань	вста́ньте
дви́нуть *to move*	он дви́нет	двинь	дви́ньте
бро́сить *to throw*	он бро́сит	брось	бро́сьте

Будь гото́в!	*Be prepared!* (slogan of the Pioneers, the Communist organization for children)
Бу́дьте здоро́вы!	*Bless you!* (lit. 'Be healthy', said when somebody sneezes)
Бу́дьте во́время на вокза́ле!	*Be at the station in time.*
Сядь сюда́! Ся́дьте на стул!	*Sit over here. Sit on the chair.*
Брось мне мяч.	*Throw me the ball.*

The verb **бро́сить** also means *to drop* or *stop doing* something:

Брось э́ту газе́ту! Дава́й поговори́м.	*Drop that newspaper. Let's have a talk.*
Да бро́сьте ссо́риться!	*Oh, do stop quarrelling!*
Бро́сьте кури́ть!	*Give up smoking.*

4. 'LET'

To let, to allow **пусти́ть** perfective, **пуска́ть** imperfective, has a rather unusual consonant difference, **ст – ск**, between the two aspects. The conjugations are:

fut. pfv.	*pres.*
я пущу́	я пуска́ю
ты пу́стишь	ты пуска́ешь
он пу́стит	он пуска́ет

and the imperatives:

пусти́, пусти́те	пуска́й, пуска́йте

Ты меня́ никуда́ не пуска́ешь. *You don't let me go anywhere.*
Пусти́ меня́ на у́лицу. Я не пущу́ тебя́ на у́лицу.
Ве́чером я не пуска́ю дете́й на у́лицу. Не пуска́йте дете́й на у́лицу.
Пусти́ соба́ку на двор.

With the third pers. of the verb in the present or future perfective (according to what the situation requires) **пуска́й** or **пусть** (derived from **пусти́**) assumes the meaning of 'let him/them do such-and-such'. This is known as the *third person imperative*.

> Пуска́й/Пусть он поёт, не меша́йте ему́.
> *Let him sing, don't worry him.*
> Пуска́й/Пусть они́ говоря́т, мы всё равно́ не слу́шаем.
> *Let them talk, we aren't listening anyway.*
> Пуска́й/Пусть Ве́ра даст ему́ ча́шку ча́я.
> *Let Vera give him a cup of tea.*

5. PERFECTIVES OF VERBS OF MOTION WITH PREFIX по-

The last words in **Мете́ль** in the preceding lesson were **поду́л ве́тер** – *a wind has got up*. **Поду́ть** is a perfective of **дуть** with the special meaning of *to begin to blow*. It is a curious fact that some perfectives denote the beginning of an action, though, as you have learnt, the function of the perfective aspect is to express completion. Such verbs as **поду́ть** express in fact the completion of the beginning of an action. They are called *inceptives*.

The prefix **по-** has this inceptive meaning with such verbs of motion as **идти́, е́хать, вести́, лете́ть** etc. When prefixed these verbs become perfective, of course. Notice that **идти́** becomes **-йти** when prefixed:

идти́	пойти́
Я иду́ домо́й.	Я пойду́ домо́й.
I am going home.	*I shall go home/I shall set off home.*
Я шла домо́й.	Я пошла́ домо́й.
I was walking home.	*I set off for/went home.*
Снег идёт.	Снег пойдёт.
It is snowing.	*It will start to snow.*
Шёл снег.	Снег пошёл.
It was snowing.	*It started to snow,* lit. 'snow began to come'.
е́хать	пое́хать
Я е́ду на грузовике́.	Я пое́ду в Пари́ж.
I am going on a lorry.	*I shall go to Paris.*
Они́ е́хали в Пари́ж.	Они́ пое́хали в Пари́ж.
They were going to Paris.	*They went to/set off for Paris.*

Везти́ (imperfective), **повезти́** (perfective) is another verb of motion which you have not met before. It means *to transport, to cart*, i.e. to take somebody or something in/on a vehicle or on horseback.

	imperfective		*perfective*
pres.	я везу́	*fut.*	повезу́
	ты везёшь		повезёшь
	он везёт		повезёт

imperfective	perfective	
мы везём	повезём	
вы везёте	повезёте	
они везу́т	повезу́т	
past. вёз *masc.*	повёз	cf. **нести́ – нёс,**
везла́ *fem.*	повезла́	**несла́** etc.
везло́ *neut.*	повезло́	
везли́ *pl.*	повезли́	

The infinitive of this verb *sounds* like the infinitive **вести́ – повести́,** since **з** before **т** is pronounced like **с,** but the spelling is different.

Мы пое́хали на да́чу и повезли́ мно́го багажа́. Позва́ли носи́льщика, да́ли ему́ все чемода́ны, а оте́ц сам понёс у́дочки и портфе́ль. Мать повела́ дете́й, я понесла́ ко́шку в корзи́нке, брат повёл соба́ку, а носи́льщик повёз чемода́ны.

The verb **везти́, повезти́** is also used in the third pers. sing., and in the neuter form of the past tense in an idiom with the dative case, meaning *to be lucky.*

> Нам повезло́. *We were lucky.*
> Вам повезло́. *You were lucky.*
> Ему́ везёт. *He is lucky.*

Such constructions, in which the verb has no grammatical subject, are known as *impersonal* constructions.

Нам повезло́ – там был носи́льщик – он повёз чемода́ны. Да, нам повезло́, а бра́ту не повезло́, он сам нёс чемода́ны.

6. READING EXERCISE

Мете́ль (*contd.*)

Вдруг пошёл ме́лкий снег.
All at once fine snow began to fall.

вдруг *suddenly, all at once;*
ме́лкий *fine (in size), small, shallow*

Внеза́пно он смени́лся кру́пными хло́пьями.
Suddenly it changed to large flakes.

lit. 'it replaced self by . . .'
хло́пья *snowflakes* is a plural of an uncommon kind ending in -ья. This particular word has no singular. *A snowflake* is снежи́нка

Ве́тер поду́л с тако́й си́лой, что лошадя́м тру́дно бежа́ть.
The wind began to blow with such strength that it (was) difficult for the horses to run.

лошадя́м тру́дно бежа́ть
a dative + infinitive construction, cf. ему́ тру́дно *it is difficult for him*

Всё смеша́лось в бе́лом ви́хре.
Everything was merged in a white whirlwind.

вихрь (m.) *whirlwind*

Во мра́ке ничего́ не ви́дно.
Nothing could be seen in the darkness.

То́лько вой в уша́х,
Only a howling in the ears,

у́хо *ear* has an irregular plural у́ши

да ре́зкий колю́чий ве́тер
бьёт в лицо́,
and the sharp stinging wind beats at (your) face,

колю́чий *prickly*

лицо́ гори́т.
your face burns.

горе́ть *to burn*

Захва́тывает дыха́ние.
You catch your breath.

lit. 'it catches breath'

Пу́тники, в овчи́нных тулу́пах
и ва́ленках,
Travellers in sheep-skin coats and felt-boots,

пу́тник *traveller*; овчи́нный *of sheep-skin*; тулу́п *fur-coat*; ва́ленки *felt-boots*

чу́вствуют, как ве́тер
прони́зывает до косте́й.
feel the wind penetrating to their bones.

чу́вствовать *to feel,*
прони́зывать *to penetrate*
кость (f.) *bone*
как ве́тер, etc., lit. 'how the wind'

Нельзя́ гляде́ть – снег с си́лой
ле́пит в лицо́.
You can't look – the snow with force (drives) into your face and sticks.

нельзя́ *it is impossible, one cannot/may not*
лепи́ть *to stick, to model* (as with clay)
в лицо́, acc., giving added meaning of motion to ле́пит

Завыва́ние вью́ги глуши́т слова́
това́рища, кото́рый сиди́т
ря́дом.
The moaning of the blizzard drowns the words of your companion, who is sitting by your side.

вью́га *blizzard*
глуши́ть *to deafen, to drown*
кото́рый *who*

7. TRANSLATION

Don't think about (your) sister. She has always been lucky and she'll be lucky this time too.[1]

Wash (your) hands now. Here is soap and a towel. And always wash (your) hands before meals.

Don't build a house by the river. It's cold and damp there. Build it by the wood.

1 И в э́тот раз.

'Sing me a little song.'[1]
'Let's sing together.'
'Play[2] the music,[3] John. Ann, you sing.[4] Ann sings so well. Give John the music.'[5]
'Let's sit by the fire and watch television.'
'No, let's listen to the radio.'
'Stop! That's too[6] loud.'
'I shall go now. Are you going?'
'No, it's snowing. I'll set off later.'[7]
'They've set off on the lorry without me.'
'I'll take you.'
Sister Suzie's sewing shirts.
'Call the waiter![8] Waiter, keep bringing[9] more[10] wine. Pour me some[11] wine.'
'Does he always drink a lot of wine?'
'Don't be afraid. Let him drink – and let them talk, it doesn't worry me. He shouts a lot but he doesn't drink much.'[12]
'Don't talk so loud. He can hear[13] you.'

1 Accusative of **пéсенка;** use perfective imperative singular.   2 Imperfective imperative.   3 **Аккомпанемéнт.**   4 Put *you* before the imperative, just as in English.
5 *Music* in the sense of *score* is **нóты,** a plural noun.   6 **Слѝшком.**   7 **Пóзже.**
8 **Официáнт.**   9 Use the imperfective imperative.   10 **Бóльше** + genitive.
11 Genitive of *wine* is enough to translate *some*.   12 Say *he drinks little*.   13 Say simply *he hears*.

SUMMARY

1 The imperative ends in **-й/-йте, -ѝ/-ѝте, -и/-ите** or **-ь/-ьте** (§§ 1, 2, 3).

Type of verb	*imperative ending*
a Vowel before third pers. sing. (also **бить** type)	-й/-йте
b First conjug. with consonant before stressed third pers. sing. / Second conjug. with one or more consonants before stressed first pers. sing. ending.	-ѝ/-ѝте
c Two or more consonants before unstressed third pers. sing.	-и/-ите
d One consonant before unstressed third pers. sing.	-ь/-ьте

2 The **и** of **бить, пить, лить, шить** changes to **ь** in the conjugation and the **ь** changes to **е** in the imperative (§ 2).

3 *Let us* is expressed by **давáй/давáйте** (§ 1), *let him/them* by **пускáй/пусть** (§ 4).

4 With some verbs, including the verbs of motion **идтѝ, нестѝ** etc., the prefix **по-** not only makes the perfective aspect but also adds the meaning of *to begin to* (§ 5).

LESSON 17 REVISION

Lesson 18

1. SHORT FORMS OF ADJECTIVES

Adjectives are words which describe nouns. They can be used in two ways in the sentence, as in *The old house stands by the river, I see a beautiful bridge over the wide river* or as in *The house is old, That bridge is beautiful, The river is wide.* In sentences of the first type the adjective is said to be an *attribute*, it is an attributive adjective. It merely stands with its noun to describe it. In sentences of the second type the adjective is used to make a new statement about the noun, the subject. The part of a sentence which makes a statement about the subject is called the predicate and an adjective which forms the gist of the predicate is called a *predicative adjective*.

Adjectives function in the same way in Russian. Attributive adjectives are declined. They agree with the noun which they describe in number, gender and case. This form of the adjective is known as the *long form*. In the predicative function you use either the long form or what is known as the *short form*. In modern Russian the long form is tending to take over the predicative function from the short form but there are still very many instances when the short form is preferable and many instances when the short form is obligatory.

Apart from a few 'fossilized' expressions, all of which are given in dictionaries, the short form is always in the nominative and agrees with its noun in gender and number. It is in the nominative because it is linked by the verb *to be* to the noun which is the subject of the sentence and therefore in the nominative case.

To form the short adjective you remove the last two letters of the nominative masculine long form to obtain the short form masculine; then add **a** for feminine, **o** for neuter and **ы** for plural. The short adjective then has endings like those of nouns of the corresponding gender:

Молодо́й *young*

| мо́лод | молода́ | мо́лодо | мо́лоды |

Сын мо́лод. Сестра́ о́чень молода́. Де́рево мо́лодо. Они́ ещё мо́лоды.

Дорого́й *dear*, both 'expensive' and 'dear to the heart'.

| до́рог | дорога́ | до́рого | до́роги |

Э́тот биле́т до́рог (биле́т *ticket*). Э́та кни́га мне дорога́. Его́ лицо́ мне до́рого.

In this lesson each set of short forms is headed by the nominative singular masculine of the long form of the adjective. For the time being simply treat them as headings. They will be discussed in the next lesson.

Ста́рый *old*

      стар   стара́   старо́   стары́

Э́тот дуб (*oak*) стар. Ба́бушка (*grandmother*) стара́. Пальто́ старо́. Сосе́ди (*neighbours*) стары́.

Бога́тый *rich*

      бога́т   бога́та   бога́то   бога́ты

Го́род бога́т. Приро́да (*nature*) бога́та. Госуда́рство (*State*) бога́то. Они́ бога́ты.

Здоро́вый *healthy*

      здоро́в   здоро́ва   здоро́во   здоро́вы

Будь здоро́в ог бу́дьте здоро́вы. *Be well* or *bless you,* said when somebody sneezes.

Хоро́ший *good*

      хоро́ш   хороша́   хорошо́   хоро́ший

Портре́т хоро́ш. Маши́на хороша́. Э́то ле́то хорошо́.

The short form for *good* can be used ironically, just as in English, meaning how awful somebody or something happens to be:

Ну и хоро́ш э́тот учени́к – ничего́ не понима́ет.
И хоро́ш же тра́нспорт в го́роде – нет ни авто́бусов, ни такси́ – ничего́ нет!

In English, however, attributive adjectives would be used in these sentences: *Well, he's a fine pupil – doesn't understand a thing. And what fine transport (we have) in this town – there are neither buses nor taxis – there's nothing.*

Плохо́й *bad*

      плох   плоха́   пло́хо   пло́хи

Э́тот актёр плох, и балери́на плоха́, вся пье́са плоха́, все пло́хи. Всё пло́хо.

Пра́вый *right*   **непра́вый** *wrong*

      прав   права́   пра́во   пра́вы
      непра́в   неправа́   непра́во   непра́вы

Он прав. Она́ права́. Прави́тельство пра́во.
Мы то́же пра́вы. Нет, вы непра́вы.

Most adjectives which have two consonants before the endings in the long form insert a mobile vowel between the two consonants *in the short form masculine only.* This mobile vowel is sometimes **o,** sometimes **e** or **ё.** If there is a soft sign between the two consonants in the long form the mobile vowel which replaces it is always **e** or **ё.**

I

Си́льный *strong*

си́лен and силён сильна́ си́льно си́льны and сильны́

Си́лен ве́тер. Мете́ль сильна́. Си́льны мете́ли. Си́льны ве́тры.
Влия́ние э́того а́втора си́льно. *The influence of this author is strong.*

Злой *angry, wicked*

зол зла зло злы

Он был зол. Она́ была́ зла. Они́ бы́ли злы.
As you see, the short form is also used after the past tense of to be.

Гру́стный *sad*

гру́стен грустна́ гру́стно гру́стны and грустны́

Э́тот напе́в (*melody*) гру́стен. Грустна́ э́та пе́сня. Гру́стны э́ти напе́вы
и пе́сни.

Бли́зкий *near*

бли́зок близка́ бли́зко бли́зки and близки́

«Уж бли́зок бе́рег, бли́зок ве́чер.» '*Already the shore is near, the evening
is near.*'

2. THE ADVERB AND SHORT FORM NEUTER ADJECTIVE

The neuter form of the short adjective is mostly identical with the adverb
though sometimes the stress is different.

The short neuter adjective for *rich*, *wealthy*, for instance, is **бога́то.**

Село́ бога́то. *The village is wealthy.*
Госуда́рство бога́то. *The State is wealthy.*

Here wealthy qualifies the *village*, the *state*, both neuter nouns in Russian.
The adverb *wealthily* or *in a wealthy way* in Russian is also **бога́то.**

Они́ живу́т бога́то. *They live wealthily.*

Here *wealthily*, the adverb, describes how they live, that is it qualifies the
verb, and it does not agree in gender and number with the subject of the
verb.

The short forms of **бе́дный** *poor* are:

бе́ден бедна́ бе́дно бе́дны

The adverb is **бе́дно.**

Они́ живу́т бе́дно. *They live in a poverty-stricken way.*

Больно́й *ill*

бо́лен больна́ больны́

114

The short form neuter of this adjective is hardly ever used.

The following examples show adjectival usage:

> Он нездоро́в, он бо́лен. *He is not well, he is ill.*
> Она́ нездоро́ва, она́ больна́.
> Они́ нездоро́вы, они́ больны́.
> Он до́ма, он бо́лен. Сего́дня он не идёт на рабо́ту.

The adverb **бо́льно** means *painful* and the following examples show the use of this adverb:

> Ой, как бо́льно! *Ooh! how painful!* or *How it hurts!*

If you want to say it hurts somebody you use the adverb with the noun or pronoun in the dative:

> Мне бо́льно.   Ему́ бо́льно.   Нам бо́льно.

Note how different the meaning is in **он бо́лен** *he is ill*, and **ему́ бо́льно** *it hurts him*.

The adverb in this construction can also be used with a verb in the infinitive.

> Ему́ бо́льно откры́ть глаза́. *It hurts him to open his eyes.*
> Ему́ бо́льно сесть. *It hurts him to sit down.*
> Вам бо́льно встать? *Does it hurt you to stand up?*

To express the fact that somebody's face etc., hurts or aches, you use the verb **боле́ть,** which in this meaning is second conjugation and has only the following forms:

Present tense	Past tense
он/она́/оно́ боли́т	боле́л, боле́ла, боле́ло
они́ боля́т	боле́ли

The part of the body that aches is the subject and the owner of the body is expressed by **у** + genitive:

> У де́вочки лицо́ боли́т. *The girl's face hurts.*
> У отца́ но́ги боля́т. *Father's legs hurt.*
> У вну́чки рука́ боли́т. *My granddaughter's hand hurts.*
> У меня́ живо́т боле́л. *My stomach ached/I had stomach-ache.*
> У де́душки голова́ боле́ла. *Grandfather's head ached/Grandfather had a head-ache.*

The verb **боле́ть** *to be/fall ill, to be suffering from* is first conjugation. It has a full conjugation, as well as all the forms of the past tense. Its perfective is **заболе́ть.**

> Оте́ц ре́дко боле́ет. *Father is seldom ill.*
> Вы ча́сто боле́ете? *Are you often ill?*
> До́ктор сам заболе́л. *The doctor himself fell ill.*

The adverb meaning *healthy/healthily* **здоро́во** is identical with the short form neuter of the adjective. Here you have the short form of the adjective:

> Сам нача́льник здоро́в? *Is the chief himself well?*
> Ну что, нача́льство здоро́во? *Well now, are the bosses well?*

Нача́льство is a *collective* noun – it is grammatically neuter singular but it expresses a group of people.

In the following sentences the adverb is used:

> На да́че ты живёшь здоро́во, а в го́роде нездоро́во.
> *In the country cottage* (i.e. in the country) *you live healthily but in town you live unhealthily* (i.e. it's healthy/unhealthy to live . . .).
> Тру́дно жить в го́роде здоро́во. *It's difficult to live healthily in town.*
> Здоро́во идти́ ра́но спать. *It's healthy to go to bed early.*
> Здоро́во ра́но встава́ть. *It's healthy to get up early.*
> Здоро́во петь, а пить нездоро́во. Ты мно́го пьёшь, э́то нездоро́во.

There is a colloquial adverb with the same spelling as **здоро́во** but different stress – **здо́рово** – meaning *very well, thoroughly, magnificently* etc.

> Ты здо́рово игра́ешь в футбо́л. *You play football very well.*
> Здо́рово порабо́тал – всё ко́нчил в оди́н день. *He's done a good bit of work – finished everything off in one day.*

Глубо́кий *deep* **глубо́к глубока́ глубоко́ глубо́ки**

> Тут река́ глубока́. Э́то о́зеро глубоко́.

The adverb is **глубоко́**. Note that one adverb can be used to qualify another adverb.

> Тут здо́рово глубоко́. *It's jolly/frightfully deep here.*
> Иди́, иди́ туда́, там совсе́м не глубоко́. Там ма́ло воды́.
> *Go, go over there, it's not at all deep there. There's little water there.*

3. 'TOO BIG,' 'TOO SMALL' ETC.

Several adjectives of size and shape when used in their short form can express the idea of '*too* big', '*too* small' etc. This is particularly so when they refer to articles of clothing and the person for whom the article of clothing is intended also figures in the context. The noun or pronoun denoting the person then goes into the dative case.

In the following sentences you have short forms of:

вели́кий *great* **вели́к велика́ велико́ велики́**

which also serve as the short forms of **большо́й** *big*

ма́лый and **ма́ленький** *small, little* **мал мала́ мало́ малы́**

116

у́зкий *narrow*   у́зок   узка́   у́зко   у́зки́
широ́кий *wide*   широ́к   широка́   широ́ко́   широ́ки́

> Эти сапоги́ мне малы́, а тебе́ они́ велики́.
> *These boots are too small for me but too big for you.*
>
> Эта шля́па вам велика́, а мне она́ мала́.
> *This hat is too big for you but it's too small for me.*
>
> Этот пиджа́к мне у́зок, а вам широ́к.
> *This jacket is too tight for me but too loose for you.*

4. THE DATIVE OF NOUNS AND ITS USES

Most of the nouns we have had so far in the masculine and neuter ended
in a hard consonant and in **o** respectively. Both types have the dative ending
in **y** in the singular:

nom. sing.	dat. sing.
оте́ц	отцу́
нача́льник	нача́льнику
ме́сто	ме́сту

Feminine nouns ending in **a** form the dative in **e**:

nom. sing.	dat. sing.
сестра́	сестре́
ко́шка	ко́шке
вну́чка	вну́чке

The dative plural, for hard-ending nouns of all genders, ends in **ам**:

nom. sing.	dat. pl.
оте́ц	отца́м
внук	вну́кам
сестра́	сёстрам
жена́	жёнам
окно́	о́кнам

The dative is used in a variety of ways:

a To express the indirect object, corresponding to the English *to* (see
Lesson 5).

b With certain verbs which have no direct object, grammatically speaking:
ве́рить *to believe*, сове́товать *to advise*, зави́довать *to envy*, помога́ть
to help.

c In impersonal expressions, with such words as на́до *necessary*, нельзя́
it is impossible/not allowed, мо́жно *it is permissible, one may*.

d To express age: Ско́лько вам лет? *How old are you?* lit. 'How many of
years (**лет** gen. pl.) to you?' Мне три́дцать лет *I am thirty*, lit. 'To
me thirty years'.

e With a few prepositions: **по** *along, on, by* etc.; **к** (**ко**) *towards, to.*

Note the expressions: к ве́черу, к у́тру, к весне́, к ле́ту, к зиме́, к за́втраку, к обе́ду, i.e. *towards evening, towards morning* etc.

5. EXERCISE ON THE DATIVE CASE

Бра́ту на́до идти́ в шко́лу.

Дру́гу э́то пальто́ мало́.

Э́ти бума́ги он даёт нача́льнику.

Мне он не ве́рит, а отцу́ он пове́рит.

Я дам ко́шке блю́дечко молока́.

Сестре́ на́до идти́ в го́род.

Э́ти башмаки́ ба́бушке малы́ – ба́бушке бо́льно.

Ей де́сять лет. – Кому́? Кому́ де́сять лет?

Вну́чке, вну́чке де́сять лет, а вну́ку пять лет. А вам ско́лько лет?

Мне три́дцать пять лет, а му́жу со́рок лет; до́чке пятна́дцать, а сы́ну двена́дцать.

Я несу́ обе́д бра́ту и сёстрам.

В авто́бусе он всегда́ даёт ме́сто да́мам.

Го́ловы рыб мы всегда́ даём ко́шке и котя́там.

Он не ве́рит до́ктору; он говори́т, что никогда́ не ве́рит доктора́м.

Ребя́там не на́до мно́го есть.

Мо́жно нам сесть тут? – Нет, нельзя́.

Мо́жно мне кури́ть? Вам кури́ть мо́жно, а бра́ту нельзя́, так как он ещё мал, он сли́шком мо́лод.

Веди́те соба́ку домо́й, соба́кам тут нельзя́ бе́гать.

Не сове́тую ученика́м игра́ть на дворе́, им нельзя́ тут игра́ть.

Я не зави́дую дире́ктору, я вообще́ (*in general*) не зави́дую нача́льникам.

Я помога́ю сестре́ и бра́ту.

Он помога́ет ученика́м чита́ть.

Я иду́ по коридо́ру.   Де́ти бе́гают по двору́.

Маши́на шла по у́лице.

Тут нельзя́ бе́гать по коридо́рам.

Я иду́ к бра́ту, а он идёт ко мне.

За́втра я пойду́ к до́ктору.

Иди́те к нача́льнику, но сперва́ пойди́те к его́ секрета́рше (секрета́рша *female secretary*).

Пойди́те к стенографи́стке (стенографи́стка *shorthand typist*).

Вре́мя идёт к весне́. *Spring is approaching*, lit. 'Time is going towards spring'.

Он встал к за́втраку.   Она́ встаёт к обе́ду.

К у́тру поду́л ве́тер.

Я пойду́ туда́ к ве́черу.

Метéль (*contd.*)

Ну, тепéрь я́сно, что мы сби́лись с доро́ги,
Well, now it's clear that we've lost our way,
    сби́ться с доро́ги *to lose one's way*; доро́га *road, way*

промелькну́ло в головé ка́ждого.
flashed through everybody's mind.
    ка́ждый *each*

Они́ бы́стро выска́кивают из санéй,
They swiftly leap out of the sledge,
    са́ни *sledge*, sing. or pl. in meaning but plural in form

стря́хивают с себя́ ку́чи снéга,
shake off from themselves heaps of snow,
    ку́ча *heap, pile*

пры́гают, чтóбы отогрéться.
jump up and down to warm themselves up.
    чтóбы *in order to/that*

Лóшади остана́вливаются.
The horses stop.

Они́ чу́вствуют, что сби́лись с твёрдой пóчвы.
They feel that they have left firm ground.
    твёрдый *hard, firm*
    пóчва *soil, ground*

Пу́тники помога́ют лошадя́м,
The travellers help the horses,
    помога́ть *to help* takes dative case

они́ подта́лкивают са́ни.
they push the sledge.

Лóшади понима́ют, что вóжжи опу́щены –
The horses understand that the reins are slack –
    вóжжи (pl. only) *reins*
    опу́щены from опуска́ть is the short form of a participle *let down*, to be dealt with later

зна́чит, лю́ди и́ми бóльше не пра́вят –
(that) means, people are no longer guiding them –
    и́ми instrumental of они́; пра́вить *to guide, conduct* takes the instrumental case
    бóльше не *no longer*

с трудóм начина́ют оты́скивать дорóгу ужé са́ми.
with difficulty they begin to seek out the road themselves.
    ужé here is a particle emphasizing са́ми

В тех места́х ужé зна́ют,
In those places they already know

что во вре́мя мете́ли ло́шадь *that during a snow-storm a horse* найдёт доро́гу домо́й сама́, *will find the way home itself,* так как она́ чу́вствует нае́зженную твёрдую по́лосу доро́ги. *since it can feel the trampled hard strip of the road.*	во вре́мя + gen. *during* найдёт future perfective, third pers. sing. of найти́ *to find,* a compound of идти́ полоса́ *strip, stripe* по́лосу and полосу́

Look through the extracts from **Мете́ль** which are in Lessons 14 to 17 and list or mark all the words which you think are adjectives. We shall return to this in the next lesson.

7. TRANSLATION

Big City Blues[1]

The city is big but the village where I live is small. Uncle works in the city and it is hard for him. He says that it is unhealthy to live in the city but he has to live there. He is right – it is not very healthy. There is too much smoke and noise. On the other hand,[2] the houses are very fine – they are tall and have many windows. You can[3] walk along a street and look into the houses. So (my) friend says.

My friend gave me an old bicycle.[4] 'Now you can ride into town and watch people working and hurrying about,'[5] he said.

Pity[6] – the bicycle is too big for me. Uncle advised me to go on the bus. I envy him – he has a car. All the directors have to travel[7] a lot, so they all have cars. They also have to eat and drink a lot. Uncle drinks an awful lot of wine.

Uncle's secretary has to travel with him. She is forty.[8] Uncle is a bachelor. I think that she hopes[9] that he will marry her.[10]

Well, I set off on the bicycle. On the way[11] I helped a lady. She had a lot of packages and she was very old. Then I lost my way and fell off[12] the bicycle. Now (my) arm hurts me. It aches when I lift it up.[13] I walked home. And I didn't see the city.

---

1 **Тоска́ по большо́му го́роду.**   2 **С друго́й стороны́.**
3 **Мо́жно идти́.**   4 **Велосипе́д.**   5 *To hurry* **торопи́ться.**
6 **Жаль.**   7 *To travel* **путеше́ствовать.**   8 *Forty* **со́рок.**
9 *To hope* **наде́яться – наде́юсь, наде́ешься** etc.
10 *To marry* **жени́ться на** + prepositional case; **жени́ться** is one of the few verbs which are both imperfective and perfective.
11 **По пути́.**   12 **Упа́л с** + genitive. Infinitive **упа́сть** (perfective).
13 *To lift up* **поднима́ть.**

SUMMARY

1 The short forms of adjectives are used predicatively; the endings are like those of hard masculine, feminine, neuter and plural nouns: hard consonant, **а, о, ы** (§ 1).

2 Many adverbs are the same in form as the corresponding neuter short adjectives but are used differently (§ 2).

3 With some adjectives of size and shape the short form expresses 'too much', 'too little' etc. (§ 3).

4 The dative singular of masculine and neuter nouns ending in hard consonants and **о** ends in **у** and of feminine nouns in **а** ends in **е;** the dative plural of nouns of these types ends in **ам** in all three genders (§ 4).

5 The dative expresses the indirect object and is used with certain verbs and prepositions and in impersonal expressions (§ 4).

Lesson 19

I. IRREGULAR PLURALS OF NOUNS

In Lesson 2 you learnt that the nominative plural ends in **ы** or **и** for feminine nouns and most masculine nouns, in **а** for neuter nouns and in stressed **á** for some masculine nouns. There are some masculine and neuter nouns which have the irregular nominative plural **ья**. This ending is unstressed in most nouns and stressed in only a few. Among common nouns which have this kind of nominative plural are:

nom. sing.		*nom. pl.*
брат	*brother*	бра́тья
стул	*chair*	сту́лья
муж	*husband*	мужья́
де́рево	*tree*	дере́вья
перо́	*feather, pen*	пе́рья
крыло́	*wing*	кры́лья
лист	*leaf*	ли́стья

Лист has a normal plural when it means *sheet* (of paper or metal): **листы́.**

Друг *friend* has this kind of plural and also changes **г** to **з: друзья́.**

Сын *son* has this kind of plural and also an additional syllable in the plural: **сыновья́.** In a metaphorical sense it has a *normal* plural: **сыны́ оте́чества** *sons of the fatherland.*

Most of these nouns have hard endings in the singular. All of them have soft endings in the plural:

dative pl.	Бра́тья иду́т к друзья́м.
(ь)ям	Друзья́ не зави́дуют сыновья́м.
	Жёны сове́туют мужья́м.

prepositional pl.	Бра́тья говоря́т о друзья́х.
(ь)ях	Друзья́ ду́мают о бра́тьях.
	Сыновья́ сиде́ли на сту́льях.

The genitive plural of these nouns varies according to the stress. Those with stress on the stem or root of the word have the genitive plural ending **ьев**, a soft equivalent, preceded by the soft sign, of the ending **ов** which you learnt in Lesson 6:

	masc.	*neut.*
genitive pl.	мно́го бра́тьев	ма́ло дере́вьев
(ь)ев	мно́го сту́льев	ма́ло пе́рьев

As you see neuter nouns with this kind of plural have the same genitive plural as the masculine nouns.

There are four nouns of this type with their stress on the ending. They form the genitive plural in **ей** (cf. Lesson 7), dropping the soft sign.

Gen. pl. in **ей**: мно́го друзе́й, мно́го сынове́й, мно́го муже́й

Друзья́ у сынове́й. Сыновья́ у друзе́й.

Друзья́ и сыновья́ у бра́тьев.

У муже́й и у сынове́й мно́го друзе́й.

Бра́тья ви́дят сынове́й и друзе́й.

2. POSSESSIVE PRONOUNS

These words behave like the long adjectives. They have a complete declension and agree in number, gender and case with the noun to which they refer. Most of their case-endings are like those of adjectives with soft endings:

	masc.		neut.	fem.	pl.
nom.	мой *my*		моё	моя́	мои́
gen.		моего́		мое́й	мои́х
dat.		моему́		мое́й	мои́м
acc.	мой/моего́[1]		моё	мою́	мои́/мои́х[1]
instr.[2]		мои́м		мое́й/мое́ю	мои́ми
prep.		моём		мое́й	мои́х

	masc.		neut.	fem.	pl.
nom.	твой *thy*		твоё	твоя́	твои́ *your*
gen.		твоего́		твое́й	твои́х
dat.		твоему́		твое́й	твои́м
acc.	твой/твоего́[1]		твоё	твою́	твои́/твои́х[1]
instr.[2]		твои́м		твое́й/твое́ю	твои́ми
prep.		твоём		твое́й	твои́х

Compare the above declensions with the declension of **он, она́, оно́, они́.**

мой друг   моя́ подру́га (*girl-friend*)
моё пальто́   мои́ друзья́
твой племя́нник (*nephew*)   твоя́ племя́нница (*niece*)
твоё зо́лото (*gold*)   моё серебро́ (*silver*)

With names of relatives you do not normally use these possessive pronouns if it is clear whose relative you are referring to:

Оте́ц е́дет в го́род. (*My*) *father is going into town.*
Я ви́дел сы́на в па́рке *I saw* (*my*) *son in the park.*

With parts of the body it is usual to express *my, thy* etc. by the construction **у меня́, у тебя́** etc., as you have already been doing. Even this may be omitted, if it is clear to whom you are referring:

1 According to whether the noun is animate or inanimate.
2 Instrumental case, to be dealt with later.

(У меня́) ру́ки боля́т. *My arm aches.*

Оте́ц до́ма. (У него́) голова́ боли́т. *Father is at home. He has a head-ache.*

У (мое́й) сестры́ мно́го друзе́й.	У твое́й сестры́ мно́го сынове́й.
Дава́й пойдём к (мое́й) ба́бушке.	Хорошо́, пойдём к твое́й ба́бушке.
Дава́й поговори́м о твое́й до́чке.	Нет, я не хочу́ говори́ть о (мое́й) до́чке.
Я ви́дел твои́х друзе́й.	Ты ви́дел мои́х друзе́й?
У твои́х друзе́й нет отца́.	У мои́х друзе́й нет отцо́в.
Я иду́ к твои́м друзья́м.	Ты идёшь к мои́м друзья́м?
Мы говори́м о твои́х друзья́х.	Они́ говоря́т о мои́х друзья́х.
Мой друг мо́лод.	Мои́ друзья́ мо́лоды.
Твой сын здоро́в.	Твои́ сыновья́ здоро́вы.

In previous lessons we have mentioned various cases of other pronouns (see Lessons 2, 4, 5, 6, 8, 12, 14). You should now look up in Part II - Grammar the declensions of the third pers. pronoun (all genders and plural), **кто, что, сам, весь, э́тот** and **тот**. You will find that you now know most of the forms. If you wish you may for the time being ignore the instrumental case.

3. LONG FORM OF THE ADJECTIVE I

The adjective *young* used at the end of the preceding section has as its long forms in the nominative case:

masc.	*neut.*	*fem.*	*pl.*
молодо́й	молодо́е	молода́я	молоды́е

In this as in the following adjectives the ending is stressed. In some of them the nominative plural ending **ые** becomes **ие** because it comes after a consonant which cannot be followed by **ы**.

gold(en)	золото́й	золото́е	золота́я	золоты́е
big	большо́й	большо́е	больша́я	больши́е
simple, ordinary	просто́й	просто́е	проста́я	просты́е
bad	плохо́й	плохо́е	плоха́я	плохи́е
dry	сухо́й	сухо́е	суха́я	сухи́е

4. EXERCISE

Note again that the long form is used attributively, i.e. it is simply attached to the noun as a description, while the short form is used predicatively, i.e. it makes a statement about the noun.

Мой молодо́й друг тут.	Мой молодо́й друг бо́лен.
Твоя́ молода́я сестра́ в больни́це (больни́ца *hospital*).	
Моё молодо́е де́рево в саду́.	Твои́ молоды́е друзья́ до́ма.
Э́то золото́е кольцо́ до́рого (кольцо́ *ring*).	Э́ти золоты́е ко́льца до́роги.

Этот большо́й дом о́чень стар.　　Э́ти больши́е дома́ о́чень стары́.

Твой просто́й расска́з о́чень интере́сен.　Твои́ просты́е расска́зы о́чень интере́сны (расска́з *tale*; интере́сный *interesting*).

Моя́ плоха́я гости́ница всё же чиста́.　Мои́ плохи́е гости́ницы всё же чи́сты (гости́ница *hotel*; всё же *nevertheless*).

Это сухо́е де́рево не мо́лодо.　　Э́ти сухи́е дере́вья не мо́лоды.

5. LONG FORM OF ADJECTIVE II

In all the long adjectives above ending in **о́й** in the masculine singular the stress is on the last syllable. The majority of adjectives, however, do *not* have the stress on the last syllable. They end in **ый** in the nominative singular masculine and are *hard-ending* adjectives.

но́вый *new*	но́вое	но́вая	но́вые
ста́рый *old*	ста́рое	ста́рая	ста́рые
холо́дный *cold*	холо́дное	холо́дная	холо́дные
опа́сный *dangerous*	опа́сное	опа́сная	опа́сные
голо́дный *hungry*	голо́дное	голо́дная	голо́дные

The long form can also be used predicatively.

Note the difference of meaning when you use the short form and the long form:

> Генера́л стар. *The General is old.*
> Собо́р (*Cathedral*) ста́рый. *The Cathedral is old.*

In **собо́р ста́рый** the long adjective suggests the repetition of the noun; the sentence therefore implies *the Cathedral is an old Cathedral*. However, you do not want to imply that *the General is an old General*, so you use the short form. Remember, the long form in the predicate suggests the repetition of the noun or implies some such word as *one, thing, person* (. . . *a big one . . . a sick person* etc.), whereas the short form simply draws attention to a quality you want to express, and this may be a new or temporary quality or characteristic. Hence the difference between: он больно́й *he is a sick person* (i.e. *an invalid*) and он бо́лен *he is ill* (at present, not permanently).

Генера́л Вороши́лов стар.　　Генера́л Конова́лов мо́лод.
Собо́р Свято́го Па́вла ста́рый.
St. Paul's Cathedral is (an) old (Cathedral).
А собо́р в Ко́вентри но́вый.
But the Cathedral in Coventry is (a) new (Cathedral).

Here are some more long forms of adjectives which have occurred in the passages from **Метéль.** In the nominative singular masculine, from which you can now derive the neuter, feminine and plural forms:

сѝльный *strong*		обшѝрный *vast*	
крýпный *large, coarse (grained)*		твёрдый *hard, firm*	
бéлый *white*		овчѝнный *(of) sheepskin*	
чёрный *black*		тёмный *dark*	

After the letters which cannot be followed by **ы** the endings **ый** and **ые** become **ий** and **ие; ое** and **ая** remain unchanged.

Again from **Метéль:**

мéлкий *fine(-grained)*	мéлкое	мéлкая	мéлкие
корóткий *short*	корóткое	корóткая	корóткие
нѝзкий *low*	нѝзкое	нѝзкая	нѝзкие
рéзкий *sharp*	рéзкое	рéзкая	рéзкие

6. 'TO HELP'

Помогáть imperfective, **помóчь** perfective *to help* takes the dative case of the person or thing helped.

Помогáть conjugates like **дýмать: помогáю, помогáешь** etc.

Помóчь conjugates like **мочь** *to be able*, from which it is derived.

я могý	помогý
ты мóжешь	помóжешь
он мóжет	помóжет
мы мóжем	помóжем
вы мóжете	помóжете
онѝ мóгут	помóгут

Я помогáю вам.	Доктора́ помогáют нам.
Брат помогáет сестрé.	Вы нам чáсто помогáете.
Я помогý брáтьям.	Брáтья помóгут сестрé.

Чтéние вслух вам óчень помóжет. *Reading aloud will help you very much.*

7. READING EXERCISE

Метéль *(concl.)*

Вот однá лóшадь спотыкáется и останáвливается. *Now one horse stumbles and stops.*	
Но нáдо двѝгаться, нельзя́ дóлго стоя́ть. *But we must move, we cannot stand about for long.*	дóлго *a long time, for long*

126

Пу́тники начина́ют крича́ть: Ау́! Ау́!
The travellers begin to shout: Oohoo! Oohoo!

Ау́! is used to call to each other in a wood, for instance

Чу́ткие ло́шади чу́ют бли́зость жилья́ и до́ма.
The sensitive horses sense the proximity of a dwelling and a house.

чу́ять: чу́ю, чу́ешь etc., *to sense*
бли́зость (fem.) *nearness, proximity*
жильё (neut.) *dwelling*

Вдруг с си́лой рву́тся вперёд.
Suddenly they rush violently forward.

рвать: рву, рвёшь etc., *to tear*
рва́ться *to rush, to tear away*

Им жа́рко, от них идёт пар, а мете́ль всё не унима́ется.
They are hot, steam rises from them, but the storm has still not abated.

унима́ть *to calm down, to soothe, to assuage*

Ну, что э́то? Кто́-то кричи́т.
Now what's this? Somebody is calling out.

Зву́ки всё бли́же; а вот что́-то черне́ет.
The sounds (come) nearer and nearer; and now something shows up black.

звук *sound*
черне́ть *to turn black/be black*

Из темноты́ слы́шен смех, а вот и огонёк.
Out of the darkness laughter can be heard, and now there's a little light.

темнота́ *darkness;* слы́шный *audible*
смех *laughter*
ого́нь *fire, light,* огонёк *diminutive of* ого́нь

– Что, жа́рко? Вот так мете́ль! Ох, и хороша́ мете́ль.
What, is it hot? Well, it's some snowstorm! Oh it's a fine snowstorm.

Совсе́м ря́дом стоя́т лю́ди, верхо́м на лошадя́х,
Quite near people are standing, mounted on horses,

верхо́м *on horseback, mounted*

с фонаря́ми и па́лками в рука́х.
with lanterns and sticks in their hands.

фона́рь (masc.) *lantern*
па́лка *staff, stick*

– Далеко́ ли мы от села́? И на доро́ге ли мы?
'*Are we far from the village? And are we on the road?*'

ли interrogative particle, i.e. it is used to form questions

– Ва́ши ло́шади иду́т пра́вильно, а до до́му всего́ пятьсо́т ме́тров.
'*Your horses are going in the right direction and it's only 500 metres to the house.*'

пра́вильный *correct, right*
пра́вильно *correctly*
(до) до́му: an alternative genitive of дом after certain prepositions
всего́ *altogether, in sum*
метр *metre*

С весёлым шу́мом добра́лись до до́му.
Merrily and noisily we have reached the house.

lit. 'with merry noise' (instrumental case)
добира́ться (imperfective), добра́ться (perfective) *to make one's way to*

Всю ночь бушу́ет пурга́.
All night the blizzard rages.
Лю́ди пережида́ют её в свои́х ую́тных, тёплых дома́х.
People wait in their cosy, warm houses until it is over.

бушева́ть (бушу́ет) *to storm, to rage*
пережида́ть *to wait till something is over;* свой *one's own*
ую́тный *comfortable, cosy;* тёплый *warm*

А у́тром ина́я карти́на!
But in the morning the picture is different.

ино́й *other, different*

Со́лнце и моро́з.
Sun and frost.

Прекра́сное у́тро.
A wonderful morning.

Взро́слые и де́ти принима́ются за расчи́стку доро́г.
The grown-ups and children set about cleaning the roads.

взро́слый *grown-up, adult*
принима́ться за + accusative *to set about*
расчи́стка *cleaning*

Вы́шли тра́кторы и бульдо́зеры.
Tractors and bulldozers have come out.

Детвора́ ката́ется на са́нках, валя́ется в пуши́стом снегу́.
The children are sledging, rolling about in the fluffy snow.

детвора́ *children, kids* is a collective noun; ката́ться на са́нках/саня́х *to sledge*
валя́ться *to roll about, to romp*
пуши́стый *downy, fluffy*

Снег прия́тно похру́стывает под ва́ленками, щёки румя́нит моро́з. *The snow crunches pleasantly under (one's) felt boots, the frost reddens (one's) cheeks.*	похру́стывать *to crunch* ва́ленками is instrumental case controlled by под щека́ *cheek* румя́нить *to redden, to rouge*
Недалеко́ зама́нчиво темне́ет лес. *Not far away is the dark and luring shape of the wood.*	lit. 'Not far away temptingly the wood shows dark' темне́ть *to go dark, to be dark, to show up dark*
На лы́жи! В лес! крича́требя́та. *On to (your) skis! Into the wood! Cry the children.* <div align="right">Н. Ефи́мова</div>	лы́жи (pl.) *skis* лы́жа (sing.) <div align="right">(Mrs.) N. Efimov</div>

8. TRANSLATION

There are many friends and relatives[1] at our house[2] today. My brothers and sons have come[3] because I am going to the Soviet Union tomorrow. All (my) brothers and sons have many friends and the friends have come too.

There is no snow, the roads are dry but it is dangerous on the roads because of[4] the frost. However[5] they were all able to come. Outside it is cold but the flat is warm and cosy.

The old wives are sitting by the fire. Their husbands are sitting on chairs and playing cards.[6] The wives advised (their) husbands to play cards. They sit and play and say little. A group of young[7] wives and husbands is standing in the middle[8] of the room. A young woman is telling[9] a short, interesting tale and all the husbands are listening. The other[10] wives are all talking loudly.

Through[11] the window you can see[12] the big, old trees in the garden. There are no leaves on the trees. I stand and look at the trees and I can no longer hear[13] (my) brothers and sons, (their) wives and friends. I am thinking: 'Tomorrow I shall set off for[14] the Soviet Union.'

---

1 *Relative* **ро́дственник.**   2 **У нас до́ма.**
3 *To come* (in a vehicle) **прие́хать** (perfective).   4 **Из-за** + genitive.
5 **Всё-таки.**   6 **В ка́рты.**   7 **Гру́ппа молоды́х** (genitive plural).
8 *Middle* **середи́на,** *in the middle* **посереди́не** or **посреди́не** + genitive.
9 *To tell, relate* **расска́зывать** (first conjugation).   10 *Other* **друго́й.**
11 **В** + accusative.   12 Say 'are visible', short form plural **видны́.**
13 Say 'I no longer hear'.   14 **В** + accusative.

129

SUMMARY

1 Some masculine and neuter nouns with a hard declension in the singular have nominative plural in **ья.** The genitive plural of these nouns is **ьев** (unstressed) or **ей** (stressed) (§ 1).

2 Declension of possessive pronouns **мой** and **твой** is similar to that of adjectives (§ 2).

3 The basic forms of the nominative case endings of the long adjective are (stressed) **ой, ое, а́я, ы́е;** (unstressed) **ый, ое, ая, ые** (§§ 3 and 5).

4 The long adjective can be used predicatively as well as the short (§ 5).

5 The verb *to help* takes the dative case (§ 6).

Lesson 20

I. POSSESSIVE PRONOUNS (*contd.*)

The possessive pronouns **наш** *our* and **ваш** *your* decline like **мой** and **твой** (Lesson 19) but since **я** and **ю** cannot occur after **ш** the nominative singular and accusative singular feminine end in **а** and **у** respectively. The stress remains on the root.

	masc.	neut.	fem.	pl.
nom.	наш *our*	на́ше	на́ша	на́ши
gen.	на́шего		на́шей	на́ших
dat.	на́шему		на́шей	на́шим
acc.	наш/на́шего	на́ше	на́шу	на́ши/на́ших
instr.	на́шим		на́шей/на́шею	на́шими
prep.	на́шем		на́шей	на́ших

	masc.	neut.	fem.	pl.
nom.	ваш *your*	ва́ше	ва́ша	ва́ши
gen.	ва́шего		ва́шей	ва́ших
dat.	ва́шему		ва́шей	ва́шим
acc.	ваш/ва́шего	ва́ше	ва́шу	ва́ши/ва́ших
instr.	ва́шим		ва́шей/ва́шею	ва́шими
prep.	ва́шем		ва́шей	ва́ших

наш уро́к	*lesson*	ваш уро́к	
на́ша равни́на	*plain*	ва́ша равни́на	
на́ше ра́дио[1]	*radio*	ва́ше ра́дио	
на́ши са́ни[2]	*sledge*	ва́ши са́ни	

Ваш интере́с к на́шим уро́кам нас о́чень ра́дует. *Your interest in our lessons pleases us very much.*

NB интере́с к *interest in*; ра́довать: ра́дую, ра́дуешь etc.

От на́шей реки́ до ва́шего о́зера недалёко. *From our river to your lake is not far.*

Ва́шу рабо́ту де́лайте и конча́йте са́ми. *Do your own work and finish it yourself.*

О ва́ших дела́х мы ничего́ не зна́ем. *We know nothing about your affairs.*

2. LONG FORMS OF ADJECTIVES (*contd.*)

Here are some more adjectives with final stress in the long form. Remember that **ы** is replaced by **и** after **к, г, х, ш, ж, ч, щ.**

---

1 Indeclinable.
2 Plural in form, singular or plural in meaning, according to context.

Чужо́й *foreign, alien*

	чужо́е	чужа́я	чужи́е
чужо́й бе́рег	чужо́е лицо́	чужа́я страна́	чужи́е лю́ди

The opposite of alien is:

Родно́й *near, related by birth, native, own, dear*

	родно́е	родна́я	родны́е

родно́й брат *own/blood brother*   родно́е село́ *native village*
родна́я страна́[1] *native land*   родно́й край *native region/land*

Прямо́й *straight* and **криво́й** *crooked*

прямо́й/криво́й нос *straight/crooked nose*
прямо́е/криво́е де́рево *straight/crooked tree*
пряма́я/крива́я нога́ *straight/crooked leg*
прямы́е/кривы́е па́льцы *straight/crooked fingers* (па́лец *finger*)

Где апте́ка? *Where's the chemist?*
Иди́те пря́мо – по той прямо́й доро́ге до моста́, а пото́м нале́во. Там
вокза́л, и напра́во бу́дет апте́ка. *Go straight on – along that straight road
to the bridge and then to the left. The station is there and on the right will be
the chemist's.*

3. ADJECTIVAL NOUNS

Some long forms of adjectives are used as nouns, i.e. they stand on their
own without a noun. They are called *adjectival nouns*.

мой родны́е (pl. only) *my relatives*
на́ши родны́е *our relatives* (ро́дственник also means *relative*)
больно́й *a sick man, a patient*   больна́я *a sick woman*
больны́е *sick people, patients*

Наш до́ктор о́чень мно́го рабо́тает. У него́ зимо́й мно́го больны́х.

Other common adjectival nouns are:

рабо́чий *worker* (cf. рабо́чий стол *work-table*)
столо́вая *dining-room* (cf. столо́вое бельё *table linen*)
живо́тное *animal* (cf. живо́тные инсти́нкты *animal instincts*)
слепо́й *blind man* (cf. слепо́й ма́льчик *blind boy*)
гости́ная *drawing-room*

Some adjectival nouns are no longer used as adjectives:

портно́й *tailor*   насеко́мое *insect*
вселе́нная *the universe*   пиро́жное *cake*

---

1 Cf. **ро́дина** *motherland; fatherland* is **оте́чество** (cf. **оте́ц**).

4. LONG FORMS OF ADJECTIVES II

Here are some more long adjectives in which the unstressed ending is preceded by **к, г** or **x** and is therefore written **ий**:

ма́ленький *small*   ма́ленькое   ма́ленькая   ма́ленькие

The short form, derived from a related adjective, is **мал** etc. (Lesson 18).

больша́й го́род   ма́ленький городо́к (городо́к is the diminutive of го́род)
большо́е село́   ма́ленькое месте́чко (*hamlet*, derived from ме́сто *place*)
больша́я у́лица   ма́ленькая ла́вка (*shop; bench*)
больши́е леса́   ма́ленькие тропи́нки (тропи́нка *path*).

велиќий *great*   вели́кое   вели́кая   вели́кие

> Пу́шкин вели́кий поэ́т. *Pushkin is a great poet.*
> Пётр Вели́кий *Peter the Great*
> Екатери́на Вели́кая *Catherine the Great*
> вели́кое де́ло *a great cause*

A compound form of the same adjective is found in:

> Великобрита́ния *Great Britain*

The short form is **вели́к, вели́ко, велика́, вели́ки.**

The same forms serve as the short forms for **большо́й** but with certain stress differences:

вели́к   велико́   велика́   велики́ (and вели́ки)

high or *tall* and its opposite *low*

высо́кий бе́рег   ни́зкая стена́ (бе́рег *bank*, стена́ *wall*)
высо́кое де́рево   ни́зкие кусты́ (куст *bush*)
высо́кая берёза   ни́зкие го́ры (берёза *birch*)

broad, wide and its opposite *narrow*

широ́кий бульва́р   у́зкая у́лица

> Иди́те пря́мо по широ́кому бульва́ру до кана́ла. Отту́да нале́во по у́зкой у́лице.

deep and *shallow*

глубо́кий кана́л   ме́лкая река́

> От глубо́кого кана́ла до ме́лкой реки́ не́сколько шаго́в (шаг *step, pace*). Кана́л глубо́кий – он о́чень глубо́кий.

far and *near*

далёкий бе́рег   бли́зкое село́
Far and *near*, the adverbs, are далеко́, бли́зко.

> Далеко́ до вокза́ла? – Нет, отсю́да (*from here*) недалеко́, совсе́м бли́зко.

severe, strict

стро́гие роди́тели (*parents*)

> У меня́ стро́гий оте́ц и стро́гая мать; стро́гие роди́тели.

loud and *quiet*

гро́мкий го́лос   ти́хий го́лос (*voice*)

Ти́хий Дон *Quiet Flows the Don* (lit. 'Quiet Don').

    Я слы́шу гро́мкие голоса́.

heavy and *light* (in weight), *easy*, *slight*

тяжёлый, лёгкий (in this word **г** before **к** has the value of **х**)

тяжёлая и лёгкая промы́шленность (*industry*)

тяжёлый сон (*sleep*) лёгкая просту́да (*chill*)

тяжёлое пальто́ и лёгкий плащ (*cloak, coat, raincoat*)

лёгкое одея́ло *lightweight blanket*, pl. лёгкие одея́ла.

The neuter form of **лёгкий** and the plural are used as adjectival nouns:

лёгкое *lung*; лёгкие *lungs* (cf. Eng. *lights*)

    У вас си́льные лёгкие, а у него́ сла́бые (*weak*) лёгкие

hard and *soft*

твёрдый, мя́гкий (in this word **г** before **к** has the value of **х**).

твёрдый дива́н и мя́гкое кре́сло.

твёрдая поду́шка и мя́гкие ковры́ (поду́шка *pillow, cushion*; ковёр *carpet*).

5. NATIONALITIES

Adjectives denoting peoples' nationality mostly end in **ский**:

англи́йский язы́к *the English language.*

англи́йский флот. *British fleet* (NB Russians use **англи́йский** to mean both *English* and *British*. There is also the word **брита́нский** *British*).

> ру́сский наро́д *the Russian people*
> ру́сское сло́во *Russian word*
> сове́тская столи́ца Москва́ *the Soviet capital, Moscow*
> сове́тское прави́тельство *the Soviet government*
> францу́зская литерату́ра *French literature*

In the general sense, for German you use **неме́цкий** (NB no **с**):

> неме́цкий язы́к   неме́цкая му́зыка   неме́цкие лю́ди

When referring to the state you use **герма́нский**:

> герма́нский наро́д   герма́нское прави́тельство

To say an Englishman or Englishwoman, a German, a Frenchman etc., you use the following nouns:

> англича́нин   англича́нка
> не́мец (mobile **е**)   не́мка
> францу́з   францу́женка

For a Russian you use the adjective as a noun:

Вот ру́сский офице́р. *Here is a Russian officer* (**ру́сский** used as adjective).

В клу́бе вчера́ бы́ли англича́не, не́мцы, францу́зы и ру́сские (used as a noun).

Yesterday at the club there were Englishmen, Germans, Frenchmen and Russians.

Э́тот челове́к ру́сский, а его́ жена́ францу́женка.

This man is a Russian but his wife is a Frenchwoman.

На́ши роди́тели англича́не,[1] а его́ роди́тели ру́сские.

Our parents are English, but his parents are Russians.

The names of the countries in which these people live are:

А́нглия or Великобрита́ния

Росси́я or СССР, pronounced as initials эс-эс-эс-э́р.

In full this is Сою́з Сове́тских Социалисти́ческих Респу́блик.

Фра́нция

Герма́ния:

Федерати́вная Респу́блика Герма́нии *German Federal Republic*

Герма́нская Демократи́ческая Респу́блика *People's Democracy of Germany*

Here are some more countries together with adjectives and names of nationalities. The ending **ец** has a mobile vowel.

Ита́лия	италья́нский	италья́нец	италья́нка
Испа́ния	испа́нский	испа́нец	испа́нка
Португа́лия	португа́льский	португа́лец	португа́лка
Шотла́ндия	шотла́ндский	шотла́ндец	шотла́ндка
Финля́ндия	финля́ндский	финля́ндец	финля́ндка
Швейца́рия *Switzerland*	швейца́рский	швейца́рец	швейца́рка
Норве́гия *Norway*	норве́жский	норве́жец	норве́жка
Да́ния *Denmark*	да́тский	датча́нин	датча́нка
Шве́ция *Sweden*	шве́дский	швед	шве́дка
Ве́нгрия *Hungary*	венге́рский	венге́рец	венге́рка
Голла́ндия *Holland*	голла́ндский	голла́ндец	голла́ндка
Бе́льгия	бельги́йский	бельги́ец	бельги́йка
Ирла́ндия	ирла́ндский	ирла́ндец	ирла́ндка
Гре́ция *Greece*	гре́ческий	грек	греча́нка
Ту́рция *Turkey*	туре́цкий	ту́рок	турча́нка
Чехослова́кия *Czechoslovakia*	че́шский (*Czech*)	чех	че́шка
Болга́рия	болга́рский	болга́рин	болга́рка
По́льша *Poland*	по́льский	поля́к	по́лька
Аме́рика	америка́нский	америка́нец	америка́нка
Кита́й *China*	кита́йский	кита́ец	кита́янка

Note that the names of the countries begin with a capital but *not* the adjectives and the names of the peoples. In nouns ending in **ец** with a vowel before the ending, the **е** changes to **й** in the other cases: hence кита́йцы *the Chinese*.

---

[1] Nouns ending in **анин/янин** have an unusual plural in **ане/яне.** See Part II – Grammar.

6. READING EXERCISE

a   *Совéтская пéсня (song)*

Широка́ страна́ моя́ родна́я,	*Broad is my native land,*
Мно́го в ней поле́й, лесо́в и рек,	*There are many fields, forests and rivers in it,*
Я друго́й тако́й страны́ не зна́ю,	*I do not know another such country,*
Где так во́льно ды́шит челове́к.	*Where man breathes so freely.*

b   *Зима́, стихи́ Фéта (verses by Fet)*

Чу́дная карти́на	*Wonderful picture*
Как ты мне родна́!	*How dear you are to me!*
Бе́лая равни́на,	*The white plain,*
По́лная луна́.	*The full moon.*
Свет небе́с высо́ких	*The light of the high heavens*
И блестя́щий снег,	*And the sparkling snow,*
И сане́й далёких	*And of the distant sledge*
Одино́кий бег.	*The lonely run.*

7. 'THIS KIND OF' AND 'WHAT KIND OF'

The following sentences show you how to use:

тако́й *such, this kind of*	така́я	тако́е	таки́е
како́й *what kind of*	кака́я	како́е	каки́е

which decline like adjectives and agree with the noun they qualify in gender, number and case.

Вот како́й рассе́янный	*What an absentminded (man)*
С у́лицы Бассе́йной.	*From Basseynaya Street.*

Како́й рассе́янный челове́к.	*What an absentminded man.*
Кака́я рассе́янная студе́нтка.	Каки́е рассе́янные ученики́.

– Како́й он челове́к? Он стар? *What sort of person is he? Is he old?*

– Нет, не стар, а то́лько рассе́янный. *No, not old, but only absentminded.*
Он тако́й рассе́янный. *He is so absentminded.*

– Кака́я у вас студе́нтка? Молода́я?

– Моя́ студе́нтка и молода́я и така́я рассе́янная!

– Ах! кака́я она́ рассе́янная! *Oh, how absentminded she is!*

– Каки́е у вас ученики́? – Мои́ ученики́ таки́е рассе́янные! Про́сто невозмо́жно! *It's simply impossible!*

8. FEMININE NOUNS ENDING IN ь

In the Reading Exercises you have met several feminine nouns ending in ь in the nominative singular:

метéль *snowstorm*   лóшадь *horse*

Here are some more common nouns of this type:

дверь *door*   The plural **двéри** means either *doors* or *door*.
   Вот наш дом, вот и нáша дверь.

ночь *night*   ночь тúхая
óсень *autumn*   óсень холóдная
пáмять *memory*   Пáмять у меня́ плохáя.
жизнь и смерть   *life and death*
   Какáя жизнь, какáя смерть! *What a life, what a death!*

ость is a common ending of abstract nouns:

рáдость *joy*   Cf. я рад *I am glad*, онá рáда *she is glad*, an adjective which has no long form; рáдовать *to gladden*.

нóвость *news*, used in the singular or plural.
хорóшая нóвость *a good piece/item of news*
   Какúе нóвости? Плохúе, плохúе нóвости. Нет трáнспорта, всю́ду снег, всё стоúт – вот какúе у нас нóвости!

мóлодость и стáрость *youth and old age*
Вéчная мóлодость – мечтá. *Eternal youth is a dream.*
Стáрость не рáдость. *Old age is no joy.*

The declension of feminine nouns ending in ь is fairly simple. Points to note are that nominative and accusative singular are the same, all other singular cases except the instrumental end in **и,** and the plural cases are simply the *soft* equivalents of the *hard* declension endings, except for the genitive plural, which ends in **ей.**

	sing.	*pl.*
nom.	метéль	метéли
gen.	метéли	метéлей
dat.	метéли	метéлям
acc.	метéль	метéли
instr.[1]	метéлью	метéлями
prep.	метéли	метéлях

After **ч, щ, ш, ж** you write **a** not **я,** so the dative, instrumental and prepositional plural of **ночь** are **ночáм, ночáми, ночáх,**

Similarly **мышь** *mouse* (in which the soft sign has *no* effect on the pronunciation of **ш**) declines in the plural **мы́ши, мышéй, мышáми, мышéй** (animate, hence genitive-accusative), **мышáми, мышáх.**

---

1 The use of the instrumental case will be dealt with in Lesson 21.

Мать *mother* and **дочь** *daughter* belong to this declension but are odd since in all cases except nominative and accusative singular the syllable **-ер-** is inserted before the case endings (cf. English moth*er*, daught*er*). Hence the genitive, dative and prepositional singular of these nouns is **ма́тери** and **до́чери**. The instr. plural of **дочь** is **дочерьми́**.

Где моя́ ло́шадь? Вы ви́дите мою́ ло́шадь? – Да, я ви́жу ва́шу ло́шадь.

Ма́ленькая се́рая мышь бе́гала по ко́мнате. *A little grey mouse ran about the room.*

Я слы́шу мышь. Карау́л! (*Help!* lit. 'Guard'!)

У ло́шади дли́нный хвост (*long tail*).

От две́ри до две́ри два шага́.

К о́сени мы е́дем домо́й.

Идёт ва́ша мать. Я ви́жу ва́шу мать на у́лице.

Твоя́ дочь мне всё говори́т. Я понима́ю твою́ дочь.

У ма́тери мно́го сынове́й.

Я иду́ к до́чери.

Она́ говори́т о на́шей ма́тери – они́ говоря́т о ва́шей до́чери.

9. DIALOGUE

– Ну посмотри́те, куда́ вы идёте! Вы совсе́м не смо́трите, куда́ вы идёте!
– Я смотрю́, но ничего́ не ви́жу!
– Ну почему́ же вы кричи́те? Не кричи́те, пожа́луйста!
– Вы са́ми кричи́те!
– Успоко́йтесь, пожа́луйста! (успоко́иться perfective, успока́иваться imperfective, *to calm down*).
– Да, да, дава́йте успоко́имся (*let us calm down*). Вы мо́жете мне помо́чь?
– Коне́чно я вам помогу́, е́сли я смогу́ (*if I can* смогу́ being first pers. sing. future perfective of мочь, смочь. NB after **е́сли** Russian must have future tense if the future is referred to).
– Я спешу́ на вокза́л, но в э́тих тёмных у́лицах, в э́том жёлтом тума́не я не ви́жу доро́ги.
– Вы идёте на вокза́л? Но вы идёте не в ту сто́рону (*not in the right direction*; сторона́ *side, direction*).
– Как э́то так?
– Посмотри́те нале́во – там у́гол. Вы ви́дите тот у́гол?
– Я ничего́ не ви́жу.
– Да вы не туда́ смо́трите (*you are not looking in the right direction*). Не смотри́те напра́во. Посмотри́те нале́во. Вот туда́. Пойди́те обра́тно (*back*) до угла́, от угла́ пойди́те напра́во.
– Тепе́рь я всё ви́жу и по́мню! (*remember*) На́до идти́ нале́во.
– Нет, не иди́те нале́во. От угла́ иди́те пря́мо – от угла́ нале́во, а пото́м иди́те пря́мо на вокза́л.

– Я ничего́ не понима́ю. Я же сказа́ла, что мне на́до пойти́ напра́во, а пото́м нале́во и пото́м пря́мо на вокза́л.
– Вы меня́ не слу́шаете! Послу́шайте! Иди́те обра́тно до угла́, от угла́ иди́те напра́во – нет, я сама́ пу́таюсь (*I'm getting confused myself*). Дава́йте начнём снача́ла! (*Let's begin again from the beginning*). Éсли хоти́те, дава́йте мы пойдём вме́сте, я же сама́ иду́ на вокза́л.

10. TRANSLATION

Native Village

My native village is a very old village and, they say, very pretty.[1] English villages are usually[2] very pretty. In our village (there is) a chemist and two shops, where they sell[3] everything. In the middle of the village (there is) a little old bridge over[4] the river. The river here is shallow but not far away it is very deep.

We hear the news on the radio or read it[5] in the newspapers but there is little (that is) new[6] in the village itself. A white horse is working in[7] the field, children are playing in the street and what[8] joy is on the faces of these children. People open[9] (their) doors and windows in the summer, the old men and women sit on chairs outside, the young people stand and talk. Youth[10] has its[11] joys and so[12] does old age but young and old live harmoniously[13] in our village. And they all have such[14] quiet voices.

That is how[15] I remember[16] my native village: distant mountains, a little bridge, a shallow river, white doors and, in the fields, white horses, green trees and, towards autumn the golden harvest;[17] my mother's quiet voice, my father's strict face, and the deep silence[18] at night.

1 **Краси́вый.**   2 **Обы́чно.**   3 **Продава́ть** a compound of **дава́ть.**
4 **Че́рез** + accusative.   5 Remember *news* is plural.   6 Genitive of **но́вый.**
7 **На.**   8 **Како́й** *what* (*a*).   9 **Открыва́ть.**
10 Say: in youth and so in old age one's own joys.
11 **Свой** *one's own* declines like **мой.**   12 **Как и.**   13 **Дру́жно.**
14 **Тако́й.**   15 **Вот как.**   16 **По́мнить.**   17 **Урожа́й.**   18 **Тишина́.**

SUMMARY

1 The declension of the possessive pronoun **наш** and **ваш** is like that of **мой** and **твой** but without stress on the endings (§ 1).
2 Some adjectives are used as nouns (§ 3).
3 Adjectives denoting nationality mostly end in **ский** (§ 5).
4 Use of **тако́й** and **како́й** (§ 7).
5 Declension of feminine nouns in **ь** including **мать** and **дочь** (§ 8).

Lesson 21

I. ADJECTIVES WITH SOFT ENDINGS

The adjectives you have met so far have all had hard endings. Because of the spelling conventions **и** not **ы** is written after certain consonants. So some adjectives had **ий** in the nominative singular masculine, **ие** in the nominative plural but **ое** in the nominative singular neuter and **ая** in the nominative singular feminine (Lesson 20, § 2).

Some adjectives have soft endings throughout, i.e. the final consonant is soft, so the nominative case endings for example are spelt:

masc.	neut.	fem.	pl.
ий	ее	яя	ие

Soft ending adjectives never have the stress on the ending.

An example of a soft ending adjective occurred in **Метéль**:

Жи́тели прокла́дывают зи́мние коро́ткие доро́ги.
The inhabitants lay down winter short roads.

masc.	fem.	neut.	pl.
зи́мний *winter('s)*	зи́мняя	зи́мнее	зи́мние

Compare this with the endings of the following hard adjectives which also have **н** before their endings:

у́мный *wise*	у́мная	у́мное	у́мные
по́лный *full, plump*	по́лная	по́лное	по́лные
больно́й *sick*	больна́я	больно́е	больны́е

зи́мний ве́чер *winter evening*
зи́мняя доро́га *winter road*
зи́мнее у́тро *winter morning*
зи́мние вечера́ *winter evenings*

All the adjectives for the seasons of the year have soft endings:

ле́то *summer*	ле́тний	ле́тняя	ле́тнее	ле́тние

ле́тний во́здух *summer air*
ле́тняя жара́ *summer heat*
ле́тнее у́тро *summer morning*
ле́тние кани́кулы *summer holidays*

весна́ *spring*	весе́нний	весе́нняя	весе́ннее	весе́нние
о́сень *autumn*	осе́нний	осе́нняя	осе́ннее	осе́нние

Весе́нний ве́тер тёплый. *The spring wind is warm.*
Осе́нний тума́н холо́дный. *The autumn mist is cold.*
Весе́нняя рабо́та тяжёлая. *The spring work is heavy.*

Осе́нняя ночь бу́рная. *The autumn night is stormy.*
Весе́ннее со́лнце жа́ркое. *The spring sun is hot.*
Осе́ннее у́тро се́рое. *The autumn morning is grey.*
Весе́нние ме́сяцы ра́достные. *The spring months are joyous.*
Осе́нние ве́тры си́льные. *The autumn winds are strong.*

The adjectives from **у́тро** *morning* and **ве́чер** *evening* also have soft endings:

у́тренний и вече́рний моро́з (моро́з *frost*)
у́тренняя и вече́рняя пого́да (пого́да *weather*)
у́треннее и вече́рнее со́лнце
у́тренние и вече́рние моро́зы

The adjectives from **ночь** *night* and **день** *day* have hard endings:

ночно́й по́езд *the night-train*
дневно́й по́езд *the day-train.*

2. SENTENCES

– Како́й по́езд лу́чше? *Which train is better?*
– Како́й по́езд? Ночно́й, коне́чно, мо́жно спать.
– Нет, по-мо́ему не так. *No, in my (opinion) it is not so.*   Нет, по-мо́ему дневно́й по́езд лу́чше.
– Нет, уж лу́чше е́хать у́тром, у́тренний по́езд ско́рый *fast.*
  No, really it's better to go in the morning, the morning train is an express.
– Ночно́й по́езд о́чень ме́дленный (*slow*).
– Но тогда́ вече́рний по́езд лу́чше всего́. Вот вам ско́рый по́езд.
  But then the evening train is best of all. There's the express (train) for you.
– Вече́рний по́езд всегда́ по́лон,[1] ма́сса люде́й е́дут ве́чером.
– Да, но у́тренний по́езд то́же по́лон, вот (transl. here as *while*) ме́дленные, дневны́е поезда́ почти́ всегда́ пусты́е. Е́сли я могу́, я всегда́ е́ду днём, днём и́ли у́тром.
– А я е́ду ве́чером и́ли но́чью, осо́бенно (*especially*) зимо́й. Зимо́й ваго́ны днём о́чень холо́дные, а но́чью и зимо́й тепло́.
– А я наоборо́т – ле́том е́хать днём в жару́ оди́н у́жас, у́тром ещё мо́жно, а днём и́ли ве́чером така́я жара́ в по́езде, так ду́шно.
  And I (do) the contrary – in the summer travelling by day in the heat is horrible (lit. 'a single horror'), *in the morning one can just bear it* (lit. 'it is still possible'), *but in the daytime or evening there is such heat in the train, it is so stuffy.*
– Ещё весно́й и́ли о́сенью мо́жно е́хать и днём и но́чью, а ле́том дневны́е и вече́рние поезда́ – э́то оди́н у́жас.

Notice the idiom **оди́н у́жас** above. The adjective is **ужа́сный,** *horrible* and the adverb **ужа́сно.**

Ле́том е́хать днём и́ли ве́чером – э́то ужа́сно. Ужа́сные, ду́шные, по́лные поезда́ битко́м наби́ты.

[1] Short form of **по́лный.**

3. INSTRUMENTAL CASE

You have learnt the following as adverbs:

у́тром	*in the morning*	ве́чером	*in the evening*
ле́том	*in the summer*	зимо́й	*in the winter*
	весно́й *in the spring*		

The corresponding forms for *at night* and *in the autumn* are **но́чью** and **о́сенью.**

All these are forms of the instrumental case. The instrumental case for masculine nouns ending in a hard consonant and neuter nouns in **o** ends in **ом**:

ве́чер	ве́чером
у́тро	у́тром
ле́то	ле́том

Feminine nouns ending in **a** form the instrumental in **ой**:

зима́	зимо́й
весна́	весно́й

Feminine nouns ending in the soft sign form the instrumental by adding **ю**:

о́сень	о́сенью
ночь	но́чью

The instrumental plural ends in **ами** for hard-ending nouns and in **ями** for soft-ending nouns:

зо́нтик	*umbrella*	зо́нтиком	зо́нтиками
одея́ло	*blanket*	одея́лом	одея́лами
па́лка	*stick*	па́лкой	па́лками
но́вость	*news*	но́востью	новостя́ми
ночь	*night*	но́чью	ноча́ми[1]

4. THE USE OF THE INSTRUMENTAL CASE WITH VERBS

The instrumental case expresses the means or instrument with which an action is performed – hence its name, as in **бить молотко́м** *to strike with a hammer.*

In Russian certain actions, such as waving, shaking, nodding etc., are thought of as being carried out by means of a stick, the arm, the head etc., while in English we use a direct object in the corresponding expressions.

Он маха́л зо́нтиком. *He waved his umbrella.*

Они́ маха́ли зо́нтиками. *They waved their umbrellas.*

Я маха́ла руко́й, а он маха́л па́лкой. *I waved my hand and he waved his stick.*
Мы маха́ли рука́ми, а они́ маха́ли па́лками.

1 Since after **ж, ш, ч** and **щ** one writes **a** not **я**.

142

Here are some more examples of verbs which normally take the instrumental in Russian while some of the English equivalents may have a direct object:

стуча́ть кулако́м *to bang (with) one's fist*
Он стуча́л кулако́м по_столу́. *He banged his fist on the table.*

то́пать нога́ми *to stamp (with) the feet*
Они́ то́пали нога́ми по_полу. *They stamped their feet on the floor* (пол *floor*).

бить молотко́м по желе́зу *to strike with a hammer on iron*
(молото́к with mobile vowel *hammer*; желе́зо *iron*).
Он бил молотко́м по желе́зу. Они́ би́ли молотка́ми по желе́зу.

The instrumental of:

кто *who* is кем	никто́ *no-one*	нике́м
что *what* is чем	ничто́ *nothing*	ниче́м

– Чем вы бьёте по желе́зу? – Я бью молотко́м.
– Чем он стучи́т в дверь? – Он стучи́т па́лкой. Нет, не па́лкой, а зо́нтиком. Он всегда́ стучи́т в дверь зо́нтиком.

To trade is **торгова́ть**: торгу́ю, торгу́ешь etc., and you express *to trade in* by means of the instrumental.

– Чем вы торгу́ете? – Мы торгу́ем молоко́м, хле́бом, сы́ром, ма́слом, я́йцами.
– Чем торгу́ет ваш сосе́д? – Сосе́д торгу́ет сапога́ми и башмака́ми.

To risk is **рискова́ть**: риску́ю, риску́ешь etc.
It takes the instrumental case, not a direct object: **рискова́ть чем** *to risk what*.

– Чем он риску́ет? – Ниче́м, ниче́м он не риску́ет. А вот мы риску́ем капита́лом.
Я риску́ю иму́ществом (иму́щество *property*).

To interest is **интересова́ть**: интересу́ю, интересу́ешь etc.
You express to *interest somebody in* by means of the instrumental. *To be interested in* is the same verb in its reflexive form **интересова́ться: интересу́юсь, интересу́ешься** etc.

– Чем вы интересу́етесь?
– Жена́ интересу́ется му́зыкой, а я интересу́юсь фи́льмами. Брат интересу́ется матема́тикой и фи́зикой. А сестра́ ча́сто в библиоте́ке.
– Чем она́ интересу́ется?
– На́до спроси́ть (*one should ask*) не чем она́ интересу́ется, а кем. Она́ интересу́ется не кни́гами, а студе́нтами.
– Сосе́ди нике́м не интересу́ются. Нике́м и ниче́м они́ не интересу́ются.

To occupy is **занима́ть.** *To be occupied with, engaged in* is **занима́ться** with the instrumental.

– Чем ты занима́ешься ле́том?
– Ле́том я занима́юсь спо́ртом.
– Каки́м (instrumental of како́й) спо́ртом? (the verb ты занима́ешься is understood).
– Я занима́юсь ра́зными (instrumental of ра́зный *various*) ви́дами спо́рта – я пла́ваю (*I swim*). Я игра́ю в те́ннис.
– Вы занима́етесь альпини́змом (альпини́зм *mountaineering*) и игра́ете в футбо́л?
– Ра́зве (*really*) вы не зна́ете, что ле́том футбо́лом не занима́ются?

See Lesson 26 and Part II – Grammar, for the instrumental and other cases of adjectives.

5. FEMININE NOUNS ENDING IN ь (*contd.*)

In Lesson 20 (§ 6) you had the complete declension of feminine nouns in ь. Read that paragraph again, noting particularly that the genitive plural is in **ей,** and then read the following sentences for comprehension:

У э́тих люде́й нет дете́й.
У э́тих дете́й нет сане́й (са́ни *sledge*).
У на́ших матере́й нет новосте́й.
Я откро́ю две́ри.
Я слы́шал все ва́ши но́вости.
Мы ви́дели ва́ших дочере́й.
Я иду́ к дверя́м.
Я не ве́рю ва́шим новостя́м.
Дочеря́м не на́до кури́ть – нельзя́ им кури́ть, а матеря́м мо́жно.
Он не спит по ноча́м (*at nights*).
Вы говори́те об э́тих новостя́х, но я то́лько ду́маю о де́тях.
А он ду́мает о тёмных холо́дных ноча́х на да́че.
На ра́достях (*for joy, in her joy*) она́ позвала́ всех друзе́й.

The instrumental plural is **ями,** and after **ж, ш, ч, щ** – **ами.**

Лю́ди *people* and **де́ти** *children* have exceptional instrumental plural in **ьми: людьми́, детьми́.**

Ло́шадь *horse* and **дочь** *daughter* usually have this instrumental plural: **лошадьми́, дочерьми́** though the less preferable forms **лошадя́ми, дочеря́ми** are sometimes found.

– Детьми́ он совсе́м не интересу́ется, а вот людьми́ сосе́днего (сосе́дний *neighbouring*) до́ма он о́чень интересу́ется.
– Да нет, он да́же не интересу́ется людьми́. Он не лю́бит дете́й, он не лю́бит люде́й, и не интересу́ется ни детьми́, ни людьми́. Он то́лько лю́бит лошаде́й и соба́к, и он то́лько занима́ется лошадя́ми.

144

6. EXERCISE

a Put the correct endings on the adjectives:

(ле́тний)	у́тро	(осе́нний)	вечера́
(зи́мний)	ночь	(весе́нний)	ве́тры
(у́тренний)	со́лнце	(вече́рний)	газе́та

b Put the words in brackets in the correct cases:

Он маха́л (зо́нтик). Они́ то́пали (но́ги).

(Что) он бьёт по_столу́? Он бьёт (молото́к).

Са́ша (ничто́) не интересу́ется. Ма́ша маха́ла (па́лка).

Лю́ди торгу́ют (хлеб, я́йца, па́лки, зо́нтики).

Они́ торгу́ют (тра́кторы, маши́ны) и (са́ни).

Кто рискова́л (жизнь)?

Сын занима́ется (фи́зика), а дочь (ничто́) не занима́ется.

Мать (никто́) не интересу́ется.

У (мать) нет (друзья́).

У фе́рмера мно́го (коро́ва), но нет (ло́шадь).

Он не интересу́ется (ло́шадь).

У (тётя) нет (де́ти).

Оте́ц занима́ется (му́зыка) по (но́чи).

(О́сень) мы е́дем домо́й.

(Ночь) я не спала́.

На (пло́щадь *square*) стоя́т (дом).

До́ктор интересу́ется (боле́знь *illness*) (ваш) (дочь).

SUMMARY

1 Some adjectives have soft endings throughout (§ 1).
2 The instrumental singular ends in **ом** for masculine and neuter nouns with hard endings; in **ой** for feminine nouns ending in **а**; in **ью** for feminine nouns ending in **ь**; and in **ами/ями** in the plural (§ 3).
3 Certain verbs control the instrumental case (§ 4).

Lesson 22

I. INSTRUMENTAL CASE AFTER THE PREPOSITION с

When the preposition **с** means *with* it is followed by the instrumental case of the noun it controls.

Я пью чай с молоко́м. *I take* (lit. 'drink') *tea with milk.*

А он пьёт чай с лимо́ном.

Они́ пьют ко́фе с молоко́м и с са́харом.

Я ем хлеб с ма́слом и сы́ром. *I am eating bread with butter and cheese.*

Он ест хлеб с со́лью (соль *salt*) и огу́рчиками (огу́рчик *gherkin*).

Они едя́т хлеб с пови́длом (пови́дло *marmalade* type of jam).

Она́ лю́бит есть чёрный хлеб с икро́й (икра́ *caviar*, lit. 'roe').

In these sentences *with* does not express the means or instrument with which something is done. It expresses *together with* and to render this meaning the instrumental is not enough. You must have the preposition **с** as well.

2. VERB FORMS – FIRST PERS. SING., SECOND CONJUGATION

You have seen (Lesson 13) that some consonants change in the first pers. sing. of second conjugation verbs:

буди́ть *to wake, rouse*	я бужу́	ты бу́дишь
спроси́ть *to ask*	я спрошу́	ты спро́сишь
чи́стить *to clean*	я чи́щу	ты чи́стишь

If the consonant is formed with the lips then it does not change but has a soft **л** added after it.

So б becomes бл

п	,,	пл
в	,,	вл
ф	,,	фл
м	,,	мл

in the first pers. sing. of second conjugation verbs.

люби́ть	спать	гото́вить	корми́ть
to love	*to sleep*	*to prepare*	*to feed*
я люблю́	сплю	гото́влю	кормлю́
ты лю́бишь	спишь	гото́вишь	ко́рмишь
он лю́бит	спит	гото́вит	ко́рмит
они́ лю́бят	спят	гото́вят	ко́рмят

146

ста́вить	терпе́ть	лови́ть
to put	*to bear*	*to catch*
я ста́влю	терплю́	ловлю́
ты ста́вишь	те́рпишь	ло́вишь
он ста́вит	те́рпит	ло́вит
они́ ста́вят	те́рпят	ло́вят

Compare the endings of the above verbs in a and b below:

a По́мните (по́мнить *to remember*), как мы буди́ли бра́та ра́но у́тром? Он лю́бит спать, он до́лго спит, он храпи́т (храпе́ть *to snore*), он да́же иногда́ груби́т (груби́ть *to be rude*). Я его́ до́лго буди́ла, а мне на́до бы́ло гото́вить за́втрак.

b Ты меня́ бу́дишь о́чень ра́но. Я люблю́ спать. Я люблю́ до́лго спать. Да, я сплю до́лго. Коне́чно я храплю́ и гровлю́, когда́ ты меня́ бу́дишь. Не на́до меня́ буди́ть так ра́но. Ты гото́вишь за́втрак, я не гото́влю. Я могу́ спать. Не буди́ меня́ так ра́но.

c Я люблю́ тебя́, жизнь,
   I love you, life,
   Что само́ по себе́ и не но́во.
   Which in itself is not new.
   Я люблю́ тебя́, жизнь,
   I love you, life,
   Я люблю́ тебя́ сно́ва и сно́ва.
   I love you again and again.
   Вот уж о́кна зажгли́сь,   зажѐчь *to light up; past tense*
   See, the windows are lit up,   зажёг, зажгла́ etc.
   Я шага́ю с рабо́ты уста́ло.   шага́ть *to stride*
   I stride from work wearily.   **c** + gen. = *from;* уста́лый *tired*
   Я люблю́ тебя́, жизнь,
   I love you, life,
   Я хочу́, чтобы лу́чше ты ста́ла.   стать *to become*
   I want you to become better.   lit. 'that better you become'

NB instrumental case after **стать** *to become*.

The perfective of some of these verbs is as follows:

Люби́ть – полюби́ть, which has the meaning of *to come to love*.
Он до́лго не люби́л свою́ рабо́ту, пото́м он полюби́л её.

Корми́ть – накорми́ть
– Она́ меня́ ча́сто корми́ла ве́чером. – Вчера́ она́ нас всех накорми́ла, хорошо́ накорми́ла, а за́втра я её накормлю́.

Гото́вить – пригото́вить
– Они́ до́лго гото́вили обе́д. Наконе́ц пригото́вили и нас всех накорми́ли.
– За́втра я пригото́влю обед.

147

3. THE PREPOSITION при

The preposition **при** takes the prepositional case and means either *in the presence of* or *in the time of, under:*

Они́ гото́вили обе́д при мне и наконе́ц пригото́вили.
При Петре́ Вели́ком на́чали стро́ить Петербу́рг.
They began to build Petersburg in the time of Peter the Great.
При Ста́лине начала́сь коллективиза́ция.
In Stalin's time collectivisation began.

4. VERBS OF MOTION WITH PREFIXES

In **пригото́вить** above the prefix **при-** simply makes the verb perfective and adds nothing else to the meaning. With verbs of motion the prefix **при-** adds the meaning 'towards the speaker'.

Идти́ ходи́ть
When prefixed **идти́** changes to **-йти.**

So **прийти́** means *to come, to arrive*; i.e. 'to move on foot towards the place where the speaker is' and it is perfective. In conjugating, the **и** of the prefix **при-** and the **и** of **иду́** etc. merge into one:

я приду́	мы придём
ты придёшь	вы придёте
он придёт	они́ приду́т

За́втра они́ все приду́т. *They will all come tomorrow.*
Сего́дня они́ уже́ не приду́т. *They won't come today now.*

The imperfective of **прийти́** is formed with **ходи́ть: приходи́ть,** second conjugation, like **буди́ть:**

он прихо́дит	они́ прихо́дят

– Я к вам ча́сто прихожу́, а вы к нам не прихо́дите. Ну, приди́те за́втра к обе́ду (приди́, приди́те is the *imperative* of прийти́; к обе́ду *for dinner*).
– Хорошо́, мы придём, и мы придём ра́но.

The past tense of **идти́** is exceptional: **шёл, шла, шло, шли.** The past tense of **прийти́** and all compounds is the same with the addition of the prefix:

пришёл	пришла́	пришло́	пришли́

– Кто пришёл вчера́?
– Еле́на пришла́ вчера́.
– Нет, никто́ не пришёл вчера́, они́ все пришли́ сего́дня.

148

Éхать -езжáть

If you add **при-** to **éхать** you get **приéхать** *to come, to arrive* by some form of transport, which is perfective. **Éхать** has **д** not **x** in its conjugation and so have **приéхать** and all compounds of **éхать**.

я приéду	мы приéдем
ты приéдешь	вы приéдете
он приéдет	они́ приéдут

The imperfective of compounds of **éхать** is formed with **-езжáть,** which never occurs without a prefix. **Приезжáть** is a first conjugation verb, like **дýмать.**

> я приезжáю, ты приезжáешь, он приезжáет etc.

Do not try to pronounce the **з** and **ж** as separate sounds. **З** before **ж** has the same value as **ж** (see Part II – Pronunciation), so **зж** sounds just like a long **ж.**

The past tense of **приéхать** perfective, and **приезжáть** imperfective, is regular:

приéхал	приéхала	приéхало	приéхали
приезжáл	приезжáла	приезжáло	приезжáли

– Кто приéхал?
– Брат и сестрá приéхали.
– А дя́дя приéхал?
– Тётя дýмает, что он приезжáет сегóдня. Я дýмаю, что он приéдет зáвтра.

Нести́ носи́ть

Нести́ means *to carry*; **принести́** means *to bring* and is perfective. Its imperfective is **приноси́ть.**

fut. pfv.	*pres.*
я принесý	приношý
ты принесёшь	принóсишь
он принесёт	принóсит
мы принесём	принóсим
вы принесёте	принóсите
они́ принесýт	принóсят

The past tense masculine of **принести́,** like that of **нести́** and all its compounds, has no **л** in the masculine singular:

принёс	принеслá	принеслó	принесли́

– У вас нет газéты?
– Нет, газéту всегдá принóсят óчень пóздно.
– Тогдá я вам принесý нáшу газéту.
– Большóе спаси́бо (*thank you very much*), не приноси́те её. Мáльчик сейчáс принесёт её. Он всегдá принóсит нáшу газéту. Вот я ви́жу, мáльчик идёт. Он пришёл и принёс газéту.

With verbs of motion and some others the prefix **у-** means *away*, the opposite of **при-**.

при-	*up to, towards*
у-	*away, off, from*

pfv.	*impfv.*
уйти́ *to go away* (on foot)	уходи́ть
уе́хать *to go away* (not on foot)	уезжа́ть
унести́ *to take away*	уноси́ть

— Мы придём к вам за́втра, но мы уйдём ра́но.
— Вы ре́дко прихо́дите и когда́ вы прихо́дите, вы ухо́дите о́чень ра́но.
— До́ма де́ти, нам на́до ра́но уходи́ть. Но за́втра мы уйдём по́здно. Тётя живёт у нас не́сколько ме́сяцев. Поэ́тому за́втра мы придём ра́но и уйдём по́здно.
— Это о́чень хорошо́. Пожа́луйста (*please*) приходи́те ра́но и уходи́те по́здно...

— Ты уезжа́ешь?
— Да, уезжа́ю сейча́с.
— Муж уже́ уе́хал?
— Нет, он уезжа́ет сего́дня.
— А де́ти то́же уезжа́ют сего́дня?
— Нет, де́ти уе́дут за́втра; у́тром уе́дет дочь, а ве́чером уе́дет сын.

— Где газе́та?
— Па́па унёс её на рабо́ту.
— Он всегда́ уно́сит газе́ту.
— Непра́вда, он никогда́ ра́ньше (*before*) не уноси́л газе́ту.
— Он унёс её вчера́, и в сре́ду унёс – ка́ждый день он уно́сит газе́ту. Сего́дня унёс – и за́втра унесёт.
— Я сама́ унесу́ газе́ту за́втра, но принесу́ её обра́тно (*back*).

The verbs *to fly to, to come flying, to arrive* (by flying) and *to fly away* are:

pfv.	*impfv.*
прилете́ть	прилета́ть
улете́ть	улета́ть

Прилета́ть and **улета́ть** are first conjugation verbs, like **ду́мать.**

Прилете́ть and **улете́ть** are second conjugation verbs with a consonant change: **т** > **ч** in the first pers. sing.:

я прилечу́	улечу́
ты прилети́шь	улети́шь
он прилети́т	улети́т

Весно́й пти́цы прилета́ют в А́нглию.
Ско́ро прилети́т пти́цы на се́вер.
Ната́ша не прилета́ет из Москвы́ сего́дня. Она́ прилети́т за́втра.

Ско́ро бе́лые мете́ли	Soon the white snow-storms
Снег подыму́т от земли́.	Snow will raise from the ground.
Улета́ют, улете́ли,	Are flying away, have flown away,
Улете́ли журавли́.	Have flown away the cranes.

5. MASCULINE NOUNS ENDING IN ь AND й

The nominative singular of **журавли́** in the last line of § 4 is **жура́вль**. It is a *masculine* noun ending in a soft sign. The declension of masculine nouns ending in **ь** is straightforward. Apart from the genitive plural the endings are simply the soft equivalents of the endings of masculine nouns ending in a hard consonant.

The difference between soft and hard endings is shown by the vowel letters. You have noticed the correspondences in the vowels between the hard-ending and soft-ending adjectives:

у́мный *hard*	у́мная	у́мное	у́мные
зи́мний *soft*	зи́мняя	зи́мнее	зи́мние

The full table of hard–soft correspondences in the vowel letters is:

hard a	*soft* я
у	ю
о	e or ё
ы	и

Endings which already have **e** in the hard ending declension, such as the prepositional singular, remain the same. Compare the declension of **конь** horse with that of **кот** tomcat:

	hard	*soft*	*hard*	*soft*
	sing.		*pl.*	
nom.	кот	конь	коты́	ко́ни
gen.	кота́	коня́	кото́в	коне́й (NB)
dat.	коту́	коню́	кота́м	коня́м
acc.	кота́	коня́	кото́в	коне́й
instr.	кото́м	конём	кота́ми	коня́ми
prep.	коте́	коне́	кота́х	коня́х

Notice that the genitive plural like that of feminine nouns in **ь** ends in **ей**. We have already pointed out that masculine nouns ending in **ж** (Lesson 7, § 1) and masculine nouns with the nominative plural in stressed **ья́** (Lesson 19, § 1) have genitive plural in **ей**. This also applies to nouns ending in **ш**, **ч** and **щ**:

	nom. pl.	*gen. pl.*
нож *knife*	ножи́	ноже́й
каранда́ш *pencil*	карандаши́	карандаше́й
врач *doctor*	врачи́	враче́й
това́рищ *comrade*	това́рищи	това́рищей
сын *son*	сыновья́	сынове́й
друг *friend*	друзья́	друзе́й
муж *husband*	мужья́	муже́й

Here is another pair of masculine nouns contrasted by hard and soft endings. Both have a mobile vowel:

	hard	*soft*		*hard*	*soft*
	sing.			*pl.*	
nom.	сон *dream*	день *day*		сны	дни
gen.	сна	дня		снов	дней
dat.	сну	дню		снам	дням
acc.	сон	день		сны	дни
instr.	сном	днём		сна́ми	дня́ми
prep.	сне	дне		снах	днях

Снег шёл днём и но́чью.   *Snow fell day and night.*
Дождь шёл днём и но́чью.   *Rain fell day and night.*

You can also say:

Снег шёл день и ночь.
Дождь шёл день и ночь.
Снег пошёл у́тром и шёл весь день и всю ночь.
Дождь пошёл у́тром и шёл весь день и всю ночь.

Here **пошёл** means *began to fall*. Rain and snow *come* in Russian.

Он рабо́тает днём и не спит но́чью.
Он рабо́тает дня́ми и не спит ноча́ми.

Both these sentences are translated the same way into English. The first one simply contrasts day-time with night-time. The second contrasts day and night and also suggests the individual days and nights: 'during the days' and 'during the nights'.

Masculine nouns ending in **й** in the nominative singular also have soft endings, identical with those of nouns ending in **ь** except in the genitive plural. In the genitive plural they have **ев** unstressed and **ёв** stressed.

	sing.	*pl.*	*sing.*	*pl.*
nom.	слу́чай *incident*	слу́чаи	слой *layer*	слои́
gen.	слу́чая	слу́чаев	сло́я	слоёв
dat.	слу́чаю	слу́чаям	сло́ю	слоя́м
acc.	слу́чай	слу́чаи	слой	слои́
instr.	слу́чаем	слу́чаями	сло́ем	слоя́ми
prep.	слу́чае	слу́чаях	сло́е	слоя́х

If the nominative singular ends in **ий** the prepositional singular ends in **ии**:

ра́дий *radium*   в ра́дии *in radium*

6. EXERCISES

a *Comprehension*

На аэропо́рте ежеча́сно (*every hour*) прилета́ют и улета́ют самолёты.
Пассажи́ры приезжа́ют сюда́ на авто́бусах и на автомоби́лях (*cars*).

Тут и мно́го зри́телей (*spectators*). Зри́тели приезжа́ют на автомоби́лях, на велосипе́дах, на мотоци́клах и на моторо́ллерах (*motor-scooters*). Среди́ (*among*) зри́телей мно́го ма́льчиков. Ма́льчики прихо́дят и пешко́м (*on foot*). Вот э́тот ма́льчик пришёл сего́дня у́тром. Он принёс с собо́й тетра́дь (*exercise-book*, fem.) и запи́сывает (*notes down*) все ти́пы самолётов. По́здно ве́чером он уйдёт домо́й и унесёт с собо́й тетра́дь.

Его́ друг прие́хал на велосипе́де. Он уе́дет ра́ньше, потому́ что он хо́чет пое́хать на ста́нцию. Ведь (*you see*) он интересу́ется и поезда́ми.

Каки́е у нас ра́зные (*different*) ви́ды (*kinds*) тра́нспорта! Ра́ньше не́ было ни поездо́в, ни автомоби́лей, ни самолётов, ни да́же велосипе́дов, а бы́ло мно́го лошаде́й.

Днём лю́ди рабо́тали и́ли путеше́ствовали (*travelled*) верхо́м на лошадя́х и́ли же в каре́тах, а но́чью они́ спа́ли. В на́ши дни лю́ди путеше́ствуют и но́чью. Мо́жно слы́шать как самолёты прилета́ют и улета́ют но́чью. День и ночь тури́сты приезжа́ют, уезжа́ют.

b *Translation*
At the airport the aeroplanes arrive and depart every hour. The passengers come by car. There are many cars here but there are no horses. There are many spectators at the airport. The (small) boys come on foot. They bring note-books with them. That boy will go home in the evening. His friend will go to the station on his bicycle.
The tourists arrive and depart by day and by night.

SUMMARY
1 When **c** means *with* it controls the instrumental (§ 1).
2 In the first pers. sing. of second conjugation verbs with lip consonants, **б** changes to **бл**, **п** to **пл**, **м** to **мл**, **в** to **вл** and **ф** to **фл** (§ 2).
3 The preposition **при** takes the prepositional case.
4 When prefixed the verbs of motion **-йти** (= **идти́**), **е́хать, нести́** and **лете́ть** are perfective, their corresponding imperfectives being formed with **ходи́ть, -езжа́ть, носи́ть** and **лета́ть** respectively (§ 4).
5 The case endings of masculine nouns ending in **ь** in the nominative singular are simply the soft equivalents of those of masculine nouns ending in a hard consonant in the nominative singular, except for the genitive plural, which ends in **ей** (§ 5).
Masculine nouns ending in **й** also have soft endings, with genitive plural in **ев** or **ёв**.

Lesson 23

I. NEUTER NOUNS ENDING IN е

There are only three nouns ending in **е** immediately after a consonant other than **ш, ж, ч, ц** or **щ** but two of them are very common. The nouns are **мо́ре** *sea,* **по́ле** *field,* **го́ре** *grief.*

The case endings are simply the soft equivalents of the case endings of nouns ending in **о,** except in the genitive plural, which ends in **ей.**

	sing.	*pl.*
nom.	мо́ре *sea*	моря́
gen.	мо́ря	море́й
dat.	мо́рю	моря́м
acc.	мо́ре	моря́
instr.	мо́рем	моря́ми
prep.	мо́ре	моря́х

Neuter nouns ending in **е** after **ш, ж, ч, ц** or **щ** have the same endings as neuter nouns ending in **о,** except in the nominative-accusative singular and the instrumental singular.

	sing.	*pl.*
nom.	се́рдце *heart*	сердца́
gen.	се́рдца	серде́ц (mobile vowel)
dat.	се́рдцу	сердца́м
acc.	се́рдце	сердца́
instr.	се́рдцем	сердца́ми
prep.	се́рдце	сердца́х

Neuter nouns ending in **ие** have endings like those of **мо́ре** except in the prepositional singular, which ends in **и,** and the genitive plural, which ends in **ий.**

	sing.	*pl.*
nom.	зда́ние *building*	зда́ния
gen.	зда́ния	зда́ний
dat.	зда́нию	зда́ниям
acc.	зда́ние	зда́ния
instr.	зда́нием	зда́ниями
prep.	зда́нии	зда́ниях

2. FEMININE NOUNS ENDING IN я

By and large the endings of feminine nouns in **я** are simply the soft equivalents of the endings of feminine nouns in **а** but there are one or two small points to notice.

154

	sing.	pl.
nom.	земля́ *earth, land*	зе́мли
gen.	земли́	земе́ль (mobile vowel)
dat.	земле́	зе́млям
acc.	зе́млю	зе́мли
instr.	землёй/ёю	зе́млями
prep.	земле́	зе́млях

Notice that the genitive plural ends in a soft sign, to show the softness of the last consonant. One or two nouns ending in **ня**, however, do not have the soft sign: **пе́сня** *song*, genitive plural **пе́сен**.

Some nouns ending in **я** have the genitive plural in **ей**:

до́ля *portion*	до́лей	ноздря́ *nostril*	ноздре́й
дя́дя *uncle*	дя́дей	тётя *aunt*	тётей

Feminine nouns ending in stressed **ья** have genitive plural in **ей**:

семья́ *family*	семе́й	статья́ *article*	стате́й

Feminine nouns ending in **я** after a vowel (other than **и**) decline like **земля́,** the genitive plural ending in **й** when the vowel of the nominative singular is dropped:

иде́я *idea*	иде́й	струя́ *spurt, jet*	струй

Feminine nouns ending in **ия** have genitive plural in **ий** and dative and prepositional singular in **ии**:

	sing.	pl.
nom.	фами́лия *surname*	фами́лии
gen.	фами́лии	фами́лий
dat.	фами́лии	фами́лиям
acc.	фами́лию	фами́лии
instr.	фами́лией/ею	фами́лиями
prep.	фами́лии	фами́лиях

3. NEUTER NOUNS ENDING IN **МЯ**

Nouns ending in **мя** are *not* feminine but neuter. They all take up an additional syllable **-ен-** in cases other than the nominative-accusative singular. They have soft endings in the singular but hard endings in the plural:

	sing.	pl.	sing.	pl.
nom.	и́мя *name*	имена́	вре́мя *time*	времена́
gen.	и́мени	имён	вре́мени	времён
dat.	и́мени	имена́м	вре́мени	времена́м
acc.	и́мя	имена́	вре́мя	времена́
instr.	и́менем	имена́ми	вре́менем	времена́ми
prep.	и́мени	имена́х	вре́мени	времена́х

Сéмя *seed* is one of these nouns: **сéмени** etc., but genitive plural **семя́н**. Do not confuse it with **семья́** a feminine noun with soft endings (§ 2 above).

There are seven more neuter nouns ending in **-мя**. They are given in Part II – Grammar.

Как его́ и́мя? *What is his name?* (lit. 'How is his name').

Его́ и́мя Ива́н.   Я вам дам имена́ всех ва́ших ученико́в.

А как ва́ше и́мя и ва́ша фами́лия?

Моё и́мя Э́мми и моя́ фами́лия Вознесéнская. Я ду́маю, что на́ши ученики́ зна́ют и моё и́мя и мою́ фами́лию.

Но я игра́ю роль (*part* fem.) сестры́ Пéти, и её и́мя Ни́на.

Моё и́мя Ви́ктор, моя́ фами́лия Грéгори. У меня́ больша́я семья́ – жена́, пять детéй, тётя и ба́бушка. У меня́ мно́го рабо́ты и ма́ло врéмени.

Я игра́ю роль бра́та Ни́ны, и его́ и́мя Пéтя.

Каки́е у нас всех тру́дные времена́!

Да, врéмя тру́дное для всех. Я иногда́ ду́маю, что никогда́ ра́ньше не бы́ло таки́х времён.

4. FOR LEARNING BY HEART

«Мойдоды́р» К. Чуко́вского

Одея́ло	
The blanket	
Убежа́ло,	убежа́ть pfv., убега́ть impfv.
ran away	*to run away*
Улетéла простыня́,	простыня́ (fem.) *sheet.*
the sheet flew away,	
И поду́шка,	
and the pillow	
Как лягу́шка,	
like a frog,	
Ускака́ла от меня́.	ускака́ть pfv., уска́кивать impfv.
hopped away from me.	*to hop, gallop away*
Я за свéчку,	
I (made) for the candle,	
Свéчка в пéчку!	пéчка *stove*
the candle (rushed) into the stove.	
Я за кни́жку,	
I (made) for the book,	
Та – бежа́ть	бежа́ть and бéгать *to run* are both
It (started) to run	impfv. (see Lessons 29 and 30)
И вприпры́жку	прыжо́к *jump.*
and at a hop, skip and jump	
Под крова́ть.	
(went) under the bed.	

5. THE PREPOSITIONS за AND под

The basic meaning of **за** is *behind, beyond*; of **под** *below, under*. Both **за** and **под** take two cases: the accusative and the instrumental.

When they take the accusative they imply motion, i.e. motion into a position behind or below.

When they take the instrumental they imply location, i.e. location in a position behind or below.

Я ста́влю чемода́н за дива́н. *I am putting the suitcase behind the divan.*
   Чемода́н стои́т за дива́ном. *The suitcase is standing behind the divan.*
Я сажу́сь за стол. *I am sitting down at the table* (lit. 'behind the table').
   Я сижу́ за столо́м. *I am sitting at the table.*
Я е́ду за́_город. *I am going into the country* (lit. 'beyond the town').
За́втра мы пое́дем за́_город. *Tomorrow we shall go out into the country.*
   Я живу́ за́_городом. *I live out of town.*

In **за́_город** and **за́_городом** the stress is attracted to the preposition from the noun, which has no stress.

Я кладу́ поду́шку под одея́ло. *I am putting the pillow under the blanket.*
   Поду́шка лежи́т под одея́лом. *The pillow is (lying) under the blanket.*
Он поста́вил чемода́н под стол. *He put the suitcase under the table.*
   Чемода́н стоя́л под столо́м. *The suitcase was standing under the table.*

6. VERBS OF MOTION WITH PREFIXES (*contd.*)

Another common verb of motion is *to run*.

Бежа́ть   бе́гать

убежа́ть perfective, **убега́ть** imperfective, *to run away* (NB stress)

убега́ть is a normal **ду́мать**-type verb.

Бежа́ть is exceptional: it is first conjugation in the first pers. sing. and third pers. pl., where the root ends in **г,** and second conjugation elsewhere. Its compounds behave in the same way.

fut. pfv.

убегу́	Я убегу́ от них.
убежи́шь	Ты убежи́шь из шко́лы.
убежи́т	Он убежи́т и́з_дому (*out of the house*).
убежи́м	Мы убежи́м от вас.
убежи́те	Вы убежи́те из тюрьмы́ (тюрьма́ *prison*).
убегу́т	Они́ убегу́т из ла́геря (ла́герь masc. *camp*).

To come running, to run up is of course **прибежа́ть** perfective: **прибегу́, прибежи́шь... прибегу́т; прибега́ть** imperfective (NB stress).

Do take careful note of this verb **бежа́ть** and its compounds. Its conjugation pattern is unique.

7. THE VERBS звать AND брать

The verbs **звать** *to call* and **брать** *to take* are very common verbs and have some very common compounds. They have a mobile vowel in the conjugation but not in the infinitive or past tense:

я зову́	беру́
ты зовёшь	берёшь
он зовёт	берёт
мы зовём	берём
вы зовёте	берёте
они́ зову́т	беру́т
я звал, звала́, мы зва́ли	ты брал, брала́, вы бра́ли

With prefixes these verbs are perfective:

назва́ть *to name*	назову́, назовёшь
призва́ть *to call up*	призову́, призовёшь
вы́звать *to call forth, provoke, cause*	вы́зову, вы́зовешь
собра́ть *to gather*	соберу́, соберёшь
прибра́ть *to tidy*	приберу́, приберёшь
вы́брать *to pick out, choose*	вы́беру, вы́берешь

Вы́звать and **вы́брать** illustrate the following rule about stress: perfective forms with the prefix **вы-** are always stressed on **вы-**.
This takes precedence over all other rules to do with stress.

The imperfectives of the compounds of **звать** and **брать** are formed with an *expanded* root and are first conjugation **ду́мать**-type:

pfv.	*impfv.*
назва́ть	называ́ть, называ́ю, называ́ешь
призва́ть	призыва́ть, призыва́ю, призыва́ешь
вы́звать	вызыва́ть,[1] вызыва́ю, вызыва́ешь
собра́ть	собира́ть, собира́ю, собира́ешь
прибра́ть	прибира́ть, прибира́ю, прибира́ешь
вы́брать	выбира́ть,[1] выбира́ю, выбира́ешь

— Пе́тя, беги́ домо́й. (NB Imperative formed from *first* pers. sing.)
— Почему́ (*why*) ты меня́ зовёшь домо́й?
— Не я тебя́ зову́. Тётя Ли́за тебя́ зовёт.
— Почему́ вы меня́ зовёте?
— Пото́м тебе́ ска́жем, почему́ мы зовём тебя́ домо́й.
— Ве́ра, мне на́до бежа́ть домо́й. Они́ меня́ зову́т домо́й.
— Ты берёшь бума́ги домо́й?
— Я беру́ больши́е чертежи́ (*sketches*) и два письма́.

1 Note that it is *only the perfective forms* that are stressed on **вы.**

– Он берёт больши́е чертежи́, и два письма́ с собо́й (*with himself*). Мы несём пи́сьма на по́чту.

– Бери́те остальны́е (adj. *remaining*) пи́сьма. Вот вам пять пи́сем и оди́н паке́т (*parcel*). Вы берёте паке́ты?

– Да, мы берём паке́ты.

– Хорошо́, что они́ беру́т паке́ты.

– Э́тот тяжёлый (*heavy*) паке́т я не беру́.

– Нет, бери́те э́тот паке́т. Паке́т большо́й, но не тяжёлый. Паке́т совсе́м лёгкий.

– С э́тим больши́м паке́том на по́чту мы не идём.

– Вы собра́ли все пи́сьма и паке́ты?

– Мы всё собра́ли. Но у Пе́ти большо́й, тяжёлый паке́т. Э́тот тяжёлый паке́т на по́чту мы не берём.

– Меня́ сестра́ зовёт домо́й и я не могу́ нести́ э́тот паке́т на по́чту.

– Тебя́ нача́льник вызыва́ет.

– Пуска́й он назна́чит вре́мя свида́ния (*fix a time of meeting*) за́втра у́тром.

– Он не мо́жет назна́чить вре́мя свида́ния за́втра у́тром. За́втра у нас кани́кулы (*holidays*).

– Тогда́ пуска́й он назна́чит вре́мя сего́дня по́сле (*after* + gen.) обе́да. Я приду́ в конто́ру по́сле обе́да.

– Е́сли ты не придёшь, он тебя́ назовёт лентя́ем (instr. of лентя́й *lazybones*).

– Коне́чно я приду́.

– Тогда́ тебе́ не на́до брать с собо́й твои́ больши́е чертежи́ и э́ти два письма́.

– Нет, не на́до, и я не беру́. Я ничего́ не беру́. Мне на́до бежа́ть.

– Беги́, беги́! Я приберу́ конто́ру. Я соберу́ все твои́ бума́ги и положу́ их на э́тот дли́нный (adj. *long*) стол. Они́ бу́дут на э́том дли́нном столе́. Что ты всё стои́шь?

– Я бегу́! Я бегу́!

8. VERBS OF THE FIRST CONJUGATION WITH CONSONANT CHANGE

You have seen already (Lesson 13) that many second conjugation verbs have a consonant change in the first pers. sing., for example:

проси́ть to ask   прошу́, про́сишь, про́сит

A complete list of all the regular consonant changes is at the beginning of the verb section of Part II – Grammar.

Some verbs of the first conjugation with a consonant before the endings **-у, -ешь, -ет** etc. also have a consonant change. This consonant change runs *throughout the conjugation* and is not just confined to the first pers. sing. like the consonant change of second conjugation verbs.

There are about sixty verbs which have this change. Some of them are rare but some of them are very common verbs.

How do we know that there is a consonant change if it runs through the entire conjugation? Because the basic consonant – without change – is found in the infinitive, the past tense and other forms of the verb.

infin.	писа́ть *to write*		написа́ть *pfv.*
pres.	я пишу́	*fut. pfv.*	напишу́
	ты пи́шешь		напи́шешь
	он пи́шет		напи́шет
	мы пи́шем		напи́шем
	вы пи́шете		напи́шете
	они́ пи́шут		напи́шут
past tense	писа́л		написа́л

The other common verbs that have this are:

пла́кать *to weep*	пла́чу, пла́чешь
маха́ть *to wave*	машу́, ма́шешь
пря́тать *to hide*	пря́чу, пря́чешь
иска́ть *to seek, look for*	ищу́, и́щешь
чеса́ть *to comb, to scratch*	чешу́, че́шешь
вяза́ть *to bind, to knit*	вяжу́, вя́жешь
сказа́ть (pfv.) *to say*	скажу́, ска́жешь
показа́ть (pfv.) *to show*	покажу́, пока́жешь
ма́зать *to smear, to grease*	ма́жу, ма́жешь
ре́зать *to cut*	ре́жу, ре́жешь
колеба́ться *to hesitate*	колéблюсь, колéблешься

Here are some sentences with **писа́ть: пишу́, пи́шешь** etc., followed, for purposes of comparison, by some sentences with **проси́ть: прошу́, про́сишь** etc.

– За́втра я напишу́ им письмо́. Хорошо́, что ты пи́шешь сего́дня. Оте́ц то́же напи́шет ему́ за́втра. И так мы все напи́шем. Вы пи́шете подро́бно? Они́ нам пи́шут о́чень подро́бно.

– Я писа́ла им вчера́ ве́чером. Сади́лась, писа́ла, писа́ла, но так и не написа́ла.[1] А вот мой брат уме́ет пи́сьма писа́ть – в две мину́ты письмо́ напи́шет.[2] Вчера́ в полчаса́ два письма́ написа́л – и не написа́л каки́е-то пустяки́ – написа́л интере́сно.

– Я попрошу́ дире́ктора дать мне э́ту кни́гу.

– Ты о́чень ча́сто его́ про́сишь. И он то́же про́сит. Мы все проси́ли, а дире́ктор нам не даёт э́ту кни́гу.

– Éсли вы попро́сите, мо́жет быть он даст.

– Éсли мы попро́сим, он не даст; он даст, е́сли вот[3] они́ попро́сят.

1 The verbs in the first part of the sentence are imperfective; *I kept sitting down and writing* – and the verb in the second part is perfective; *but somehow I didn't write it.*

2 The future perfective is used here in the sense of *can*, just as we say in English *he'll write a letter in two minutes*, meaning 'he can etc.'.

3 **Вот** here lends emphasis to **они́.**

9. говори́ть – сказа́ть AND SIMILAR PAIRS

Сказа́ть: скажу́, ска́жешь etc. is the perfective of *to say, to tell*.

To say, to tell

я говорю́ *I say*	я скажу́ *I shall say*
он вам говори́т *he is telling you*	он вам ска́жет *he will tell you*

– Не говори́те мне. Не на́до говори́ть. Я не хочу́ слы́шать.

– Нет, я тебе́ скажу́ – на́до сказа́ть.

– Ты ска́жешь, а пото́м ты пожале́ешь, что мне сказа́ла об э́том (пожале́ть is perfective of жале́ть *to be sorry*). Я же зна́ю тебя́. Ты пожале́ешь, что сказа́ла.

– Е́сли я не скажу́ – дире́ктор ска́жет. И́ли други́е твои́ колле́ги тебе́ ска́жут. Мы все тебе́ ска́жем.

– Что ты мне говори́шь? Что вы мне ска́жете? В чём де́ло? (*What is the matter?*)

– Де́ло в том (*The matter/point is*), что ты о́чень по́здно прихо́дишь у́тром на рабо́ту.

– Вот что сказа́ла! (*Now you've told me something!*). Я э́то сам зна́ю.

– А пото́м сра́зу ухо́дишь.

– Но я тебе́ сказа́л, что меня́ позва́ли (позва́ть perfective of звать) домо́й.

The other common verbs which have imperfective and perfective formed from completely different roots are:

impfv.	*pfv.*
брать *to take*	взять
лови́ть *to catch*	пойма́ть
класть *to put*	положи́ть

When **говори́ть** means *to talk, to speak*, it forms its perfective normally by adding a prefix. The perfective is **поговори́ть,** which has the additional meaning of *for a little while*, like **постоя́ть** perfective *to stand (about) for a while*.

Друзья́ встре́тились на углу́, постоя́ли, поговори́ли и пошли́ домо́й.
The friends met on the corner, stood and talked for a while and then went home.

10. DIALOGUE

– Вот за́втра начина́ются[1] кани́кулы.

– Дверь закро́й[2] и закро́й окно́. Кани́кулы ещё не начали́сь.

– Почти́ все ушли́ домо́й и за́втра на рабо́ту не приду́т. Я то́же не приду́.

[1] **Начина́ть, нача́ть** means 'to begin *something*' or 'to begin *doing something*'. When you say *the holidays begin* in Russian you have to say 'the holidays begin themselves'.

[2] Imperative of **закры́ть** *to close*.

– А я тебе́ говорю́ – закро́й дверь.

– Ну, ти́ше,¹ не говори́ так гро́мко!

– Все твои́ бума́ги улетя́т на у́лицу. Закро́й окно́!

– Да что ты!

– Закро́й окно́! Одна́ бума́га уже́ улете́ла!

– Вот оби́дно²!

– На́до поговори́ть с тобо́й серьёзно!

– Ты о́чень мно́го говори́шь. Ты о́чень гро́мко говори́шь. Кака́я беда́! Бума́га улете́ла! Я не люблю́ э́ти дра́мы. Я то́же ухожу́. Сиди́³ одна́ тут. До свида́ния.

II. EXERCISE

Напиши́те почему́ Ни́на и тётя Ли́за позва́ли Пе́тю домо́й.
Мы вам не сказа́ли причи́ну (причи́на *reason*).

1 *More quietly.* 2 *What a shame!* 3 Imperative of **сиде́ть**.

SUMMARY

1 The declension of neuter nouns ending in **e** in the nominative singular is either identical with that of neuter nouns ending in **o** or consists of the equivalent soft endings. The principal point of difference is in the genitive plural (§ 1).

2 The declension of feminine nouns ending in **я** in the nominative singular consists largely of the soft equivalents to the case-endings of nouns ending in **a**. The principal point of difference is in the genitive plural (§ 2).

3 Nouns ending in **мя** are neuter. There are ten of them and they have a special declension (§ 3).

4 **За** and **под** take the accusative when motion is implied and the instrumental when location is implied (§ 5).

5 **Звать** and **брать** have a mobile vowel in the root when conjugated (§ 7).

6 Some verbs of the first conjugation have a consonant change running through the entire conjugation (§ 8).

7 The members of a few imperfective-perfective pairs of verbs are formed from entirely different roots (§ 9).

LESSON 24 REVISION

Lesson 25

I. USE OF THE INSTRUMENTAL CASE WITH PREPOSITIONS

You have seen already that the instrumental is used with certain prepositions (Lessons 22 and 23). **C,** for instance, means (*together*) *with* when it takes the instrumental case. **За** with the instrumental means *behind*, *beyond*, and **под** with the instrumental means *under*, *beneath*.

За and **под** also take the accusative case, as you have seen, when motion into a position behind or under is implied. Here are some examples of **за** and **под** with instrumental and accusative:

Instrumental

Он стоя́л за сто́йкой. *He was standing behind the bar.*

Он сиде́л за столо́м. *He was sitting at* (lit. 'behind') *the table.*

Чемода́н стоя́л под сто́йкой. *The suitcase was* ('stood') *under the bar.*

Соба́ка сиде́ла под столо́м. *The dog was sitting under the table.*

Accusative

Слу́жащий[1] сел за сто́йку. *The official sat down behind the bar.*

Он сел за стол. *He sat down at the table.*

Он поста́вил чемода́н под сто́йку. *He put the suitcase under the bar.*

Соба́ка се́ла под стол. *The dog sat (down) under the table.*

Ме́жду *between* is a preposition that always takes the instrumental, whether location or motion is implied.

Я сиде́ла ме́жду сы́ном и до́черью. *I was sitting between (my) son and (my) daughter.*

Я се́ла ме́жду сы́ном и до́черью. *I sat down between (my) son and (my) daughter.*

Ме́жду is also used, just like *between*, in an *abstract* sense, when neither location nor motion is implied, as in:

Разгово́р ме́жду слу́жащим и одни́м челове́ком. *Conversation between an official and a certain* ('one') *man.*

Мы говори́ли ме́жду собо́й. *We were talking between ourselves.*

Вы говори́ли ме́жду собо́й. *You were talking between yourselves.*

(собо́й instrumental of **себя́,** reflexive pronoun)

2. EXERCISE

Вот э́тот разгово́р я услы́шал в па́спортном отделе́нии ме́жду слу́-жащим и одни́м челове́ком, кото́рый стоя́л ря́дом со мной: – Вы

1 **Слу́жащий** declines like an adjective.

163

не написа́ли ни ва́шего и́мени,[1] ни ва́шей фами́лии,[2] сказа́л слу́жащий. – Ся́дьте за стол и напиши́те ва́ше и́мя вот тут и ва́шу фами́лию тут. Без и́мени и без фами́лии я не могу́ дать па́спорт. – Он говори́л ме́дленно и гро́мко, как с глухи́м.[3] Да, он говори́л, как с глухи́м. Он о́тдал ему́ анке́ту. Он о́тдал ему́ анке́ту и опя́ть сказа́л: – На́до написа́ть ва́ше и́мя и фами́лию. – Хорошо́, хорошо́, я напишу́ моё и́мя, я напишу́ мою́ фами́лию, сказа́л челове́к почти́ про себя́.[4] – Не люблю́ э́тих анке́т. Одна́ анке́та с двумя́[5] ко́пиями, одна́ анке́та с тремя́[6] ко́пиями, он всё говори́л про себя́. – Ну вот, я написа́л и и́мя и фами́лию, сказа́л он слу́жащему. – Вы написа́ли о́чень пло́хо. На и́мя поста́вили кля́ксу, гро́мко сказа́л ему́ слу́жащий. – Тепе́рь у вас на и́мени кля́кса. – Э́то ва́ше перо́ тако́е,[7] сказа́л ему́ челове́к. – Не люблю́ анке́ты, не люблю́ паспорта́.[8] Мой дед всю́ду разъезжа́л без па́спорта. Не люблю́ но́вые на́ши времена́. Мно́го люде́й не лю́бит но́вые времена́. Паспорта́, нало́ги, анке́ты. Дава́йте, поговори́м о ста́рых времена́х, сказа́л он мне вдруг. А я то́лько посмотре́л на него́ и убежа́л!

– А кто он был? Англича́нин, францу́з, ру́сский?

– Англича́нин. Францу́зы, италья́нцы, ру́сские тут иностра́нцы. Да, иностра́нцы так не говоря́т с слу́жащими в чужо́й стране́. Так мо́жно говори́ть то́лько с слу́жащим на ро́дине. В чужо́й стране́ нельзя́ так говори́ть. Вот чуда́к!

3. THE PREPOSITION за (contd.)

За with the instrumental means *behind* (location), as we have seen. It also means *after* (motion) in such sentences as:

Я побежа́л за сы́ном. *I ran after my son.*

Сын побежа́л за ма́мой. *The son ran after his mother.*

Маши́на шла за авто́бусом. *The car followed* (lit. 'went after') *the bus*

За with the instrumental also means *for* in the sense of *to fetch, to get,* as in:

Я иду́ за газе́той. *I'm going for a newspaper.*

Она́ идёт за до́ктором. *She is going for the doctor* or *she is going to fetch the doctor.*

In such sentences you do not need anything other than **за** + instrumental to express *to fetch*.

1 Genitive of **и́мя** (*Christian*) *name* (see Lesson 23).
2 Genitive of **фами́лия** *surname.* In Russian you must always distinguish between *Christian name* **и́мя** and *surname* **фами́лия**.
3 Instrumental of **глухо́й** *deaf,* hence *as with a deaf person.*   4 **Про себя́** *to himself.*
5 Instrumental of **два** and **две**. See § 5 below. Notice that when a number is controlled by a word requiring a case other than the accusative both the number and the noun are in the same case.   6 Instrumental of **три**. Cf. preceding note.
7 *It's your pen that's at fault* or *Your pen's to blame,* lit. 'It is your pen (that) is such'.
8 Nominative-accusative plural of **па́спорт**.

Here is part of the poem **Мойдодыр** in which there are several examples of **за** + instrumental meaning *after*:

Бóже, бóже	*Good Lord, Good Lord*
Что случилось?	*What has happened?*
Отчегó же всё кругóм	*Why has everything around*
Завертéлось, закружилось	*Started to turn and spin*
И помчáлось колесóм?	*And cartwheeled off?*
Утюги за сапогáми,	*The irons (went) after the boots,*
Сапоги за пирогáми,	*The boots after the pies,*
Пироги за утюгáми,	*The pies after the irons,*
Кочергá за кушакóм.	*The poker after the belt.*
Всё вертится	*Everything is turning*
И кружится	*And spinning*
И несётся кувыркóм.	*And rushing topsy turvy.*

4. THE PREPOSITION c (contd.)

In the following passage you will find many examples of **c** + instrumental meaning *with* (see Lesson 22). You will also find three reflexive verbs followed by **c** + instrumental. They are:

ссóриться, поссóриться с	*to quarrel with*
здорóваться, поздорóваться с	*to say hello to, to greet*
прощáться, попрощáться с	*to say goodbye to*

Russian has **c** *with* after the last two verbs, where English has *to*, because the Russian verbs mean literally 'to exchange greetings with' and 'to exchange farewells with' respectively. The passage also has several negated verbs. Remember that when there is a negated verb in a sentence then pronouns, certain adverbs etc., *must* be in the negative form. So while English has *I don't see anybody* Russian has **Я не вижу никогó,** lit. 'I don't see nobody'.

When the words **никтó** *nobody* and **ничтó** *nothing* are controlled by a preposition they split into two parts and the preposition is inserted between them. So **ни с кем** *with nobody* or *not with anybody*, **ни от чегó** *from nothing* or *not from anything* etc.

– Я никогдá ни с кем не ссóрюсь. Дáже с нáшей стáрой сердитой домрабóтницей я не ссóрюсь.

– С домрабóтницей ты не ссóришься, так как ты её боишься, вы все её боитесь, – а со всéми другими ты ссóришься.

– Непрáвда, я с другими не ссóрюсь, это прóсто дрýгие со мной ссóрятся.

– Никтó с тобóй не ссóрится, а ты сам и с друзьями[1] ссóришься и вчерá

1 Instrumental plural of **друг** (Lesson 18, § 1).

с ма́ленькой сестро́й поссо́рился, и с на́шей но́вой жили́чкой ссо́ришься.

– Я с на́шей но́вой жили́чкой не ссо́рюсь; с э́той жили́чкой я вообще́ ни[1] сло́ва не говорю́. Я её не люблю́ и она́ меня́ терпе́ть не мо́жет. Я э́ту на́шу но́вую жили́чку терпе́ть не могу́, и она́ нас всех терпе́ть не мо́жет. Я терпе́ть не могу́ таки́х люде́й, как она́. Она́ никогда́ ни с кем не здоро́вается, не говори́т «здра́вствуйте» и́ли «до́брый день».

– Она́ не здоро́вается ни[2] с отцо́м, да́же с ма́ленькой сестро́й не здоро́вается, то́лько иногда́ с ма́терью здоро́вается, но о́чень ре́дко, – да́же с на́шей ста́рой домрабо́тницей не здоро́вается – одни́м сло́вом[3] – ни с кем, ни[4] с на́ми, ни[4] с ва́ми.

– Ни с на́ми, ни с ва́ми не здоро́вается, не проща́ется, ни с кем никогда́ не[5] проща́ется. Не проща́ется, никогда́ не ска́жет[6] «до свида́ния». А вот на́ша ста́рая жили́чка, кото́рая тут жила́ у нас в про́шлом году́, она́ нас всех люби́ла, и мы её люби́ли, она́ всегда́ со все́ми и здоро́валась и проща́лась. И когда́ она́ уезжа́ла[7] – она́ уе́хала[7] год тому́ наза́д – когда́ она́ уезжа́ла год тому́ наза́д, да, э́то бы́ло в про́шлом году́, то[8] она́ со все́ми проща́лась и да́же пла́кала. Она́ пла́кала и говори́ла: «Я то́лько потому́ пла́чу,[9] что уезжа́ю, я не хочу́ уезжа́ть». Она́ пла́кала и всех целова́ла, да́же на́шу ста́рую домрабо́тницу поцелова́ла.

– Наде́юсь, что она́ и швейца́ра поцелова́ла.

1 **Ни** is an emphatic negative particle, i.e. a little word which helps to strengthen a negative – *not a (single) word.*

2 Here **ни** has the meaning of English *neither*, but since English does not pile up negatives, translate it *either.*

3 *In a (single) word.*

4 When repeated, **ни** means *neither . . . nor. . . .*

5 This illustrates well the Russian way of negating everything possible in a negative sentence, lit. 'with nobody never not exchanges farewells', i.e. *she never says goodbye to anybody.*

6 NB not present tense but future perfective, just as in English we say *she will never say 'goodbye'.*

7 Notice that first we have imperfective past **уезжа́ла,** then the perfective past **уе́хала,** i.e. *when she was leaving – she left a year ago. . . .* This sentence illustrates one of the major differences between the imperfective and the perfective. As you see, the imperfective can describe a background event, the circumstances in which something else happened. It does not move the narrative forward. The perfective, on the other hand, tells us of the act which was actually performed; it is not *descriptive*: it moves the narrative forward another step.

8 **То** often introduces the main clause in sentences beginning with а **когда́** or **е́сли** clause. Its equivalent is *then* or you can ignore it.

9 **Пла́кать** *to weep* **пла́чу, пла́чешь** etc. is one of the first conjugation verbs that change the consonant throughout the conjugation, like **писа́ть, пишу́, пи́шешь** (see Lesson 23, § 8).

– Что за глу́пости, что за ерунду́ ты говори́шь! Она́ была́ до́брая же́нщина. Она́ прие́хала с како́й-то корзи́нкой, с одни́м ма́леньким чемода́ном, с одно́й канаре́йкой в кле́тке и с каки́м-то ужа́сным кра́сным абажу́ром. Она́ прие́хала мно́го лет тому́ наза́д, а когда́ она́ уезжа́ла, то она́ уе́хала с двумя́[1] больши́ми чемода́нами, с той же корзи́нкой битко́м наби́той всем,[2] что мать и куха́рка пригото́вили. Она́ уе́хала с варе́ньем, с пече́ньем, с ка́ктусом в горшке́, с канаре́йками – в кле́тке уже́ не одна́, а две канаре́йки – и всё с тем же ужа́сным кра́сным абажу́ром. Вот так она́ уезжа́ла от нас и уе́хала. И мы ча́сто ду́маем о ней и о том, как она́ уезжа́ла и как мы все проща́лись.

5. DECLENSION OF THE NUMBERS два/две, три, четы́ре

In §§ 2 and 4 above we had the instrumental of два/две and три. These numbers together with четы́ре have a unique declension, which has some similarities to the declension of the plural of adjectives.

nom.	два/две	три	четы́ре
gen.	двух	трёх	четырёх
dat.	двум	трём	четырём
acc.	as *nom.* or *gen.*	as *nom.* or *gen.*	as *nom.* or *gen.*
instr.	двумя́	тремя́	четырьмя́
prep.	двух	трёх	четырёх

You already know that два/две, три and четы́ре (and, note, all higher numbers ending in два/две, три or четы́ре) take the genitive singular (Lesson 6, § 13b). This, however, is true only when the number itself is in the nominative case or the nominative-accusative (i.e. the form of the accusative that is the same as the nominative):

Там два сту́ла.
Да́йте мне две ча́шки (*cups*).
Прошло́ три го́да.
Он написа́л четы́ре письма́.

If the number is controlled by a word – a preposition or a verb or a noun, which requires some case other than the nominative-accusative, then the number and its noun (and any adjective) all go into the same case, which will be plural for the noun and adjective:

от двух до четырёх часо́в
с двумя́ рубля́ми
Я дал конфе́ты (*sweets*) э́тим трём де́вушкам.
Она́ всегда́ здоро́вается с э́тими четырьмя́ ма́льчиками.
Мы говори́ли об э́тих двух но́вых кни́гах.

---

1 Instrumental of два/две (see § 5 below).
2 **Битко́м наби́тый**, in the appropriate case, is an idiom meaning (*stuffed*) *full of* and the *of* is expressed by the *plain instrumental*, here the instrumental of всё.

The same applies when the numbers 2, 3, 4 qualify an animate noun which is the direct object of a verb. As you know, animates have an accusative plural which is identical with the genitive. The numbers 2, 3 and 4 have to follow the same rule:

> Я позва́л двух докторо́в.
> Мать лю́бит свои́х трёх сынове́й.
> Он встре́тил четырёх краси́вых де́вушек.

6. CONGRATULATIONS, GREETINGS AND GOOD WISHES WITH THE PREPOSITION **с**

The verb *to congratulate* is **поздравля́ть, поздра́вить.** It takes a direct object:

> Поздравля́ю вас! *I congratulate you* or *Congratulations!*

The cause for congratulation is expressed by **с** + instrumental. This is an idiomatic use of **с** + instrumental.

Поздравля́ю вас с ва́шим успе́хом. *I congratulate you on your success.*

Учи́тель поздра́вил ученико́в со зна́нием ру́сского языка́. *The teacher congratulated the pupils on their knowledge of Russian.*

Certain kinds of greetings and good wishes in Russian are in fact expressed as congratulations. For instance, you do not *wish* people a happy New Year, you congratulate them on the occasion of the New Year. Nearly always in such instances the verb is left out but the preposition **с** is retained:

С Но́вым Го́дом – с но́вым сча́стьем! *Happy New Year and Good Luck!* (lit. 'new/fresh happiness/luck').

С пра́здником! *Happy Holiday!* (a greeting used on a festival).

С пра́здником Рождества́ Христо́ва! *Happy Christmas!*

С днём рожде́ния! *Happy Birthday!*

In Russian you can congratulate people on various other things too:

С прие́здом! *Glad to see you!* ('Congratulations on your arrival').

С переéздом! Used to express good wishes to somebody who is about to or has just moved house.

Some kinds of wishes, however, take the form of the genitive case, since *underlying* them is the expression **жела́ю вам/тебе́** *I wish you*, which takes the genitive case of what you wish.

> Всего́ до́брого! *All the best!*
> Счастли́вого пути́! *Bon Voyage!*
> Споко́йной но́чи! *Good night!*

but the plain nominative-accusative is used in

> До́брое утро! *Good morning!*
> До́брый день! *Good-day!*
> До́брый ве́чер! *Good evening!*

7. TRANSLATION
A Trip to Moscow

When we went to Moscow we were met[1] at[2] the airport by our Soviet colleagues. They greeted us in a very friendly fashion.

'Glad to see you,' said one.

'(I wish you) a happy stay[3] in the U.S.S.R.,' said another.

I was able to answer them in Russian[4] and soon we were talking quite freely among ourselves.

In the Customs Office an official asked me to open my luggage.

'With pleasure,' I said. 'But I can't see[5] my luggage.'

Then I saw a porter with four suitcases. I thought that two of[6] them were[7] mine. My friend who was standing at my side and talking to[8] two interpreters said that they were[7] his. I found my suitcases under two trunks. Finally we set off for the city.

In Moscow we concluded[9] a contract with three Soviet firms. We also visited theatres and exhibitions and bought souvenirs in GUM.[10]

When we were leaving our Soviet colleagues gave us presents and wished us *bon voyage*.

1 Make *our Soviet colleagues* the subject, saying lit. 'us at the airport met our Soviet colleagues'.   2 **На** + prepositional case.   3 **Счастли́во пребыва́ть** or **счастли́вого пребыва́ния.**   4 **По-ру́сски.**   5 Say *I do not see it.*   6 **Дво́е из** + genitive. **Дво́е** is a collective numeral meaning (*a group of*) *two*; see Part II – Grammar.   7 Omit the verb. See Lesson 27.   8 Remember Russian has **говори́ть с.** 9 **Заключи́ть** perfective, **заключа́ть** imperfective.   10 **ГУМ** (the large State Stores in Moscow).

SUMMARY

1 The instrumental case with **за** *behind* and **под** *under* implies location, the accusative case with these prepositions implies motion into a position (§ 1).

2 **За** + instrumental also means *after* and *for, to fetch* (§ 3).

3 One of the meanings of **с** + instrumental is *with, together with* (§ 4).

4 When there is a negated verb everything else that can be negated must be negated (§ 4).

5 With prepositions, the words **никто́** *nobody* and **ничто́** *nothing* divide into two parts and the preposition is inserted between the parts (§ 4).

6 The imperfective is often *descriptive*, the perfective is always *narrative* (§ 4, note 8).

7 Declension of **два/две, три** and **четы́ре** (§ 5).

8 When a number is not in the nominative or nominative-accusative it and its noun go into the same case (§ 5).

9 **С** + instrumental is used in congratulations, greetings and good wishes (§ 6).

10 The genitive is used in some expressions of good wishes (§ 6).

Lesson 26

I. ADJECTIVES WITH HARD AND SOFT ENDINGS

You remember that hard adjectives end in:

masc.	fem.	neut.	pl.
ый	ая	ое	ые
ой	áя	óе	ы́е
но́вый	но́вая	но́вое	но́вые
молодо́й	молода́я	молодо́е	молоды́е

and that soft adjectives end in:

masc.	fem.	neut.	pl.
ий	яя	ее	ие
зи́мний	зи́мняя	зи́мнее	зи́мние

Here are two more soft-ending adjectives:

после́дний *last*

после́дний по́езд *the last train*
после́дняя наде́жда *the last hope*
после́днее сло́во *the last word*
после́дние дни ме́сяца *the last days of the month*

пре́жний *former*

Пре́жний дире́ктор терпе́ть не мог шу́ма. Пре́жняя секрета́рша дире́ктора писа́ла все пи́сьма на на́шей маши́нке в на́шей ко́мнате, так как он терпе́ть не мог сту́ка маши́нки. Моё пре́жнее ме́сто бы́ло у окна́ в друго́й ко́мнате, тепе́рь мы все сиди́м на но́вых места́х.

Below is a complete set of declensions both for hard-ending and soft-ending adjectives. The neuter shares the same endings as the masculine, except in the nominative-accusative; the masculine accusative is like the genitive if it refers to an animate being. This applies to the plural too.

Hard Endings

	masc.		neut.	fem.	pl.
nom.	но́вый	*new*	но́вое	но́вая	но́вые
gen.		но́вого		но́вой	но́вых
dat.		но́вому		но́вой	но́вым
acc.	*as nom.* or *gen.*		но́вое	но́вую	*nom.* or *gen.*
instr.		но́вым		но́вой/ою	но́выми
prep.		но́вом		но́вой	но́вых

In the instrumental feminine **но́вой** is commoner than **но́вою**. An adjective like **молодо́й** has the same endings except in the nominative singular masculine.

170

Soft Endings

	masc.	neut.	fem.	pl.
nom.	зи́мний *wintery*	зи́мнее	зи́мняя	зи́мние
gen.	зи́мнего		зи́мней	зи́мних
dat.	зи́мнему		зи́мней	зи́мним
acc.	*as nom.* or *gen.*	зи́мнее	зи́мнюю	*nom.* or *gen.*
instr.	зи́мним		зи́мней/ею	зи́мними
prep.	зи́мнем		зи́мней	зи́мних

In the instrumental feminine **зи́мней** is commoner than **зи́мнею**.

2. ADJECTIVES WITH MIXED ENDINGS

шой, жой, кой, гой, хой

You know that after **ш, ж, ч, щ, к, г, х** you cannot write **ы** but must write **и** instead. So adjectives ending in the nominative singular masculine in **жой, кой** etc. (see Lesson 20, § 2) have endings like those of **молодо́й**, but wherever the latter has **ы** in the case-ending they have **и**:

	masc.	neut.	fem.	pl.
nom.	чужо́й *alien*	чужо́е	чужа́я	**чужи́е**
gen.	чужо́го		чужо́й	**чужи́х**
dat.	чужо́му		чужо́й	**чужи́м**
acc.	*as nom.* or *gen.*	чужо́е	чужу́ю	*nom.* or *gen.*
instr.	**чужи́м**		чужо́й/о́ю	**чужи́ми**
prep.	чужо́м		чужо́й	**чужи́х**

Adjectives ending in **кий, гий, хий** (Lesson 20, § 4) have the same endings as **но́вый**, but again wherever the latter has **ы** in the case-ending they have **и**:

	masc.	neut.	fem.	pl.
nom.	у́зкий *narrow*	у́зкое	у́зкая	**у́зкие**
gen.	у́зкого		у́зкой	**у́зких**
dat.	у́зкому		у́зкой	**у́зким**
acc.	*as nom.* or *gen.*	у́зкое	у́зкую	*nom.* or *gen.*
instr.	**у́зким**		у́зкой/ою	**у́зкими**
prep.	у́зком		у́зкой	**у́зких**

ший, жий, чий, щий

There are also adjectives ending in **ший, жий, чий** and **щий** and these have endings like those of **зи́мний**. However, after **ш, ж, ч** and **щ** you never write **я** and **ю** but **а** and **у**, so in two case-endings these adjectives differ from **зи́мний**.

	masc.	neut.	fem.	pl.
nom.	хоро́ший *good*	хоро́шее	**хоро́шая**	хоро́шие
gen.	хоро́шего		хоро́шей	хоро́ших
dat.	хоро́шему		хоро́шей	хоро́шим
acc.	*as nom.* or *gen.*	хоро́шее	**хоро́шую**	*nom.* or *gen.*
instr.	хоро́шим		хоро́шей/ею	хоро́шими
prep.	хоро́шем		хоро́шей	хоро́ших

At first glance it looks as if there is a bewildering variety of declensions for the adjective. However, there are in fact only *two* basic patterns: hard and soft. The variations are brought about by the rules, which you already know, concerning the vowel letters that cannot appear after **ш, ж, ч, щ, к, г** and **х.**

– Сего́дня хоро́шая пого́да. Со́лнце све́тит. Я люблю́ хоро́шую пого́ду.
– Тут нет хоро́шей пого́ды. Тут то́лько плоха́я (*bad*) пого́да. А там у вас на ю́ге нет плохо́й пого́ды.

Настоя́щий *real, present* (cf. стоя́ть *to stand*)
Мой брат настоя́щий разбо́йник (*a real brigand*).
Ва́ша сестра́ настоя́щая кулина́рка (*culinary expert*), она́ так вку́сно гото́вит (*she cooks so 'tastily'*).
В (*At*) настоя́щее вре́мя у нас мно́го пла́нов, но ма́ло де́нег (де́нег genitive plural of де́ньги *money*).
В настоя́щее вре́мя у нас нет но́вых пла́нов.

Бу́дущий *future, next* (cf. я бу́ду *I shall be*)
В бу́дущем году́ бу́дут де́ньги и мы ку́пим дом.

Сле́дующий *next* (cf. сле́довать *to follow*: я сле́дую, ты сле́дуешь etc.)
В сле́дующем году́ (*next year*) мы ку́пим дом.
Когда́ сле́дующий по́езд? – Нет сле́дующего по́езда, после́дний по́езд уже́ ушёл.
Сле́дующий уро́к сле́дует че́рез неде́лю (*in a week's time*).

3. 'THE PRESENT,' 'THE FUTURE' AND 'THE PAST'
To express *the present* and *the future* you use the adjectival nouns **настоя́щее** and **бу́дущее.**

Что вы ду́маете о бу́дущем?
Я не зна́ю, что в бу́дущем (*what (will happen) in the future*), я да́же не зна́ю, что в настоя́щем (*what (is happening) in the present*).

Past, last, in the sense of 'which has just passed' is **про́шлый,** a hard-ending adjective.

про́шлое вре́мя	*past time*	про́шлые го́ды	*past years*
про́шлое	*the past*	О про́шлом я не ду́маю.	
про́шлый уро́к	*last lesson*	про́шлая неде́ля	*last week*

Cf. после́дний уро́к ку́рса   *the last lesson of the course*
после́дняя неде́ля ме́сяца *the last week of the month*

4. SUPERLATIVES
The following two adjectives act as comparatives (*more . . .*) or superlatives (*most . . .*) and belong to the last group of declensions with mixed endings (§ 2).

ста́рший *eldest* or *elder* (i.e. the one born first)
мла́дший *youngest* or *younger* (i.e. the one born last)

172

In the following examples we use the verb **назва́ть,** perfective *to name*, imperfective **называ́ть** or **звать** (see Lesson 23, § 6). This verb takes a direct object but the name or thing by which you call somebody or something usually goes into the instrumental case.

Ста́ршую дочь роди́тели (*parents*) назва́ли Ве́рой, мла́дшего сы́на назва́ли Константи́ном. Ста́ршие де́ти в шко́ле, мла́дшие ещё до́ма. У мои́х ро́дственников (ро́дственник *relative*) три до́чери – ста́ршую дочь, пе́рвую, то́же назва́ли Ве́рой и так и зову́т Ве́рой (*and that is what they call her,* i.e. that is how they address her); втору́ю, сре́днюю (сре́дний *middle*), назва́ли Наде́ждой, а зову́т всегда́ На́дей, да, про́сто говоря́т На́дя, зову́т На́дей, а мла́дшую дочь назва́ли Любо́вью, а зову́т Лю́бой. Имена́ до́черей – Ве́ра, Наде́жда, Любо́вь, и имени́ны тридца́того сентября́.

Любо́вь *Lyubov* means *love* and is the equivalent of the English name *Charity*. The last part of the last sentence means *and their nameday is on the thirtieth of September. Nameday* is the day of the saint whose name you bear. **Имени́ны** is one of a group of nouns which are plural in form but singular in meaning.

Note that the date is expressed by the genitive case standing without a preposition:

пе́рвое ма́я *the 1st of May*; пе́рвого ма́я *on the 1st of May.*

второ́е декабря́ *the 2nd of December*; второ́го декабря́ *on the 2nd of December.*

У крестья́нина три сы́на.	*A peasant (had) three sons.*
Ста́рший у́мный был дети́на,[1]	*The eldest was a clever lad,*[1]
Сре́дний сын и так и сяк,	*The middle son so-so,*
Мла́дший во́все был дура́к.	*The youngest was quite a fool.*

There are a few more adjectives having the meaning *more . . .* and/or *most . . .* like **ста́рший** and **мла́дший**:

лу́чший *better, best*
    икра́ лу́чшего со́рта *best quality caviar*
    икра́ хоро́шего со́рта *good quality caviar*

ху́дший *worse, worst*
    в ху́дшем настро́ении *in the worst mood*
    в плохо́м настро́ении *in a bad mood*
    лу́чшие дни и ху́дшие дни *the best days and the worst days*
    хоро́шие дни и плохи́е дни *good days and bad days*

В ху́дшем слу́чае, в лу́чшем слу́чае are idioms meaning *at worst, at best*, lit. 'in the worst event, in the best event'.

1 **Дети́на** is feminine in form but masculine in meaning.

вы́сший *superior, higher, supreme*

    вы́сшая честь *the supreme honour*

    высо́кая честь *high honour*

ни́зший *lower, inferior, lowest*

    ни́зшие слой *the lower/lowest layers*

    ни́зкий слой *low layer*

These adjectives are somewhat limited in use. To form a true superlative, i.e. an adjective meaning . . . *est* or *most* . . . you simply put **са́мый** in front of the adjective. **Са́мый** itself goes into the appropriate case.

Сего́дня са́мый холо́дный день э́того го́да.	*Today is the coldest day of this year.*
У́тром са́мого холо́дного дня...	*On the morning of the coldest day . . .*
Она́ са́мая краси́вая же́нщина, кото́рую я знал.	*She is the most beautiful woman I have known.*
Это дочь са́мой краси́вой же́нщины в э́том го́роде.	*This is the daughter of the most beautiful woman in this town.*
Это са́мое удо́бное ме́сто.	*This is the most comfortable place.*
Они́ сиде́ли в са́мом удо́бном ме́сте.	*They were sitting in the most comfortable place.*

There is also a form of the superlative in one word. It ends in **ейший** (or **айший** after **ш, ж, ч, щ**). Not all adjectives have this form, which often has the meaning *a most* . . . instead of *the most* . . . (see Part II – Grammar, for further details).

    кратча́йший путь *the shortest way*

    длинне́йшая доро́га, *the longest road, a most long road*

    интере́снейший вопро́с *a most interesting question*

5. VERBS WITH THE INFINITIVE ENDING IN -ереть

There are a few verbs with infinitive ending in **-ереть**. They and their compounds all form the past tense masculine by lopping off **-еть**:

умере́ть pfv. *to die*	у́мер	умерла́	у́мерло	у́мерли
тере́ть *to rub*	тёр	тёрла	тёрло	тёрли
запере́ть pfv. *to lock*	за́пер	заперла́	за́перло	за́перли

The imperfective of the prefixed forms ends in **-ирать: умира́ть, запира́ть, стира́ть** *to rub off* (perfective **стере́ть**).

The **-ереть** verbs are first conjugation of the type which have a consonant before the ending, and the **e** before the **p** disappears in conjugation:

fut. pfv.	я умру́	*pres.*	тру
	ты умрёшь		трёшь
	он умрёт		трёт

мы умрём	трём
вы умрёте	трёте
они умрут	трут

The **-ирать** verbs are first conjugation **думать**-type: **умираю, умираешь** etc.

6. IMPERSONAL EXPRESSIONS

You have already met some impersonal expressions: **надо** *it is necessary one must;* **нельзя** *it is impossible, one cannot;* **можно** *it is permissible, one may.* In the following passage from a modern poem there are two more impersonal expressions which we will talk about in more detail.

«Памяти Бориса Горбатова» К. Симонова
To the Memory of Boris Gorbatov by K. Simonov

Умер друг у меня – вот какая беда...	My friend has died – that is the calamity . . .
Как мне быть – не могу и ума приложить.	How am I to live – I cannot grasp it.
Я не думал, не верил, не ждал никогда,	I never thought, never believed, never expected,
Что без этого друга придётся мне жить.	That I should have to live without this friend.
Был в отъезде, когда хоронили его,	I was away when they buried him,
В день прощанья у гроба не смог постоять.	I was unable to stand beside his coffin on the day of farewell.
А теперь вот приеду – и нет ничего.	But now I shall arrive – and there is nothing.
Нет его. Нет совсем. Нет. Нигде не видать.	He does not exist. Does not exist at all. No, he is nowhere to be seen.

In the last line **видать** *to see* is a less common form of the verb **видеть**. It is used only in the infinitive and past tense. It is most common with **не**:

Его нигде не видать. *He is nowhere to be seen.*
Я вас давно не видал. *I haven't seen you for a long time.*
Я никогда не видал такое чудо – чёрные розы! *I have never seen such a marvel – black roses!*

When it is not negated **видать** usually means *to see often, to see a lot of*:

Он виды видал. *He's seen a thing or two,* lit. 'he has seen sights (and lots of them)'.

Как мне быть consists of the infinitive with the dative of the *logical* subject and means *what am I to do*, lit. 'How to me to be'.

Another way of saying this is: **Что мне де́лать?**

Here are some more examples of this infinitive + dative construction:

Как мне жить? *How am I to live?*
Что ему́ чита́ть? *What is he to read?*

Another impersonal expression occurs in the fourth line:

Мне придётся. *I shall have to.*

This impersonal verb is used only in the third pers. sing. and the neuter forms of the past tense, and the logical subject is again in the dative case:

Ему́ придётся жить скро́мно. *He will have to live modestly.*
Ему́ прихо́дится жить скро́мно. *He has to live modestly.*
Нам придётся постоя́ть. *We shall have to stand (for a while).*
Нам придётся стоя́ть. *We shall have to stand.*
Нам прихо́дится стоя́ть. *We have to stand.*
Им пришло́сь постоя́ть. *They had to stand (for a while).*
Им пришло́сь стоя́ть. *They had to stand.*

The imperfective past is **приходи́лось** and is used when one had to do something often:

Им приходи́лось стоя́ть. *They had to stand.*

Вам ча́сто прихо́дится ждать авто́буса? *Do you often have to wait for the bus?*

Ра́ньше мне приходи́лось ждать недо́лго, мину́ты две-три; но во вре́мя забасто́вки (*At the time of the strike*) мне пришло́сь идти́ пешко́м (*to go on foot*). И вчера́ мне пришло́сь пойти́ пешко́м. *And yesterday (or yesterday too) I had to go on foot.*

У нас нет ни одно́й спи́чки в до́ме. Нам придётся попроси́ть спи́чек у сосе́дей. *We haven't a single match (*спи́чка*) in the house. We shall have to ask our neighbours for some matches.*

Notice the construction **проси́ть** imperfective, **попроси́ть** perfective plus accusative or genitive of the thing asked for and **у** + genitive of the person asked.

Сосе́д *neighbour* is a very unusual noun. It has hard endings in the singular but soft endings in the plural.

sing. nom.	сосе́д		*pl.*	сосе́ди
acc.	сосе́да			сосе́дей
dat.	сосе́ду etc.			сосе́дям etc.

Чёрт *devil* is the only other noun that declines in the same way:

sing	чёрт		*pl.*	че́рти
	чёрта			чертей
	чёрту etc.			чертя́м etc.

7. Должен

Another way of saying that somebody has to do something is to use the short adjective:

до́лжен   должна́   должно́   должны́

which agrees with the gender and number of the subject of the sentence, the verb being in the infinitive. This adjective is connected with the noun **долг** *duty*.

> Я должна́ помога́ть роди́телям – э́то мой долг.
> *I must help my parents – it is my duty.*
>
> Он не мо́жет прийти́ к вам за́втра, он до́лжен идти́ на уро́к.
>
> Мы должны́ быть ра́но на вокза́ле.
>
> Всё на земле́ должно́ измени́ться мало-пома́лу.
> *Everything on earth must gradually change.*
>
> Э́то должно́ вы́йти. *It must succeed/come off.*

The past tense is formed by putting **был** etc. *after* **до́лжен** and the future by putting **бу́ду** etc. after it.

> Он до́лжен был идти́ на уро́к. *He had to go to his lesson.*
>
> Мы должны́ бы́ли быть ра́но на вокза́ле.
>
> Я должна́ бу́ду пойти́ туда́. *I shall have to go there.*
>
> Они́ должны́ бу́дут сказа́ть нам. *They will have to tell us.*

NB The word order is important, since **до́лжен** also means *owe* and in its past and future tenses the verb **был/бу́ду** goes in front:

> Я вам должна́ рубль. *I owe you a ruble.*
>
> Он был мне́ до́лжен фунт. *He owed me a pound.*
>
> Тогда́ вы бу́дете мне должны́. *Then you'll owe me (something),*
>   i.e. *you'll be in my debt.*

There is also an expression **должно́ быть** which never changes its form. It is a sort of adverbial expression meaning *probably*, *it must be so*, *I suppose* etc. Compare this with **мо́жет быть** *perhaps*, lit. 'it can/may be'.

– Он хоте́л прийти́, но не пришёл. Мо́жет быть он пошёл к бра́ту.

– Нет, должно́ быть у него́ мно́го рабо́ты. *No, he must have a lot of work.*

Note that this is not the same as *he has to have* etc.

Ему́ ча́сто прихо́дится по́здно рабо́тать, должно́ быть ему́ пришло́сь *(he probably had to, he must have had to)* и сего́дня рабо́тать по́здно, вот он и не смог прийти́ к нам.

Смог is past tense masculine *perfective* of **смочь**, **мочь** *to be able*:

смог	смогла́	смогло́	смогли́
impfv. мог	могла́	могло́	могли́

8. VERBS OF MOTION WITH THE PREFIX вы-

The prefix **вы-** means *out*.

In the preceding section we had:

$$\text{Э́то должно́ вы́йти.} \quad \textit{It must succeed/come off.}$$

If it had succeeded we should have said: **Э́то вы́шло.**

Вы́йти is a compound of **идти́,** so **вы́йти** literally means *to come/go out*.
The imperfective is **выходи́ть.**

pfv.	вы́йти		*impfv.*	выходи́ть
fut.	я вы́йду		*pres.*	выхожу́
	ты вы́йдешь			выхо́дишь
past	вы́шел вы́шла вы́шло		*past*	выходи́л выходи́ла выходи́ло
	вы́шли			выходи́ли

To express *of* in *to come/go out of* you use the preposition **из,** which takes the genitive case:

$$\text{вы́йти/выходи́ть из теа́тра, из шко́лы, из зда́ния } (\textit{building}).$$

Я вы́шел из теа́тра.

Сестра́ вы́шла из шко́лы.

Я вы́йду ра́но и́з_дому.[1] *I shall go out of the house early.*

Ка́ждый день я выхожу́ в одно́ и то же вре́мя из конто́ры.
I come out of my office at one and the same time every day.

Notice that *same* is **тот, та, то, те** (*that*) followed by **же. Са́мый** (*most, very*) and **сам** (*self*) do *not* mean *same*.

– Вот тут вы́ход (*exit*).

– Нет, вы́хода тут нет.

– Нет вы́хода, вы́хода нет?

– У э́того теа́тра то́лько два вы́хода: оди́н вы́ход сле́ва, друго́й вы́ход спра́ва. Лю́ди о́чень до́лго выходи́ли из теа́тра, наконе́ц все вы́шли.

You can also come out *into* the field, for instance:

Я вы́йду в по́ле. *I shall go out into the field.*

вы́йти на опу́шку ле́са *to go out into the fringe of a forest*

Мы до́лго шли в лесу́,[2] доро́га вела́ че́рез лес, наконе́ц мы вы́шли
на опу́шку ле́са.

To drive out is **вы́ехать, выезжа́ть.**

pfv.	вы́ехать		*impfv.*	выезжа́ть
fut.	я вы́еду		*pres.*	выезжа́ю
	ты вы́едешь			выезжа́ешь
past	вы́ехал вы́ехала		*past*	выезжа́л выезжа́ла

---

[1] There are some masculine nouns which have an alternative genitive ending in **y** (see next section).

[2] **В лесу́** *in the forest*, see Lesson 13, § 9.

The exit by which you drive out is **вы́езд.**

Грузови́к выезжа́л из воро́т; наро́д стоя́л круго́м и смотре́л, вы́езд был о́чень у́зкий, шофёр осторо́жно вёл маши́ну, грузови́к ме́дленно выезжа́л из воро́т. – Что, вы́едет и́ли нет? ка́ждый ду́мал про себя́. Грузови́к е́хал о́чень ме́дленно и, наконе́ц, благополу́чно вы́ехал из воро́т на у́лицу.

Воро́т is genitive plural of the neuter plural **воро́та** *gate/gates*, a word which has no singular form.

Вёл past tense of **вести́** *to lead* in the sense of *to drive* (a vehicle).

Про себя́ *to himself.*

9. GENITIVE ENDING IN **y**

There are some masculine nouns which have an extra genitive case ending in **y** or **ю.**

With some of these nouns the genitive in **y/ю** is used only when quantity is expressed (it is called a *partitive genitive*):

фунт ча́ю *a pound of tea,* cf. за́пах ча́я *the smell of tea*
кусо́к са́хару *a lump,* lit. 'a piece of sugar', cf. цена́ са́хара *the price of sugar*
ско́лько ле́су *how much timber,* cf. опу́шка ле́са *the edge of the wood*

With some nouns the genitive in **y** is used after certain prepositions as an alternative to the genitive in **a.** Often the stress is then moved to the preposition and the noun is left without stress:

и́з‿дому *out of the house* (and из до́ма)
и́з‿лесу *out of the wood* (and из ле́са)
и́з‿виду *out of sight* (and из ви́да)

There are also some fixed expressions in which the genitive in **y** occurs, such as:

ни ра́зу *not once*
ни ша́гу (наза́д, вперёд, в сто́рону) *not a step (back, forward, to the side)*

10. TRANSLATION

Our former director's secretary typed[1] all the letters on that old typewriter. She used to sit in the small room because he could not bear the rattle of the typewriter.

He died last week.[2] His last words were: 'Has she typed[3] my last letter?

---

1 Say *wrote.*   2 **На** + prepositional case.   3 Perfective.

I told her I could not bear the rattle of the typewriter. You will lock up my house when I am dead.'[1] And then he died.

They have indeed[2] locked up the house. It is the tallest house on the longest street in our most interesting town. Nobody wanted to live in that big old house.

The eldest son of the family always lived in that house but now the house is empty. Our director wanted to give it to (his) eldest son but (his) son works in France and he must live there.

When they told the middle son that he could live there he said he did not like to live in a big old house. The youngest son gave the same[3] answer. He told the solicitor he would have to sell it.

The old director used to come out[4] of the house and stand[5] in the garden. It was[6] the most beautiful garden in the town. Then he drove out[4] of the gates, across town to the new office.

One day he came out of the house and set off on foot across the park. He stood for a while on the bank of the river. Then he returned to the house and never[7] came out.

1 Future perfective of **умере́ть.** 2 Insert **и** before the verb. 3 **Тот же** (see § 8). 4 Imperfective. 5 Imperfective. 6 The verb agrees with **сад,** not with **э́то** in this kind of sentence. 7 **Бо́льше не.**

SUMMARY

1 Declension of adjectives (§§ 1 and 2).

2 A few adjectives have the same form for the superlative and comparative (§ 4).

3 **Са́мый** is put in front of an adjective to make the superlative; there are also some superlatives in **ейший/айший** (§ 4).

4 Verbs with the infinitive in **-ереть** form the past tense masculine without **л** and lose the **е** before the **р** in conjugation (§ 5).

5 *Have to* and *must* are expressed by the impersonal verb **прихо́дится, придётся** etc. or the short adjective **до́лжен** etc. (§§ 6 and 7).

6 Prefix **вы-** with verbs of motion (§ 8).

7 Some masculine nouns have an additional genitive in **у/ю** (§ 9).

Lesson 27

I. SEQUENCE OF TENSES

Compare the tenses in these Russian sentences with the tenses in the English translations:

Я спроси́л его́, кото́рый час. *I asked him what time it was.*
Он сказа́л, что уже́ два часа́. *He said that it was already two o'clock.*
Мы ду́мали, что уже́ по́здно. *We thought it was already (too) late.*

As you see, with verbs meaning *to say, to ask, to think,* and with other verbs that serve to introduce one's words or thoughts, you use in Russian the tense which you would actually use at the time of saying or thinking. In the first sentence above, for example, my actual words were **кото́рый час** *what time is it?* In the second sentence he actually said **уже́ два часа́** *it is already two o'clock.* In the third sentence we actually thought **уже́ по́здно** *it is already (too) late.*

In Russian these tenses must be carried over into the indirect statements or questions introduced by **спроси́л, сказа́л, ду́мали.**

In the sentences above the Russian has no verb in the indirect statement or question. The verb *to be* is understood. The same rule about tenses applies when there *is* a verb:

Я спроси́л его́, кто идёт. *I asked him who was coming.*
Он сказа́л, что Ве́ра не идёт, потому́ что она́ рабо́тает. *He said that Vera was not coming because she was working.*
Мы ду́мали, что она́ сиди́т до́ма и чита́ет. *We thought that she was sitting at home and reading.*

As you see the tenses in the indirect statements and questions are the ones actually used at the time of speaking or thinking.

If the speaker's actual statement or question was or is about the future then you have to have the future in the indirect statement or question where English sometimes has *would*:

Я спроси́л его́, кто придёт. *I asked him who would come.*
Я спрошу́ его́, кто придёт. *I shall ask him who will come.*
Он сказа́л, что Ве́ра не придёт. *He said that Vera would not come.*
Он говори́т, что Ве́ра не придёт. *He says that Vera will not come.*

As you see, the main tense makes no difference. The tense in the indirect statement or question has to be future, if the future is referred to. This is why in the poem in the last lesson you had **придётся** a future perfective, after **ду́мал** etc., where the English equivalent is *would have to.*

It follows that if you have the past tense in an indirect statement or question then the tense actually used at the time of speaking or thinking must have been the past tense, which corresponds to English *had done* etc.:

Я спроси́л его́, кто был там. *I asked him who had been there.*
(but я спроси́л его́, кто там. *I asked him who was there.*)
Он спроси́л меня́, кто пришёл. *He asked me who had come.*
Я сказа́л, что Ве́ра пришла́. *I said that Vera had come.*
Мы ду́мали, что она́ сиде́ла до́ма и чита́ла. *We thought she had been sitting at home and reading.*

2. VERBS OF MOTION WITH THE PREFIX вы- (*contd.*)

In the last lesson (§ 8) we had two verbs of motion with the prefix вы- meaning *out*. Here are some more verbs of motion with the prefix вы-:

pfv.	вы́вести *to lead out, to bring out*		*impfv.*	выводи́ть
fut.	я вы́веду		*pres.*	вывожу́
	ты вы́ведешь			выво́дишь
past	вы́вел вы́вела		*past*	выводи́л выводи́ла

Лошаде́й выводи́ли из коню́шни. Вы́вели всех лошаде́й, то́лько ста́рого осла́ не вы́вели. Заче́м выводи́ть его́? На нём никто́ не хоте́л е́хать верхо́м и его́ не вы́вели.

Лошаде́й, genitive-accusative, is object of **выводи́ли. Осла́,** genitive-accusative of **осёл,** is object of **вы́вели.**

Вы не зна́ете как вы́йти на на́бережную? Я сам иду́ туда́, дава́йте пойдём вме́сте и я вас вы́веду из э́того лабири́нта у́лиц.

pfv.	вы́везти *to export* or *to convey out*		*impfv.*	вывози́ть
fut.	я вы́везу		*pres.*	вывожу́
	ты вы́везешь			выво́зишь
past	вы́вез вы́везла		*past*	вывози́л вывози́ла

Из А́нглии выво́зят мно́го маши́н, да, А́нглия выво́зит мно́го маши́н. Из Голла́ндии выво́зят ма́сло и сыр, а Финля́ндия выво́зит мно́го ле́са.

pfv.	вы́нести *to carry out*		*impfv.*	выноси́ть
fut.	я вы́несу		*pres.*	выношу́
	ты вы́несешь			выно́сишь
past	вы́нес вы́несла		*past*	выноси́л выноси́ла

Из сосе́днего до́ма выноси́ли ме́бель, на́ши сосе́ди уезжа́ли в Австра́лию, весь день выноси́ли ве́щи из до́ма и к ве́черу всё вы́несли.

к ве́черу *towards evening, by evening*

The prefix вы- does not exist on its own as a preposition. As a prefix it is used not only with verbs of motion, идти́, е́хать, вести́, везти́, нести́, but with many other verbs.

182

pfv.	вы́дать *to give out, to hand out*	*impfv.*	выдава́ть
fut.	я вы́дам	*pres.*	выдаю́
	ты вы́дашь		выдаёшь
past	вы́дал вы́дала	*past*	выдава́л выдава́ла

Во вре́мя войны́ нам выдава́ли хлеб по ка́рточкам. *During the war bread was given out to us on (ration) cards*, lit. '(they) gave out to us'.

Они́ is never used in this type of construction where the subject is people in general.

Хлеб, мя́со, ма́сло, са́хар нам выдава́ли по ка́рточкам.

Вы́дать, выдава́ть also meant *to betray, to give away*.

Они́ вы́дали та́йные све́дения врага́м.
They gave away secret information to the enemy, lit. 'enemies'.

pfv.	вы́бросить *to throw away*	*impfv.*	выбра́сывать
fut.	я вы́брошу	*pres.*	выбра́сываю
	ты вы́бросишь		выбра́сываешь
past	вы́бросил	*past*	выбра́сывал

Э́ти ста́рые газе́ты на́до вы́бросить. Я всегда́ выбра́сываю ста́рые газе́ты.

The prefix **вы-** in **вы́мыть,** a compound of **мыть** *to wash*, gives it the meaning of to wash thoroughly, i.e. to wash all the dirt out or off.

pfv.	вы́мыть *to wash out*	*impfv.*	вымыва́ть
fut.	я вы́мою	*pres.*	вымыва́ю
	ты вы́моешь		вымыва́ешь
past	вы́мыл	*past*	вымыва́л

Ты не вы́мыл ру́ки по-настоя́щему (по-настоя́щему *properly*).
У тебя́ но́гти гря́зные. Ты то́лько поигра́л мы́лом и водо́й и помы́л ладо́ни. Тепе́рь пойди́ и вымо́й ру́ки по-настоя́щему.

Notice that to play *with* the soap etc. is simply **игра́ть** plus instrumental since the soap etc. is the instrument or thing with which you are playing. The same construction is used with abstract nouns and people if the meaning is *not to take seriously* or *to be frivolous with*:

> Он игра́ет свое́й жи́знью. *He is playing with his life.*
> Она́ про́сто игра́ет им. *She is just playing with him.*

If *to play with somebody* means that the somebody is a partner in the game you use **с** with the instrumental:

> С кем де́ти игра́ют? *Who are the children playing with?*
> Они́ игра́ют с друзья́ми. *They are playing with (their) friends.*

С + instrumental is also used in the phrases:

> игра́ть с огнём *to play with fire* (ого́нь m. *fire*)
> игра́ть с судьбо́й *to play with fate*

To win is a compound of **игра́ть – вы́играть** a perfective verb, from which the imperfective **вы́игрывать** has been formed.

> Она́ вы́играла в ка́рты. *She won at cards.*
> Он вы́играл па́ртию в ша́хматы. *He has won a game of chess.*
> Он всегда́ выи́грывает. *He always wins.*

To lose is also a compound of **игра́ть – проигра́ть, прои́грывать.**

вы́думать *to invent, to think up*		выду́мывать

Ну, что ты опя́ть вы́думала? Э́то непра́вда – где же ты ви́дел адмира́ла на коне́? Что ты всё выду́мываешь!

pfv.	вы́брать *pick out, to choose*	*impfv.*	выбира́ть
fut.	я вы́беру	*pres.*	выбира́ю
	ты вы́берешь		выбира́ешь
past	вы́брал	*past*	выбира́л

Choice is **вы́бор.**

У вас хоро́ший вы́бор, я не зна́ю, что вы́брать.
Он вы́берет я́блоко, он всегда́ выбира́ет я́блоко.

All *perfective* verb forms with the prefix **вы-** are always stressed on the **вы-**. All other rules for stress are superseded by this one.

3. VERBS OF MOTION WITH THE PREFIX **В-**

The opposite of *out of* is *into* and to add this idea to a verb you use the preposition **в** or **во** as a prefix.

pfv.	войти́ *to go in, come in*	*impfv.*	входи́ть
fut.	я войду́	*pres.*	вхожу́
	ты войдёшь		вхо́дишь
past	вошёл вошла́	*past*	входи́л

Notice the contrast of stress between **войти́** and **вы́йти:**

	fut.	я войду́	вы́йду
		ты войдёшь	вы́йдешь
		он войдёт	вы́йдет
	past	он вошёл	вы́шел
		она́ вошла́	вы́шла
		они́ вошли́	вы́шли

Куда́ вы идёте? Тут вы́ход, а не вход. Тут лю́ди выхо́дят, а не вхо́дят. Вы должны́ входи́ть не тут, а там, у фонаря́, там вы должны́ войти́, там вход и лю́ди вхо́дят там, а тут то́лько выхо́дят.

Здра́вствуйте, как вы пожива́ете? Войди́те, пожа́луйста, э́то хорошо́, что вы пришли́; да, входи́те, входи́те – мы давно́ вас не ви́дели.

This is a very usual way to greet and to invite the person to come in, using the imperfective imperatives:

Входи́те, входи́те, пожа́луйста. Мы так ра́ды вас ви́деть. Мы вас давно́ не ви́дели.

pfv.	въе́хать *to drive in*	*impfv.*	въезжа́ть
fut.	я въе́ду	*pres.*	въезжа́ю
	ты въе́дешь		въезжа́ешь
past	въе́хал	*past*	въезжа́л

Pronounce **e** after the hard sign as if it were at the beginning of a word, i.e. with a *y* sound in front of it.

въезд *drive in* or (*carriage-*)*entrance*

– Как мне въе́хать в э́ти у́зкие воро́та? Мы ника́к не въе́дем с э́тим больши́м грузовико́м, он сюда́ не въе́дет.

– Въезд в гара́ж тут напра́во, тут на́до въезжа́ть; а там нале́во вы́езд, там выезжа́ют. Куда́ вы е́дете? На́до смотре́ть, куда́ вы е́дете. Э́то вы́езд, а не въезд. Въезд напра́во.

The difference between **прийти́** and **уйти́** on the one hand and **войти́** and **вы́йти** on the other is the difference between arrival and departure and coming in and going out.

Come tomorrow is: – Приди́те за́втра.

Come in, when somebody knocks at the door or stands in the doorway, is: Войди́те!

To visitors, who are preparing to leave, you would say: – Вы уже́ ухо́дите? and they would reply: – Да, нам пора́ идти́.

To someone living in the same house, you would say: – Ты выхо́дишь? – Да, мне на́до вы́йти на два–три часа́.

> NB in expressions of time **на** is used with the accusative to mean *for* in the sense of a period of time starting at the moment you are talking about and going on into the future.
>
> Он уе́хал на не́сколько дней. *He has gone away for a few days.*
> Я получи́л о́тпуск на це́лый ме́сяц. *I've received leave for a whole month.*

This is different from *for* in the sense of *during a period of time*, which is expressed by the accusative without a preposition:

Он был це́лый год в Москве́. *He was in Moscow for a whole year.*

In **на сле́дующий день** the preposition **на** means *on*:

На сле́дующий день он уе́хал.

The contrast to *to lead out* **вы́вести, выводи́ть** is:

pfv.	ввести́ *to lead in*	*impfv.*	вводи́ть
fut.	я введу́	*pres.*	ввожу́
	ты введёшь		вво́дишь
past	ввёл	*past*	вводи́л

You can use **ввести** in the sense of leading a horse into the stables: Он ввёл лóшадь в конюшню, or in the sense of showing guests into the sitting room: Он привёл гостéй домóй и ввёл их в гостúную.

In the following sentence **ввести в**, lit. 'to lead into', is the equivalent of English *introduce to*: Нáдо вас ввести в круг нáших друзéй. *You have to be introduced to our circle of friends.*

> NB You use **познакóмить с** + genitive or more formally **предстáвить** + dative when you mean *to introduce to X or Y*. You do not use **ввести** in this way.

Ввести, вводить is also used in relation to the introduction of a new law or a new order of things or a new way of life.

Говорят, что у нас хотят ввести нóвые порядки – дирéктор выдумал какúе-то нóвые прáвила и вот их скóро введýт у нас. Óчень обúдно. Я терпéть не могý нововведéний.

It's said ('they say') that they want to introduce a new order (of things) at our place. The director has thought up some new rules and soon they are going to introduce them at our place. It's very annoying. I can't stand innovations.

Я не люблю нововведéний, терпéть не могý. Люблю стáрый порядок.

pfv.	ввезти *to import* or *to convey in*	*impfv.*	ввозúть
fut.	я ввезý	*pres.*	ввожý
	ты ввезёшь		ввóзишь
past	ввёз ввезлá	*past*	ввозúл

Áнглии прихóдится ввозúть мнóго зернá, поэтому Áнглия должнá вывозúть промышленные товáры (*manufactured goods*).

(*Importation*) is **ввоз**

Ввоз валюты запрещáется. *The importation of currency is forbidden.*

Other prefixed verbs of motion are:

pfv.	влезть *to climb in*	*impfv.*	влезáть
fut.	я влéзу	*pres.*	влезáю
	ты влéзешь		влезáешь
past	влез влéзла	*past*	влезáл

pfv.	вылезть *to climb out*	*impfv.*	вылезáть
	внести *to carry in*		вносúть
	вынести *to carry out*		выносúть

Побежáл он на перрóн,	*He ran on to the platform,*
Влез в отцéпленный вагóн,	*Climbed into an uncoupled coach,*
Внёс узлы и чемодáны...	*Brought in the bundles and suit-cases . . .*

За́втра я внесу́ де́ньги в банк, я всегда́ вношу́ де́ньги по среда́м; в про́шлом году́ я вноси́л де́ньги по вто́рникам, а тепе́рь я вношу́ по среда́м.

> Here **внести́, вноси́ть в банк** *means to take to the bank* for the purpose of paying into one's account.
>
> **По** plus dative plural of the days of the week means *on . . . s,* as in **по среда́м** *on Wednesdays.*

4. VERBS OF MOTION WITH THE PREFIX **от-**

In the poem in the last lesson we had the noun **отъе́зд** *departure* in the phrase **был в отъе́зде** *was absent.* The prefix **от-** is used with verbs of motion. It implies movement away, or setting off.

The prefix **у-** with verbs of motion also means *away* but it implies complete departure, disappearance from view etc. The prefix **от-** does not have this implication, so it is often used when somebody or something moves away for a certain distance:

> отойти́ *to move away*   отходи́ть

По́езд отошёл от вокза́ла на три киломе́тра и останови́лся.

In expressions of distance **на** + accusative means *for* in the sense of distance to be covered from the point of departure.

Я отошла́ в сто́рону. *I moved to one side.*

> отнести́ *to take away*   относи́ть

Отнеси́ э́ти цветы́ тёте, она́ лю́бит цветы́.
Ве́тер отно́сит ло́дку от бе́рега.

> отвезти́ *to take away in a vehicle*   отвози́ть

Чемода́ны на́до во́время отвезти́ на вокза́л.

> отвести́ *to lead away, to take away*   отводи́ть

Отведи́ дете́й домо́й, они́ меша́ют.

> отъе́хать *to drive away, to set off*   отъезжа́ть

Мы уже́ отъе́хали от до́ма, когда́ вспо́мнили про соба́ку.
We had already driven away from home, when we remembered about the dog.

5. VERBS OF MOTION WITH THE PREFIX **до-**

The opposite of **от-** is the prefix **до-** *up to:*

> дойти́ *to go/come up to, to reach*   доходи́ть

Мы дошли́ до теа́тра, посмотре́ли афи́ши и реши́ли войти́.
We walked up to the theatre, looked at the posters and decided to go in.

доéхать *to go/come up to, to reach* (not on foot)   доезжáть

Они́ ужé доéхали до гóрода, когдá вспóмнили про собáку.

довести́ *to lead/take up to*   доводи́ть

Он довёл слепóго до останóвки. *He led the blind man up to the stop.*

6. THE USE OF есть

Пáмяти Бори́са Горбáтова (*contd.*)

На кварти́ру пойду́ к нему́ – там егó нет.	*I shall go to his flat – he is not there.*
Есть та у́лица, дом, есть подъéзд тот и дверь.	*That street is there, the house, that entrance is there and the door.*
Есть дощéчка, где и́мя егó и тепéрь.	*The plate is there, where his name still is.*
Есть на вéшалке пáлка егó и пальтó.	*On the coat-hanger are his stick and his coat.*
Есть налéво, за двéрью, егó кабинéт...	*To the left, behind the door, is his study . . .*
Всё тут есть. Тóлько всё э́то вóвсе не то,	*Everything is here. Only it is all quite wrong,*
Потому́ что он был, а тепéрь егó нет!	*Because he was and now is not!*

The word **есть** appears six times in the passage above. In modern Russian **есть** is the only form of the present tense of the verb *to be* in use and it means *there is*, *there are* or simply *is*, *are*. In the latter sense it is usually used for emphasis.

Всё тут есть. *Everything is really here.*
Всё тут. *There is everything here.*
Хлеб есть? *Is there any bread?*
Есть хлеб у нас? *Have we any bread?*

The answer would be: **Да, есть** or **Хлéба нет.**

Notice the difference between the following questions:

Гарáж там? *Is the garage there?*
Есть там гарáж? *Is there a garage there?*

The answer might be:

Нет там гаражá. Пéрвый гарáж на перекрёстке (*at the crossroads*).

Есть is occasionally used with the first, second and third pers. for emphasis:

– Зови́те дирéктора! *Call the director!*
– Я и есть дирéктор! *I am the director!*
– Ах, вы и есть дирéктор? *Oh, you are the director?*
Прости́те! *Excuse me!*
– Он и есть дирéктор. *He is the director.*

7. POSSESSIVE PRONOUNS: HIS, HER, THEIR

You have already learnt the possessive pronouns **мой, твой** (Lesson 19, § 2) and **наш, ваш** (Lesson 20, § 1), which decline and agree with the noun they qualify according to gender and number:

мой дом   твоё и́мя   ва́ша па́лка   на́ши ко́мнаты

To say *his, her, their* you use the genitive singular and plural of **он, она́, оно́, они́:**

его́ дом *his house*	её дом *her house*	их дом *their house*
его́ и́мя	её и́мя	их имена́

These words do not change, whatever the case and number of the thing possessed, since they are simply the genitive case of the pronoun referring to the possessor.

его́ имена́ his names   её имена́ her names

Notice in the last few lines of the poem:

па́лка его́ и пальто́ his stick and coat

As you see, **его́** agrees in gender with the person to whom the stick and the coat belong, *not* with the things that belong to him. This also applies to **её** and **их.**

его́ па́лка his stick   её пальто́ her coat   их кабине́т their study

8. TRANSLATION

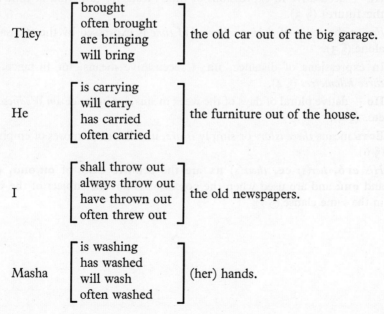

They	brought often brought are bringing will bring	the old car out of the big garage.
He	is carrying will carry has carried often carried	the furniture out of the house.
I	shall throw out always throw out have thrown out often threw out	the old newspapers.
Masha	is washing has washed will wash often washed	(her) hands.

We	⎡ have driven often drove will drive are driving ⎤	⎡ into out of ⎤ the narrow gates.

The train	⎡ left is leaving will leave always left ⎤	the station at three o'clock.

We	⎡ reached will reach always reach never reached ⎤	the station in time.

SUMMARY

1 The sequence of tenses (§ 1).

2 The prefix **вы-** means *out* (§ 2), **в/во-** means *in(to)* (§ 3), **от-** means *away* (§ 4), **до-** means *up to* (§ 5).

3 All perfective verb forms with the prefix **вы-** are stressed on **вы́-** (§ 2).

4 **На** + accusative in expressions of time means *for* (a period of time into the future) (§ 3).

5 *For* in the sense of *during a period of time* is expressed by the accusative alone (§ 3).

6 In expressions of distance, **на** + accusative means, for instance, *for three kilometres* (§ 4).

7 **По** + dative plural of days of the week means, for instance, *on Wednesdays* etc. (§ 3).

8 **Есть** means *there is/are* or simply *is/are*, usually for purposes of emphasis (§ 6).

9 *His* **его́**, *her(s)* **ёе**, *their(s)* **их** are the genitive cases of **он/оно́**, **она́** and **они́** and are used when the possessor is not the subject of the verb in the same clause (§ 7).

Lesson 28

I. POSSESSIVE PRONOUN свой

You have already met and used several possessive pronouns: **наш** *our*, **ваш** *your*, **мой** *my*, **твой** *thy, your* (Lessons 18 and 19).

You have also seen that the third person possessive pronoun consists of the genitive case of the appropriate pronoun (Lesson 27), as in:

его новости *his news*
её новости *her news*
их новости *their news*

There is another possessive pronoun, called the *reflexive possessive pronoun* **свой**, which declines like **мой** and **твой: свой, своя, своё, свой.**

This reflexive possessive pronoun can only be used when it refers to the subject of the verb in the same clause, whatever the subject is. So **свой** corresponds to *my (own), your (own), his, her, its (own), our (own), their (own)*, depending on the context.

When the subject is the first pers. sing. or pl. you may use *either* the reflexive possessive pronoun **свой** *or* the possessive pronouns **мой** or **наш.**

Я ношу моё старое платье только дома.
Я ношу своё старое платье только дома.
Мы забыли наш долг. Мы забыли свой долг.

The same applies to the second pers. pl.:

Вы хорошо помните вашу родину?
Вы хорошо помните свою родину?

To express possession with the second pers. sing., if **ты** is the subject of the verb, you use only the reflexive pronoun.

Ты увезла свои вещи? *Have you taken your things away?*
Да, я увезла свои вещи.

Ты позвонишь своему приятелю? *Will you ring your friend?* (звонить, позвонить *to ring* takes the dative case).
Я уже позвонила ему.

Ты отнесла своё пальто в чистку? *Have you taken your coat to the cleaners?* (чистка *cleaning*).
Нет, я всё ношу моё пальто. *No, I am still wearing my coat.*

You use **твой** only if the possessor is *not* the subject of the verb:

Я увёз твои вещи.
Кто позвонит твоему приятелю?

Note above the use of **ношу́** from **носи́ть** imperfective *to wear*. There will be a further explanation of this verb in Lesson 29.

To express that so-and-so is/was wearing something on a specific occasion, you say 'the garment is/was on so-and-so' or 'so-and-so is/was in such-and-such a garment':

> На нём чёрная шля́па. *He is wearing a black hat.*
> Она́ была́ в но́вом костю́ме. *She was wearing a new suit.*

When speaking of the third pers. sing. or pl. you must always use the reflexive pronoun if the possessor is the subject of the verb:

> Они́ всегда́ во́дят свои́х госте́й по го́роду.
> *They always take their guests around the town.*

> Своё но́вое пла́тье она́ бу́дет носи́ть всю зи́му.
> *She will wear her new coat all winter.*

> Наш учи́тель везёт свою́ ма́ленькую дочь в шко́лу.
> *Our teacher is taking his little daughter to school.*

> Мой муж ста́вит свою́ но́вую маши́ну на_ночь в гара́ж.
> *My husband is putting his new car in the garage for the night.*

If you say: **Учи́тель поста́вил ЕГО́ велосипе́д в гара́ж** it means that the teacher has put somebody else's bike into the garage.

The situation might be as follows:

> Учени́к был в кла́ссе, его́ велосипе́д стоя́л на дворе́ и учи́тель поста́вил его́ велосипе́д в гара́ж.

> У нас о́чень ми́лый сосе́д и вот брат везёт ка́ждое у́тро его́ ма́ленькую дочь в шко́лу на свое́й маши́не. Да, он себе́ купи́л маши́ну на про́шлой неде́ле и вот на свое́й маши́не он везёт его́ дочь, дочь сосе́да.

Своя́ маши́на – его́ дочь: *his car*, but not *his daughter* – it is the neighbour's daughter.

To sum up:

subject	possessive pronoun
я	мой *or* свой
мы	наш *or* свой
вы	ваш *or* свой
ты	свой
он, она́, оно́, они́	свой

Since **свой** always refers back to the subject of the verb in the clause in which it occurs it always qualifies the object of a verb or it appears after a preposition. The nominative case therefore should not occur.

192

However, the nominative *does* occur:

a In 'have' constructions where the logical subject in Russian is in the genitive.

У до́ктора свои́ пробле́мы. *The doctor has his own problems.*
У меня́ бы́ли свои́ пла́ны. *I had my own plans.*

b In a few idioms:

Бу́дьте как до́ма – здесь все свои́. *Make yourself at home – we're all friends here.*

Он для нас свой челове́к. *He is one of us.*

Своя́ руба́шка бли́же к те́лу. *Charity begins at home* (lit. 'One's own shirt is nearer to one's body').

2. 'YOU AND I,' ETC.

The brother in the preceding section who bought the car and who takes his neighbour's daughter to school might say:

> На про́шлой неде́ле я купи́л маши́ну и тепе́рь ка́ждое у́тро мы с до́чкой сосе́да е́дем в шко́лу на мое́й маши́не.
> *Last week I bought a car and now every morning my neighbour's little daughter and I go to school in my car.*

Notice that *my neighbour's daughter and I* is lit. 'we with the daughter'. This is an example of a Russian idiom in which instead of saying 'she and I', 'he and I', 'you and I' you say:

> мы с ней   мы с ним   мы с ва́ми

You express in fact, 'we, the two of us, counting her/him/you.'

You also use this construction when there are more than two people involved:

> мы с ва́ми *you* (pl.) *and I*
> мы с ни́ми *they and I*

and with nouns as well as pronouns:

> мы с му́жем *my husband and I*
> мы с жено́й *my wife and I*

Мы с бра́том вы́шли на прогу́лку. *My brother and I went out for a walk.*
Мы с сестро́й вы́ехали за́_город. *My sister and I went out into the country.*
Мы с му́жем за́втра уезжа́ем за грани́цу. *My husband and I are going abroad tomorrow.*

If the speaker and the other person or people are not the subject of the action, you can use the same construction, simply putting **мы** into the appropriate case:

Они́ ви́дели нас с ва́ми в па́рке. *They saw us* (including you) *in the park.*
У нас с ней свида́ние. *She and I have a rendezvous.*

o   193

The same construction can also be used when the speaker is not in the group, i.e. when two nouns are linked by **c**:

Доктор с женой всегда уезжают в это время. *The doctor and his wife always leave at this time.*

Мы видели доктора с женой в поезде. *We saw the doctor and his wife on the train.*

3. MOVEMENT TO AND FROM

In Lesson 5 you were given the expressions *from the north and east,* as in:

ветер дует с севера, с востока

These are masculine nouns in the genitive singular.

You have also had *to go south, north* etc. (Lesson 12):

Судно идёт на юг. *The boat is going south.*

Пароход идёт на север. *The steamer is going north.*

Поезд идёт на восток. *The train is going east.*

Мы едем на запад. *We are going west.*

The point is that when you use **на** with the accusative to indicate movement to some place, you use **c** with the genitive to indicate movement from that place. Remember: **на – c.**

Дети вышли на улицу.
The children went out on to the street.

С улицы дети побежали на набережную.
From the street the children ran to the embankment.

С набережной они поехали на вокзал.
From the embankment they went to the station.

На вокзале они долго любовались локомотивами.
At the station they gazed with admiration at the engines for a long time.

С вокзала они поздно вернулись домой.
From the station they returned home late.

Я поехал на кирпичный завод за_городом.
I went to the brick-works (that is) out of town.

С кирпичного завода брат поехал в контору.
From the brick-works (my) brother went to the office.

You remember that while with some nouns you use **на** with the accusative to express movement to or into, with others you use **в** with the accusative.

With these nouns, you use **из** with the genitive to say movement from, or out of. Remember: **в – из.**

С кирпичного завода брат поехал в контору. Из конторы мне надо было поехать в библиотеку. Из библиотеки я пошёл в ресторан. Из ресторана я вернулся в библиотеку. В библиотеке я занимался два-три часа. Из библиотеки я пошёл в аптеку, из аптеки на рынок, а с рынка поехал домой с покупками. Да, с рынка он вернулся домой с покупками.

4. THE IMPERFECTIVE FUTURE

In Lesson 13 we saw that the perfective conjugation has a future meaning.

The imperfective future tense consists of the conjugation of the verb *to be*, which has a future meaning *I shall be, you will be* etc., plus the imperfective infinitive.

> я бу́ду де́лать
> ты бу́дешь де́лать
> он бу́дет де́лать
> мы бу́дем де́лать
> вы бу́дете де́лать
> они́ бу́дут де́лать

The difference between the perfective future and the imperfective future is the same as that between the perfective past and the imperfective past:

pfv. я сде́лаю — *I shall do* – once, and I expect to complete whatever it is.

impfv. я бу́ду де́лать — *I shall be doing* – something that will go on for some time and I do not have completion in mind.
or
I shall do – several times, a series of acts of which I do not have the completion in mind.

Что ты бу́дешь де́лать сейча́с? *What are you going to do now?*
Ты сде́лаешь э́то сейча́с? *Will you do it now?* i.e. will you get it done now?

– Что вы бу́дете де́лать ве́чером? *What are you going to do this evening?*
– Мы с бра́том бу́дем писа́ть пи́сьма. Но до э́того я бу́ду гото́вить обе́д.
– Ты пригото́вь обе́д, а я прочту́ докла́д.
– Нет, сего́дня мы с тобо́й пообе́даем ра́ньше (*we shall dine earlier*). Чита́й свой докла́д по́сле обе́да.

5. THE COMPARATIVE ADVERB AND ADJECTIVE

Towards the end of the preceding paragraph we had **ра́ньше** *earlier*. This is a *comparative adverb*. The comparative adverb or adjective, and they are mostly identical in Russian, expresses the state of being earlier or later, more or less, better or worse, higher, lower, faster, slower, and so on.

The following adverbs and adjectives have their comparative ending in **ше**:

adverb	comparative	adjective
ра́но *early*	ра́ньше	ра́нний
ти́хо *quietly*	ти́ше	ти́хий
су́хо *drily*	су́ше	сухо́й
до́лго *for a long time*	до́льше	до́лгий
далеко́ *far, distant*	да́льше	далёкий

The words *much* or *plenty* and the comparative *more* are:

мно́го   бо́льше

Бо́льше is also the comparative adjective of *big* **большо́й.**

Here are some sentences with comparatives:

– Ти́ше, ти́ше! не говори́те так гро́мко!
– Да (*but*) мы говори́м ти́хо.
– Но на́до говори́ть ещё (*still*) ти́ше. Де́ти спят в сосе́дней ко́мнате.
– У меня́ ти́хий го́лос, я говорю́ ти́хо, могу́ говори́ть ещё ти́ше. На́до мне то́лько сказа́ть...
– Бо́льше не говори́те! Я вас прошу́ бо́льше не говори́ть.
– Ну что с тобо́й! (*What's the matter with you?*) Ты ду́маешь, что мы бу́дем так сиде́ть це́лый ве́чер?
– Игра́йте в ка́рты, игра́йте в ша́хматы.
– Я не хочу́ игра́ть в ка́рты. Я не бу́ду игра́ть в ша́хматы! Я не бу́ду сиде́ть без де́ла. Сиде́ть я тут бо́льше не хочу́ и не бу́ду. Я иду́ в кино́!

You will find more details about the comparative in Part II – Grammar; but first learn the comparative of some of the common adjectives which we shall keep introducing in the next lessons.

6. READING EXERCISE

Па́мяти Бори́са Горба́това (*contd.*)

Ра́ньше как говори́ли друг дру́гу мы с ним?	*Formerly ('earlier') how did he and I talk to each other?*
Говори́ли: «Споём. Посиди́м. Позвони́м».	*We would say: 'Let's sing. Let's sit for a while. Let's ring up.'*
Говори́ли: «Скажи́». Говори́ли: «Прочти́».	*We would say: 'Tell (me)' We would say: 'Read'.*
Говори́ли: «Зайди́ ко мне за́втра к пяти́».	*We would say: 'Come round to my place tomorrow towards five.'*
А тепе́рь привыка́ть на́до к сло́ву: «Он был».	*And now one must grow accustomed to the word: 'He was.'*
Привыка́ть говори́ть про него́: «говори́л.»	*Grow accustomed to say of him: 'He used to say.'*
Говори́л, приходи́л, помога́л, выруча́л,	*He used to say, used to come, used to assist, used to help out,*
Что́бы я не грусти́л, до́лго жить обеща́л.	*And so that I should not grieve, he promised to live for a long time.*
Ещё в па́мяти все твои́ жи́вы черты́,	*All your features are still alive in my memory,*
А уже́ не могу́ я сказа́ть тебе́ «ты».	*And yet I can no longer say to you 'you'.*

Говоря́т: раз ты у́мер, – тако́в уж закóн, –	They say: since you're dead – and such is the law (of things) –
Вме́сто «ты», про тебя́ говори́ть на́до: «он»;	Instead of 'you' I must say of you 'he';
Вме́сто слов, что люблю́ тебя́, на́до: «люби́л»;	Instead of the words 'I love you', I must say 'loved';
Вме́сто слов, что есть друг у меня́, на́до: «был».	Instead of the words 'I have a friend', I must say 'had'.

7. 'EACH OTHER'

In the first line of the reading passage we had the phrase **друг дру́гу** *to each other*. The words are connected with the adjectival pronoun **друго́й** *other*.

In this expression the first word never changes, the second word goes into the appropriate case and any preposition there may be goes between the two words. The expression has no plural forms – the singular forms are used with a subject in the plural.

Мы говори́ли друг с дру́гом. *We talked with each other.*
Мы ча́сто звони́ли друг дру́гу. *We often phoned each other.*
Мы ча́сто заходи́ли друг к дру́гу. *We often dropped in on each other.*
Они́ помога́ют друг дру́гу. *They help each other.*
Вы обеща́ете друг дру́гу. *You promise each other.*
Мы привы́кли друг к дру́гу. *We got used to each other.*

A curious feature of this expression is that even when it refers to inanimate objects it has a genitive-accusative. This is the only instance in the language, other than the third pers. pronoun and reflexive pronoun, where an inanimate has a genitive-accusative:

Небе́сные тела́ притя́гивают друг дру́га. *Heavenly bodies attract one another.*

8. VERBAL PREFIXES

In the fourth line of the reading passage we had **про него́** *about him.* **Про** is a preposition meaning *about, concerning* and it takes the accusative case.

Про- is also common as a verbal prefix, with quite a different meaning: it adds to the verb the meaning *through*.

Дава́йте прочтём э́то вме́сте. *Let's read this together.*

Here **прочтём** is first pers. plural future perfective of **чита́ть,** perfective **прочесть: прочту́, прочтёшь** etc. If you read a thing completely, you read it *through* and that is why the perfective of **чита́ть** is formed with the prefix **про-.**

When added to verbs of motion **про-** gives them the meaning of *through*, *across* or *past*.

пройти́   проходи́ть

Я ждала́ тебя́ на углу́ и ты прошёл ми́мо меня́.

прое́хать   проезжа́ть

Мы прое́хали ми́мо толпы́ и бы́стро прое́дем че́рез пло́щадь (*across the square*).

As you see, the preposition associated with **про-** is **ми́мо** + genitive when **про-** means *past* and **че́рез** + accusative when **про-** means *through*, *across*.

The prefix **под-** means *up to* and corresponds to the preposition **к,** which never occurs as a prefix. **Под-** can also mean *under*, corresponding to the preposition **под.**

Подойти́ pfv. **подходи́ть** impfv. means *to walk up to, to come up to*.

Мы подъе́хали во́время к вокза́лу. Тётя Ли́за уже́ ждала́ у подъе́зда. Она́ уви́дела нас и подошла́ к маши́не. Её чемода́н стоя́л на тротуа́ре. Я вы́шла из маши́ны. Мы поцелова́ли друг дру́га. Она́ се́ла ря́дом со мной и мы пое́хали.

Подъе́зд is a *porch, a main entrance*, which is covered over.

Вход is any entrance.

– Ты ждала́ меня́ у подъе́зда музе́я, а я ждал тебя́ у вхо́да напра́во, поэ́тому мы и не встре́тились. *You waited for me by the main entrance of the museum and I waited for you by the entrance on the right and that's why we didn't meet.*

– Я тебя́ никогда́ бо́льше ждать не бу́ду. *I shall never wait for you again.*

– На́до подойти́ к э́тому споко́йно. *We must approach this calmly.*

(подойти́, подходи́ть к пробле́ме *to approach a problem*)

Ваш подхо́д к э́той пробле́ме слаб. *Your approach to this problem is feeble.*

Парохо́д подхо́дит к мосту́. *The boat is approaching the bridge.*

Парохо́д подхо́дит под мост. *The boat is passing under the bridge.*

To sum up:

prefix		takes	preposition (if needed)
про-	*through*		че́рез + acc.
про-	*past*		ми́мо + gen.
под-	*up to*		к + dat.
под-	*under*		под + acc.

9. DIALOGUE

ВЕ́РА Ну вот, наконе́ц ты пришёл – я уже́ ду́мала, что ты опя́ть не придёшь. Что за невозмо́жный челове́к!

ПЕ́ТЯ То-есть как так... опя́ть не пришёл – когда́ э́то[1] я не пришёл?

1 *When was it that.*

198

ВЕ́РА Про́шлый раз я тебя́ ждала́, ждала́ – позавчера́ я стоя́ла у подъе́зда музе́я, ждала́ тебя́ у гла́вного вхо́да, а ты не пришёл.

ПЕ́ТЯ Я не пришёл? Я подъе́хал на мое́й чу́дной, но́вой маши́не ро́вно полови́на пя́того[1] к гла́вному вы́ходу, там уже́ стоя́ло мно́го маши́н, я с трудо́м нашёл ме́сто для свое́й маши́ны, поста́вил её ме́жду како́й-то ужа́сной ста́рой легково́й с одно́й стороны́[2] и о́чень элега́нтной мо́дной спорти́вной маши́ной с друго́й стороны́,[2] и на́чал тебя́ иска́ть...

ВЕ́РА Иска́л, иска́л, и не нашёл, как всегда́! Я тебе́ про́сто не ве́рю; я стоя́ла у гла́вного вхо́да, пря́мо про́тив университе́та.

ПЕ́ТЯ Одну́ мину́точку,[3] одну́ мину́точку! Ты говори́шь у вхо́да про́тив университе́та? и ты говори́шь у гла́вного вхо́да?

ВЕ́РА Ну да, ну да, у гла́вного вхо́да про́тив университе́та –

ПЕ́ТЯ Дорога́я моя́, ми́лая моя́, про́тив университе́та не гла́вный вход, а се́верный вход музе́я, се́верный вход му́зея про́тив университе́та, э́то совсе́м не гла́вный вход, наоборо́т, э́то ма́ленький вход, э́то же не подъе́зд. Понима́ешь? – ты стоя́ла у одного́ вхо́да, а я стоя́л у друго́го! – и вот мы друг дру́га не нашли́! Гла́вный вход в музе́й с ю́га, там больша́я пло́щадь, больши́е воро́та[4] и у воро́т стои́т швейца́р. Когда́ я подъезжа́л к воро́там музе́я, из воро́т выезжа́л большо́й си́ний авто́бус с иностра́нными тури́стами, они́ прое́хали ми́мо меня́, а я всё смотре́л нет ли тебя́[5] среди́ толпы́. Лю́ди выходи́ли из музе́я, сходи́ли по ступе́нькам подъе́зда, а ты в то вре́мя стоя́ла у друго́го вы́хода. Так и́ли не так?

ВЕ́РА Мо́жет быть я и стоя́ла у друго́го вхо́да, а про́шлый раз, когда́ я тебя́ ждала́ у вы́хода из кино́, ты то́же не пришёл.

ПЕ́ТЯ Я зна́ю, я винова́т, я пришёл с опозда́нием,[6] но я пришёл – я пришёл, и стоя́л у вхо́да, а ты стоя́ла у вы́хода, ты стоя́ла за угло́м у вы́хода, а я стоя́л пря́мо у вхо́да на большо́й пло́щади. А вот э́тот раз мы с тобо́й встре́тились. Не на́до серди́ться, пожа́луйста не серди́сь.

ВЕ́РА Пе́тя, ми́лый, я бо́льше не сержу́сь.

ПЕ́ТЯ Ну хорошо́! Вот мы и пришли́, вот мы и дошли́ до самого́ зда́ния вы́ставки.

1 *At exactly half-past four.* Half of the hour is expressed by **полови́на** + genitive of the ordinal number (**пе́рвый, второ́й** etc.) denoting the next hour. At half past four you are halfway towards five o'clock – hence **полови́на пя́того** 'half of the fifth (hour)', or, less colloquially, **в полови́не пя́того.**

2 Note that *on one side, on the other side* is **с одно́й/друго́й стороны́.** The same expressions also mean *on one/the other hand.*

3 *Just a minute!* **Мину́точка** is the diminutive form of **мину́та.**

4 **Воро́та** *gate/gates* is always plural in form.

5 *I was looking all the time to see if you were.*

6 *I was late,* lit. 'I came with a delay'.

10. TRANSLATION

'What are you going to do (this) summer?'[1]

'My husband and I are going[2] abroad.'

'Ah, how interesting! My sister and I are going abroad too. Where are you going?'

'We shall be spending[3] the summer in the U.S.S.R.'[4]

'What a coincidence! We are going to the Soviet Union too.'

'How will you go?[5] We shall go[6] by plane.'

'We shall go by steamer. The boat goes north at first, then it goes east. It passes through the Kattegat into the Baltic. It is further by sea[7] and we shall be travelling[8] for a longer time but on the other hand it is more comfortable and my sister must rest.'

'Yes, we shall set off after you but we shall be in the Soviet Union earlier. You will probably stand on deck when the boat approaches[9] Leningrad and look at the city. They say the view is very fine.'

'What clothes will you take with you?'

'They say it will be hot in the Soviet Union this summer, so I shall take my new light coat with me and I shall wear it all the time.'

'Let us write to each other before setting off[10] and decide where we shall meet.'

1 Use instrumental of summer. 2 Use **éхать.** 3 Future imperfective of **проводить.**
4 **СССР** – words represented by and pronounced as initials do not decline.
5 Use **поéхать.** 6 **На** + prepositional case. 7 Say 'By sea (instrumental without preposition) – further'. 8 Use **éхать** future imperfective.
9 Remember the rule about 'sequence of tenses' in Russian (Lesson 27, § 1).
10 **Пéред поéздкой.**

SUMMARY

1 The possessive pronoun **свой** can refer only to the subject of the verb in the same clause (§ 1).

2 'You and I' etc. (§ 2).

3 Movement to and from is expressed by **на – с** with some nouns, **в – из** with others (§ 3).

4 The imperfective future consists of the conjugation of the auxiliary verb **быть, бýду** etc. plus the imperfective infinitive (§ 4).

5 Some examples of comparative adverbs and adjectives (§ 5).

6 'Each other' etc. (§ 7).

7 In verbs of motion the prefix **про-** is associated with **чéрез** when it means *across*, *through*, and with **мймо** when it means *past*; the prefix **под-** is associated with **к** when it means *up to*, and with **под** when it means *under* (§ 8).

8 'Half of the hour' is **половйна** plus the ordinal number denoting the coming hour (§ 9, note 2).

Lesson 29

I. VERBS OF MOTION WITHOUT A PREFIX — I

In previous lessons we have frequently used verbs of motion with prefixes and you have noticed that in the root of the verb there is a difference between perfective and imperfective:

прийти́	приходи́ть *to come, to arrive*
увести́	уводи́ть *to lead, to take away*
отнести́	относи́ть *to carry away/off*
подвезти́	подвози́ть *to bring up*

You have also used the *imperfective* verbs without prefixes: **идти́** (which becomes **-йти́** when prefixed), *to go on foot*, **вести́** *to lead*, **нести́** *to carry*, **везти́** *to cart*.

If you remove the prefix from the imperfectives of the pairs given above you have another set of verbs which are also imperfective and also have the same basic or 'dictionary' meanings as **идти́** etc.:

ходи́ть	*to go on foot*
води́ть	*to lead*
носи́ть	*to carry*
вози́ть	*to cart*

There is, however, a difference in meaning between these two sets of imperfective verbs and it is a very important difference.

The verbs **идти́, вести́, нести́, везти́** indicate movement in one direction. One name given to them by grammarians is 'determinate' verbs and we shall use that term in this book.

The verbs **ходи́ть, води́ть, носи́ть, вози́ть** indicate a movement in more than one direction: walking about a room, a return trip to school or to work, or movement in general. One name given to them by grammarians is 'indeterminate' verbs and this is the term we shall use in this book.

Here are some examples of the determinate and indeterminate verbs, both sets being, remember, imperfective with the idea of continuing action or repetition of action.

Two friends meet – one asks the other: *Where are you going?* Куда́ ты идёшь?

Я иду́ в политéхникум. *I am going to the polytechnic.*

And the friend asks: *Do you attend the polytechnic? I didn't know this.*

Ты хо́дишь в политéхникум! Я э́то не знал.

Now here the speaker uses the indeterminate verb **ходи́ть,** because he is no longer asking 'where are you going now, in what single direction are you moving?' He is asking: 'Do you attend, do you go regularly?' The verb carries the idea of *coming back* and, of course, if you are attending a school or an institute you do not just go there – you go at intervals and come back.

The conversation continues:

Нет, я в политéхникум бóльше не хожý; я прóсто идý тудá сегóдня вéчером, потомý что мой друг там даёт урóки матемáтики и мы встрéтимся пóсле урóка и пойдём в кинó. Ужé прошлó два гóда с тех пор как я ходи́ла в политéхникум.	*No, I no longer go to the polytechnic; I am simply going there this evening* ('today in the evening') *because my friend is giving maths lessons there and we shall meet after the lesson and go to the cinema. It is two years since* ('Already two years have passed since') *I attended the polytechnic.*

Notice that when she says *we shall go to the cinema* she uses the prefixed perfective **пойдём** 'we shall set off and go'. She is not thinking either of the movement of walking in one direction – **идём** – and certainly not of regular return visits – **хóдим**.

The conversation might continue:

А ты кудá идёшь? *And where are you going?*

Я идý к тёте, я к ней хожý по пя́тницам. *I am going to (my) aunt; I visit her on Fridays.*

Again **ходи́ть** is used and it conveys the same precise information that on Fridays he makes a habit of going to his aunt and returning home.

Я дýмала, что ты хóдишь к ней по четвергáм.

Да, я ходи́л к ней по четвергáм, но вот ужé два мéсяца как я хожý к ней по пя́тницам.

Notice the use of the present tense *but it's now two months since I've been visiting her on Fridays*. The present tense is used because he still goes at the time of speaking.

Я шла и о чём-то дýмала. *I was walking along and thinking about something.*

Notice the difference in meanings of:

Я ходи́л к ней по четвергáм and Я шла и о чём-то дýмала.

Here she was walking along in a single direction and she must use the past tense of **идти́** because she wants to say quite simply that she was in the process of walking. She is not saying that she went somewhere regularly or that she was going there and back: one direction only and therefore **шла**.

If you want to say:

From next week I'll be visiting her on Saturdays, you use **бýду ходи́ть**.

Со слéдующей недéли я бýду ходи́ть к ней по суббóтам.

Again, you are going to go there and back regularly.

But if you want to add: *And I shall walk on this side of the street*, you use **бýду идти́:**

Я бу́ду идти́ по э́той стороне́ у́лицы,

because now you are thinking of the process of walking in the direction of your aunt's. So, as you see, both **ходи́ть** and **идти́** have an imperfective future.

Here is another conversation:

- Ты сего́дня не пошёл на рабо́ту?
- Нет, сего́дня я не пошёл на рабо́ту.
- Но ты же хо́дишь на рабо́ту по суббо́там? (The force of **же** here is 'but you *do* go to work' etc.)
- Да, я хожу́, коне́чно я хожу́! Но сего́дня я бо́лен и не пошёл на рабо́ту, и в понеде́льник я то́же не пойду́.
- Како́й ты лентя́й! *What a lazy person you are!*

If he had wanted to say from *Monday onwards I shall not be going to work*, i.e. I shall not be attending daily and so going back and forth, he would have said **с понеде́льника я не бу́ду ходи́ть на рабо́ту.**

To pace up and down the room is **ходи́ть по ко́мнате** – the movement is in more than one direction.

Он хо́дит по ко́мнате. *He is walking up and down the room.*

But *he is going to the door* is: **Он идёт к две́ри,** – he is moving in one direction.

For *he is going to the window* you can either say: **Он идёт к окну́** or **он подхо́дит к окну́,** lit. 'he is approaching the window'.

Here you are using a prefixed verb of motion **подходи́ть** and in the prefixed verbs of motion there is *no* distinction between movement in a single direction and movement in different directions. There is just the one imperfective (Lesson 26).

In the past tense *he went to the window* you would say: **Он подошёл к окну́,** past perfective, because the action is completed.

Now supposing you want to say *he was going to the window when he heard the bell*, the points to bear in mind are: (*a*) the action was going on, it was not completed when he heard the bell, so an imperfective is needed; (*b*) the movement was in a single direction; (*c*) *heard* is a completed action, so this must be perfective.

Он шёл к окну́, когда́ он услы́шал звоно́к,

or:

Он подходи́л к окну́, когда́ . . . *He was approaching the window, when . . .*

2. VERBS OF MOTION WITHOUT A PREFIX – II

What has been said above about **идти́ – ходи́ть** applies equally to the other verbs of motion without prefixes. Below are examples of **вести́ – води́ть, нести́ – носи́ть** and **везти́ – вози́ть.**

вести́ – води́ть *to lead, to take a person or animal* (on foot)

Я веду́ ребёнка в де́тский сад.

А я веду́ соба́ку в парк. Я её всегда́ вожу́ в парк. Я не зна́ю, соба́ка меня́ ведёт и́ли я веду́ соба́ку.

I am taking the dog to the park.	Moving in a single direction.
I always take her/it to the park.	Regular movement there and back.
I don't know whether the dog is taking me or I am taking the dog.	Again movement going on now in a single direction.

If we had:

Я не зна́ю, соба́ка меня́ во́дит, и́ли я вожу́ соба́ку

this would mean: *I don't know whether the dog takes me or I take the dog.*

нести́ – носи́ть *to carry, to take*

– Что вы несёте? *What are you carrying?*
– Я несу́ торт племя́ннику. *I am taking a flan to my nephew.*
– Торт племя́ннику? Ра́зве сего́дня день его́ рожде́ния? *Surely it isn't his birthday today?*
– Нет, не день рожде́ния, а про́сто так. ('But simply so,' i.e. for no particular reason.) Я ча́сто хожу́ к племя́ннику и приношу́ ему́ то́рты, бискви́ты и пече́нье.

Notice: **хожу́,** because a return trip is implied, but **приношу́,** meaning simply *bring* or *take.* Obviously she does not carry the flans etc., back home with her.

Он лю́бит сла́дости. *He loves sweetmeats.* Я люблю́ приноси́ть ему́ сла́дости.

What one carries to and fro, in all directions, as one walks about, is clothes. That is why **носи́ть** means *to wear* as well as *to carry.* The determinate verb **нести́** however, cannot be used in the meaning *to wear* (see Lesson 28).

– До́ма я ношу́ ста́рое пла́тье. Я э́то пла́тье купи́ла пять лет тому́ наза́д. Оно́ удо́бное и я его́ люблю́, но носи́ть его́ на рабо́ту я уже́ не могу́.
– А я ношу́ до́ма свои́ но́вые брю́ки.
– Ты да́же носи́л свои́ но́вые брю́ки когда́ ты ходи́л в саду́ рабо́тать. А тепе́рь они́ гря́зные. Но́вые твои́ брю́ки уже́ на́до отда́ть в чи́стку.
– Где они́?
– Да тут, я их как раз несу́ в чи́стку. *Here they are, I am just taking them to the cleaners.*

вози́ть – везти́ *to cart*

Ра́ньше вози́ли дрова́ на саня́х, а тепе́рь во́зят у́голь на грузовика́х (грузови́к *lorry*) да́же зимо́й.

– А что вы везёте на вашей машине?

– Это – это ничего, это капуста и картофель.

– Капуста и картофель, хорошо. А тут что? Ага! Тут вино, вы везёте вино. Итак вы везёте капусту и картофель, а под капустой и под картофелем – вино. Вы везёте контрабанду.

3. READING EXERCISE

Памяти Бориса Горбатова (concl.)

Так ли это? Не знаю. По-моему, нет!	*Is it so? I do not know. In my opinion, it is not!*
Свет погасшей звезды ещё тысячу лет	*The light of an extinguished star for a thousand years still*
К нам доходит. А что ей, звезде, до людей?	*Reaches us. And what does it, the star, care about people?*
Ты добрей был её, и теплей, и светлей.	*You were kinder than a star, and warmer, and brighter.*
Да и срок не велик: тыщу лет мне не жить,	*And (our allotted) time is not great: I shall not live a thousand years.*
На мой век тебя хватит – мне по дружбе светить.	*You will be enough for my lifetime – to shine on me in friendship.*

Notice in this passage the following expressions:

по-моему *in my opinion, I think.* You can also say, more formally, **по моему мнению** *in my opinion,* in which case **моему** has its normal stress on the last syllable. Note also:

> по-твоему *in your opinion*
> по-вашему *in your opinion*
> по-нашему *in our opinion*

These expressions can also mean *in my/your/our way* or *fashion* and there is also **по-своему:**

> Хорошо, делайте по-своему! *All right, do it your own way.*

Что до (line 3), used with the dative and the genitive as in:

> Что мне до подробностей? *What do I care about details?*

A similar construction is used without **что** as in

> Ему не до нас. *He has no time for us, he doesn't care about us.*

As you see, the person who does not care is in the dative case and the person or thing not cared about is in the genitive after **до.**

Срок means an allotted period of time and can be translated *time, period, span.*

Тысяцу лет мне не жить *I am not (going) to live a thousand years, I shall not live a thousand years,* lit. 'it is not for me to live' etc.

Тысяцу represents the colloquial pronunciation of **тысячу**. The other cases are pronounced in a similar way: **тысяча – тысща** etc.

Век means *age, century* or as here *lifetime*.

Хватит is perfective future of **хватить** perfective, **хватать** *to snatch*. In impersonal use as here this verb means *to suffice, to be enough* and the thing of which there is or is not enough goes into the genitive case.

> Дров хватит на целый месяц. *That will be/There will be enough firewood for a whole month.*

> Мне не хватает сил. *I haven't enough strength, I can't go on.*

You can also use this verb with an infinitive:

> Ну, хватит ерунду говорить! *That will be enough talking nonsense!*

4. THE COMPARATIVE IN **ee** AND **более**

In Lesson 28, § 5, you were introduced to a few comparatives ending in **ше**. There are only a few comparatives ending in a single **e** (see Part II, Grammar). Much more numerous are the comparatives ending in **ee,** which colloquially and in poetry is often reduced to **ей**.

Three such comparatives occurred in l. 4 of the Reading Passage above. Here they are again, together with the comparative of **поздний**.

	adj.	adv.	comparative adj. and adv.	colloquial form
kind	добрый	добро	добрее	добрей
warm	тёплый	тепло	теплее	теплей
bright	светлый	светло	светлее	светлей
late	поздний	поздно	позднее	позднéй

As a general rule the stress in the comparative in **ee** is the same as in the short form feminine of the adjective: **добра, тепла, светла**. Cf. **красивее** comparative of **красивый**, short form feminine **красива**.

As soft-ending adjectives rarely have short forms and **поздний** has no short forms, the stress on such words as **позднее** has to be learnt separately.

Than is expressed by putting the person or thing with which the comparison is drawn into the genitive case.

> Ты добрее её. *You are kinder than she.*

You can also use **чем** followed by the nominative case:

> Ты добрее, чем она.

There are certain circumstances when you have to use **чем**:

> Идти кругом не всегда дальше, чем идти прямо. *To go round is not always further than to go straight.*

Here are some examples using the comparative adjectives with the regular **ee** endings:

Брат добрéе сестры́.
Брат добрéе, чем сестрá. } *The brother is kinder than the sister.*

Спáльня светлéе столóвой.
Спáльня светлéе, чем столóвая. } *The bedroom is lighter than the dining room* (столóвая adjectival noun).

А кýхня дáже светлéе спáльни.
А кýхня дáже светлéе, чем спáльня. } *And the kitchen is even lighter than the bedroom.*

Here are some similar sentences with superlatives (Lesson 26):

Кýхня сáмая свéтлая кóмната. *The kitchen is the lightest room.*
Кýхня сáмая свéтлая из всех кóмнат в этой квартúре. *The kitchen is the lightest of all the rooms in this flat.*

Note that here you must have **из** + genitive, not the genitive alone. You must also use **из** + genitive to say 'one of . . .', 'two of . . .' etc.

Столóвая сáмая тёмная из всех кóмнат. *The dining room is the darkest room of all.*
Столóвая однá из сáмых тёмных кóмнат в квартúре. *The dining room is one of the darkest rooms in the flat.*
Нáша лéстница темнéе вáшей лéстницы. *Our staircase is darker than your staircase.*

There is another way of forming the comparative and that is by putting the word **бóлее** *more* in front of the appropriate form of the adjective or adverb: **бóлее тёплый, бóлее красúвая, бóлее холóдное.**

The converse of this is **мéнее** *less.* These forms are usually followed by **чем.**

Вáша убóрная бóлее холóдная, чем нáша убóрная. *Your lavatory is colder than ours.*
Нáша вáнная мéнее холóдная, чем вáша вáнная. *Our bathroom is less cold than yours.*

In sentences such as these, however, and with such common adjectives you would be more likely to use the forms in **ee.**

Нáша вáнная теплéе вáшей. Нáша вáнная теплéе, чем вáша.
Вáша убóрная холоднéе нáшей. Вáша убóрная холоднéе, чем нáша.

The adjective **стáрый** *old* has two comparatives:

стáрше used of people, the opposite of **молóже** *younger*, which is the comparative of **молодóй** (see § 6).

старéе (and less commonly **бóлее стáрый**) used of things, the opposite of **новéе** *newer*, which is the comparative of **нóвый.**

Отéц мой стáрше твоегó отцá. *My father is older than yours.*

Моя́ мать то́же ста́рше, чем твоя́ мать. *My mother is also older than your mother.*

Мой оте́ц моло́же твоего́, но вы́глядит ста́рше. *My father is younger than yours but looks older* (вы́глядеть *to look, seem*; вы́гляжу, вы́глядишь).

Я бу́ду носи́ть э́тот пиджа́к в дере́вне. *I shall wear this jacket in the country.*

Он старе́е друго́го. *It's older than the other.*

Он бо́лее ста́рый и удо́бнее. *It's older and more comfortable* (удо́бнее is comparative of удо́бный *comfortable*).

Much more is expressed by **гора́здо** or **мно́го** + comparative.

Да, э́тот ста́рый пиджа́к гора́здо/мно́го удо́бнее друго́го. *Yes, this old jacket is much more comfortable than the other one.*

5. 'MORE AND LESS'

As you have noticed, there are apparently two words meaning *more*, **бо́льше** and **бо́лее,** and there are two words meaning *less*, **ме́ньше** and **ме́нее**.

Бо́льше is the comparative of **большо́й** *big* and also of **мно́го** *much, many.*

Ме́ньше is the comparative of **ма́ленький/ма́лый** *small* and also of **ма́ло** *little, few.*

Бо́лее and **ме́нее** in modern Russian are used almost exclusively with an adjective or adverb to produce comparative *adverbs* and *adjectives,* as for instance **бо́лее краси́вый** *more beautiful,* **ме́нее холо́дный** *less cold* or **бо́лее краси́во** *more beautifully,* **бо́лее хо́лодно** *more coldly.*

In the following sentences you use **бо́льше** or **ме́ньше:**

По э́той доро́ге бо́льше движе́ния. *There is more traffic on this road.*
По э́той доро́ге ме́ньше движе́ния, чем обыкнове́нно (*than usual*).
По э́той доро́ге бо́льше движе́ния у́тром.
По э́той доро́ге ме́ньше движе́ния у́тром, чем ве́чером.
По э́той доро́ге бо́льше движе́ния в а́вгусте.
По э́той но́вой доро́ге ме́ньше движе́ния, чем по ста́рой доро́ге.

In the following sentence you use **бо́лее** plus the adjective to express the comparative meaning *more direct:*

Э́та но́вая доро́га бо́лее пряма́я, чем ста́рая доро́га. *This new road is more direct than the old road.*

Or you can use the comparative in **ee** formed from **прямо́й:**

Э́та но́вая доро́га пряме́е ста́рой доро́ги.
Э́та но́вая доро́га пряме́е, чем ста́рая доро́га.

6. THE COMPARATIVE IN же

There are some common adjectives with the comparative ending in a single
e preceded by ж. They all have a root ending in д, з or г (see Part II,
Grammar):

adj.	adv.	comparative adv. and adj.	
молодо́й *young*	мо́лодо	моло́же	
ре́дкий *rare*	ре́дко	ре́же	(NB loses к)
бли́зкий *near*	бли́зко	бли́же	(NB loses к)
у́зкий *narrow*	у́зко	у́же	(NB loses к)
ни́зкий *low*	ни́зко	ни́же	(NB loses к)
дорого́й *dear*	до́рого	доро́же	

and **ху́же** *worse* comparative of the adjective **плохо́й** *bad* and the adverb
пло́хо *badly*.

Notice the difference in stress between **у́же** *narrower* and **уже́** *already*.

Ста́рая доро́га у́же но́вой.
Но́вая доро́га ху́же ста́рой.
Да нет, но́вая доро́га лу́чше ста́рой.

7. DIALOGUE

Peter and Vera finally manage to meet and are approaching the exhibition
entrance when . . .

Ве́ра Отчего́ так мно́го наро́ду?[1] Посмотри́, они́ как бу́дто[2] ждут
кого́-то.

Пе́тя Ну и пуска́й ждут. Я куплю́ биле́ты.

Ве́ра Нет, подожди́,[3] дава́й узна́ем, кого́ э́то ждут, кто́-то до́лжен
прие́хать.[4]

Пе́тя Да не всё ли равно́ кого́ ждут.[5] Ве́ра, Ве́ра, где ты? Опя́ть
тебя́ нет. Ве́ра...

Ве́ра (*взволно́ванно*) Пе́тя, Пе́тя, да ты зна́ешь, кого́ ждут? Гага́рина!
Ю́рия Гага́рина! Он же как раз прие́хал в Ло́ндон и, коне́чно,
он прие́дет сюда́ на вы́ставку, ведь э́то сове́тская вы́ставка.

Пе́тя Ну хорошо́, тогда́ войдём.[6]

1 **Наро́д** *people* has genitive in у after **мно́го**.   2 *As if* transl. *they seem to be waiting.*
3 Imper. of **подожда́ть** perfective of **ждать** *to wait*.   4 *Somebody must be coming.*
5 *Well, does it matter who they're waiting for?* lit. 'well, is it not all the same etc.'.
6 First pers. plural future perfective of **войти́** *let's go in*.

Ве́ра Да нет, я хочу́ ви́деть, как он прие́дет;[1] ви́дишь, все тут стоя́т, и
мы то́же постои́м. Вот – вот маши́на подъезжа́ет – нет, прое́хала,
э́то не он... Вот он... Нет, э́то мотоци́кл...

Пе́тя На мотоци́кле он не прие́дет, и на велосипе́де вряд ли прие́дет.

1 *I want to see him arrive*, lit. 'I want to see how he will arrive'.

ВЕ́РА   Е́сли ты бу́дешь издева́ться надо² мно́й... Вот е́дет маши́на...

ПЕ́ТЯ   Да э́то про́сто такси́; с аэропо́рта Гага́рин не прие́дет на такси́!

ВЕ́РА   Да ты посмотри́! вот маши́на с кра́сными флажка́ми – э́то из посо́льства.

ПЕ́ТЯ   Да, э́то маши́на сове́тского посо́льства.

ВЕ́РА   Они́ то́же ждут. Мо́жет быть и нам придётся до́лго ждать. Дава́й, ся́дем на ступе́ньки, мне ту́фли жмут.³

ПЕ́ТЯ   Хорошо́, дава́й ся́дем на ступе́ньки. Я но́вые брю́ки наде́л, а тут прихо́дится на ступе́ньках сиде́ть! Ой, Ве́ра! Ве́ра...

ВЕ́РА   Да сади́сь на газе́ту. Ты сам хо́чешь его́ ви́деть? Как мы счастли́во попа́ли⁴ на сове́тскую вы́ставку, то́чно в тот же день, как и Гага́рин! Я всем расскажу́, что я его́ ви́дела. Ра́зве ты не рад? Ты то́же смо́жешь всем рассказа́ть, как ты его́ ви́дел.

---

2 **Надо** – the form which **над** *over* takes before **мной** and some other words beginning with two consonants. **Издева́ться над** *to make fun of.*

3 *My shoes are hurting me*, lit. 'to me the shoes press'; **жать** *to press* **жму, жмёшь** etc. See Part II, Grammar.   4 *How lucky that we came*, lit. 'How fortunately we got to....'

ПЕ́ТЯ   Я ви́дел? Я ничего́ не ви́дел! Ты то́чно влюблена́ в¹ э́того Гага́рина!

ВЕ́РА   Ах како́й ты глу́пый – я ни в кого́² не влюблена́! Э́то ты, как дура́к влюблён уж не зна́ю в кого́.³

ПЕ́ТЯ   А ты да́же его́ не вида́ла и уже́ влюблена́. Как влюблённая говори́шь – «вот он», «вот он», в ка́ждом мотоцикли́сте ви́дишь Гага́рина.

ВЕ́РА   Я про́сто хочу́ его́ ви́деть, так как э́то прогре́сс челове́чества.

ПЕ́ТЯ   Да, прогре́сс челове́чества!

ВЕ́РА   А ты про́сто ревну́ешь!⁴ Ты ревни́в, я э́то зна́ю! Ты всегда́ ревну́ешь. Вот, вот маши́на...

ПЕ́ТЯ   Да, вот, вот маши́на. Э́то везу́т молоко́,⁵ а не Гага́рина.

ВЕ́РА   Да переста́нь,⁶ ты всё смеёшься! Excuse me, do you know when Yuriy Gagarin is expected?

НЕЗНАКО́МЫЙ   But he's arrived. He's in there. They won't let you in now, if you are not the press.

ПЕ́ТЯ   Thank you. Ну вот, он уже́ тут, отто́го и маши́ны из посо́льства, тут. Да что ты, Ве́ра, в са́мом де́ле, ну, не плачь.⁷ Ничего́, ничего́,⁸ не на́до пла́кать – мы его́ ещё уви́дим, я ведь то́лько

---

1 Short form feminine of a participle **влюблённый** *in love*. Notice the construction: **в** + acc.

2 *I'm not in love with anybody* (see Lesson 25, § 4).

3 *It's you, like a fool, you're in love with Heaven knows who* (lit. 'with I don't know who').

4 Second pers. singular present tense of **ревнова́ть** *to be jealous.*

5 *It's the milk-van*, lit. 'It's the milk they are bringing'.

6 Imper. of **переста́ть**, perfective, *to stop;* **переста́ну, переста́нешь.**

7 Imper. of **пла́кать** *to weep;* **пла́чу, пла́чешь** (Lesson 16, §§ 1 and 3, Lesson 23, § 7).

8 *Never mind, it's nothing.*

пошути́л. Ну, ну, Ве́рочка, я же пошути́л, прости́, я зна́ю, что ты не влюблена́ в Гага́рина. Да ведь ты не в него́ влюблена́ – да? Да ведь ты меня́ лю́бишь, хоть немно́жко – да? Да я действи́тельно ревну́ю, я не хочу́, что́бы друго́й, да́же Гага́рин – ведь ты меня́ лю́бишь, да? Я то́лько тебя́ люблю́, то́лько тебя́.

8. TRANSLATION

'Where are you going (е́дете)?'
'I'm going to the exhibition and I am taking my son with me.'
'Isn't he wearing a new jacket?'
'It isn't a new jacket. It's older than the one he wears when he goes to school.'
'Oh, does he go to school now?'
'Yes, he has been going to school for a year[1]. – No, more than a year – or is it less than a year? By the way,[2] is John also going to school now? But he's younger than Peter, isn't he?'[3]
'No, he is older than Peter – nearly a year[4] older, but he hasn't started to go to school yet. I am giving him lessons at home. One of his friends comes to our house[5] and they read together.'
'Can you tell me where the exhibition is?'
'Well, this road[6] is more direct, it's nearer this way.[6] I am taking my aunt home in the car. If you like,[7] we'll take you in the car. It's further but it will be much more comfortable.'
'Thank you very much.[8] I am very grateful to you.'[9]
'Not at all.[10] Hop in.'[11]

1 Lit. 'It's a year how he is going to school'.　　2 Кста́ти.
3 Не так ли? or не пра́вда ли?　　4 Го́дом (instr.).　　5 К нам.
6 По э́той доро́ге.　　7 Е́сли хоти́те.　　8 Большо́е спаси́бо.
9 Я вам о́чень благода́рен/рна.　　10 Не́ за что or Ничего́.　　11 Влеза́йте.

SUMMARY

1 The unprefixed verbs of motion fall into two sets of imperfective verbs: *determinate* (motion in a single direction), *indeterminate* (motion in more than one direction, §§ 1 and 2).
2 Many comparatives are formed in **ее** or by means of **бо́лее** and **ме́нее** plus the appropriate form of the adjective or adverb (§ 4).
3 *Than* is expressed by the genitive or by **чем** (§ 4).
4 'One of,' 'two of ' etc. is **оди́н из, два из** etc. plus genitive (§ 4).
5 **Бо́льше** and **ме́ньше** are comparative adjectives and adverbs, **бо́лее** and **ме́нее** are only used to form comparative adjectives and adverbs (§ 5).
6 There are some comparatives ending in **же** (§ 6).

Lesson 30

1. VERBS OF MOTION (*contd.*)

Here are some more imperfective verbs of motion with the same difference in meaning as those given in the last lesson:

determinate	*indeterminate*
('one direction')	('more than one direction')
éхать *to go* (in a vehicle)	éздить
плыть *to swim, to sail*	плáвать
летéть *to fly*	летáть
бежáть *to run*	бéгать

Éхать   éздить

The prefixed forms of this verb which you have met are:

приéхать	приезжáть
уéхать	уезжáть
подъéхать	подъезжáть

Note that when prefixed, **éздить** is replaced by **-езжáть,** which does not occur without a prefix.

– Ты хóдишь на рабóту; мне нáдо éздить на рабóту. Я éзжу пóездом.

Notice the instrumental of **пóезд,** lit. 'by means of the train'.

– Почемý ты не éздишь автóбусом? *Why don't you go by bus?*

– Éздить автóбусом удóбно, но берёт мнóго врéмени. Éздить автóбусом на рабóту кáждый день невозмóжно. *To travel by bus is comfortable but takes a lot of time. To travel by bus to work every day is impossible.*

The indeterminate **éздить** like **ходúть** has this multidirectional meaning. That is why you use it in the context of travelling to work every day and obviously returning from work.

– Вы хорошó знáете Совéтский Союз?

– Нет, но я éздила в Москвý, в Ленингрáд и на Чёрное мóре, в Крым. (NB на Чёрное мóре *to the Black Sea.*)

– Вы éздили на Кавкáз? (NB на Кавкáз *to the Caucasus.*)

– К сожалéнию нет, на Кавкáз я не éздила.

In these contexts you would not use **éхать** because you went in various directions and you also returned home. But if you met someone on a train, or at the airport or if you were hitch-hiking and had stopped a car on the road, you might well ask:

– Кудá вы éдете?

And the answer might be:

– Я éду в Со́чи *or* Я éду в Оде́ссу *or* Я éду в Ха́рьков.

Плыть пла́вать

Да, са́мый лу́чший спорт э́то пла́вать. (*The very best sport is swimming.*) Я о́чень люблю́ пла́вать. Я пла́ваю дово́льно хорошо́, я всегда́ пла́ваю ле́том в мо́ре, а сейча́с зимо́й мне не́где пла́вать, в на́шем го́роде нет бассе́йна.

> Notice мне не́где пла́вать *I have nowhere to swim*, lit. 'there is nowhere to/for me to swim'. There are several adverbs and pronouns with the negative prefix **не**. They are used in a special construction with the infinitive and if a logical subject is expressed, it goes into the dative case; the meaning is: *I have nowhere/nobody/nothing etc. to . . .* or *There is nowhere/nobody/nothing etc. for me to. . . .*
>
> Не́чего де́лать. *There is nothing to do* or *There is nothing can be done (about it).*
>
> Нам не́куда идти́. *There is nowhere for us to go.*
>
> Де́тям не́_с_кем игра́ть. *The children have nobody to play with.*
>
> **Не́чего** (*there is*) *nothing* and **не́кого** (*there is*) *nobody* split into two parts when controlled by a preposition, and the preposition is inserted between them (see Part II, Grammar – Negative Pronouns).

– Посто́йте, подожди́те! тут что-то пла́вает у вас в стака́не, э́то му́ха? *Stop, wait! There's something swimming about in your glass. Is it a fly?*

If you were in a rowing boat and thought that a medium swimmer had swum out too far, you might pull up and say to the swimmer:

– Куда́ вы плывёте? *Where are you swimming to?*

Вам на́до плыть к бе́регу, а вы плывёте от бе́рега. *You should be swimming towards the shore but you're swimming away from the shore.*

When prefixed, the verb **пла́вать** is replaced by **-плыва́ть,** which never occurs without a prefix:

pfv.	*impfv.*	
переплы́ть	переплыва́ть	*to swim across*
приплы́ть	приплыва́ть	{ *to swim up (to)* *to float up (to)*

Лете́ть лета́ть

Мы живём недалеко́ от аэродро́ма, у нас весь день лета́ют самолёты над голово́й. Шум ужа́сный, но мы привы́кли,[1] мы да́же не смо́трим вверх, когда́ они́ летя́т над на́ми. Мла́дший сын сосе́дей весь день

---

1 Past tense plural of **привы́кнуть** perfective of **привыка́ть** *to get used to.* **Привы́к-нуть** has past tense **привы́к** (no л), **привы́кла** etc.

стоѝт, смóтрит и считáет. «Вот, вот, летѝт – смотрѝ, какóй большóй летѝт, а тут другóй летѝт, а там ещё одѝн летѝт, тут большóй летѝт – пассажѝрский, а вот там летѝт бомбардирóвщик – э́то бомбардирóвщик, я знáю, вот летѝт бомбардирóвщик.»

«Довóльно, хвáтит! Онѝ тут весь день летáют и ты сам полетѝшь (*you will fly yourself*), ты сам бýдешь летáть на самолётах.»
«Пáпа чáсто летáет, пáпа лю́бит летáть. А ты лю́бишь летáть, ты летáла?»
«Да, я летáла, немнóго, но летáла. Я обыкновéнно éздила на канѝкулы пóездом ѝли парохóдом, я не люблю́ летáть.»

Бежáть   бéгать

Бéгать conjugates like **дýмать: бéгаю, бéгаешь** etc., but **бежáть** has an unusual mixed conjugation:

я бегý
ты бежѝшь
он бежѝт
мы бежѝм
вы бежѝте
онѝ бегýт

– Кудá вы бежѝте? Кудá вы, кудá вы так бежѝте?
– На вокзáл, на пóезд, прощáйте! Бегý, бегý, пóезд отхóдит.
– Да, он бежѝт, бежѝт со всéми своѝми чемодáнами, а пóезд ведь ужé отхóдит. Я не люблю́ бéгать, я никогдá не бéгаю, я хожý мéдленно и спокóйно. Совсéм не нáдо (*There is no need at all*) бéгать. Когдá я былá молодá я любѝла бéгать на стадиóне, и óчень бы́стро бéгала, но тепéрь я старá.
– Бéдная моя́ стáренькая сестрѝца! *My poor old little sister!*
– Я слѝшком старá, чтóбы бéгать. *I am too old to run.*

Here you have the conjunction **чтóбы** meaning *in order to*.

2. THE CONDITIONAL

The word **чтóбы** at the end of the preceding section is made up of the words **что** and **бы**. The word **бы** on its own is called by grammarians *the conditional particle*. Together with the past tense it forms the conditional mood of the verb, that is the forms which express *would do, would have done* etc.:

он сдéлал бы   *he would do/have done*
онá сдéлала бы   *she would do/have done*
онѝ сдéлали бы   *they would do/have done*

Do not confuse these 'would' forms in English with the 'would' forms that occur in such sentences as *she would go to the post-office every Thursday*, where *would go* means *used to go*. The 'would' forms we are discussing here

214

are the ones you find in sentences with the conjunction *if,* as in *she would go to the post-office if she had the time.*

In English the *if* clause in such a sentence has the verb in the past tense. In Russian *both* parts of such a sentence must have the conditional particle.

Éсли бы я имéла мой дождевѝк, я бы не беспокóилась.
If I had my raincoat I would not worry.

As you see, the particle **бы** does not necessarily follow the past tense form. It is simply associated with it in the same clause to express the conditional. It is very usual to put **бы** as the second word in the clause (it can never stand as the first word) and especially to put it immediately after **éсли.**

The Russian sentence we have just had could also be the equivalent of the English *If I had had my raincoat I would not have worried.*

There is no difference of tense in the Russian conditional. The time to which it refers is seen from the context. But there *is* a difference in aspect, just as there is in the past tense and the future tense:

Éсли бы нé_было так пóздно, я бы сидéл и писáл пѝсьма.
If it were not so late I would be sitting and writing letters or *If it had not been so late I would have been sitting and writing letters.*

Here no completion is implied. The business of writing letters would go on for some indefinite time. But in the following sentence you have in mind the completion of a single letter:

Éсли бы нé_было так пóздно, я бы написáл емý письмó.
If it were not so late, I would write him a letter or *If it had not been so late, I would have written him a letter.*

In the next example the second sentence makes it clear that you are referring to the present:

Éсли бы у вас бѝли дéти, вы бы так не говорѝли, вы бы нас пóняли. Вы нас не понимáете.
If you had children, you would not talk like that – you would understand us. You don't understand us.

To understand is **понимáть** imperfective, **понять** perfective, and in the preceding example the perfective conditional **пóняли бы** was used in the sense 'you would reach an understanding' (completed act) and therefore *would understand.*

In the next example the word **зáвтра** *tomorrow* makes it clear that you are referring to the future:

Éсли бы я былá свобóдна, я бы, конéчно, пришлá зáвтра.
If I were free I should of course come tomorrow.

Without **зáвтра** this sentence could also mean:

If I had been free I should of course have come.

Sometimes **бы** is clipped to **б** colloquially and sometimes **éсли** is omitted, just as *if* may be omitted in English:

Был бы он там, он бы сдéлал э́то.
Had he been there he would have done it.

The particle **бы** is not only found in *if* clauses:

Ты бы побóльше читáл. *You should read a little more.*
Вам бы отдохнýть. *You ought to rest.*
Дождь бы! *If only it would rain!* or *I wish it would rain.*

3. THE USE OF **чтóбы**

Чтóбы can be followed either by the infinitive or by the past tense forms of the verb. Its meaning is *in order to, in order that, so as to, so that.*

Профéссор получи́л óтпуск, чтобы поéхать в Москвý. *The professor has received leave in order to go to Moscow.*
Профéссору дáли две недéли óтпуска, чтóбы он мог поéхать в Москвý. *They have given the professor leave so that he may go to Moscow* or *They gave etc., so that he might etc.*
Не нáдо имéть мнóго дéнег, чтóбы хорошó жить. *You don't need to have a lot of money to live well.*
Чтóбы вы пóняли нáше положéние, я вам всё расскажý. *In order that you should understand our position, I shall tell you everything.*

Чтóбы is also used after certain verbs where English does not have *in order to* etc. The commonest of these verbs is **хотéть** *to want.*

Я не хочý, чтóбы вы дýмали э́то. *I do not want you to think that.*
Я бы не хотéла, чтóбы вы дýмали э́то. *I should not like you to think that,* lit. 'that you should think this'.
Я бы не хотéла, чтóбы вы дýмали, что мне не интерéсно. *I should not like you to think that I am not interested.*

The third part of the sentence is put into the past or the present or the future, whichever is appropriate: *that I was not interested* would be:

Я бы не хотéла, чтóбы вы дýмали, что мне нé_было интерéсно,

and *I should not like you to think that I shall not be interested* would be:

Я бы не хотéла, чтóбы вы дýмали, что мне не бýдет интерéсно.

And if you want to introduce an even more tentative note you use the conditional in the third part:

Я бы не хотéла, чтóбы вы дýмали, что мне не бы́ло бы интерéсно.
I should not like you to think that I might not be interested.

216

4. QUESTIONS

You learnt in the first lesson that questions can be put using the same words in the same order as in a statement.

> Пе́тя до́ма? *Is Peter at home?*

A somewhat tentative note or a shade of politeness is added to questions by the *interrogative particle* **ли,** which always stands after the first important word in the sentence:

> До́ма ли Пе́тя? *Is Peter at home?*
> Ве́ры нет до́ма? *Is Vera not at home?* or Нет ли Ве́ры до́ма?
> Он не́_был до́ма? *He wasn't at home?* Не́_был ли он до́ма?

The word **есть,** we have seen, means *there is* or, in questions, *is there.*
Ли may be associated with **есть** too.

> Есть до́ма хлеб?   *Is there any bread at home?*
>   or
> Есть ли у нас хлеб?   *Have we any bread?*
> Нет ли у нас хле́ба?⎫ *Isn't there any bread at home?*
> У нас нет хле́ба? ⎬ or
> До́ма нет хле́ба? ⎭ *Haven't we any bread at home?*

You do not usually add **ли** when you ask somebody if he understands.

> Вы понима́ете? *Do you understand*
> Вы по́няли? *Have you understood?*
> Вы не понима́ете? *Don't you understand?*
> Вы не по́няли? *Didn't you understand?*

With the last two questions you expect the answer *No, I don't understand.*

If you add **ли** and invert the sentence you add a tentative note:

> Не понима́ете ли вы?
> Не по́няли ли вы?

You are not quite so sure that the answer will be *No.*

Similarly, when asking about a third person:

> Она́ поймёт? (see § 5) *Will she understand?*
> Поймёт ли она́? *Will she understand?*
>   or *I wonder if she will understand?*

In English, when you want to invite agreement with a statement, you have to say *isn't it, won't they, didn't he* etc., as for instance in:

> *It's late, isn't it?*
> *They'll be late, won't they?*
> *He came late, didn't he?*

217

In many languages there is a fixed phrase which covers all these contingencies: Fr. *n'est-ce-pas*, Germ. *nicht wahr*, Ital. *non è vero* etc. Russian has two such phrases, with the same meaning:

не пра́вда ли and не так ли

Поздно, {не пра́вда ли? *It's late, isn't it?*
{не так ли?

Они́ приду́т с опозда́нием, {не пра́вда ли? *They'll come late, won't they?*
{не так ли?

Он опозда́л, {не пра́вда ли? *He came late, didn't he?*
{не так ли?

Нет затрудне́ний в отве́тах на вопро́сы, {не пра́вда ли?
{не так ли?

Answers to questions present no difficulties, do they? lit. 'There are no difficulties in answers, isn't that so?'

5. VERBS OF THE -нять, -нимать GROUP

The verb **поня́ть – понима́ть** belongs to a small group of verbs with the perfective infinitive in **-нять** and the imperfective in **-нимать**. The original root meant *to take* but now it occurs only with prefixes. The meanings are varied, though in some of them the idea of *taking* can still be seen.

prefix **по-**	поня́ть *to understand*	понима́ть
при-	приня́ть *to accept*	принима́ть
на-	наня́ть *to hire*	нанима́ть
за-	заня́ть *to occupy, to borrow*	занима́ть

In these four verbs the prefix ends in a vowel and the conjugation of the perfective verb, **поня́ть, приня́ть, наня́ть, заня́ть** drops the middle **н**:

я пойму́	приму́	найму́	займу́
ты поймёшь	при́мешь	наймёшь	займёшь
он поймёт	при́мет	наймёт	займёт

NB No **й** in **приму́** etc.

In four other verbs of this same group the prefix ends in a consonant.

prefix **от-**	отня́ть *to take from*	отнима́ть
под-	подня́ть *to lift, to raise*	поднима́ть
с-	снять *to remove*	снима́ть

One also says

снять, снима́ть кварти́ру *to take a flat*
снять, снима́ть *to take a photograph* (сни́мок)

and the person photographed goes into the accusative.

| prefix **об-** | обня́ть *to embrace* | обнима́ть |

In these verbs the conjugation of the perfective verb retains the **н** of the infinitive:

я отниму́	подниму́	сниму́	обниму́
ты отни́мешь	подни́мешь	сни́мешь	обни́мешь
он отни́мет	подни́мет	сни́мет	обни́мет

NB In these verbs the stress shifts as in **приня́ть.**

The perfective verb **взять** *to take* originally belonged to this group. Its imperfective **брать** is from a completely different root. Notice the mobile vowels **о** and **е** that appear in the conjugation:

взять *to take*	брать
я возьму́	беру́
он возьмёт	берёт
они́ возьму́т	беру́т

6. SHOPPING

In the following passage on shopping various numbers are used. Here are the numbers used in the first paragraph:

ты́сяча *thousand* declines like a feminine noun
два *two*, see Lesson 25, § 5 for declension
че́тверть *quarter*, a feminine noun ending in **ь**
четы́реста *four hundred*, see Part II, Grammar, for declension
две́сти *two hundred*, see Part II, Grammar, for declension
полфу́нта *half a pound*

Ходи́ть за поку́пками[1] удово́льствие сре́днее. Всё зави́сит от того́, что вы хоти́те купи́ть, где, в каки́х магази́нах, ско́лько де́нег[2] в карма́не— э́то о́чень ва́жный вопро́с. Ходи́ть за хле́бом, и́ли ма́слом, э́то не сло́жно. Купи́ть са́хар, соль, пе́рец, я́йца, сыр, макаро́ны, бискви́ты, не́сколько консе́рвов, э́то вся́кий[3] мо́жет. Но и тут быва́ют[4] неожи́данные осложне́ния. Я о́чень забы́вчива. Я мно́го лет жила́ за грани́цей. Везде́ всё продаётся на[5] килогра́ммы и гра́ммы. Ты́сяча грамм[6] — оди́н килогра́мм, а по сравне́нию[7] с англи́йскими фунта́ми оди́н килогра́мм равня́ется бо́лее и́ли ме́нее двум с че́твертью[8] фунта́м. Два с че́твертью англи́йских фу́нта – э́то о́коло одного́[9] килогра́мма. Оди́н англи́йский фунт приблизи́тельно четы́реста пятьдеся́т грамм, а две́сти пятьдеся́т

---

1 *To go shopping;* **поку́пка** is the thing bought.   2 Genitive plural of **де́ньги** *money.*
3 *Anybody.*   4 **Быва́ть** imperfective *to be* (frequently, regularly).   5 *In* or *by.*
6 **Грамм** normally has genitive plural **грамм.** The genitive plural **гра́ммов** is rather bookish.   7 *In comparison.*
8 Notice how you say *and a quarter.* This phrase remains unchanged, no matter what case the other numbers may be in. The same applies to *and a half* **с полови́ной** (**полови́на** *half*).
9 **Оди́н** omits the **и** in declension and declines like **э́тот,** with the stress on the end. See Part II, Grammar.

грамм и́ли че́тверть килогра́мма – э́то немно́го бо́льше полуфу́нта.[10] В ста́рое вре́мя в Росси́и то́же взве́шивали фу́нтами,[11] но ста́рый ру́сский фунт немно́го ме́ньше англи́йского фу́нта, ста́рый ру́сский фунт равня́ется четы́реста гра́ммам,[12] и ро́вно два с полови́ной ру́сских фу́нта – оди́н килогра́мм.

10 Words formed with the prefix **пол** *half* decline normally, the **пол** changing to **полу** in all the other cases: **полуфу́нта, полуфу́нту, полуфу́нтом** etc.
11 *By* or *in pounds.*
12 In a more formal style one would also put **четы́реста** into the dative: **четырёмста́м.**

Among the numbers in the second paragraph are: **де́сять** *ten,* which declines like a feminine noun in **ь,** with stress on the endings; **дю́жина** *dozen,* feminine noun; **три че́тверти** *three-quarters;* **во́семь** *eight,* which declines like a feminine noun in **ь,** with stress on the endings, **е** being a mobile vowel: genitive, dative, prepositional **восьми́,** instrumental **восемью́** and **восьмью́.**

Я до́лго не могла́ привы́кнуть к англи́йским деньга́м и к англи́йским ме́рам ве́са. Наконе́ц привы́кла. И вот одна́жды иду́ я в моло́чную ла́вку.

«Что вам уго́дно?»[1] спра́шивает ла́вочник. Беру́, что на́до на[2] обе́д и на у́жин. Всё что-то[3] вздорожа́ло! – «Отчего́ ма́сло так до́рого?» – спра́шиваю его́. – «На про́шлой неде́ле я плати́ла за фунт ма́сла три ши́ллинга и де́сять пе́нсов, а сего́дня я плачу́ четы́ре ши́ллинга и два пе́нса». Он отвеча́ет: – «Это потому́, что тако́е вре́мя го́да;[4] в э́то вре́мя го́да ма́сло всегда́ доро́же, я́йца то́же доро́же; во всём го́роде вы не найдёте ма́сла по[5] бо́лее дешёвой цене́. А я́йца в мое́й ла́вке мно́го деше́вле, чем в други́х магази́нах – три с полови́ной пе́нса ма́ленькие, а больши́е по[6] четы́ре с полови́ной пе́нса. Ско́лько вам дать и каки́е?» – «Да́йте дю́жину за[7] четы́ре с полови́ной ши́ллинга, да, да, больши́е – дю́жину за четы́ре ши́ллинга и шесть пе́нсов, да ещё да́йте колбасы́.»[8] – «Ско́лько вам отре́зать?» – «Да отре́жьте[9] мне, ска́жем, сто...» Я стою́ и ду́маю, а ла́вочник молчи́т и на меня́ смо́трит. – «Да́йте сто, и́ли нет, да́йте две́сти. Да, отре́жьте мне две́сти». Он с мину́ту молчи́т и неуве́ренно говори́т: «Что? Ско́лько?» – «Две́сти, да́йте две́сти». – «Две́сти чего́?» – «Да колбасы́, две́сти колбасы́», и тут я наконе́ц понима́ю, – ведь я говорю́ ему́ вес гра́ммами, а он, коне́чно, ду́мает, что я говорю́ о фунта́х, что хочу́ купи́ть сто и́ли две́сти фу́нтов колбасы́. В его́ глаза́х ти́хий у́жас, он наве́рно реши́л, что я с ума́ сошла́.[10]

1 *What can I do for you?*   2 *For* **на** + accusative.   3 *Somewhat, rather.*
4 *It's because of the time of year/season,* lit. 'It's because such is the time of the year'.
5 *At* **по** + prepositional.   6 Here *at . . . each.*   7 *At, for* **за** + accusative.
8 Genitive alone renders *some.*   9 Imperative of **отре́зать** *to cut off.*
10 *Gone out of my mind/off my head;* **сходи́ть** imperfective, **сойти́** perfective, **с ума́.**

– «Извини́те, я хоте́ла сказа́ть: полфу́нта колбасы́ и три че́тверти фу́нта ветчины́».

– «По како́й цене́? по три ши́ллинга во́семь пе́нсов за фунт, и́ли э́ту тут, полу́чше,[1] четы́ре ши́ллинга де́сять пе́нсов за фунт? А вот тут са́мая лу́чшая – пять ши́ллингов и четы́ре пе́нса. Хоти́те це́лый фунт ветчины́, и́ли три че́тверти?» – «Ну ла́дно, да́йте це́лый фунт са́мой лу́чшей».

1 **По** added to comparatives means *somewhat, rather*, as here, and sometimes *as . . . as possible.*

Да, пу́тать гра́ммы и фу́нты не сле́дует![1] А знако́мые из Москвы́ пошли́ в Ло́ндоне покупа́ть про́стыни и на́волочки и перепу́тали дю́ймы и сантиме́тры. Ведь у нас всё по[2] дю́ймам и по фу́там и я́рдам, а на́ши бе́дные знако́мые называ́ют разме́р по сантиме́трам. Прика́зчик в магази́не ме́рит дю́ймами, а дюйм мно́го бо́льше сантиме́тра – в[3] два с полови́ной ра́за бо́льше, два с полови́ной сантиме́тра – э́то оди́н дюйм. Вот они́ из магази́на иду́т домо́й. Что-то[4] о́чень тяжёлый паке́т! Пришли́ домо́й, разверну́ли паке́т – и что же?! – на́волочки и про́стыни грома́дные. «На что нам таки́е больши́е? Са́мый большо́й разме́р! Вот отчего́ так тяжело́ бы́ло нести́, вот отчего́ так до́рого!»

1 **Сле́дует** – impersonal verb *one ought.*   2 *In,* i.e. in inches etc.
3 Notice that to say how many times bigger you must use the preposition **в – в два ра́за бо́льше** *twice as big as* and note too that Russian says lit. 'twice, three times bigger than' etc.
4 Here **что-то** means *somehow,* 'for some unknown reason.'

7. EXERCISES

a Cover up the Russian and translate from English into Russian all the examples with translation given in §§ 1, 2, 3 and 4.

b Learn the conjugations in § 5 and write out from memory the conjugations of:

поня́ть	заня́ть	приня́ть
снять	взять	брать

c Write a short composition of 200–300 words on going shopping.

SUMMARY

1 Some more unprefixed verbs of motion (§ 1).
2 The use of **не́где** etc. (§ 1).
3 The conjugation of **бежа́ть** (§ 1).
4 The form and use of the conditional (§ 2).
5 The use of **чтобы** (§ 3).
6 The use of **ли** (§ 4).
7 Verbs of the **-нять, -нима́ть** group and **взять** (§ 5).
8 The use of certain numbers (§ 6).

Lesson 31

I. TELLING THE TIME

To express the hours you simply say, for instance:

> час *one o'clock*
> два часá *two o'clock*
> три часá *three o'clock*
> пять часóв *five o'clock*
> дéсять часóв *ten o'clock*

Notice that in *one o'clock* the number is not expressed. If you say **одúн час** you are saying *one hour*, not *one o'clock*.

To express *at* what hour you simply put **в** in front of the clock hour:

> в час *at one o'clock*
> в два часá *at two o'clock*
> в три часá *at three o'clock*
> в пять часóв *at five o'clock*
> в дéсять часóв *at ten o'clock*

Most of the other times on the clock are based on the hour in progress, *not* the hour that has just been completed, as in English.

Half past is expressed by **половúна** *half* followed by the genitive of the ordinal number denoting the hour in progress. At *half past one*, then, the second hour is in progress, so you say:

> половúна вторóго, lit. 'half of the second (hour)'

At *half-past twelve* the first hour is in progress, so you say:

> половúна пéрвого, lit. 'half of the first (hour)'

Similarly *quarter past* is 'quarter of', as in

> чéтверть пéрвого *quarter past twelve*
> чéтверть вторóго *quarter past one*

You use the same means of expression for 'minutes after':

> пять минýт пéрвого *five (minutes) past/after twelve*
> двáдцать минýт седьмóго *twenty (minutes) past six*

You can also say, for example:

> час с чéтвертью *quarter past one*, lit. 'one o'clock
>   with a quarter'
> час и пять минýт *one o'clock and five minutes*

though this is rarer.

222

Quarter to/of is **без че́тверти** followed by the number of the hour that is about to be completed:

> без че́тверти два *quarter to two*, lit. 'without
> (i.e. less) a quarter two'

You use the same means of expression for 'minutes to':

> без пяти́ шесть *five (minutes) to six*
> без десяти́ де́вять *ten (minutes) to nine*

You usually omit the word *minutes*, though it is not wrong to include it: **без пяти́ мину́т шесть.** Remember that numbers ending in **ь** decline like feminine nouns ending in **ь.**

– Кото́рый час? *What time is it?* lit. 'which hour?'
– Час.
– Нет, не мо́жет быть, у тебя́ часы́ останови́лись. *No, it can't be, your watch has stopped.*

Remember **часы́** is always plural in the sense of *watch* or *clock*.

– Да, ка́жется, так и есть. Часы́ стоя́т, я их заведу́. *Yes I think it has*, lit. 'it seems so it is'. *My watch has stopped*, lit. 'is standing'. *I'll wind it up.*

– На́до узна́ть кото́рый час.
– Мне ка́жется (*I think*, lit. 'it seems to me'), что полови́на второ́го. Да, полови́на второ́го.
– По-мо́ему ра́ньше. По-мо́ему то́лько че́тверть второ́го (or час с че́твертью).
– Нет, по-мо́ему гора́здо по́зже. По-мо́ему без че́тверти два. Да, без че́тверти два *a quarter to two* (lit. 'less a quarter two').
– Нет, ещё по́зже. Без пяти́ два. Да, без пяти́ два.
– Ты про́сто уга́дываешь вре́мя. Мне на́до то́чно узна́ть, кото́рый час. *You're simply guessing the time. I must find out the exact time*, lit. 'I need exactly to know what time it is'.

To say at what time in terms of minutes or quarters of the hour, you use **в** + accusative as follows:

> в че́тверть второ́го *at a quarter past one*
> в два́дцать мину́т шесто́го *at twenty past five*

or **без** + genitive:

> без че́тверти де́сять *at a quarter to ten*

but with the half-hour you use **в** + prepositional:

> в полови́не восьмо́го *at half past seven*

or, colloquially, simply полови́на восьмо́го.

223

2. USE OF **на** IN EXPRESSIONS OF TIME

One of the uses of **на** in expressions of time is to express *by* how long somebody is late:

– На ско́лько вре́мени ты опозда́ла? *How late were you?* lit. 'By how much time etc.'
– Я опозда́ла на час. А вчера́ я опозда́ла на полчаса́, а позавчера́ – на два часа́.

Another use of **на** in expressions of time is to express *for* how long an action or process is going to go on from the time mentioned or implied:

Он прие́хал к нам вчера́ на неде́лю. *He came to us yesterday for a week.*
Брат пое́хал в Москву́ на це́лый год. *(My) brother has gone to Moscow for a whole year.*

3. THE DATE AND THE DAY

To give the date you use the ordinal number, that is the number in the form of an adjective, just as you do in English. It goes into the nominative singular neuter because **число́** *number, date* is understood.

пе́рвое ма́я *the first of May*
тре́тье ию́ня *the third of June*
два́дцать шесто́е сентября́ *the twenty-sixth of September*
тридца́тое ноября́ *the thirtieth of November*

To express *on* a particular date you put the number into the genitive case:

пе́рвого ма́я *on the first of May*
шесто́го февраля́ *on the sixth of February*

Notice that no preposition is used.

To express on a *day* of the week you use the preposition **в** followed by the accusative case:

в понеде́льник *on Monday*
в сре́ду *on Wednesday*
в суббо́ту *on Saturday*

Note again that names of months, days of the week, names of nationalities and adjectives of nationality (Lesson 19, § 5) are *not* written with a capital letter.

To express what year it is you use cardinal and ordinal numbers followed by the word **год** *year*:

Ты́сяча девятьсо́т шестьдеся́т тре́тий год *1963*
Ты́сяча восемьсо́т девяно́сто девя́тый год *1899*

Only the last of the numbers, no matter how many there are, goes into the ordinal form.

To say *in* a particular year you use **в** with the prepositional case:

в ты́сяча девятьсо́т шестьдеся́т тре́тьем году́ *in 1963*

году́ being the special locative form of **год.**

When you give a complete date, however, i.e. date, month and year, the year goes into the *genitive* case:

пе́рвое ма́я ты́сяча девятьсо́т шестьдеся́т тре́тьего го́да *May the first, 1963*

пе́рвого ма́я ты́сяча девятьсо́т шестьдеся́т тре́тьего го́да *on May the first, 1963*

в апре́ле ты́сяча девятьсо́т пятьдеся́т шесто́го го́да *in April, 1956*

In *writing* the year, just as in English, you use figures and the word **год** or the abbreviation **г.** is added:

1963 год, 1963 г.

в 1963 году́ (or в 1963-ом году́, with the prepositional case ending added to the figures)

в 1963 г.

In conversation, when it is clear which *century* you are talking about, it is very common to use only the last two parts of the number of the year:

в шестьдеся́т пе́рвом году́ *in 1961*

and certain historic years are habitually referred to in this way:

семна́дцатый год *1917*
со́рок пе́рвый год *1941*

– Кото́рое/Како́е число́? *What's the date?*
– Сего́дня пе́рвое ма́я. *It's the first of May today.*
– Сего́дня двена́дцатое апре́ля. *It's the twelfth of April today.*

– Когда́ ты е́дешь в Эдинбу́рг?
– Я е́ду в Эдинбу́рг трина́дцатого ма́я.

– Когда́ ты же́нишься? *When are you getting married?*
– Мо́жет быть двадца́того ию́ня, а мо́жет быть в конце́ (*at the end*) ию́ля – два́дцать девя́того, и́ли тридца́того. Мы ещё не вы́брали день сва́дьбы. Мо́жет быть она́ состои́тся в а́вгусте – в нача́ле (*at the beginning*) а́вгуста – я то́чно не зна́ю.
– В како́й день неде́ли? (*On*) *which day of the week?*
– Как ты ду́маешь? *What do you think?* lit. 'how do you think?'
– По-мо́ему хорошо́ бы́ло бы в суббо́ту. *I think it would be fine on a Saturday.*
– Да, хорошо́ бы́ло бы в суббо́ту и́ли воскресе́нье. А по-тво́ему?
– Мы с Ве́рой хоте́ли, чтобы сва́дьба состоя́лась в пя́тницу у́тром (*on Friday morning*, lit. 'on Friday in the morning').

– В пя́тницу у́тром никто́ не смо́жет прийти́ на сва́дьбу.
– Есть ещё вре́мя ду́мать об э́том. *There is still time to think about that.*

– Кото́рый год? *What year is it?*
– Ты́сяча девятьсо́т шестьдеся́т тре́тий год.

– Когда́ произошла́ Ру́сская Револю́ция? В како́м году́? *When did the Russian Revolution take place? In what year?*
– Ру́сская Револю́ция произошла́ в ты́сяча девятьсо́т семна́дцатом году́.
– Когда́ то́чно начала́сь Револю́ция? *When did the Revolution begin exactly?*
– Револю́ция начала́сь двена́дцатого ма́рта семна́дцатого го́да.

4. REVISION OF NUMBERS

Here are a few simple sentences which will help you to revise numbers and rules for cases with numbers (Lessons 6, § 13, 9, § 2, 25, § 5).

Briefly the rules are:

a Оди́н/одно́/одна́ and any bigger number ending in оди́н/одно́/одна́ always agree with the noun, which is always in the singular.

b When the other numbers are in the nominative-accusative then два, три, четы́ре and higher numbers ending in два, три, четы́ре take the genitive singular, while all other numbers take the genitive plural.

c When the number and its noun are controlled by a word which requires a case other than the nominative-accusative then number and noun agree: they are in the same case and the noun is in the plural, except with оди́н and numbers ending in оди́н, when the noun remains in the singular.

Óба/óбе *both* behave like два/две.

After полови́на, че́тверть, треть and the other fractions you always have the genitive singular or plural, whichever is required.

Я опозда́ла на три че́тверти часа́.
Я опозда́ла на четы́ре часа́.
Я опозда́ла на два го́да.
Прошло́ четы́ре го́да. *Four years have passed.*

Notice the neuter singular ending of the verb.

Прошло́ пять, шесть, семь часо́в. *Five, six, seven hours have passed.*
Прошло́ семь, во́семь, де́вять, де́сять дней. (. . . *days*).
Прошло́ де́сять, оди́ннадцать, двена́дцать лет. (. . . *years*).

You use год *year* with два, три, четы́ре and higher numbers ending in these elements, as well as with fractions. *One year* is simply год or somewhat emphatically, оди́н год. With other numbers, *year* is expressed by the plural cases of ле́то *summer, year*.

226

Ско́лько ему́ лет? *How old is he?*

Ему́ два́дцать оди́н год.

Нет, ему́ два́дцать два го́да, а мо́жет быть, что ему́ два́дцать пять лет.

Тут нет двух фу́нтов.

Тут нет шести́ рубле́й.

Приба́вьте три фу́нта к двум фу́нтам. *Add three pounds to two pounds.*

Приба́вьте семь рубле́й к шести́ рубля́м.

Я не говорю́ о четырёх фу́нтах. *I am not talking about four pounds.*

Я говорю́ о семи́ рубля́х.

В кла́ссе со́рок оди́н ма́льчик. *There are forty boys in the class.*

В кла́ссе со́рок две де́вочки.

В кла́ссе со́рок пять ма́льчиков.

У пяти́десяти одно́й де́вочки нет мест. *Fifty-one girls have no seats.*

У шести́десяти двух ма́льчиков нет мест.

У семи́десяти шести́ ма́льчиков и де́вочек нет мест.

5. CASES OF ADJECTIVES WITH NUMBERS

You should now learn the following rules for the use of the cases of adjectives with numbers.

With **оди́н** and higher numbers ending in **оди́н** the adjective is in the same case and number as the noun:

> два́дцать оди́н большо́й стол *twenty-one big tables*
> со́рок одна́ но́вая копе́йка *forty-one new copecks*
> от сорока́ одно́й но́вой копе́йки *from forty-one new copecks*

Other numbers – when the number is in the nominative or nominative-accusative:

a With **два, три, четы́ре** and higher numbers ending in **два, три, четы́ре** the adjective is in the genitive *plural* or the nominative plural. The genitival plural is more usual with masculine and neuter nouns, the nominative plural with feminine nouns:

> четы́ре но́вых фу́нта *four new pounds*
> три но́вые копе́йки *three new copecks*

b With other numbers the genitive plural of the adjective is used:

> пять краси́вых де́вушек *five beautiful girls*
> сто ста́рых сту́льев *a hundred old chairs*

When the number and noun are in some other case, then the adjective goes into the same case:

> двух краси́вых де́вушек *of two beautiful girls*
> с пятью́ но́выми рубля́ми *with five new rubles*

The same rules apply to adjectival nouns and to adjectives standing on their own, when a noun is understood.

6. DIALOGUE

п é т я Вы зна́ете, Ве́ра хо́дит за поку́пками со спи́ском. Снача́ла она́ хо́дит по[1] ку́хне, открыва́ет и закрыва́ет все я́щики и шкафы́. Она́ смо́трит на по́лки и де́лает спи́сок.

н и́ н а Ми́лый мой бра́тец, я то́же де́лаю спи́ски... на ста́рых конве́ртах, на откры́тках, на оборо́тной стороне́ како́го-нибу́дь ста́рого письма́, но ты э́тим никогда́ не интересова́лся.

п é т я Я нахожу́ э́ти ста́рые конве́рты, пи́сьма и откры́тки в ва́нне, в убо́рной, на полу́ в пере́дней, на ле́стнице и да́же нашёл оди́н из твои́х спи́сков у себя́[2] в посте́ли ме́жду простыня́ми. У нас до́ма нет поря́дка, как ты э́то не понима́ешь!

н и́ н а По́сле сва́дьбы ты поймёшь, что мужчи́не то́же на́до помога́ть до́ма. Ве́ра тебе́ ска́жет – Пе́тя, сними́ э́ти брю́ки со стола́ – и ты их сни́мешь. – Пе́тя, ты бро́сил полоте́нце на_пол, подними́ его́ – и ты подни́мешь. А пото́м она́ ска́жет – Пе́тя, пойди́ купи́ два биле́та на[3] суббо́ту – ты пойдёшь и ку́пишь э́ти биле́ты. – Пе́тя, звоно́к в две́рь, прими́ бельё из сти́рки. – Пе́тя, отнеси́ бельё в сти́рку – ты и при́мешь и отнесёшь. – Пе́тя, до́ма так мно́го рабо́ты, нам на́до наня́ть прислу́гу, дава́й наймём прислу́гу – вы и прислу́гу наймёте!

п é т я Кака́я ерунда́! А ты что – ревну́ешь? Ты ревну́ешь, что ли?

н и́ н а Я тебя́ про́сто жале́ю. Я и себя́ жале́ю. Что я де́лала в про́шлом году́ и в позапро́шлом году́? Я то́лько всё поднима́ла и снима́ла за тобо́й. Принима́ла твои́х друзе́й! То́лько занима́лась до́мом и тобо́й. Тепе́рь ты же́нишься и ты да́же не познако́мил меня́ с э́той Ве́рой. Да, ты про́сто не поду́мал нас познако́мить!

п é т я Ни́на, что ты! Вы же встре́тились не́сколько ме́сяцев тому́ наза́д!

н и́ н а Но тогда́ я не зна́ла, что она́ бу́дет твое́й жено́й! Я да́же не по́мню как она́ вы́глядит! И с тех пор ты ни сло́ва не сказа́л о ней.

п é т я Ни́на, ду́шечка, дай мне объясни́ть...

Ни́на хло́пает две́рью Nina slams the door

7. VERBS OF MOTION WITH THE PREFIX за-

With verbs of motion the prefix за- has by and large the idea of a casual diversion from an original course.

---

1 *About.*   2 **Себя́** here translated *my.*   3 *For.*

Зайти, заходить к *to pop round* somewhere or to somebody's house, *to call in on* casually

Я иду́ на вокза́л, но вот я зашёл к тебе́ на мину́тку, зашёл то́лько на мину́тку – ду́маю, «зайду́ к тебе́, давно́ я тебя́ не вида́л» – так вот я и зашёл то́лько на одну́ мину́тку, у меня́ о́чень ма́ло вре́мени, спешу́ на вокза́л. По́езд мой отхо́дит в четы́ре часа́, я бою́сь опозда́ть на по́езд. Да, я бою́сь опозда́ть на по́езд и зашёл то́лько на мину́тку. Ведь ты сама́ никогда́ ко мне не захо́дишь.

You can also use **зае́хать, заезжа́ть** to say for instance:
They went to Rome but they will call at Florence on the way.

Они́ пое́хали в Рим, но они́ зае́дут по доро́ге во Флоре́нцию.
Из Ло́ндона по пути́ в Москву́ мы зае́дем в Варша́ву. Мы там бу́дем три дня.

Занести́, заноси́ть *to drop something in in passing*

У вас нет газе́ты? Ну, я вам занесу́ мою́ газе́ту по доро́ге на рабо́ту.
Да, я вам занесу́ газе́ту по доро́ге.

The prefix **за-** with verbs of motion can also mean *too far, in the wrong direction*, though it may not be necessary to translate these meanings into English. So you can also use these verbs to say: *where have we got to*, if you lose your way.

Куда́ мы зашли́?
Куда́ мы зае́хали?
Куда́ э́тот ма́льчик занёс на́шу газе́ту? *Where has that boy taken our paper?*
Куда́ он завёз на́ши чемода́ны? (завезти́, завози́ть *to take* by transport, and too far or to the wrong place is implied.)

Зайти́, заходи́ть also has a completely different meaning, in which much of the meaning of the preposition **за** is retained, i.e. *behind*. It is used of the sun, moon and stars setting, since they go *behind* or *beyond* the horizon.

Со́лнце захо́дит на за́паде. *The sun sets in the west.*

To rise, when referring to the sun, moon and stars, is: **взойти́, восходи́ть** or **всходи́ть** with a prefix meaning *up.* The prefix has five forms: **вос-** and **вс-** before voiceless consonants, **взо-** before two consonants, **вз-** and **воз-** otherwise.

Со́лнце взошло́, но луна́ не зашла́. *The sun has risen but the moon has not set.*

8. TRANSLATION
(Write out dates in full, for practice.)
'Do you remember in what year we visited Peter's aunt?'
'I think it was in 1959.'

'No, I think it was earlier. John had a free day. We sat about[1] at home for a couple of hours.[2] Then we went round to your place in the car on the off-chance.[3] Peter called in and . . .'

'Yes, it was on a Wednesday. You arrived at 11 o'clock and said you had come for half an hour. Then Peter came and we all went to his aunt's because it was her birthday.'

'Yes. Her birthday is on the first of April and the first of April 1959 was on Wednesday. It was half past eleven when we set off. We were two hours late and arrived at half past two.'

'His aunt thought we had had lunch,[4] so she gave us coffee. By the way, why did you ask about that trip?'

'Well, I forgot to tell her that I don't take milk with my coffee.'

1 **Посиде́ли.**
2 If the number is placed *after* the noun, it expresses an approximate quantity: so say **часа́ два.**   3 **На аво́сь.**   4 Use **пообе́дать.**

SUMMARY

1 Clock-time (§ 1).
2 **На** in expressions of time (§ 2).
3 Dates (§ 3).
4 The use of cases with numbers and nouns (§ 4).
5 The use of cases with numbers and adjectives (§ 5).
6 The prefix **за-** with verbs of motion often means 'casual diversion' (§ 7).

Lesson 32

I. THE PREFIX за- (*contd.*)

We saw in the last lesson that the prefix **за-** with verbs of motion means *too far, in the wrong direction, astray*. This is the meaning inherent in the verb **завести́, заводи́ть:**

Они́ завели́ дете́й в лес и там оста́вили их. *They led the children into the forest and left them there.*

Куда́ вы нас заво́дите? *Where are you taking us?*

implying that you are not being taken to the right place, or that you are being led on a roundabout journey.

Завести́, заводи́ть also has quite a different meaning *to wind (up)*:

– Часы́ не иду́т. На́до завести́ их. *My watch has stopped. I must wind it up.*
Э́ти часы́ на́до заводи́ть раз в неде́лю.   Ты их завёл вчера́?

– Нет, я не завел, я забы́л (*forgot*) их завести́ вчера́ ве́чером. Скажи́ мне кото́рый час и я их заведу́.

– Ты всегда́ забыва́ешь (*forget*) заводи́ть часы́. Не забу́дь (*don't forget*).

Here you have another verb formed with the prefix **за-,** the verb **забы́ть, забыва́ть** *to forget*. This is a compound of **быть** perfective, **быва́ть** imperfective.

Забыва́ть is a verb of the **ду́мать** type, so it is quite straight-forward.

Забы́ть behaves exactly like **быть,** so:

fut. pfv.	*imper.*
забу́ду	забу́дь
забу́дешь	забу́дьте
забу́дет	

The imperfective imper. **забыва́й(те)** is uncommon, even after the negative particle **не.** So *don't forget* is nearly always **не забу́дь(те).**

– Бу́дьте гото́вы в семь часо́в. Не забу́дьте! Мы так ре́дко быва́ем у тёти Ли́зы и она́ уже́ давно́ не быва́ла у нас. Мы мо́жем забы́ть, что мы е́дем к ней сего́дня ве́чером.

– Я не забу́ду. Я куплю́ ей цветы́. Ах нет, я забы́ла, она́ не лю́бит цветы́, она́ лю́бит шокола́д.

The converse of *to forget* is *to remember* **по́мнить,** which is imperfective and has perfective **вспо́мнить.** From this another imperfective has been created: **вспомина́ть** *to recall, to recollect*.

Another verb derived from **по́мнить** is **запо́мнить,** with its imperfective **запомина́ть** *to memorise, to commit to memory*.

The verb **писа́ть** also has a compound with the prefix **за-: записа́ть,** imperfective **запи́сывать** meaning *to note down.*

– Как хорошо́, что ты по́мнишь таки́е ме́лочи.

– Э́то совсе́м не ме́лочь, э́то о́чень ва́жно. Хорошо́, что я вспо́мнила. И она́ не лю́бит моло́чный шокола́д.

– Я то́же э́то по́мню. Е́сли хо́чешь, я сам ей куплю́ большу́ю коро́бку шокола́дных конфе́т.

– Ты не забу́дешь?

– Нет, я бу́ду по́мнить об э́том.

– Запиши́ её но́вый а́дрес.

– Я запо́мнил его́. Я легко́ запомина́ю и адреса́ и телефо́нные номера́.

– А я всё тако́е забыва́ю, но хорошо́ по́мню ме́лочи, как ты говори́шь.

2. THE PREFIX **за-** MEANING 'TO BEGIN'

As we have seen in the preceding section **за-** has several meanings besides the meaning *too far* when it is added to verbs of motion.

За- also has the meaning of beginning an action and this is common with verbs of *emotion.* Of course, these verbs also become perfective when the prefix **за-** is added.

Хоте́ть *to want*   **захоте́ть** *to want, to conceive a desire to*

– Ся́дьте за стол. Мы пообе́даем ра́но. Е́сли хоти́те, по́сле обе́да мы пойдём в кино́. Я ду́маю вы не захоти́те сиде́ть це́лый ве́чер с ва́шей ста́рой тётей.

This idea of starting is very evident with *to laugh, to cry, to worry, to doze, to be excited, to be ill:*

смея́ться, пла́кать, беспоко́иться, дрема́ть, волнова́ться, боле́ть.

   Все засмея́лись, когда́ кло́ун появи́лся на экра́не.

   Она́ прочла́ письмо́ и го́рько запла́кала (прочла́ past tense fem. of
      perfective of чита́ть, проче́сть *to read*).

   Пу́блика забеспоко́илась, когда́ арти́ст упа́л.

   С кни́гой в рука́х тётя задрема́ла.

   Толпа́ заволнова́лась, когда́ мини́стр вы́шел на балко́н.

   Вы не заболе́ете от мои́х блино́в.

The normal English equivalent of **засмея́лись** and **запла́кала** is *began to laugh* and *began to cry* respectively.

Беспоко́иться has a plain perfective **обеспоко́иться,** and **волнова́ться** has a plain perfective **взволнова́ться.**

All these verbs also have perfectives with the prefix **по-** meaning *for a little* or *slightly*, like the verbs *to talk a little, to sing a little, to shout a little, to keep quiet for a little time:*

             поговори́ть, попе́ть, покрича́ть, помолча́ть

If you add **за-** to:

             говори́ть, петь, крича́ть, молча́ть

232

then you create verbs meaning *to start talking, to burst into song, to start shouting, to shut up.*

Заговори́ть Вдруг все заговори́ли, ничего́ нельзя́ бы́ло поня́ть, все заговори́ли сра́зу.

Запе́ть «Ну, пой!» сказа́ли ему́ и он запе́л.

Закрича́ть Ребёнок упа́л и закрича́л.

3. DIALOGUE

говя́дина *beef*	теля́тина *veal*
свина́я котле́та *pork chop*	свини́на *pork*
бара́нья котле́та *mutton chop*	бара́нина *lamb, mutton*

Дава́йте я вам расскажу́, как я составля́ла спи́сок поку́пок в тот день, когда́ Ве́ра пришла́ к нам на обе́д. Это была́ суббо́та.[1] В суббо́ту я не хожу́ на рабо́ту. Я вста́ла ра́но, бы́стро оде́лась и начала́ ду́мать – что купи́ть – что пригото́вить на обе́д: мя́со и́ли ры́бу? По-мо́ему мя́со, не́которые лю́ди не лю́бят ры́бу. Да, но како́е мя́со, что лу́чше купи́ть – кусо́к говя́дины – бифште́кс, что ли? Я люблю́ теля́тину, но Пе́тя лю́бит говя́дину. А мо́жет быть бы́ло бы лу́чше купи́ть свины́е и́ли бара́ньи котле́ты? Не зна́ю – пойду́ в мясну́ю, поговорю́ с мяснико́м.

Мне ну́жен лук, карто́фель.[2] До́ма ничего́ нет; я куплю́ четы́ре фу́нта того́ и друго́го[3] – четы́ре фу́нта лу́ка и четы́ре фу́нта карто́феля. Нет, шесть фу́нтов карто́феля, э́то хва́тит на неде́лю. Что ещё? Пе́тя не лю́бит цветну́ю капу́сту, фасо́ли пока́ нет и горо́ха нет. Я могла́ бы пригото́вить сала́т. Не сто́ит[4] ничего́ запи́сывать, пока́ я не[5] реши́ла како́е мя́со купи́ть. На про́шлой неде́ле, в суббо́ту, в мясно́й висе́ли цыпля́та[6] и у́тки. Да, мо́жет быть я так и сде́лаю – куплю́ у́тку. Не на́до говя́дины, не на́до бара́нины, я пригото́влю у́тку с я́блоками. Пе́тя тако́й жа́дный, что мне на́до бу́дет купи́ть соси́ски – оди́н фунт соси́сок. У́тка ве́сом семь-во́семь фу́нтов. Ско́лько она́ бу́дет сто́ить? Я ду́маю о́коло восемна́дцати-девятна́дцати ши́ллингов, а мо́жет быть да́же фунт и два–три ши́ллинга. Я вы́бежала из_до́му, побежа́ла за поку́пками и забы́ла спи́сок на столе́.

1 When **э́то** is linked by the past tense of *to be* with a noun, as here, the past tense takes the gender of the noun and does *not* agree with **э́то**:

Это была́ суббо́та.	*It was a Saturday.*
Это была́ моя́ сестра́.	*That was my sister.*
Это был наш врач.	*That was our doctor.*
Это бы́ли на́ши друзья́.	*That was/Those were our friends.*
but Это бы́ло в суббо́ту.	*It was on a Saturday.*

2 **Карто́фель**, masculine, means *potato* or *potatoes.*

3 *Of one* ('that') *and the other*, i.e. *of both.*   4 **Сто́ить** means *to be worth* as well as *to cost.*

5 **Пока́... не** *until*. The element **не** in this conjunction always comes immediately before the verb which is always perfective, past or future.

6 *Chickens*; remember that nouns ending in **ёнок** have the plural ending in **я́та/а́та** (Lesson 9).

– И я пошёл за са́харом, за ри́сом, за консе́рвами, за ча́ем, за ко́фе,[7] за хле́бом и так да́лее, и так да́лее!

– Каки́м ты стал до́брым![8]

7 **Ко́фе** is indeclinable.

8 *How kind you have become.* After **стать** you must have the instrumental. The word order here, with **каки́м** at the beginning and **до́брым** at the end is normal for this kind of remark.

4. THE GENITIVE WITH A NEGATIVE

We have seen that with **нет** *there is/are not* the genitive is obligatory. The same applies to the past **не́_было** *there was/were not* and the future **не бу́дет** *there will not be.*

Here are some examples with animate nouns:

Тётя до́ма? Тёти нет до́ма, тёти до́ма не́_было, тёти до́ма не бу́дет.

Есть ли у вас секрета́рша в конто́ре? *Have you a secretary in the office?*

Нет, нет секрета́рши в конто́ре. Секрета́рши в конто́ре не́_было. Секрета́рши в конто́ре не бу́дет.

У гла́вного архите́ктора нет стенографи́стки, а в бухгалте́рии нет счетово́да.

Here are some examples with inanimate nouns:

В до́ме есть отопле́ние зимо́й. Ле́том нет отопле́ния; ле́том отопле́ния не́_было и не бу́дет.

В ва́нной ко́мнате у́тром бы́ло полоте́нце; сейча́с полоте́нца нет.

Полоте́нца не́_было у́тром и ве́чером не бу́дет.

Почему́ нет полоте́нец в ва́нной ко́мнате? У́тром там полоте́нца бы́ли, а тепе́рь полоте́нец нет.

Полоте́нец не́_было и не бу́дет.

Како́й беспоря́док! В буфе́те нет ни ло́жек, ни ви́лок, ни ноже́й – ничего́ нет. Нет таре́лки, нет салфе́тки, нет ска́терти.

Ло́жки, ви́лки, ножи́, таре́лка, салфе́тка, ска́терть бы́ли на ку́хне, а тепе́рь всё на столе́.

This rule in fact applies to *all* nouns and pronouns so it also affects nouns for abstract ideas like **ра́дость** *joy*, **любо́вь** *love* and quantitative nouns like **са́хар** *sugar*, **таба́к** *tobacco*, **чай** *tea.*

We pointed out in Lesson 15, § 3, that with a negated verb the direct object is sometimes in the genitive and sometimes in the accusative. You should read those remarks again now, bearing in mind that they represent a guide to usage, not a rigid rule.

There are one or two further points to be made. The negative genitive, i.e genitive in a negative sentence, affects only the direct object. If some verb or preposition normally requires the genitive, the dative, the instrumental or the prepositional, it makes no difference whether the statement is a positive or a negative one.

234

За са́харом remains in the instrumental whether you say:

> Я не ходи́л за са́харом. *I did not go for the sugar*
> or Я ходи́л за са́харом. *I went for the sugar.*

Тебе́ remains in the dative whether Nina says to Peter:

> Я тебе́ не ве́рю. *I don't believe you*
> or Я тебе́ ве́рю. *I believe you.*

If Peter says: *I am thinking about Vera, I am not thinking about Nina*, both Vera and Nina are in the prepositional after **о**.

> Я ду́маю о Ве́ре, я не ду́маю о Ни́не.

If the direct object is a masculine noun denoting an animate being (unless it ends in **а/я**) or a noun of any gender in the plural denoting animate beings then the case used must be the genitive (genitive-accusative), whether the verb is negated or not. This rule you already know.

> Я понима́ю бра́та. *I understand my brother.*
> Я не понима́ю бра́та. *I don't understand my brother.*
> Я жду докторо́в. *I am waiting for the doctors.*
> Я не жду докторо́в. *I am not waiting for the doctors.*
> Я слы́шу сестёр. *I hear my sisters.*
> Я не слы́шу сестёр. *I don't hear my sisters.*

With an animate noun which is feminine and singular and denotes a specific person the general tendency is to use the accusative.

> Я слы́шу домрабо́тницу. *I hear the domestic help.*
> Я не слы́шу домрабо́тницу. *I don't hear the domestic help.*
> Я понима́ю ма́му. *I understand Mummy.*
> Я не понима́ю ма́му. *I don't understand Mummy.*
> Мы не лю́бим сестру́ сосе́да.

But after the verb *to see* in the negative, the genitive is very common:

> Где тётя? Я тёти не ви́жу. Где Ве́ра? Я Ве́ры не ви́жу.

Па́па and **дя́дя** decline like feminine nouns:

> Я звал и па́пу и дя́дю. *I called both my father and uncle.*
> Я не звал ни па́пу ни дя́дю.

But after the verb *to see*:

> Я ви́жу и па́пу и дя́дю. Я не ви́жу ни па́пы, ни дя́ди.

The accusative with a negated verb tends to imply definiteness – a specific thing or person – and, in sentences such as those above, you do have a specific person in mind. Here are examples with nouns denoting things:

> Ты но́сишь свою́ ста́рую шля́пу? *Do you wear your old hat?*
> Я ста́рую шля́пу не ношу́.

In terms of Lesson 15, § 3, this would be interpreted as Я не [ношу́ ста́рую шля́пу].

If she goes on to say that she does not wear hats in summer, she uses the genitive plural, because she is no longer referring to a specific hat:

> Ле́том я шляп не ношу́, i.e.
>
> Ле́том я [не ношу́] [шляп].

In: Где твой си́ний га́лстук? *Where's your blue tie?*

> Я не зна́ю. Си́него га́лстука я давно́ не ви́дел,

he uses the genitive, because although he is referring to a particular tie – the blue tie, he does not see it.

I don't buy my ties in this shop is:

> Свои́х га́лстуков я никогда́ не покупа́ю в э́том магази́не.

Again genitive because ties in general is meant.

The distinction between the specific and the general is very evident with the quantitative nouns:

> Муку́ я не покупа́ю сего́дня. *I am not buying the flour today.*
>
> Муки́ я не покупа́ю сего́дня. *I am not buying flour today.*

Both accusative and genitive are correct, but if you use the genitive you imply *any*.

> Я не покупа́ю муки́. *I am not buying any flour.*
>
> Я не пью молока́. *I don't drink milk.*
>
> Я не пью молоко́. *I am not drinking the milk.*
>
> Я не ем ры́бы. *I don't eat fish.*
>
> Я не съел ры́бу. *I did not eat the fish.*

The accusative is somewhat less common with negative verbs when the direct object is a feminine noun ending in **ь,** and, as you know, many feminine nouns ending in **ь** are abstract nouns.

> Ты слы́шала но́вость? (*sing.*) *Have you heard the news?*
>
> Я но́вости не слы́шала (*gen. sing.*).
>
> Ты слы́шала но́вости? (*pl.*) *Have you heard the news?*
>
> Никаки́х новосте́й я не слы́шала. *I haven't heard any news.*
>
>   (see § 5 below)
>
> Новосте́й нет.   Новосте́й я не слы́шала.

Again, however, when a definite piece of news is meant the accusative tends to predominate:

> Э́ту но́вость я не слы́шала. *I haven't heard this piece of news.*

5. INTENSIVE NEGATION

In Lesson 8, § 3, you were given the expression **ни оди́н** *not a single.* Another common word expressing such 'intensive negation' is **никако́й, никака́я, никако́е, никаки́е,** *none, not any.*

236

In negative sentences with such intensive negative words you nearly always find the genitive. The accusative is very rare.

Они́ не беру́т ни одно́й кни́ги. *They are not taking a single book.*
Он не понима́ет ни одного́ сло́ва. *He doesn't understand a single word.*
Я не могу́ запо́мнить ни одно́й ци́фры. *I can't remember a single number.*
Я не пью никаки́х напи́тков. *I don't drink anything* (напи́ток *a drink*).
Никако́й му́зыки я не слы́шу. *I don't hear any music.*
Не гото́вьте обе́д – обе́да нам не на́до. *Don't prepare dinner; we don't need any dinner.* Никако́го обе́да нам не на́до.

In this last example the genitive depends on **не на́до,** which cannot be followed by the accusative.

6. EXERCISE

a Write out the following passage, making all the positive sentences negative and all the negative sentences positive:

Я не купи́ла мя́са – ни говя́дины, ни теля́тины, ни свины́х, ни бара́ньих котле́т. Нет, я не купи́ла ни свини́ны, ни бара́нины. Я купи́ла у́тку.
У нас не́_было ни лу́ка, ни карто́феля. У нас ничего́ не́_было до́ма.
Я сде́лала дли́нный спи́сок того́, что мне на́до бы́ло купи́ть. Но спи́сок я не взяла́ с собо́й. Спи́сок я оста́вила на столе́. Я ходи́ла за поку́пками без спи́ска. Спи́ска с собо́й не́_было.

b Make all the negative sentences (except **У нас ничего́ не́_было до́ма**) intensive negatives by inserting in the appropriate case and gender **никако́й** or **ни оди́н,** whichever is suitable.

SUMMARY

1 The prefix **за-** with verbs has other meanings besides *too far* and one of these meanings is *to begin to* (§§ 1 and 2).
2 The past tense of **быть** agrees with the noun and not with **э́то** in such sentences as **э́то была́ суббо́та** (§ 3, note 1).
3 After **пока́...не** *until* the perfective is obligatory (§ 3, note 5).
4 With negated verbs the direct object is in the genitive or the accusative (§ 4).
5 With intensive negatives the direct object is almost always in the genitive (§ 5).

LESSON 33 REVISION

Lesson 34

I. VERBS OF MOTION WITH THE PREFIX **раз-**

The prefix **раз-**, which does not occur as a preposition, means *asunder*, i.e. it means dispersion, division, opening and bursting out, in contrast to gathering, closing up. Before voiceless consonants it is spelt **рас-**, before **-йти** it is spelt **разо-** and also before some roots beginning with two or more consonants.

To carry to different places, to distribute, to deliver: **разнести, разносить** газеты, листки (*leaflets*), выборную литературу (*election literature*)

Что этот человек там разносит? Газеты он разносит, что ли? Нет, не газеты, газеты у нас разносят рано утром, он разносит какие-то листки, ах да, у нас ведь скоро выборы, вот он и разносит пропагандные листки своей партии.

Рано утром много шума – разносят газеты,	*Early in the morning there is a noise – the papers are delivered* ('they distribute the papers'),
молочник развозит молоко, он разъезжает на своей странной маленькой машине, и потом разносит бутылки по домам.	*the milkman brings* ('carts around') *the milk, he rides around in his funny little car and then delivers the milk to the houses* (NB **по** + dative, in the sense of 'to each in turn').
Каждый раз, когда он проезжает, он разгоняет стаю воробьёв перед домом, – они разлетаются во все стороны.	*Every time he passes, he scatters a flock of sparrows in front of the house – they fly away in all directions.*

The intransitive verbs of motion, which describe the actual movement of persons or animals, are reflexive when prefixed with **раз-**. (The exception is **разъезжать,** which furthermore has no perfective.)
Hence **разлететься, разлетаться** *to fly away, apart.*

Воробьи разлетаются, когда проезжает машина, а мои бумаги тоже разлетаются, когда ты открываешь окно. Вот теперь на улице все птицы разлетелись, а на моём столе все мои бумаги разлетелись.

To run in different directions: **разбежаться, разбегаться**
Note that the *imperfective* compounds of **бегать** are stressed on the **a**.

Шко́льники о́чень боя́лись своего́ дире́ктора (*headmaster*) – ка́ждый раз, когда́ он приходи́л на двор, где ученики́ игра́ли, они́ разбега́лись по ра́зным сторона́м. Так и вчера́ – дире́ктор вы́шел на двор, где они́ ссо́рились и крича́ли и при ви́де его́ все разбежа́лись.

To part (after a gathering), *to go in various directions, to go one's* (*various*) *ways*: **разойти́сь, расходи́ться** (*on foot*), **разъе́хаться, разъезжа́ться** (*not on foot*)

Вот и ко́нчилась на́ша вечери́нка, бы́ло о́чень ве́село, но тепе́рь нам на́до расходи́ться по дома́м (*go home*), мы все разойдёмся тепе́рь, мы все разъе́демся, неизве́стно, когда́ мы опя́ть уви́димся... И вот мы все разошли́сь, разъе́хались по дома́м, кто куда́, а когда́ мы опя́ть сойдёмся, съе́демся, – неизве́стно. *...And now we have all separated, gone home, each in a different direction* (NB this idiom), *and when we shall again meet, come together, is unknown.*

2. VERBS OF MOTION WITH THE PREFIX c-

The last sentence above showed two examples of verbs of motion with the prefix **c-** meaning *together*, which thus corresponds to the preposition **c** + instrumental, meaning (*together*) *with*.

Notice that these verbs are also reflexive:

сойти́сь, сходи́ться со всех сторо́н *to meet, to come together from all sides*
съе́хаться, съезжа́ться со всех стран *to come together from all countries*
сбежа́ться, сбега́ться со всех концо́в *to run together from all parts, sides* (lit. 'ends').
слете́ться, слета́ться со всех сторо́н *to fly together from all sides*

Мы все сошли́сь опя́ть в пя́тницу, мы съе́хались и́менно в э́том предме́стье, так как э́то бы́ло удо́бнее всего́ для большинства́ из нас. *We all got together again on Friday; we met (precisely) in this suburb because it was most convenient for the majority of us.*

В го́роде бы́ло беспоко́йно, наро́д сбежа́лся на гла́вной пло́щади и до́лго стоя́л пе́ред дворцо́м президе́нта. *There was anxiety in the town* (lit. 'it was restless'); *a crowd had collected* ('run together') *on the main square and stood for a long time in front of the president's palace.*

Когда́ я вы́шла в сад и ста́ла разбра́сывать кро́шки хле́ба, пти́цы ста́ли слета́ться со всех сторо́н – они́ все слете́лись у нас в саду́. *When I went out into the garden and begun to scatter crumbs of bread, the birds began to fly up from all sides; they all met in our garden.*

To drive apart and *to drive together* are transitive verbs and therefore not reflexive:

разогна́ть; разгоню́, разго́нишь *to drive away, apart* **разгоня́ть**

239

гнать (and compounds) conjugates **гоню́, го́нишь** (Part II, Grammar)
согна́ть; сгоню́, сго́нишь *to drive together, to herd* **сгоня́ть**

Что вы де́лаете, что вы? сперва́ согна́ли всё ста́до (*herd*), а тепе́рь опя́ть разгоня́ете коро́в (*cows*). Отчего́? Почему́?

Мы согна́ли коро́в сюда́ на двор (*yard*) чтобы их пересчита́ть (*to count over*), а тепе́рь мы их разгоня́ем, нам на́до счита́ть (*to count*) бара́нов (*rams*), вот мы их всех сюда́ сго́ним и посчита́ем, а пото́м опя́ть разго́ним. И так вот они́ свой скот, коро́в, бара́нов, свине́й сгоня́ли, счита́ли и опя́ть разгоня́ли.

3. OTHER VERBS WITH THE PREFIXES раз- AND с-

To press is **жать,** with **м** in the conjugations:

жму, жмёшь, жмёт, жмём, жмёте, жмут

Сапоги́ мне жмут, ту́фли жмут тут, они́ таки́е у́зкие. *My (heavy) shoes pinch, my (light) shoes pinch here; they are so tight* (lit. 'narrow').

Here **мне** expresses to whom the shoes are causing discomfort, the word **но́гу** (*foot*) or **па́лец** (*toe*) being understood.

сжать *to press together, tighten*	сжима́ть
я сожму́	сжима́ю
ты сожмёшь	сжима́ешь
они́ сожму́т	сжима́ют
разжа́ть *to release pressure, to relax the grip*	разжима́ть
я разожму́	разжима́ю
ты разожмёшь	разжима́ешь
они́ разожму́т	разжима́ют

У меня́ всё па́льцы боля́т. Не могу́ ни сжать, ни разжа́ть. Вот когда́ я па́лец так разжима́ю, то у меня́ все му́скулы боля́т. Вот я их сжима́ю и разжима́ю – и мне бо́льно, так сожму́ – не бо́льно, а разожму́, и опя́ть му́скулы боля́т.

связа́ть *to tie together*	свя́зывать

Вот все э́ти паке́ты на́до связа́ть вме́сте, э́то са́мое лу́чшее (*it's the very best thing*) все паке́ты связа́ть вме́сте.

развяза́ть *to untie, to undo*	развя́зывать
развяза́ть у́зел (*knot*), развя́зывать паке́ты	

Не на́до свя́зывать паке́ты – пото́м не развяза́ть, потому́ что бу́дет о́чень тру́дно развяза́ть верёвку. Твои́ узлы́ я зна́ю, их никогда́ не развяза́ть. *Don't tie the parcels together – it will be impossible to untie them afterwards* (lit. 'then not to untie') *because it will be very difficult to undo the string. I know your knots; one can never undo them.*

When you tie several things together, you use **связа́ть,** but although **развяза́ть** means to untie or undo a bundle of parcels or a knot, you use a different prefix to denote tying a *knot*: **завяза́ть, завя́зывать.**

Ты всегда́ так кре́пко завя́зываешь узлы́, что мне их ника́к не развяза́ть. Не завя́зывай так кре́пко, пожа́луйста, завяжи́ осторо́жно, тогда́ мне не так тру́дно бу́дет развя́зывать верёвку.

You can also use **завяза́ть** in a figurative sense **завяза́ть спор** *to start an argument;* while **связа́ть** has a wide variety of uses in the sense of 'to connect' etc.

На́до связа́ть э́то с тео́рией. *You must connect that (up) with the theory.*
Она́ связа́ла себя́ обеща́нием. *She bound herself with a promise.*
Он связа́лся с контрабанди́стами. *He got mixed up with some smugglers.*

> собра́ть *to gather, to collect*   собира́ть

Remember that **брать** and its compounds conjugates **беру́, берёшь.**

– Мы собира́ем почто́вые ма́рки (*postage stamps*).
– А я ничего́ не собира́ю, ни ма́рок, ни номеро́в локомоти́вов, ни ста́рых моне́т (*coins*), ни спи́чечных коро́бок (*match-boxes*). Я то́лько собира́ю грибы́ (*mushrooms*) в лесу́, грибы́ я собира́ю, а бо́льше ничего́. За́втра у́тром я бу́ду собира́ть грибы́, соберу́ мно́го и дам вам. И́ли хоти́те – соберём вме́сте?

> разобра́ть *to sort out, to disentangle, to decipher*   разбира́ть

– В э́том письме́ я ничего́ разобра́ть не могу́, ничего́ не понима́ю. Я с трудо́м разбира́ю э́тот ужа́сный по́черк, но смысл письма́ я разобра́ть не могу́.
– Да́йте мне – я ско́ро разберу́.

The verb **разосла́ть, рассыла́ть** *to send out, to send in different directions, to distribute, to deliver* has no counterpart that means 'to send together'.

Слать (and its compounds) conjugates **шлю, шлёшь.**

– На́до разосла́ть все э́ти пи́сьма по ра́зным адреса́м, разошли́ их, пожа́луйста, не забу́дь разосла́ть.
– Хорошо́, я их разошлю́ за́втра у́тром.

The verb **разброса́ть, разбра́сывать** *to throw about, to scatter* has a counterpart **сбро́сить, сбра́сывать** *to pile up, to throw together* but the latter verb usually means *to throw down,* the prefix **с-** then having its other meaning of *off* or *down.*

– Кака́я ты неаккура́тная, ты все мои́ бума́ги разброса́ла.
– Ты сам неаккура́тный, ты сам всё разбра́сываешь, всё разброса́л, и сапоги́, и кни́ги, и носки́ (*socks*), всё ты разброса́л по ко́мнате.

– Нет, э́то ты неаккура́тная. Ты всегда́ сбра́сываешь свои́ ве́щи в ку́чу (*into a heap*).

разложи́ть *to lay out* (*tidily*)   раскла́дывать
сложи́ть *to fold up, to pack*   скла́дывать

These are compounds of a verb meaning *to put* (in a lying position). As you see, the perfective and imperfective are formed from different roots. Verbs of putting will be dealt with in more detail in the next chapter.

На́до свои́ ве́щи аккура́тно раскла́дывать, отчего́ ты не мо́жешь аккура́тно и опря́тно (*neatly*) разложи́ть свои́ ве́щи? Тогда́ и мно́го ле́гче скла́дывать, мо́жно всё в две мину́ты сложи́ть, а так я вот скла́дываю полчаса́ все твои́ ве́щи, потому́ что ты лентя́й (*lazy person*) и всё то́лько разбра́сываешь, а не раскла́дываешь аккура́тно.

To cut is **ре́зать: ре́жу, ре́жешь.** It has the peculiarity that its imperfective compounds are formed either with **-ре́зывать** or **-реза́ть** (NB stress difference), conjugated **-реза́ю, -реза́ешь.**

разре́зать *to cut up*   разре́зывать/разреза́ть

Я разреза́ю бума́гу но́жницами (*with scissors*), что́бы разре́зать э́ту то́лстую бума́гу нужны́ о́стрые но́жницы.

руби́ть *to hack, to chop*   рублю́, ру́бишь
разруби́ть *to chop up*   разруба́ть

Я рублю́ дрова́. *I am chopping firewood.*
Ты ру́бишь дрова́. *You are chopping firewood.*
Лес ру́бят, ще́пки летя́т. *When they chop wood, the chips fly;* a proverb, equivalent to *You can't make an omelette without breaking eggs.*
Я разрублю́ э́то поле́но (*piece of wood*), а ты разруби́ то бревно́ (*log*).
Не люблю́ руби́ть брёвна, их о́чень тру́дно разруби́ть.

In the verbs **сре́зать, сре́зывать** or **среза́ть** and **сруби́ть, сруба́ть** the prefix **с-** has the meaning *off, down:*

сре́зать цвето́к *to cut* (*off*) *a flower*
сруби́ть де́рево *to chop down a tree*
сруби́ть ветвь *to chop off a branch*

раскры́ть *to open up, to uncover*   раскрыва́ть

Remember that **крыть** (and its compounds) conjugates **кро́ю, кро́ешь.**

разры́ть *to dig up, to unearth*   разрыва́ть

Remember that **рыть** (and its compounds) conjugates **ро́ю, ро́ешь.**

раскопа́ть *to dig out, to excavate*   раска́пывать

The converse of these verbs is formed with the prefix **за-: закры́ть** *to close, to cover,* **зары́ть** and **закопа́ть** *to bury, to dig in, to fill up.*

Раскро́й газе́ту и посмотри́, что там написа́ли об э́том.
Закро́йте кни́гу и смотри́те на меня́.

242

– Э́ту я́му (*hole, pit*) давно́ пора́ зары́ть, разры́ли вы тут большо́й кусо́к земли́ – и для чего́? Пора́ зары́ть э́ту я́му, тут мо́жно упа́сть в темноте́.

– Мы тут в своё вре́мя закопа́ли больши́е ка́мни, и они́ нам нужны́ для са́да, вот мы их и раскопа́ли. Настоя́щие раско́пки (*excavations*).

With certain verbs of emotion which are reflexive, the prefix **раз-** means a sudden bursting out, giving full vent to the emotion, not just beginning it, as is indicated by the prefix **за-**. One could, for instance, translate **распла́каться** and **рассмея́ться** as *to dissolve into tears, to dissolve into laughter.*

Пришла́ телегра́мма – тётка-миллионе́рша не е́дет к нам, на́чался крик – все раскрича́лись, распла́кались – а пото́м все рассмея́лись, ведь её прие́зда хоть и жда́ли и жела́ли, всё же её о́чень боя́лись. Попла́кали, покрича́ли, а пото́м рассмея́лись.

A telegram arrived: our aunt, who is a millionairess, was not coming to us. There was shouting (lit. 'shouting began'), *everybody burst out shouting, dissolved into tears; and then we all burst out laughing. You see, though we were waiting and longing for her visit, still we were very afraid of her. (So) we had a bit of a cry and shouted a bit and then we all had a good laugh.*

Sometimes with certain emotions **раз-** implies 'annihilation', i.e. that something has ceased to be. For instance, *to fall in love* is **влюби́ться, влюбля́ться в** + accusative, and *to love* is **люби́ть**. But *to stop loving, to fall out of love with* is **разлюби́ть.**

Ра́ньше я люби́л есть в рестора́нах, но тепе́рь я разлюби́л обе́дать в рестора́нах.

Ра́ньше мы все люби́ли телеви́зор, но тепе́рь разлюби́ли.

Она́ влюби́лась в меня́, до́лго люби́ла меня́, пото́м вдруг разлюби́ла меня́ – она́ узна́ла, что у меня́ в ба́нке ма́ло де́нег.

научи́ться/вы́учиться *to learn* учи́ться

разучи́ться *to forget (what one has learnt)* разу́чиваться.

Давны́м давно́ я научи́лся говори́ть по-италья́нски, но тепе́рь я совсе́м разучи́лся, ничего́ не понима́ю. Так как у меня́ нет пра́ктики, то я разучи́лся.

Вы научи́лись понима́ть и немно́го говори́ть по-ру́сски, смотри́те, практику́йте (*see that you practise*) ва́ши зна́ния и не разу́чивайтесь, не разу́чивайтесь понима́ть и чита́ть и да́же говори́ть по-ру́сски.

4. TEXT

Read the following continuous passage for comprehension. The necessary vocabulary is at the end of the book. Difficult phrases and new grammatical forms are annotated and there is a translation in the Key to the Exercises and Texts.

Scenes from Russian Life

Весе́нняя охо́та на глухаря́[1]

В густо́м и тёмном ура́льском лесу́ охо́тник де́лает каки́е-то стра́нные и непоня́тные движе́ния. Он бы́стро шага́ет два ра́за, остана́вливается и соверше́нно замира́ет. Одна́ нога́ его́ в глубо́ком снегу́, а друга́я е́ле каса́ется[2] сне́жного покро́ва. Так он стои́т не́которое вре́мя. Зате́м опя́ть сле́дуют два скачка́ и сно́ва замира́ние, иногда́ на[3] продолжи́тельное вре́мя. Э́то он охо́тится на глухаря́. Но почему́ охо́тник как-то необы́чно приближа́ется к э́той кру́пной пти́це?

1 Note the construction: **на** + accusative English *for*.
2 Takes genitive case.   3 See Lesson 31, § 2.

Глуха́рь, хотя́ и на́званный[1] от сло́ва «глухо́й», в са́мом де́ле о́чень чу́ткая пти́ца. Он прекра́сно слы́шит. Весно́й же, когда́ он поёт, в э́ти коро́ткие мгнове́ния он действи́тельно не слы́шит. Он проха́живается по ве́рхним сучка́м большо́й е́ли, току́ет – подзыва́ет са́мку – сле́дующим о́бразом.[2]

1 *Called, named.*
2 Idiomatic use of instrumental, cf. **таки́м о́бразом** *thus, in this way*, **каки́м о́бразом** *how, in what way.*

Внача́ле раздаю́тся зву́ки, похо́жие не треск сухи́х па́лочек: тэкэ... тэкэ... Охо́тник не дви́жется,[1] замира́ет, ждёт... Пото́м слы́шится бормота́нье: бур-бур-бур... не бо́льше одно́й секу́нды. Вот в э́то-то вре́мя стрело́к мгнове́нно де́лает два шага́ – бо́льше не успе́ть[2] – и застыва́ет в том положе́нии, в како́м его́ застаёт[3] э́тот сигна́л, т.е. прекраще́ние бормота́ния.

1 **Дви́гаться,** *to move* conjugates **дви́жусь, дви́жешься** and also **дви́гаюсь, дви́гаешься.**   2 *There's no time for (any more),* lit. 'more not to manage'.
3 **Застава́ть** *to catch* (unawares) is a compound of **става́ть,** hence **застаю́, застаёшь.**

Глуха́рь замолка́ет, замира́ет и охо́тник. Иногда́ пти́ца молчи́т мину́т де́сять[1] и бо́лее. Она́ чу́тко и внима́тельно прислу́шивается к тому́, что де́лается в лесно́й тишине́. Но вот он сно́ва току́ет. Опя́ть начина́ются коро́ткие прыжки́ охо́тника. До де́рева, на кото́ром он сиди́т, остаётся не бо́лее пяти́десяти ме́тров. Мо́жно уже́ стреля́ть.

1 The number after the noun indicates approximate quantity. See Lesson 31, § 8, note 2.

Но вот беда[1]: рассвёт тóлько начинáется и в лесно́й темноте́ не ви́дно, где, на какóм сучкé большóй éли сиди́т глухáрь. Ещё нéсколько скачкóв. Тепéрь ви́дно, что концы́ вéток одногó вéрхнего сукá тёмной éли качáются. Но крýпная пти́ца прохáживается бли́же к стволý дéрева и её не ви́дно. Стреля́ть наугáд рискóванно – мóжно промахнýться и потеря́ть такýю огрóмную дичь – гóрдость молодóго охóтника.

А охóтник молодóй и неóпытный. Он пры́гает, но не успевáет сдéлать вторóй шаг. Ногá повисáет в вóздухе. Постáвить её на снег нельзя́. Веснóй вéрхний слой егó обы́чно обледенéлый. Э́то – наст. Под лучáми сóлнца он тáет днём, а нóчью замерзáет. В лесý он óчень хрýпкий. Малéйшее прикосновéние к[2] немý производит шум и треск. Как стеклó.

1 *But here's a stroke of bad luck*, lit. 'But here is a misfortune'.
2 Note that, while the verb **касáться, коснýться** *to touch* takes the genitive, the verb **прикасáться, прикоснýться** *to touch* and the related noun **прикосновéние** *touching, a touch* take **к** + dative.

Но дóлго баланси́ровать на однóй ногé, котóрая утонýла в снегý, трýдно. Егó немнóго наклоня́ет в стóрону.[1] Чтóбы не упáсть, он слегкá касáется пáльцами обледенéвшего[2] покрóва. Раздаётся слáбый треск... И все пропáло. Какáя жáлость! Глухáрь бы́стро взлетáет и скрывáется за дерéвьями. Слы́шен тóлько шум егó кры́льев.[3]

1 Impersonal use of the verb: 'it tilts him slightly to the side,' i.e. *he begins to overbalance.*
2 *Frozen.*   3 **Крылó** *wing* is one of the neuter nouns with plural in **ья.**

Расстрóенный[1] охóтник выхóдит на леснýю поля́нку, сади́тся на бревнó и решáет закури́ть и послýшать, где поёт другóй глухáрь. На другóй сторонé поля́нки раздаётся лёгкий хруст снéга. Выбегáет зáяц. Вдруг чтó-то большóе, сéрое с горя́щими в темнотé глазáми[2] бросáется свéрху, с дéрева на зáйца. Тот дéлает рéзкий скачóк в стóрону. Зверь приготовля́ется к[3] нóвому прыжкý. Вы́стрел. Некрýпная дробь, пригóдная для глухаря́, тóлько рáнит звéря. Он хромáет и пытáется убежáть. Стрелóк спéшно заряжáет ружьё картéчью. Вторóй вы́стрел, и рысь, похóжая на ди́кую кóшку, а размéром с крýпную собáку[4], растянýлась на снегý. Э́то óчень опáсный зверь, он бросáется с дéрева не тóлько на живóтных, но и на человéка.

Для молодóго охóтника э́то большáя удáча. Шкýра ры́си лежи́т тепéрь в кóмнате в ви́де коврá и напоминáет о пéрвой охóте на глухаря́.

А. Ефи́мов

1 *Upset, put out, put off.*
2 *With eyes burning/blazing in the dark.* It is not uncommon in literary Russian to put a lengthy description in front of the noun to which it refers.
3 NB **к** + dative, *makes ready for.*
4 Notice the use of the instrumental to express *size*, followed by **с** + accusative, expressing the actual measurement, in this case a comparison with *a large dog.* **С** + accusative can also occur on its own as an adverbial phrase:
Мы прошли́ с полчасá. *We walked for half an hour.*

5. TRANSLATION

Early in the morning the milkman delivers the milk in his van.[1] The birds scatter when he passes. Then the postman delivers the letters and a boy delivers the newspapers. The children in our street meet[2] on the corner and then go to school.

You say that you studied Russian ten years ago and have quite forgotten (it). Well, you have to keep on learning a foreign language, otherwise you forget (it) quickly. So close that paper and open (your) book.

My wife went shopping. She tied all (her) parcels together with string. When she came home she burst into tears because it took her such a long time to undo[3] the bundle. We had to cut the string with scissors.

John collects engine-numbers. He notes them down in an exercise-book but his handwriting is so bad that nobody can decipher them.

The tourists unpacked their things and at once went off to various parts of the town[4] to look at the sights.

1 **Маши́на.**   2 **Сходи́ться.**
3 Say 'for a long time she could not undo'.   4 Say 'went various ways through (**по**) the town.'

SUMMARY

1 Verbs with the prefixes **раз-** and **с-** (§§ 1, 2, 3).
2 Conjugation of **слать** (§ 3).
3 Conjugation of **дви́гаться** (§ 4, para. 3, note 1).
4 Expression of size and dimensions (§ 4, final para., note 4).

Lesson 35

I. VERBS OF LYING AND PUTTING IN A LYING POSITION

You have already met various verbs denoting the actions of lying, sitting and standing. This lesson amplifies and revises what you have learnt about these verbs. We take first the verbs of lying.

pfv.	**лечь** *to lie down*	*impfv.*	**ложи́ться**
fut.	ля́гу NB change of vowel.	*pres.*	ложу́сь
	ля́жешь		ложи́шься
	ля́жет		ложи́тся
	ля́жем		ложи́мся
	ля́жете		ложи́тесь
	ля́гут		ложа́тся
past	лёг, легла́, легло́, легли́		ложи́лся, ложи́лась
imper.	ляг, ля́гте		ложи́сь, ложи́тесь

Что ты тепе́рь бу́дешь де́лать?

Я ля́гу на полчаса́, да, на полчаса́ я ля́гу. По́сле тако́го сы́тного (*full, satisfying*) обе́да на́до лечь, хоть (*if only*) на полчаса́.

Когда́ ва́ши де́ти ложа́тся спать?

Обыкнове́нно они́ ложа́тся в полови́не девя́того. Но по суббо́там я им позволя́ю ложи́ться попо́зже (*a little later*). По суббо́там они́ ложа́тся в де́вять и́ли да́же в полови́не деся́того.

Когда́ мы бы́ли детьми́, нам не позволя́ли ложи́ться поздне́е девяти́, мы всегда́ ложи́лись до девяти́.

лежа́ть *to lie, to be lying* (second conjugation): лежу́, лежи́шь, лежи́т
pfv. **полежа́ть** *to lie for a while*

Он лёг на полчаса́ и всё лежи́т.

Кни́га лежа́ла на полу́.

Отчего́ на полу́? Кни́га должна́ лежа́ть на столе́, а не на полу́, но в э́том до́ме всё всегда́ лежи́т на полу́.

Ты до́лго бу́дешь лежа́ть? – У меня́ голова́ боли́т, я ещё полежу́.

When you put something somewhere you may put it in a lying, standing or sitting position. Russian always distinguishes between these three ways of putting things and has therefore three verbs for *to put*.

pfv. **положи́ть** *to put* (in a lying position), *to lay*
The imperfective **класть** is a verb from an entirely different root and conjugates:

кладу́, кладёшь, кладёт, кладём, кладёте, кладу́т

past клал, кла́ла, кла́ло, кла́ли   *imper.* клади́, клади́те

247

Я всегда кладу газету под ноги, когда я ложусь на диван в туфлях, так и ты положи газету вот сюда у ног. Да не эту газету – что же (*why*) ты сегодняшнюю газету кладёшь, ты положи вчерашнюю газету, вот она – среда, восьмого мая.

The compounds of the verb *to put* (*lying*) are formed from **-ложить** (*pfv.*) and **-кладывать** (*impfv.*).

<blockquote>сложить to fold up, to pack   складывать</blockquote>

Ваня очень быстро складывает свои вещи, таким образом он скоро сложит всё в чемодан.

<blockquote>разложить to put out, to place   раскладывать</blockquote>

Что ты раскладываешь свои игрушки на полу под ногами? Гости приходят, а ты разложил свой поезд под столом.

<blockquote>отложить to put off, to postpone   откладывать</blockquote>

Саша всегда откладывает всё до последней минуты. Он и сегодня отложил упаковку (*packing*) до последней минуты, вот почему он опоздал на поезд.

2. VERBS OF SITTING AND PUTTING IN A SITTING POSITION

pfv.	**сесть** *to sit down*	*impfv.*	**садиться**
fut.	сяду NB vowel change.	*pres.*	сажусь
	сядешь		садишься
	сядет		садится
	сядем		садимся
	сядете		садитесь
	сядут		садятся
past	сел, села, село, сели		садился
imper.	сядь, сядьте		садись, садитесь

сидеть *to sit, to be in a sitting position* (second conjugation), сижу, сидишь
pfv. **посидеть** *to sit for a while*

– А, здравствуйте! Входите, садитесь!
– Нет, спасибо, я на минутку только (*I've only come for a moment*), не буду сидеть.
– Ну, пожалуйста, посидите хоть минут пять. Что с вами? (*What is the matter with you?*)
– Я, кажется, сел на что-то.
– Ах, да. Это пружина торчит (*It's a spring sticking up*). Сядьте на диван. Удобнее сидеть на диване чем в этом кресле.
– Хорошо, я туда и сяду.
– Осторожно, не садитесь на иголку. *Careful! Don't sit on the needle.*

посади́ть *to put* (in a sitting position) **сажа́ть**

Посади́ ребёнка на высо́кий стул. Не сажа́й его́ сюда́, тут сли́шком ни́зко для него́. И положи́ э́тот большо́й а́тлас на стул, тогда́ ему́ бу́дет доста́точно высоко́, что́бы удо́бно сиде́ть.

The same verb also means *to plant*.

Вот на́ши цвето́чные горшки́ (цвето́чный горшо́к *flowerpot*).

В э́тих горшка́х мы всегда́ сажа́ем ка́ктусы. В э́том году́ я посади́ла три но́вых ка́ктуса, а о́сенью я посажу́ ещё пять ма́леньких ка́ктусов.

Compounds of this verb are formed in **-сади́ть** perfective, **-са́живать** imperfective.

Когда́ ка́ктусы подрасту́т (*grow bigger*), я их пересажу́ в горшо́к побо́льше. На́до переса́живать их, что́бы они́ лу́чше росли́ (*so that they will grow better*).

The reflexive verb **переса́живаться** means *to change* (trains, seats) and its perfective is **пересе́сть.**

– Вам на́до переса́живаться.

– Как? Я уже́ раз пересе́ла. Мне сказа́ли, что э́тот по́езд без переса́дки (*that this is a through train*, lit. 'without change' **переса́дка** fem.).

– Прости́те, вы пересе́ли не в тот по́езд. *You changed to the wrong train.*

В Ленингра́д по́езд без переса́дки че́рез пять мину́т.

3. VERBS OF STANDING AND PUTTING IN A STANDING POSITION

pfv.	**стать** *to stand, to take up a*	*impfv.*	**станови́ться**
fut.	ста́ну *standing position;*	*pres.*	становлю́сь
	ста́нешь *to become*		стано́вишься
	ста́нет		стано́вится
	ста́нем		стано́вимся
	ста́нете		стано́витесь
	ста́нут		стано́вятся
past	стал, ста́ла, ста́ло, ста́ли		станови́лся
imper.	стань, ста́ньте		станови́сь, станови́тесь

Я ста́ну здесь, а ты ста́нешь там, ита́к мы ста́нем о́ба, ка́ждый на своём ме́сте. Ты ста́нешь о́коло кали́тки (*gate*), а я ста́ну у подъе́зда, и таки́м о́бразом мы бу́дем ждать почтальо́на (*postman*).

Да заче́м же ты стано́вишься пря́мо посереди́не доро́ги? Так никому́ не пройти́, ты ведь так други́м пройти́ не даёшь (*let*), е́сли ты тут стано́вишься. Ты лу́чше стань сюда́, напра́во, вот так, там ты мо́жешь стоя́ть и никому́ не меша́ешь.

Гра́ждане, станови́тесь в о́чередь (*stand in line*)! Вы, гражда́нка, почему́ сто́йте вне (*out of*) о́череди? Ста́ньте вме́сте с други́ми и сто́йте там, ско́ро о́чередь дойдёт и до вас (*it will soon be your turn*).

И вот я ста́ла вме́сте с други́ми, стою́, жду, все мы ждём. Те, кто по́сле меня́ приходи́ли, станови́лись за мной в о́череди, и ме́дленно, ме́дленно де́ло ста́ло дви́гаться (*things began to move*).

When **кто** is a relative pronoun, referring to a plural noun or pronoun, as in the sentence above (. . . *those who* . . .), it can have a singular *or* a plural verb, i.e. either **те, кто... приходи́ли** or **те, кто приходи́л.** The last sentence also illustrates another meaning of **стать** – *to begin.*

Станови́ться cannot have this meaning. **Стать** meaning *to begin* is then followed by an imperfective verb to express what someone will begin to do. Sometimes this is scarcely distinguishable from the imperfective future.

– Я ста́ну учи́ться (*to learn*) испа́нскому языку́.
– А я ста́ну изуча́ть (*to study*) кита́йский язы́к.
– Ста́нешь изуча́ть, а пото́м бро́сишь (*you'll give up, 'chuck' it*). Я тебя́ зна́ю, – ты уже́ не раз изуча́л иностра́нный язы́к – начина́л, а пото́м броса́л. «Я ста́ну изуча́ть» – ничего́ ты не бу́дешь изуча́ть.

The last sentence gives you the difference between **я ста́ну изуча́ть** *I'll start studying/to study* and the future imperfective **я бу́ду, ты бу́дешь изуча́ть.** *I shall be studying, you will be studying.*

Notice further the difference in meaning of

учи́ть *to teach*
учи́ться *to learn, to be learning*
изуча́ть *to study, to be studying*

although **учи́ться** can also be translated *to study* when it does not have an object.

стоя́ть *to stand, to be standing* (second conjugation): стою́, стои́шь, стои́т
imper. стой, сто́йте
pfv. **постоя́ть** *to stand for a while, imper.* посто́й, посто́йте

И вот я стоя́ла в о́череди бо́лее получа́са, а как дошла́ о́чередь до меня́, то оказа́лось (*it turned out*), что я стоя́ла не в том хвосте́ (*in the wrong queue*). Я хоте́ла купи́ть продово́льственные проду́кты (*groceries*), а стоя́ла в о́череди за фотографи́ческими аппара́тами и про́чим. Напра́сно я ста́ла в э́ту о́чередь, напра́сно стоя́ла и ждала́. Пришло́сь (*I had to*) стать в другу́ю о́чередь и за́ново стоя́ть и ждать!

Пришло́сь is an impersonal verb meaning *have to.* If the logical subject is expressed it goes into the dative case:

мне пришло́сь *I had to*

The past imperfective is **приходи́лось,** the present **прихо́дится,** the future **придётся** and the conditional **пришло́сь бы** and **приходи́лось бы.**

The imperative **стой**(**те**) is often used in the sense of *stop!* The perfective imperative **постой**(**те**) has the same meaning but is less abrupt, and you can also use it to mean *just a moment* as in:

Постойте, вы же не по́няли меня́. *Just a moment, you haven't understood me.*

Стать can also mean *to stop* in the sense of *to stop moving*. But the imperative is not used in that sense.

Маши́на ста́ла. *The car stopped.*

Compounds of **стать**

      переста́ть *to stop doing something, to cease*   переставать

Он учи́лся ру́сскому языку́, пото́м бро́сил, переста́л ходи́ть на уро́ки.

Notice that the compounds of **стать** form their imperfective in **-ставать**.

      встать *to get up, to rise*   вставать
      заста́ть *to catch (someone in)*   заставать

Пе́тя всегда́ встаёт о́чень по́здно, потому́ что о́чень по́здно ложи́тся спать, но сего́дня он встал ра́но. Он хоте́л заста́ть своего́ дру́га до́ма.

Compounds of **станови́ть**(**ся**)

The verb **останови́ть** means *to stop (something that is moving)*, the reflexive **останови́ться** *to stop (moving oneself), to come to a halt.* The imperfectives are **остана́вливать** and **остана́вливаться**.

Маши́на шла всё ме́дленнее (*slower and slower*).

– Остана́вливается! сказа́л Ми́тя.
– Чепуха́! (*rubbish*), возрази́л (*retorted*) Са́ша, но на са́мом де́ле маши́на остана́вливалась. Вдруг мото́р переста́л рабо́тать и маши́на останови́лась.
– Вот, ви́дишь, – ста́ла, сказа́л Ми́тя.

поста́вить *to put (in a standing position), to stand (something)* **ста́вить**

pfv.	поста́влю	*impfv.*	ста́влю
	поста́вишь		ста́вишь
imper.	поста́вь, поста́вьте		ставь, ста́вьте

Ты всегда́ всё ста́вишь не туда́ (*in the wrong place*) и вчера́ ты поста́вила ва́зу на мой бума́ги.

Compounds of **ста́вить**

Compounds of this verb form the perfective in **-ста́вить** and the imperfective in **-ставля́ть**:

      переста́вить *to change the order, to transpose* переставля́ть
      заста́вить *to compel*   заставля́ть

– Почему́ ты переставля́ешь ме́бель?
– Ведь, ты же сказа́ла – переста́вь!
– Я же сказа́ла? Нет, я сказа́ла – переста́нь!

– Переста́нь? То́-есть, как переста́ть?

– Переста́нь подпева́ть (*to hum*) – у тебя́ тако́й го́лос, что во́лосы ды́бом стоя́т (*one's hair stands on end*). Ну, раз ты стал переставля́ть, мо́жно всё переста́вить.

– Почему́ ты заставля́ешь меня́ переставля́ть всю ме́бель?

– Я же не заставля́ю тебя́. Сам стал переставля́ть, зна́чит (*so, therefore*), сам себя́ заста́вил.

4. DIALOGUE

н и́ н а Ты хо́чешь полежа́ть по́сле обе́да? Хорошо́, ляг на дива́н, и́ли хо́чешь лечь на крова́ть?

п е́ т я Нет, я ля́гу не дива́н.

н и́ н а Хорошо́, ляг, но смотри́, не запа́чкай (*stain, dirty*) дива́н сапога́ми, ты их лу́чше сними́.

г о́ л о с т ё т и л и́ з ы   Где Пе́тя?

н и́ н а Лежи́т на дива́не, чита́ет газе́ту и́ли спит. Ах нет, газе́та лежи́т тут на сту́ле. Он, ка́жется, засну́л, тётя Ли́за. Пе́тя, а Пе́тя (вдруг серди́тый го́лос) – Пе́тька, ты опя́ть лёг с нога́ми на дива́н и в сапога́х. Ну, встава́й, встава́й с дива́на.

п е́ т я Гммм...

н и́ н а Всегда́ я говорю́, что на́до ложи́ться на дива́н без сапо́г, и́ли положи́ себе́ газе́ту под но́ги, а ты про́сто так, в сапога́х ложи́шься и лежи́шь и спишь.

п е́ т я Гммм – и полежа́ть не даю́т споко́йно, и спать не даю́т.

н и́ н а Что тако́е – полежа́ть не даю́т? Кто тебе́ лежа́ть не даёт, хоте́ла бы я знать? Ты лёг на но́вый дива́н в сапога́х, а я тебе́ всегда́ говорю́, – ложи́сь на дива́н, но сперва́ сними́ сапоги́, а ты мне на зло (*you do it to spite me*).

п е́ т я Э́то кто кому́ на зло что де́лает?[1] Я на зло ложу́сь на дива́н в сапога́х, да? А ты на зло ста́вишь каки́е-то ва́зы с цвета́ми пря́мо на мои́ чертежи́ (*plans*), так и поста́вила вчера́ ва́зу с фиа́лками на мои́ бума́ги, пря́мо на бума́ги.

5. TEXT

Read the following continuous passage for comprehension. The necessary vocabulary is at the end of the book. Difficult phrases and new grammatical forms are annotated and there is a translation in 'Key to Exercises and Texts', also at the end of the book.

Scenes from Russian Life
Охо́та на волко́в с флажка́ми

Охо́та на волко́в с флажка́ми – интере́сный вид спо́рта в Росси́и. Обы́чно э́то происхо́дит зимо́й и де́лается так.

---

1 *Who is spiting who?* lit. 'Who is doing what to whom for spite?'.

Моско́вские охо́тники получа́ют телегра́мму. В ней говори́тся,[1] что на се́вере Кали́нинской о́бласти, т.е. киломе́тров четы́реста от столи́цы, появи́лась ста́я волко́в. Бли́же их нет,[2] потому́ что давно́ уже́ всех истреби́ли. Э́та ста́я пришла́ туда́ из больши́х лесо́в сосе́дней, бо́лее се́верной о́бласти. Вся́кий зна́ет, что во́лки опа́сны, осо́бенно зимо́й. Они́ уничтожа́ют ове́ц, напада́ют на коро́в, лошаде́й и да́же на люде́й. Их на́до неме́дленно уничто́жить. За ка́ждого уби́того[3] во́лка госуда́рство в ви́де пре́мии пла́тит пятьдеся́т рубле́й, т.е. о́коло двадцати́ фу́нтов сте́рлингов.

1 *It says*, lit. 'in it is said'.   2 *Nearer at hand there are none.*   3 *Killed.*

И вот охо́тники собира́ют всё необходи́мое, е́дут снача́ла по́ездом, а пото́м на саня́х к тому́ ме́сту, где в лесу́ ночева́ли во́лки. Ме́стный е́герь, кото́рый отправля́л в Москву́ телегра́мму, пока́зывает на берёзовую ро́щу, куда́ веду́т следы́ волко́в. На снегу́ они́ хорошо́ видны́. На́до знать интере́сную привы́чку волко́в: они́ иду́т большо́й ста́ей[1] по снегу́ друг за дру́гом и ступа́ют в одно́ и то же ме́сто. Получа́ется так, бу́дто[2] идёт оди́н волк, а в са́мом де́ле их шесть.

1 *In a large pack.* NB use of instrumental.   2 *The effect is as if/though.*

Охо́тники в бе́лых хала́тах иду́т на специа́льных, широ́ких лы́жах по глубо́кому снегу́ вокру́г э́той ро́щи. У одного́ из них на спине́ больша́я кату́шка, с кото́рой[1] разма́тывается то́нкая верёвка с кра́сными флажка́ми. Верёвку разве́шивают на кусты́, на дере́вья на высоте́ ме́тра от земли́. Во́лки боя́тся кра́сных флажко́в, кото́рые вися́т на расстоя́нии не́скольких[2] ме́тров друг от дру́га. Поэ́тому они́ не бу́дут пры́гать че́рез верёвки.

1 *Genitive, not instrumental, hence* **с** *here* = *from.*   2 *Genitive of* **не́сколько** *several.*

С трёх сторо́н окружи́ли лес флажка́ми, а с четвёртой стороны́ остаётся[1] свобо́дный вы́ход. Здесь охо́тники распределя́ются по жре́бию. Они́ стано́вятся на свои́ номера́.[2] Охо́тники схо́дят с лыж[3] и выбира́ют ме́сто за де́ревом и́ли в куста́х, что́бы бы́ло удо́бно ви́деть волко́в и стреля́ть. Снег под нога́ми на́до утопта́ть, он до́лжен быть пло́тным. Лю́ди стано́вятся так, что́бы ве́тер дул на них,[4] тогда́ во́лки не чу́вствуют за́паха челове́ка и по́роха.

1 **Оста́ться, остава́ться** *to remain* is a compound of **стать**, hence future **оста́нусь, оста́нешься** etc., present **остаю́сь, остаёшься** etc.
2 *They take up their positions according to their numbers.*
3 *The hunters remove their skis*, lit. 'come off the skis'.   4 i.e. 'down wind'.

Тепе́рь всё гото́во. Раздаётся[1] вы́стрел е́геря, кото́рый стреля́ет с противополо́жной стороны́, для того́, что́бы испуга́ть волко́в. Во́лки

1 A compound of **дать, дава́ть** – **разда́ться, раздава́ться** *to resound, to ring out.* Hence future **разда́стся, раздаду́тся**, present **раздаётся, раздаю́тся.**

бегу́т к стрелка́м. Е́герь кричи́т, опя́ть стреля́ет, шуми́т трещо́ткой.[2] Во́лки устремля́ются в ра́зные сто́роны, но ви́дят флажки́ и опя́ть бегу́т в направле́нии к охо́тникам.

И вот за дере́вьями пока́зывается снача́ла оди́н волк, пото́м друго́й, тре́тий. Они́ броса́ются к охо́тникам скачка́ми по глубо́кому снéгу. Бежа́ть по тако́му снéгу о́чень тру́дно да́же волка́м.[3] С трево́гой они́ огля́дываются наза́д и по сторона́м.

2 *Makes a noise with a rattle.*   3 *For wolves.*

Вы с нетерпе́нием смо́трите и ждёте. Вот вы́стрел спра́ва, пото́м не́сколько вы́стрелов сле́ва, и раздаётся вой ра́неного[1] во́лка. Сра́зу два во́лка бегу́т на вас. Пе́рвый – ста́рый, о́пытный, са́мый большо́й и опа́сный; он величино́й с по́ни.[2] Волк ви́дит чёрный ствол ружья́ и глаза́ охо́тника, ре́зко броса́ется в сто́рону, в кусты́ и карте́чь то́лько слегка́ задева́ет его́ спи́ну. Он успева́ет скры́ться в лесу́. Второ́й же волк па́дает по́сле то́чного вы́стрела. Всего́ уби́то пять волко́в.[3] Подъезжа́ют са́ни, ло́шади боязли́во кося́тся на уби́тых звере́й, храпя́т. Охо́тники возвраща́ются домо́й. На друго́й день в газе́те «Вече́рняя Москва́» даётся сообще́ние об успе́шной охо́те на волко́в.

А. Ефи́мов

1 *Wounded.*   2 Cf. Lesson 34, § 4, last para. note 4.
3 *Altogether five wolves have been killed.* **Всего́** *in all* (in summing up). In such constructions as this, where a number is the grammatical subject, the adjective (or participle, as here) expressing the predicate is either *neuter*, agreeing with **пять** (the cardinal numbers are regarded as neuter, whatever their endings), or *plural*, agreeing with the logically plural subject 'wolves'. The neuter agreement implies that you are thinking of the objects as a group, a mass, while the plural agreement implies that you are thinking of the objects as separate individuals or items. The same applies when there is a verb in the predicate: **пять волко́в бы́ло уби́то/бы́ли уби́ты.**

6. EXERCISE

a Write out the conjugations of **сесть, стать** and **лечь.**

b Write out the passage in § 4, transposing all the verbs – and also pronouns and nouns, where appropriate – into the plural.

c Write out a translation of the passage in § 4 and then translate it back into Russian, first in written form and then orally.

SUMMARY

1 Verbs of lying and laying (§ 1).
2 Conjugation of **лечь** and **лежа́ть** (§ 1).
3 Verbs of sitting and setting (§ 2).
4 Conjugation of **сесть** and **сиде́ть** (§ 2).
5 Verbs of standing and putting in a standing position (§ 3).
6 Conjugation of **стать** and **стоя́ть** (§ 3).
7 Agreement of verb with **кто** (§ 3).
8 Agreement of predicate when subject is a number (§ 5, para. 6, note 3).

Lesson 36

I. THE VERB деть

As well as the verbs given in Lesson 35, corresponding to the English *to put*, there is also the verb **деть** *to put*. It is used when the idea of laying, setting down or standing something is not appropriate and also in the sense of *putting* something away so that it cannot be found.

pfv.	**деть**	*impfv.*	**дева́ть**
	я де́ну		дева́ю
	ты де́нешь		дева́ешь
	он де́нет		дева́ет
	они́ де́нут		дева́ют

The past tense of **дева́ть** can also be perfective, and is used like the past tense of **деть,** which is **дел, де́ла, де́ло, де́ли.**

– Ве́ра, Ве́ра, куда́ ты де́ла мои́ футбо́льные купо́ны, где они́, куда́ ты их де́ла?

– Никуда́ я их не де́ла, никуда́ я их не дева́ла, я и не вида́ла их. Мо́жет быть Ни́на их взяла́, спроси́ её, куда́ она́ их де́ла.

Он не знал, куда́ деть свои́ си́лы. *He did not know on what to expend* ('where to put') *his energy.*

Я не зна́ю, куда́ деть мою́ семью́ на ле́то. *I don't know where to send* ('put') *my family for the summer.*

The reflexive is also used:

Куда́ дева́ются его́ де́ньги? *What does he do with his money?*

Пе́тя куда́-то де́лся. Пе́тя куда́-то дева́лся. *Peter has gone off somewhere.*

Я не зна́ла, куда́ де́ться от замеша́тельства. *I didn't know where to put myself from embarrassment.*

Compounds of **деть** include the *dressing* verbs:

наде́ть *to put on* (clothes, etc.)	надева́ть
оде́ть *to dress* (somebody)	одева́ть
оде́ться *to dress* (oneself)	одева́ться
разде́ть *to undress* (somebody)	раздева́ть
разде́ться *to undress* (oneself)	раздева́ться
разоде́ться *to dress up*	разодева́ться

Когда́ я была́ ма́ленькой де́вочкой, мы всегда́ разодева́лись по воскресе́ньям. Ма́ма одева́лась, надева́ла своё лу́чшее пла́тье, па́па надева́л свой лу́чший костю́м. Пото́м ма́ма одева́ла нас, дете́й, надева́ла на нас лу́чшие пла́тья, костю́мы и ту́фли. Одно́ воскресе́нье она́ оде́ла нас, мы все пошли́ гуля́ть в парк и прохо́жие (*passers by*) смотре́ли на нас дете́й. Ве́чером я не хоте́ла разде́ться, и по́сле э́того всегда́ о́чень ме́дленно раздева́лась.

2. Сказа́ть AND SIMILAR VERBS

Сказа́ть *to say*, perfective of **говори́ть**, is a verb of the **писа́ть** type (Lesson 23, § 7), first conjugation. It drops the vowel **a** in the conjugation and has a change of consonant throughout the conjugation:

я скажу́
ты ска́жешь
он ска́жет
мы ска́жем
вы ска́жете
они́ ска́жут

A reflexive derivative of **сказа́ть** is **ска́зываться** used as follows:

Хоро́шее воспита́ние ска́зывается. *A good up-bringing tells.*
Боле́знь ска́зывалась на нём. *His illness told on him.*

There are several other verbs historically related to **сказа́ть** with the same type of conjugation:

каза́ться *impfv. to seem* ка́жется *it seems* каза́лось *it seemed*
показа́ться *pfv.* показа́лось *it seemed, it appeared*

In the following pairs the perfective is given first:

оказа́ть *to render, to exert* ока́зывать

Серёжа оказа́л нам значи́тельную по́мощь в э́том де́ле. *Seryozha rendered us considerable help in this matter.*

Достое́вский оказа́л большо́е влия́ние на э́того писа́теля. *Dostoyevsky exerted great influence on this writer.*

оказа́ться *to turn out to be* ока́зываться (see § 3)
показа́ть *to show* пока́зывать

Я вам (NB dative) покажу́ сад. *I'll show you the garden.*

заказа́ть *to order* зака́зывать

Закажи́те себе́ но́вый костю́м. *Order yourself a new suit.*

наказа́ть *to punish* нака́зывать

Престу́пников нака́зывают за преступле́ния. *Criminals are punished* ('they punish criminals') *for their crimes.*

приказа́ть *to order, to command* прика́зывать

Прикажу́ ему́ (NB dative) приходи́ть ра́но. *I shall order him to come early.*

доказа́ть *to prove* дока́зывать

Он хо́чет доказа́ть, что мо́жно жить на луне́. *He wants to prove that one can live on the moon.*

рассказа́ть *to tell (a story), to relate* расска́зывать

Не расска́жете ли нам что́-нибудь о свое́й пое́здке в СССР? *Won't you tell us something about your trip to the U.S.S.R.?*

256

вы́сказать *to express, to speak out* выска́зывать

Ми́тя всегда́ ре́зко выска́зывает своё мне́ние. *Mitya always speaks his opinion frankly* ('sharply').

указа́ть *to point out, to indicate* ука́зывать

Ма́льчик нам указа́л доро́гу к да́че. *The boy pointed out to us the way to the villa.*

Дире́ктор ука́зывал на то, что ни одного́ ученика́ не́ было там в то вре́мя. *The headmaster pointed out that none of the pupils was there at that time.*

отказа́ть *to refuse, to reject* отка́зывать

Нача́льник отказа́л мне в о́тпуске. *The boss refused to give me leave.*

Пе́тя сде́лал ей предложе́ние, а она́ отказа́ла ему́ (NB dative). *Petya proposed to her but she turned him down.*

отказа́ться *to give up, to renounce* отка́зываться

Он отказа́лся от до́лжности. *He has given up his job.*

Я никогда́ не откажу́сь от своего́ мне́ния. *I shall never renounce my opinion.*

3. THE USE OF THE INSTRUMENTAL WITH CERTAIN VERBS

When you say that somebody or something becomes, turns into this or that, as in *This student is turning into a real scholar*, the phrase 'a real scholar' is the *complement* of the verb. In Russian the complement of **стать, станови́ться** and other verbs is in the instrumental case:

Э́тот студе́нт стано́вится настоя́щим учёным.
Его́ брат стал до́ктором, а он сам стал архите́ктором.
Вы стано́витесь настоя́щей кулина́ркой (*culinary expert*).

Another verb meaning *to become* is **де́латься,** perfective **сде́латься.**
Он сде́лался необходи́мым. *He has become indispensible.*

The verb **оказа́ться** has a complement in the instrumental in such sentences as these:

Он оказа́лся о́чень о́пытным счетово́дом. *He turned out to be a very experienced accountant.*

Актёр оказа́лся о́чень тала́нтливым. *The actor turned out to be very talented.*

Вот вы её хва́лите, а она́ ока́жется глу́пенькой де́вочкой. *Here you are, praising her, and she will turn out to be a stupid little girl.*

When, however, **оказа́ться** is used in such sentences as:

Я оказа́лся на пло́щади. *I found myself (turned out to be) in the square,*

the instrumental is not used, since there is no complement but only the adverbial phrase **на пло́щади,** denoting place where.

S
257

Here are some examples of other verbs with a complement in the instrumental case:

показа́ться *to seem* **каза́ться**

Я кажу́сь сорокале́тним, а на са́мом де́ле мне то́лько три́дцать четы́ре го́да. *I look like a forty-year old but in fact I am only thirty-four.*

А я кажу́сь мальчи́шкой, а мне уже́ два́дцать два го́да. *And I look like a little boy but I'm already twenty-two.*

Он мне показа́лся немно́го гру́стным сего́дня. *He seemed to me rather sad today.*

Шофёр мне показа́лся пья́ным. *The driver looked drunk to me.*

Она́ мне показа́лась о́чень взволно́ванной. *She seemed very upset to me.*

роди́ться *to be born* **рожда́ться**
умере́ть *to die* **умира́ть**

Рожда́ются бедняка́ми – умира́ют богача́ми, рожда́ются богача́ми – умира́ют бедняка́ми. Вот и э́тот челове́к – роди́лся сы́ном ма́ленького ла́вочника, а у́мер миллионе́ром. *People are born poor ('poor people') and die rich ('rich men'), others are born rich and die poor. This man for example – he was born the son of a small shopkeeper and died a millionaire.*

вы́глядеть, imperfective, *to look, to appear*

There is no perfective to this verb and it is the only verb with a stress on **вы-** which is not perfective.

Он вы́глядит настоя́щим бродя́гой в э́той шля́пе. *He looks a real tramp in that hat.*

> Note that **бродя́га** is a noun like **дя́дя;** it is masculine, though it belongs to the **а/я** declension.

To say *to look well* or *better* you use an adverb:

Ни́на хорошо́ вы́глядит. *Nina looks well.*

Сего́дня он вы́глядит лу́чше. *He is looking better today.*

служи́ть *to serve* **прослужи́ть**

Он слу́жит сержа́нтом в артиллери́йской брига́де (*brigade*).

Он на́чал служи́ть просты́м солда́том, а ко́нчил слу́жбу полко́вником. *He began his service as an ordinary soldier and finished his service as a colonel.*

Всю жизнь она́ прослужи́ла куха́ркой бога́тых ро́дственников. *All her life she served as the cook of some rich relations.*

4. THE VERB 'TO BE' AND THE INSTRUMENTAL CASE

a *Present tense*

In the present tense, when the verb *to be* is not expressed, subject and predicate are both in the nominative case:

> Брат – официа́нт. *My brother is a waiter.*
> Сестра́ – парикма́херша. *My sister is a hairdresser.*
> Муж – офице́р. *My husband is an officer.*

Sometimes the predicate may be in the instrumental if it denotes an occupation and is also qualified by some adverb or adverbial phrase:

Наш сын инженéром на завóде. *Our son is an engineer in a factory.*

The instrumental predicate is usual with **винá** *fault* and **причи́на** *cause, reason*:

Всемý винóй – вáша лень. *Your laziness is to blame for it all.*

Причи́ной нáшей отстáлости – невнимáние к подрóбностям. *The cause of our backwardness is inattention to detail.*

When two contrasting clauses stand side by side and in each the subject and the predicate are expressed by the same noun, the predicate is in the instrumental:

Дрýжба дрýжбой, а слýжба слýжбой. *Friendship is friendship, but duty is duty.*

b *Future tense*

In modern Russian the predicate is in the instrumental after the future tense of **быть**:

Я бýду учи́телем. *I shall be a teacher.*

Мой сын бýдет инженéром. *My son will be an engineer.*

c *Past tense*

With the past tense of **быть** both the instrumental and the nominative are found in the predicate.

The instrumental here implies a temporary state or partial activity, the nominative a permanent state or total devotion to some calling. 'Permanent state' would include not only family relationships but, say, the vocation of a poet, especially when talking of a dead poet. To say, using the instrumental, **он был поэ́том** would imply either that he was a poet at one time and then gave up being a poet, or that he was a poet but being a poet was not his entire vocation – it was just a part of his activities.

Sentences with the instrumental:

Мой брат был в то врéмя официáнтом, тепéрь он кондýктор.

Неужéли вáша сестрá бýдет парикмáхершей?

Что вы, что вы, онá бýдет студéнткой, онá хóчет стать врачóм.

Её муж был офицéром-танки́стом, до тогó как они́ уéхали в Ю́жную Амéрику.

Ты никогдá хорошéнько не мóешь рýки, стáнешь взрóслым (*grown-up*) бýдешь трубочи́стом (*chimney-sweep*).

Когдá мы жи́ли в столи́це (*capital*), нáша племя́нница (*niece*) былá стенографи́сткой.

Sentences with the nominative:

Он был сын генерáла.

Алексéй Толстóй был поэ́т, а Лев Толстóй был писáтель.

259

In statements like the following one might find either case:

> Наш дéдушка был землевладéлец/землевладéльцем. *Our grandfather was a landowner.*

When **чтóбы** introduces the past tense form of **быть** the predicate is usually in the instrumental:

> Мой отéц не хóчет, чтóбы я был дóктором.

When the predicate is an abstract noun it is usual to put it in the instrumental case:

> Причúной запоздáния парохóда был тумáн. *The reason for the ship's belated arrival was a fog.*
>
> На канúкулах глáвной забóтой бы́ло бельё. *On holiday the main worry was the laundry.*
>
> Этот чудéсный подáрок был сюрпрúзом. *This marvellous present was a surprise.*

When the predicate is an adjective, the instrumental is not common: it is only used when it is clear from the situation that the characteristic is definitely temporary as in:

> Он был молоды́м, когдá кóнчилась войнá. Cf. Он был ещё óчень мóлод.

5. VERBS WITH THE INFINITIVE IN **-нуть**

We have had the verbs *to get used to* **привыкáть,** imperfective, **привыкáю, привыкáешь,** and once or twice we have used the perfective past tense **привы́к** *he got used to*. This verb belongs to a small group of first conjugation verbs with a consonant before **-е-** and the infinitive ending in **-нуть**. The infinitive of **привы́к** is **привы́кнуть,** perfective.

Verbs with infinitive in **-нуть** can be divided into two groups:

a Those which drop the **-нуть** ending in the past and form the past tense masculine without **-л** like **привы́кнуть: он привы́к, онá привы́кла, онú привы́кли.**

b Those which retain the **-нуть** ending in all their verbal forms, so that they are no different from any first conjugation verb with consonant followed by **-е-** (see Lesson 38).

The verbs that drop the **-нуть** ending in the past generally denote transition from one state to another, like getting used to something, growing deaf etc.

привыкáть *to get used to*   **привы́кнуть**   *past* привы́к, привы́кла
отвыкáть *to get out of a habit*   **отвы́кнуть**   *past* отвы́к, отвы́кла

– Вот я привы́к курúть двáдцать папирóс в день и никáк не могý отвы́кнуть.

– Ничегó, Пéтя, отвы́кнешь. Тётя Лúза курúла не мéнее сорокá сигарéт в день – пря́мо ýжас – а потóм всё-таки отвы́кла.

– То́-есть, как так отвы́кла? Прихожу́ к ней неда́вно, у неё сигаре́та торчи́т во рту как всегда́.
– Ну да, она́ ку́рит о́коло двадцати́ пяти́ сигаре́т в день.
– Вот и отвы́кла! Зна́чит я то́же отвы́к кури́ть! Отвы́к кури́ть и курю́ два́дцать!

исчеза́ть *to vanish* **исче́знуть** *past* исче́з, исче́зла

Кот укра́л ры́бу и сам исче́з.
Исче́зли мои́ пи́сьма. Я их положи́л на стол, а вот они́ исче́зли.
В э́том до́ме всё исчеза́ет.

умолка́ть *to fall silent* **умо́лкнуть** *past* умо́лк, умо́лкла
замолка́ть **замо́лкнуть** *past* замо́лк, замо́лкла

Of these two verbs the former simply expresses the idea of growing silent, the latter emphasizes the suddenness with which, say, people fall silent when a conversation stops.

До́лго шли спо́ры, но бы́ло уже́ по́здно и ма́ло-пома́лу разгово́р на́чал умолка́ть и наконе́ц умо́лк. *The arguments went on for a long time but gradually the conversation began to falter and finally broke off.*
Внеза́пно все замо́лкли и бо́льше ни сло́ва никто́ не сказа́л. *Suddenly everybody fell silent and nobody said a word more.*

достига́ть + gen. *to achieve, to attain* **дости́гнуть**

Дости́г я вы́сшей вла́сти, шесто́й уж год я ца́рствую споко́йно. *I have attained the highest power, five years and more have ruled in peace.*

(Пу́шкин: Бори́с Годуно́в)

Косми́ческий кора́бль достига́ет о́чень высо́кой ско́рости. *A space-ship reaches a very high velocity.*

па́хнуть *to smell* **запа́хнуть**

Па́хло ры́бой. *There was a smell of fish.*

Notice the construction: impersonal use of the verb, with the instrumental case.

Па́хнет ры́бой. *There is a smell of fish.*
Дом пах/па́хнул све́жими берёзовыми ли́стьями. *The house smelt of fresh birch-leaves.*

A few verbs of this type have an alternative past tense masculine formed in the normal way from the infinitive, as the example shows. The same idea could equally well be expressed by an impersonal use of the verb:

В до́ме па́хло бензи́ном. *The house smelt of petrol.*
В ко́мнате запа́хло духа́ми. *A smell of scent pervaded the room.*

A good proportion of the verbs in **-нуть** of this type are, like **па́хнуть**, imperfective and they denote the passage from one condition or state to another. Their perfectives are formed with various prefixes. Here are a few of the commoner ones, first imperfective, then perfective:

мёрзнуть *to freeze, to be/become cold* **замёрзнуть** and **промёрзнуть** *to become frozen through*

Я мёрзла весь день, бы́ло о́чень хо́лодно.

Вода́ в кувши́не (*ewer*) замёрзла за́_ночь.

Я весь промёрз на стадио́не, я был без пальто́ (*coat* indeclinable).

га́снуть *to dim, to be extinguished* **пога́снуть**

Электри́ческий свет га́снул и пога́с, мы зажгли́ свечу́ и она́ пога́сла.
The electric light dimmed and went out, we lit a candle and the candle went out.

ги́бнуть *to perish, to be lost* **поги́бнуть**

Он поги́б на войне́.

Вся библиоте́ка поги́бла от пожа́ра.

мо́кнуть *to be soaked* **промо́кнуть**

Я стоя́л и мо́кнул на углу́, и весь промо́к до косте́й. *I stood getting wet on the corner, and got completely soaked to the skin* (lit. 'to the bones').

Де́ти совсе́м промо́кли. *The children got absolutely soaked.*

со́хнуть *to get dry* **засо́хнуть, вы́сохнуть**

До́лго не́ было дождя́, засо́хнут молоды́е дере́вья, а не́которые уже́ засо́хли.

Клён (*maple*) засо́х.

Бельё (*washing*) со́хнет в саду́ и ско́ро вы́сохнет на со́лнце.

Мне ну́жен носово́й плато́к (*handkerchief*). Плато́к вы́сох?

Руба́шки и носовы́е платки́ уже́ вы́сохли.

сле́пнуть *to go blind* **осле́пнуть**

Дя́дя под ста́рость (*in old age*) осле́п.

Мы едва́ не (*nearly*) осле́пли от я́ркого све́та.

гло́хнуть *to go deaf* **огло́хнуть**

Де́душка огло́х под ста́рость.

Мы все огло́хли от шу́ма.

6. TEXT

Scenes from Russian Life
Подлёдный лов ры́бы

Моро́зный зи́мний день. Огро́мная сне́жная равни́на залита́[1] со́лнцем. Везде́, куда́ ни[2] взгля́нешь, гру́ппами сидя́т на я́щичках лю́ди... Э́то рыбаки́, люби́тели подлёдного ло́ва. Они́ прие́хали сюда́, на Большу́ю

1 *Flooded.*
2 *Wherever.* **Ни** with pronouns and adverbs such as **где, куда́,** adds the meaning of *-ever.*

Во́лгу. Большинство́ их[3] – москвичи́, хотя́ от столи́цы до э́тих мест сто три́дцать киломе́тров. Здесь о́чень мно́го ры́бы разли́чных поро́д.

На автомоби́лях и в больши́х авто́бусах они́ е́дут пря́мо по засне́женным[4] доро́гам. Доро́ги прокла́дываются по льду, и рыбаки́ остана́вливаются там, где лу́чше клюёт[5] ры́ба. То́лстый и о́чень кре́пкий лёд выде́рживает больши́е авто́бусы с сорока́[6] рыбака́ми.

3 Usually **большинство́ из них.**   4 *Snowed-up, snow covered.*
5 **Клева́ть** *to bite, to nibble, to peck* **клюю́, клюёшь.**
6 **Со́рок** *forty* has **сорока́** for all its other cases.

Пре́жде всего́ на́до разброса́ть ного́й в ра́зные сто́роны снег, проби́ть во льду отве́рстие, кото́рое называ́ется лу́нка. После́дние уда́ры. Пе́ред ва́ми глубо́кая пуста́я дыра́ во льду. Ещё оди́н си́льный уда́р, и вода́ с шу́мом бы́стро заполня́ет лу́нку.

Тепе́рь на́до пригото́вить у́дочку. Рыба́к достаёт[1] её из специа́льного я́щика, в кото́рый пото́м скла́дывается ры́ба. На нём же и сидя́т, потому́ что ло́вля продолжа́ется не́сколько часо́в. У́дочка о́чень коро́ткая, всего́ о́коло двух фу́тов. С неё разма́тывается ле́ска разме́ром в не́сколько ме́тров. На конце́ ле́ски ма́ленький крючо́к. На нём дроби́нка гру́за. На коне́ц крючка́ на́до наде́ть одного́-двух мотыле́й. Э́то я́рко-кра́сные червячки́ длино́й о́коло двух сантиме́тров. Они́ продаю́тся в рыболо́вных магази́нах. Храни́ть коро́бочку с мотыля́ми прихо́дится в карма́не, а то[2] они́ мо́гут бы́стро замёрзнуть.

1 A compound of **стать: доста́ть, достава́ть** *to get, to fetch;* future **доста́ну, доста́нешь,** present **достаю́, достаёшь.**   2 **А то,** *otherwise.*

Всё в поря́дке? Мо́жно начина́ть? Начнём.

Крючо́к вме́сте с нейло́новой то́нкой ле́ской опуска́ется до дна.[1] Зате́м рыба́к начина́ет ме́дленно поднима́ть её, он ритми́чно потря́хивает руко́й и поднима́ет у́дочку на[2] полме́тра. Пото́м опуска́ет вновь и повторя́ет движе́ние. Живы́е кра́сные червячки́ – хоро́шая прима́нка. Ведь зимо́й ры́ба бо́льше спит. Её на́до дразни́ть краси́вой прима́нкой. На конце́ ма́ленькой у́дочки приде́лан[3] на ги́бкой про́волочке специа́льный поплаво́к. Как то́лько ры́ба клю́нет, поплаво́к дёрнется[4] вниз. На́до сра́зу тащи́ть. И вот на сверка́ющем[5] снегу́ появля́ется пе́рвый о́кунь. Он зелёно-серебри́стый с я́рко кра́сными плавника́ми и ре́зко выделя́ется на бе́лом фо́не. За ним – друго́й. Хоро́ший уло́в – э́то четы́ре и́ли пять килогра́мм ры́бы за[6] не́сколько часо́в.

1 Genitive of **дно** *bottom.*   2 NB *by* or omit in translation.   3 *Attached.*
4 **Клю́нуть** and **дёрнуть** are instantaneous perfectives (see Lesson 38) of **клева́ть** *to bite* and **дёргать** *to tug.*   5 *Glittering.*   6 *In.*

Вдруг что́-то происхо́дит. Мно́гие рыбаки́ вска́кивают со свои́х я́щиков и бегу́т в сто́рону, где сиди́т старичо́к – о́пытный рыба́к. Он то́лько что вы́тащил из воды́ огро́мную щу́ку. Да, таку́ю на ма́ленький крючо́к с мотылём не пойма́ешь.¹ Стари́к ло́вит други́м спо́собом. Он приво́зит с собо́й в ведре́ с водо́й² деся́тка два ме́лких рыб. Осторо́жно прока́лывает им³ гу́бы крючко́м и на дли́нной про́чной ле́ске отправля́ет их в во́ду. Подо_льдо́м э́ти ры́бки пла́вают вме́сте с крючко́м, похо́жим на я́корь. Све́рху у лу́нки рыба́к ста́вит в снегу́ па́лочку. На неё он кладёт ле́ску с кра́сным флажко́м. Таки́х у́дочек он приво́зит не ме́нее десяти́. Зате́м он прогу́ливается о́коло э́тих па́лочек и следи́т, где упада́ет флажо́к. Па́дает он тогда́, когда́ живца́ взяла́⁴ и потащи́ла⁴ кру́пная ры́ба. Он бы́стро дёргает ле́ску. На́до схвати́ть моме́нт зацепи́ть за⁵ щёку кру́пную ры́бу крючко́м, что́бы она́ не ушла́. Тогда́ рыба́к выта́скивает её на снег.

А. Ефи́мов

1 The perfective of **лови́ть** *to catch* is formed from a different root: **пойма́ть: пойма́ю, помйа́ешь.**

2 *In a bucket of water*, NB construction.   3 *Their*, lit. 'to them'.

4 The subject is **ры́ба** at the end of the sentence.   5 *By.*

7. TRANSLATION

My father was a writer and we lived in the country. Earlier we had lived in the town but it was so noisy that papa could only work at night when everything had gone quiet. He got used to working at night and did not give up this habit even in the country.

Before her marriage mother was an actress but looking after¹ a large family occupied too much of her time. When we were small, she used to dress us in turn.² Later we were able to dress ourselves. Once we had dressed ourselves and had breakfast we would set off for school.

At that time it seemed that we were rich. I thought we had been born rich. Now it seems that in fact³ we were not very rich. Still, we were happy. We did not freeze at night and we ate well. In the morning the house smelt of tasty food and at one o'clock we all sat down to dinner.⁴ If there was too much noise father pretended⁵ that he had gone deaf and gradually we fell silent.

Last week⁶ I went back to the village. Everything is changing. Mother and father look well but, it seems, old age is beginning to tell on them.

1 Use infinitive **ходи́ть за** + instrumental.   2 **По о́череди.**   3 **На са́мом де́ле.**

4 Use infinitive.   5 Use past tense of **де́лать вид.**   6 **На про́шлой неде́ле.**

SUMMARY

1 The verb **деть** and its compounds (§ 1).

2 Verbs derived from **-каза́ть** (§ 2).

3 The instrumental after verbs of becoming etc. (§ 3).

4 The instrumental and the nominative with the verb 'to be' (§ 4).

5 The first type of verbs in **-нуть** denoting transition (§ 5).

6 Wherever etc. (§ 7, para. 1, note 2).

Lesson 37

1. PARTICIPLES

To describe an action that a person or thing is doing and which is not the main action of the sentence you can use a clause introduced by *who* or *which*:

The man who is reading the news is my brother.
I have just bought that new book which is lying on the table over there.

Instead of *who is reading* and *which is lying* you can also say simply *reading* and *lying*:

The man reading the news is my brother.
I have just bought that new book lying on the table over there.

The words *reading* and *lying* in these sentences are *participles*: i.e. single words describing the action performed by the noun. They are not verbs.

You could call them verbal adjectives.

Participles describing the action which the noun performs are *active* participles.

You can also have participles which describe the action performed on a noun. Take, for instance, the following sentences:

The man who was elected yesterday is my brother.
I have just bought the book which was praised by all the critics.

Instead of *who was elected* and *which was praised* you could have the single words *elected* and *praised*.

The man elected yesterday is my brother.
I have just bought the book praised by all the critics.

In these sentences *elected* and *praised* are also participles, i.e. single words describing the action performed on the noun. They are not verbs.

Participles describing the action performed on the noun are *passive participles*.

Participles in Russian are verbal adjectives: they are derived from verbs and they have the meaning of the verb from which they are derived but they have adjectival endings and they agree in number, gender and case with the noun which they describe.

2. THE PAST PASSIVE PARTICIPLE IN -НН- I

This participle is the commonest of the Russian participles. It states that an action has been performed on the noun which it describes and that the action is completed. It should strictly be called, therefore, the perfective passive participle but we shall use the traditional term *past passive participle* and abbreviate it to p.p.p.

It is formed, of course, from perfective verbs only.

For verbs of the first conjugation with the infinitive ending in **-ать** you replace the **-ть** by **-нн-** and add the hard adjectival endings.

прочита́ть *to read through,* прочита- прочи́танный, прочи́танная, прочи́танное, прочи́танные *read*
прочи́танный лист *the sheet read,* прочи́танная страни́ца *the page read*
прочи́танное сло́во *the word read,* прочи́танные стихи́ *the verses read*

написа́ть *to write,* написа- напи́санный, напи́санная, напи́санное, напи́санные *written*
напи́санный план *the plan written,* напи́санная поэ́ма *the poem written*
напи́санное сло́во *the word written,* напи́санные пе́сни *the songs written*

вы́играть *to win* выигра- вы́игранный, -ая, -ое, -ые,
проигра́ть *to lose* проигра- прои́гранный, -ая, -ое, -ые·
Вы́игранная игра́ нас ра́дует. *A game won cheers us up.*
Прои́гранная игра́ нас всегда́ огорча́ет. *A lost game always vexes us.*

посла́ть *to send* посла- по́сланный, -ая, -ое, -ые

Мы ещё не получи́ли паке́т, по́сланный на про́шлой неде́ле. *We still haven't received the parcel sent last week.*

You have probably noticed a difference in stress between the infinitive and the p.p.p. in some of these verbs. There is a simple rule governing the stress of the p.p.p. in **-анный**.

If the stress is not on the **-ать** of the infinitive, then it stays in the same place in the p.p.p. Hence **вы́играть** *to win,* **вы́игранный** *won;* **приду́мать** *to think up,* **приду́манный** *thought up.*

If the stress is on the **-ать** of the infinitive, then it moves back one syllable in the p.p.p. Hence **прочита́ть – прочи́танный, посла́ть – по́сланный, образова́ть** *to educate,* **образо́ванный** *formed, educated.*

An exception is **жела́ть** *to wish, to desire,* **жела́нный** *desired.*

In **пе́реданный** *transferred* the stress [moves back two syllables (cf. **переда́ть**) but not in any other **-анный** participle with the prefix **пере-** (**пересла́ть – пере́сланный** *sent across,* **перебра́ть – пере́бранный** *sorted out* etc.).

3. THE PAST PASSIVE PARTICIPLE IN **-нн-** II

Verbs of the second conjugation also form the p.p.p. in **-нн-**. However, in these the **-нн-** is preceded by **-е-** so the full ending is **-енный,** and any consonant change in the first pers. sing. is also found in the p.p.p. of these verbs.[1] A simple rule, therefore, for forming the p.p.p. of these verbs is to take the first pers. sing. and replace the **-ю** or **-у** by **-енный.**

1 The p.p.p. of **уви́деть** *to see, to catch sight of* is exceptional in not having the consonant change: **уви́жу** but **уви́денный.**

приговори́ть *to sentence*	приговорю́
приговор-	приговорённый, приговорённая etc.

Престу́пника, приговорённого сего́дня у́тром, уже́ посади́ли в тюрьму́. *The criminal sentenced this morning has already been put in prison ('they have put the criminal etc.').*

покра́сить *to paint*	покра́шу
покраш-	покра́шенный, -ая, -ое, -ые

Покра́шенный забо́р вы́глядит мно́го лу́чше. *The painted fence looks much better.*

посади́ть *to plant*	посажу́
посаж-	поса́женный, -ая, -ое, -ые

Цветы́, поса́женные в э́тих горшка́х, не расту́т. *The flowers planted in these pots are not growing.*

вы́чистить *to clean*	вы́чищу
вы́чищ-	вы́чищенный, -ая, -ое, -ые

Хорошо́ вы́чищенные сапоги́ блестя́т как зе́ркало. *Well cleaned boots shine like a mirror.*

купи́ть *to buy*	куплю́
купл-	ку́пленный, -ая, -ое, -ые

Мно́ю ку́пленный га́лстук гора́здо деше́вле, чем га́лстук, кото́рый ты сам купи́л. *The tie bought by me is much cheaper than the tie which you bought yourself.*

Note that the agent who performs the action on the noun goes into the instrumental case.

Verbs of the first conjugation with the infinitive ending in **-ти, -чь** or **-ть** preceded by a consonant also form the p.p.p. in **-енный**. In these verbs it is formed by replacing the **т** of the third pers. sing. by **-нный**.

унести́ *to carry off*	он унесёт, унесённый

Чемода́н, унесённый тури́стами, мы нашли́ на ста́нции. *The suitcase carried off by the tourists we found at the station.*

перевести́ *to translate*	он переведёт, переведённый

Я купи́ла кни́гу, переведённую мои́м дру́гом. *I have bought a book translated by my friend.*

сбере́чь *to save*	он сбережёт, сбережённый

Ва́ня потеря́л де́ньги, сбережённые за це́лый год. *Johnny has lost the money (which he had) saved up for a whole year.*

укра́сть *to steal*	он украдёт, укра́денный

Поли́ция уже́ нашла́ ве́щи, укра́денные сего́дня у́тром. *The police have already found the things stolen this morning.*

There is also a simple rule for the stress of the p.p.p. in **-енный**.
The stress falls on the same vowel as in the third pers. sing. of the conjugation and **-енный** when stressed is pronounced **-ённый**.

приговори́т	приговорённый
покра́сит	покра́шенный
поса́дит	поса́женный
вы́чистит	вы́чищенный
ку́пит	ку́пленный
сбережёт	сбережённый
унесёт	унесённый
переведёт	переведённый

There are a few exceptions to this stress rule. The commonest p.p.p.'s which are exceptional in this respect are:

изменённый *changed*   cf. изме́нит
    (and other compounds of **-мени́ть**)
оценённый *evaluated*   cf. оце́нит
    (and other compounds of **цени́ть**)
осуждённый *condemned*   cf. осу́дит
    (and other compounds of **суди́ть**)
отделённый *separated*   cf. отде́лит
    (and other compounds of **дели́ть**)
остри́женный *cut, bobbed*   cf. острижёт
    (and other compounds of **стричь**)
укра́денный *stolen*   cf. украдёт

4. THE PAST PASSIVE PARTICIPLE IN **-ТЫЙ**

Some verbs form the p.p.p. by replacing the infinitive ending **-ть** by **-тый, -тая, -тое, -тые.**

Many verbs whose infinitive when not prefixed is monosyllabic have the p.p.p. in **-тый**. For instance, a compound of:

крыть has откры́тый *open*   p.p.p. of откры́ть
    and закры́тый *closed*   p.p.p. of закры́ть
мыть has вы́мытый *washed*   p.p.p. of вы́мыть
рыть has вы́рытый *dug*   p.p.p. of вы́рыть
петь has спе́тый *sung*   p.p.p. of спеть
брить has вы́бритый *shaven* p.p.p. of вы́брить

Закро́йте все откры́тые две́ри и откро́йте все закры́тые о́кна. *Close all the open doors and open all the closed windows.*
Я поста́вила вы́мытую посу́ду на ни́жнюю по́лку. *I have put the washed crockery on to the lower shelf.*
Ва́ми вы́рытую я́му посреди́не са́да нам на́до зары́ть. *We have to fill in the pit dug by you in the middle of the garden.*

268

Ва́ми то́лько что спе́тая пе́сня нам о́чень нра́вится. *We very much like the song just sung by you.*

Нра́виться *to like* is used in impersonal constructions with the dative of the person who likes:

Нам нра́вилась его́ мане́ра. *We liked his manner.*
Нам понра́вилась карти́на. *We took a liking to the picture.*
Вам нра́вится э́та карти́на? *Do you like this picture?*
Карти́на вам понра́вится. *You will like the picture.*

Чи́сто вы́бритый подборо́док нра́вится де́вушкам лу́чше чем щети́на. *Girls like a cleanly shaven chin better than bristles.*

Another group that forms the p.p.p. with the **-тый** ending are the perfectives of the verbs:

бить *to strike*   пить *to drink*   лить *to pour*   шить *to sew*

Из-за разби́той ча́шки не сто́ит пла́кать. *It's not worth crying over a broken cup.*

Тут всю́ду проли́тое молоко́, бу́дьте осторо́жны. *There is spilt milk everywhere – be careful.*

Пальто́, сши́тое в про́шлом году́ в Пари́же, никуда́ не годи́тся, оно́ мне мало́, хотя́ и ши́ли его́ в Пари́же. Вот э́то пальто́, сши́тое до́ма в Англии, мно́го лу́чше сиди́т. *The coat made ('sewn') last year in Paris is no good at all – it's too small for me, although it was made in Paris. But this coat, made at home in England, fits ('sits') much better.*

The verb **прожи́ть** *to live, to live through (a certain period)* and other compounds of **жить** also form their p.p.p. with **-тый.**

Вре́мя, про́житое в столи́це, бы́стро пролете́ло. *The time lived in the capital passed swiftly.*

Perfective compounds of the **-нять** group of verbs, and also **взять**, all form the p.p.p. in **-тый.**

взять *to take*   взя́тый

Де́ньги, взя́тые в долг, на́до возвраща́ть. *Borrowed (lit. 'taken in debt') money must be returned.*

отня́ть *to take away*   о́тнятый

У нас отня́ли большо́й кусо́к земли́ и на земле́, о́тнятой у нас, тепе́рь стро́ят мно́го домо́в. *They have taken a large piece of land from us and on the land taken from us they are now building many homes.*

снять *to take off*   сня́тый

Большо́е спаси́бо вам за фотогра́фию, сня́тую ва́ми во вре́мя кани́кул. *Thank you very much (lit. 'a big thank you to you') for the photograph taken by you during the holidays.*

занять *to occupy*　　　 за́нятый

Террито́рия, за́нятая не́мцами во вре́мя войны́, до́лгое вре́мя голода́ла. *The territory occupied by the Germans during the war went hungry for a long time.*

Note the following verbs which are compounds of **жать** and **-чать** with monosyllabic stems ending in **-ать,** and which form their p.p.p. in **-тый**:

сжать *to squeeze, to clench*　　 сжа́тый
разжа́ть *to unclench, to release*　 разжа́тый
нача́ть *to begin*　　　 на́чатый

Что ты де́ржишь в сжа́том кулаке́? *What are you holding in your clenched fist?*

Мо́жно испра́вить э́ту разжа́тую пружи́ну в замке́? Йли нам ну́жен но́вый замо́к? *Can one mend this spring that's gone* (lit. 'released spring') *in the lock. Or do we need a new lock?*

На́чатую кни́гу на́до ко́нчить. *A book begun should be finished.*

Она́ уже́ прочла́ кни́гу, на́чатую е́ю вчера́ ве́чером. *She has already finished the book she began* ('begun by her') *last night.*

The point to note about these compounds of **жать** and the verb **нача́ть** is that **-ать** is preceded by **ж** or **ч** and, as you know, you cannot write **я** after **ж** and **ч.** These infinitives are, so to speak, not 'genuine' **-ать** infinitives and bearing this in mind one can say that all **-ать** verbs form the p.p.p. in **-нный.** Hence compounds of **дать, знать, ждать** and verbs ending **-ть** preceded by a consonant do not form their p.p.p. in **-тый,** but follow the rules given in § 2 above.

The few verbs with infinitive ending in **-оть** and **-ереть** also have the p.p.p. in **-тый,** for example:

проколо́ть *to pierce* (impfv. коло́ть) проко́лотый

The stress in the p.p.p. of such verbs moves back one syllable as compared with the infinitive.

запере́ть *to lock* (impfv. запира́ть) за́пертый (NB one **е**)

The stress in the p.p.p.'s of these verbs moves on to the prefix.

5. THE SHORT FORM OF THE PAST PASSIVE PARTICIPLE

The p.p.p. is used with the appropriate tense of *to be* to form the *passive voice.* This is the form of the verb which expresses the fact that the subject is undergoing, has undergone or will undergo some action.

Used like this the p.p.p. has to be in the short form.

In the short form the p.p.p. in **-нн-** has only one **н**:

прочи́танный	прочи́тан	прочи́тана	прочи́тано	прочи́таны
напи́санный	напи́сан	напи́сана	напи́сано	напи́саны
вы́чищенный	вы́чищен	вы́чищена	вы́чищено	вы́чищены
ку́пленный	ку́плен	ку́плена	ку́плено	ку́плены

270

In the short forms of nearly all p.p.p.'s in **-анный** the stress stays on the same syllable as in the long form. In one or two verbs only the stress moves on to the ending in the short form feminine, just as it does in the past tense feminine. This happens with the compounds of **-данный**:

при́данный *added*   при́дан, придана́ (cf. придала́), при́дано, при́даны

ро́зданный (NB spelling) *distributed*   ро́здан, раздана́ (cf. раздала́), ро́здано, ро́зданы

In the short forms of **данный** itself the stress moves on to the endings throughout:

дан, дана́, дано́, даны́

The stress moves on to the ending in the feminine short form in:

со́званный *convoked*   со́зван, созвана́, со́звано, со́званы

but *not* in:

при́званный *called up, invoked*   при́зван, при́звана, при́звано, при́званы

In the short forms of p.p.p.'s in **-енный** (i.e. with **-е-** unstressed) the stress remains as in the long form (see examples above) but in the short forms of p.p.p.'s in **-ённый** it moves on to the endings:

приговорённый *condemned*   приговорён, приговорена́, приговорено́, приговорены́

унесённый *carried off*   унесён, унесена́, унесено́, унесены́

изменённый *changed*   изменён, изменена́, изменено́, изменены́

Програ́мма изменена́. *The programme has been changed.*
Програ́мма была́ изменена́. *The programme was/had been changed.*
Програ́мма бу́дет изменена́. *The programme will be changed.*
Э́та кни́га была́ напи́сана в девятна́дцатом ве́ке и переведена́ два го́да тому́ наза́д. *This book was written in the nineteenth century and translated two years ago.*
Ту́фли бы́ли уже́ вы́чищены. *The shoes had already been cleaned.*
Забо́р покра́шен, а дом бу́дет покра́шен на сле́дующей неде́ле. *The fence has been painted, and the house will be painted next week.*

The short forms of the p.p.p. in **-тый** are formed in the same way as the short forms of adjectives:

откры́тый *open*   откры́т, откры́та, откры́то, откры́ты

The stress shifts on to the ending in the feminine only of:

за́нятый *occupied*   за́нят, занята́, за́нято, за́няты (and the other compounds of **-нятый**)

про́житый *lived through, spent*   про́жит, прожита́, про́жито, про́житы

на́чатый *begun*   на́чат, начата́, на́чато, на́чаты

271

Иди́, поигра́й, я о́чень занята́. *Go and play, I'm very busy.*
Дверь откры́та, о́кна закры́ты. *The door is open, the windows closed.*
Австра́лия была́ откры́та в семна́дцатом ве́ке. *Australia was discovered in the seventeenth century.*
Молоко́ бы́ло про́лито, а вино́ бы́ло вы́пито. *The milk had been spilt but the wine had been drunk.*

6. текст

This is a more difficult version of the story which appeared in Lesson 35, with an additional piece at the end.

Scenes from Russian Life

Охо́та на волко́в с флажка́ми

Охо́та на волко́в с флажка́ми – интере́сный и своеобра́зный вид спо́рта в Росси́и. Обы́чно э́то происхо́дит зимо́й и де́лается так.

Моско́вские охо́тники получа́ют телегра́мму. В ней говори́тся, что на се́вере Кали́нинской о́бласти, т.е. киломе́тров четы́реста от столи́цы, появи́лась ста́я волко́в (бли́же их нет, потому́ что давно́ уже́ всех истреби́ли). Она́ пришла́ туда́ из больши́х лесо́в сосе́дней, бо́лее се́верной о́бласти. Вся́кий зна́ет, что во́лки опа́сны, осо́бенно зимо́й.

Они́ уничтожа́ют ове́ц, напада́ют на коро́в, лошаде́й и да́же на люде́й. Их на́до неме́дленно уничто́жить. За ка́ждого уби́того во́лка госуда́рство в ви́де пре́мии пла́тит пятьдеся́т рубле́й, т.е. о́коло двадцати́ фу́нтов сте́рлингов.

И вот, бы́стро собра́в[1] всё необходи́мое, гру́ппа охо́тников-люби́телей (четы́ре–пять челове́к) е́дет снача́ла по́ездом, а пото́м на саня́х к тому́ ме́сту, где в лесу́ ночева́ли во́лки. Ме́стный е́герь (кото́рый отправля́л в Москву́ телегра́мму) пока́зывает на берёзовую ро́щу, куда́ веду́т следы́ волко́в. На снегу́ они́ хорошо́ видны́. На́до знать интере́сную привы́чку волко́в: чтобы не выдава́ть себя́, они́ иду́т большо́й ста́ей по снегу́ друг за дру́гом, ступа́я[2] в одно́ и то же ме́сто. Получа́ется так, бу́дто идёт оди́н волк, а в са́мом де́ле их шесть.

1 *Having collected.*   2 *Stepping.*

Охо́тники в бе́лых хала́тах иду́т на лы́жах по глубо́кому снегу́ вокру́г э́той ро́щи. У одного́ из них на спине́ больша́я кату́шка, с кото́рой разма́тывается то́нкая верёвка с кра́сными флажка́ми. Верёвку разве́шивают на кусты́, стволы́ дере́вьев на высоте́ ме́тра от земли́. Во́лки боя́тся кра́сных флажко́в, располо́женных друг от дру́га на расстоя́нии не́скольких ме́тров. Поэ́тому они́ не бу́дут пры́гать че́рез верёвку.

272

Когда́ с трёх сторо́н окружи́ли лес флажка́ми, в четвёртой стороне́ оста́лся свобо́дный прохо́д. Здесь, распредели́вшись по жре́бию,[1] стано́вятся на свои́ номера́ замаскиро́ванные охо́тники. Они́ схо́дят с лыж и выбира́ют ме́сто за де́ревом и́ли в куста́х, что́бы бы́ло удо́бно ви́деть волко́в и стреля́ть. Снег под нога́ми на́до утопта́ть. Тепе́рь всё гото́во. Раздаётся вы́стрел е́геря, кото́рый с противополо́жной от охо́тников стороны́, пуга́ет волко́в и го́нит[2] их к стрелка́м. Он кричи́т, опя́ть стреля́ет, шуми́т трещо́ткой. Во́лки устремля́ются в ра́зные сто́роны, но уви́дев[3] флажки́ опя́ть бегу́т в направле́нии к охо́тникам.

1 *Having taken up their places according to the draw.*
2 Third pers. sing. of **гнать** *to drive* **гоню́, го́нишь.**   3 *Having seen/seeing.*

И вот за дере́вьями пока́зывается снача́ла оди́н волк, пото́м друго́й, тре́тий, кото́рые бегу́т к охо́тникам скачка́ми по глубо́кому сне́гу. Они́ с трево́гой огля́дываются наза́д и по сторона́м.

Раздаётся вы́стрел спра́ва, пото́м не́сколько вы́стрелов сле́ва, вой ра́неного во́лка. Наконе́ц, сра́зу два во́лка бегу́т на вас. Пе́рвый – матёрый, т.е. ста́рый, о́пытный, о́чень большо́й и опа́сный. Его́ на́до бить в пе́рвую о́чередь.[1] Уви́дев[2] чёрный ствол ружья́ и глаза́ охо́тника, он ре́зко броса́ется в сто́рону, в кусты́ – и карте́чь то́лько слегка́ задева́ет его́ спи́ну. Он успева́ет скры́ться в лесу́. Второ́й же волк па́дает по́сле то́чного вы́стрела. Всего́ уби́то пять волко́в. Их кладу́т на подъе́хавшие[3] са́ни, ло́шади боязли́во кося́тся на уби́тых звере́й, храпя́т. Охо́тники возвраща́ются домо́й.

1 *First.*   2 *Having seen/seeing.*   3 *Which have come up* ('having come up').

Э́то оди́н вид охо́ты на волко́в. Существу́ет ещё не́сколько. Охо́та с борзы́ми соба́ками, кото́рые ло́вко хвата́ют во́лка за ␣уши и го́рло. Иногда́ ро́ют в лесу́ во́лчьи[1] я́мы, т.е. глубо́кие, величино́й с ко́мнату, кана́вы с прямы́ми отве́сными сте́нами. Све́рху их прикрыва́ют то́нкими пру́тьями и ве́тками, в це́нтре кладу́т на них прима́нку – кусо́к мя́са. Направля́ясь[2] к нему́, волк прова́ливается в я́му. Старики́ расска́зывают, что в их вре́мя, когда́ волко́в бы́ло мно́го, сме́лые охо́тники де́лали так: запряга́ют в са́ни тро́йку си́льных лошаде́й, выбира́ют в лесу́, где мно́го волко́в, доро́гу, выбра́сывают поса́женного в мешо́к ма́ленького поросёнка. Мешо́к привя́зан верёвкой и воло́чится в пяти́ ме́трах сза́ди сане́й. Тро́йка бе́шено несётся, поросёнок визжи́т, охо́тники непреры́вно стреля́ют в выска́кивающих[3] из ле́са волко́в.

А. Ефи́мов

1 Nominative plural of **во́лчий** *wolf's, wolf* (adjective). See Part II, Grammar, for such 'relative' adjectives.   2 *Making its way.*   3 *Leaping out.*

7. TRANSLATION

Moscow and the Kremlin

We do not know exactly when Moscow was founded. In all probability[1] it was built by Prince Yuri Vladimirovich, nicknamed Yuri Long-Arm.[2]

The town was sacked by the Tatars in 1237. There was a great fire in 1337 and Moscow was burnt almost to the ground.[3] The first stone buildings were built in the following century.

In the fifteenth century Italian architects were engaged to build new cathedrals and a new wall. The Kremlin[4] wall built at that time is more or less the same as the one we know. In 1600 water was laid on[5] in pipes from the River Moskva.

The great bell which now stands in the Kremlin was cast at the beginning of the eighteenth century. It was called the Tsar of Bells[6] although it was broken and has never been hung.

Towards the end of the eighteenth century a building was erected in which the Senate was housed. Today the Soviet of Ministers is housed there.

The new city of Petersburg,[7] built by Peter the Great, was made into the administrative centre. Renamed[8] Petrograd during the first World War, it was again renamed Leningrad after the death of Lenin in 1924. Already before that Moscow had been made the administrative centre of the new Soviet Republic.

On 20th July, 1955, the Kremlin was opened to the public. Recently a new building has been built – a great hall in which thousands of people can meet.

1 По всей вероя́тности.　　2 Долгору́кий.
3 До тла.　　4 Use the adjective кремлёвский.
5 Use the p.p.p. of провести́.　　6 Царь-Ко́локол.
7 NB no 's' in Russian Петербу́рг.　　8 Переимено́вать в + accusative.

SUMMARY

1 The p.p.p. ends in **-анный, -енный** or **-тый** (§§ 2, 3, 4).
2 The p.p.p. must be in the short form when it is the predicate (§ 5).
3 The short forms of the p.p.p. in **-нный** have only one **н** (§ 5).

Lesson 38

I. VERBS WITH THE INFINITIVE IN **-нуть** (*contd.*)

The group of verbs in **-нуть** which we examined in Lesson 36 is strictly limited in number and no new verbs of this type are formed.

The other group of verbs in **-нуть** consists largely of verbs which denote an instantaneous action – an action performed once and taking only a very brief moment. More verbs of this type are constantly created. They are all perfective, even those without a prefix. You have already met the imperfective of some of them.

This group retains the element **-ну-** in the past tense.

Like the other group of verbs in **-нуть** they are first conjugation, of the type with a consonant (in this case **н**) before the endings.

> **кри́кнуть** *to cry out, to shout*   крича́ть

fut. кри́кну, кри́кнешь; *past* кри́кнул, кри́кнула; *impfv. pres.* кричу́, кричи́шь.

Крича́ть also has the perfective **закрича́ть,** which you have met, meaning *to start shouting,* and **покрича́ть** *to shout a little.*

Ма́льчик кри́кнул, пото́м закрича́л «Помоги́те!» *The boy let out a cry and then began to shout 'Help'!*
Он покрича́л и умо́лк. *He shouted a little and fell silent.*

> **шагну́ть** *to step, to stride*   шага́ть

Non-instantaneous perfectives **зашага́ть, пошага́ть**

Он шагну́л че́рез поро́г. *He stepped over the threshold.*
Он шага́л больши́ми шага́ми. *He was taking big strides.*
Солда́ты зашага́ли в сто́рону га́вани. *The soldiers began to march towards the harbour.*

> **ки́нуть** *to throw*   кида́ть

Он ки́нул нам мяч. *He threw us the ball.*
Мяч на́до так кида́ть. *You must throw a ball like this.*

> **дро́гнуть** *to tremble*   дрожа́ть

Non-instantaneous perfectives **задрожа́ть, подрожа́ть**

При э́тих слова́х она́ дро́гнула. *At these words she gave a shudder.*
Она́ задрожа́ла всем те́лом и до́лго дрожа́ла. *Her whole body began to shake and continued to shake for a long time.*

> **улыбну́ться** *to smile*   улыба́ться

Он так ра́достно улыба́лся, что младе́нец вдруг улыбну́лся, пото́м

275

опя́ть-таки запла́кал. *He was smiling so happily that the baby suddenly broke into a smile, and then began to cry again.*

косну́ться *to touch*   **каса́ться** + gen.
прикосну́ться   **прикаса́ться** к + dat.

Он то́лько слегка́ косну́лся э́того вопро́са. *He only touched slightly on this question.*

Э́то меня́ не каса́ется. *That does not concern me.*

Он прикосну́лся к э́тому стака́ну и стака́н упа́л. *He touched this glass and it fell down.*

сту́кнуть *to knock*   **стуча́ть**

Non-instantaneous perfectives **застуча́ть** and **постуча́ть**

Кто стуча́л в дверь? *Who was knocking at the door?*

Кто́-то сту́кнул в дверь и ушёл. *Somebody gave a knock at the door and went away.*

Учи́тель сту́кнул по столу́ и разгово́р умо́лк. *The teacher tapped (once) on his desk and the conversation died down.*

Учи́тель постуча́л по столу́ и разгово́р умо́лк. *The teacher tapped (several times) on his desk etc.*

Вдруг кто́-то гро́мко застуча́л в дверь. *Suddenly somebody began hammering at the door.*

These few examples will give you an inkling of the wide possibilities of expression that the Russian verb system has because of its prefixes and suffixes.

A few verbs of this type are perfective without being instantaneous and the most important of them is:

верну́ть *to return, to give back*   **возвраща́ть**

There is also the perfective **возврати́ть,** having the same meaning as **верну́ть,** but it is less common.

Он никогда́ не возвраща́ет книг, бо́льше я ему́ не дам ни одно́й кни́ги, ведь он их не возвраща́ет.

Брать кни́ги в долг и пото́м не возвраща́ть, типи́чно студе́нческая черта́. Непра́вда, – я студе́нт и я всегда́ возвраща́ю кни́ги, и вчера́ ещё я верну́л вам ва́шего Достое́вского.

Да, но моего́ Пу́шкина вы мне не верну́ли. Собра́ние сочине́ний Го́голя (*Gogol's collected works*) вы мне то́же не верну́ли.

When reflexive, this verb means *to return, to come/go back*:

верну́ться (and возврати́ться) *impfv.* возвраща́ться

Мы верну́лись по́здно ве́чером домо́й, мы о́чень ре́дко возвраща́емся так по́здно, обыкнове́нно мы возвраща́емся мно́го ра́ньше, и за́втра мы вернёмся совсе́м ра́но.

повернýть *to turn* (something) *round*   повора́чивать (NB different form of imperfective).

Гла́вная соли́стка поверну́ла компози́тора лицо́м к пу́блике. Э́то бы́ло в Ве́не, бо́лее чем сто лет тому́ наза́д, компози́тор был глух, он огло́х на ста́рости лет и не слы́шал рукоплеска́ний (*applause*), пока́ пе́рвая соли́стка не поверну́ла его́ лицо́м к пу́блике. Компози́тор был Бетхо́вен, игра́ли его́ девя́тую симфо́нию.

Поверну́ть маши́ну на э́том у́зком ме́сте о́чень тру́дно, но я всегда́ повора́чиваю её о́чень осторо́жно.

повернýться *to turn* (oneself)   повора́чиваться

Ты всегда́ повора́чиваешься так неуклю́же (*clumsily*), смотри́, ты опроки́нул (*upset*) стул.

Одна́жды слон вошёл в фарфо́ровую ла́вку и поверну́лся там...
One day an elephant went into a china-shop and turned round . . .

переверну́ть *to turn over*   перевора́чивать

(alternative impfv. – перевёртывать, obligatory in the meaning *to turn over a page*).

переверну́ться *to overturn, be overturned*   перевора́чиваться

Я переверну́ла матра́сы на крова́тях, они́ переверну́ли сту́лья вверх нога́ми (*upside down*) и поста́вили их на столы́.

Тепе́рь мо́жно разверну́ться (*to turn round*) и нача́ть чи́стку.

Са́ша перевёртывал страни́цы кни́ги и нашёл э́то письмо́.

Ма́ня чита́ла, переверну́ла две страни́цы сра́зу и не заме́тила (*did not notice*).

Маши́на на по́лном ходу́ нае́хала на столб (*ran into a post*) и переверну́лась три ра́за.

сверну́ть *to turn, to change direction*   свора́чивать

Вот тут нам на́до свора́чивать, – да свора́чивай же! *That is where we should turn – well, go on, turn!*

Я уже́ сверну́л нале́во мину́ту тому́ наза́д. Ты хо́чешь, что́бы я опя́ть сверну́л нале́во? *I turned left a minute ago. Do you want me to turn left again?*

заверну́ть *to wrap up, to roll up*   завора́чивать

Пожа́луйста, заверни́те мою́ колбасу́ хороше́нько, заверни́те её вот в э́тот хоро́ший кусо́к бума́ги.

Гражда́нка, мы всегда́ завора́чиваем това́р в лу́чшую бума́гу, мо́жете не беспоко́иться, мы завернём ва́шу колбасу́ как сле́дует.

Finally, there are four verbs of this type which, when not prefixed, are imperfective. Of these, the two commonest are:

тяну́ть *to pull*	**тону́ть** *to drown, to sink*
pres. тяну́	*pres.* тону́
тя́нешь	то́нешь

Ло́шадь тя́нет теле́гу. *The horse pulls a cart.*

Он потяну́л теле́жку на́_го́ру. *He pulled the little cart up the hill.*

Смотри́, ло́дка то́нет! – по́здно, она́ уже́ потону́ла. *Look, there's a boat sinking! – too late, it's sunk.*

The verb **гнуть** *to fold, to bend*: **гну, гнёшь** etc. is usually prefixed, the prefix showing the manner of bending:

загну́ть *to fold over, back*	согну́ть *to fold together*
обогну́ть *to bend round*	перегну́ть *to twist*

These prefixed verbs are, of course, perfective. Their imperfectives are: **загиба́ть, сгиба́ть, огиба́ть, перегиба́ть.**

Note that the perfective **-нуть** verbs form their p.p.p. by replacing **-ть** with **-тый**:

перевёрнутая маши́на
завёрнутая колбаса́
со́гнутая спина́ (*back* cf. spine)

2. THE PRESENT ACTIVE PARTICIPLE

The present active participle (pres. act. p.) describes the action which the noun is performing. It is formed, therefore, only from imperfective verbs.

More strictly it could be called the imperfective active participle but we shall use the traditional term.

The pres. act. p. is very easy to form. Remove the **-т** of the third pers. plural and add **-щий, -щая, -щее, -щие.**

сле́довать *to follow* они́ сле́дую/т

сле́дую-щий, -щая, -щее, -щие

following сле́дующий, сле́дующая, сле́дующее, сле́дующие

На сле́дующей неде́ле всё бу́дет в поря́дке. *Next week/The following week everything will be in order.*

бежа́ть *to run* они́ бегу́/т

running бегу́щий, -щая, -щее, -щие

Бегу́щая де́вочка несёт газе́ту. *The girl (who is) running is carrying a newspaper.*

> As you see, it is often convenient to translate the Russian pres. act. p. by a *who/which* clause in English. In conversation Russians also use *who/which* clauses very often, except of course where the pres. act. p. has in effect become an adjective, as in the first example above.

говори́ть *to speak* они́ говоря́/т

speaking говоря́щий, говоря́щая, говоря́щее, говоря́щие

Учи́тель, говоря́щий по-францу́зски, вас поймёт. *The teacher who speaks/is speaking French will understand you.*

278

Я поздоро́вался по-неме́цки с учи́телем, говоря́щим по-францу́зски. *I said 'hello' in German to the teacher who speaks French.*

игра́ть *to play*   они́ игра́ю/т
playing игра́ющий, -щая, -щее, -щие

Скажи́ де́тям, игра́ющим в саду́, что́бы они́ не шуме́ли так. *Tell the children playing in the garden not to make so much noise.*

NB **что́бы** after **сказа́ть** when it means 'to pass on an order'

шуме́ть *to make a noise*   они́ шумя́/т
making a noise, noisy шумя́щий, -щая, -щее, -щие

Де́ти, шумя́щие в саду́, игра́ют в жму́рки. *The children (who are) making a noise in the garden are playing at blind man's buff.*

спать *to sleep*   они́ спя/т
sleeping спя́щий, -щая, -щее, -щие

Спя́щие де́ти не шумя́т. *Sleeping children do not make a noise.*

ви́деть *to see*   они́ ви́дя/т
seeing ви́дящий, -щая, -щее, -щие

Челове́к, не ви́дящий свои́х оши́бок, ча́сто су́дит други́х о́чень стро́го. *A person who does not see his own mistakes is often a very severe judge of others.*
Не люблю́ люде́й не ви́дящих свои́х оши́бок. *I don't like people who don't/can't see their own mistakes.*

люби́ть *to love, to like*   они любя́/т
loving, liking лю́бящий, -щая, -щее, -щие

Лю́ди, лю́бящие одино́чество, о́чень ча́сто быва́ют хоро́шими това́рищами. *People who like solitude are often good companions.*

NB instrumental after **быва́ть** imperfective *to be*

With verbs of the first conjugation the stress in the pres. act. p. is the same as in the third pers. plural. An exception is **могу́щий** *(being) able* (cf. **они́ мо́гут**).

With verbs of the second conjugation having a fixed stress the stress in the pres. act. p. is the same as in the third pers. plural. With verbs of the second conjugation in which the stress moves back after the first pers. sing. (e.g. **хожу́ – хо́дишь**) there is some variety in the stressing of the pres. act. p. In some it coincides with that of the third pers. plural, in others it coincides with that of the infinitive:

ходи́ть – ходя́щий, носи́ть – нося́щий, води́ть – водя́щий

дели́ть *to divide*   они́ де́лят – деля́щий
терпе́ть *to suffer*   они́ те́рпят – те́рпящий

The word **бу́дущий**, formed like a pres. act. p. from the third pers. plural **бу́дут** *they will be*, is an adjective meaning *future*.

Reflexive verbs can also have a pres. act. p.:

laughing смею́щийся, смею́щаяся, смею́щееся, смею́щиеся

Note that in the pres. act. p. the reflexive particle is always **-ся,** whereas in other verb forms where it occurs it is **-ся** after consonants and **-сь** after vowels: **смеющаяся** but **смеюсь.**

3. THE PRESENT GERUND

The pres. act. p. is *descriptive* of the *noun* – it behaves like an adjective, though it is derived from a verb. It can be replaced by or translated by a descriptive clause beginning with *who* or *which,* followed by the verb from which it is derived.

> Игра́ющие де́ти шумя́т. } *The children (who are) playing are*
> Де́ти, кото́рые игра́ют, шумя́т. } *making a noise.*

In English the present participle can be used adverbially:

> *While playing, the children make or made a noise.*
> *When playing, the children make or made a noise.*

In these sentences playing does not describe the children, but tells you what background action was going on, while the children made a noise. It qualifies the verb and not the noun.

Russian has a special kind of participle to express this adverbial idea. It is formed from imperfective verbs, since it expresses an action going on in the past, present or future, as a background action to some other action denoted by the main verb. The traditional name for it is *the present gerund.*

The present gerund in Russian is easily formed. For most verbs which have a present gerund you remove the last two letters of the third pers. plural and add **-я** after a vowel or any consonant except **ш, ж, ч** or **щ,** after which you must add **-а.**

ду́мать *to think*	ду́ма/ют	– ду́мая (*while*) *thinking*
чита́ть *to read*	чита́/ют	– чита́я (*while*) *reading*
атакова́ть *to attack*	атаку́/ют	– атаку́я (*while*) *attacking*
име́ть *to have*	име́/ют	– име́я (*while*) *having*
стоя́ть *to stand*	сто/я́т	– сто́я (*while*) *standing*
говори́ть *to speak*	говоря́т	– говоря́ (*while*) *speaking*
сиде́ть *to sit*	сидя́т	– си́дя (*while*) *sitting*
жить *to live*	живу́т	– живя́ (*while*) *living*
дыша́ть *to breathe*	ды́шат	– дыша́ (*while*) *breathing*
молча́ть *to keep silent*	молча́т	– мо́лча (*while*) *keeping silent*
лежа́ть *to lie*	лежа́т	– лёжа (*while*) *lying*

The stress is generally the same as in the third pers. plural, but there are a few exceptions, as some of the examples show.

The verbs in **-ава́ть** form the present gerund from the infinitive:

> дава́ть *to give* дава́я   встава́ть *to get up* встава́я

Ду́мая о свои́х дела́х, она́ се́ла не в тот по́езд. *Thinking about her own affairs, she got into the wrong train.*

280

Отéц заснýл читáя газéту. *Father fell asleep reading the paper.*

Атакýя нóвое движéние в литератýре, мóжно всё-таки сказáть, что есть в нём и хорóшие чертьí. *While attacking the new movement in literature, one can nevertheless say that it has some good features.*

Не имéя новостéй, он поéхал домóй. *Not having any news, he went home.*

Стóя у дверéй, собáка нас ждалá весь вéчер. *Standing by the door, the dog waited for us the whole evening.*

Онú стоя́ли у окнá, не говоря́ ни слóва. *They were standing by the window without saying a word.*

Мы провелú весь вéчер, сúдя у камúна. *We spent the whole evening sitting by the fire.*

Живя́ в глухóй дерéвне, как онú моглú услы́шать эти нóвости? *Living in the depths of the country, how could they hear this news?*

Чуть дышá, я вошёл в кóмнату. *Scarcely breathing, I entered the room.*

Вставáя кáждое ýтро в шесть часóв, я óчень устаю́ к концý недéли. *Getting up every morning at six, I became very tired towards the end of the week.*

Several points emerge from these examples:

a The present gerund never changes its form. It behaves like an adverb and is not declinable.

b The person (or thing) performing the action expressed by the gerund is the subject of the verb in the same sentence. In the third example above there is no grammatical subject but the logical subject of the impersonal construction **мóжно сказáть** is *one* or 'people in general' and *one* is also the person who is doing the attacking expressed by the gerund **атакýя.**

An apparent exception to this last point is the word **говоря́.** In addition to sentences like the sixth example above, it is commonly used with adverbs to make an introductory adverbial phrase which expresses an attitude towards the statement as a whole:

Он, сóбственно говоря́, не дóлжен быть здесь. *Properly/strictly speaking, he ought not to be here.*

Инáче говоря́, ракéту доставля́ют на орбúту. *Putting it in another way, they place the rocket in orbit.*

See Part II, Grammar, for verbs which do *not* form a present gerund.

4. THE PRESENT PASSIVE PARTICIPLE

There is another present participle – the present passive participle, as it is traditionally called. Like the pres. act. p. the present passive participle (pres. p.p.) is descriptive: it looks like and functions as an adjective. Again, like the pres. act. p., it is also formed only from imperfective verbs.

The pres. p.p. means that the person or thing which it describes is undergoing the action which it denotes. Note this difference: the *past* passive participle means that the action has, had been or will have been performed on the person or thing – the action is completed. The *present* passive participle means that the action is being, was being or will be being performed on the person or thing – the action is not completed, it is going on.

The pres. p.p. is formed by adding hard adjective endings to the first pers. plural of the verb:

чита́ть, мы чита́ем – чита́емый (*being*) *read*
атакова́ть, мы атаку́ем – атаку́емый (*being*) *attacked, under attack.*

Not all verbs form this participle. It is commonest in first conjugation verbs with prefixes which conjugate like **ду́мать.**

убежда́ть *to convince*	убежда́емый (*being*) *convinced*
разреша́ть *to solve*	разреша́емый (*being*) *solved*
выполня́ть *to perform, carry out*	выполня́емый (*being*) *performed*
обвиня́ть *to accuse*	обвиня́емый (*being*) *accused*

Verbs of the **-ывать/-ивать** type:

усѝливать *to reinforce, intensify*	усѝливаемый (*being*) *intensified*
подпѝсывать *to sign*	подпѝсываемый (*being*) *signed*

The **-овать** verbs:

организова́ть *to organize*	организу́емый (*being*) *organized*
рекомендова́ть *to recommend*	рекомендуемый (*being*) *recommended*

and in some of the indeterminate verbs of motion (usually prefixed):

ввози́ть *to import*	ввози́мый (*being*) *imported*
уноси́ть *to carry off*	уноси́мый (*being*) *carried off.*

It is not common with other verbs of the second conjugation. The words **люби́мый** *favourite* and **ви́димый** *visible* were originally participles of this kind.

The same participle has also provided the opening phrases for formal letters:

уважа́ть *to respect*   уважа́емый (*being*) *respected*

Уважа́емый Граждани́н. *Dear Sir.*
Многоуважа́емый Алекса́ндр Серге́евич. *Dear Alexander Sergeyevich.*
Глубокоуважа́емый Колле́га. *Dear Colleague.*

A very few intransitive verbs also form this participle:

угрожа́ть *to threaten* (+ dative) угрожа́емый (*being*) *threatened.*
предше́ствовать *to precede* (+ dative) предше́ствуемый (*being*) *preceded.*

Это кни́га чита́емая все́ми детьми́. *It is a book read by all children.*
Атаку́емые со всех сторо́н, мы всё же бу́дем отста́ивать своё положе́ние.
     Though attacked from all sides, we shall still go on defending our position.
Обвиня́емый стоя́л понуря́ го́лову. *The accused stood with bowed head*
     (понуря́ is a 'fossilized' gerund).

Я, к сожалéнию, ещё не читáл рекомендýемую литератýру. *Unfortunately I have not yet read the recommended literature.*

Предшéствуемые духовы́м оркéстром, шахтёры шагáли в парк. *Preceded by a brass band, the miners marched to the park.*

The pres. p.p. gives rise to adjectives corresponding to English adjectives ending in -*able*, -*ible*:

забывáть *to forget*   незабывáемый *unforgettable*
сгорáть *to burn*   несгорáемый *non-inflammable*

Short forms of the pres. p.p. are sometimes found in literary Russian but they are rare in spoken Russian.

5. TEXT

This is a more difficult and fuller version of *The Snowstorm* which was serialized in earlier lessons.

Scenes from Russian Life

Метéль

Метéль – э́то густóй снегопáд, сопровождáющийся штормовы́м вéтром. Снег, пáдающий и лежáщий на землé, нахóдится в непреры́вном круговóм движéнии. Днём всё белó и в[1] двух шагáх ничегó не ви́дно, как во врéмя густы́х лóндонских тумáнов. Но ещё хýже ви́димость нóчью. Передвижéние по больши́м шоссéйным дорóгам си́льно затрудненó. В такýю порý просёлочные дорóги совсéм занóсит,[2] так как вéхи (высóкие елóвые вéтки), котóрые устанáвливаются по бокáм дорóги, си́льным вéтром сбивáет[2] и занóсит[2] снéгом.

1 *At.*
2 Impersonal use of verb: 'it covers up' (with snow) and 'it knocks down' (by means of the wind). Translated *the roads are . . . snowed up* and *are knocked down by the . . . wind.*

Сильнá метéль на ю́жном Урáле. Начинáется онá внезáпно. Сначáла идёт мéлкий снег, он сменя́ется крýпным. Вéтер, с нарастáющей си́лой, перехóдит в ви́хрь, вóет,[1] свисти́т, крýжит пáдающий снег, поднимáя огрóмные бéлые столбы́ снéга с земли́. Станóвится темнó. В снéжном мрáке ничегó не ви́дно.

Местá обши́рные. Селéния нахóдятся на расстоя́нии пяти́ киломéтров и бóлее. Жи́тели проклáдывают зи́мние корóткие дорóги чéрез болóта и рéчки, котóрые замерзáют в ноябрé мéсяце и покрывáются снéгом.

Вéсело быть в гостя́х, но порá и домóй. Отдохнýвшие[2] лóшади бы́стро проéхали небольшóй берёзовый лесóк. Но чтó-то хмýрится нéбо; нависáют ни́зкие облакá, они́ бы́стро сгущáются в тýчи; подýл вéтер. Вдруг пошёл мéлкий снег. Внезáпно он смени́лся крýпными хлóпьями.

1 Third pers. sing. of **выть** *to howl*, **вóю, вóешь.**
2 'Having rested' (see Lesson 39), i.e. *which have rested.*

Ве́тер поду́л с тако́й си́лой, что лошадя́м тру́дно бежа́ть. Всё смеша́лось в бе́лом ви́хре. Во мра́ке ничего́ не ви́дно. То́лько вой в уша́х, да ре́зкий колю́чий ве́тер с неи́стовой си́лой бьёт в лицо́, обжига́я его́. Захва́тывает дыха́ние. Пу́тники, тепло́ оде́тые в овчи́нные тулу́пы и ва́ленки, чу́вствуют как ве́тер прони́зывает до косте́й. Нельзя́ гляде́ть – снег с молниено́сной быстрото́й ле́пит в лицо́. Завыва́ние вьюги глуши́т слова́ ря́дом сидя́щего челове́ка.

– Ну тепе́рь я́сно, что мы сби́лись с доро́ги – промелькну́ло в голове́ ка́ждого.

Они́ бы́стро выска́кивают из сане́й. Стря́хивают с себя́ ку́чи сне́га. Пры́гают, что́бы отогре́ться. Ло́шади встаю́т, они́ чу́вствуют, что сби́лись с твёрдой по́чвы. Пу́тники помога́ют лошадя́м, подта́лкивая са́ни. Ло́шади, поня́в, что во́жжи опу́щены, лю́ди и́ми не пра́вят, с трудо́м выбира́ются и начина́ют оты́скивать доро́гу са́ми.

В тех места́х уже́ зна́ют, что во вре́мя мете́ли ло́шадь найдёт сама́ доро́гу домо́й, нащу́пывая нога́ми твёрдую нае́зженную по́лосу́ доро́ги.

Вот одна́ ло́шадь спотыка́ется и остана́вливается. Но на́до дви́гаться, нельзя́ до́лго стоя́ть. Ло́шади са́ми устремля́ются вперёд. Продвиже́ние стано́вится всё ме́дленнее: одну́ но́гу вы́тащишь – друга́я увяза́ет в глубо́ком снегу́. Пу́тники начина́ют крича́ть: Ау́! Ау́! Мо́жет быть селе́нье бли́зко? Вьюга глуши́т их голоса́. Наступа́ют су́мерки. Мрак впереди́ сгуща́ется. Чу́ткие ло́шади, почу́яв[1] бли́зость жилья́ и до́ма, вдруг с си́лой рву́тся вперёд. Им жа́рко,[2] от них идёт пар, а мете́ль всё не унима́ется.

– Ну что э́то? Кто́-то кричи́т?

Зву́ки всё бли́же. А вот что́-то черне́ет? Из темноты́ слы́шен смех, а вот и огонёк.

– Что, жа́рко? Вот так мете́ль! Ох, и хороша́!

Совсе́м ря́дом стоя́т лю́ди, верхо́м на лошадя́х с фонаря́ми и па́лками в рука́х. Это встреча́ют возвраща́вшихся из госте́й.[3]

– Далеко́ ли мы от села́? И на доро́ге ли мы?

– Ва́ши ло́шади иду́т пра́вильно, а до до́му[4] всего́ пятьсо́т ме́тров.

С весёлым шу́мом добрали́сь до до́му.

---

1 *Having sensed* or *sensing* (see Lesson 39).   2 *They are hot.*
3 *People returning from visiting* (see Lesson 39).   4 Alternative gen. of **дом.**

Всю ночь бушу́ет пурга́, но лю́дям хорошо́ пережида́ть её в свои́х ую́тных тёплых дома́х. А у́тром ина́я карти́на. Со́лнце и моро́з. Прекра́сное у́тро. Вокру́г така́я тишь, тру́дно пове́рить, что всю ночь бушева́ла мете́ль. Снег волна́ми и ослепи́тельной белизно́й блиста́ет под я́ркими луча́ми со́лнца. Сло́вно в ска́зке, стоя́т е́ли и со́сны в бе́лом убо́ре.

Взро́слые и де́ти принима́ются за расчи́стку доро́г. Вы́шли тра́кторы и бульдо́зеры. Детвора́ ката́ется на са́нках, валя́ется в пуши́стом снегу́.

Снег прия́тно похру́стывает под ва́ленками, щёки румя́нит моро́з. Недалёко зама́нчиво темне́ет лес.

– На лы́жи! В лес! – крича́т ребя́та.

Лю́бит ру́сский челове́к свою́ краса́вицу-зиму́ с её мете́лями, с её бодря́щим моро́зом.

Н. Ефи́мова

6. EXERCISE

Replace each phrase in brackets by a single, appropriate participle (pres. act. p., pres. p.p.) or gerund.

[Когда́ я путеше́ствовал] по Сове́тскому Сою́зу, я ви́дел мно́го интере́сных веще́й. [Сопровожда́ть[1]] о́чень уме́лой перево́дчицей, я смог познако́миться с людьми́ [кото́рые жи́ли] в весьма́ разли́чных усло́виях.

На восто́ке я был на гидроста́нции, [кото́рая стро́илась] ещё. Грома́дные глы́бы земли́ [вырыва́ть[1]] бульдо́зерами, дли́нные стальны́е ба́лки [поднима́ть[1]] высо́кими кра́нами, рабо́чие [кото́рые бе́гали] туда́-сюда́, молоды́е инжене́ры [кото́рые стоя́ли] с пла́нами в рука́х и оживлённо [обсужда́ли] ход рабо́ты – всё э́то произвело́ на меня́ [не забыва́ть[2]] впечатле́ние.

[Когда́ мы возвраща́лись] в Москву́, мы посети́ли колхо́з [кото́рый нахо́дится] недалёко от го́рода и там я разгова́ривал со ста́рым крестья́нином. [Когда́ он расска́зывал] нам о жи́зни крестья́н и [когда́ он вспомина́л] слу́чаи из вое́нного и послевое́нного пери́ода, он сказа́л, что во мно́гом жизнь крестья́нина ста́ла гора́здо лу́чше.

В Москве́ само́й я познако́мился с молоды́м писа́телем [кото́рый по́льзуется] широ́кой популя́рностью у молодёжи. Он познако́мил меня́ с други́ми писа́телями и худо́жниками [кото́рые мы́слят] на но́вый лад. [Когда́ мы разгова́ривали] об иску́сстве и литерату́ре, мы нашли́, что есть в на́ших взгля́дах бо́льше [что объединя́ет] нас, чем [что отделя́ет] нас друг от дру́га.

[Когда́ я отправля́лся] домо́й, я обеща́л друзья́м, [кото́рые сопровожда́ли] меня́, верну́ться в Сове́тский Сою́з в ближа́йшем бу́дущем.

1 Pres. p.p.   2 Pres. p.p. with prefix не-.

SUMMARY

1 Instantaneous action verbs in -путь (§ 1).
2 The present active participle ends in -ущий, -ющий, -ащий or -ящий (§ 2).
3 The present gerund ends in -я or -а (§ 3).
4 The present passive participle ends in -мый (§ 4).

285

Lesson 39

I. THE PAST ACTIVE PARTICIPLE

The past active participle (p. act. p.) has two forms: perfective and imperfective.

We shall take the perfective form first. It means that the person or thing described by the p. act. p. has done, had done or will have done the action it denotes. In other words it is the perfective parallel to the pres. act. p., which we said would be more accurately described if called the imperfective act. p.

With most verbs the p. act. p. is formed by taking the past tense masculine, removing the **л** and adding **-вший, -вшая, -вшее, -вшие**.

дать	он дал	да́вший *having given*
прочита́ть	он прочита́л	прочита́вший *having read*
уговори́ть	он уговори́л	уговори́вший *having persuaded*

Э́тот челове́к, да́вший нам э́ти кни́ги, друг моего́ дя́ди. *The man who gave ('having given') us these books is a friend of my uncle.*

Мы подошли́ к же́нщине, то́лько что прочита́вшей докла́д. *We went up to the woman who had just read ('having just read') the report.*

Са́ша, уговори́вший её не идти́ в кино́, пошёл с ней в теа́тр. *Sasha, who had persuaded her not to go to the cinema, went with her to the theatre.*

Verbs without **л** in the past tense masculine form the p. act. p. by adding **-ший, -шая, -шее, -шие** to the past tense masculine.

перенести́	он перенёс	перенёсший *having carried across*
привезти́	он привёз	привёзший *having brought*
иссо́хнуть	он иссо́х	иссо́хший *having dried up*
поги́бнуть	он поги́б	поги́бший *having perished*
умере́ть	он у́мер	уме́рший *having died*
постри́чь	он постри́г	постри́гший *having cut* (hair)

Verbs of this type with **т** or **д** in the conjugation but not in the past tense reinstate the **т** or **д** in the p. act. p.

я переведу́	он перевёл	переве́дший *having translated*
я вы́мету	он вы́мел	вы́метший *having swept out*

The following verbs have an irregular p. act. p.:

укра́сть *to steal*	я украду́	он укра́л	укра́вший
упа́сть *to fall*	я упаду́	он упа́л	упа́вший
сесть *to sit down*	я ся́ду	он сел	се́вший

The compounds of **идти́** have **-ше́дший**:

войти́	воше́дший *having entered*	
уйти́	уше́дший *having left*	

Они́ все пошли́ на борт корабля́, привёзшего делега́цию. *They have all gone on board the ship which brought the delegation.*

Э́то па́мятник поги́бшим на войне́. *That is a monument to those who fell in the war.*

В Сове́тском Сою́зе господи́н Макдо́нальд познако́мился с С. Мар-ша́ком, переве́дшим Бе́рнса на ру́сский язы́к. *In the Soviet Union Mr. MacDonald made the acquaintance of S. Marshak, who has translated Burns into Russian.*

Воше́дшее уже́ в си́лу постановле́ние не спасёт положе́ние. *The decree which has already gone into force will not save the situation.*

This participle can also be reflexive. The reflexive particle, as in the case of the pres. act. p., is always **-ся,** never **-сь.**

Скрыва́вшийся за занаве́ской ребёнок вдруг запла́кал. *The child who had hidden behind the curtain suddenly burst into tears.*

Охо́тник иска́л скрыва́вшегося за кусто́м за́йца. *The hunter was looking for the hare, which had hidden itself behind a bush.*

The stress in the p. act. p. is the same as in the past tense masculine of the same verb, except for **уме́рший,** cf. past tense **у́мер.**

The imperfective p. act. p. is formed from imperfective verbs in the same way as the p. act. p. perfective is formed from perfective verbs, except that the unprefixed **-нуть** verbs which lose the **-ну-** in the past tense usually keep it in forming the imperfective p. act. p.:

> со́хнуть *to dry up* сох со́хнувший

The meaning of the imperfective form of this participle is that the person or thing described was performing the action, which was not completed. It is found only in sentences with the verb in the past tense and is very much a literary form. Even in literary Russian it is tending to be replaced by the pres. act. p., which can appear in sentences with the verb in the past, present or future.

The word **бы́вший** is the p. act. p. of **быть.** It usually has adjectival meaning – *former.*

Команди́р разгова́ривает с бы́вшими чле́нами полка́. *The commanding officer is conversing with some former members of the regiment.*

2. THE PAST GERUND – I

The past gerund functions like the present gerund but means that the action has been, had been or will be completed before that of the main verb and so it is formed from perfective verbs.

Like the p. act. p. it is formed from the past tense or the infinitive. Remove the **-л** or **-ть** (or **-сть**) and add **-в** or **-вши:**

он дал	дав/да́вши *having given*
он прочита́л	прочита́в/прочита́вши *having read*
он уговори́л	уговори́в/уговори́вши *having persuaded*
он сел	сев/се́вши *having sat down*
он упа́л	упа́в/упа́вши *having fallen*
он укра́л	укра́в/укра́вши *having stolen*

The form in **-вши** is less 'literary' than the form in **-в** but reflexive verbs must have the **-вши** ending:

простил   прости́лся   прости́вшись *having said goodbye*

Verbs with the infinitive in **-зть** or **-чь** form the past gerund by adding **-ши** to the past tense masculine.

перелéзть	перелéз	перелéзши *having crawled across*
постри́чься	постри́гся	постри́гшись *having had a hair-cut*

Verbs in **-ереть** do the same or replace the **-ть** of the infinitive by **-в/-вши**:

запере́ть *to lock*	за́пер	за́перши or запере́в(ши) *having locked*
умере́ть *to die*	у́мер	у́мерши or умере́в(ши) *having died*

Дав нам пода́рки, дя́дя прости́лся со все́ми. *Having given us presents, uncle said goodbye to everybody.*

Прочита́в докла́д, он вы́шел, не дожда́вшись вопро́сов. *Having read his lecture, he went out without waiting for questions.*

Сев у роя́ля, тётя начала́ игра́ть вальс. *Having sat down/sitting down at the grand piano, auntie began to play a waltz.*

The last example shows that it is sometimes better to translate the p. act. p. into English by a 'doing' form, instead of a 'having done' form. Be careful in translating such expressions back into Russian, which is very precise in this respect: if the action is, was or will be completed before the action of the main verb you must have the past gerund, not the present gerund:

Покрасне́в, она́ начала́ обясня́ть. *Blushing, she began to explain* – past gerund because the Russian verb means *to turn red*. Hence **покрасне́в** *having turned red* – and therefore with a blush on her cheeks. You could have **красне́я** (present gerund) in such a sentence as: **Она́ объясня́ла, красне́я** – *She was blushing as she explained* ('She explained, blushing').

Укра́вши все карти́ны, вор верну́лся и за серебро́м. *Having stolen all the pictures, the thief returned for the silver as well.*

Ива́н уе́хал, не прости́вшись ни с кем. *Ivan left without saying goodbye to anybody.*

From these examples, it can be seen that, like the present gerund, the past gerund is not a declinable word and that the action it denotes must be performed by the grammatical subject of the main verb – or the logical subject, as in:

288

Нельзя́ уе́хать не прости́вшись. *One cannot go without having said goodbye.*
Remember the rule:

> present gerund = simultaneous or background action
> past gerund = prior action

3. THE PAST GERUND — II

The past gerund of verbs with the infinitive in **-ти** has exactly the same function as the past gerund described above. It ends, however, in **-я**, which is added to the stem of the conjugation:

пройти́ *to pass through*	пройд/у́	пройдя́ *having passed through*
увести́ *to lead away*	увед/у́	уведя́ *having led away*
изобрести́ *to invent*	изобрет/у́	изобретя́ *having invented*

Ошиби́ться *to make a mistake* and **проче́сть** *to read* (and other compounds of **-честь**) form the past gerund in the same way:

ошиб/у́сь	ошибя́сь *having made a mistake*
прочт/у́	прочтя́ *having read*
вы́чту	вы́чтя *having subtracted*

You are unlikely to confuse this past gerund with the present gerund in **-я** since the past gerund is made from perfective verbs, and the present gerund from imperfective verbs. In any case, the context usually makes it clear whether it is a past or present gerund.

Пройдя́ мост, вы вы́йдете на на́бережную. *If you go past ('having passed') the bridge, you will come out on to the embankment.*

Изобретя́ телеско́п-рефле́ктор, Нью́тон сде́лал большо́й вклад в разви́тие астроно́мии. *By inventing ('having invented') the reflector-telescope Newton made a great contribution to the development of astronomy.*

Прочтя́ (or прочита́в) докла́д, профе́ссор спроси́л: «Есть ли у вас вопро́сы?» *Having read his lecture, the professor asked: 'Have you any questions?'*

4. THE EXPRESSION OF THE PASSIVE VOICE

The passive voice consists of verb forms which express the fact that something is being done to the subject of the verb. In the course of these lessons you have met several ways of expressing the passive voice: reflexive verbs, passive participles, the third pers. plural or the past tense plural of the verb when no subject is expressed, and the impersonal use of the neuter past tense.

These various ways of expressing the passive are not freely interchangeable: there are certain differences between them.

The past passive participle can only be used when the action has been completed, not if the subject is still undergoing the action.

U

By using the p.p.p. it is possible to differentiate between the recent past and the remoter past, which is otherwise impossible in Russian.

Он уво́лен. *He has been dismissed.*

Он был уво́лен сами́м дире́ктором. *He was dismissed by the director himself.*

As you see, if the person or thing performing the action on the subject is expressed, the agent goes into the instrumental case.

Волк уби́т. *The wolf has been killed.*

Волк был уби́т ме́тким вы́стрелом. *The wolf was killed/had been killed by an accurate shot.*

Все во́лки в э́том райо́не бу́дут уби́ты. *All the wolves in this area will be killed.*

Дом был постро́ен за оди́н ме́сяц. *The house was built in one month.*

Дом бу́дет постро́ен на берегу́ реки́. *The house will be built on the river bank.*

All the above ideas could be expressed by making the subject into the object and using the past tense plural or the third pers. plural of the verb or, in two of the sentences, making the agent expressed in the instrumental into the subject. This way of expressing the passive is slightly less *impersonal*, even though in most of these sentences no subject is named.

Во́лка уби́ли. *The wolf has been/was/had been killed.*

Во́лка уби́ли ме́тким вы́стрелом.

Во́лка уби́л о́чень ме́ткий вы́стрел. *The wolf was killed by a very accurate shot.*

Всех волко́в убью́т в э́том райо́не. *All the wolves will be killed in this area.*

Его́ уво́лили. *He has been/was/had been dismissed.*

Его́ уво́лил сам нача́льник. *He has been/was/had been dismissed by the director himself. The director himself has/had sacked him.*

Постро́или дом за оди́н ме́сяц. *The house has been/was/had been built in one month. They built the house. . . .*

Постро́ят дом на берегу́ реки́. *The house will be built on the river bank.*

As you see, the differentiation of the past tense which is possible with the p.p.p. is not possible with this construction.

When the action is not completed, it is sometimes possible to express the passive voice by means of the short form of the pres. p.p.:

Влади́мир был уважа́ем все́ми. *Vladimir was respected by everybody.*

But **все уважа́ли Влади́мира** is more usual.

You would be more likely, however, to find the pres. p.p. in an adjectival phrase, as in two of the sentences in § 4 of Lesson 38:

Атаку́емые со всех сторо́н, мы всё же бу́дем отста́ивать своё положе́ние.

Предше́ствуемые духовы́м орке́стром, шахтёры шага́ли в парк.

Some reflexive verbs can be used to express the passive:

> У них продаётся кровáть. *They have a bed for sale.*
>
> Здесь продаю́тся пти́цы. *Birds sold here.*

The agent can be expressed in the instrumental if the action is an 'abstract' one:

> Он счита́ется все́ми тала́нтливым ма́льчиком. *He is considered a gifted boy by everybody.*

The impersonal use of the past tense neuter to express the passive voice is used only when the (logical) agent is inanimate. The logical agent, if expressed, goes into the instrumental case. The same construction is found with the third pers. sing. of the verb used impersonally.

Самолёт качну́ло. *The aeroplane was bumped about.*

Все доро́ги занесло́ сне́гом. *All the roads were snowed up.*

Ло́дку кача́ет. *The boat is being rocked about.*

В таку́ю пору́ просёлочные доро́ги совсе́м зано́сит. *At such a time the country roads are entirely snowed up* (see Lesson 38, § 5).

> The agent is not expressed, since it is obvious that it must be snow which has blocked the roads.

5. EXERCISE

Rewrite the following passages, using as many different ways as possible to express the passive voice:

– Он уво́лен.

– Да нет, не мо́жет быть!

– Да, да, он уво́лен, ста́рший счетово́д уво́лен. Вчера́ он был уво́лен. И касси́ра то́же уво́лят – он бу́дет за́втра уво́лен.

У нас отнима́ют кусо́к земли́.

Вот весь э́тот кусо́к бу́дет о́тнят у нас. У нас уже́ два го́да тому́ наза́д о́тняли зе́млю. Вот тот кусо́к, где постро́ена шко́ла, был о́тнят у нас два го́да тому́ наза́д. Сказа́ли нам, что там бу́дет постро́ена больни́ца, а постро́или шко́лу. Тепе́рь хо́дят слу́хи, что и на той стороне́ бу́дет стро́иться шко́ла, а нам больни́ца нужна́ – шко́ла уже́ есть.

Тут хо́дят ра́зные слу́хи. Разнёсся слух, что постро́ят не шко́лу, а гидроэлектри́ческую ста́нцию, вот каки́е слу́хи тут хо́дят.

Дя́дя Са́ша был ра́нен во вре́мя второ́й мирово́й войны́, его́ ра́нили в ру́ку и в спи́ну, а его́ оте́ц был уби́т во вре́мя пе́рвой мирово́й войны́, его́ уби́ли в боя́х в Карпа́тах.

6. TEXT

This is the same story as in Lesson 36, with more participles and gerunds and a wider vocabulary.

Подлёдный лов рыбы

Морóзный зи́мний день. Огрóмная снéжная равни́на зали́та сóлнцем. Кругóм, куда́ ни взгля́нешь, гру́ппами сидя́т на я́щичках лю́ди...

Но почему́ такóй необы́чный пейза́ж?

Это рыбаки́, люби́тели подлéдного лóва. Они́ приéхали сюда́, на Большу́ю Вóлгу – водоём, образова́вшийся пóсле тогó, как рéку перекры́ла плоти́на гидроэлектроста́нции. Большинствó их – москвичи́, хотя́ от столи́цы до э́тих мест сто три́дцать киломéтров. Здесь óчень мнóго ры́бы разли́чных порóд.

Есть и други́е водохрани́лища, нéкоторые óчень бли́зко от Москвы́.

Но стра́стных рыболóвов тя́нет на вóлжские простóры.

На автомоби́лях и в больши́х автóбусах они́ éдут пря́мо по заснежённому льду и располага́ются там, где лу́чше клюёт ры́ба.

Зимóй подо_льдóм лóвят ры́бу на у́дочку слéдующим óбразом.

Прéжде всегó на́до, разброса́в ногóй в ра́зные стóроны снег, проби́ть во льду отвéрстие, котóрое называ́ется лу́нка. Тóлстый (не мéнее двух фу́тов) и óчень крéпкий лёд, выдéрживающий больши́е автóбусы с сорока́ рыбака́ми, пробура́вливается специа́льным сверлóм и́ли же пробива́ется желéзной пéшней.

Конéц у неё óстрый, а ру́чка деревя́нная с верёвочной пéтлей на концé. Её надева́ют на_руку, чтóбы пéшня не вы́скочила и не утону́ла подо_льдóм. Когда́ пробива́ют лу́нку, осóбой рыба́цкой лóжкой с отвéрстиями для стека́ния воды́ выбра́сывают куски́ льда.

Послéдние уда́ры, и вода́, вы́рвавшись, момента́льно заполня́ет всю лу́нку. Размéр её такóй, что мóжно вы́тащить кру́пную ры́бу.

Тепéрь на́до приготóвить у́дочку. Рыба́к достаёт её из специа́льного я́щика, в котóрый потóм скла́дывается ры́ба. На нём же сидя́т, потому́ что лóвля продолжа́ется нéсколько часóв. У́дочка óчень корóткая, всегó óколо двух фу́тов. С неё разма́тывается лéска размéром в нéсколько мéтров, в зави́симости от глубины́. На концé лéски ма́ленький крючóк с припа́янным к нему́ в фóрме дроби́нки гру́зом. На остриé крючка́ на́до надéть однóго-двух мотылéй. Это кра́сные, длинóй óколо двух сантимéтров червячки́ – личи́нки комара́. Они́ продаю́тся в рыболóвных магази́нах. Храни́ть корóбочку с мотыля́ми прихóдится в карма́не, а то они́ мóгут бы́стро замёрзнуть.

Всё в поря́дке. Мóжно начина́ть. Крючóк вмéсте с нейлóновой тóнкой лé１ской опуска́ется до дна. Затéм рыба́к начина́ет мéдленно поднима́ть её, слегка́ потря́хивая ритми́чно рукóй, не бóлее как на полмéтра.

Пото́м опуска́ет вновь и повторя́ет движе́ние. Живы́е кра́сные чер-
вячки́, потря́хиваемые ле́ской – хоро́шая прима́нка. На конце́ ма́лень-
кой у́дочки приде́лан на ги́бкой про́волочке небольшо́й рези́новый
поплаво́к. Как то́лько ры́ба клю́нет, поплаво́к неме́дленно дёрнется
вниз. На́до бы́стро тащи́ть.

И вот на сверка́ющем от со́лнца снегу́ появля́ется пе́рвый о́кунь. Он
ре́зко выделя́ется на бе́лом фо́не свои́ми кра́сными плавника́ми и
пёстрой раскра́ской. За ним – друго́й. Хоро́ший уло́в – э́то четы́ре или
пять килогра́ммов ры́бы за не́сколько часо́в.

Вдруг что́-то происхо́дит. Мно́гие рыбаки́ вска́кивают со свои́х я́щиков
и бегу́т в сто́рону, где сиди́т старичо́к – о́пытный рыба́к. Он то́лько что
вы́тащил из воды́ огро́мную щу́ку. Да, таку́ю на ма́ленький крючо́к с
мотылём не пойма́ешь. Стари́к ло́вит други́м спо́собом. Он привози́т
с собо́й в бидо́нчике с водо́й деся́тка два ме́лких рыб. Их называ́ют –
живцы́. Осторо́жно прока́лывает им гу́бы крючко́м и на дли́нной
про́чной ле́ске отправля́ет их в во́ду. Све́рху у лу́нки он ста́вит в снегу́
па́лочку, на кото́рую кладёт ле́ску с привя́занным к ней кра́сным
флажко́м. Таки́х у́дочек он привози́т не ме́нее десяти́. Зате́м он прогу́ли-
вается о́коло э́тих па́лочек и следи́т, где па́дает флажо́к. Па́дает же он
тогда́, когда́ живца́ взяла́ и потащи́ла кру́пная ры́ба. На́до бы́стро
дёрнуть ле́ску – подсе́чь ры́бу и тащи́ть.

Профессиона́льные же рыбаки́ ло́вят зимо́й сетя́ми, иску́сно рас-
ставля́я их подо_льдо́м.

А. Ефи́мов

7. TRANSLATION

In the following translation all the phrases underlined are to be translated
by constructions with participles or gerunds.

Having gone by train from Edinburgh to London, we set off by plane for
Moscow. The delegates who had arrived earlier in London had already
left. They went by ship to Leningrad and after spending a day and a half
there they flew to Moscow.

We arrived at the airport late at night. Among the people who had come
to meet[1] us was Vavilov, who had visited my factory last year. When we
had exchanged greetings,[2] we went into Moscow by car.

Though it was late, our hosts, who had waited more than two hours, insisted
that[3] we should have supper. When we had had supper, we went to bed at
once. On the following day, after getting up early, we went to the Ministry.

---

1 Imperfective.　　2 Use поздоро́ваться.　　3 Настоя́ть на том, что́бы...

The managers and engineers <u>who had assembled</u>[1] were waiting for us. The negotiations lasted for three days. <u>When we had reached an agreement,</u>[2] we spent three more days in Moscow <u>visiting</u> theatres and exhibitions. On the last day, <u>having bought</u> presents the day before,[3] we set off for the airport. My friend Vavilov was again among <u>those who were seeing us off.</u>[4] <u>Leaving</u>[5] the airport at 11 a.m.[6] we were in London at 2 p.m.[7]

1 Put this in front of the nouns.   2 Use **прийти́ к соглаше́нию.**
3 *The day before* – **накану́не.**
4 Omit *those* and use pres. act. p. of **сопровожда́ть,** followed by **нас.**
5 Past gerund of **вы́лететь,** followed by **из.**   6 *a.m.* **утра́.**   7 *p.m.* – **дня.**

SUMMARY

1 The past active participle (§ 1).
2 The past gerund in **-в/-вши** and **-ши** (§ 2).
3 The past gerund in **-я** (§ 3).
4 The expression of the passive voice (§ 4).

LESSONS 40 AND 41 REVISION

На́ша семья́ – Ни́на, Ве́ра, Пе́тя, тётя Ли́за – появи́лась в ва́ших уро́ках без объясне́ния и так же пропа́ла без объясне́ния, вро́де де́йствующих лиц в совреме́нных пье́сах и́ли в совреме́нных францу́зских рома́нах и фи́льмах. Но вы найдёте объясне́ние их коро́ткой и ча́сто спу́танной жи́зни в грамма́тике.

Part II

ALPHABET AND SPELLING

ALPHABET

Below are the letters of the Russian alphabet, in the order of that alphabet. Except for **ы** and **э** the names of the vowel letters are simply the sounds represented by the letters. The names of all the other letters are given under each letter. The names of some of the consonant letters have two, slightly different spellings.

А а	Б б бе/бэ	В в ве/вэ	Г г ге/гэ	Д д де/дэ
Е е (and Ё ё)		Ж ж же	З з зе/зэ	И и
Й й и кра́ткое (short и)	К к ка	Л л эль	М м эм	Н н эн
О о	П п пе/пэ	Р р эр	С с эс	Т т те/тэ
У у	Ф ф эф	Х х ха	Ц ц це	Ч ч че
Ш ш ша	Щ щ ща	Ъ ъ твёрдый знак (hard sign)	Ы ы еры́	Ь ь мя́гкий знак (soft sign)
Э э э оборо́тное (backwards э)	Ю ю	Я я		

ITALICS (курси́в)

Most of the italic letters in Russian are easily recognizable. All the capital and most of the small letters are like the normal letters in general outline, but a few of the small italics are more like cursive letters. Here is the complete italic alphabet, small letters only:

*а б в г д е ж з и й к л м
н о п р с т у ф х ц ч ш щ
ъ ы ь э ю я*

А а	*Й й*	*У у*	*Э э*
Б б	*К к*	*Ф ф*	*Ю ю*
В в	*Л л*	*Х х*	*Я я*
Г г	*М м*	*Ц ц*	
Д g д	*Н н*	*Ч ч*	
Е е	*О о*	*Ш ш*	
Ё ё	*П п*	*Щ щ*	
Ж ж	*Р р*	– *ъ*	
З з	*С с*	– *ы*	
И и	*Т т (т)*	– *ь*	

Of the two forms of **д** – *g*, *д* – either is correct. It is not good practice to use the two forms in one word and in general it is better to use only one. The same applies to the two forms of **т** – *m*, *т*.

g and *m*, have the advantage that they run easily into the next letter; *д* and *т*, while lacking this advantage, have the advantage of being more immediately recognizable as representations of 'd' and 't'.

Do not reduce the upper loop of **в** to a single line – *б* is wrong, *б* is right.

Do not use a diaeresis (two dots) instead of a curl over **й**.

In writing **ш** make sure that the last stroke comes right down – it is *not* like English w (*w*).

Make the soft sign the same height as *a, e, c* etc.

The initial 'hook' of **л, м, я** is an integral part of the cursive forms of these letters and must always be written, no matter what precedes.

ж is formed like this:

ЖС ЖС ЖС ЖС ЖС

ф is formed like this:

ф ф ф ф ф ф

This is an 'exploded' version of **ф**:

ᴄ∕Ɔ

A bar may be placed over *п̄* and *т̄* and under *ш̲*. This is optional – its sole purpose is to help distinguish these letters from other, similar ones.

As you will see from the examples below, some of the cursive letters cannot conveniently be joined to their neighbours.

бак, зуб, вас, равно, год/год, да/да,

дуб/дуб, нагой, рог, ест/ест, жена,

муж, ива, вид/вид, кот/кот, как,

майор, узкий, лампа, лодка/лодка,

голод/голод, клал, знал, дама, рама,

нас, рано, пара, лапа, утка/утка,

тут/тут, фон, графа, ход/ход,

мох, цинк, цена, нация, час, бочка,

шар, ноша, наше, щека, ещё, роща,

мать/мать, третье/третье, мы, сын,

столы/столы, съезд/съезд, этот/этот,

эхо, юг, люк, ключ, яма, язык, красная,

снять/снять,

фотограф/фотограф, атомная энергия,

большевистский/большевистский,

типичный/типичный,

национальный, микроскопический,

биология, Ленинград/Ленинград,

Москва, Харьков, Туполев, Хрущёв,

Кремль, английский, французский,

Франция, Германия,

Соединенные Штаты Америки,

Организация Объединённых Наций,

Союз Советских Социалистических

Республик.

OLD LETTERS

In books published before 1918 (and in some published since that date
outside the Soviet Union) you will find certain letters which are no longer
used:

i has the same value as и
ɵ has the same value as ф
ѣ has the same value as e

The rare letter ѵ had the same value as и.

1 The letters **к, г, х, ш, ж, ч** and **щ** cannot be followed by **ы**. They can be and are followed by **и**.

2 The letter **ц** can be followed by both **ы** and **и**. It is followed by **ы** when **ы** is a case-ending or the beginning of a case-ending or the beginning of the suffix **ын**. It is also followed by **ы** in a handful of words, of which the commonest are **цыга́н** *gypsy*, **цыплёнок** *chicken*, **на цы́почках** *on tip-toe*. Otherwise **ц** is followed by **и**.

3 The letters **к, г, х, ш, ж, ч, щ** and **ц** are not usually followed by **я** and **ю**. They can be and are followed by **а** and **у**. There are very few exceptions to this, e.g. **маникю́р** *manicure*, **Кя́хта** (a place-name), **парашю́т** *parachute*, **жюри́** *jury*. In the last two **ю** has the value of **у**. **Ц** is followed by **ю** and **я** only in foreign names, such as **Цю́рих** *Zurich*.

4 The use of the apostrophe instead of the hard sign was current at one time after the revolution. It is not used now. Before 1918 the hard sign appeared at the end of every word which did not end in a vowel or the soft sign.

5 The letter **г** has the value of **в** in the adjective and pronoun endings **ого, его** and in one or two words, such as **сего́дня** *today*, **итого́** *altogether*. Before 1918 the genitive singular masculine and neuter of the adjective was spelt **аго** and **яго,** corresponding to the modern spellings **ого** and **его**. Some works published outside the Soviet Union may still use these older spelling conventions.

PRONUNCIATION

You cannot learn to pronounce a foreign language completely correctly simply by reading a description of the pronunciation of the language. You must listen to a native speaker, either in person or on the radio, records, or magnetic tape. Written descriptions can, however, give you a rough idea of the sounds or help you towards a better pronunciation, in conjunction with listening to a native speaker.

The remarks given below are a rough guide to the sounds of Russian. If you want further information consult one or more of the books listed in Recommended Reading.

1. STRESS

In Russian, just as in English, one syllable in each word is pronounced with greater force than the other syllables. The greater force with which that syllable is pronounced is called the 'stress' and the syllable pronounced with stress is called the 'stressed syllable'. Hence the vowel in a stressed syllable is the 'stressed vowel' of the word. The other syllables and vowels are 'unstressed'. Sometimes one says that a vowel is in 'stressed position' or 'unstressed position'. This is the same as saying the vowel is stressed or unstressed.

In this book an acute accent marks the stressed vowel: ло́дка, столы́. Words with one vowel, however, are not provided with a stress-mark: it is to be understood that in most instances (see next para.) the vowel is stressed. The vowel ё is always stressed and so may be written without a stress-mark.

The common prepositions, especially the monosyllabic ones, the word не and the particles бы, же, -то, -нибудь, ли etc. are usually unstressed. As far as stress is concerned all these words form a unit with the word which they precede or (in the case of the particles) follow – they are attached as unstressed syllables to that word.

You can, however, put stress on the prepositions and не for emphatic purposes.

With the past tense masculine, neuter and plural of a few verbs the word не, while still forming a unit with the verb, is itself stressed and the verb has no stress: cf. они́ да́ли *they gave* with они́ не́‿дали *they did not give*, or Са́ша был *Sasha was* with Са́ша не́‿был *Sasha was not*. Here the ligature is used to bring out the fact that the two words are a unit as far as stress is concerned. This rule does not apply to the feminine form: не дала́, не была́.

Some of the prepositions do this too in combination with some nouns, e.g. на́‿гору *up the mountain, uphill,* из‿дому *out of the house,* на́‿пол *on to the floor.*

Some long compound words, especially new technical words, and some numbers, may have more than one stressed syllable. When this occurs, it is the last of the stressed syllables which is more heavily stressed, as in карто́фелекопА́лка *potato-harvester,* моро́зоустО́йчивый *frost-resistant.*

2. SPEECH ORGANS

The speech organs which we are concerned with are shown in the diagram below, representing a longitudinal cross-section through the mouth.

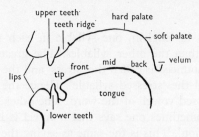

The lips can be pressed together, as in *p, b, m,*
or spread, as in *ee*
or half rounded, as in *aw*
or fully rounded, as in *oo.*

The lower lip can make contact with the upper teeth, as in *f, v.*

The tongue tip can touch the teeth-ridge as in *t, d, n;*
or the angle between the upper teeth and the teeth-ridge, as in Russian
т, д, н.

The tongue tip can approach the palate just behind the teeth-ridge, as in *r.*

The front of the tongue can touch the fore part of the hard palate, as in
ch, j, ч,
or nearly touch it, as in *sh.*

The back of the tongue can touch the soft palate, as in *k, g.*

The tongue can be almost completely flat, as in *ah.*

The back of the tongue can be raised slightly, as in *aw,* which is accompanied
by half-rounded lip position;
or raised slightly more than halfway, as in Scots or North country *no,*
which is accompanied by a greater degree of lip-rounding;
or raised very high, without touching the palate, as in *oo,* which is accompanied by fully rounded lip-position.

The tongue can be raised so that a point just between front and mid is
highest. This point is quite low down in *cat,*
is higher in *get,*
higher still in Scots *game,*
and highest (for English) in *ee,* which is accompanied by spread lip-position.

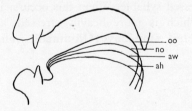

Vowels of this type are called back
vowels.

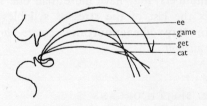

Vowels of this type are called front
vowels.

3. STRESSED VOWELS

a As a general rule stressed vowels are slightly longer than unstressed vowels in Russian. This, however, is 'accidental' – it just happens because the vowels are stressed. There is no grammatical *significance* in vowel length in Russian. There is no *intrinsic* difference in length as for instance between the vowels in *caught* and *cot*.

b **И** is a front vowel, like English *ee*, but the tongue position is even higher. This vowel must not be prolonged nor the tongue and lips allowed to slip from the one position that must be held throughout the sound. Spread the lips well (see also **ы**).

c **А** is not like the *a* in *father* or *ah*: it is not a back vowel but a front vowel. The tongue is not raised as much as in the pronunciation of *a* in *cat*. It is more like the Scots or North country *a* in this word.

Я has the same vowel value as **a** but when it does not follow a consonant it has an initial **ў**, as in *yam*.

When **я** is followed by a soft consonant (see below) and when **a** is followed by a soft consonant *and* preceded by **ч** or **щ** they both represent a sound more like *a* in English *cat*, as in **пять, начáть, прощáть**.

d **О** is a back vowel. The back of the tongue is raised slightly higher than it is for the English vowel *aw* and the lips are slightly more rounded. When it is not followed by a soft consonant **o** is often finished off by a very slight suggestion of the vowel heard at the end of the word *china*.

Ё has the same value as **o** but when it does not follow a consonant it has a *y*-sound, as in *your*, in front of it, as in **ёлка, моё**.

When **ё** is followed by a soft consonant the highest point of the tongue is slightly further forward.

e **Ы** is not a front vowel nor is it a back vowel. The highest point of the tongue varies slightly according to the consonants around it but in the 'average' **ы** it is the middle of the tongue which is raised high. The lips are spread. Try to pronounce *ee* with the tongue rather drawn back, or say *book* with the lips spread (pull the corners of the mouth sideways with the little fingers, if necessary). *Book* pronounced in this way will sound very much like Russian **бык** *bull*.

Ы has a 'muffled **и**' quality about it.

When it comes after **ж, ш** and **ц** the letter **и** has the vowel value of **ы**, so **жить, шúло, цинк** are pronounced as though spelt with **ы**.

И also has this value when it is the initial letter of a word and the preceding word is a preposition ending in a hard consonant. So **из Úндии** is pronounced as if spelt '**из_ы́нд...**'.

f **Е** is a front vowel.

Э is a front vowel.

Both these letters represent two different kinds of *e*. When not followed by a soft consonant they represent a vowel like that in *men* though the tongue is slightly lower than for the vowel in *men*. (It is not, however, so low that it sounds like *a* in *cat*.) When they have this value **e** and **э** are often finished off by a very slight suggestion of the vowel at the end of *china*, as in **э́то, сел.**

When followed by a soft consonant, both **e** and **э** represent a vowel with a tongue position slightly higher than that in *men*. It is like the French *é*. When they have this value **e** and **э** do not have the slight suggestion of the vowel at the end of *china*: tongue and lips, which are slightly spread, must be kept in the same position throughout the sound, as in **э́ти, се́ли. E,** but not **э,** has an initial *y*, as in *yes*, when it does not follow a consonant.

g **У** is a back vowel.

Ю is a back vowel.

Both these letters represent a vowel like English *oo*, the back of the tongue being higher than in English *oo*. In fact the back of the tongue is raised as high as possible. The vowel must not be prolonged nor must tongue or lips, which are fully rounded, be allowed to slip from their position throughout the sound.

When it does not follow a consonant **ю,** but not **у,** has an initial *y*, as in *you*. When **ю** is followed by a soft consonant the high point of the tongue is further forward – and the vowel sounds like some varieties of Scots *u*, as in *tune* (but *not* like French *u* or German *ü*). **У** has the same value when it comes after **ч** or **щ** and is followed by a soft consonant. Examples: **тюль, чуть-чу́ть, щу́рить.**

4. UNSTRESSED VOWELS

a **а, о** and **я**

In unstressed positions the letters **а** (with one set of exceptions – see below) and **о** have the same values.

Immediately before the stress and when initial they represent a sound like *u* in *cup*.

Examples (vowels with the value *u* are underlined):
н<u>а</u>го́й, в<u>о</u>да́, <u>а</u>дв<u>о</u>ка́т, <u>о</u>дн<u>о</u>го́.

A and **o** also tend to have this value in any position in front of the stress when next to **а, о** or **у.**

Examples: **с<u>о</u>образ<u>о</u>ва́л, н<u>а</u>обо́рот, н<u>а</u>уга́д.** (In other words, these are pronounced as if spelt **саабразава́л, наабаро́т, науга́д.**)

In other positions in front of the stress and in any position after the stress **a** and **o** have a value like that of *a* in *china*. We shall indicate this sound by means of a double underlining.

Examples: **с<u><u>а</u></u>м<u><u>о</u></u>лёт, г<u><u>о</u></u>л<u><u>о</u></u>ва́, мно́г<u><u>о</u></u>, ко́мн<u><u>а</u></u>т<u><u>а</u></u>.**

Notice that it is precisely in the syllable *immediately* before the stress that **a** and **o** do not have the value of *a* in *china*. In Russian this is the next most strongly stressed position in comparison with the stressed position, whereas in English this position is a weakly stressed position, where the *a*-sound of *china* frequently occurs.

Take care, therefore, not to say **голова́** (as it might be, English *gallavá*) but **голова́**; not **самолёт** (*sammalyót*) but **самолёт** etc.

Я has the *a* in *china* value *after the stress only*, retaining of course its initial *y* when not preceded by a consonant.

Examples: **кра́сная, зна́я, сосе́дям, чужа́я.**

b **и, е, э, я** and **а**

И sounds more like *i* in *bit* when it is unstressed.

Examples: **чистота́, ру́ки.**

In a careful pronunciation unstressed **и** tends to sound more like stressed **и**, though it is not so 'tense'.

Е and **э** sound like *i* in *bit* before the stress. **Е** has this value after the stress too (**э** does not occur after the stress).

Examples: **река́, щека́, эква́тор, мо́ре, кра́сное.**

In a careful pronunciation unstressed **э** tends to sound more *e*-like.

Я sounds like *i* in *bit* before the stress (but *not* after the stress; see above).

А also has this value before the stress when it follows **ч** or **щ**.

Examples: **тяну́ть, язы́к, часы́, щади́ть.**

c **ы, и** and **е**

Unstressed **ы** is simply **ы** pronounced in a less 'tense' fashion. The middle of the tongue is not so high as in stressed **ы**.

Examples: **быки́, сыновья́, ко́мнаты.**

И also has this value in unstressed positions when it follows **ш, ж** or **ц**.

Examples: **широко́, она́ жила́, цикло́н.**

И also has this value in unstressed position when it is the initial letter of a word following a preposition ending with a hard consonant.

Examples: **от Ива́на** = '**от_ыва́на**', **с игру́шками** = '**с_ыгру́ш-ками**'.

Е also has this value in unstressed position after **ш, ж** or **ц**.

Examples: **шесто́й** = '**шысто́й**', **жена́** = '**жына́**', **цена́** = '**цына́**', **вы́ше** = '**вы́шы**', **ху́же** = '**ху́жы**', **полоте́нце** = '**полоте́нцы**'. It must be pointed out, however, that some speakers pronounce **е** *after* the stress when it follows **ш, ж** or **ц**, like *a* in *china*.

d **У** and **ю** when unstressed sound more like the *u* in English *butcher* or *book*. They are less 'tense' than stressed **у** and **ю**.

Examples: **ума́, го́лову, юбиле́й, зна́ю.**

303

5. DIPHTHONGS

A dipthong is a sequence of two vowels composing one syllable or, to put it another way, a diphthong is a vowel glide which starts as one vowel and glides in the direction of another. The vowel elements in the following English words are diphthongs: *how, boy, high*.

In Russian all diphthongs end in **й**, representing here a sound like Russian **и** rather than the *i* in *bit* but *not* forming a separate syllable. All other vowel sequences in Russian form *two* syllables.

Diphthongs may be stressed or unstressed. The value of the vowel letters is as described above. **Й** has the same effect as a soft consonant on the vowels which it follows. This is to say that stressed **е** and **э,** for example, have the higher tongue position before **й** (see § 3f above).

In the stressed diphthong **ий** the tongue rises from the high position of **и** to a slightly higher position for **й,** i.e. to the position of a very 'tense' English *y*.

In the stressed diphthong **ый** the high point of the tongue moves forward from the **ы** position to the **и** position.

In the unstressed diphthongs **ий** and **ый** the **й** element is heard only in a careful pronunciation: at normal conversation speed it is dropped.

Examples: **узна́йте, валя́йте, де́лайте, яйцо́, Чайко́вский, ду́йте, испо́льзуйте, дюйм, дюймо́вка, пе́йте, эй!, вы́лейте, бой, пойду́, с да́мой, с землёй, вы́йду, англи́йский, кра́сный, си́ний.**

6. CONSONANTS

a Consonants: **п, б, м, ф, в, с, з, к, г, ч, ц, й**

Apart from the details below these twelve consonants are like, respectively, English *p, b, m, f, v, s, z, k, g, ch, ts* (e.g. in *bits*) and *y* (e.g. in *yield*).

Before stressed vowels *p* and *k* in English are slightly aspirated, i.e. there is a slight puff of air between the consonant and the vowel. (You can test this by holding the back of your hand close to your mouth while saying *park* and *cart*). This aspiration must be avoided in Russian.

In the adjective and pronoun endings **ого** and **его** (genitive singular masculine and neuter) **г** represents the sound **в**. It also represents **в** in one or two words in which there is a 'fossilized' pronoun, e.g. **сего́дня** *today* ('of this day'), **итого́** *altogether, in sum*.

In all forms of the words **мя́гкий** *soft* and **лёгкий** *light, easy* and words derived from them **г** represents **х** (see below) whenever it occurs before **к** and also before **ч** (as in **мя́гче** *softer*).

In a few words **ч,** when it occurs before a consonant, has the value of **ш** (see below). These include **что** *what, that* and derivatives such as **что́-то, что́-нибудь,** *something* (but not **не́что** *something*). **Ничто́** *nothing* is pronounced as spelt or as **'ништо́'.** Other words in which **ч** has the value of **ш** before a consonant are **чтобы** *in order that,* **конечно** *of course,* **скучный** *boring* and feminine patronymics such as **Никитична.**

The *s* element of **ц** is short, though quite unmistakable.

As a consonant **й** occurs before vowels and is like the *y* in English *yield,* as in **майор** *major.*

b **т, д, н**

In English *t, d* and *n* are formed with the tip of the tongue against the teeth-ridge. In Russian **т, д,** and **н** are formed with the tip of the tongue further forward – in the angle formed by the upper teeth and the teeth-ridge.

Т, like **к** and **п,** must not be aspirated.

c **x**

X is formed in the same place as **к** and **г** but the back of the tongue does not touch the soft palate: a space is left for the air stream to pass through and cause a light friction. There is a similar sound in Scots *loch* and German *ach* but the Russian sound has less friction than the Scots and German sounds, which are 'noisier' than the Russian sound.

d **р**

Р is a 'rolled' or 'tapped' consonant. The tongue taps once or twice against the teeth-ridge. Many Scots speakers use this kind of *r.* Do not exaggerate the 'roll'.

e **ш** and **ж**

In English, *sh* and '*zh*' (the sound represented by *s* in *leisure*) are formed with the front of the tongue raised.

In Russian the tip of the tongue is *behind* the teeth-ridge and the body of the tongue is hollowed or depressed. It may help in pronouncing the Russian sounds to round the lips well.

The English sounds have more of a sharp hissing quality, the Russian sounds more of a dull hushing quality.

f **л**

In many kinds of English pronunciation there are two kinds of *l,* a 'clear' *l* heard before vowels (in this *l* most of the tongue is raised), and a 'dark' *l* heard after vowels (in this *l* the middle of the tongue is slightly depressed). In Russian too there are two kinds of **л.** The dark or hard **л** has an even more 'hollow' quality than English dark *l.*

To pronounce hard **л** put the tip of your tongue in the angle where the upper teeth enter the gums and, still keeping the tip in this position, put the rest of the tongue in the position for English *oo.* In profile your tongue is now roughly in the shape of a saddle. The lips should not be

x

too rounded, even though the back of the tongue is in the *oo*-position. Now say an *l*-sound without letting it slip into an ordinary English *l*. Use some of the words given in Lesson 11 for practice. See the diagram in that lesson.

7. SOFT CONSONANTS

a Most of the consonants described above have 'soft' counterparts. (Another term used instead of 'soft' is 'palatalized'.)

Broadly speaking, a soft consonant is one in the articulation of which you try to pronounce the sound **й** (*y* in *yield*) at the same time. With some soft consonants this means that two articulations – the 'normal' and the **й** articulation – are made at the same time. With others it means that the 'normal' way of articulating the consonant is modified.

Ч, described above, is in fact a soft consonant, since the front of the tongue is in the **й** position to form this consonant. **Щ** is also a soft consonant – it consists in one type of pronunciation of a sound like English *sh* (a soft consonant – see the description in § 6e above) followed by **ч**, or in another type of pronunciation of a long or double *sh*. The letter sequences **сч, зч, стч, здч, шч** and **жч** have the same value as the single letter **щ.**

As far as **ч** and **щ** are concerned the softness is, so to speak, intrinsic – it is shown by the letters themselves. The softness of other consonants is shown by writing the consonant letter followed by one of the vowel letters **и, е, ё, ю, я** or the soft sign **ь.** The vowel letters of course also have their vowel value.

Sometimes the softness of one consonant influences preceding consonants and then the preceding consonants become soft too (see Lesson 6).

When a consonant is followed by the soft sign **ь,** which is then followed by **и, е, ё, ю** or **я,** this means that not only is the consonant soft but also that the vowel keeps its initial *y*, as **лью, бьёт, счастье** etc.

The hard sign, **ъ,** acts as a 'separating sign'. It separates a consonant from the softening effect of a following **и, е, ё, ю** or **я:** the consonant letter has its normal (i.e. not soft) value and the vowel is preceded by the *y*-sound. Thus **отъе́зд** is pronounced with a normal **т** and a *y* in front of **е,** whereas **оте́ц** is pronounced with a soft **т** and no *y*-sound before the **е.** The letters **с** and **з** may or may not be affected by the hard sign. Thus the **с** in **съезд** may be soft or normal but in either case the **е** has an initial *y*-sound.

b *Soft Consonants* **п, б, м, ф, в**

In forming these soft consonants the normal articulation of the consonant and the **й** articulation are made simultaneously. The tongue is lowered from the **й** position a fraction of a second after the consonant articulation is finished so that there is a *faint* suggestion of *y* after the consonant.

Examples: **пел, пёк, пять, бил, бес, бюст, мя́та, фи́ник, фе́ска, вист, век, вяз.**

The *y* element is more obvious before **ё, ю, я** than before **и** and **е**.

c *Soft Consonants* **с, з, т, д, н**

In forming these soft consonants the tongue tip is approximately in the same position as in forming English *t*, *d*, *n* (i.e. slightly further back than in forming hard **т, д, н**, see § 7 above), and at the same time the front of the tongue is pushed up against the hard palate, making a single, combined articulation. Again there is a slight suggestion of *y* as these consonants are released but it is less evident than in the case of the consonants described in § 7b.

These soft consonants may also be made with the tip of the tongue lowered to a position behind the lower teeth.

Examples: **сел, ся́ду, зима́, газе́та, те, тётя, дед, дя́дя, ни́зко, ня́ня.**

In the reflexive particles **ся** and **сь** the modern tendency is to pronounce soft **с**, while the older pronunciation had hard **с** here. As a result the current pronunciation of these particles varies. A rough guide is this: after **т, ть, з** and **с** the particle has a hard **с**, after other letters a soft **с**. The combinations **тся** and **ться** sound alike: 'тса' or 'ца'.

d *Soft Consonant* **р**

The front of the tongue is raised slightly towards the **й** position while the tip stays in the 'trill' position. A faint suggestion of *y* follows the consonant. It is extremely difficult to prolong soft **р**, since the raising of the front of the tongue changes the attitude of the tongue which is necessary for the tapping of the tip against the teeth-ridge.

Examples: **ритм, ре́ки, рёв, рю́мка, ряд.**

e *Soft Consonants* **к, г, х**

The effect of softening on **к, г** and **х** is to move forward the point of articulation, i.e. the back of the tongue makes a contact or near-contact with the soft palate at a point somewhat further forward than in forming normal **к, г** and **х**.

Examples: **ки́нуть, с кем, ткёт, маникю́р, Кя́хта, ноги́, на ноге́, духи́, в дохе́.**

f *Soft* **ж**

Some speakers use a long soft **ж** like the *s* in *leisure* prolonged, where the letters **зж** or **жж** occur *within* a root, as in **е́зжу** or **во́жжи**. When the letters **зж** belong one to a prefix and the other to a root as in **изжо́га** they represent long *hard* **ж** as described in § 6e and this pronunciation is now spreading to words like **éзжу, вóжжи** etc. (see also § 9).

g *Soft* **л**

In forming soft **л** the tip of the tongue is in the angle where the upper teeth enter the gums (or it may be lowered to a position behind the lower teeth), while the front of the tongue is pushed up into the **й** position, producing a single combined articulation.

Compare these diagrams of the tongue-positions of hard **л** and soft **л**.

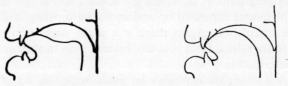

Examples: **лúпа, лес, ляг, лёд, люк.**

8. VOICED AND VOICELESS CONSONANTS

Some consonants are 'voiced', i.e. the vocal chords vibrate while they are being pronounced. In English, voiced consonants include *b*, *d*, *g*, *z* etc. Other consonants are 'voiceless', i.e. the vocal chords do not vibrate while they are being pronounced. In English, voiceless consonants include *p*, *t*, *k*, *s* etc.

Twelve of the Russian consonant letters form six pairs, such that in each pair one member normally represents a voiced consonant and the other a voiceless consonant. The pairs are given in this table, together with four consonants which are voiceless and have no regular voiced counterparts:

voiced	Б	В	Д	З	Ж	Г	
	|	|	|	|	|	|	
voiceless	П	Ф	Т	С	Ш	К	(Х Ц Ч Щ)

When a consonant letter from the upper line appears at the end of a word it takes on the value of its voiceless counterpart. This process is some-times called 'devoicing'. The same thing happens when a letter from the upper line appears before any letter (including the four in brackets) from the lower line. Thus:

боб	pronounced as if spelt	'боп'
ров	,,	,,	'роф'
год	,,	,,	'гот'
раз	,,	,,	'рас'
муж	,,	,,	'муш'
рог	,,	,,	'рок'
юбка	,,	,,	'юпка'

308

девчо́нка	pronounced as if spelt		'дефчо́нка'
ло́дка	,,	,,	'ло́тка'
везти́	,,	,,	'вести́'
ло́жка	,,	,,	'ло́шка'
тягча́йший	,,	,,	'тякча́йший'

Conversely, when a consonant letter from the lower line appears within a word before a consonant letter from the upper line (*except* в) it takes on the value of its voiced counterpart. This process is sometimes called 'voicing'. Notice that в does *not* have this effect. Thus:

Афганиста́н	pronounced as if spelt		'Авганиста́н'
отбо́р	,,	,,	'одбо́р'
сдава́ть	,,	,,	'здава́ть'

These rules for devoicing and voicing also apply to the common prepositions.

под столо́м	pronounced as if spelt		'пот_столо́м'
с горы́	,,	,,	'з_горы́'
к до́му	,,	,,	'г_до́му'

The bracketed consonants from the lower line appear before the voiced consonants of the upper line in one or two words only, such as **плацда́рм** *military base*, where ц has the value of 'voiced ц' (like English *dz*).

Voicing and devoicing are, as you see, not registered in the spelling. The only set of exceptions concerns the prefixes ending in з: **без/обез, воз/вз, из, низ, раз** and **через,** which are spelt with final с whenever they occur in front of a root beginning with one of the consonants from the lower line. Thus **издава́ть** but **исходи́ть, раздира́ть** but **распуска́ть** etc.

9. OTHER CONSONANT CHANGES

We have noted above (§ 7a) that сч and зч, among other combinations, have the value of щ. С and з are also affected by ш and ж – not only does voicing or devoicing occur but the consonants с and з are completely assimilated to ш and ж, so that:

сш	has the value		шш
зш	,,	,,	шш
сж	,,	,,	жж
зж	,,	,,	жж

as in

сшить	pronounced as if spelt		'шшить'
вёзший	,,	,,	'вёшший'
сжёг	,,	,,	'жжёг'
разжёчь	,,	,,	'ражжёчь'.

Grammar

After **к, г, х, ш, ж, ч** and **щ** write **и**, not **ы**.
After **ш, ж, ч, ц** and **щ** write **а, у**, not **я, ю**.

A. NOUNS

MASCULINE NOUNS

Masculine nouns denoting animate beings – people, animals, birds, reptiles, fishes, insects etc. – have genitive-accusative singular and plural, e.g.

nom. sing.	*acc. sing.*	*nom. pl.*	*acc. pl.*
кот *tom-cat*	котá	коты́	котóв

Other masculine nouns have nominative-accusative singular and plural.

Nominative ending in:

	hard consonant		soft sign **ь**	
	singular	plural	singular	plural
nom.	тумáн *mist*	тумáны	дождь *rain*	дожди́
gen.	тумáна	тумáнов	дождя́	дождéй
dat.	тумáну	тумáнам	дождю́	дождя́м
acc.	тумáн	тумáны	дождь	дожди́
instr.	тумáном	тумáнами	дождём	дождя́ми
prep.	тумáне	тумáнах	дождé	дождя́х

1 When preceded by **ш, ж, ч, ц** or **щ** the *unstressed* instrumental singular ending becomes **ем: мýжем** *husband* (but **ножóм** *knife*).

2 Some nouns have nominative plural in **á: гóрод** *town* – **городá, дóктор** *doctor* – **докторá.**

3 Some nouns have an alternative genitive singular in **у** used in partitive expressions and after some prepositions: **сáхару** *of sugar*, **из_лесу** *out of the wood.*

4 Some nouns have a locative (i.e. prepositional after **в, на**) in **ý: на берегý** *on the shore.*

5 The genitive plural ends in **ей** after **ш, ж, ч** and **щ: луч** *ray* – **лучéй, ножéй**; and in **ев**, if unstressed, in **ов**, if stressed, after

1 Some nouns have nominative plural in **я: учителя́** *teachers.*

2 When unstressed, the instrumental singular is **ем: гóстем** *guest.*

3 The nouns **лю́ди** *people* and **дéти** *children*, which have no singular form, have exceptional instrumental plural: **людьми́, детьми́.**

4 The two nouns **сосéд** *neighbour* and **чёрт** *devil* have a hard-ending singular declension *but a soft-ending plural declension*, like **дождь: сосéди, сосéдей** etc., **чéрти, чертéй** etc.

ц: ме́сяц *month* – ме́сяцев, оте́ц *father* – отцо́в.

6 Some nouns have genitive plural with no ending: глаз *eye*, солда́т *soldier*.

nominative ending in й

	singular	plural
nom.	обы́чай *custom*	обы́чаи
gen.	обы́чая	обы́чаев
dat.	обы́чаю	обы́чаям
acc.	обы́чай	обы́чаи
instr.	обы́чаем	обы́чаями
prep.	обы́чае	обы́чаях

1 Some nouns have nominative plural in я́: кра́я́ *edges*.
2 Some nouns have an alternative genitive singular in ю, used in partitive expressions: ча́шка ча́ю *a cup of tea*.
3 Some nouns have a locative (i.e. prepositional after в, на) in ю́: на краю́ *on the edge*.
4 When stressed, the genitive plural becomes ёв: краёв.
5 The few nouns in which й is preceded by и have prepositional singular in и: о ра́дии *about radium*.

with plural ья

	singular	plural
nom.	стул *chair*	сту́лья
gen.	сту́ла	сту́льев
dat.	сту́лу	сту́льям
acc.	стул	сту́лья
instr.	сту́лом	сту́льями
prep.	сту́ле	сту́льях

1 A few common nouns of this type have final stress in the plural and the genitive plural ends in ей: муж *husband*, мужья́, муже́й; князь *prince*, князья́, князе́й; друг *friend*, друзья́ (NB з), друзе́й.
2 Two nouns, with final stress in the plural, also have the additional syllable ов: сын *son*, сыновья́, сынове́й; кум '*gossip*', *kinsman*, кумовья́, кумовьёв (NB).

with mobile vowel

	singular	plural	singular	plural
nom.	сон *sleep, dream*	сны	день *day*	дни
gen.	сна	снов	дня	дней
dat.	сну	снам	дню	дням
acc.	сон	сны	день	дни
instr.	сном	сна́ми	днём	дня́ми
prep.	сне	снах	дне	днях

1 When the mobile vowel follows another vowel it changes to й in the other cases: бое́ц *warrior* бойца́, заём *loan* за́йма.
2 In за́яц *hare* the mobile vowel я is unique. It too changes to й: за́йца. The genitive plural follows the rule for nouns ending in ц, hence за́йцев.

3 The mobile vowel **e** in the ending **ей** changes to **ь**: **ручей** *stream* **ручья́**. The genitive plural is the soft equivalent of **ов**, hence **ручьёв**.

4 Nouns denoting the young of animals etc., ending in **ёнок**, have a mobile vowel: **ребёнок** *child* **ребёнка**, **жеребёнок** *foal* **жеребёнка**, but in the plural the ending changes and these nouns follow a neuter declension (see below).

	ending in **анин/янин**		the noun **путь**[1]	
	singular	*plural*	*singular*	*plural*
nom.	англича́нин *Englishman*	англича́не	путь *way*	пути́
gen.	англича́нина	англича́н	пути́	путе́й
dat.	англича́нину	англича́нам	пути́	путя́м
acc.	англича́нина	англича́н	путь	пути́
instr.	англича́нином	англича́нами	путём	путя́ми
prep.	англича́нине	англича́нах	пути́	путя́х

Rules for genitive plural of masculine nouns:

1 Nouns with nominative singular ending in **й**,
   ,,   ,,   ,,   ,,   ,,   ,, **ц** and not having final stress,
   ,,   ,, nominative plural ending in unstressed **ья**

have a genitive plural ending spelt **ев**:

слу́чай	слу́чаев
край	краёв
ручей	ручьёв
ме́сяц	ме́сяцев
сту́лья	сту́льев

2 Nouns with nominative singular ending in **ь**,
   ,,   ,,   ,,   ,,   ,, **ш, ж, ч, щ,**
The commoner nouns with nominative plural ending in stressed **ья**
have a genitive plural ending spelt **ей**:

дождь	дожде́й
путь	путе́й
луч	луче́й
мужья́	муже́й

3 A limited number of nouns with nominative singular ending in a hard consonant have no ending in the genitive plural.

Nouns with nominative singular ending in **анин/янин** drop the **ин** in the plural and have no ending in the genitive plural:

глаз	глаз
солда́т	солда́т
англича́нин	англича́н

1 **Путь** has a unique singular declension among masculine nouns.

4 With very few exceptions, all other nouns have a genitive plural ending spelt **ов**:

тума́н	тума́нов
до́ктор	докторо́в
сон	снов

NEUTER NOUNS

Neuter nouns, with the exception of one group, have the same endings as masculine nouns except in the nominative-accusative singular and plural. The genitive plural zero-ending, however, is very common in neuter nouns, whereas it is restricted to a few masculine nouns.

nominative ending in

	hard consonant + **o**		*hard consonant* (**ш, ж** or **ц**) + **e**	
	singular	*plural*	*singular*	*plural*
nom.	ме́сто *place*	места́	се́рдце *heart*	сердца́
gen.	ме́ста	мест	се́рдца	серде́ц
dat.	ме́сту	места́м	се́рдцу	сердца́м
acc.	ме́сто	места́	се́рдце	сердца́
instr.	ме́стом	места́ми	се́рдцем	сердца́ми
prep.	ме́сте	места́х	се́рдце	сердца́х

Nouns with the nominative singular ending in **ко** usually form the nominative-accusative plural in **ки**: **я́блоко** *apple* **я́блоки, око́шко** *little window* **око́шки, ве́ко** *eyelid* **ве́ки** but a few which shift the stress have the 'normal' nominative-accusative plural ending **a**:

о́блако	облака́
во́йско	войска́

(**о́блако** has genitive plural **облако́в**)

Nouns with the root ending in two consonants usually insert a mobile vowel, **o** or **e,** between these two consonants in the genitive plural with zero-ending: **окно́** *window* **о́кон, число́** *number* **чи́сел.** This does not happen when the two consonants are **с** followed by **т** or **к**: **ме́сто** *place* **мест, во́йско** *army* **войск;** nor does it happen in the consonant cluster **ств**: **чу́вство** *feeling* **чувств.**

	soft consonant + **e** (1)		*soft consonant* + **e** (2)	
	singular	*plural*	*singular*	*plural*
nom.	жили́ще *dwelling*	жили́ща	по́ле *field*	поля́
gen.	жили́ща	жили́щ	по́ля	поле́й
dat.	жили́щу	жили́щам	по́лю	поля́м
acc.	жили́ще	жили́ща	по́ле	поля́
instr.	жили́щем	жили́щами	по́лем	поля́ми
prep.	жили́ще	жили́щах	по́ле	поля́х

In nouns of this type the soft consonant is **щ**.

Some nouns of this type have an alternative nominative-accusative plural in **и**: **доми́ще** *big house* **доми́щи/доми́ща.**

There are only three neuter nouns ending in a soft consonant, other than **щ**, followed immediately by **е**: **по́ле, мо́ре** *sea* and **го́ре** *grief*.

Nouns ending in **ьё** have similar endings but stressed: **питьё** *drink* instrumental **питьём.** If the stress is on the ending in the genitive plural, the **ь** changes to **é**: **пите́й.** Otherwise it becomes **и** (see below). **Ружьё** *rifle* is exceptional: genitive plural **ру́жей** (cf. nominative plural **ру́жья**).

The genitive plural **ей** is not found outside this group.

soft ие and ье

	singular	plural
nom.	зда́ние *building*	зда́ния
gen.	зда́ния	зда́ний
dat.	зда́нию	зда́ниям
acc.	зда́ние	зда́ния
instr.	зда́нием	зда́ниями
prep.	зда́нии	зда́ниях

Nouns ending in **ье** (unstressed) have the same endings, except in the prepositional singular. Hence **муче́нье** *torment* **муче́нья** etc., prepositional singular **муче́нье**, nominative plural **муче́нья**, genitive plural **муче́ний**, dative plural **муче́ньям** etc.

There is one masculine noun with the ending **-ье**: **подмасте́рье** *apprentice*. Being a masculine animate it has genitive-accusative singular **подмасте́рья** and genitive-accusative plural **подмасте́рьев.**

вре́мя and similar nouns

singular	plural
вре́мя *time*	времена́
вре́мени	времён
вре́мени	времена́м
вре́мя	времена́
вре́менем	времена́ми
вре́мени	времена́х

There are nine other neuter nouns ending in **мя** and all have this type of declension:

бре́мя *burden*	вы́мя *udder*
зна́мя *banner*	и́мя *name*
пла́мя *flame*	пле́мя *tribe*
се́мя *seed*	стре́мя *stirrup*
те́мя *crown of the head*	

Се́мя and **стре́мя** have exceptional genitive plural **семя́н** and **стремя́н.** The nouns **вы́мя, пла́мя** and **те́мя** are not used in the plural.

All the others are stressed on the endings in the plural, except **зна́мя** which has plural: **знамёна, знамён, знамёнам** etc.

ребёнок, ребя́та and similar nouns

singular	plural
ребёнок *child*	ребя́та
ребёнка	ребя́т
ребёнку	ребя́там
ребёнка	ребя́т
ребёнком	ребя́тами
ребёнке	ребя́тах

Nouns of this type, denoting the young of animals, are *masculine* but in the plural the suffix changes and the declension is a neuter type, retaining however the genitive-accusative plural typical of masculine animates.

Other exceptions and anomalies

a Some neuter nouns have a declension in the plural of the masculine type ending in unstressed **ья**:

крыло́ *wing*	кры́лья
	кры́льев
	кры́льям
	кры́лья
	кры́льями
	кры́льях

Other common nouns of this type are **перо́** *feather, pen* **пе́рья, де́рево** *tree* **дере́вья, звено́** *link* **зве́нья**.

b **Коле́но** *knee* has a plural declension of the soft masculine type:

коле́ни
коле́ней
коле́ням
коле́ни
коле́нями
коле́нях

Коле́но *joint, node* has a plural declension of the unstressed **ья** type, like **кры́лья** (above).

c Some nouns ending in **ье** in the nominative singular also have a plural declension of the **кры́лья** type, hence genitive plural in **ев**:

пла́тье *dress* пла́тья, пла́тьев
верхо́вье *upper reaches* верхо́вья, верхо́вьев

d **Ружьё** *gun*, while belonging to the **ие/ьё** declension, has exceptional genitive plural **ру́жей**.

e The plural of **плечо́** *shoulder* is **пле́чи**, genitive **плеч** etc. The plural of **у́хо** *ear* is **у́ши**, genitive plural **уше́й** etc. The plural of **о́ко** *eye* (arch.) is **о́чи**, genitive plural **оче́й** etc.

f The plural of **нéбо** *sky* and **чýдо** *miracle, marvel* has an additional syllable **-ес-**: небесá, небéс, небесáм etc.

    чудесá, чудéс, чудесáм etc.

g In the genitive plural of **яйцó** *egg* the **й** changes to **и**: **яиц** (nominative plural **йца** etc.).

FEMININE NOUNS

Feminine nouns denoting animate beings have a genitive-accusative in the plural only.

Masculine nouns ending **а** or **я** are animates. They have the endings of feminine nouns of the **а/я** declension but behave otherwise like masculine nouns:

> Ваш дя́дя был там. *Your uncle was there.*
> Я ви́дел твоегó дя́дю. *I saw your uncle.*

Nouns with the nominative singular ending in **а/я** and having two consonants before this ending usually insert a mobile vowel between these consonants before the genitive plural zero-ending. After a soft consonant and **ш, ж** it is usually **е**, otherwise it is usually **о**, though there are exceptions to this:

> тюрьмá *prison*   тю́рем
> лóжка *spoon*   лóжек
> лóдка *boat*   лóдок
> (but соснá *pine*   сóсен)

nominative ending in

	а		**я**	
	singular	*plural*	*singular*	*plural*
nom.	мину́та *minute*	мину́ты	недéля *week*	недéли
gen.	мину́ты	мину́т	недéли	недéль
dat.	мину́те	мину́там	недéле	недéлям
acc.	мину́ту	мину́ты	недéлю	недéли
instr.	мину́той/ою	мину́тами	недéлей/ею	недéлями
prep.	мину́те	мину́тах	недéле	недéлях

1 After **ш, ж, ч, щ, ц** the instrumental singular ends in **ой/ою** if stressed, **ей/ею** if unstressed: **межá** *boundary, hedge* **межóй, кóжа** *skin* **кóжей.**

2 **Й** before the ending **к** changes to the mobile vowel **е** in the genitive plural **чáйка** *sea-gull* **чáек.**

1 A few nouns of this type have genitive plural in **ей**:
> дя́дя *uncle*   дя́дей
> тётя *aunt*   тётей
> ноздря́ *nostril* ноздрéй

2 Nouns with a vowel before **я** in the nominative singular form the genitive plural in **й**:
> стáя *flock*   стай
> ли́ния *line*   ли́ний
> идéя *idea*   идéй

3 Nouns having nominative singular ending in **ья** also form the genitive plural in **й**, the **ь** changing to the mobile vowel **е**:

статья́ *article* стате́й
свинья́ *pig* свине́й

The sole exception is **го́стья** *guest*, genitive plural **го́стий.**

4 Nouns having nominative singular ending in **ия** have prepositional singular in **и**:

ли́ния *line* на ли́нии

5 Nouns ending in **ня** with a consonant or **й** before this ending have the genitive plural in *hard* **н**:
пе́сня *song* genitive plural **пе́сен,** **бо́йня** *slaughterhouse* genitive plural **бо́ен.** An exception is **дере́вня** *village* genitive plural **дереве́нь.**

	nominative ending in -ь	
	singular	*plural*
nom.	кость *bone*	ко́сти
gen.	ко́сти	косте́й
dat.	ко́сти	костя́м
acc.	кость	ко́сти
instr.	ко́стью	костя́ми
prep.	ко́сти	костя́х

	the noun **мать**	
	singular	*plural*
nom.	мать *mother*	ма́тери
gen.	ма́тери	матере́й
dat.	ма́тери	матеря́м
acc.	мать	матере́й
instr.	ма́терью	матеря́ми
prep.	ма́тери	матеря́х

Ло́шадь *horse* has instrumental plural **лошадьми́,** less commonly **лошадя́ми; дверь** *door* and **плеть** *whip* have instrumental plural **дверя́ми, плетя́ми** and also **дверьми́, плетьми́.**

Дочь *daughter* declines like **мать** but has instrumental plural **до-черьми́,** less commonly, **до-черя́ми.**

DECLENSION OF SURNAMES

Surnames ending in **ый, ой, ий** and the feminine forms **ая, яя** are adjectives and decline like the appropriate adjectives (see below).

Surnames ending in **ов/ев, ин** and the feminine forms **ова/ева, ина** were originally possessive adjectives and have mixed adjectival and substantival endings (cf. possessive adjectives below).

	masculine	feminine	plural
nom.	Пу́шкин	Пу́шкина	Пу́шкины
gen.	Пу́шкина	Пу́шкиной	Пу́шкиных
dat.	Пу́шкину	Пу́шкиной	Пу́шкиным
acc.	Пу́шкина	Пу́шкину	Пу́шкиных
instr.	Пу́шкиным	Пу́шкиной	Пу́шкиными
prep.	Пу́шкине	Пу́шкиной	Пу́шкиных

Place-names ending in **ов/ев, ин, ово/ево, ино** are declined exactly like hard ending masculine and neuter nouns. Hence **перед‿Пу́шкиным** *in front of Pushkin* (the poet), but **перед‿Пу́шкином** *before Pushkin* (the place).

B. ADJECTIVES

SHORT FORMS

Short forms of adjectives do not decline. They have nominative masculine, neuter, feminine and plural only. The masculine ends in a consonant letter or a soft sign, the feminine in **a** or **я,** the neuter in **o** or **e/ё,** and the plural in **ы** or **и.**

Most adjectives with more than one consonant before the ending in the long form insert a mobile vowel before the last consonant in the short form masculine.

	masculine	neuter	feminine	plural
young	мо́лод	мо́лодо	молода́	мо́лоды
old	стар	ста́ро	стара́	ста́ры
dear	до́рог	до́рого	дорога́	до́роги
bad	плох	пло́хо	плоха́	пло́хи
high	высо́к	высо́ко	высока́	высоки́
short	коро́ток	коро́тко	коротка́	коро́тки
near	бли́зок	бли́зко	близка́	бли́зки
cold	хо́лоден	хо́лодно	холодна́	хо́лодны
clever	умён	у́мно	умна́	у́мны
blue	синь★	си́не★	синя́★	си́ни★

After **ш, ж, ч, щ,** and **ц** the neuter ending is **o** if stressed, **e** if unstressed:

hot	горя́ч	горячо́	горяча́	горячи́
comely	приго́ж	приго́же	приго́жа	приго́жи

Й occurring before the last consonant in the long form changes to the mobile vowel **e** in the short form masculine:

| calm | споко́йный | споко́ен, споко́йно, споко́йна, споко́йны |
| chance | случа́йный | случа́ен, случа́йно, случа́йна, случа́йны |

The adjective **досто́йный** *worthy* (and **недосто́йный** *unworthy*) is exceptional, having **и** as a mobile vowel instead of **e:**

досто́ин, досто́йно, досто́йна, досто́йны.

★ Soft ending short forms are rare. Rare forms are marked by an asterisk.

Masculine and neuter adjectives have the same case endings except in the nominative-accusative.

Adjectives describing masculine animates have a genitive-accusative singular and plural, adjectives describing feminine animates have a genitive-accusative in the plural only.

hard ending: nominative singular masculine **ый**

	masculine	*neuter*	*feminine*	*plural*
nom.	кра́сный *red*	кра́сное	кра́сная	кра́сные
gen.	кра́сного		кра́сной	кра́сных
dat.	кра́сному		кра́сной	кра́сным
acc.	as nom. or gen.	кра́сное	кра́сную	as nom. or gen.
instr.	кра́сным		кра́сной/ою	кра́сными
prep.	кра́сном		кра́сной	кра́сных

soft ending: nominative singular masculine **-ий**

	masculine	*neuter*	*feminine*	*plural*
nom.	си́ний *blue*	си́нее	си́няя	си́ние
gen.	си́него		си́ней	си́них
dat.	си́нему		си́ней	си́ним
acc.	as nom. or gen.	си́нее	си́нюю	as nom. or gen.
instr.	си́ним		си́ней/ею	си́ними
prep.	си́нем		си́ней	си́них

hard ending stressed: nominative singular masculine **-ой**

	masculine	*neuter*	*feminine*	*plural*
nom.	молодо́й *young*	молодо́е	молода́я	молоды́е
gen.	молодо́го		молодо́й	молоды́х
dat.	молодо́му		молодо́й	молоды́м
acc.	as nom. or gen.	молодо́е	молоду́ю	as nom. or gen.
instr.	молоды́м		молодо́й/о́ю	молоды́ми
prep.	молодо́м		молодо́й	молоды́х

Adjectives in which the last consonant before the endings is **к, г, х, ш, ж,** or **ц** belong to the *hard* ending declension but since one must write **и** not **ы** after all of these letters, except **ц,** some of the case endings begin with **и,** not **ы.** Hence **высо́кий** *high*, instrumental masculine and neuter **высо́ким,** plural **высо́кие, высо́ких** etc., but **высо́кого, высо́кое, высо́кая, высо́кой** etc.

Стро́гий *severe, strict*, instrumental masculine and neuter – **стро́гим,** pl. **стро́гие, стро́гих** etc., but **стро́гого, стро́гое, стро́гая, стро́гой** etc. End-stressed adjectives of this type have, like normal end-stressed adjectives, **ой** in the nominative singular masculine – **дорого́й** *dear*, instrumental masculine and neuter **дороги́м,** pl. **дороги́е, дороги́х** etc., but **дороѓого, дорогое, дорога́я, дорогой** etc.

In adjectives not stressed on the ending the endings beginning with **o** (**ого, ому** etc.) are replaced by the endings beginning with **e** (**его, ему** etc). after **ш, ж, ч, щ,** or **ц.**

	masculine	*neuter*	*feminine*	*plural*
nom.	хоро́ший *good*	хоро́шее	хоро́шая	хоро́шие
gen.	хоро́шего		хоро́шей	хоро́ших
dat.	хоро́шему		хоро́шей	хоро́шим
acc.	as nom. or gen.	хоро́шее	хоро́шую	as nom. or gen.
instr.	хоро́шим		хоро́шей/ею	хоро́шими
prep.	хоро́шем		хоро́шей	хоро́ших

	masculine	*neuter*	*feminine*	*plural*
nom.	бледноли́цый *pale-faced*	бледноли́цее	бледноли́цая	бледноли́цые
gen.	бледноли́цего		бледноли́цей	бледноли́цых
dat.	бледноли́цему		бледноли́цей	бледноли́цым
acc.	as nom. or gen.	бледноли́цее	бледноли́цую	as nom. or gen.
instr.	бледноли́цым		бледноли́цей/ею	бледноли́цыми
prep.	бледноли́цем		бледноли́цей	бледноли́цых

Relative adjectives derived from names of animals and occasionally from nouns denoting persons have a soft declension differing somewhat from the normal soft declension. Note the presence of **ь** in all cases except nominative singular masculine. **Тре́тий** *third* also belongs to this declension.

	masculine	*neuter*	*feminine*	*plural*
nom.	во́лчий *wolf's*	во́лчье (NB)	во́лчья (NB)	во́лчьи (NB)
gen.	во́лчьего		во́лчьей	во́лчьих
dat.	во́лчьему		во́лчьей	во́лчьим
acc.	as nom. or gen.	во́лчье (NB)	во́лчью (NB)	as nom. or gen.
instr.	во́лчьим		во́лчьей/ею	во́лчьими
prep.	во́лчьем		во́лчьей	во́лчьих

Possessive adjectives ending in **ин** denoting 'belonging to so-and-so' have a mixed declension, partly adjectival, partly substantival.

	masculine	*neuter*	*feminine*	*plural*
nom.	ма́мин *mama's*	ма́мино	ма́мина	ма́мины
gen.	ма́мина or ма́миного		ма́миной	ма́миных
dat.	ма́мину or ма́миному		ма́миной	ма́миным
acc.	as nom. or gen.	ма́мино	ма́мину	as nom. or gen.
instr.	ма́миным		ма́миной/ою	ма́миными
prep.	ма́мином		ма́миной	ма́миных

Possessive adjectives in **ов/ев** (e.g. **отцо́в** *father's*) have a similar declension but are now obsolescent.

Compound Comparative

shorter бо́лее коро́ткий... коро́ткая etc.
longer бо́лее дли́нный... дли́нная etc.

Compound Superlative

shortest са́мый коро́ткий, са́мая коро́ткая etc.
longest са́мый дли́нный, са́мая дли́нная etc.

Simple (indeclinable) Comparative

a Many adjectives form a simple ('one-word') comparative, which is indeclinable, by adding **ee** to the stem. The first **e** is stressed if the short form feminine is stressed on the **a**, otherwise the stress is on the stem:

дли́нн-ый *long* дли́нне́е (cf. длинна́)
краси́вый *beautiful* краси́вее (cf. краси́ва)
у́мный *clever* умне́е (cf. умна́)

ee can be reduced to **ей: длинне́й, краси́вей,** etc.

b A limited number of adjectives (about sixty) form the simple comparative by adding **e** to the stem. The last consonant of the stem changes in nearly all instances and the stress is always on the stem. Here are comparatives of this type:

к changes to **ч** in:

вя́зкий *sticky*	вя́зче	го́рький *bitter*	го́рче (NB no ь)
гро́мкий *loud*	гро́мче	е́дкий *caustic*	е́дче
жа́ркий *hot*	жа́рче	жёсткий *hard*	жёстче
зво́нкий *sonorous*	зво́нче	кра́ткий *short*	кра́тче*
кре́пкий *strong*	кре́пче	лёгкий *easy, light*	ле́гче
ме́лкий *fine, shallow*	ме́льче (NB soft sign)	мя́гкий *soft*	мя́гче
ре́зкий *sharp*	ре́зче	те́рпкий *tart*	те́рпче
хру́пкий *brittle*	хру́пче	я́ркий *vivid*	я́рче

г changes to **ж** in:

дорого́й *dear*	доро́же	стро́гий *strict*	стро́же
туго́й *tight, stiff*	ту́же		

т changes to **ч** in:

бога́тый *rich*	бога́че	круто́й *steep*	кру́че

д changes to **ж** in:

молодо́й *young*	моло́же	твердый *firm*	тве́рже

ст changes to **щ** in:

густо́й *dense*	гу́ще	просто́й *simple*	про́ще
то́лстый *fat*	то́лще	ча́стый *frequent*	ча́ще
чи́стый *clean*	чи́ще		

Y

x changes to **ш** in

сухо́й *dry*	су́ше	ти́хий *quiet*	ти́ше

в changes to **вл** in

дешёвый *cheap*   деше́вле

к is dropped and the remaining consonant changes in

га́дкий *nasty*	га́же	гла́дкий *smooth*	гла́же
жи́дкий *liquid*	жи́же	ре́дкий *rare*	ре́же
коро́ткий *short*	коро́че		
бли́зкий *near*	бли́же	ни́зкий *low*	ни́же
у́зкий *narrow*	у́же		

An entire syllable is dropped in

высо́кий *high*	вы́ше	широ́кий *wide*	ши́ре

No consonant change occurs in

большо́й *big*   бо́льше

Various changes occur in

глубо́кий *deep*	глу́бже	далёкий *far*	да́льше (and да́лее)
до́лгий *long* (in time)	до́льше (and до́лее)	по́здний *late*	по́зже (and поздне́е)
ра́нний *early*	ра́ньше (and ра́нее★)	сла́дкий *sweet*	сла́ще
ста́рый *old*	ста́рше (and старе́е)	то́нкий *fine, thin*	то́ньше

The comparative is formed from a different root in

ма́ленький ма́лый	} *small*	ме́ньше (and ме́нее)
плохо́й *bad*		ху́же
хоро́ший *good*		лу́чше

The simple form of the comparative adjective also serves as a comparative adverb. Today the forms **бо́лее, да́лее, до́лее, ме́нее** and **поздне́е** are used almost exclusively as comparative adverbs, not adjectives. *More* and *less* before another adjective or adverb can only be **бо́лее** and **ме́нее** (cf. compound comparative above).

Simple (declinable) Comparatives

бо́льший *greater*   ме́ньший *less(er)*

The following are comparatives *or* superlatives:

вы́сший *higher, supreme*	лу́чший *better, best*
мла́дший *younger, youngest*	ни́зший *lower, inferior*
ста́рший *elder, oldest*	ху́дший *worse, worst*

322

Simple (declinable) Superlatives

Only adjectives which form a simple comparative may form the simple superlative – and not all of them do so. The ending is **ейший** and, after **ж, ш, ч, щ, айший**. This form usually has the meaning *a most...* rather than *the ... -est*.

ва́жный *important*	(важне́е)	важне́йший
		вопро́с *a most important question*
у́мный *clever*	(умне́е)	умне́йший
		учени́к *the cleverest pupil*
бога́тый *rich*	(бога́че)	богате́йший
		челове́к *an extremely rich man*

As can be seen from the last example, these superlatives are formed not from the comparative but direct from the adjective stem. Final **к** of this stem changes to **ч**, final **г** to **ж**, final **х** to **ш**.

кратча́йший путь *the shortest way* (cf. кра́ткий)
строжа́йший учи́тель *a most strict teacher* (cf. стро́гий)
редча́йший слу́чай *the rarest event* (cf. ре́дкий)

but

ближа́йший го́род *the nearest town* (cf. бли́зкий)
нижа́йший покло́н *a very low bow* (cf. ни́зкий)

C. PRONOUNS

PERSONAL PRONOUNS

nom.	я *I*	мы *we*	ты *thou, you*	вы *you*
gen.	меня́	нас	тебя́	вас
dat.	мне	нам	тебе́	вам
acc.	меня́	нас	тебя́	вас
instr.	мной/-о́ю	на́ми	тобо́й/-о́ю	ва́ми
prep.	мне	нас	тебе́	вас

	masculine	*neuter*	*feminine*	*plural*
nom.	он *he, it*	оно́ *it*	она́ *she*	они́ *they*
gen.	его́		её	их
dat.	ему́		ей	им
acc.	его́		её	их
instr.	им		е́ю	и́ми
prep.	нём		ней	них

Whenever it is governed by a preposition the third person pronoun has an initial **н**. Hence the prepositional case always has an initial **н**. The alternative instrumental of **она́** is found only with the prepositions: **с ней.**

REFLEXIVE PRONOUN

nom.   –
gen.   себя́
dat.   себе́
acc.   себя́
instr. собо́й/о́ю
prep. себе́

INTERROGATIVE AND RELATIVE PRONOUNS ETC.

nom.	кто *who*	что *what*
gen.	кого́	чего́
dat.	кому́	чему́
acc.	кого́	что
instr.	кем	чем
prep.	ком	чём

The compounds **никто́** *nobody,* **ничто́** *nothing* decline in the same way. When governed by a preposition the pronouns **никто́** and **ничто́** split into two parts and the preposition is inserted between them: ни‿у‿кого́, ни‿с‿ ке́м, ни‿от‿чего́, ни‿о‿чём etc.

This does not happen when **никто́** means *a nobody* and **ничто́** means (*a mere*) *nothing* – **Мно́го шу́ма из ничего́** *Much ado about nothing.* The first elements in the compounds **кто́-то** *somebody,* **кто́-нибудь** *somebody, anybody,* **кто́-либо** *anybody,* **что́-то** *something,* **что́-нибудь** *something, anything,* **что́-либо** *anything* decline like **кто** and **что** respectively, the second elements remaining unchanged.

The pronouns **кое-кто́** (**кой-кто́**) *somebody, some,* and **кое-что́** (**кой-что́**) *something, some things* decline the second elements only. When governed by a preposition these pronouns usually behave in the same way as **никто́** and **ничто́** – **ко́е с ке́м, ко́е от чего́.** The pronoun **не́кто** *somebody* has only a nominative case and the pronoun **не́что** *something* has only a nominative-accusative case.

The following two pronouns have no nominative case:

nom.	–	
gen.	не́кого (*there is*) *nobody*	не́чего (*there is*) *nothing*
dat.	не́кому	не́чему
acc.	не́кого	не́чего, не... что
instr.	не́кем	не́чем
prep.	не... ком	не... чем

Like **никто́** and **ничто́,** these two pronouns split into two parts when governed by a preposition and the preposition is inserted between them, **не́‿с‿кем, не́‿к‿чему** etc. Hence the prepositional case is always split into two parts – **не́ о ко́м, не́_в_чем.** The accusative **не...что** is used only with a preposition, as in **не́_на_что бу́дет со́ли купи́ть** (Turgenev) *there will be nothing with which to buy salt*.

POSSESSIVE PRONOUNS

Most of the endings of the possessive pronouns are like those of soft-ending adjectives, but most of these pronouns have stress on the ending.

	masculine	neuter	feminine	plural
nom.	наш *our*	на́ше	на́ша	на́ши
gen.	на́шего		на́шей	на́ших
dat.	на́шему		на́шей	на́шим
acc.	like nom. or gen.	на́ше	на́шу	like nom. or gen.
instr.	на́шим		на́шей/-ею	на́шими
prep.	на́шем		на́шей	на́ших

Ваш *your* is declined in the same way.

	masculine	neuter	feminine	plural
nom.	мой *my*	моё	моя́	мои́
gen.	моего́		мое́й	мои́х
dat.	моему́		мое́й	мои́м
acc.	like nom. or gen.	моё	мою́	like nom. or gen.
instr.	мои́м		мое́й/-е́ю	мои́ми
prep.	моём		мое́й	мои́х

Твой *thy, your*, **свой** *one's own*, **чей** *whose*, **ничей** *nobody's* are declined in the same way. In **чей** and **ничей** the letter **e** is a mobile vowel, which becomes **ь** in the other cases:

	masculine	neuter	feminine	plural
nom.	чей *whose*	чьё	чья	чьи
gen.	чьего́		чьей	чьих
dat.	чьему́		чьей	чьим
acc.	like nom. or gen.	чьё	чью	like nom. or gen.
instr.	чьим		чьей/-е́ю	чьи́ми
prep.	чьём		чьей	чьих

DEMONSTRATIVE AND DETERMINATIVE PRONOUNS

Э́тот *this, that* and **сам** *self* have similar declensions, **сам** having stress on the endings except in the nominative plural.

	masculine	neuter	feminine	plural
nom.	э́тот	э́то	э́та	э́ти
gen.	э́того		э́той	э́тих
dat.	э́тому		э́той	э́тим
acc.	like nom. or gen.	э́то	э́ту	like nom. or gen.
instr.	э́тим		э́той/-ою	э́тими
prep.	э́том		э́той	э́тих

	masculine	neuter	feminine	plural
nom.	сам	само́	сама́	са́ми (NB)
gen.	самого́		само́й	сами́х
dat.	самому́		само́й	сами́м
acc.	like nom. or gen.	само́	само́ё (NB) or саму́	like nom. or gen.
instr.	сами́м		само́й/-о́ю	сами́ми
prep.	само́м		само́й	сами́х

The declension of **тот** *that* and **весь** *all* is noteworthy in that the instrumental singular masculine and neuter and all the plural cases have the letter **е,** not **и** in the ending. (Note that **кто** and **что** (above) have this feature too in the instrumental.) In **весь** the **e** is a mobile vowel.

	masculine	neuter	feminine	plural
nom.	тот	то	та	те (NB)
gen.	того́		той	тех
dat.	тому́		той	тем
acc.	like nom. or gen.	то	ту	like nom. or gen.
instr.	тем (NB)		той/-о́ю	те́ми
prep.	том		той	тех

	masculine	neuter	feminine	plural
nom.	весь	всё	вся	все (NB)
gen.	всего́		всей	всех
dat.	всему́		всей	всей
acc.	like nom. or gen.	всё	всю	like nom. or gen.
instr.	всем (NB)		всей/е́ю	все́ми
prep.	всём		всей	всех

RECIPROCAL PRONOUN

In the reciprocal pronoun **друг дру́га** *each other, the one... the other* only the second word declines. It declines like a *masculine animate noun,* **дру́га** being accusative (and genitive) *even if the subject of the verb is inaminate* (cf. **себя́**).

nom.		–
gen.	друг	дру́га
dat.	друг	дру́гу
acc.	друг	дру́га
instr.	друг	дру́гом
prep.	друг	дру́ге

Prepositions are placed between the two words:

друг от дру́га, друг с дру́гом, друг о дру́ге etc.

QUANTITATIVE PRONOUNS

Ско́лько *how much, how many,* **сто́лько** *so much, so many,* **не́сколько** *a few, several* are nominative-accusative. Their other cases are like the plural cases of adjectives ending in **кий:**

nom.	сто́лько
gen.	сто́льких
dat.	сто́льким
acc.	like nom. or gen.
instr.	сто́лькими
prep.	сто́льких

The pronouns **мно́гие** *many* and **немно́гие** *few* have complete plural declensions, like that of adjectives, and these serve as the declensions of **мно́го** *many* and **немно́го** *a few*.

У мно́гих недостаёт пи́щи. *Many people do not have enough food.*
с немно́гими това́рищами *with a few friends*

The pronouns **мно́гое** *much* and **немно́гое** *little* have complete singular declensions, like those of neuter adjectives, and these serve as the declensions of **мно́го** *much* and **немно́го** *a little*.

Во мно́гом он прав. *He is right in many things* (lit. 'in much').

The words **ско́лько, сто́лько, не́сколько, мно́го** and **немно́го** may also be called *indefinite numerals*.

ADJECTIVAL PRONOUNS

These have declensions, including the nominative case, exactly like those of adjectives and are therefore brought together in one group, though from the point of view of meaning they may be interrogative, relative, demonstrative etc. They include:

вся́кий *each, every, any*	ка́ждый *each*
како́й *what sort of, what a*	кото́рый *which*
не́который *a certain*	не́которые *several*
никако́й ⎱ *not one, not a (single)* никото́рый ⎰	
са́мый *very*	тако́й *such*

When **никако́й** is governed by a preposition it splits into two parts and the preposition is inserted between them: **ни_у_како́го ученика́ нет карандаша́** *not a single pupil has a pencil.*

D. NUMERALS

CARDINALS AND ORDINALS

cardinals	*ordinals*
1 оди́н, одно́, одна́	пе́рвый *first*
2 два, две	второ́й *second*
3 три	тре́тий (declines like во́лчий, see above)
4 четы́ре	четвёртый

327

	cardinals	ordinals
5	пять	пя́тый
6	шесть	шесто́й
7	семь	седьмо́й
8	во́семь	восьмо́й
9	де́вять	девя́тый
10	де́сять	деся́тый
11	оди́ннадцать	оди́ннадцатый
12	двена́дцать	двена́дцатый
13	трина́дцать	трина́дцатый
14	четы́рнадцать	четы́рнадцатый
15	пятна́дцать	пятна́дцатый
16	шестна́дцать	шестна́дцатый
17	семна́дцать	семна́дцатый
18	восемна́дцать	восемна́дцатый
19	девятна́дцать	девятна́дцатый
20	два́дцать	двадца́тый
21	два́дцать оди́н/одно́/одна́	два́дцать пе́рвый
22	два́дцать два/две	два́дцать второ́й
23	два́дцать три	два́дцать тре́тий
30	три́дцать	тридца́тый
40	со́рок	сороково́й
50	пятьдеся́т	пятидеся́тый
60	шестьдеся́т	шестидеся́тый
70	се́мьдесят	семидеся́тый
80	во́семьдесят	восьмидеся́тый
90	девяно́сто	девяно́стый
100	сто	со́тый
101	сто оди́н/одно́/одна́	сто пе́рвый
102	сто два	сто второ́й
200	две́сти	двухсо́тый
300	три́ста	трёхсо́тый
400	четы́реста	четырёхсо́тый
500	пятьсо́т	пятисо́тый
600	шестьсо́т	шестисо́тый
700	семьсо́т	семисо́тый
800	восемьсо́т	восьмисо́тый
900	девятьсо́т	девятисо́тый
1,000	ты́сяча	ты́сячный
1,000,000	миллио́н	миллио́нный

Compound numbers such as 25, 36, 148, 1,567 consist simply of the separate elements written down in sequence:

два́дцать пять, три́дцать шесть, сто со́рок во́семь,
ты́сяча пятьсо́т шестьдеся́т семь

The only numbers which distinguish gender are **одúн, однó, однá;**
два (masculine and neuter), **две** (feminine); any larger number ending in
одúн etc., or **два/две;** and **óба/óбе** *both* (see below).
Одúн has a plural form **однú** *some*.

All numbers decline.
Одúн etc. declines like a pronoun, similar to **сам** but with stress on the
endings throughout. Note that **и** occurs only in the nominative singular
masculine.

	masculine		*neuter*	*feminine*	*plural*
nom.	одúн		однó	однá	однú
gen.		одногó		однóй	однúх
dat.		одномý		однóй	однúх
acc.	like nom. or gen.		однó	однý	like nom. or gen.
instr.		однúм		однóй/-óю	однúми
prep.		однóм		однóй	однúх

Два/две, три and **четы́ре** have a peculiar declension, not unlike that of
plural adjectives:

nom.	два/две	три	четы́ре
gen.	двух	трёх	четырёх
dat.	двум	трём	четырём
acc.	like nom. or gen.	like nom. or gen.	like nom. or gen.
instr.	двумя́ (NB)	тремя́ (NB)	четырьмя́
			(NB soft sign)
prep.	двух	трёх	четырёх

Both is **óба** (masculine and neuter), **óбе** (feminine). It has endings like those
of a plural adjective and has a masculine-neuter declension and a feminine
declension, being the only word in the language which distinguishes gender
in the plural declension.

	masculine and neuter	*feminine*
nom.	óба	óбе
gen.	обóих	обéих
dat.	обóим	обéим
acc.	like nom. or gen.	like nom. or gen.
instr.	обóими	обéими
prep.	обóих	обéих

Numbers ending in **ь** decline like feminine nouns ending in **ь,** having
'singular' forms only. In the teens the stress is fixed, otherwise the stress
shifts on to the end (but see below):

329

	masculine and neuter	*feminine*
nom.	пять	двена́дцать
gen.	пяти́	двена́дцати
dat.	пяти́	двена́дцати
acc.	пять	двена́дцать
instr.	пятью́	двена́дцатью
prep.	пяти́	двена́дцати

Во́семь *eight* has instrumental **восьмью́** or **восемью́**.

The instrumental of *all* numbers ending in **ь** has stress on the stem when it means 'times': **пя́тью пять** 5 × 5, **во́семью** (not **во́сьмью**) **шесть** 8 × 6, **два́дцатью семь** 20 × 7.

50, 60, 70 and 80 decline both elements, the second element being treated as a feminine noun in **ь**:

nom.	пятьдеся́т	во́семьдесят
gen.	пяти́десяти	восьми́десяти
dat.	пяти́десяти	восьми́десяти
acc.	пятьдеся́т	во́семьдесят
instr.	пятью́десятью	восьмью́десятью
prep.	пяти́десяти	восьми́десяти

Со́рок and **девяно́сто** have respectively **сорока́** and **девяно́ста** for all other cases.

Сто has **ста** for all other cases in the singular and also has a plural declension, like that of a neuter noun in **о**, used only as part of 200, 300 etc., which decline both parts:

nom.	две́сти	семьсо́т
gen.	двухсо́т	семисо́т
dat.	двумста́м	семиста́ми
acc.	две́сти	семьсо́т
instr.	двумя̀ста́ми	семьюста́ми
	(with secondary stress on **я**)	
prep.	двухста́х	семиста́х

Восемьсо́т is unusual in having instrumental **восьмиста́ми** (and also less commonly **восьмьюста́ми, восемьюста́ми**).

Ты́сяча declines like a feminine noun ending in **ча** but has two instrumentals: **ты́сячью** when used as a number, **ты́сячей** when used as a noun. 2,000, 3,000, 4,000, 5,000 etc., are **две ты́сячи, три ты́сячи, четы́ре ты́сячи, пять ты́сяч** etc.

The ordinals are **двухты́сячный, трёхты́сячный, четырёхты́сячный, пятиты́сячный** etc.

Миллио́н, биллио́н are masculine nouns and are declined as such. The higher ordinals are **двухмиллио́нный, пятимиллио́нный** etc.

Compound numbers, i.e. numbers consisting of separate words, decline all parts but when there are more than three parts it is permissible to decline only the thousands and the units:

двум ты́сячам пятьсо́т шестьдеся́т четырём солда́там.

In compound ordinals only the last part is put into the ordinal form:

два́дцать пе́рвый, сто пятьдеся́т шесто́й.

FRACTIONS

половина $\frac{1}{2}$, declined like a noun in **a**

че́тверть $\frac{1}{4}$
треть $\frac{1}{3}$ } declined like a feminine noun in **ь**

Other fractions are expressed by the feminine form of the appropriate ordinal:

одна́ восьма́я $\frac{1}{8}$ одна́ деся́тая $\frac{1}{10}$
две пя́тых $\frac{2}{5}$ семь восьмы́х $\frac{7}{8}$

one-and-a-half is **полтора́** (masculine and neuter), **полторы́** (feminine), the form **полу́тора** serving for all other cases.

The 'half' in $2\frac{1}{2}$, $3\frac{1}{2}$ etc. is expressed by **с полови́ной** *with a half*, the 2, 3 etc. being **два/две, три** etc. in the appropriate case. The word-order of the number as shown in these examples is obligatory:

два с полови́ной часа́ $2\frac{1}{2}$ *hours*
пять с полови́ной часо́в $5\frac{1}{2}$ *hours*
бо́лее двух с полови́ной часо́в *more than* $2\frac{1}{2}$ *hours* etc.

Полтора́ста means *one hundred and fifty*. It has the form **полу́тораста** for all other cases.

Полчаса́ means *half an hour, half-hour*. It declines in singular and plural as follows:

	singular	*plural*
nom.	полчаса́	получасы́ *half-hours*
gen.	получа́са	получасо́в
dat.	получа́су	получаса́м
acc.	полчаса́	получасы́
instr.	получа́сом	получаса́ми
prep.	получа́се	получаса́х

Полго́да *half a year* and **полмину́ты** *half a minute* decline in a similar way: **полуго́да, полуго́ду** etc., **полумину́ты, полумину́те** etc.

COLLECTIVES

дво́е 2, тро́е 3, че́тверо 4, пя́теро 5, ше́стеро 6, се́меро 7, во́сьмеро 8, де́вятеро 9, де́сятеро 10.

The last three are now rare and 5, 6 and 7 are much less common than 2, 3, 4.

nom.	двóе	чéтверо
gen.	двоúх	четверы́х
dat.	двоúм	четверы́м
acc.	like nom. or gen.	like nom. or gen
instr.	двоúми	четверы́ми
prep.	двоúх	четверы́х

Трóе declines like **двóе**, the rest like **чéтверо**.

E. VERBS

1 In certain forms of the verb the final consonant of the root changes to another consonant. These consonant changes also occur in other parts of speech. The only possible consonant changes are:

Т	to Ч, less often to Щ	
Д	to Ж, slightly less often to ЖД	
С	to Ш	
З	to Ж	
К	to Ч	
Г	to Ж	
Х	to Ш	
СТ ⎫ СК ⎭	to Щ	
П	to ПЛ	
Б	to БЛ	
М	to МЛ	
Ф	to ФЛ	
В	to ВЛ	

2 All other rules concerning stress are nullified by the rule that *perfective* forms with the prefix **вы-** are stressed on this prefix.

INFINITIVE

There are three types of infinitive:

1 Ending in **-ть**

    (*a*) Preceded by a vowel

дéлать *to do*	образовáть *to form*
стрелять *to shoot*	краснéть *to blush*
умерéть *to die*	дуть *to blow*
мыть *to wash*	колóть *to pierce*
говорúть *to speak*	

332

(*b*) Preceded by **-с-** or **-з-**

    сесть *to sit down*   лезть *to climb*

2 Ending in **-ти́**

    нести́ *to carry*   вести́ *to lead*

    везти́ *to convey*   идти́ *to go*

3 Ending in **-чь**

    мочь *to be able*   жечь *to burn*

    бере́чь *to look after*   печь *to bake*

The basic root of all verbs with this type of infinitive ends in **г** or **к,** which changes to **ч** in the infinitive.

CONJUGATION

Endings. The present tense and the future perfective have the same endings. The auxiliary **буду,** used to form the future imperfective, shares the same endings. The endings of the conjugated forms of verbs are:

1st pers. sing.	-у or -ю	1st pers. pl.	-м
2nd pers. sing.	-шь	2nd pers. pl.	-те
3rd pres. sing.	-т	3rd pers. pl.	-ут or -ют, and
			-ат or -ят

There are two types of conjugation:

First conjugation. All the endings except the first pers. sing. and third pers. pl. have **e** in front of them; the third pers. pl. ends in **-ут** or **-ют.**

Second conjugation. All the endings except the first pers. sing. and third pers. pl. have **и** in front of them; the third pers. pl. ends in **-ат** or **-ят.**

Hence the full endings of the two conjugations are:

first conjug.	*second conjug.*
-у/ю	-у/ю
-ешь	-ишь
-ет	-ит
-ем	-им
-ете	-ите
-ут/ют	-ат/ят

Classes[1]

The *first conjugation* is divided into four broad classes:

Class (*a*) those with a vowel or **ь** before the endings:

    ду́маю, ду́маешь etc., *think*

---

1 This classification is derived from a *phonological* classification of Russian conjugation made by K. H. Albrow, Lecturer in Phonetics, University of Edinburgh, to be published in *Archivum Linguisticum*. It has been converted here, with some modifications, into orthographic terms.

читáю, читáешь etc., *read*
гуля́ю, гуля́ешь etc., *stroll*
краснéю, краснéешь etc., *blush*
дýю, дýешь etc., *blow*
адресýю, адресýешь etc., *address*
жую́, жуёшь etc., *chew*
плюю́, плюёшь etc., *spit*
мóю, мóешь etc., *wash*
пью, пьёшь etc., *drink*

(The infinitive ends in **-ть** preceded by a vowel.)

Class (*b*) those with a consonant before the endings, this consonant not undergoing any change.

несý, несёшь etc., *carry*
везý, везёшь etc., *convey*
ведý, ведёшь etc., *lead*

(The infinitive ends in **-ти.**)

гúбну, гúбнешь etc., *perish*
стýкну, стýкнешь etc., *will knock* (fut. pfv.)

(The infinitive ends in **-нуть.**)

умрý, умрёшь etc., *will die* (fut. pfv.)

(The infinitive ends in **-ерéть.**)

and the unique verb
ткý, ткёшь etc., *weave* (infin. ткать)

Class (*c*) those with a consonant before the endings, this consonant changing except in the first pers. sing. and third pers. pl.

могý, мóжешь... мóгут *be able*
берегý, бережёшь... берегýт *look after*
пекý, печёшь... пекýт *bake*
жгу, жжёшь... жгут *burn*

(The infinitive ends in **чь.**)

and one verb with the infinitive in **-ать**
лгу, лжёшь... лгут *lie* (infin. лгать)

Class (*d*) those with a consonant before the ending, this consonant having changed, as compared with the infinitive, and the change running throughout the conjugation:

пишý, пúшешь etc., *write*, cf. infin. писáть
скажý, скáжешь etc., *will say* (fut. pfv.),
cf. infin. сказáть
пря́чу, пря́чешь etc., *hide*, cf. infin. пря́тать
плáчу, плáчешь etc., *weep*, cf. infin. плáкать

334

ищу́, и́щешь etc., *seek*, cf. infin. иска́ть

сы́плю, сы́плешь etc., *strew*, cf. infin. сы́пать

(The infinitive ends in **-ать**.)

Verbs of the first three classes, with very few exceptions, have no stress-shift: the stress remains on the same syllable throughout.

There are no exceptions in Class (*a*).

The exceptions in Class (*b*) include, **стону́, сто́нешь** *groan* (**стона́ть**); **стелю́, сте́лешь** *spread* (**стлать**); verbs with the infinitive in **-оть: коло́ть** *pierce* – **колю́, ко́лешь; тяну́, тя́нешь** *pull* (**тяну́ть**) and **тону́, то́нешь** *sink, drown* (**тону́ть**).

The exception in Class (*c*) is **могу́, мо́жешь** *be able* (**мочь**).

Verbs of Class (*d*) have a stress-shift only if the first pers. sing. is stressed on the ending, after which the stress shifts off the ending:

пишу́, пи́шешь

скажу́, ска́жешь

колéблю, колéблешь *shake* is exceptional in having a stress-shift in the first pers. sing. (i.e. as compared with the infinitive **колеба́ть**).

The *second conjugation* has only one class. In this conjugation the final consonant before the endings changes in the *first pers. sing. only*, if it is one of the consonants which can undergo a change.

Most verbs of this conjugation keep the stress fixed (on the ending or on the root), some shift the stress after the first pers. sing.:

хожу́, хо́дишь *go*

INFINITIVE AND CONJUGATION

The relation between infinitive and type and class of conjugation is set out in the following tables:

infinitive in	*1st conjugation*	*conjugation classes*
-ать	all except *ca*. 25, which are second conjugation	mostly (*a*), some (*d*); also **стлать** and **ткать** of class (*b*) and **лгать** of class (*d*)
-ять	all except two, which are second conjugation (see below)	(*a*)
-уть (incl. -нуть)	all	(*a*) verbs in **-уть**; (*b*) verbs in **-нуть**
-ыть	all	(*a*) and (*b*)
-оть	all	(*b*)
-ти	all	(*b*)
-чь	all	(*c*), except **дости́чь**, which is class (*b*) – **дости́гну, дости́гнешь**

-еть (incl. **-ереть**)	most	(a), most are derived from adjectives, a few from nouns (b) verbs in **-ере́ть,** losing the first **e** in conjugation
-ить	a few	(a) пить – пью, бить – бью, вить – вью, лить – лью, шить – шью; брить – бре́ю, бре́ешь, гнить – гнию́, гниёшь; (b) жить – живу́, живёшь; ошиби́ться – ошибу́сь, ошибёшься

infinitive in	2nd conjugation
-ить	most
-еть	some (*ca.* 40)
-ать	some (*ca.* 25)
-ять	two – **стоя́ть** and **боя́ться**

ANOMALOUS CONJUGATIONS

The verbs in this section either do not fit entirely into any of the conjugation classes or have anomalous features which make them difficult.

All verbs in **-овать/-евать** except those below change **ов/ев** to **у/ю** in the conjugation: **адресова́ть** to *address* **адресу́ю, адресу́ешь** etc. Seven verbs of this type have stress on the endings: **кова́ть** to *forge* **кую́ куёшь** and **снова́ть** to *shuttle*, **сова́ть** to *thrust*, **блева́ть** to *vomit* (vulg.), **жева́ть** to *chew*, **клева́ть** to *nibble, peck*, **плева́ть** to *spit*.

The following verbs do *not* change **ов/ев** to **у/ю**:

сомнева́ться	сомнева́юсь	*doubt*
здоро́ваться	здоро́ваюсь	*greet*
намерева́ться	намерева́юсь	*intend*
недоумева́ть	недоумева́ю	*be at a loss*
дева́ть	дева́ю	*put* (and compounds)
успева́ть	успева́ю	*have time, make progress*
затева́ть	затева́ю	*contrive, think up*

дать *to give* (pfv.)	**есть** *to eat*
дам	ем
дашь	ешь
даст	ест
дади́м	еди́м
дади́те	еди́те
даду́т (NB)	едя́т

хоте́ть *to want*

хочу́	⎫ 1st conjug.
хо́чешь	⎬ class (d)
хо́чет	⎭
хоти́м	⎫
хоти́те	⎬ 2nd conjug.
хотя́т	⎭

бежа́ть *to run*

бегу́	1st conjug.
бежи́шь	⎫
бежи́т	⎬ 2nd conjug.
бежи́м	⎬
бежи́те	⎭
бегу́т	1st conjug.

бить *beat,* **вить** *twine,* **лить** *pour,* **пить** *drink,* **шить** *sew,* conjugate like this:

бью
бьёшь
бьёт
бьём
бьёте
бьют

мыть *wash,* **выть** *howl,* **крыть** *cover,* **ныть** *mope, ache,* **рыть** *dig, delve,* conjugate like this:

мо́ю
мо́ешь
мо́ет
мо́ем
мо́ете
мо́ют

петь *to sing*

пою́
поёшь
поёт
поём
поёте
пою́т

е́хать *to go* (not on foot)

е́ду
е́дешь
е́дет
е́дем
е́дете
е́дут

Verbs ending in **-ава́ть** omit **-ва-** in the conjugation, as for instance: **дава́ть** *to give* (impfv.):

даю́
даёшь
даёт
даём
даёте
даю́т

жить *to live* and **плыть** *to swim, sail* have a **в** in the conjugation and belong to the first conjugation:

живу́
живёшь
живёт
живём
живёте
живу́т

(But *not* verbs ending in **-а́вать** **пла́вать, пла́ваю** *sail, swim.*)

(Also the archaic verb **слыть, слыву́** *to be known as, to have the reputation of.*)

Лечь *lie down* (perfective) and **сесть** *to sit down* (perfective) change the **е** to **я** and conjugate like this:

ля́гу (class (c))	ся́ду (class (b))
ля́жешь	ся́дешь
ля́жет	ся́дет
ля́жем	ся́дем

ля́жете   ся́дете
ля́гут   ся́дут

Five verbs have a mobile vowel in the conjugation but not in the infinitive:

mobile vowel **e**

брать to take (class (b))	**стлать** to spread (class (b))
беру́	стелю́
берёшь	сте́лешь
берёт	сте́лет
берём	сте́лем
берёте	сте́лете
беру́т	сте́лют

Драть *to flay, tear* conjugates like **брать.**

mobile vowel **o**

звать to call (class (b))	**гнать** to chase (second conj.)
зову́	гоню́
зовёшь	го́нишь
зовёт	го́нит
зовём	го́ним
зовёте	го́ните
зову́т	го́нят

A few verbs have a mobile vowel in the infinitive but not in the conjugation:[1]

жечь to burn (class (c))	**проч́есть** to read, pfv. (class (b))
жгу	прочту́
жжёшь	прочтёшь
жжёт	прочтёт
жжём	прочтём
жжёте	прочтёте
жгут	прочту́т
similarly compounds.	similarly other compounds of the root verb **-честь.**

тер́еть to rub (class (b))	**толо́чь** to pound (class (c))
тру	толку́
трёшь	толчёшь
трёт	толчёт
трём	толчём
трёте	толчёте
трут	толку́т

similarly compounds and also **уме-
р́еть** *to die* (and other compounds

1 The mobile vowel reappears in the past tense masculine **жёг – жгла, прочёл –
прочла́, толо́к – толкла́** and with the **-ереть** verbs throughout the past tense –
у́мер – умерла́.

338

of **-мере́ть**), **запере́ть** *to lock* (and other compounds of **-пере́ть**), and **простере́ть** *to stretch forth*. The imperfective of these verbs is formed in **-ирать**: **стере́ть** – **стира́ть** *to rub off*; **умира́ть, запира́ть, простира́ть**: these are class (a).

Verbs ending in **-оть** belong to class (b), one of them having **o** in the infinitive root but **e** in the conjugation.

коло́ть *to pierce*	**моло́ть** *to grind*
колю́	мелю́
ко́лешь	ме́лешь
ко́лет	ме́лет
ко́лем	ме́лем
ко́лете	ме́лете
ко́лют	ме́лют

similarly **поло́ть** *to weed*,
поро́ть *to rip, flog*,
боро́ться *to fight*.

Расти́ *to grow* belongs to class (b) and has **т** in the conjugation:

расту́
растёшь
растёт
растём
растёте
расту́т

(past tense **рос, росла́** etc. NB spelling)

Слать belongs to class (b), or class (d), the **c** changing to **ш** in the conjugation:

шлю
шлёшь
шлёт
шлём
шлёте
шлют

Брить *to shave*, **гнить** *to rot*, **ушиби́ть** (perfective) *to knock, bruise* belong to the first conjugation:

брить (class (a))	**гнить** (class (a))	**ушиби́ть** (class (b))
бре́ю (NB e!)	гнию́	ушибу́
бре́ешь	гниёшь	ушибёшь
бре́ет	гниёт	ушибёт
бре́ем	гниём	ушибём
бре́ете	гниёте	ушибёт
бре́ют	гнию́т	ушибу́т

similarly other compounds, such as **ошиби́ться** (*pfv.*) *to make a mistake*.

Реве́ть to roar is first conjugation, class (b).

ревý
ревёшь
ревёт
ревём
ревёте
ревýт

Дости́чь (*pfv.*) to achieve, reach, is first conjugation, class (b), and conjugates like this:

дости́гну
дости́гнешь
дости́гнет
дости́гнем
дости́гнете
дости́гнут

(cf. the alternative infinitive **дости́гнуть**)

Several verbs, all first conjugation, class (b), have an **н** in the conjugation but not in the infinitive:

нача́ть (pfv.) *to begin*	**жать** (1) *to reap*	**мять** *to crush*
начнý	жну	мну
начнёшь	жнёшь	мнёшь
начнёт	жнёт	мнёт
начнём	жнём	мнём
начнёте	жнёте	мнёте
начнýт	жнут	мнут

similarly **зача́ть** (pfv.)
to conceive

стать (pfv.) *to become, to begin*	**деть** (pfv.) *to put*	**клясть** *to curse (something, somebody)*
ста́ну	де́ну	клянý
ста́нешь	де́нешь	клянёшь
ста́нет	де́нет	клянёт
ста́нем	де́нем	клянём
ста́нете	де́нете	клянёте
ста́нут	де́нут	клянýт

similarly in the compounds **наде́ть** to put on (a garment), **оде́ть(ся)** to dress, **разде́ть(ся)** to undress etc. The imperfective of these verbs is formed from **дева́ть** to put, imperfective (class (a)).

similarly the reflexive **кля́сться** to swear (an oath).

распя́ть (pfv.) *to crucify*	**стыть** *to freeze, to congeal*
распнý	сты́ну
распнёшь	сты́нешь

распнёт	сты́нет
распнём	сты́нем
распнёте	сты́нете
распну́т	сты́нут

Some verbs, all first conjugation, class (*b*), have **м** in the conjugation but not in the root:

жать (2) *to press*
жму
жмёшь
жмёт
жмём
жмёте
жмут

This group includes the compounds of the verb **-нять/-ять** *to take*, which is no longer used without a prefix. In the conjugation the root appears as **-йм-**, **-ним-**, **-ьм-** or **-ым-**.

-йм-	**поня́ть** (pfv.) *to under-stand*	-ним-	**снять** (pfv.) *to take off, to take a photograph*
	пойму́		сниму́
	поймёшь		сни́мешь
	поймёт		сни́мет
	поймём		сни́мем
	поймёте		сни́мете
	пойму́т		сни́мут

similarly **доня́ть** *to annoy*, **заня́ть** *to occupy*, **наня́ть** *to hire*, **уня́ть** *to calm down*, all perfective. No stress-shift. Note that in this group all the prefixes end in a vowel.

similarly **обня́ть** *to embrace*, **отня́ть** *to take away*, **подня́ть** *to raise*, **приня́ть** *to receive*, **разня́ть** *to take apart*, all perfective. Stress-shift. **Приня́ть** loses the **ни** in conjugation **приму́**, **при́мешь** etc. Note that in this group all the prefixes except **при-** end in a consonant.

The imperfective of all the **-нять** verbs is formed in **-нима́ть**, class (a).

-ьм-	**взять** (pfv.) *to take*	-ым-	**изъя́ть** (pfv.) *to take out* (e.g. of circulation)
	возьму́ (NB о!)		изыму́
	возьмёшь		изы́мешь
	возьмёт		изы́мет
	возьмём		изы́мем
	возьмёте		изы́мете
	возьму́т		изы́мут

Imperfective **брать,** class (*b*) (see above).

Some of the **-им-** type have alternatives with **-ым-** (e.g. **подыму́**) which are now either archaic or quite obsolete.

FUTURE

The conjugation of a perfective verb is the future perfective of that verb: **сде́лаю** *I shall do*, **сде́лаешь** *you will do* etc.

The imperfective future consists of the imperfective infinitive and the auxiliary:

> бу́ду
> бу́дешь
> бу́дет
> бу́дем
> бу́дете
> бу́дут

(These forms also occur alone meaning *I shall be, you will be* etc.)

Hence **бу́ду де́лать/де́лать бу́ду** *I shall do*, **бу́дешь де́лать/де́лать бу́дешь** *you will do* etc.

PAST

The past tense is not conjugated. It changes according to gender and number. The masculine ends in **-л**, the neuter in **-ло**, the feminine in **-ла** and the plural in **-ли.** In most verbs these endings simply replace the infinitive ending **-ть.**

impfv. де́лать				*pfv.* сде́лать			
де́лал	де́лало	де́лала	де́лали	сде́лал	сде́лало	сде́лала	сде́лали

Verbs with infinitive in **-сти** or **-сть** and having **т** or **д** in the present or future perfective tense do not have **т** or **д** in the past tense. In other words they drop the last three letters of the infinitive in forming the past tense:

вести́ *to lead* (веду́)	вёл	вело́	вела́	вели́
плести́ *to weave* (плету́)	плёл	плело́	плела́	плели́
прясть *to spin* (пряду́)	прял	пря́ло	пря́ла	пря́ли
сесть *to sit down*, pfv. (ся́ду)	сел	се́ло	се́ла	се́ли

Идти́ *to go* has past tense **шёл, шло, шла, шли.**

Вя́нуть *to fade* has past tense **вял** etc., less commonly **вя́нул** etc.

Some verbs do not have **л** in the past tense masculine. Such verbs include:

a those with infinitive in **-сти** and **з, с** or **б** in the present tense:

нести́ *to carry* (несу́)	нёс	несло́	несла́	несли́
везти́ *to convey* (везу́)	вёз	везло́	везла́	везли́
грести́ *to row* (гребу́)	грёб	гребло́	гребла́	гребли́

b all verbs with infinitive in **-чь,** the first pers. sing. of the present tense of which has **г** or **к:**

мочь *to be able* (могу́)	мог	могло́	могла́	могли́
жечь *to burn* (жгу́)	жёг	жгло	жгла	жгли
печь *to bake* (пеку́)	пёк	пекло́	пекла́	пекли́
толо́чь *to pound* (толку́)	толо́к	толкло́	толкла́	толкли́

c all verbs with infinitive in **-ереть.** These drop the last three letters of the infinitive in forming the past tense:

умере́ть *to die*	у́мер	у́мерло	умерла́	у́мерли
запере́ть *to lock*	за́пер	за́перло	заперла́	за́перли

d Verbs with infinitive in **-нуть,** which in their simple form are imperfective. These drop the **-нуть** in forming the past tense. The past tense masculine of these verbs ends in **к, г, х, с, з, п** or **б:**

со́хнуть *to dry up*	сох	со́хло	со́хла	со́хли
ки́снуть *to go sour*	кис	ки́сло	ки́сла	ки́сли
ги́бнуть *to perish*	гиб	ги́бло	ги́бла	ги́бли

e The verb **расти́** *to grow*, past tense **рос, росло́, росла́, росли́.**

f The verb **ушиби́ть** *to knock*, *bruise*, past tense **уши́б, уши́бло, уши́бла, уши́бли** and other compounds of the same root verb, e.g. **ошиби́ться** *to make a mistake*, **оши́бся, оши́блась** etc.

CONDITIONAL

The conditional consists of the past tense, imperfective or perfective, and the particle **бы,** which either immediately follows the past tense form or some other *earlier* word in the sentence.

impfv.	*pfv.*
де́лал бы	сде́лал бы
де́лало бы	сде́лало бы
де́лала бы	сде́лала бы
де́лали бы	сде́лали бы

PARTICIPLES

The *present active* participle ends in **-ущий/-ющий** for first conjugation verbs and **-ащий/-ящий** for second conjugation verbs. It is formed by replacing the **-т** of the third pers. pl. of the present tense by **-щий:**

де́лают	де́лающий	*doing*
несу́т	несу́щий	*carrying*
говоря́т	говоря́щий	*speaking*
дрожа́т	дрожа́щий	*trembling*

The *present passive* participle ends in **-емый** for first conjugation verbs and **-имый** for second conjugation verbs. A convenient way of forming it is by adding **-ый** to the first pers. pl. of the present tense:

де́лаем	де́лаемый (*being*) *done*
хвали́м	хвали́мый (*being*) *praised*

A few verbs of classes (*b*) and (*c*) form this participle; the **ё** of the present tense is changed to **o** and the consonant change of class (*c*) is nullified:

несём	несо́мый (*being*) *carried*
влечём	влеко́мый (*being*) *attracted*

This participle may have a short form **де́лаем, де́лаемо, де́лаема, де́лаемы.**

The *past active* participle ends in **-вший** after vowels and **-ший** after consonants. It is formed for most verbs by adding one of these endings to the past tense masculine after the **л,** if there is one, has been removed. It may be imperfective or perfective.

impfv.	де́лал	де́лавший (*was*) *doing*
	говори́л	говори́вший (*was*) *speaking*
	нёс	нёсший (*was*) *carrying*
	писа́л	писа́вший (*was*) *writing*
	пёк	пёкший (*was*) *baking*
pfv.	у́мер	у́мерший *having died, dead*
	сказа́л	сказа́вший *having said*
	зати́х	зати́хший *having fallen silent*

Verbs of the type **вести́, вёл** reinstate the final consonant of the root as in **ве́дший** (cf. веду́):

плести́	плёл	плётший (cf. плету́) (*was*) *weaving*

The verb **вя́нуть** *to fade* and its compounds reinstate the consonant **д** which has disappeared from all other forms:

увя́нуть	увя́л	увя́дший (*having*) *faded*

The verb **идти́** and its compounds have past active participle **(-)ше́дший.**

The *past passive* participle ends in **-нный** or **-тый.** Verbs of the first conjugation with infinitive in **-ать** (including **-овать/-евать**) or **-ять** and verbs of the second conjugation with infinitive in **-ать** form this participle by replacing the **-ть** of the infinitive with **-нный**:

сде́лать	сде́ланный *done*	
расстреля́ть	расстре́лянный *shot*	
образова́ть	образо́ванный *formed; educated*	
задержа́ть	заде́ржанный *delayed*	

344

If the **-ать/-ять** ending of the infinitive is stressed the stress moves back one syllable in the past passive participle. Two exceptions to this are:

жела́ть	жела́нный *wished for* (no shift)
переда́ть	пе́реданный *transferred* (moves two syllables)

Verbs of the second conjugation with the infinitive ending in **-ить** or **-еть** and verbs of the first conjugation with the infinitive ending in **-ти, -сть** or **-чь** form this participle by adding **-енный** to the verb root. Second conjugation verbs and first conjugation verbs in **-чь** have the consonant change which is found in the conjugation.

уговори́ть	уговорённый *persuaded*
запрети́ть	запрещённый (cf. запрещу́) *forbidden*
пересмотре́ть	пересмо́тренный *revised*
отвертеть	отве́рченный (cf. отверчу́) *turned back*
принести́	принесённый *brought*
перевести́	переведённый (cf. переведу́) *translated*
спрясть	спрядённый (cf. спряду́) *spun*
сбере́чь	сбережённый (cf. сбережёшь) *saved up*

Уви́денный *seen*, from **уви́деть** does not have the consonant change (cf. **уви́жу**) and is thus exceptional.

The stress is as in the third pers. sing., the ending becoming **-ённый** when stressed.

Exceptions to this include:

изменённый *changed* (cf. изме́нит)
оценённый *evaluated* (cf. оце́нит)
разделённый *divided* (cf. разде́лит)
осуждённый *condemned* (cf. осу́дит)

and, of course, other compounds of the same verbs.

The past passive participle ends in **-тый** for verbs with infinitive in **-уть, -ыть, -оть, -ереть** and verbs whose simple infinitive is a monosyllable ending in **-ить, -еть**. The verbs **жать, нача́ть, зача́ть** and compounds of the verb **-нять/-ять** (always prefixed) form this participle in the same way. The ending **-тый** replaces the past tense ending, except in verbs of the **-нуть** type having past tense masculine without **л**: here **-тый** replaces the infinitive ending.

наду́л	наду́тый *inflated*
сти́снул	сти́снутый *squeezed*
протяну́л	протя́нутый *stretched forth*
дости́гнуть (дости́чь)	дости́гнутый *achieved*
отве́ргнуть	отве́ргнутый *rejected*
вы́мыл	вы́мытый *washed*

345

прокол́ол	проќолотый	*pierced*
з́апер	з́апертый	*locked*
в́ыбрил	в́ыбритый	*shaved*
уб́ил	уб́итый	*killed*
нал́ил	нал́итый	*poured*
нагр́ел	нагр́етый	*heated*
сжал	сж́атый	*compressed*
н́ачал	н́ачатый	*begun*
з́анял	з́анятый	*occupied*

The stress is the same as in the past tense masculine except for verbs in stressed **-н́уть** and **-оть,** which move the stress back one syllable.

This participle is sometimes formed from imperfective verbs but such forms tend to have adjectival meaning, **бр́итый** *shaven.*

This participle has short forms, the **-нн-** of the **-нный** type being reduced to one **н.** When the long form is stressed **-ённый** the short form has the stress on the very last syllable:

> **уговорённый, уговорён, уговорен́а, уговорен́о, уговорен́ы.**

GERUNDS

The *imperfective* (or 'present') gerund ends in **-я** or **-а** (after **ш, ж, ч** and **щ**). It is formed by replacing the last two letters of the third pers. pl. present tense by **-я/-а.** Verbs of the **-ав́ать** type replace the last two letters of the infinitive with **-я.**

зн́ают	зн́ая	*knowing*
говор́ят	говор́я	*saying*
дрож́ат	дрож́а	*trembling*
адрес́уют	адрес́уя	*addressing*
дав́ать	дав́ая	*giving*

In modern Russian the 'present' gerund is not formed from the following verbs:

1 Verbs with no vowel in the root of the present tense:

врать – вру *to lie*	ждать – жду *to wait*
лгать – лгу *to lie*	жать – жму *to press*
тер́еть – тру *to rub*	бить – бью *to strike*
пить – пью *to drink* etc.	

An exception is **мчась** from **мч́аться** *to rush, to hurtle.*

2 Verbs of class (c), i.e. those with the infinitive in **-чь.**

The exception is **толч́а** from **тол́очь** *to pound.*

3 Verbs of class (d), i.e. those first conjugation verbs which have a consonant change throughout the conjugation.

An exception is **пр́яча** from **пр́ятать** *to hide.*

346

4 Verbs in **-нуть** which lose the **-ну** in the past tense.

5 Various common verbs, including **бежа́ть** *to run*, **е́хать** *to go*, **хоте́ть** *to want*, **звать** *to call*, **петь** *to sing*, **гнить** *to rot*, **драть** *to tear*, **лезть** *to climb*, **тону́ть** *to drown*, **тяну́ть** *to pull*.

The *perfective* (or 'past') gerund ends in **-в/-вши, -ши,** or **-я. -в/-вши** occurs after vowels and replaces the infinitive ending **-ть.**

узна́ть	узна́в(ши)	*having found out*
покрасне́ть	покрасне́в(ши)	*having blushed, blushing*
уговори́ть	уговори́в(ши)	*having persuaded*
запере́ть	запере́в (and за́перши)	*having locked*

The ending **-ши** occurs after consonants and is added to the past tense masculine ending in **г, к, з, р:**

сберёг	сберёгши	*having saved up*
перелёз	перелёзши	*having climbed across*
за́пер	за́перши	*having locked*

Verbs in **-нуть** which are perfective in their unprefixed form behave like **узна́ть** etc.: **сту́кнуть, сту́кнув(ши)** *having knocked.*

Verbs in **-нуть** which are imperfective in their unprefixed form either do the same or add **-ши** to the past tense masculine:

  вы́сохнуть, вы́сохнув(ши)/вы́сохши *having dried up*

The form of the perfective gerund in **-вши** or **-ши** is obligatory before the reflexive particle:

  сде́лавшись *having become*
  запе́ршись *locked (having been locked)*

Verbs with infinitive in **-ти** and also compounds of **-честь** form the gerund in **-я,** which replaces the **-у** of the first person singular:

привести́	приведу́	приведя́ *having brought*
проче́сть	прочту́	прочтя́ *having read*
принести́	принесу́	принеся́ *having brought*
пройти́	пройду́	пройдя́ *having passed through*

IMPERATIVE

The imperative singular ends in **-й, -и** or **-ь,** the imperative plural in **-йте, -ите** or **-ьте.**

a Verbs with a vowel before the conjugational endings (but not when the infinitive is in stressed **-и́ть**) replace the ending of the third pers. sing. with **-й/-йте:**

де́лает	де́лай	де́лайте *do*
образу́ет	образу́й	образу́йте *form*
поёт	пой	по́йте *sing*
бре́ет	брей	бре́йте *shave*
стои́т	стой	сто́йте *stop*

Verbs of the **пить** type form the imperative in **-й/-йте,** changing **ь** to **е:**

пью, пьёт – пей, пейте *drink*

Verbs of the **-ава́ть** type replace the **-ть** of the infinitive with **-й/-йте:**

дава́ть (даю́, даёт)   дава́й, дава́йте *give*

b Verbs with one or more consonants before the conjugational endings and stress on the ending of the first pers. sing. form the imperative by replacing the third pers. sing. ending with **-й/-йте:**

принесу́, принесёт	принеси́, принеси́те *bring*
напишу́, напи́шет	напиши́, напиши́те *write*
говорю́, говори́т	говори́, говори́те *speak*
скажу́, ска́жет	скажи́, скажи́те *say, tell*
кормлю́, ко́рмит	корми́, корми́те *feed*
хожу́, хо́дит	ходи́, ходи́те *go*

Note that verbs of class (*c*) form the imperative by replacing the ending of the *first* pers. sing. with **-й/-йте:**

помогу́, помо́жет	помоги́, помоги́те *help*
жгу, жжёт	жги, жги́те *burn*
лгу, лжёт	лги, лги́те *lie*

Verbs with a vowel before the conjugational endings have this type of imperative *if the infinitive is in stressed* **-йть:**

затаи́ть: затаю́, затаи́т   затаи́, затаи́те *hide, conceal*

c Verbs with two or more consonants before the conjugational endings and no stress on the ending of the first pers. sing. form the imperative in unstressed **-и/-ите:**

сту́кну, сту́кнет	сту́кни, сту́кните *give a knock*
коле́блю, коле́блет	коле́бли, коле́блите *shake*

d Verbs with *one* consonant before the unstressed first pers. sing. ending form the imperative by replacing the ending of the third pers. sing. with **-ь/-ьте:**

ре́зать: ре́жу, ре́жет	режь, ре́жьте *cut*
встать: вста́ну, вста́нет	встань, вста́ньте *stand up, get up*
быть: бу́ду, бу́дет	будь, бу́дьте *be*
бро́сить: бро́шу, бро́сит	брось, бро́сьте *throw, give up*
сесть: ся́ду, ся́дет	сядь, ся́дьте *sit down*

There are some exceptions to this rule.

The imperatives of **лечь** *to lie down,* **дать** *to give* and **есть** *to eat* are **ляг, ля́гте** (cf. **ля́гу**), **дай, да́йте** and **ешь, е́шьте.**

REFLEXIVE VERB FORMS

All verb forms except the passive participles may have the reflexive particle

348

-ся/-сь attached; **-ся** occurs after consonants, **-сь** after vowels, except in the participles, which always have **-ся**:

смеющийся, смеющегося etc. laughing

ASPECTS

The basic notion of the perfective aspect is completed action.

It expresses an act carried out, or the result of an act, or an action that goes on for a limited time, or a single act.

The imperfective aspect does not emphasize the notion of completion.

It expresses action going on, or action attempted, or action repeated, or habitual action, or the abstract idea of the action in general.

(There is a special use of the perfective future to express repeated action in past, present or future. The time of the action is indicated by adverbs, by other main verbs or by the context in general.)

Nearly all simple verbs are imperfective. When prefixed they nearly always become perfective.

impfv.	pfv.
де́лать *to do, make*	сде́лать
писа́ть *to write*	написа́ть
чита́ть *to read*	прочита́ть

When the suffix **-ну-** is added to simple verbs it also makes them perfective.

impfv.	pfv.
дуть *to blow*	ду́нуть
шага́ть *to step*	шагну́ть
стуча́ть *to knock*	сту́кнуть

Perfective verbs, nearly all of them prefixed, are made imperfective by means of the suffixes **-á-/-я́-**, **-вá-** and **-ыва-/-ива-**.

Suffix **-á-/-я́-**

pfv.	impfv.
спасти́ *to save*	спаса́ть
пережи́ть *to survive*	пережива́ть (cf. переживу́)
встре́тить *to meet*	встреча́ть
объясни́ть *to explain*	объясня́ть
укра́сить *to adorn*	украша́ть
запрети́ть *to forbid*	запреща́ть
ко́нчить *to finish*	конча́ть
прости́ть *to forgive*	проща́ть
бро́сить *to throw*	броса́ть

Note that verbs of the **-ить** type forming the imperfective by means of **-á-/-я́-** usually have the consonant changes listed above.

Suffix **-ва-**

pfv.	*impfv.*
дать *to give*	дава́ть
узна́ть *to find out*	узнава́ть
встать *to rise*	встава́ть
уби́ть *to kill*	убива́ть

This is the rarest suffix for forming imperfective verbs.

Suffix **-ыва-/-ива-**

переде́лать *to alter*	переде́лывать
прописа́ть *to prescribe*	пропи́сывать
спроси́ть *to ask*	спра́шивать
останови́ть *to stop*	остана́вливать
просмотре́ть *to look through*	просма́тривать

This is a very common way of forming imperfective verbs. Note that (1) verbs of the **-ить** type undergo consonant change in forming this kind of imperfective. (2) **o** in the last syllable of the root in the perfective becomes **a** and is stressed in the imperfective. This does not apply to **-овать** verbs, since **o** in these verbs is not part of the root:

переобразова́ть *to re-form*   переобразо́вывать

Some verbs have imperfective-perfective pairs formed from variants of the same root:

impfv.	*pfv.*
сади́ться *to sit down*	сесть (ся́ду, ся́дет)
ложи́ться *to lie down*	лечь (ля́гу, ля́жет)
станови́ться *to become*	стать (ста́ну, ста́нет)
па́дать *to fall*	упа́сть (упаду́, упадёт)
покупа́ть *to buy*	купи́ть
предлага́ть *to propose*	предложи́ть

Some verbs have imperfective-perfective pairs from different roots:

impfv.	*pfv.*
брать *to take*	взять
говори́ть *to say*	сказа́ть
лови́ть *to catch*	пойма́ть
класть *to put*	положи́ть
скла́дывать *to fold up,*	сложи́ть
to put together	

(But in a 'non-physical' sense **-ложить** verbs usually form the imperfective from **-лагать,** a variant of the same root: **предлага́ть** *to propose* **предложи́ть.**)

A few verbs are *either* imperfective *or* perfective:

веле́ть *to order*

жени́ть *to marry*

жени́ться *to get married*
казни́ть *to execute*
крести́ть *to baptize*
роди́ть *to give birth to*
ра́нить *to wound*

Many of the unprefixed verbs in **-овать/-евать** are also imperfective and perfective but prefixes and the suffix **-ыва-** make it possible to avoid these anomalies:

impfv. and pfv.	pfv. only
арестова́ть *to arrest*	заарестова́ть
телефони́ровать *to telephone*	протелефони́ровать
диктова́ть *to dictate*	продиктова́ть
ночева́ть *to spend the night*	переночева́ть
	impfv. only
образова́ть *to form*	образо́вывать
организова́ть *to organize*	организо́вывать

VERBS OF MOTION

In the following pairs of verbs both members are imperfective. The *determinate* or *specific* verb means motion in a single direction. The *indeterminate* or *generalized* verb does not mean this and hence means motion in more than one direction, or repeated motion, or habitual motion, or the abstract idea of the motion. The conjugation of those marked * is given above under *Anomalous Conjugations*.

indeterminate	determinate
ходи́ть *to go* (on foot)	идти́
е́здить *to go* (not on foot)	е́хать*
носи́ть *to carry* (on foot)	нести́
води́ть *to lead*	вести́
вози́ть *to convey*	везти́
лета́ть *to fly*	лете́ть
бе́гать *to run*	бежа́ть*
пла́вать *to swim, sail*	плыть*
ла́зить *to climb*	лезть
по́лзать *to crawl*	ползти́
гоня́ть *to chase*	гнать*
таска́ть *to drag*	тащи́ть
ката́ть *to roll*	кати́ть

The following points regarding the compounds of these verbs should be noted:

1 When the same prefix is added to both members of a pair and *retains the*

same meaning it turns them into an ordinary imperfective-perfective pair, i.e. the indeterminate verb remains imperfective, the determinate verb becomes perfective.

impfv.	*pfv.*
переноси́ть *to carry across*	перенести́
улета́ть *to fly away*	улете́ть

2 **идти́** changes to **-йти** when prefixed:

impfv.	*pfv.*
уходи́ть *to go away*	уйти́
входи́ть *to enter*	войти́

3 The basic forms of some of the indeterminate verbs are changed when prefixed, but only if they become the imperfective member of an imperfective-perfective pair.

	impfv.	*pfv.*
е́здить	уезжа́ть *to ride away*	уе́хать
бе́гать	выбега́ть *ro run out*	вы́бежать
пла́вать	переплыва́ть *to sail across*	переплы́ть
ла́зить	вылеза́ть *to climb out*	вы́лезть
по́лзать	вполза́ть *to crawl in*	вползти́
таска́ть	отта́скивать *to drag away*	оттащи́ть
ката́ть	отка́тывать *to roll away*	откати́ть

All verbs in **-езжа́ть** are imperfective. Hence, **разъезжа́ть** *to ride about*, though it has no paired member in **-éхать,** is imperfective.

4 If a prefixed indeterminate verb (other than **разъезжа́ть**) does not form a pair with a prefixed determinate verb, the form of the basic verb is not changed and *the verb is perfective.* Some of these perfective verbs may then form imperfectives by means of the suffix **-ыва-/-ива-.**

pfv.	*impfv.*
налета́ть *to fly* so many hours	налётывать
or miles	

    (cf. налета́ть impfv., налете́ть pfv. *to raid*)
сходи́ть *to pop round somewhere*
    (cf. сходи́ть, сойти́ *to come down*)
съе́здить *to pop round* in a vehicle
    (cf. съезжа́ть, съе́хать *to drive down*)

5 The prefix **по-** does not give the same meaning to indeterminate and determinate verbs, therefore these verbs prefixed with **по-** do not form imperfective-perfective pairs and the indeterminate verbs prefixed with **по-** become perfective.

    по- + indeterminate verb 'to do a bit of', 'to do for a while'.
    по- + determinate verb 'to start doing' or plain perfective.

352

полета́ть	pfv.	*to fly a little*
полете́ть	pfv.	*to set off flying*
походи́ть	pfv.	*to walk about a little*
пойти́	pfv.	*to set off, to go*
попла́вать	pfv.	*to swim about a little*
поплы́ть	pfv.	*to swim, to set off swimming*

6 The verbs **ката́ть, кати́ть** are tending to lose in part the indeterminate-determinate contrast and to become fixed, one in some expressions, the other in other expressions. Both become perfective when prefixed and do not therefore form imperfective-perfective pairs. The imperfective for both is formed in **-ка́тывать** (see above).

TWO TYPICAL VERBS

The forms of a typical first conjugation and a typical second conjugation verb:

	impfv.	*pfv.*
infin.	де́лать *to do, make*	сде́лать
pres.	де́лаю	
	де́лаешь	
	де́лает	
	де́лаем	
	де́лаете	
	де́лают	
fut.	бу́ду де́лать	сде́лаю
	бу́дешь ,,	сде́лаешь
	бу́дет ,,	сде́лает
	бу́дем ,,	сде́лаем
	бу́дете ,,	сде́лаете
	бу́дут ,,	сде́лают

past де́лал де́лало де́лала де́лали   сде́лал сде́лало сде́лала сде́лали

imper. де́лай де́лайте   сде́лай сде́лайте

participles:

pres. act.	де́лающий	
pres. pass.	де́лаемый	
past active	де́лавший	сде́лавший
past pass.		сде́ланный
gerund	де́лая	сде́лав(-ши)

	impfv.	*pfv.*
infin.	твори́ть *to create, do*	сотвори́ть
pres.	творю́	
	твори́шь	
	твори́т	

	impfv.	
	твори́м	
	твори́те	
	творя́т	
		pfv.
fut.	бу́ду тво́рить	сотворю́
	бу́дешь ,,	сотвори́шь
	бу́дет ,,	сотвори́т
	бу́дем ,,	сотвори́м
	бу́дете ,,	сотвори́те
	бу́дут ,,	сотворя́т

past твори́л твори́ло твори́ла   сотвори́л сотвори́ло сотвори́ла
твори́ли   сотвори́ли

imper. твори́ твори́те   сотвори́ сотвори́те

participles:

pres. act.	творя́щий	
pres. pass.	твори́мый	
past act.	твори́вший	сотвори́вший
past pass.		сотворённый
gerund	творя́	сотвори́в(-ши)

F. ADVERBS

Adverbs in **o/e** are formed from descriptive adjectives. The ending **o** may be stressed or unstressed; the ending **e** occurs when the ending is unstressed and the original adjective has soft endings or ends in **жий** or **ший**.

холо́дный *cold*	хо́лодно
высо́кий *high*	высо́ко́
кра́йний *extreme*	кра́йне

Adverbs of this type have comparatives identical with the comparative of the corresponding adjective **холодне́е, вы́ше**.

Adverbs in **и** are formed from adjectives ending in **ский/цкий**.

| ритми́ческий *rhythmic* | ритми́чески |
| молоде́цкий *valiant* | молоде́цки |

Adverbs in **e** are formed from some present active participles.

| поража́ющий *striking* | поража́юще |
| угрожа́ющий *menacing* | угрожа́юще |

Adverbs are formed with **по-**

a   with adverbs in **ки** meaning *in the manner of*

по-де́тски *childishly*
по-учи́тельски *in the manner of a teacher*
по-ру́сски *in the Russian manner, à la russe* also *in Russian*
по-англи́йски *in the English manner*, also *in English*

b plus forms in **ьи** from relative adjectives in **ий**

> по-пти́чьи *like a bird*
> по-ба́бьи *like a woman* (an expression of contempt)

c plus dative singular masculine-neuter of an adjective or pronoun

> по-ста́рому *in the old way*
> по-настоя́щему *really, thoroughly*
> по-мо́ему *in my (own) way*, also *in my opinion*

The instrumental singular of some nouns is used adverbially:

> у́тром *in the morning*
> ве́чером *in the evening*
> днём *in the day-time/afternoon*
> но́чью *at night*
> весно́й *in the spring*
> ле́том *in the summer*
> о́сенью *in the autumn*
> зимо́й *in the winter*
> ша́гом *at walking pace*
> по́лем *through the fields*

G. PREPOSITIONS

With genitive:

без (безо) *without*	ми́мо *by, past*
близ *near*	накану́не *on the eve of*
вдоль *along*	о́коло *around*
вме́сто *instead of*	от (ото) *from*
вне *outside, without*	относи́тельно *concerning*
внутри́ *inside, within*	по́дле *beside*
во́зле *beside*	позади́ *behind*
вокру́г *round*	по́сле *after*
впереди́ *in front of*	посреди́ *in the middle of, among*
для *for (the sake of)*	про́тив *opposite, against*
до *up to, till*	ра́ди *for the sake of*
из (изо) *out, from (a place)*	сверх *above*
из-за *from behind, because of*	свы́ше *above, beyond*
из-под *from underneath*	с (со) *from, off*
кро́ме *besides*	среди́ *among*
круго́м *round*	у *at*
меж *among*	

With dative:

благодаря́ *thanks to*	подо́бно *like*
вопреки́ *contrary to*	навстре́чу *towards*

355

вслед *after*
к *towards*
наперекóр *counter to*

по *according to, along, by, in*
соглáсно *according to*

With accusative:

в *into*
на *on to*
по *up to, till; for*
про *about, concerning*
сквозь *through*

за *behind*
о (об) *against*
под (подо) *under*
с (со) *about, approximately*
чéрез *through*

With instrumental:

за *behind, after, for*
над (надо) *above*
под (подо) *below*

мéжду *between*
пéред (передо) *in front of*
с (со) *with*

With prepositional:

в *in*
о (об, обо) *about, concerning*
при *in the presence of, in the time of, given, with, by*

на *on*
по *after*

Broadcast Texts for some Lessons

Listeners to the broadcasts are asked to listen to these texts and not to follow them in the book.

ВОТ КАКÓЙ РАССÉЯННЫЙ

Жил человéк рассéянный	*There lived an absent-minded man*
На ýлице Бассéйной.	*In Basseynaya Street.*
Сел он ýтром на кровáть,	*In the morning he sat down on the bed,*
Стал рубáшку надевáть,	*Began to put on his shirt,*
В рукавá просýнул рýки –	*Slipped his arms into the sleeves –*
Оказáлось э́то брю́ки.	*They turned out to be trousers.*
Вот какóй рассéянный	*What an absent-minded man*
С ýлицы Бассéйной!	*From Basseynaya Street!*
Надевáть он стал пальтó –	*He began to put on his coat –*
Говоря́т емý: не то.	*They tell him: It's the wrong one.*
Стал натя́гивать гамáши –	*He began to pull on his gaiters –*
Говоря́т емý: не вáши.	*They tell him: They're not yours.*
Вот какóй рассéянный	*What an absent-minded man*
С ýлицы Бассéйной!	*From Basseynaya Street!*

Вместо ша́пки на ходу́ Он наде́л сковороду́. Вместо ва́ленок перча́тки Натяну́л себе́ на пя́тки. Вот како́й рассе́янный С у́лицы Бассе́йной!	*Instead of a hat, in a hurry* *He put on a frying-pan.* *Instead of felt boots, gloves* *He pulled on his heels.* *What an absent-minded man* *From Basseynaya Street!*
Он отпра́вился в буфе́т Покупа́ть себе́ биле́т. А пото́м помча́лся в ка́ссу	*He set off for the buffet* *To buy himself a ticket.* *And then he rushed to the ticket* *office*
Покупа́ть буты́лку ква́су. Вот како́й рассе́янный С у́лицы Бассе́йной!	*To buy a bottle of kvas.* *What an absent-minded man* *From Basseynaya Street!*
Побежа́л он на перро́н, Влез в отце́пленный ваго́н, Внёс узлы́ и чемода́ны, Рассова́л их под дива́ны, Сел в углу́ перед окно́м	*He ran on to the platform,* *Got into an uncoupled coach,* *Brought in his bundles and cases,* *Distributed them under the seats,* *Sat down in the corner by the* *window*
И засну́л споко́йным сном... – Это что за полуста́нок? – Закрича́л он спозара́нок. А с платфо́рмы говоря́т: – Это го́род Ленингра́д.	*And fell into a peaceful sleep . . .* *'What sort of a halt is this?'* *He shouted early in the morning.* *And from the platform they say:* *'This is the town of Leningrad.'*
Он опя́ть поспа́л немно́жко И опя́ть взгляну́л в око́шко,	*Again he slept a little* *And again he looked out of the* *window,*
Увида́л большо́й вокза́л, Удиви́лся и сказа́л: – Это что за остано́вка – Болого́е иль Попо́вка? – А с платфо́рмы говоря́т: – Это го́род Ленингра́д.	*Saw a large station,* *Was amazed and said:* *'What sort of station is this –* *Bologoe or Popovka?'* *And from the platform they say:* *'This is the town of Leningrad.'*
Он опя́ть поспа́л немно́жко И опя́ть взгляну́л в око́шко,	*Again he slept a little* *And again he looked out of the* *window,*
Увида́л большо́й вокза́л, Потяну́лся и сказа́л: – Что за ста́нция така́я – Дибуны́ или Ямска́я?	*Saw a large station,* *Stretched himself and said:* *'What sort of station is this –* *Dibuny or Yamskaya?'*

357

А с платфо́рмы говоря́т:
– Э́то го́род Ленингра́д.

Закрича́л он: – Что за шу́тки!

Éду я вторы́е су́тки,
А прие́хал я наза́д,
А прие́хал в Ленингра́д!

Вот како́й рассе́янный
С у́лицы Бассе́йной!

С. Марша́к

And from the platform they say:
'This is the town of Leningrad.'

He began to shout: 'What jokes are these!

I am travelling for the second day
But I have arrived back,
But I have arrived in Leningrad!'

What an absent-minded man
From Basseynaya Street!

S. Marshak

МОЙДОДЫ́Р

Одея́ло
Убежа́ло,
Улете́ла простыня́,
И поду́шка,
Как лягу́шка,
Ускака́ла от меня́.

The blanket
Ran away,
The sheet flew away,
And the pillow,
Like a frog,
Galloped away from me.

Я за све́чку,
Све́чка – в пе́чку!
Я за кни́жку,
Та – бежа́ть
И вприпры́жку
Под крова́ть!

I (made) for the candle,
The candle (rushed) into the stove!
I (made) for the book,
It (started) to run
And at a hop, skip and jump
(Rushed) under the bed!

Я хочу́ напи́ться ча́ю,
К самова́ру подбега́ю,
Но пуза́тый от меня́
Убежа́л, как от огня́.

I want to drink some tea,
And run to the samovar,
But the pot-bellied one from me
Ran away, as from fire.

Бо́же, Бо́же,
Что случи́лось?
Отчего́ же
Всё круго́м
Заверте́лось,
Закружи́лось,
И помча́лось колесо́м?

Good Lord, good Lord,
What's happened?
Why
Everything all round
Has started to turn,
Has started to go round,
And cart-wheeled off?

Утюги́
   за
      сапога́ми,

The irons (went)
   after
      the boots,

Сапоги́
   за
      пирога́ми,
Пироги́
   за
      утюга́ми,
Кочерга́
   за
      кушако́м –
Всё верти́тся,
И кру́жится,
И несётся кувырко́м.
	The boots
	   after
	      the pies,
	The pies
	   after
	      the irons,
	The poker
	   after
	      the belt –
	Everything is turning,
	And spinning
	And rushing topsy turvy.

Вдруг из ма́миной из спа́льни, *Suddenly out of mother's bedroom,*
Кривоно́гий и хромо́й, *Bandy-legged and lame,*
Выбега́ет умыва́льник *Runs out the wash-stand*
И кача́ет голово́й: *And shakes his head:*

– Ах ты га́дкий, ах ты гря́зный, *'Oh you horrid, oh you dirty,*
Неумы́тый поросёнок! *Unwashed piglet!*
Ты черне́е трубочи́ста, *You're blacker than a chimney-sweep,*
  Полюбу́йся на себя́: *Take a look at yourself:*
У тебя́ на ше́е ва́кса, *You have polish on your neck,*
  У тебя́ под но́сом кля́кса, *You have a blot under your nose,*
У тебя́ таки́е ру́ки, *You have such hands,*
  Что сбежа́ли да́же брю́ки, *That even your trousers have run away,*

Да́же брю́ки, да́же брю́ки *Even your trousers, even your trousers*

Убежа́ли от тебя́. *Have run away from you.*

Ра́но у́тром на рассве́те *Early in the morning at dawn*
  Умыва́ются мыша́та, *Baby mice wash themselves,*
И котя́та, и утя́та, *And kittens, and ducklings,*
  И жучки́, и паучки́. *And baby beetles and spiders.*

Ты оди́н не умыва́лся *Only you haven't been washing yourself,*

И грязну́лею оста́лся, *And have remained a filthy little creature,*

И сбежа́ли от грязну́ли *And from the filthy little creature have run away*

И чулки́ и башмаки́. *Both stockings and shoes.*

Я – Вели́кий Умыва́льник,
Знамени́тый Мойдоды́р,
Умыва́льников Нача́льник
И моча́лок Команди́р!

Е́сли то́пну я ного́ю,
Позову́ мои́х солда́т,
В э́ту ко́мнату толпо́ю
Умыва́льники влетя́т
И зала́ют, и заво́ют,
И нога́ми застуча́т,
И тебе́ головомо́йку,
Неумы́тому, даду́т –

Пря́мо в Мо́йку,
Пря́мо в Мо́йку

С голово́ю окуну́т! –

Он уда́рил в ме́дный таз
И вскрича́л: – Кара́-бара́с! –
И сейча́с же щётки, щётки
Затреща́ли, как трещо́тки,
И дава́й меня́ тере́ть,
Пригова́ривать:
– Мо́ем, мо́ем трубочи́ста
Чи́сто, чи́сто, чи́сто, чи́сто!
Бу́дет, бу́дет трубочи́ст
Чист, чист, чист, чист! –

Тут и мы́ло подскочи́ло
И вцепи́лось в волоса́,
И юли́ло, и мыли́ло,
И куса́ло, как оса́.

А от бе́шеной моча́лки
Я помча́лся, как от па́лки,
А она́ за мной, за мной
По Садо́вой, по Сенно́й.

Я к Таври́ческому са́ду,
Перепры́гнул чрез огра́ду,
А она́ за мно́ю мчи́тся
И куса́ет, как волчи́ца.

I am the Great Wash-stand,
The famous Moydodyr,
Boss of washstands,
And Commander of loofahs!

If I stamp my foot,
To call my soldiers,
Into this room in a crowd
The wash-stands will fly in,
And start barking and howling,
And stamping their feet,
And to you a dressing down,
To unwashed you, they will
*   give –*
Right into the Moyka (river),
Right into the Moyka (a pun on
*   мо́йка washing)*
They will totally immerse (you)!

He hit the copper basin
And shouted: 'Kara-baras!'
And at once the brushes, the brushes
Began rattling like rattles,
And began rubbing me,
Saying:
'We wash, we wash the chimney-sweep
Clean, clean, clean, clean!
The chimney-sweep will be, will be
Clean, clean, clean, clean!'

And now the soap leaped up
And seized me by the hair,
And bustled, and soaped,
And stung like a wasp.

But from the mad face-cloth
I rushed away, as from a stick,
And it (rushed) after me, after me
Along Sadovaya, along Sennaya.

I (rushed) to the Tavrichesky garden,
Leapt over the fence,
But it (the face-cloth) races after me
And bites like a she wolf.

Вдруг навстре́чу мой хоро́ший,	Suddenly I ran into my good, good,
Мой люби́мый Кокоди́л.	My beloved Crocodile.
Он с Тото́шей и Коко́шей	He with Totosha and Kokosha
По алле́е проходи́л	Was walking down the avenue
И моча́лку, сло́вно га́лку,	And the face-cloth, as though (it were),
Сло́вно га́лку, проглоти́л.	As though (it were) a jackdaw, he swallowed.

А пото́м как зарычи́т
  На меня́,
Как нога́ми застучи́т
  На меня́:
– Уходи́-ка ты домо́й,
  Говори́т,
Да лицо́ своё умо́й,
  Говори́т,
А не то как налечу́,
  Говори́т,
Растопчу́ и проглочу́! –
  Говори́т.
Как пусти́лся я по у́лицам
  бежа́ть,
Прибежа́л я к умыва́льнику
  опя́ть,
    Мы́лом, мы́лом,
    Мы́лом, мы́лом,
  Умыва́лся без конца́,
    Смыл и ва́ксу
    И черни́ла
  С неумы́того лица́.

И сейча́с же брю́ки, брю́ки

Так и пры́гнули мне в ру́ки,
А за ни́ми пирожо́к:
– Ну́-ка, съешь меня́, дружо́к! –
А за ним и бутербро́д:
Подбе́жал – и пря́мо в рот!

Вот и кни́жка вороти́лась,
Вороти́лася тетра́дь,
И грамма́тика пусти́лась
С арифме́тикой пляса́ть.

And then how he began to roar
  At me,
How he began to stamp (his) feet
  At me:
'You go away home,'
  He says,
'And wash your face,'
  He says,
'Or else I may rush upon (you),'
  He says,
'Stamp upon and swallow (you)!'
  He says.
How I set off running along the
  streets,
I ran to the wash-stand again,

    With soap, with soap,
    With soap, with soap,
  I washed myself without stopping,
  I washed off both the polish
  And the ink
  From (my) unwashed face.

And immediately (my) trousers, (my)
  trousers
Simply jumped into my hands,
And after them a small pie:
'Now then, eat me, little friend!'
And after it a sandwich too:
Ran up – and straight into (my)
  mouth!

And now the book returned,
The exercise-book returned,
And the grammar-book set off
To dance with the arithmetic-book.

Тут Вели́кий Умыва́льник,	*Hereupon the Great Wash-stand,*
Знамени́тый Мойдоды́р,	*The Famous Moydodyr,*
Умыва́льников Нача́льник	*Boss of wash-stands*
И моча́лок Команди́р,	*Commander of face-cloths,*
Подбежа́л ко мне, танцу́я,	*Ran up to me, dancing,*
И целу́я, говори́л:	*And, kissing (me), said:*
– Вот тепе́рь тебя́ люблю́ я,	*'So now I love you,*
Вот тепе́рь тебя́ хвалю́ я!	*So now I praise you!*
Наконе́ц-то ты, грязну́ля,	*At last, you filthy little creature,*
Мойдоды́ру угоди́л! –	*You have pleased Moydodyr!'*
На́до, на́до умыва́ться	*One has to, one has to wash oneself*
По утра́м и вечера́м,	*In the mornings and the evenings,*
А нечи́стым	*And to dirty*
Трубочи́стам –	*Chimney-sweeps –*
Стыд и срам!	*Shame and disgrace!*
Стыд и срам!	*Shame and disgrace!*
Да здра́вствует мы́ло души́стое,	*Long live fragrant soap,*
И полоте́нце пуши́стое,	*And the fluffy towel,*
И зубно́й порошо́к,	*And tooth powder,*
И густо́й гребешо́к!	*And the fine-toothed comb!*
Дава́йте же мы́ться, плеска́ться,	*Let us wash ourselves, let us splash about,*
Купа́ться, ныря́ть, кувырка́ться	*Bathe, dive, somersault*
В уша́те, в коры́те, в лоха́ни,	*In the tub, in the trough, in the basin,*
В реке́, в ручейке́, в океа́не,	*In the river, in the stream, in the ocean,*
И в ва́нне, и в ба́не,	*And in the bath and in the bath-house,*
Всегда́ и везде́!	*Always and everywhere!*
Ве́чная сла́ва воде́!	*Everlasting glory to water!*
К. Чуко́вский	*K. Chukovsky*

Key to Exercises and Texts

Most of the sentences and passages not translated in the lessons are translated here.

Brackets before and after words in the English translation indicate that these words are either implied in the Russian context or are necessary in English usage.

'Who is there?'
'We're here. I'm here, brother Mark and Mary.'
'Well, how (goes it)?'
'How (goes it) here? (It's) torture here – (there are) mosquitoes here.'
'(There are) mosquitoes here, because (there is) mist here, (it is) wet, but (there is a) pub here.'

§ 12a

I am not eating. He is not here. The chimneys are not here but there.
The bouquet is not there but here. Not so! – Not so? Then how? – So!
The house isn't here? – The house is not here but there.
Will the doctors give (it)? – No, the doctors will not, but I shall give (it).
Who is rolling (it)? Is she rolling (it)? – No, he, the brother, is rolling (it).
Who smokes/is smoking? She smokes/is smoking but (her) brother does/is not.
They smoke/are smoking. We do not smoke/are not smoking.

§ 12b

(My) brother is at home. The banker is at home. The lady is at home. Mama is at home.
Yes, the lady is at home, Mama is at home, (my) brother and the banker are at home, and the cat is at home!
The houses are here. – What? Are the houses here? How is that? – The houses are here because the river is here.
Is the lady at home? – Yes, she is at home. Are the ladies at home? – Yes, they are at home.
Who is he? – He is a doctor. – Are you a doctor? – No, I am not a doctor but my brother is a doctor.

LESSON 3, § 2

I shall be there. I shall be there early in the morning. I shall not be at home in the morning.
They will be at home in the morning. Early in the morning they are at home.

'Where are they going? There?'
'They are not going there, but I am going there.'
'How is it that they are not going?'
'They are not going there.'
'But how is it that they are not going there?'
'Well, it just is so – they are not going there. They are at home, they are smoking.'
'Where are they going to?'
'They are going there, and I am going there.'

The ships are going there. Knock! Knock! – Who's there? – We! Me! We are here!

They will be there but not soon.

How strange! (It is) damp here so quickly. Yes, (there are) mists here.

§ 6

Ann's garden is here. Here stands banker Smith's house.

The house of old man Brown stands over there and the doctor's house is alongside.

The windows of the house are here. The window of the booth is here and the window of the kiosk is there.

And here are brother Mark's socks. No, (it's) not (my) brother's socks (which) are here, but (my) son's.

(My) son is a sailor. He himself is on board (his) ship – but (his) socks are here.

Brother Mark's socks are there. Yes, yes – they are there.

§ 8

There is no pub here, and no tobacco. Neither pub nor tobacco!

There is no bridge here, because there is no river. Neither bridge nor river.

Is the window here? Yes, the window is here but there is no window-frame.

There is neither dog nor cat here. There is a fish here.

And over there is a dog and a cat but no fish.

The cat and the dog are not here but over there.

Is the doctor at home? – The doctor is not at home but on board ship.

The doctor is not at home but on board ship.

No, the doctor is not at home.

There is no place here. – Is there a place there? – No, there is no place there either.

They are standing there and we are standing here.

Who is standing there? – The doctors are standing there.

And the doctor's brother is not at home. The doctor's brother is standing here.

Is Ivan here? – No, Ivan is not here. Victor and I are here.

That's not true! – Ivan and Victor are here.

§ 9

Тут сад до́ктора?

Нет, сад до́ктора там, но сад бра́та тут.

Тут таба́к, а не там.

Тут нет табака́!

Кто стои́т там?

Там стоя́т матро́сы, а директора́ стоя́т тут.

Неве́рно! Матро́сы тут. Ива́н и Ви́ктор там.
Тут нет соба́ки, но кот наве́рно тут.
Окно́ ко́мнаты тут.
Нет, нет, о́кна там.
Они́ иду́т туда́, а я не иду́.
Доктора́ е́дут туда́.
Тут ме́сто? – Нет, тут нет ме́ста.
Тут каба́к? – Нет, тут нет кабака́.
Вино́ тут, во́дка и вода́ стоя́т там.

LESSON 4, § 4

The garden is here. In the garden stand oak trees. In the morning it is damp
in the garden. Since it is damp and wet here, there are mists here. The mists
seem to grow, they grow like oak-trees. But oak-trees do not grow fast and
mists do grow fast. There are mists both here and there. No, I am not going
there in the morning. I am at home in the morning. I am not going there.
Early in the morning it is damp and wet in the garden – there are oak-trees
standing there and there are mists there.

§ 9

I think a lot. They talk a lot but they do not think much.
And he neither thinks nor speaks.
I run quickly and play a lot. He does not play, does not run, but stands (still).
They do not stand (still) – they run, but they do not run as fast as I (do).
They are going south. They are dining on board ship. I am not going
anywhere (by any manner of means). I am dining at home in the garden.

§ 12

– Доктора́ стоя́т и говоря́т и говоря́т, в то вре́мя как банки́р стои́т там
  и ку́рит папиро́сы. Ему́ ду́рно ра́но у́тром.
– Ива́н не говори́т, но он мно́го ду́мает...
– Тут рю́мки?
– Рю́мки тут, а вина́ нет.
– Как? Нет вина́/Вина́ нет?
– Там стои́т ГУМ и там мно́го вина́.
– Тут мно́го тума́на. Да, тут мно́го тума́на, так как тут река́.
– Тут мно́го воды́. Да, мно́го воды́ – а вина́ нет.
– Куда́ они́ е́дут? Я е́ду на юг.
– Они́ е́дут домо́й, так как обе́дают до́ма.
– До́ктор, говоря́т, обе́дает на борту́ су́дна.
– А! Вино́ там! Ивано́в гре́ет вино́.
– Как?! Я иду́ домо́й. До свида́ния!

Is it clean here? No, it is not clean here.

It is always clean here. Of course, it is clean here.

You are pupils – yes, you are pupils. The pupils are reading the lesson.

The country-house is in the south.

(My) daughter is at home now – (my) daughter is dining at home.

(My) daughter and grand-daughter are going home. (My) daughter and grand-daughter are going home in the evening.

It is pitching (lit. 'rocking') now. The ship is pitching and we don't feel well.

How is it (that it is) pitching? – It is pitching because there is an east wind blowing.

No, it's a north wind.

Who is there? – The banker himself is there. I think he is reading.

What is (that) there? There is a convoy and there are railway carriages over there.

What is here? – The river is here and a bridge stands here, and alongside is Westminster.

. . . .

Westminster, both Bank and Bridge and Abbey.

Wrong! Wrong!

Now, now – we are talking (too) loudly!

§ 3

Ivan himself is not here, but (his) friend is here.

What is not here? That paper is not here, that book is not here.

That market is not here, those goods (sing. in Russian) are not here.

There is no one here. There is nothing here.

What is there? – Why, there is nothing there.

– Well now, there is nothing! How do you mean – there is nothing?

– Just that – nothing at all, there is nothing there – neither wine nor tobacco, it's so tiresome!

Well, never mind, never mind – you see, I'm going home and at home there's tobacco and wine and books and papers. You're offended that there's no tobacco, but I'll give you (some) and I'll give you a glass of wine.

§ 6

Сейча́с два часа́. Я иду́ домо́й, так как я обе́даю в три часа́. И сего́дня я обе́даю до́ма. Вну́чка всегда́ обе́дает до́ма. Да, сего́дня я ра́но иду́ домо́й. Ду́ет с восто́ка.

Она́ стару́ха? – Нет, она́ не стару́ха. До́ктор стари́к, и вот он! Я ду́маю, что он бу́дет до́ма сего́дня ве́чером.

Брат мно́го чита́ет? – Да, брат мно́го чита́ет, но тут нет кни́ги. Тут нет ничего́ – ни кни́ги, ни бума́ги.

366

Что он нам даст? Он даст нам а́дрес? – Да, он вам даст а́дрес. – Нет, я не ду́маю, что он даст нам а́дрес до́ма. Я ду́маю, что он даст нам а́дрес конто́ры.

LESSON 6, § 9

The tourists are standing by the gate. They are ready. They are hiring a bus. They drive quickly as far as the town. There are many tourists, many suitcases, many bags, many books, many papers. But the tourists' suitcases, their bags, their books, their papers are at home. They are carrying nothing. They must (go) to the bank. From the bank they go to the restaurant. There they dine and I dine there (too). We finish dinner. From the restaurant the tourists go to the bridge. There is a market by the bridge. There they stand, talk, smoke. They find it interesting there. And in the evening they all go to the cinema and from there they go home. I too go to the cinema and from there I go home. I often have that sort of break (lit. 'I often rest so').

LESSON 7, § 3a

'Can you live here?'
'You are able to live like this but I can't. I live differently.'
'We live by the bridge. There are buses around.'
'(My) husband lives very quietly. He works hard and he must rest at home. You live differently but he cannot live like that.'
'We live as we can. And they live as they can.'

§ 3b

'Can one smoke here?' 'No, one must not smoke here.'
'May one talk here?' 'Yes, one can, one can.'

§ 6

The house is on fire. The houses are on fire. The people are/a crowd is standing and watching.
He is standing in the garden and shouting. They are standing in the garden and shouting.
Don't shout so loudly! Don't shout!
(My) wife is standing by (my) side. She is holding both papers and a suitcase.
They are holding both papers and suitcases.

§ 7

Fishes eat mosquitoes. Grandfather is eating crayfish. The cat is holding a crayfish.
I am holding (my) son and grandfather is leading (his) grandson. He is carrying the cat.

367

We are going home and are taking grandfather and (his) grandsons and (our) brother and a friend.

The wife is leading (her) husband. He is carrying a turkey. They are taking the tourists and the sailors home.

§ 10

I must go. I often have to work in the evening.

You must read. You must not go to the cinema today.

He has to be here in the morning. He does not have to/he must not go to Moscow. He must rest.

She has to be there early in the morning. She must not go to the theatre now. She must not go anywhere.

Today we must play tennis. We don't have to dine at home. We must go now.

You must play and you must run about. You must eat and rest a lot.

They have to take (some) coffee home. They don't need to take (any) meat. They have to take coffee and tea home (нести *to take, to carry*; брать *to take, to pick up*).

Who has to go home? Who has to go?

§ 12

In the evening the fire is warm (lit. 'warms'). I am warming myself by the fire. Two dogs are warming themselves by the fire. I can go to the cinema but I do not have to move (i.e. myself). The cat keeps moving about all the time – he is hot. In the morning I often take my son (out) and we go for a ride on horse-back.

And now in the evening it's not at all bad to warm oneself quietly by the fire.

§ 14

Всё кругóм идём!

– Вчерá бы́ло жáрко, а сегóдня ужé нет той жары́.

– Нет, ужé вéчер, а вéчером не так жáрко.

– Где багáж?

– Там, у гаражá.

– У гаражá? А там мнóго гаражéй. Я так не могу́ жить – вы не знáете, где багáж.

– Мы живём, как мóжем. Не нáдо сердúться.

– Мы живём инáче. Мы живём тúхо.

– И тут тúхо.

– Как?! Кругóм автóбусы и гаражú!

– Тепéрь вы кричúте. Не нáдо кричáть.

– Я не кричу́. Женá стоúт там, онá дéржит чемодáн и ждёт.

– Как так?

– Ей нáдо жить тúхо. Ей нáдо отдыхáть.

368

– Она́ мо́жет отдыха́ть тут.
– Нет, нам на́до е́хать.
– Никуда́ не на́до е́хать. Вы мо́жете сиде́ть у ками́на и гре́ться и ти́хо чита́ть. У́тром вы мо́жете ката́ться верхо́м.
– Нет, мне на́до е́хать в Москву́.
– В Москву́? Но там не ти́хо.
– Нам на́до е́хать. Где бага́ж?
– Там у гаража́…

LESSON 8, § 3

All I have is (a lot of) books, but no actual lessons.
Only they have stamps, while he has envelopes but no stamps.
The sisters themselves have no country cottage, they have only a flat.
She herself has no work.

§ 4

Here is a map of the region, but the whole of the town is not here (on the map).
There are no books here – all the books are at home.
We are all at home in the evening.
In the morning none of us will be at home (lit. 'we all shall not be') – only Ivan will be at home.
None of you will be at home in the morning – only the children will be at home.
None of them are at home – only Nina is at home.
We all have children. You all have a lot of work.
They all have grand-daughters.

§ 10

Она́ чита́ет письмо́.
Та́ня понима́ет ту де́вочку.
Де́вочка мо́ет кота́.
Сего́дня я жду до́ктора.
Я дам ему́ коро́бки.
Вы ждёте Ни́ну?
Кто несёт дива́ны сюда́?
Сы́на я жду до́ма.
Вну́чка всегда́ говори́т всю пра́вду.
Я сама́ мо́ю до́чку.

Я чита́ю откры́тку.
Сын понима́ет тех докторо́в.
Они́ мо́ют ру́ки.
До́ктор даст мне коро́бку.
Он ку́рит папиро́су.
Нет, я жду па́пу.
До́ктор ведёт тех дам туда́.
Мы зна́ем тех де́вочек.
Друг чита́ет все пи́сьма.
Жена́ мо́ет до́чек.

LESSON 9, § 1a

There is so much noise here. It is so noisy here.
No, it is not noisy here, it is quiet here – there is a lesson (going on) here.

There is no noise here, it is quiet here – there is silence, yes, silence.
And is it noisy now in your home? Is it noisy at your (place)? Are your children playing and making a noise?
Yes, the children are playing and making a noise – it's difficult for us.
One must not make a noise. If they make a noise, of course it is difficult for you.
That's what I'm saying – that it's very difficult for me. They make a noise all the time.

§ 1b

'Have you a fur coat?' 'No, I haven't a fur coat but a certain lady ('one lady') – that lady there – is buying a fur coat. She is buying a fur coat today but I am not buying (one).

§ 1c

'Misha, Sasha, Masha – it's time to go. Well, chaps/folks, let's go home.'
'You must not bother us, it's bad to bother (people).' (нам is controlled by мешáть not by не нáдо.)
'Am I bothering you?'
'No, you are not bothering me, but the children here are bothering (me). There is a noise at home all the time, always a noise; they make a noise all the time. Yes, the children always prevent me from working.'
'Children are always bothering somebody. Why do children always bother somebody?'
'Children are always a nuisance because they make a noise all the time. Where there are children, there is noise.'

§ 1d

'Here is the car tyre. The car won't go. Here is the car tyre, but where is the mechanic? There's no mechanic. Where is he? Why is he not here? Where's the driver?'
'The mechanic is coming now.'
'He has a cigarette. One must not smoke here, but he is smoking. No smoking here.'

§ 6

'Are you going home?'
'No, I am not; I have to work. You are hindering me. You are smoking all the time and talking and making a noise here; how (is it that) you don't understand that you are simply hindering me? I am mixing everything up.'
'Why are you talking like that? What do you want to eat?'
'I am not hungry at all. Now, what do you want?'
'(If) you want, I'll give you . . .'
'I don't want anything!'

370

'Don't you want a cigarette?'
'Well, yes, cigarettes. . . . Can you give me two or three cigarettes?'
'Here you are, I'll give you the packet.'
'Thank you! Thank you! But I tell you, you are hindering me. You stand here all the time.'
'All right! All right! I'm going.'

§ 8a

The domestic help is going to the market to buy fish. We know that she eats it herself in the evening. We are eating chicken – we must finish it today. They are having ('eating') chicken. Yes, they are having it for dinner.

§ 8b

We hire a workman. We hire him early in the morning but we often have to wait for him. He is beginning the redecorating at our house. He is always beginning it. The work has already been going on for a month. He begins it but doesn't finish anything. First ('now') he hasn't any paint, then ('now') he hasn't any lime. 'You know, you must work systematically,' we say to him. 'Yes, yes, one must, one must – I know. Of course, one must!' He talks quietly and behaves nicely but the work does not get finished. It's inconvenient for us to live like this. It's impossible! 'Yes, yes, I know, I know, I understand – of course, I understand you! And today I am working systematically and fast,' he says, but he doesn't care.

§ 8c

My husband's brother is living with us too. Because there is chaos in our home, we take him to the office. He takes a novel and reads it all day. He can (spend) the whole day reading one book. He finishes it at home in the evening. That way he reads many books. He begins them and finishes them all. Not all the books are novels. He finishes novels quickly. He reads them quickly.

§ 9

Тихий уголóк

м у ж   Шум, шум, всё врéмя шум. Мне он мешáет. Как я могý рабóтать?

ж е н а   Дéти, вы шумúте.

м у ж   Я не могý рабóтать. Тут так шýмно.

ж е н а   Конéчно тебé трýдно, когдá онú шумя́т.

м у ж   Я и говорю́, что мне трýдно.

ж е н а   Всё-таки, онú не всё врéмя шумя́т.
          (Шум.)

ж е н а   Что э́то?

м у ж   Машúны. Когдá дéти не шумя́т, то машúны шумя́т.

ж е н а   Да, но не всё врéмя. Сейчáс машúны не идýт мúмо.

м у ж Нет, но вот э́тот машини́ст – он ря́дом живёт – идёт домо́й и кричи́т.

ж е н а Машини́стка живёт ря́дом, а не машини́ст, я ду́маю.

м у ж Да, э́то пра́вда. Она́ идёт домо́й ра́но и начина́ет рабо́тать. Она́ рабо́тает и ве́чером.

ж е н а Куда́ ты идёшь? Ты не хо́чешь есть?

м у ж Нет, я ничего́ не хочу́. Мо́жет быть ты дашь мне две–три папиро́сы?

ж е н а Вот. Я тебе́ дам всю па́чку. Но куда́ ты идёшь?

м у ж Спаси́бо. Куда́ я иду́? Я иду́ в парк. Там ти́хо.

ж е н а Но де́ти игра́ют там.

м у ж Да, но они́ не меша́ют мне. До свида́ния.

ж е н а До свида́ния.

LESSON II, § I

'You have chaos here – you are bachelors, there is disorder here in your place and it's cold.'

'That's not true, we don't have any chaos here at all. There's no chaos, no disorder in our place at all. We have order here – everything is fine and tidy. Yes, tidy.'

'It's not tidy at all – right here there are boots and cheese, and over here there are papers and socks, and here, yes, here there is a pair of stockings. Petya, where do they come from? Why is there a pair of stockings in a bachelor's place?'

'Here, here – it's nothing. . . .'

'What do you mean – nothing?'

'There's nothing here, no stockings at all; it's paper here, not stockings. . . . What a calamity! (Let's put) everything into the corner here and on to the floor and everything will now be tidy – see, the shoes here, and the socks here, and the stockings – my sister's stockings right here.'

'And now you say that that is not paper, but stockings?'

'Yes, yes – my sister Nina's stockings – (I'll put) the stockings here. Vera, don't you believe me?'

'How can I believe you? How can I not believe you? It's just chaos you have here and I'm cold. I'm going home.'

'What do you mean – cold? My fire warms (the place) (very) well. Don't go/there's no need to go home. Here is an armchair. It's warm here, not cold at all.'

'The armchair is full of books.'

'And the books (can go) into the corner and on to the floor.'

'You've got everything in the corner and on the floor. Disorder everywhere. There's always chaos in bachelors' (quarters).'

'It's not true, there's order in bachelors' (quarters). Women have chaos – yes,

that's it, it's women that have chaos. It's fine, warm here in my place. There, now the lamp is lit. I've two bottles of wine and two bottles of beer. Four bottles will be enough. Here is a bottle of wine. I'll give you a glass of wine now. Misha and Nina will soon be here. Dinner will be soon. See how well the wine warms (you up). There, you see how fine everything is here.'
'Yes, I don't feel cold now. It's true, the fire does warm (the room) well. I'm not cold at all, I'm warm.'

§ 3a

I was standing, taking the soap and washing my hands and thinking.
Yes, you were standing, taking the soap and washing your hands and thinking.
He was standing, taking the soap and washing his hands and thinking.

§ 3b

In the morning I was at home. I was listening to the radio. The radio was playing something. Papa did not speak at all. I said little and did my lessons.
In the morning you were at home. You were listening to the radio. The radio was playing something. Papa did not speak at all. You said little and did your lessons.
In the morning she was at home. She was listening to the radio. She said little and did her lessons.

§ 3c

Uncle was building a hut in the garden. But he was not working much (lit. 'he was working little') – he stood and looked and smoked a lot.
Uncle, when you were building the hut in the garden, you were not working much – you stood and looked and smoked a lot.

§ 7

Кто де́лал что, и кто шёл куда́?

– Же́нщина стоя́ла там, а брат стоя́л тут.
– Нет, Пе́тя стоя́л там.
– Пе́тя был до́ма у́тром, я ду́мал(а).
– Я не зна́ю – но его́ сестра́ была́ до́ма ве́чером.
– Да, она́ мы́ла во́лосы.
– Нет, я слу́шала ра́дио, но оте́ц всё вре́мя говори́л.
– Непра́вда – он ма́ло говори́л. Ни́на всё вре́мя говори́ла.
– И Алекса́ндр мыл ру́ки и о́чень шуме́л.
– Да, я стро́ил до́мик в саду́.
– Ты до́мик стро́ил?! Когда́ Та́ня тебя́ ви́дела, ты стоя́л и кури́л.
– Кто? Я? Я не курю́. Ири́на мно́го ку́рит – она́ вчера́ вы́курила все папиро́сы. Она́ кури́ла мно́го папиро́с.
– Она́ мно́го рабо́тает.

– Мо́жет быть. Она́ ра́но шла домо́й, когда́ я её ви́дел.

– Она́ не шла домо́й. Она́ шла в конто́ру.

– Ве́чером?! Я её ви́дел и у́тром и она́ не шла в конто́ру.

– Оте́ц шёл в парк и вёл соба́ку.

– Ве́ра шла в конто́ру, ты говори́шь?

– Нет, Ма́ша шла в конто́ру.

– Ты ви́дела Со́ню? Она́ вела́ сы́на домо́й?

– Я её не ви́дела. Я ви́дела Та́ню. Она́ несла́ зо́нтик и сын то́же был там. Он нёс её су́мку.

– Но оте́ц ждал их до́ма!

– Кого́ он ждал?

– Ну, я не зна́ю… ты меня́ спу́тала.

LESSON 12, § 4

They used to give me coffee and go to work. They used to get up early in the morning and they advised me to get up early.

They lived there for a long time. They said that the neighbours did not recognize them.

Husband and wife drove together to the market. They carried on (their) trade there. The market was by the bridge. People used to stand there, talk loudly, laugh and buy a lot of all sorts of things. Children ran about, played and shouted. It was fun.

§ 10

'What's this?'

'It's (some) parcels.'

'Well, of course, it's (some) parcels. They're parcels! I can see for myself that it's (some) parcels. You buy a lot (of things).'

'It's all for dinner. Vanya, Sasha, Misha and Masha are coming. This morning I ran down to the market. I was buying (and) carrying a lot (of things). You weren't (here) in the morning and I had to take the dog too.'

'Well, all right, all right! I was working after all. And what's for dinner? Is this tin for dinner?'

'It's soup.'

'Is this soup for dinner?'

'Well, what of it? Is that bad?'

'No, why (should it be) bad? It's not bad at all, in fact it's good. And what's this?'

'It's fish.'

'That's fish? It's not meat?'

'Of course, it's not meat. I spent a long time buying fish this morning – this fish here.'

'You think that it's fish – that it isn't meat?'

374

'Why do you keep on? – it's meat, it's not meat – it's fish, it's not fish! I was carrying fish, this fish here. And this evening you'll eat this fish.'
'But it's not fish. You must look what you're carrying.'
'I don't understand anything! This morning I was buying fish and I carried the fish. Where is that parcel? It's the wrong parcel!'
'Well, there you are!'

§ 11

Они дают нам стул.
Я вам советую не идти в понедельник.
Ему надо рано вставать, потому что он идёт на службу.
Он идёт на станцию, потому что он организует поездку в Лондон.
Доктор не узнавал меня.
Саша кладёт книги и бумаги на полку.
Судно шло на восток. Они ехали в Европу.
Это жена, а это дети. Они идут на концерт.
Таня дала мне эти книги – это «Анна Каренина» и это «Три сестры».
Этих/Тех книг тут мало, но этих газет много.

LESSON 13, § 4

Early in the morning I have to wake my brother. He often gets up very late and so I must wake him. The alarm-clock rings at seven o'clock, rings so loudly that everybody around hears (it), everybody – only not (my) brother. He, of course, does not hear. The alarm-clock rings, rattles, the cat (jumps) on to the cupboard in fright, sits and looks and is afraid, but my brother goes on sleeping and snoring as though nothing (had happened).
So I go into his room: 'Time to get up, lazybones, why are you asleep? You'll catch it for always being late.' But he (says) not a word, turns on to his side and (goes on) sleeping. I continue to wake (him): 'Time to get up. I always have to drive you to the office. Really, don't you hear (me)? Later it will be too late. The alarm-clock has already gone, it's been ringing and ringing, rattling and rattling. Really, don't you believe me? It's already late!' He keeps silent and sleeps – no, he turns over, begins to yawn, to grumble – he yawns and grumbles. 'That's enough grumbling from you, you must get up, but you just go on lying and snoring.'
I go into the kitchen to make breakfast, I stand and stand – he does not appear. I go into his room and look – he's still lying there and the cat is lying asleep there too. 'Aren't you ashamed? Are you (doing) this on purpose?' He grumbles again, I wake him again: 'And aren't you ashamed to sleep so long? Aren't you at all ashamed that you are always late?' And he (says) to me in reply: 'I am not ashamed at all, and what is it to you?' Well, there you are – he starts using coarse language, I start to get angry. I get angry (and) shout: 'You're a fool, you're just a fool.' Now the cat is also yawning and actually getting up. The cat is getting up but he is still lying (there).

I go downstairs. Eight o'clock – my brother has not appeared. I go upstairs: 'Well, are you getting up, you fool?' And he, insolent creature, answers me: 'You're a fool yourself. You like to sleep late yourself. You get up late yourself. You sleep till ten and you won't let me sleep.' 'And all you (do) is argue. I'm simply afraid because you're always late. I tell you (this), I ask you, I beg you (to get up), but you don't care. You have to get up – and you're arguing!' 'What's it to you? You like arguing yourself, arguing and quarrelling.' 'It's you who are quarrelling, not me – I'm only waking you up.' 'I don't want to get up and I shan't get up. So there!' 'All right, if you like, you can sleep all day. And I shan't wake you early in the morning. I don't want to and I shan't!'

And that's how it is with us always – I go on waking him, he goes on sleeping, he uses coarse language, I get angry – and the cat just sits and looks at us.

§ 4

буди́ть	– бужу́	бу́дит	бу́дят
звони́ть	– звоню́	звони́т	звоня́т
слы́шать	– слы́шу	слы́шит	слы́шат
треща́ть	– трещу́	трещи́т	треща́т
сиде́ть	– сижу́	сиди́т	сидя́т
смотре́ть	– смотрю́	смо́трит	смо́трят
боя́ться	– бою́сь	бои́тся	боя́тся
спать	– сплю	спит	спят
храпе́ть	– храплю́	храпи́т	храпя́т
гнать	– гоню́	го́нит	го́нят
ве́рить	– ве́рю	ве́рит	ве́рят
молча́ть	– молчу́	молчи́т	молча́т
ворча́ть	– ворчу́	ворчи́т	ворча́т
лежа́ть	– лежу́	лежи́т	лежа́т
гото́вить	– гото́влю	гото́вит	гото́вят
стоя́ть	– стою́	стои́т	стоя́т
стыди́ться	– стыжу́сь	стыди́тся	стыдя́тся
груби́ть	– грублю́	груби́т	грубя́т
серди́ться	– сержу́сь	се́рдится	се́рдятся
крича́ть	– кричу́	кричи́т	крича́т
люби́ть	– люблю́	лю́бит	лю́бят
спо́рить	– спо́рю	спо́рит	спо́рят
говори́ть	– говорю́	говори́т	говоря́т
проси́ть	– прошу́	про́сит	про́сят
моли́ть	– молю́	мо́лит	мо́лят
ссо́риться	– ссо́рюсь	ссо́рится	ссо́рятся

§ 7

I shall not offend you. We shall not offend you.

They always offend (my) brother, and (my) neighbour's son offends him too.

We shall solve this problem to-morrow.
We often solve these problems, but we do not always solve them correctly.

We shall not finish this work so soon/quickly – we shall finish it to-morrow.
Here we are – we are always working and working, we are always finishing and finishing – but we can never finish everything.

It's dangerous to play here now – I shall forbid them to play here.
I always forbid them to shout but I do not forbid them to talk loudly.

I shall give you this book to-morrow.
I am always giving them tickets.

§ 11

Разговор по телефону

Я сижу́ в ко́мнате и смотрю́ в окно́. На дворе́ тепло́ и де́ти игра́ют в саду́... Ива́н? – нет, я не ви́жу Ива́на, но я слы́шу его́. Он про́сто стои́т и кричи́т... я запреща́ю им крича́ть в до́ме... Па́па рабо́тает в лесу́. Он гру́зит дрова́ на та́чку. Он бро́сит дрова́ в у́гол двора́, но я ему́ прощу́. Дрова́ треща́т так ве́село в ками́не, когда́ на дворе́ хо́лодно и ла́мпа гори́т на столе́ и мы все сиди́м в кре́слах и чита́ем... Тепе́рь де́ти стуча́т в дверь. Они́ про́сят меня́ игра́ть на дворе́. Мне на́до идти́, а то я их оби́жу... Мы ко́нчим разгово́р за́втра. Мы говори́ли о сестре́. Мы всё реша́ем зада́чу – мо́жет быть за́втра реши́м её.

LESSON 14, § 3

And so here I am, going home. . . .
I am going home, it's already late, I take a seat in the bus – there is only one seat free, I sit down quickly – I sat down, I'm sitting (there), – we are going along, we go for a very long time, when suddenly (my) neighbour, the man at my side, says:
'Excuse me, but you sat down on (my) hat.'
'How do you mean, I sat down on (your) hat? What hat (do you mean)?'
'Well, this one here, there's a hat here – you sat down on (my) hat and you're sitting on (my) hat.'
I get up quickly – yes, indeed, here is his hat. I had sat down on his hat and have been sitting on his hat all the time, all the way.
'Yes, one must not sit down on (people's) hats.'
Well, how was I to know that I was sitting (lit. 'am sitting') down on his hat; and he could at once have called (my) attention to the fact that I was sitting down on his hat, but he kept quiet (lit. 'keeps quiet'); I sat down on his hat, I sit on his hat all the way, and he keeps quiet.
'Well, you should look where you are sitting down, that's all. If you don't look where you are sitting down, you may sit on a hedgehog!'
We do not advise you to sit down on a hedgehog, – you'd better sit down on a hat.

'It's so cold here – that's not good. When the boss will sit down here. . . .'
'Well, so what? The boss will grumble a bit, that's all.'
'He'll not only grumble but he'll shout too and bang his fist on the table.'
'Well, so *what*? He bangs his fist on the table and already you're afraid and you're trembling.'
'When you hear how he shouts/him shouting . . .'
'He shouts! Imagine! You're even afraid to breathe, when he's just silent. Now our boss grumbles and growls and shouts, (and) not only bangs his fist on the table but bangs his feet too – stamps his feet – and there's shouting and noise – (and) I'm never afraid, I never tremble – I shall shout a little myself and I'll bang a little with my fist. So there!'
'You know what? You'd better keep quiet, you just keep quiet a bit!'

§ 8

– Они́ стро́ят дом.
– Они́ стро́или его́, когда́ я был тут два го́да тому́ наза́д.
– Да, они́ стро́ят его́ уже́ два го́да. Э́та фи́рма то́же постро́ила две больни́цы.

– Ты потеря́ешь э́ти перча́тки, е́сли я дам их тебе́?
– Я всегда́ теря́ю перча́тки – в теа́тре, в авто́бусе, на у́лице.

Ты уже́ позвала́ дете́й домо́й? Ма́ма звала́ их полчаса́.

Ты ве́ришь в де́да-моро́за? Мари́я ве́рила в де́да-моро́за, но она́ бо́льше не ве́рит в него́.

Ива́н пове́рил до́ктору, хотя́ обы́чно он ему́ совсе́м не ве́рил.

– Потуши́ли уже́ пожа́р?
– Нет, ту́шат его́ уже́ два часа́, но ещё не потуши́ли его́.

До́ктор смотре́л, смотре́л, но не ви́дел биле́та. Он посмотре́л на стол, но биле́та не́ было на столе́.

Оте́ц посто́ял в саду́, пото́м сел на стул. Он посиде́л там и покури́л тру́бку.

Нача́льник покричи́т и постучи́т по̮столу́, но секрета́рши не боя́тся его́.

We set off for the country cottage and took a lot of luggage. We called a porter, gave him all the suitcases, and father carried the fishing rods and brief case himself. Mother took the children, I carried the cat in (her) basket, (my) brother had the dog on its lead, and the porter transported the cases.

Не ду́майте о сестре́. Ей всегда́ везло́, ей повезёт и в э́тот раз.

Помо́й ру́ки сейча́с. Вот мы́ло и полоте́нце. И всегда́ мой ру́ки пе́ред обе́дом.

Не стро́йте дом у реки́. Там хо́лодно и сы́ро. Постро́йте его́ у ле́са.

– Спо́йте мне пе́сенку.
– Дава́йте петь вме́сте.
– Ива́н, ты игра́й аккомпанеме́нт, А́ня, ты пой. А́ня так хорошо́ поёт. Дай Ива́ну но́ты.

– Дава́йте посиди́ у ками́на и посмо́трим телеви́дение/телеви́зор.
– Нет, дава́йте послу́шаем ра́дио.
– Стой! Э́то сли́шком гро́мко.

– Я сейча́с пойду́. Вы идёте?
– Нет, снег идёт. Я пойду́ по́зже.
– Они́ пое́хали на грузовике́ без меня́.
– Я вас повезу́.

Сестра́ Сю́зи/Сюза́нна шьёт руба́шки.

– Позови́ официа́нта! Официа́нт, неси́те бо́льше вина́. Нале́йте мне вина́.
– Он всегда́ пьёт мно́го вина́?
– Не бо́йтесь. Пусть он пьёт – и пусть они́ говоря́т, э́то меня́ не беспоко́ит. Он мно́го кричи́т, но он ма́ло пьёт.
– Не говори́те так гро́мко. Он вас слы́шит.

LESSON 18, § 5

(My) brother has to go to school.
This coat is too small for (my) friend.
He is giving these papers to the boss.
He does not believe me but he will believe (his) father.
I shall give the cat a saucer of milk.
(My) sister has to go to town.
These shoes are too small for grandmother – they hurt grandmother.
She is ten. – Who is? Who is ten?
(My) granddaughter, (my) granddaughter is ten and (my) grandson is five. And how old are you?
I am thirty-five, and (my) husband is forty; (my) daughter is fifteen and (my) son is twelve.
I am taking dinner to (my) brother and (my) sisters.
He always gives his seat to ladies in the bus.

We always give the fish-heads to the cat and (her) kittens.
He does not believe the doctor; he says that he never believes doctors.
Children must not eat (too) much.
May we sit here? – No, you may not.
May I smoke? – You may smoke, but (your) brother may not, since he is still small – he is too young.
Take the dog home – dogs aren't allowed to run about here.
I do not advise the pupils to play outside/in the yard. They are not allowed to play here.
I do not envy the director – in general I do not envy the bosses.
I help (my) sister and brother.
He helps the pupils to read.
I am going along the corridor. The children are running about the yard.
The car was going along the street.
One is not allowed to run about the corridors here.
I am going to (my) brother's and he is coming to my place.
Tomorrow I shall go to the doctor's.
Go to the chief, but first go to his secretary.
Go to the shorthand typist.
Spring is approaching.
He got up for breakfast. She gets up for dinner.
Towards morning a wind got/blew up.
I shall go there towards evening.

§ 7
Тоска́ по большо́му го́роду

Го́род большо́й, но село́, где я живу́, ма́ленькое. Дя́дя рабо́тает в го́роде и ему́ тру́дно. Он говори́т, что жить в го́роде нездоро́во, но ему́ на́до жить там. Он прав – там не о́чень здоро́во. Там сли́шком мно́го ды́ма и шу́ма. С друго́й сторны́, дома́ о́чень краси́вые – они́ высо́кие и у них мно́го о́кон. Мо́жно идти́ по у́лице и смотре́ть в дома́. Так говори́т друг.

Друг дал мне ста́рый велосипе́д. – Тепе́рь ты мо́жешь е́хать в го́род и смотре́ть, как лю́ди рабо́тают и торо́пятся, сказа́л он.

Жаль – велосипе́д мне вели́к. Дя́дя посове́товал мне е́хать на авто́бусе. Я зави́дую ему́ – у него́ маши́на. Всем директора́м на́до мно́го путеше́ствовать, поэ́тому у них всех маши́ны. Им на́до то́же мно́го есть и пить. Дя́дя пьёт здо́рово мно́го вина́.

Секрета́рше дя́ди на́до путеше́ствовать с ним. Ей со́рок лет. Дя́дя – холостя́к. Я ду́маю, что она́ наде́ется, что он же́нится на ней.

Ну, я пое́хал на велосипе́де. По пути́ я помо́г (одно́й) да́ме. У неё бы́ло мно́го паке́тов и она́ была́ о́чень ста́ра. Пото́м я сби́лся с доро́ги и упа́л с велосипе́да. Тепе́рь у меня́ боли́т рука́. Боли́т, когда́ поднима́ю её. Я пошёл домо́й пешко́м, и го́рода я не ви́дел.

My young friend is here. My young friend is ill.
Your young sister is in hospital.
My young tree is in the garden. Your young friends are at home.
This gold ring is dear. These gold rings are dear.
This big house is very old. These big houses are very old.
Your simple tale is very interesting. Your simple tales are very interesting.
My bad hotel is nevertheless clean. My bad hotels are nevertheless clean.
This dry tree is not young. These dry trees are not young.

§ 8

У нас до́ма мно́го друзе́й и ро́дственников сего́дня. Мои́ бра́тья и сыновья́ прие́хали, потому́ что я е́ду за́втра в Сове́тский Сою́з. У всех бра́тьев и сынове́й мно́го друзе́й и друзья́ то́же прие́хали.

Сне́га нет, доро́ги сухи́е, но на доро́гах опа́сно из-за моро́за. Всё-таки, они́ все могли́ прие́хать. На дворе́ хо́лодно, но в кварти́ре тепло́ и ую́тно.

Ста́рые жёны сидя́т у ками́на. Их мужья́ сидя́т на сту́льях и игра́ют в ка́рты. Жёны посове́товали мужья́м игра́ть в ка́рты. Они́ сидя́т, игра́ют и ма́ло говоря́т. Гру́ппа молоды́х жён и муже́й стои́т посреди́не ко́мнаты. Молода́я же́нщина расска́зывает коро́ткий интере́сный расска́з и все мужья́ слу́шают. Други́е жёны все гро́мко говоря́т.

В окно́ видны́ больши́е, ста́рые дере́вья в саду́. На дере́вьях нет ли́стьев. Я стою́ и смотрю́ на дере́вья и я бо́льше не слы́шу бра́тьев и сынове́й, их жён и друзе́й. Я ду́маю: – За́втра я уе́ду в Сове́тский Сою́з.

LESSON 20, § 9

'Do look where you're going! You aren't looking at all where you're going!'
'I am looking but I can't see anything!'
'Well, why are you shouting? Please don't shout.'
'You're shouting yourself!'
'Calm down, please!'
'Yes, yes, let's calm down. Can you help me?'
'Of course, I'll help you, if I can!'
'I'm hurrying to the station but in these dark streets, in this yellow fog I cannot see (my) way.'
'Are you going to the station? But you're going in the wrong direction.'
'How is that?'
'Look to the left – there's the corner. Do you see that corner?'
'I can't see anything.'
'But you're not looking in the right direction! Don't look to the right. Look left. Over there. Go back to the corner and from the corner go right.'

'Now I can see and remember everything! I must go left.'

'No, don't go left. Go straight on from the corner – left from the corner, and then go straight on to the station.'

'I don't understand a thing. I *said* I had to go right and then left and then straight on to the station.'

'You aren't listening to me! Listen! Go back to the corner, from the corner go right – no, I'm getting confused myself. Let's begin again from the beginning! If you like let's go together – I'm going to the station myself.'

§ 10

Родно́е село́

Моё родно́е село́ – о́чень ста́рое село́ и, говоря́т, о́чень краси́вое. Англи́йские сёла обы́чно о́чень краси́вые. В на́шем селе́ – апте́ка и две ла́вки, где всё продаю́т. Посреди́не села́ – ма́ленький ста́рый мост/мо́стик че́рез реку́. Тут река́ мелка́ но недалеко́ отсю́да она́ о́чень глубока́.

Мы слы́шим но́вости по ра́дио и́ли чита́ем их в газе́тах, а в само́м селе́ ма́ло но́вого. Бе́лая ло́шадь рабо́тает на по́ле, де́ти игра́ют на у́лице – и кака́я ра́дость на ли́цах э́тих дете́й. Ле́том лю́ди открыва́ют две́ри и о́кна, старики́ и стару́шки сидя́т на сту́льях на дворе́ у двере́й, молоды́е лю́ди стоя́т и разгова́ривают. В мо́лодости, как и в ста́рости, свои́ ра́дости, но молоды́е со ста́рыми дру́жно живу́т у нас в селе́. И у них всех таки́е ти́хие голоса́.

Вот как я по́мню родно́е село́: далёкие го́ры, ма́ленький мост/мо́стик, ме́лкая река́, бе́лые две́ри и, на поля́х, бе́лые ло́шади, зелёные дере́вья и, к о́сени, золото́й урожа́й, ти́хий го́лос ма́тери, стро́гое лицо́ отца́, и но́чью глубо́кая тишина́.

LESSON 21, § 6a

ле́тнее у́тро	осе́нние вечера́
зи́мняя ночь	весе́нние ве́тры
у́треннее со́лнце	вече́рняя газе́та

§ 6b

Он маха́л зо́нтиком. Они́ то́пали нога́ми.

Чем он бьёт по̲_столу? Он бьёт молотко́м.

Са́ша ниче́м не интересу́ется. Ма́ша маха́ла па́лкой.

Лю́ди торгу́ют хле́бом, я́йцами, па́лками, зо́нтиками.

Они́ торгу́ют тра́кторами, маши́нами и саня́ми.

Кто рискова́л жи́знью?

Сын занима́ется фи́зикой, а дочь ниче́м не занима́ется.

Мать нике́м не интересу́ется.

У ма́тери нет друзе́й.

У фéрмера мнóго корóв, а нет лошадéй.

Он не интересýется лошадьми́.

У тёти нет детéй.

Отéц занимáется мýзыкой по ночáм.

Óсенью мы éдем домóй.

Нóчью я не спалá.

На плóщади стоя́т домá.

Дóктор интересýется болéзнью вáшей дóчери.

LESSON 22, § 4

'We shall come to you tomorrow but we shall leave early.'

'You rarely come and, when you do come, you leave very early.'

'There are children at home, we have to leave early. But tomorrow we shall leave late. Auntie is staying with us for several months. So tomorrow we shall come early and leave late.'

'That's fine. Please come early and leave late.'

'Are you going away/leaving?'

'Yes, I'm leaving now.'

'Has your husband already left?'

'No, he is leaving today.'

'And the children are also leaving today?'

'No, the children will leave tomorrow; (our) daughter will leave in the morning, and in the evening (our) son will leave.'

'Where is the newspaper?'

'Daddy took it to work.'

'He always takes the newspaper away.'

'That's not true, he has never taken the paper away before.'

'He took it yesterday and he took it on Wednesday – everyday he takes the paper away. He took it today – and he'll take it tomorrow.'

'I shall take the paper myself tomorrow but I'll bring it back.'

§ 6a

At the airport planes arrive and depart hourly. The passengers come here in buses and cars. There are many spectators here too. The spectators come in cars, on bicycles, on motorcycles and on motor-scooters. Among the spectators there are many boys. The boys also come on foot. This boy here came this morning. He brought an exercise book with him and he notes down all the types of aircraft. Late in the evening he will go home and will take his exercise book with him.

His friend came on a bicycle. He will leave earlier because he wants to go to the station. You see, he is interested in trains too.

What different forms of transport we have! Formerly there were neither trains, nor cars, nor aeroplanes, nor even bicycles, but there were many horses. In the day-time people worked or travelled on horses or in carriages, and at night they slept. In our day people travel at night too. You can hear the aeroplanes arriving and departing at night. Day and night the tourists arrive (and) depart.

§ 6b

На аэропóрте самолёты прилетáют и улетáют ежечáсно. Пассажѝры приезжáют на автомобѝлях/машѝнах. Тут мнóго автомобѝлей/машѝн, а лошадéй нет. На аэропóрте мнóго зрѝтелей. Мáльчики прихóдят пешкóм. Онѝ принóсят с собóй тетрáди. Тот/Вот э́тот мáльчик уйдёт домóй вéчером. Егó друг уéдет на стáнцию на велосипéде.

Турѝсты приезжáют/прилетáют и уезжáют/улетáют днём и нóчью.

LESSON 23, § 10

'Tomorrow the holidays begin.'

'Close the door and close the window. The holidays haven't begun yet.'

'Nearly everybody has gone home and won't come to work tomorrow. I shan't come either.'

'And I tell you – close the door.'

'Now, quietly, don't talk so loudly!'

'All your papers will fly away on to the street. Close the window!'

'What's the matter with you?!'

'Close the window! One paper has already flown away!'

'What a shame!'

'I must speak to you seriously.'

'You talk a great deal. You talk very loudly. What a calamity! A paper has flown away! I don't like these dramas. I'm going away too. Sit here on your own. Goodbye.'

LESSON 25, § 2

I heard this conversation in the Passport Office between an official and a man who was standing by my side: 'You haven't written either your Christian name or your surname,' said the official. 'Sit down at the table and write your Christian name here and your surname here. I can't give (you) a passport without (your) Christian name and surname.' He spoke slowly and loudly, as if to a deaf person. Yes, he spoke as if to a deaf person. He gave him the form back. He gave him the form back and again said: 'You must write your Christian name and surname.'

'All right, all right, I'll write my Christian name; I'll write my surname,' said the man, almost to himself. 'I don't like these forms. One form with two copies, one form with three copies . . . ,' he kept saying to himself. 'Well now, I've written both my Christian name and my surname,' he said to the official. 'You've written (them) very badly. You've put a blot on (your) Christian name,' said the official loudly. 'Now there's a blot on your Christian name.'

'Your pen's to blame,' the man said to him. 'I don't like forms, I don't like passports. My grandfather travelled everywhere without a passport. I don't like these modern times of ours. Many people don't like (our) modern times. Passports, taxes, forms. – Let's talk about the old times,' he suddenly said to me. And I just looked at him and ran away.

'And who was he? An Englishman, a Frenchman, a Russian?'

'An Englishman. The French, the Italians and the Russians are foreigners here. Yes, foreigners don't talk like that to officials in a foreign country. You can talk like that to an official only in your own country. In a foreign country you can't talk like that. What an eccentric!'

§ 4

'I never quarrel with anybody. I don't quarrel even with our angry old domestic help.'

'You don't quarrel with the domestic help because you're afraid of her – you're all afraid of her – but you quarrel with everybody else.'

'That's not true – I don't quarrel with others (people), it's just that others quarrel with me.'

'Nobody quarrels with you but you yourself quarrel even with your friends and yesterday you quarrelled with your little sister, and you quarrel with our new lodger.'

'I don't quarrel with our new lodger; as a rule I don't exchange a single word with this lodger. I don't like her and she can't stand me. I can't stand this new lodger of ours and she can't stand any of us. I can't stand people like her. She never greets anybody, never says "hello" or "good-day".'

'She doesn't say "hello" to father either, she doesn't even say "hello" to (our) little sister. Just sometimes she says "hello" to mother, but very rarely – she doesn't even say "hello" to our old domestic help – in a word, she doesn't say "hello" to anybody, neither to us nor to you.'

'She doesn't say "hello", she doesn't say "goodbye" either to us or to you – she never says "goodbye" to anybody. She doesn't say "goodbye" – she'll never say "goodbye". Now our old lodger – the one who lived here with us last year – she liked us all and we liked her. She always said "hello" and "goodbye" to everybody. And when she was leaving – she left a year ago – when she was leaving a year ago – yes, it was last year – she said "goodbye" to everybody and even wept. She wept and said: "I'm only crying because I'm leaving. I don't want to leave!" She wept and kissed everybody, even kissed our old domestic help.'

'I hope she kissed the hall porter as well!'

'What rubbish, what nonsense you talk! She was a kind woman. She came with some sort of basket, with one small suitcase, with a canary in a cage and some sort of awful red lampshade. She came many years ago and, when she was leaving, she left with two large suitcases, with the same basket stuffed full of everything that mother and the cook had prepared. She left with jam, with pastries, a cactus in a pot, canaries – not one canary in the cage but two – and still with the same awful red lampshade. That's how she took her leave of us and left. And we often think of her and how she took her leave of us and how we all said goodbye.'

§ 7
Поéздка в Москвý

Когдá мы éхали в Москвý, нас встречáли на аэропóрте совéтские коллéги. Они поздорóвались óчень дрýжески с нáми.

– С приéздом, сказáл одúн.

– Счастлúво пребывáть в СССР, сказáл другóй.

Я мог отвечáть им по-рýсски и скóро мы разговáривали мéжду собóй совсéм свобóдно.

На тамóжне слýжащий попросúл меня открýть багáж.

– С удовóльствием, сказáл я. – Но я не вúжу своегó багажá.

Потóм я увúдел носúльщика с четырьмя чемодáнами. Я дýмал/Мне казáлось, что двóе из них мой. Мой друг, котóрый стоял рядом со мной и говорúл с двумя перевóдчиками, сказáл, что это егó чемодáны. Я нашёл свой чемодáны под двумя сундукáми. Наконéц мы поéхали/ отпрáвились в гóрод.

В Москвé мы заключúли контрáкт с тремя совéтскими фúрмами. Мы тóже посещáли теáтры и выставки и в ГУМ купúли сувенúры.

Когдá мы уезжáли, нáши совéтские коллéги дáли нам подáрки и пожелáли нам счастлúвого путú.

LESSON 26, § 1

Our former director could not bear noise. The director's former secretary typed all the letters on our typewriter in our room, since he could not bear the clatter of the typewriter. My former place was by the window in the other room but now we all sit in new places.

§ 8

The lorry was coming out of the gate. A crowd was standing around and watching. The exit was very narrow. The driver drove the vehicle carefully. The lorry slowly came out of the gate. 'Now, will it get out or not?' each thought to himself. The lorry was going very slowly and finally it came safely out of the gate on to the street.

§ 10

Секретáрша нáшего прéжнего дирéктора писáла все пúсьма на той стáрой машúнке. Онá сидéла в мáленькой кóмнате, потомý что он терпéть не мог стук машúнки.

Он ýмер на прóшлой недéле. Егó послéдние словá были: – Онá написáла

моё после́днее письмо́? Я сказа́л ей, что не могу́ терпе́ть стук маши́нки…
Вы запрёте мой дом, когда́ я умру́. – Пото́м он и у́мер.

Они́ и за́перли дом. Э́то са́мый высо́кий дом на са́мой дли́нной у́лице в на́шем интере́снейшем го́роде. Никто́ не хоте́л жить в том большо́м ста́ром до́ме.

Ста́рший сын семьи́ всегда́ жил в том до́ме, но тепе́рь дом пуст. Наш дире́ктор хоте́л дать его́ ста́ршему сы́ну, но сын рабо́тает во Фра́нции и он до́лжен там жить.

Когда́ сказа́ли сре́днему сы́ну, что он мо́жет там жить, он отве́тил/ сказа́л, что не лю́бит жить в большо́м ста́ром до́ме. Мла́дший сын дал тот же отве́т. Он сказа́л адвока́ту, что ему́ придётся прода́ть его́.

Когда́ дире́ктор выходи́л и́з_дому, он стоя́л в саду́. Э́то был са́мый краси́вый сад в го́роде. Пото́м он выезжа́л из воро́т, че́рез го́род в но́вую конто́ру.

В оди́н день он вы́шел и́з_дому и пошёл пешко́м че́рез парк. Он постоя́л на берегу́ реки́. Пото́м он верну́лся в дом и бо́льше не выходи́л.

LESSON 27, § 2

They were bringing the horses out of the stable. They brought out all the horses – only the old ass was not brought out. Why bring him out? Nobody wanted to ride on him and they did not bring him out.

Don't you know how to come out on to the embankment? I am going there myself. Let's go together and I will lead you out of this labyrinth of streets.

Many machines are exported from England – yes, England exports many machines. Butter and cheese are exported from Holland, while Finland exports much timber.

They were carrying the furniture out of the next house. Our neighbours were going to Australia. They were carrying the furniture out all day and towards evening had carried it all out.

(You) must throw out these old newspapers. I always throw out old newspapers.

You haven't washed your hands properly. Your nails are dirty. You've just played with the soap and water and washed your palms. Now go and wash your hands properly.

Now, what have you thought up this time ('again')? It's not true – where did you see an admiral on a horse? The things you are always thinking up!

You have a good choice – I don't know what to choose. He will choose an apple – he always chooses an apple.

§ 3

Where are you going? This is the exit here, not the entrance. People come

out here, they don't go in. You should not go in here but there, by the lamp.
That's where you should go in – the entrance is there and people go in there.
They only come out here.

Hello, how are you? Come in, please. It's good that you came. Yes, come in,
come in – we haven't seen you for a long time.
Come in, come in, please. We are so glad to see you. We haven't seen you
for a long time.

How can I drive into this narrow gate? We shall never get in with this big
lorry – it will not go in here.
The entrance to the garage is here on the right. That's where you must go in.
But on the left there is the exit – that's where they come out. Where are you
going to? You must watch where you are going. That is the exit, not the
entrance. The entrance is on the right.

Are you leaving? – Yes, it's time for us to go.
Are you going out? – Yes, I must go out for two or three hours.

England has to import much grain, so England must export industrial goods.

Tomorrow I shall pay the money into the bank – I always take the money in
on Wednesdays. Last year I used to pay the money in on Tuesdays but now
I take it in on Wednesdays.

§ 4

The train moved three miles out of the station and stopped.
Take these flowers to auntie. She loves flowers.
The wind is taking the dinghy away from the shore.
The suitcases must be taken to the station in time.
Take the children off home – they are a nuisance.

§ 8

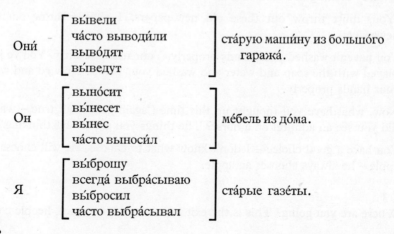

Они	вы́вели ча́сто выводи́ли выво́дят вы́ведут	ста́рую маши́ну из большо́го гаража́.
Он	выно́сит вы́несет вы́нес ча́сто выноси́л	ме́бель из до́ма.
Я	вы́брошу всегда́ выбра́сываю вы́бросил ча́сто выбра́сывал	ста́рые газе́ты.

388

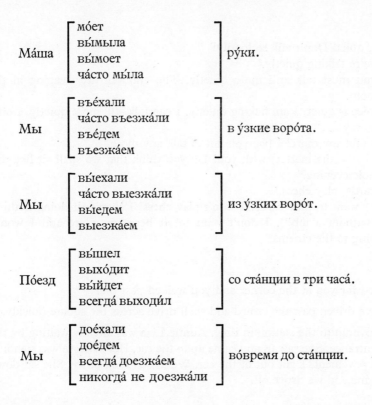

Ма́ша	мо́ет вы́мыла вы́моет ча́сто мы́ла	ру́ки.
Мы	въе́хали ча́сто въезжа́ли въе́дем въезжа́ем	в у́зкие воро́та.
Мы	вы́ехали ча́сто выезжа́ли вы́едем выезжа́ем	из у́зких воро́т.
По́езд	вы́шел выхо́дит вы́йдет всегда́ выходи́л	со ста́нции в три часа́.
Мы	дое́хали дое́дем всегда́ доезжа́ем никогда́ не доезжа́ли	во́время до ста́нции.

LESSON 28, § 1

The pupil was in class, his bicycle stood in the yard and the teacher put the pupil's bicycle into the garage.

We have a very nice neighbour and so (my) brother takes his small daughter every morning to school in his car. Yes, he bought the car last week and so he takes his daughter – the neighbour's daughter in his car.

§ 3

From the office I had to go to the library. From the library I walked to a restaurant. From the restaurant I returned to the library. In the library I worked for two or three hours. From the library I went to the chemist, from the chemist to the market, and from the market I drove home with the shopping. Yes, from the market he returned home with the shopping.

§ 4

'My brother and I will write letters. But before that I shall prepare dinner.'
'You prepare the dinner, and I shall read through the report.'
'No, today we shall dine earlier. Read your report after dinner.'

389

§ 5

'Quiet, quiet! Don't talk so loudly!'

'But we're talking quietly.'

'But you must talk still more quietly. The children are sleeping in the next room.'

'My voice is quiet, I am talking quietly. I can talk still more quietly. I only want to say . . .'

'Don't talk any more! I beg you not to talk any more.'

'But what's (the matter) with you! Do you think that we shall sit like this the whole evening?'

'Play cards, play chess.'

'I don't want to play cards. I won't play chess! I shan't sit doing nothing (lit.: "without a job"). I don't want to sit here any more and I won't. I'm going to the cinema.'

§ 8

I waited for you at the corner and you walked past me.

We have driven past the crowd and shall drive across the square quickly.

We drove up to the station in time. Auntie Liza was already waiting by the main entrance. She saw us and came up to the car. Her suitcase was standing on the pavement. I got out of the car. We kissed each other. She sat down beside me and we drove off.

§ 9

VERA Well, you've come at last – I was already thinking that again you wouldn't come. What an impossible man!

PETYA How's that – wouldn't come again – when was it that I didn't come?

VERA The last time I waited and waited – the day before yesterday I stood by the entrance of the museum, I waited for you by the main entrance, and you didn't come.

PETYA I didn't come? I drove up in my wonderful new car at exactly half past four to the main exit. There were already lots of cars there and I found a place for my car with difficulty, parked it between some sort of awful old (lit. 'lightweight') car on one side and a very elegant fashionable sports car on the other side, and started looking for you. . . .

VERA You looked and looked and did not find (me) as usual! I simply don't believe you. I was standing by the main entrance, right opposite the university.

PETYA One moment, one moment! You say by the entrance opposite the university? And you say by the main entrance?

VERA Well, yes, yes, by the main entrance opposite the university . . .

PETYA My dear, my darling, it is not the main entrance opposite the university, it is the north entrance of the museum. The north entrance of the museum is opposite the university, it is not the main entrance at all, on the contrary, it is a little entrance, it really is not the main entrance. Do you understand? You were standing by one entrance and I was standing by another! And so we did not find each other. The main entrance into the museum is from the south, there is a large square, large gates and a commissionaire stands by the gates. When I was driving up to the gates of the museum, out of the gates came a large blue 'bus with foreign tourists. They drove past me and I kept looking (to see) if you were not in the middle of the crowd. People were coming out of the museum, walking down the steps of the main entrance, but at the time you were standing by a different exit. Is that so or isn't it?

VERA Perhaps I really was standing by a different entrance. But last time when I waited for you by the cinema exit, you didn't come either.

PETYA I know, I am to blame. I was late, but I came – I came and stood by the entrance, and you stood by the exit. You were standing round the corner by the exit, and I was standing right by the entrance on the big square. But now this time we have met. You mustn't be cross, please don't be cross.

VERA Petya darling, I am not cross any more.

PETYA Well, that's fine! And now we have arrived, now we have reached the exhibition building itself.

§ 10

– Что вы бу́дете де́лать ле́том?
– Мы с му́жем е́дем за грани́цу.
– А, как интере́сно! Мы с сестро́й то́же е́дем за грани́цу. Куда́ вы е́дете?
– Мы бу́дем проводи́ть ле́то в СССР.
– Како́е совпаде́ние! Мы то́же е́дем в Сове́тский Сою́з.
– Как вы пое́дете? Мы пое́дем на самолёте.
– А мы пое́дем на парохо́де. Парохо́д сперва́ идёт на се́вер, пото́м идёт на восто́к. Он прохо́дит че́рез Каттега́т в Балти́йское мо́ре. Мо́рем – да́льше, и мы бу́дем до́льше е́хать, но с друго́й стороны́ удо́бнее, моя́ сестра́ должна́ отдыха́ть.
– Да, мы пое́дем по́сле вас, но бу́дем ра́ньше в Сове́тском Сою́зе. Вы наве́рно бу́дете стоя́ть на па́лубе, когда́ су́дно бу́дет подходи́ть к Ленингра́ду, и смотре́ть на го́род. Говоря́т, вид прекра́сный.
– Каку́ю оде́жду вы возьмёте с собо́й?

– Говоря́т, бу́дет жа́рко в Сове́тском Сою́зе ле́том, поэ́тому я возьму́ с собо́й своё но́вое лёгкое пальто́ и бу́ду всё вре́мя носи́ть его́.
– Дава́йте напи́шем друг дру́гу пе́ред пое́здкой и реши́м, где мы встре́тимся.

LESSON 29, § 1

'Didn't you go to work today?'
'No, I didn't go to work today.'
'But you do go to work on Saturdays, (don't you)?'
'Yes, I go, of course I go! But today I am ill and did not go to work, and I shan't go on Monday either.'

§ 2

'At home I wear an old frock. I bought this frock five years ago. It is comfortable and I like it, but I cannot wear it to work any more.'
'I wear my new trousers at home.'
'You even wore your new trousers when you went to work in the garden. And now they are dirty. Your new trousers have to be handed in to the cleaners already.'
'Where are they?'

'What are you carrying in your car?'
'This – this is nothing, it's cabbages and potatoes.'
'Cabbages and potatoes, good. And what's here? Aha! There's wine here. You are carrying wine. So you are carrying cabbages and potatoes, but under the cabbages and under the potatoes there is wine. You are carrying contraband.'

§ 5

There is more traffic on this road in the morning.
There is less traffic on this road in the morning than in the evening.
There is more traffic on this road in August.
There is less traffic on this new road than on the old road.

§ 7

VERA   Why are there so many people? Look, they seem to be waiting for someone.

PETYA   Well, let them wait. I'll buy the tickets.

VERA   No, wait, let's find out who it is that they are waiting for. Somebody must be coming.

PETYA   Well, does it matter who they are waiting for? Vera, Vera, where are you? You've vanished again (lit.: 'Again you are not'). Vera. . . .

VERA   (*excitedly*) Petya, Petya, do you know who they are waiting for? Gagarin! Yury Gagarin! He has just arrived in London and, of course, he'll come here to the exhibition, since it's a Soviet Exhibition.

PETYA   Well, that's fine, let's go in then.

VERA   Well, no, I want to see him arrive. You see, everyone's standing (about) here and we too shall stand (about) a bit. Here – here's a car driving up – no, it's gone past, it's not him. . . . There he is. . . . No, it's a motorcycle.

PETYA   He won't arrive on a motorcycle, and he is unlikely to arrive on a bicycle.

VERA   If you're going to make fun of me. . . . There's a car coming. . . .

PETYA   Well, that's just a taxi. Gagarin won't come from the airport in a taxi!

VERA   Do look! Here's a car with red pennants – it's from the Embassy.

PETYA   Yes, it is a Soviet Embassy car.

VERA   They're also waiting. Perhaps we'll also have to wait a long time. Let's sit down on the steps, my shoes are hurting me.

PETYA   All right, let's sit down on the steps. I put my new trousers on, and here we have to sit on the steps! Oh, Vera, Vera. . . .

VERA   Then sit down on the newspaper. You yourself want to see him? How lucky that we came to the Soviet Exhibition exactly on the very same day as Gagarin! I'll tell everyone that I saw him. Aren't you glad? You'll also be able to tell everyone how you saw him.

PETYA   I saw him? I saw nothing! It's as though you were in love with this Gagarin!

VERA   Oh, how silly you are – I am not in love with anybody. It's you, like a fool, you're in love with I don't know who.

PETYA   And you haven't even seen him and you're already in love. Like a (girl) in love you keep saying – 'Here he is', 'here he is'. You see Gagarin in every motorcyclist.

VERA   I simply want to see him, because it is human progress (lit.: 'progress of humanity').

PETYA   Yes, human progress!

VERA   And you are simply jealous! You are jealous. I know it! You are always jealous. Here, here's the car. . . .

PETYA Yes, here, here's the car. It's the milk van and not Gagarin.

VERA Do stop it, you're laughing all (the time)!

PETYA There you are, he's here already, that is why the Embassy cars are here. Why, what's the matter with you, Vera, really, well, don't cry. Never mind, it's nothing, you mustn't cry – we'll see him yet – I was only joking, you know. Now, now, Vera, my dear, I was only joking, forgive me, I know that you are not in love with Gagarin. It isn't with him that you are in love, you know – yes (isn't that so)? Why, you love me, just a little – yes, (isn't that so)? – I am really jealous, I don't want somebody else, even Gagarin. . . . You do love me, don't you, yes? I only love you, only you.

§ 8

– Куда́ вы е́дете?

– Я е́ду на вы́ставку и везу́ с собо́й сы́на.

– Не в но́вом ли он пиджаке́?

– Это не но́вый пиджа́к. Он старе́е, чем тот, кото́рый он но́сит, когда́ хо́дит в шко́лу.

– А, он тепе́рь хо́дит в шко́лу?

– Да, он уже́ год хо́дит в шко́лу. Нет, бо́льше го́да – и́ли ме́ньше го́да? Кста́ти, Ива́н то́же хо́дит в шко́лу тепе́рь? Но он моло́же Петра́, не пра́вда ли?

– Нет, он ста́рше Петра́ – почти́ го́дом ста́рше, но он ещё не на́чал ходи́ть в шко́лу. Я даю́ ему́ уро́ки до́ма. Оди́н из его́ друзе́й хо́дит к нам и они́ чита́ют вме́сте.

– Мо́жете ли вы мне сказа́ть, где нахо́дится вы́ставка?

– Ну, по э́той доро́ге прямее́, – бли́же по э́той доро́ге. Я везу́ тётю домо́й на маши́не. Е́сли хоти́те, мы повезём вас на маши́не. Это да́льше, но бу́дет гора́здо удо́бнее.

– Большо́е спаси́бо. Я вам о́чень благода́рна.

– Не́_за_что. Влеза́йте.

LESSON 30, § 1

We live not far from the aerodrome and aeroplanes fly about over our heads all day. The noise is terrible but we are used to it – we don't even look up when they fly over us. Our neighbour's youngest son stands all day, watching and counting. 'There, there's one flying – see, what a big one (is flying) and here's another one and there's still another, here's a big one – a passenger plane – and over there there's a bomber. It's a bomber. I know it is – look, there's a bomber.'

'That's enough, that will do! They are flying about here all day and you will fly yourself – you'll fly about in aeroplanes'.

'Daddy often flies, Daddy likes flying. Do you like flying – have you flown?'
'Yes, I have flown – a little, but I have flown. I have usually gone on my holidays by train or steamer. I don't like flying'.

'Where are you running to? Where are you off to? Where are you running like that?'
'To the station, for a train – goodbye! I'm running and running – the train is leaving.'
'Yes, he's running, running with all his suitcases and the train is already leaving. I don't like to run. I never run, I walk slowly and calmly. There's no need at all to run. When I was young, I liked to run at the stadium – and I ran very fast – but now I'm too old.'

§ 6

To go shopping is a middling pleasure. It all depends on what you want to buy, where, in which shops, how much money you have in your pocket – that's a very important question. To go for bread, or butter, is not complicated. To buy sugar, salt, pepper, eggs, cheese, macaroni, spongecakes, some preserves – anybody can (do) that. But even here there are unexpected complications. I am very forgetful. I have lived abroad a long time. Everywhere everything is sold in kilograms and grammes. A thousand grammes is one kilogram, and in comparison with English pounds one kilogram is equal more or less to two and a quarter pounds. Two and a quarter English pounds is about one kilogram. One English pound is approximately four hundred and fifty grammes, and two hundred and fifty grammes or a quarter of a kilogram is a little more than half a pound. In the old days in Russia they also weighed in pounds but the old Russian pound was slightly less than the English pound – the old Russian pound is equal to four hundred grammes, and two and a half Russian pounds exactly is one kilogram.
For a long time I could not get used to English money and English measures of weight. At last I got used to them. So here I am one day going into a dairy.
'What can I do for you?' asks the shopkeeper. I take what I need for dinner and supper. Everything has become rather dear.
'Why is the butter so dear?' I ask him. 'Last week I paid three and ten for a pound of butter and today I am paying four and two.'
He answers: 'It's because of the time of year. At this time of year butter is always dearer and eggs are dearer too, you won't find butter at a cheaper price anywhere in town. And the eggs in my shop are much cheaper than in other shops – threepence halfpenny the small ones, and fourpence halfpenny the large ones. How many shall I give you and which sort?'
'Give me a dozen at four and six, yes, yes, the large ones – a dozen at four and six, and give (me) some sausage too.'

'How much shall I cut you?'

'Well, cut me, say, a hundred . . .' I stand and think and the shopkeeper says nothing but looks at me.

'Give me a hundred, or no, give me two hundred. Yes, cut me two hundred.'

He says nothing for a moment and then says uncertainly: 'What? How much?'

'Two hundred, give me two hundred.'

'Two hundred what?'

'Sausage, of course, two hundred of sausage,' and then at last I understand: I am telling him the weight in grammes, you see, and he of course thinks that I am talking about pounds, that I want to buy a hundred or two hundred pounds of sausage. There is quiet horror in his eyes – he has probably decided that I have gone out of my mind.

'Excuse me, I meant to say half a pound of sausage and three quarters of a pound of ham.'

'At what price? Three and eight a pound or this here, somewhat better, at four and ten a pound? And this is the very best – five and four. Do you want a whole pound of ham or three quarters?'

'Well, all right, give me a whole pound of the best.'

Yes, one ought not to confuse grammes and pounds! Acquaintances from Moscow went shopping in London for sheets and pillowslips and mixed up inches and centimetres. You see, we have everything in inches and feet and yards, but our poor friends give ('name') the size in centimetres. The assistant in the shop measures in inches and an inch is much bigger than a centimetre – two and a half times bigger: two and a half centimetres is one inch. So they go home from the shop. Somehow the parcel is very heavy! They arrived home, opened the parcel – and what (do they find)?! The pillowslips and sheets are enormous! 'What use are such big ones to us? The biggest size! That's why it was so heavy to carry, that's why it was so dear!'

LESSON 31, § 6

PETYA   You know, Vera goes shopping with a list. First she walks about the kitchen, opens and closes all the drawers and cupboards. She looks at the shelves and makes a list.

NINA   My dear little brother, I also make lists . . . on old envelopes, on postcards, on the back of some old letter, but you have never shown any interest in that.

PETYA   I find these old envelopes, letters and postcards in the bathroom, the lavatory, on the floor in the hall, on the stairs and I have even found one of your lists in my bed between the sheets. We have no order in our house, how is it that you don't understand that!?

NINA   After (your) wedding you'll understand that a man must also help at home. Vera will tell you: 'Petya, remove those trousers from the table,' and you'll remove them. 'Petya, you've thrown the towel on the floor, pick it up,' and you'll pick it up. Then she'll say: 'Petya, go and buy two tickets for Saturday,' you'll go and buy those tickets. 'Petya, there's a ring at the door, take the laundry in.' 'Petya, take the linen out to the laundry' – you'll take it in and you'll take it out. 'Petya, there's so much work at home, we must hire a servant, let's hire a servant,' and you'll even hire a servant!

PETYA　What nonsense! What are you (up to) – are you jealous? You aren't jealous, are you?

NINA　I'm simply sorry for you. I'm also sorry for myself. What was I doing last year and the year before last? I just picked up and tidied everything away after you. I received your guests! I occupied myself with just the house and you. Now you're getting married and you haven't even introduced me to this Vera. Yes, you just haven't thought of introducing us.

PETYA　Nina, what are (you saying)! Why, you've met several months ago!

NINA　But then I didn't know that she was going to be your wife! I don't even remember what she looks like. And since then you haven't said a word about her.

PETYA　Nina, darling, let me explain. . . .

§ 7

I am going to the station, but I've popped in to (see) you for a moment, I've popped in just for a moment – I thought: 'I'll pop in to (see) you, I haven't seen you for a long time' – so I popped in only for a moment. I have very little time, I'm hurrying to the station. My train goes at four o'clock, I'm afraid of being late for the train. Yes, I'm afraid of being late for the train and I popped in only for a moment. You know, you never pop in to see me.
On the way from London to Moscow we shall look in at Warsaw. We shall be there for three days.
You have no newspaper? Well then, I'll bring my newspaper round to you on my way to work. Yes, I'll bring the newspaper round on my way.

§ 8

– Вы помните, в каком году мы посетили тётю Пети?
– Мне кажется, это было в тысяча девятьсот пятьдесят девятом году.
– Нет, по-моему, было раньше. У Ивана был свободный день. Мы посидели часа два дома, потом поехали к вам на машине, на авось. Петя зашёл и...

– Да, э́то бы́ло в сре́ду. Вы прие́хали в оди́ннадцать часо́в и сказа́ли, что прие́хали на полчаса́. Пото́м зашёл Пе́тя и мы все пое́хали к его́ тёте, потому́ что был день её рожде́ния.

– Да. Её день рожде́ния – пе́рвого апре́ля, и пе́рвое апре́ля ты́сяча девятьсо́т пятьдеся́т девя́того го́да бы́ло в сре́ду. Бы́ло полови́на двена́дцатого, когда́ мы пое́хали. Мы опозда́ли на два часа́, и прие́хали в полови́не тре́тьего.

– Его́ тётя ду́мала, что мы уже́ пообе́дали, поэ́тому она́ дала́ нам ко́фе. Кста́ти, почему́ вы спроси́ли об э́той пое́здке?

– Ну, я забы́ла сказа́ть ей, что я пью ко́фе без молока́.

LESSON 32, § 1

'This watch/clock has to be wound up once a week. Did you wind it up yesterday?'
'No, I didn't wind (it) up. I forgot to wind it up yesterday evening.'
'Tell me what time it is and I'll wind it up. You always forget to wind up the watch/clock. Don't forget.'

'Be ready at seven o'clock. Don't forget. We visit (lit. 'are at') Aunt Liza so rarely and she hasn't visited (lit. 'been at') us for a long time. We can forget that we're going to (visit) her this evening.'
'I shan't forget. I'll buy her flowers. Oh, no, I forgot, she doesn't like flowers, she likes chocolate.'
'How splendid that you remember such trifles.'
'It's not a trifle at all, it's very important. It's good that I thought of it (lit. 'recollected'). Also she doesn't like milk chocolate.'
'I also remember that. If you like, I'll buy her a large box of chocolates myself.'
'You won't forget?'
'No, I'll remember that.'
'Write down her new address.'
'I memorised it. I can easily memorise both addresses and telephone numbers.'
'Everything like that I forget, but I have a good memory for trifles, as you put it.'

§ 2

'Sit down at the table. We'll dine early. If you want, we'll go to the cinema after dinner. I don't think that you'll want to sit a whole evening with your old aunt.'

Everyone began to laugh when the clown appeared on the screen.
She read the letter through and began to cry bitterly.
The public became anxious when the artiste fell.
Book in hand, auntie dozed off.

The crowd became excited when the minister came out on to the balcony.
You will not fall ill from my pancakes.
Suddenly everyone began to talk. One could understand nothing. Everyone began talking together.
'Well, sing!' they told him and he began singing.
The child fell and began yelling.

§ 3

Let me tell you how I made up the shopping-list ('list of purchases') on the day when Vera came to dinner. It was a Saturday. On Saturday I do not go to work. I got up early, dressed quickly and began to think – what shall I buy – what shall I do ('prepare') for dinner: meat or fish? Meat, I think – some people do not like fish. Yes, but what kind of meat, what will it be best to buy – a piece of beef – steak, hm? I like veal but Peter likes beef. But perhaps it would be best to buy pork or lamb chops? I don't know – I'll go to the butcher's and have a word with the butcher.
I need onions and potatoes. There's nothing at home. I'll buy four pounds of both – four pounds of onions and four pounds of potatoes. No, six pounds of potatoes – that will be enough for a week. What else? Peter does not like cauliflower, there are no beans yet and no peas. I could make a salad. It's not worth writing anything down until I've decided what kind of meat to buy. Last week, on Saturday, the butcher had chickens and ducks hanging up. Yes, perhaps that is what I shall do – I'll buy a duck. I won't get beef, I won't get mutton – I'll do duck with apples. Peter is so greedy that I shall have to buy sausages – one pound of sausages. A duck weighing seven or eight pounds. How much will it cost? I think about eighteen or nineteen shillings or may be even twenty-two or three shillings. I ran out of the house, ran to do the shopping and forgot the list on the table.
– And I went for the sugar, the rice, the preserves, the tea, the coffee, the bread and so on and so on!
– How kind you are ('have become')!

§ 4

The chief architect does not have a shorthand typist, and in the accounts department there is no book-keeper.

There is heating in the house in the winter. There is no heating in summer.
In summer there was no heating and there will not be (any).
In the bathroom there was a towel in the morning etc.
. . . .
What disorder! In the sideboard there are neither spoons, nor forks, nor knives – there is nothing. There is no plate, no napkin, no tablecloth. The spoons, forks, knives, plate, napkin, tablecloth were in the kitchen and now everything is on the table.

§ 6a

Я купи́ла мя́со – говя́дину, теля́тину, свины́е и бара́ньи котле́ты.
Да, я купи́ла и свини́ну и бара́нину. Я не купи́ла у́тку.
У нас бы́ли и лук и карто́фель. У нас всё бы́ло до́ма.
Я не сде́лала дли́нного спи́ска того́, что мне на́до бы́ло купи́ть.
Но спи́сок я взяла́ с собо́й. Спи́сок я не оста́вила на столе́. Я не
ходи́ла за поку́пками без спи́ска. Спи́сок был с собо́й.

b

Я не купи́ла никако́го мя́са – никако́й говя́дины, никако́й теля́тины,
никаки́х свины́х ни бара́ньих котле́т. Нет, я не купи́ла никако́й
свини́ны, никако́й бара́нины.
У нас не́ было никако́го лу́ка, никако́го карто́феля.
Ни одного́ спи́ска я не взяла́ с собо́й.
Ни одного́ спи́ска не́_было со мной.

LESSON 34, § 3

All my fingers ache. I cannot tighten them or relax them. When I unbend
the finger like that, all my muscles ache. Now I am flexing them and it
hurts me. (When) I tighten it like this, it doesn't hurt, but (when) I unbend,
all the muscles ache again.

Now all these parcels should be tied together, it's best to tie all the parcels
together.

You always tie your knots so firmly that I can never undo them. Please do
not tie so firmly, tie them carefully, then it will not be so difficult for me to
undo the string.
. . . .
'I cannot make out anything in this letter, I do not understand anything.
I am deciphering this awful writing with difficulty, but I cannot make out
the meaning of the letter.'
'Give it to me – I'll soon make it out.'

'One must send out all these letters to the different addresses. Distribute
them please, don't forget to distribute them.'
'All right, I'll send them out tomorrow morning.'

'How untidy you are, you have thrown all my papers all over (the place).'
'You're untidy yourself, you throw everything about yourself, you've thrown
everything about, your shoes and boots and socks, you've thrown everything
all over the room.'
'No, it's you who are untidy. You always throw all your things together
into a heap.'

400

'You must put your things out tidily. Why can't you put your things out tidily and neatly? Then it is a lot easier to pack, one can pack everything in a couple of minutes. But I have now been packing all your things for half an hour, because you're a lazybones and only throw everything around and don't put things out tidily.'

§ 4

Hunting for Capercaillie in the Spring

In a thick, dark wood in the Urals a hunter is making some strange, incomprehensible movements. He takes two quick steps, stops and freezes. One of his feet is in deep snow, the other barely touches the surface of the snow. He stands like that for a while. Then again two quick leaps follow and again he freezes – sometimes for a long time. He is hunting capercaillie. But why does the hunter approach this large bird in such an unusual way? The capercaillie, though it takes its name from the word глухой (*deaf*), has in fact a very acute sense of hearing. It hears very well. In spring, however, it really cannot hear in those brief moments when it sings. It walks up and down the top branches of a big fir tree, giving its mating call – in the following way. First there are sounds like the crackle of dry sticks: *tacka . . . tacka. . . .* The hunter does not move, he freezes, waits. . . . Then there is a mumbling: *brr – brr – brr . . .* not more than a second. It is in that moment that the hunter swiftly takes two steps – he has no time for more – and freezes in the position in which he is caught by the signal, i.e. by the cessation of the mumbling.

The capercaille falls silent – and the hunter freezes. Sometimes the bird is silent for ten minutes and more. It listens acutely and attentively to what is going on in the silence of the forest. But now it calls again. Again the hunter starts to make his short hops. It is not more than fifty metres to the tree where the bird is sitting. Close enough to fire.

But then – a stroke of bad luck: dawn is just beginning and in the darkness of the forest one cannot see where, on which branch of the big fir tree, the capercaillie is perched. A few more leaps. Now one can see that the ends of the branches of one of the upper boughs of the dark fir tree are swaying. But the large bird is pacing up and down nearer the tree-trunk and cannot be seen. It would be risky to take a shot at random – one might miss and lose such an enormous game-bird – a young hunter's pride.

And the hunter is young and inexperienced. He leaps but does not manage to take a second step. His foot hangs in the air. He cannot put it down on the snow. In spring the upper layer of snow is usually frozen over. That is the crust. During the day it melts under the rays of the sun and at night it freezes. In the forest it is very brittle. The slightest touch makes a cracking noise. Like glass.

But it is difficult to balance for long on one leg which has sunk into the

DD

snow. He begins to heel over a little. So as not to fall, he slightly touches with his fingers the frozen crust. There is a faint crack . . . And all is lost. What a pity! The capercaillie quickly rises and is hidden behind the trees. All one can hear is the swish of its wings.

The hunter, upset, comes out into a clearing, sits down on a log, and decides to light a cigarette and listen for another capercaillie calling. At the other side of the clearing the snow crunches slightly. A hare runs out. Suddenly something large and grey, with eyes blazing in the dark, throws itself down from above, from a tree, on to the hare. The hare makes an abrupt jump to one side. The beast makes ready for a second jump. A shot. The fine shot, suitable for the capercaillie, only wounds the beast. It limps and tries to run away. The hunter hastily loads his gun with large shot. A second shot and the lynx, which looks like a wild-cat but is the size of a large dog, lies stretched out on the snow. It is a very dangerous beast, for it throws itself from the tree not only on to animals but also on to man.

This is a great success for the young hunter. The lynx's pelt now lies in (his) room as a rug and reminds him of his first hunt for capercaillie.

§ 5

Ра́но у́тром моло́чник развози́т молоко́ на свое́й маши́не. Пти́цы разлета́ются, когда́ он проезжа́ет. Пото́м почтальо́н разно́сит пи́сьма и ма́льчик разно́сит газе́ты. Де́ти на на́шей у́лице схо́дятся на углу́ и пото́м иду́т в шко́лу.

Вы говори́те, что вы учи́лись ру́сскому языку́ де́сять лет тому́ наза́д и совсе́м разучи́лись. Ну, на́до продолжа́ть учи́ться иностра́нному языку́, а то ско́ро разу́чиваетесь. Ита́к, закро́йте э́ту газе́ту и откро́йте кни́гу.

Моя́ жена́ пошла́ за поку́пками. Она́ связа́ла верёвкой все паке́ты. Когда́ она́ верну́лась домо́й, она́ запла́кала, потому́ что она́ так до́лго не могла́ развяза́ть свя́зку (паке́тов). На́до бы́ло разре́зать верёвку но́жницами.

Ива́н собира́ет номера́ парово́зов. Он их запи́сывает в тетра́дь, но у него́ тако́й плохо́й по́черк, что никто́ не мо́жет разобра́ть их.

Тури́сты разложи́ли свои́ ве́щи и сра́зу же разъе́хались по го́роду, что́бы смотре́ть достопримеча́тельности.

LESSON 35, § 4

NINA Do you want to have a lie (down) after dinner? All right, lie down on the settee – or do you want to lie down on the bed?

PETYA No, I'll lie down on the settee.

NINA All right, lie down, but see that you don't dirty the settee with your shoes – you'd better take them off.

AUNT LIZA'S VOICE OFF Where's Petya?

NINA   He's lying on the settee, reading the paper or sleeping. Oh no, the paper is lying here on the chair. I think he has fallen asleep, Aunt Liza. Peter, oh Peter (*suddenly (in an) angry voice*) – Petka, you've lain down again with your feet on the settee and your shoes on. Come on, get up, get off the settee.

PETYA   Hmmm. . . .

NINA   I'm always saying that you must lie down on the settee with your shoes off, or put a paper under your feet, and you simply lie down with your shoes on and lie and sleep.

PETYA   Hmm – and they won't let you have a quiet little lie (down) and sleep.

NINA   What's that – won't let you have a little lie (down)? Who doesn't let you lie, I'd like to know? You've lain down on the new settee with your shoes on and I'm always telling you – lie down on the settee but take your shoes off first – but you do it to spite me.

PETYA   Who's doing what to spite who? I lie down on the settee with my shoes on to spite you, eh? And you put some vases of flowers straight on my plans to spite me – why, you went and put a vase of violets on my papers yesterday, straight on to my papers.

§ 5

A Wolf-hunt with Pennants

Hunting wolves with pennants is an interesting Russian sport. It usually takes place in winter and is carried out as follows.

The Moscow hunters receive a telegram. It says that in the north of the Kalinin *Oblast*, i.e. about 400 kilometres from the capital, a pack of wolves has appeared. There are none nearer at hand because they have all been wiped out long ago. This pack has come there from the big forests of the neighbouring, more northerly *oblast*. Everybody knows that wolves are dangerous, especially in winter. They destroy sheep, attack cattle, horses and even people. They must be destroyed at once. For every wolf killed the government pays a premium of fifty rubles, i.e. about twenty pounds sterling.

So the hunters collect everything they need and go, at first by train and then by sledge, to the place where the wolves have spent the night in the forest. The local professional hunter, who had sent the telegram to Moscow, points out the birch copse, where the tracks of the wolves lead. They are clearly visible in the snow. One should know an interesting habit of the wolves: they move in a big pack over the snow, one after the other, stepping into the same prints. So it looks as if there is only one wolf whereas in fact there are six.

403

The hunters in white smocks move on special broad skis across the deep snow round the copse. One of them has a large reel on his back and a thin rope with red pennants is wound out from this reel. The rope is hung on bushes and trees at a height of one metre from the ground. The wolves are afraid of the red pennants, which hang at a distance of several metres one from the other. So they will not jump over the rope.

On three sides the wood has been surrounded by the pennants while on the fourth side there remains a free exit. Here the hunters draw lots for their positions. They take up their positions according to their numbers. The hunters step off their skis and choose a place behind a tree or among the bushes, so that they can conveniently see the wolves and fire. One must stamp down the snow under one's feet – it has to be firm. The men stand down-wind so that the wolves do not sense the smell of men and powder. Everything is now ready. A shot is heard, fired by the professional hunter from the opposite side to frighten the wolves. The wolves run towards the hunters. The professional shouts, fires again and makes a noise with his rattle. The wolves rush off in various directions but, seeing the pennants, they again run in the direction of the hunters.

Now, behind the trees, first one wolf appears, then another, and a third. They hurl themselves in leaps across the deep snow towards the hunters. It is difficult even for wolves to run in such snow. In alarm, they look back and to the sides.

You watch and wait impatiently. There is a shot on the right, then several shots on the left and the howl of a wounded wolf is heard. Two wolves run at you at once. The first is old, experienced, the biggest and most dangerous; he is as big as a pony. The wolf sees the black barrel of the gun and the hunter's eyes, abruptly throws himself to one side, into the bushes, and the shot only slightly grazes his back. He succeeds in hiding in the wood. The second wolf falls to an accurate shot. Altogether five wolves are killed. The sledges come up and the horses timidly eye askance the dead beasts and snort. The hunters return home. The next day in the paper *Вечéрняя Москвá* (*Moscow Evening News*) there is a report about the successful wolf-hunt.

§ 6b

Вы хотúте полежáть пóсле обéда? Хорошó, ля́гте на дивáны, или хотúте лечь на кровáти?

Нет, мы ля́жем на дивáны.

Хорошó, ля́гте, но смотрúте, не запáчкайте дивáны сапогáми, вы их лýчше снимúте.

Лежáт на дивáнах, читáют газéты или спят. Ах нет, газéты лежáт тут на стýльях. Онú, кáжется, заснýли, тётя Лúза. ... вы опя́ть леглú с ногáми на дивáны в сапогáх. Ну, вставáйте, вставáйте с дивáнов.

Всегда́ мы говори́м, что на́до ложи́ться на дива́ны без сапо́г, и́ли положи́те себе́ газе́ты под но́ги, а вы про́сто так, в сапога́х ложи́тесь и лежи́те и спи́те.

Кто вам лежа́ть не даёт, хоте́ли бы мы знать? Вы легли́ на но́вые дива́ны в сапога́х, а мы вам всегда́ говори́м – ложи́тесь на дива́ны, но сперва́ сними́те сапоги́, а вы нам на зло.

Мы на зло ложи́мся на дива́ны в сапога́х, да? А вы на зло ста́вите каки́е-то ва́зы с цвета́ми пря́мо на на́ши чертежи́, так и поста́вили вчера́ ва́зы с фиа́лками на на́ши бума́ги, пря́мо на бума́ги.

LESSON 36, § 1

When I was a little girl, we always dressed up on Sundays. Mama would dress herself – she would put on her best frock. Papa would put on his best suit. Then Mama would dress us, the children, – she would dress us all in our best frocks, suits and shoes. One Sunday she got us dressed. We all went for a walk in the park and the passers-by looked at us children. In the evening I did not want to undress and since then I have always undressed very slowly.

§ 5

'Well, I've got used to smoking twenty cigarettes a day and simply cannot lose the habit.'

'Never mind, Petya, you'll lose it. Aunt Liza used to smoke not less than forty cigarettes a day – simply terrible – and then in spite of it she lost the habit.'

'How do you mean, lost the habit? I arrived at her place recently, and she had a cigarette sticking out of her mouth as usual.'

'Well yes, she smokes about twenty-five cigarettes a day.'

'There you are, lost the habit! So I've also lost the habit of smoking. I've lost the habit of smoking and smoke twenty!'

The cat stole the fish and (itself) vanished.

My letters have vanished. I placed them on the table, but they've disappeared. Everything disappears in this house.

§ 6

Fishing under the Ice

A frosty winter's day. The vast snowy plain is flooded with sunshine. Wherever you look groups of people are sitting on boxes. They are fishermen, amateurs of fishing under the ice. They have come here to *Bolshaya Volga*. Most of them are from Moscow, though it is a hundred and thirty kilometres from the capital to here. There are very many fish of different species here. They come in cars and large buses straight over the snowed-up roads. Roads are laid over the ice and the anglers stop wherever the fish bite best. The thick, very strong ice can hold large buses with forty anglers on board.

First of all one has to kick away the snow and in the ice knock a hole which is called a *lunka*. The last blows: in front of you there is a deep, empty hole in the ice. One more strong blow and the water noisily and swiftly fills the *lunka*.

Now one has to prepare one's rod. The angler gets it out of a special box, into which the fish is placed afterwards. The fishermen also sit on this box, because the fishing goes on for several hours. The rod is very short – no more than two feet. A line several metres long is wound off it. On the end of the line is a small hook. On it is a small pellet as a sinker. One or two gnat-larvae must be put on the end of the hook. These are bright red maggots about two centimetres long. They are sold by fishing-tackle suppliers. You have to keep the box of maggots in your pocket, otherwise they might quickly freeze.

Is everything in order? Can we start? Let's start.

The hook with the thin nylon line is lowered to the bottom. Then the angler begins to lift it slowly – he shakes his hand rhythmically and raises the rod about half a metre. Then he lowers it again and repeats the movement. The live red maggots are a good bait. You see, in winter the fish are mostly asleep. They have to be teased with a beautiful bait. A special float is attached to the end of the rod on a springy wire. As soon as the fish will bite, the float will be tugged downwards. One must pull in at once. And so the first perch appears on the glittering snow. It is greenish-silver with bright red fins and it stands out sharply against the white background. After that – another. A good catch is four or five kilograms of fish in several hours.

Suddenly something happens. Many of the anglers jump up from their boxes and run over to one side, where an old man – an experienced angler – is sitting. He has just pulled an enormous pike out of the water. Yes, you won't catch one like that on a small hook with a maggot. The old man fishes by a different method. He brings with him about two dozen small fish in a bucket of water. He carefully pierces their lips with a hook and puts them in the water on a long, strong line. Under the ice these fish swim about with the hook, which looks like an anchor. Up above, by the *lunka*, the old man puts a stick in the snow. On this he places a line with a red pennant. He brings not less than ten of these rods with him. Then he walks up and down by these sticks and watches for a pennant to fall. It falls when a large fish has taken and dragged the live bait. Quickly he tugs the line. One must seize the moment to gaff the big fish in the cheek with the hook so that it will not escape. Then the angler drags it out on to the snow.

§ 8

Мой отéц был писáтель и мы жи́ли в дерéвне. Рáньше мы жи́ли в гóроде но (там) бы́ло так шýмно, что пáпа мог рабóтать тóлько нóчью, когдá всё утихло. Он привы́к рабóтать нóчью и дáже в дерéвне не отвы́к от э́той привы́чки.

Пе́ред заму́жеством мать была́ актри́сой, но ходи́ть за большо́й семьёй занима́ло у неё сли́шком мно́го вре́мени. Когда́ мы бы́ли (ещё) ма́ленькими, она́ одева́ла нас по о́череди. По́зже мы могли́ са́ми одева́ться. По́сле того́ как мы оде́лись и поза́втракали, мы отправля́лись в шко́лу.

В то вре́мя (мне) каза́лось, что мы бога́ты. Я ду́мала, что мы роди́лись бога́тыми. Тепе́рь ка́жется, что на са́мом де́ле мы не́ были о́чень бога́тыми. Всё же, мы бы́ли сча́стливы. Но́чью мы не мёрзли, и мы хорошо́ е́ли. У́тром в до́ме па́хло вку́сной едо́й и в час мы все сади́лись обе́дать. Е́сли бы́ло сли́шком шу́мно, оте́ц де́лал вид, что он огло́х, и тогда́ ма́ло-пома́лу мы все умолка́ли.

На про́шлой неде́ле я верну́лся в дере́вню. Всё меня́ется. Мать и оте́ц вы́глядят хорошо́, но, ка́жется, ста́рость начина́ет ска́зываться на них.

LESSON 37, § 6

A Wolf-hunt with Pennants

Hunting wolves with pennants is an interesting and unique Russian sport. It usually takes place in winter and is carried out as follows.

The Moscow hunters receive a telegram. It says that in the north of the Kalinin *Oblast*, i.e. about four hundred kilometres from the capital, a pack of wolves has appeared (there are none nearer at hand because they have all been wiped out long ago). This pack has arrived there from the big forests of the neighbouring, more northerly *oblast*. Everybody knows that wolves are dangerous, especially in winter. They destroy sheep, attack cattle, horses and even people. They must be destroyed at once. For every wolf killed the government pays a premium of fifty rubles, i.e. about twenty pounds sterling.

So, having collected everything necessary, a group of amateur hunters (four to five men) goes, at first by train and then by sledge, to the place where the wolves have spent the night in the forest. The local professional hunter (who sent the telegram to Moscow) points out the birch copse, where the tracks of the wolves lead. They are clearly visible in the snow. One must know an interesting habit of the wolves: in order not to betray themselves they move in a large pack over the snow, one after the other, stepping into the same prints. So it looks as though there is only one wolf whereas in fact there are six.

The hunters in white smocks move on skis across the deep snow round this copse. One of them has a large reel on his back and a thin rope with red pennants is wound out from this reel. The rope is hung on bushes and tree trunks at a height of one metre from the ground. The wolves are afraid of the red pennants, placed at a distance of several metres one from the other. So they will not jump over the rope.

When they have surrounded the wood on three sides with pennants, a free passage remained on the fourth side. Here, having taken up their places by drawing lots, the camouflaged hunters take up their positions.

They step off their skis and choose a place behind a tree or among the bushes, so that they can conveniently see the wolves and fire. The snow underfoot has to be trampled down. Now everything is ready. A shot is heard, fired by the professional hunter, who, at the opposite end (of the copse) from the hunters, frightens the wolves and drives them towards the marksmen. He shouts, fires again and makes a noise with a rattle. The wolves race in different directions but seeing the flags they again run in the direction of the hunters.

Now, behind the trees first one wolf appears, then another, then a third, and they run, leaping across the deep snow towards the hunters. In alarm they look back and to the sides.

A shot rings out to the right, then several shots to the left, and the howl of a wounded wolf. Finally, two wolves run at you at once. The first is mature, i.e. old, experienced, very large and dangerous. He must be put down first. Seeing the black barrel of the gun and the hunter's eyes, he hurls himself abruptly to one side, into the bushes – and the shot only slightly grazes his back. He succeeds in hiding in the forest. The second wolf, however, falls to an accurate shot. Altogether five wolves have been killed. They are put into the sledges which have come up. The horses timidly look askance at the dead beasts and snort. The hunters return home.

That is one way of hunting wolves. There are several others. There is hunting with borzois, which skilfully seize the wolf by the ears and throat. Sometimes wolf-pits are dug in the forest, i.e. deep trenches, about the size of a room, with straight, vertical sides. They are covered on top with thin twigs and branches, and bait – a piece of meat – is put in the middle. Making its way to the meat, the wolf falls through into the pit. The old men recount that in their time, when there were many wolves, bold hunters used to do as follows: they (would) harness three strong horses to a sledge, choose a road in a forest where there were many wolves and throw out a small piglet, placed in a sack. The sack is tied on by rope and drags along five metres behind the sledge. The troika (of horses) races madly along, the piglet squeals and the hunters fire without pause at the wolves leaping out of the wood.

§ 7

Москва́ и Кремль

Мы то́чно не зна́ем, когда́ Москва́ была́ осно́вана. По всей вероя́тности, она́ была́ постро́ена кня́зем Ю́рием Влади́мировичем, кото́рый был про́зван Ю́рием Долгору́ким (про́званным Ю́рием Долгору́ким).

В ты́сяча две́сти три́дцать седьмо́м году́ го́род был разорён тата́рами. В ты́сяча три́ста три́дцать седьмо́м году́ был большо́й пожа́р и Москва́ была́ сожжена́ почти́ до тла. Пе́рвые ка́менные зда́ния бы́ли постро́ены в сле́дующем столе́тии.

В пятна́дцатом столе́тии италья́нские архите́кторы бы́ли на́няты (с тем), что́бы постро́ить но́вые собо́ры и но́вые сте́ны. Кремлёвская стена́, постро́енная в то вре́мя, бо́лее и́ли ме́нее та же са́мая, кото́рую мы зна́ем тепе́рь. В ты́сяча шестисо́том году́ была́ проведена́ в тру́бах вода́ из Москвы́-реки́.

Большо́й ко́локол, кото́рый тепе́рь стои́т в Кремле́, был отли́т в нача́ле восемна́дцатого столе́тия. Он был на́зван Царь-Ко́локол, хотя́ он слома́лся и никогда́ не был пове́шен.

К концу́ восемна́дцатого ве́ка бы́ло постро́ено зда́ние, в кото́ром был помещён Сена́т. Тепе́рь там помеща́ется Сове́т Мини́стров.

Но́вый го́род Петербу́рг, постро́енный Петро́м Вели́ким, был сде́лан администрати́вным це́нтром. Переимено́ванный в Петрогра́д во вре́мя пе́рвой мирово́й войны́ он был сно́ва переимено́ван в Ленингра́д по́сле сме́рти Ле́нина. Уже́ до того́ Москва́ была́ сде́лана администрати́вным це́нтром но́вой Сове́тской Респу́блики.

Двадца́того ию́ля ты́сяча девятьсо́т пятьдеся́т пя́того го́да Кремль был откры́т для пу́блики. Неда́вно бы́ло постро́ено но́вое зда́ние – большо́й зал, в кото́ром мо́гут собира́ться ты́сячи люде́й.

LESSON 38, § 1

The leading soloist turned the composer round to face the public. This happened in Vienna, over a hundred years ago. The composer was deaf. He had grown deaf in his old age and did not hear the applause until the first soloist turned him round to face the public. The composer was Beethoven. They were performing his ninth symphony.

It is very difficult to turn the car round in this narrow place, but I always turn it round very carefully.

I have turned the mattresses over on the beds. They have turned the chairs upside down and placed them on the tables. Now, it is possible to turn round and start cleaning.

'Please wrap my sausage up well, wrap it up in this good piece of paper.'
'Citizen, we always wrap up the goods in the best paper. You need not worry, we'll wrap your sausage up properly.'

§ 5

Snowstorm

A snowstorm is a dense fall of snow accompanied by a wind of storm force. The snow, falling and lying on the ground, is in constant circular motion. In the daytime everything is white and at two paces nothing can be seen, as during thick London fogs. But at night visibility is even worse. Traffic along the great main highways is seriously impeded. At such a time the side-roads are completely snowed up, because the landmarks (tall fir-branches), which are put up at the sides of the roads, are knocked down by the strong wind and covered by snow.

A snowstorm in the Southern Urals is violent (lit. 'strong'). It begins suddenly. Fine snow falls at first, then this is succeeded by large snowflakes. The wind, with increasing force, turns into a whirlwind – it howls, whistles, whirls the falling snow, lifting huge white columns of snow from the ground. It grows dark. Nothing can be seen in the snowy gloom.

The landscape is vast. Settlements are situated five kilometres and more apart. The inhabitants lay down short winter roads across the swamps and rivers, which freeze in the month of November and are covered with snow. It is fun to be out visiting but it is time (to go) home. The rested horses have gone swiftly through a small birch copse. But the sky looks rather lowering; low clouds hang down and quickly thicken into storm-clouds; a wind has got up. All at once fine snow has begun to fall. Suddenly it has been replaced by large snowflakes. The wind has begun to blow with such force that the horses find it difficult to run. Everything has become confused in a white whirlwind. Nothing can be seen in the dark. There's only a howling in your ears and the sharp stinging wind striking your face with furious strength, burning it. You catch your breath. The travellers, warmly dressed in sheep-skin coats and felt-boots, feel the wind piercing to their bones. You cannot look – the snow strikes at your face with lightning speed. The howling of the blizzard drowns the words of the person sitting next to you.

'Well, it's now clear that we've lost our way' flashed through everybody's head.

They quickly leap out of the sledge. They shake heaps of snow off them-selves. They jump up and down to warm themselves up. The horses stand – they feel that they have left firm ground. The travellers help the horses by pushing the sledge. The horses, knowing that the reins are slack, that they are not being guided, have difficulty in getting out and start to search for the road themselves.

In those regions they know that during a snowstorm a horse will find the road home itself by feeling with its hooves the firm, well-trodden strip of the road-surface.

Now one horse stumbles and stops. But one must keep moving, one must not stand for long. The horses themselves strain forward. Progress becomes slower and slower: you drag one foot out – the other sinks in the deep snow. The travellers begin to shout: A-ooo! A-ooo! Perhaps there is a settlement nearby? The blizzard drowns their voices. Darkness sets in. The gloom in front deepens ('thickens').

The sensitive horses, sensing the proximity of house and dwelling, suddenly tear forcefully forward. They are hot, steam is rising from them, but the snowstorm has still not abated.

'What's that? Is that someone shouting?'

Sounds come nearer and nearer. Is that a dark shape there? Laughter is heard in the darkness and then there's a light.

'Hot, eh? There's a snowstorm for you! What a fine one!'

There are people just alongside, on horseback, with lanterns and sticks in their hands. They (have come out to) meet the returning visitors.

'Are we far from the village? And are we on the road?'

'Your horses are going (in the) right (direction) and it's only five hundred metres from home.'

We reached home amid noisy laughter.

All night the blizzard rages but people comfortably wait it out in their snug, warm houses. And in the morning the picture is different. Sun and frost. A magnificent morning. There is such silence all round that it is hard to believe that the snowstorm raged all night. The snow glistens in waves and dazzling whiteness in the bright rays of the sun. Just as in a fairy-tale, the firs and pines stand in white finery.

Grown-ups and children set about clearing the roads. Tractors and bull-dozers have come out. The children are sledging and rolling about in the powdery snow. The snow crunches pleasantly under your felt-boots and the frost reddens your cheeks. Not far off is the tempting dark shape of the wood.

'To your skis! Into the wood!' the children shout.

The Russian loves his beautiful winter, with her snowstorms and her invigorating frost.

§ 6

Путешéствуя по Совéтскому Сою́зу, я ви́дел мнóго интерéсных вещéй. Сопровождáемый óчень умéлой перевóдчицей, я смог познакóмиться с людьми́, живу́щими в весьма́ разли́чных усло́виях.

На востóке я был на ещё стро́ящейся гидростáнции. Громáдные глы́бы земли́, вырывáемые бульдóзерами, дли́нные стальны́е бáлки, поднимáемые высóкими крáнами, рабóчие, бéгающие туда́-сюда́, молоды́е инженéры, стоя́щие с плáнами в рукáх и оживлённо обсуждáющие ход рабóты, – всё э́то произвелó на меня́ незабывáемое впечатлéние.

Возвращáясь в Москву́, мы посети́ли колхóз, находя́щийся недалекó от гóрода, и там я разговáривал со стáрым крестья́нином. Расскáзывая нам о жи́зни крестья́н и вспоминáя слу́чаи из воéнного и послевоéнного перио́да, он сказáл, что во мнóгом жизнь крестья́нина стáла горáздо лу́чше.

В Москвé самóй я познакóмился с молоды́м писáтелем, пóльзующимся ширóкой популя́рностью у молодёжи. Он познакóмил меня́ с други́ми писáтелями и худóжниками, мы́слящими на нóвый лад. Разговáривая об иску́сстве и литератýре, мы нашли́, что есть в нáших взгля́дах бóльше объединя́ющего нас, чем отделя́ющего нас друг от дру́га.

Отправля́ясь домóй, я обещáл сопровождáющим меня́ друзья́м верну́ться в Совéтский Сою́з в ближáйшем бу́дущем.

Attacked from all sides, we shall still defend our positions.
Preceded by a brass band, the miners were marching into the park.

§ 5

– Его́ уво́лили.
– Да нет, не мо́жет быть!
– Да, да, его́ уво́лили, ста́ршего счетово́да уво́лили. Вчера́ его́ уво́лили.
– И касси́р то́же бу́дет уво́лен – его́ уво́лят за́втра.

У нас отнима́ют кусо́к земли́. Вот весь э́тот кусо́к отни́мут у нас. У нас уже́ два го́да тому́ наза́д земля́ была́ отнята́. Вот тот кусо́к, где постро́или шко́лу, о́тняли у нас два го́да тому́ наза́д. Сказа́ли нам, что там постро́ят больни́цу, а была́ постро́ена шко́ла. Тепе́рь хо́дят слу́хи, что и на той стороне́ бу́дут стро́ить шко́лу, а нам больни́ца нужна́ – шко́ла уже́ есть.
Тут хо́дят ра́зные слу́хи. Разнесли́ слух, что бу́дет постро́ена не шко́ла а гидроэлектри́ческая ста́нция, вот каки́е слу́хи тут хо́дят.

Дя́дю Са́шу ра́нили во вре́мя второ́й мирово́й войны́, он был ра́нен в ру́ку и в спи́ну, а его́ отца́ уби́ли во вре́мя пе́рвой мирово́й войны́, он был уби́т в боя́х в Карпа́тах.

§ 6

Fishing under the Ice

A frosty winter's day. The vast snowy plain is flooded in sunshine. Around, wherever you look, groups of people are sitting on boxes.
Why such a strange scene?
They are anglers, amateurs of fishing under the ice. They have come here, to *Bolshaya Volga* – a reservoir formed after the river was blocked by the dam for a hydro-electric station. The majority of them are from Moscow, though it is 130 kilometres from the capital to here. There are very many fish of different species here.
There are other reservoirs, some of them very near to Moscow. But the keen fishermen are attracted to the open expanses of the Volga.
They drive straight over the ice in cars and big buses and take up their positions wherever the fish bite best.
In winter fish are caught under the ice by rod in the following way.
First of all, having kicked away the snow all around, you have to break in the ice which a hole is called a *lunka*. The thick (not less than two feet) and very strong ice, holding big buses with forty anglers on board, is bored through with a special bore or is broken through with a special iron implement.
Its end is sharp and it has a wooden handle with a loop of string at the end.

You put this loop on your hand so that the tool will not jump out of your hand and sink under the ice. When you are breaking the *lunka*, the pieces of ice are thrown out with a special angler's spoon that has holes in it for the water to flow through.

The last blows – and the water, having burst out, fills the whole *lunka* in a moment. Its size is such that you can pull out a large fish.

Now you must prepare the rod. The angler gets it out of a special box, into which the fish is put afterwards. You sit on the box too, for the fishing lasts several hours. The rod is very short – about two feet in all. A line – several metres in length, depending on the depth – is reeled off. At the end of the line is a small hook with a sinker in the form of a pellet soldered on to it. One or two maggots must be put on to the point of the hook. These are red maggots, about two centimetres in length – larvae of the mosquito. They are sold by fishing-tackle suppliers. You have to keep the box of maggots in your pocket, otherwise they can quickly freeze.

Everything is in order. We can start. The hook and the thin nylon line are lowered to the bottom. Then the angler starts to lift it slowly, shaking it gently and rhythmically with his hand, – but not more than half a metre. Then he lowers it again and repeats the movement. The live red maggots, shaken by the line, are a fine bait. A small rubber float is attached to the end of the little rod on a springy wire. As soon as a fish bites, the float will immediately be tugged down. Then you must pull quickly.

So, here on the snow glittering in the sun appears the first perch. It stands out sharply against the white background because of its red fins and variegated colouring. Another follows it. A good catch is four to five kilograms of fish in several hours.

Suddenly something happens. Many of the anglers jump up from their boxes and run over to one side, where an old man – an experienced angler – is sitting. He has just pulled an enormous pike out of the water. Yes, you won't catch one like that on a small hook, with a maggot. The old man fishes by a different method. He brings with him about two dozen small fish in a bucket of water. They are called live-bait. He carefully pierces their lips with a hook and puts them in the water on a long, strong line. Up above, by the *lunka*, the old man puts in the snow a stick on which he places a line with a red pennant attached to it. He brings not less than ten of these rods with him. Then he walks up and down by these sticks and watches for a pennant to fall. It falls when a large fish has taken and dragged the live bait. You have to jerk the line quickly to hook the fish and pull.

Professional anglers fish in winter with nets which they place out skilfully under the ice.

§ 7

Пое́хав по́ездом из Эдинбу́рга в Ло́ндон, мы полете́ли в Москву́ на самолёте. Делега́ты, прие́хавшие ра́ньше в Ло́ндон, уже́ уе́хали. Они́ поéхали на парохóде в Ленингрáд и, проведя́ там полторá дня, они́ полетéли в Москву́.

Мы прилетéли на аэропóрт пóздно нóчью. Среди́ людéй, приéхавших встречáть нас, был Вави́лов, посети́вший мой завóд в прóшлом году́. Поздорóвавшись, мы поéхали в Москву́ на маши́не.

Хотя́ бы́ло ужé пóздно, нáши хозя́ева, ждáвшие нас бóльше двух часóв, настáивали на том, чтóбы мы пообéдали. Пообéдав, мы срáзу легли́ спать. На другóй день, встав рáно, мы поéхали в Министéрство.

Собрáвшиеся управля́ющие и инженéры ждáли нас. Нáши переговóры продолжáлись три дня. Придя́ к соглашéнию, мы провели́ ещё три дня в Москвé, посещáя теáтры и вы́ставки. В послéдний день, купи́в подáрки наканýне, мы поéхали на аэропóрт. Мой друг Вави́лов опя́ть был среди́ провожáющих нас.

Вы́летев из аэропóрта в оди́ннадцать часóв утрá, мы бы́ли в Лóндоне в три часá дня.

Our family – Nina, Vera, Petya, Aunt Liza – appeared in your lessons without explanation and disappeared without explanation in the same way, rather like characters in modern plays or modern French novels and films. But you will find the explanation of their short and often confused life in grammar.

Recommended Reading

There are now many handbooks available for the study of Russian. Some of them are mentioned below.

GRAMMARS

If you want to work through another beginners' grammar you will find the following very useful:

N. POTAPOVA *Russian* (two vols., Foreign Languages Publishing House, Moscow).

J. L. I. FENNELL *The Penguin Russian Course* (Penguin Books). A revised version of the preceding work shortened to one volume.

A. SEMEONOFF *A New Russian Grammar* (Dent). A well proved grammar, now in its thirteenth edition.

K. BROOKE and J. FORSYTH *Russian through Reading* (Hutchinson). A book which gives continuous prose passages from the very beginning and introduces you to the grammar by deducing it for you from the texts.

S. C. BOYANUS and N. B. JOPSON *Spoken Russian* (Sidgwick & Jackson). As well as explanations of the grammar, contains several hundred illustrative sentences in good colloquial Russian, each with phonetic transcription.

REFERENCE GRAMMARS

I. M. PULKINA *A Short Russian Reference Grammar* (Foreign Languages Publishing House, Moscow). A rapid reference grammar in rules and tables.

B. O. UNBEGAUN *Russian Grammar* (Clarendon Press). The fullest description in English of Russian grammar.

SYNTAX AND USAGE

F. M. BORRAS and R. F. CHRISTIAN *Russian Syntax* (Clarendon Press). Deals with all the problems of expression which face you after you have learnt the basic grammar.

READERS

M. GREENE and D. WARD *Graded Russian Reader*, I, II and III (Oliver and Boyd). Parts I and II have passages of elementary to intermediate standard arranged in sets, each set illustrating a point of grammar. Part III consists of annotated passages from Russian literature.

PETER NORMAN and ARIADNE NICOLAEFF *Russian Readings* (BBC). Long continuous passages from nineteenth and twentieth century authors with stressed text, facing translation and notes on the authors. Written to accompany a series of broadcast lessons but can be read independently.

D. WARD *Keep Up Your Russian* (Harraps). A revised edition of a book first written to accompany a series of broadcast lessons. Short stressed texts from nineteenth and twentiety century authors, with vocabulary, detailed grammar notes and additional special vocabularies.

R. HINGLEY *Soviet Prose* (Allen and Unwin). An advanced reader – extracts from Soviet authors, with introduction, notes and select vocabulary.

Harrap Bilingual Series – Russian. A collection of pocket-size books with stressed texts from well-known authors and translation on facing page.

Bradda Books (see below) have a steadily increasing series of annotated editions of standard works.

PRONUNCIATION

S. C. BOYANUS *Russian Pronunciation* (Lund Humphries). A short but complete description, using the International Phonetic Alphabet, of the phonetics of Russian, with a section on intonation.

S. C. BOYANUS *Russian Phonetic Reader* (Lund Humphries). Short Russian passages with phonetic transcriptions and intonation diagrams, and an introduction on spelling and its relation to pronunciation. (These two works can be bought separately or in one volume.)

D. WARD *Russian Pronunciation – a practical course* (Oliver and Boyd). A progressive guide through the difficulties of Russian pronunciation, pre-supposing no previous knowledge of phonetics and using the letters of the Russian alphabet for phonetic transcription.

Áнгло-рýсский разговóрник and Рýсско-англи́йский разговóрник (Foreign Languages Publishing House, Moscow). Two phrase books for the traveller, arranged according to subject (theatre, hotel, trains etc.).

I. B. FADEN *A Book of Russian Idioms* (Methuen). A short collection of some common idioms.

LAPIDUS and SHEVTSOVA *Russian–English Dictionary for the Foreign Student* (Moscow, 1962). 10,000 entries. (At the time of going to press a companion English–Russian volume is said to be 'shortly available').

O. S. AKHMANOVA *English–Russian Dictionary* and *Russian–English Dictionary* (Moscow). Each contains 25,000 entries.

V. K. MÜLLER *English–Russian Dictionary* (Moscow). 70,000 entries.

A. I. SMIRNITSKY *Russian–English Dictionary* (Moscow). 50,000 entries. You should note that this is designed for Russian students of English and therefore may lack some of the information you need.

L. SEGAL *Russian–English Dictionary* and *English–Russian Dictionary* (Lund Humphries). About 50,000 entries in each.

The following three publishers and booksellers specialize in Russian books and will be able to give you information about prices and availability of the above and other works:

Bradda Books, Ltd., 4 Watford Way, Hendon Central, London, N.W. 4.

Collet's Russian Bookshop, 44–5 Museum Street, London, W.C. 1.

Bailey Bros. and Swinfen, Ltd., Hyde House, West Central Street, W.C. 1.

Vocabulary

RUSSIAN-ENGLISH

Normally in an imperfective/perfective pair of verbs the imperfective aspect is given first without indication. If the perfective aspect is used in lessons before the imperfective, the perfective is given first and this is indicated.

а but, and; **а то,** otherwise
абажу́р lampshade
абба́тство abbey
абстраги́ровать to abstract
а́вгуст August
автобус bus
автомоби́ль (*m.*) motor-car
а́втор author
адмира́л admiral
адмиралте́йский admiralty
а́дрес (*nom. pl.* **адреса́**) address
адресова́ть to address
аккомпанеме́нт accompaniment
аккура́тно neatly, precisely
актёр actor
Алекса́ндр Alexander
алле́я avenue
альпини́зм mountaineering
Аме́рика America
америка́нец American
америка́нка American (woman)
америка́нский American
анализи́ровать to analyse
англи́йский English
англича́нин Englishman
англича́нка Englishwoman
анке́та questionnaire
А́нна Ann(a)
А́ня Ann(a)
апре́ль (*m.*) April
апте́ка chemist's shop
Арара́т Ararat
арифме́тика arithmetic
артиллери́йский artillery
арти́ст artiste
Арту́р Arthur
архите́ктор architect
астроно́мия astronomy
атакова́ть attack
а́тлас atlas
а то otherwise
а́том atom
афи́ша poster
А́фрика Africa
аэродро́м aerodrome
аэропо́рт airport

ба́ба peasant woman, 'Gran'ma'
бага́ж luggage

бал ball
баланси́ровать to balance
балери́на ballerina
балко́н balcony
банди́т bandit
банк bank
ба́нка can, jar
банки́р banker
ба́ня bath(-house)
бараба́н drum
бара́н ram
бара́ний lamb, mutton (*adj.*)
бара́нина lamb, mutton
бас bass
баскетбо́л basketball
бассе́йн basin, pool
башма́к shoe
бе́гать to run *indet.*, **бежа́ть** *det.*
бегу́щий running
беда́ misfortune; it's a pity
бе́дный poor
бедня́к poor person
бедро́ hip
безлу́нный moonless
белизна́ whiteness
бе́лый white; *as noun*: white man
бельги́ец Belgian (man)
бельги́йка Belgian (woman)
бельги́йский Belgian
Бе́льгия Belgium
бельё linen, washing
бе́рег (*loc.* **б-у́**) shore, bank
берегово́й bank, of the bank/shore
берёза birch
берёзовый birch
беспоко́йный disturbed, worried
беспоря́док (*gen.* **б-ка**) disorder
бе́шеный mad, furious
библиоте́ка library
бидо́н(чик) small bucket
биле́т ticket
бискви́т cake
битко́м наби́то crowded out, full up
бить to beat, to strike; **бить молот-ко́м** to hammer
благополу́чно right, all right, happily
блеск glitter
блесте́ть (*2nd conj.*) to shine
бли́же (*comp. of* **бли́зкий**) nearer

бли́зкий near
близне́ц twin
бли́зость (*f.*) proximity, nearness
блин pancake
блиста́ть to sparkle
блу́зка blouse, smock
блю́дечко saucer
боб bean
бога́тый rich
бога́ч rich man
бодри́ть to stimulate, to invigorate
бо́дрый cheerful
бодря́щий bracing
бо́же good Lord, goodness
бой battle
бок side; бо́ком sideways
болга́рин Bulgarian (man)
Болга́рия Bulgaria
болга́рка Bulgarian (woman)
болга́рский Bulgarian
бо́лее more
боле́знь (*f.*) illness, disease
боле́ть, за- to be ill (*1st conj.* боле́ю,
 боле́ешь); to hurt (*2nd conj.* боли́т,
 боля́т)
боло́то swamp, bog
больни́ца hospital
больно́й sick, ill; *as noun*: patient, sick
 person
бо́льше more, bigger
большинство́ most, majority
бо́мба bomb
бомбарди́ро́вщик bomber
борза́я borzoi, Russian wolf-hound
бормота́нье mumbling, muttering,
 grumbling
бормота́ть (бормочу́, бормо́чешь)
 to mumble, to mutter, to grumble
борода́тый bearded
борт ship's side; на борту́ on board
борщ *borshch* (beetroot soup)
боязли́вый timid
боя́ться (+ *gen.*) to be afraid (of), to
 fear
брак marriage
брат (*nom. pl.* бра́тья) brother
брать (беру́, берёшь), взять *pfv.*
 (возьму́, возьмёшь) to take
бревно́ log
брига́да brigade
брить (бре́ю, бре́ешь), по- to shave
бри́ться, по- to have a shave
бродя́га tramp
броса́ться, бро́ситься to hurl oneself
бро́сить *pfv.*, броса́ть *impfv.* to throw
брю́ки trousers
буди́ть, раз- to wake, to rouse
бу́дка booth, kennel

бу́дто as if, as though
бу́дущий future; бу́дущее the future
бу́ква letter
буке́т bouquet
бу́лка loaf of white bread, roll
бульва́р boulevard
бульдо́зер bulldozer
бума́га paper
бума́жка (small) piece of paper
бутербро́д sandwich, slice of bread and
 butter
буты́лка bottle
буфе́т buffet
бухгалте́рия book-keeping, counting-
 house
бушева́ть to rage
бы (б) conditional particle, see Lesson
 30, § 2
быва́ть to be (frequently)
бы́вший former
бык bull
бы́стрый swift; *adv.* бы́стро swiftly
быт mode of life, manners and customs,
 every-day existence
быть to be
бюро́ office

в (+ *acc.* and *prep.*) in, on, at
ваго́н waggon, carriage
ва́кса (shoe) polish
ва́ленки (*gen. pl.* ва́ленок) felt boots
вальс waltz
валю́та currency
валя́ться to lie about, to roll
ва́нна bath
ва́нная, ~ ко́мната bathroom
варе́нье jam
Варша́ва Warsaw
ватт watt
ваш, -а, -е, -и your
вверх up, upwards
вводи́ть, ввести́ to lead in, to introduce
ввоз importation
ввози́ть, ввезти́ to import, to bring in
вдруг suddenly
ведро́ bucket
ведь why, you know
ве́ер fan
везде́ everywhere
везти́ *det.* to cart, to convey
век lifetime, century
вели́кий great, big
Великобрита́ния Great Britain
величина́ size
велосипе́д bicycle
Ве́на Vienna
ве́ра faith, belief
верёвка rope, string

верёвочный of rope

ве́рить, по- to believe (+ *dat.*), to believe in (в + *acc.*)

ве́рно right, correct, true

верну́ть *pfv.*, возвраща́ть *impfv.* to return, to give back

верну́ться *pfv.*, возвраща́ться *impfv.* to return, to come back

ве́рный true, faithful, correct

верте́ть to turn, spin

ве́рхний upper

верхо́м on horseback

вес weight

ве́село merrily, gaily

весе́нний spring('s)

весна́ spring, весно́й in spring

вести́ to lead, to bring

весь, вся, всё, все all

ветвь (*f.*) branch

ве́тка branch

ветчина́ ham

ве́ха landmark

ве́чер evening; ве́чером in the evening

вечери́нка evening-party

вече́рний evening('s)

ве́чный eternal

ве́шалка coat-hanger, peg

ве́ять to blow

взве́шивать, взве́сить to weigh

взволно́ванно excitedly

взволнова́ться *pfv.*, волнова́ться *impfv.* to be excited

взгляну́ть *pfv.*, взгля́дывать *impfv.* to look

вздорожа́ть *pfv.*, дорожа́ть *impfv.* to go up, to rise (of prices)

взлета́ть, взлете́ть to fly up

взро́слый adult, grown-up

вид view, aspect, form, type, species

вида́ть to see (usually only *infin.* or *past tense*, after *negative*)

ви́деть to see

ви́димость (*f.*) visibility

ви́димый visible

ви́дно can be seen

ви́дный outstanding

визжа́ть (*2nd conj.*) to squeal

ви́лка fork

вина́ blame

вино́ wine

винова́тый guilty, at fault

висе́ть (*2nd conj.*) to hang

ви́ски whisky

вихрь (*m.*) whirlwind

вклад contribution

вку́сно tasty, tastily

власть (*f.*) authority, power

влеза́ть, влезть to climb in

влия́ние influence

влюби́ться *pfv.*, влюбля́ться *impfv.* to fall in love (with в + *acc.*)

вме́сте with, together with

вме́сто (+ *gen.*) instead of

внача́ле at the beginning, at first

вне (+ *gen.*) out of

внеза́пно suddenly

внести́ *pfv.*, вноси́ть *impfv.* to bring in

вниз down, downstairs (motion)

внима́тельно attentively

вновь again

внук grandson

вну́чка grand-daughter

во вре́мя (+ *gen.*) during

во́время in time

вода́ water

во́дка vodka

водоём reservoir, water-basin

водоро́д hydrogen

водохрани́лище reservoir

вое́нный military, war (time)

во́жжи reins

возврати́ть to return

возвраща́ться, верну́ться to return, to come back

во́здух air

возрази́ть *pfv.*, возража́ть *impfv.* to retort, to object

вой moan

войти́ *pfv.*, входи́ть *impfv.* to go in, come in

вокза́л station

вол ox

во́лжский Volga, of the Volga

волк wolf

волна́ wave

во́лос hair

волочи́ться to drag

во́лчий wolf, wolf's

во́льно freely

вообража́ть, вообрази́ть to imagine

вообще́ in general

воробе́й (*gen.* воробья́) sparrow

воро́на crow

воро́та (*nom. pl.*) gate

вороти́ться *pfv.* to return

воротни́к collar

ворча́ть to grumble

во́семь eight

воскресе́нье Sunday

воспита́ние up-bringing

восто́к east; на восто́к to the east; на восто́ке in the east

восходи́ть, взойти́ to rise (sun)

вот here is/are, there is/are, that's it

вперёд forward(s)

впереди́ in front

вприпры́жку with a jump, skipping

враг enemy

вратарь (*m.*) goalkeeper

время (*gen.* времени) time

всё everything; all the time, always, constantly, steadily. всё + *comparative* = more and more

всё ещё still

всегда always

всего in all, altogether

вселенная universe

всё-таки still, yet, nevertheless

вскакивать, вскочить to jump up

вслух aloud

вспомнить *pfv.*, вспоминать and помнить *impfv.* to recall, to recollect

вставать, встать to get up

встретиться *pfv.*, встречаться *impfv.* to meet

встречать, встретить to meet

всюду everywhere

всякий any, each

вторник Tuesday

вход entrance

вцепляться, вцепиться to seize, to get hold of

вчера yesterday

въезд drive-in, (carriage) entrance

въезжать, въехать to drive in

выбираться, выбраться to get out

выбор choice

выборный election (*adj.*)

выбрать *pfv.*, выбирать *impfv.* to pick out, to choose

выбросить *pfv.*, выбрасывать *impfv.* to throw away, to throw out

выводить, вывести to lead out

вывозить, вывезти to export, to convey out

выглядеть to look, to seem

выгружать, выгрузить to unload

выдавать, выдать to betray, to give away, to give out

выделяться, выделиться to stand out

выдерживать, выдержать to endure, to bear

выдумать *pfv.*, выдумывать *impfv.* to invent, to think up

выезд exit

выезжать *indet.*, выехать *det.* to leave, to drive out

вызвать *pfv.*, вызывать *impfv.* to call forth, to provoke, to cause

выиграть *pfv.*, выигрывать *impfv.* to win

выйти *pfv.*, выходить *impfv.* to go/come out; to succeed, to have a successful outcome

выкурить *pfv.* to smoke up (all the cigarettes)

вылезать, вылезть to climb out

вымести *pfv.*, выметать *impfv.* to sweep out

вымыть (вымою, вымоешь) *pfv.*, вымывать *impfv.* to wash out, to wash thoroughly

выносить, вынести to carry out

выпасть *pfv.*, выпадать *impfv.* to fall out

выпить *pfv.*, пить *impfv.* to drink

выражать, выразить to express

вырваться *pfv.*, вырываться *impfv.* to burst out, to tear oneself free

выручать, выручить to rescue, to relieve

вырывать, вырвать to tear out

высказать *pfv.*, высказывать *impfv.* to express, to speak out

выскакивать, выскочить to jump out, to hop out

высокий high

высохнуть *pfv.*, сохнуть *impfv.* to get dry

выставка exhibition

выстрел shot

высший superior, higher, supreme

вытащить *pfv.*, вытаскивать *impfv.* to drag out, to pull out

выть (вою, воешь) to howl

выучиться *pfv.*, учиться *impfv.* (+ *dat.*) to learn

выход exit, way out

вычесть *pfv.*, вычитать *impfv.* to subtract

вычистить *pfv.*, чистить *impfv.* to clean

вьюга snowstorm, blizzard

вязать (вяжу, вяжешь) to bind, to knit

гавань (*f.*) harbour

гадкий horrid

газ gas

газета newspaper

газетчик, газетчица newspaper-seller, newsagent

галка jackdaw

галстук tie

гамаши gaiters

гараж garage

гаснуть, по- to go out, to dim, to be extinguished

где where

Германия Germany

германский German, as in Г-ая Демократическая Республика German Democratic Republic

гибкий supple

гибнуть, по- to perish, to be lost

гидроэлектри́ческий hydro-electric
гидроэлектроста́нция hydro-electric station
гла́вный main
глаго́л verb
глубина́ depth
глубо́кий deep
глу́пенький stupid
глу́пость (f.) stupidity
глуха́рь (m.) capercaillie
глухо́й deaf; a deaf person
глуши́ть, за- to choke, to stifle
глы́ба block
гляде́ть to look
гнать (гоню́, го́нишь) det., гоня́ть indet. to drive, to chase
гнуть to fold, to bend
го́вор talk; dialect
говори́тся it is said
говори́ть, по- to speak, to talk
говори́ть, сказа́ть to say, to tell
год (loc. году́, nom. pl. года́ and го́ды) year
гол goal
голки́шер goalkeeper
голла́ндец Dutchman
Голла́ндия Holland
голла́ндка Dutchwoman
голла́ндский Dutch
голова́ head
головомо́йка dressing down
го́лод hunger, famine
голода́ть, про- to go hungry
го́лодно hungrily
голо́дный hungry
го́лос (nom. pl. голоса́) voice
гольф golf
гора́ mountain, hill
гора́здо much (with comparatives)
го́рдость (f.) pride
горе́ть to burn
го́рло throat
го́род (nom. pl. города́) town; за́_городом out of town
городо́к (gen. –дка́) little town
горо́х peas
горшо́к (gen. горшка́) pot
го́рький bitter
го́спиталь (m.) hospital (usually military)
гости́ная drawing-room, living-room
гости́ница hotel
гость (m.) guest
госуда́рство state
гото́вить, при- to prepare, to cook
гото́вый ready
град hail
граждани́н, гражда́нка citizen
грамм gram

грамма́тика grammar
грани́т granite
грани́ца frontier, за грани́цу abroad (motion), за грани́цей abroad (location)
гра́фик graph
графи́чески graphically
гребешо́к (gen. –шка́) comb
грек Greek (man)
греть, ото- to warm
гре́ться, ото- to warm oneself
Гре́ция Greece
греча́нка Greek (woman)
гре́ческий Greek
гриб mushroom
гроб coffin, grave
грози́ть (+ dat.) to threaten
гром thunder
грома́да enormous mass
грома́дный enormous
гро́мкий loud; гро́мко loudly
груби́ть to be rude, to utter coarse words
груз weight, load, sinker
грузи́ть, на- to load
грузови́к lorry
гру́ппа group
грусти́ть to grieve
гру́стный sad
грязну́ля grubby creature
гря́зный dirty
губа́ lip
гул dull, humming noise
гуля́ть to stroll, to go for a walk
ГУМ State Stores
густо́й thick, dense

да yes, and; да так well
давно́ long ago
давны́м давно́ long, long ago
да́же even
далёкий far, distant
да́ма lady
да́мба dam, dike
Да́ния Denmark
да́нный given
да́ром for nothing, in vain
да́тский Danish
датча́нин, датча́нка Dane
дать pfv., дава́ть impfv. to give (see Lessons 3, § 3; 9, § 5; 12, § 1)
да́ча dacha (country house, cottage)
два /две two
два́дцать twenty
двена́дцать twelve
дверь (f.) door
две́сти two hundred
дви́гать (дви́жу, дви́жешь and дви́гаю, дви́гаешь) to move

дви́гаться to move (oneself)
движе́ние motion, movement, traffic
дво́е two
двор yard; на дворе́ outside
дворе́ц (gen. дворца́) palace
дво́рник janitor
дева́ть, деть to put
де́вочка girl
девяно́сто ninety
де́вять nine
девятьсо́т nine hundred
дед grandfather
Дед-моро́з Father Christmas
де́душка grandfather
действи́тельно really
де́лать, с- to do
де́латься, с- to happen, to go on; to
  become, to be made
дели́ть, раз-, от- to divide
де́ло affair, business; thing; в са́мом
  де́ле indeed; на са́мом де́ле in
  (very) fact; де́ло в том, что the
  point is
демократи́ческий democratic
день (gen. дня) day
де́ньги money
дере́вня village, country
де́рево tree
деревя́нный wooden
держа́вный sovereign, powerful
держа́ть (2nd conj.) to hold
дёрнуться pfv., дёргаться impfv. to
  be tugged
деся́ток (gen. -тка) 'dozen' (lit. a ten)
де́сять ten
детвора́ children
де́ти (pl. of ребёнок) children
дети́на lad
де́тский children's; ~ сад kinder-
  garten
деть pfv., дева́ть impfv. to put
де́ться pfv., дева́ться impfv. to be
  put, to go to
дешёвый cheap
дива́н settee, sofa
ди́вно marvellous
ди́во marvel
ди́кий wild
дире́ктор director, headmaster
длина́ length
дли́нный long
дневно́й day('s)
днём in the daytime
до (+ gen.) up to, till; ему́ не до...
  he has no time for . . .
доба́вить pfv., добавля́ть impfv. to
  add
добира́ться, добра́ться до (+ gen.)
  to reach, to get to

доводи́ть, довести́ to lead / take up to
дово́льно enough, somewhat
дово́льный satisfied, pleased
доезжа́ть, дое́хать to go / come up to,
  to reach (not on foot)
дожда́ться pfv., дожида́ться impfv.
  (+ gen.) to wait for
дождеви́к raincoat
дождь (m.) rain; ~ идёт it is raining
дока́зывать, доказа́ть to prove
докла́д lecture, report, paper
до́ктор (nom. pl. -á) doctor
долг duty, debt
до́лго (for) a long time
до́лжен, должна́, должно́, должны́
  must (see Lesson 26, § 7); owe
должно́ быть probably, it must be so,
  I suppose
до́ля portion
дом (nom. pl. дома́) house, home;
  до́ма at home; домо́й home(wards)
дома́шний domestic
домо́й home(wards)
домрабо́тница domestic help
доро́га road
дорого́й dear
до свида́ния goodbye
доска́ board, plank
достава́ть, доста́ть to get
доходи́ть, дойти́ (до + gen.) to go / come
  up to, to reach
дочь (gen. до́чери) daughter; до́чка
  (familiar)
дощёчка name-plate
дразни́ть to tease
дра́ка quarrel, fight
дра́ма drama
дрема́ть to doze, to drowse
дроби́нка pellet
дробь (f.) shot
дрова́ (nom. pl.) (fire)wood
дрожа́ть, дро́гнуть to tremble
друг (nom. pl. друзья́) friend
друг дру́га one another, each other (see
  Lesson 28, § 7)
друго́й another
дру́жба friendship
дружи́ть to be / make friends with
дру́жный harmonious, in accord
дуб oak
ду́мать to think
дура́к fool
дурно́й bad; ему́ ду́рно he feels bad
дуть to blow
дух (nom. pl. ду́хи) spirit
духи́ perfume
духово́й орке́стр brass band
ду́шечка my dear, sweetheart
души́стый fragrant

ду́шный stuffy, hot
дым smoke
дыра́ hole
ды́рка (small) hole
дыха́ние breathing, breath
дыша́ть (2nd conj.) to breathe
дю́жина dozen
дюйм inch
дя́дя uncle

Евро́па Europe
е́герь (m.) huntsman
его́ his
еда́ food, meal
едва́ hardly; едва́ не nearly
её her('s)
ёж hedgehog
ежеча́сно hourly, every hour
е́здить indet., е́хать det. to go (not on foot)
е́ле hardly, scarcely
Еле́на Helen
Елизаве́та, Ли́за, Ли́зочка Elizabeth, Beth, Liz etc.
ело́вый of fir, fir
ель (f.) fir-tree
Ерма́к Yermak (name of Soviet icebreaker after Cossack leader of 16th century)
ерунда́ nonsense
е́сли if
есть is, there is, there are
есть to eat (see Lessons 3, § 3; 9, § 5)
ещё more, still; ещё раз once more

жа́дный greedy
жале́ть, по- to be sorry
жа́лость (f.) pity
жаль it's a pity; with dat., as in ему́ жаль he feels sorry
жара́ heat
жа́ркий, жа́рко hot
жать (жму, жмёшь) to press
ждать to wait
же emphatic particle
жела́нный desired
желе́зо iron
жена́ wife
жени́ться на (+ prep.) to marry (of a man)
живе́ц (gen. живца́) live bait
жи́во lively, alive
живо́й (a)live, lively
живо́т belly, abdomen
живо́тное animal
жизнь (f.) life
жиле́ц (gen. жильца́) lodger (male)
жили́чка lodger

жильё dwelling, house, habitation
жир fat
жи́рно fat(ty)
жи́тель (m.) inhabitant
жить (живу́, живёшь), про- to live
жму́рки blind man's buff
жужжа́ть (2nd conj.) to buzz, to hum
жук, dim. жучо́к (gen. жучка́) beetle
жура́вль (m.) crane

за behind, beyond (+ acc. motion, + inst. location); for, to fetch (+ instr.); in (+ acc. in expressions of time)
забасто́вка strike
забеспоко́иться pfv. to begin to be uneasy
заболе́ть pfv. to fall ill; to start to ache
забо́р fence
забо́та worry
забыва́ть, забы́ть to forget
забы́вчивый forgetful
заверте́ться pfv. start to turn
зави́довать (+ dat.) to envy
зави́симость (f.) dependence; в зави́симости от depending on
заво́д factory
заводи́ть, завести́ to take too far or to the wrong place; to wind up
заволнова́ться pfv. to get excited
завора́чивать, заверну́ть to wrap up
за́втра tomorrow
за́втракать, поза́втракать to lunch, to breakfast
завыва́ние howling
завы́ть pfv., выть impfv. to start howling
завя́зывать, завяза́ть to tie a knot, to knot
загла́вие title
загну́ть pfv., загиба́ть impfv. to fold over /back
заговори́ть pfv. to start talking
за грани́цей abroad (location)
за грани́цу abroad (motion)
зада́ча task, problem
задева́ть, заде́ть to touch, to brush against
задрема́ть to doze off
задрожа́ть pfv. to start trembling
заду́мчивый pensive
заезжа́ть, зае́хать (к + dat.) to call at, to call in on
зажига́ть, заже́чь to light
зажига́ться, заже́чься to be lit, to catch fire
зака́зывать, заказа́ть to order

зака́нчивать, зако́нчить to finish (something)

зака́нчиваться, зако́нчиться to (come to an) end

заключа́ть, заключи́ть to conclude

зако́н law

закопа́ть *pfv.* to bury, to fill in

закрича́ть *pfv.* to start shouting

закружи́ться *pfv.* to start to spin, twirl

закрыва́ть, закры́ть to close, to cover

закури́ть *pfv.* to start smoking, to light up

зал hall

заля́ять *pfv.* to start barking

залива́ть, зали́ть to flood

зама́нчивый tempting, alluring

замаскиро́ванный disguised, camouflaged

замерза́ть, замёрзнуть to freeze

замеша́тельство embarrassment

замира́ние standing still, 'freezing'

замира́ть, замере́ть to stand stockstill, to 'freeze'

замо́к (*gen.* **замка́**) lock

замолка́ть, замо́лкнуть and **замолча́ть** to fall silent

занима́ть, заня́ть to occupy; to borrow

занима́ться, заня́ться (+ *instr.*) to be occupied in, to study

заноси́ть, занести́ to take too far or to the wrong place; to leave or drop in passing; **~ сне́гом** to block with snow

за́нятый occupied

за́пад west

за́пах smell, scent

запа́чкать *pfv.*, **па́чкать** *impfv.* to stain, to dirty

запере́ть *pfv.* (**запру́, запрёшь, за́пер, заперла́**), **запира́ть** *impfv.* to lock

за́пертый locked

запе́ть *pfv.* to burst into song

запи́сывать, записа́ть to note down

запла́кать *pfv.* to start crying

запозда́ние belated arrival

заполня́ть, запо́лнить to fill up

запомина́ть, запо́мнить to memorise

запреща́ть, запрети́ть to forbid, to prohibit

запреща́ться to be forbidden

запряга́ть, запря́чь to harness

зары́ть *pfv.* to bury, to dig in

зарыча́ть *pfv.* to start roaring

заряжа́ть, заряди́ть to load

засмея́ться *pfv.* to burst out laughing

заснежённый snowed-up

заснежи́ть *pfv.*, **снежи́ть** *impfv.* to cover with snow

засну́ть *pfv.*, **засыпа́ть** *impfv.* to fall asleep

засо́хнуть *pfv.*, **со́хнуть** *impfv.* to get dry

застава́ть, заста́ть to find, to catch (someone in)

заставля́ть, заста́вить to compel

застуча́ть *pfv.* to start knocking

застыва́ть, засты́ть to freeze

зате́м then

затреща́ть *pfv.* to start cracking

затрудне́ние difficulty

затрудни́ть *pfv.*, **затрудня́ть** *impfv.* to hinder, to impede

захва́тывать, захвати́ть to catch, to seize

заходи́ть, зайти́ to set (sun)

заходи́ть, зайти́ (**к** + *dat.*) to visit, to call in, to drop in on

захоте́ть *pfv.* to want, to conceive a desire

зацепи́ть *pfv.*, **зацепля́ть** *impfv.* to gaff (fish)

заче́м why, for what purpose

зашага́ть *pfv.* to begin to march

за́яц (*gen.* **за́йца**) hare

звать (**зову́, зовёшь**), **позва́ть** to call

звезда́ star

звони́ть, позвони́ть to ring; to phone (+ *dat.*)

звоно́к (*gen.* **звонка́**) bell

звук sound

звуча́ть (*2nd conj.*) to sound

зда́ние building

здоро́ваться, поздоро́ваться to greet

здо́рово magnificently, very well

здра́вствуйте hello

зелёно-серебри́стый greenish-silver

зелёный green

землевладе́лец (*gen.* **землевладе́льца**) landowner

земля́ earth, land

зе́ркало mirror

зерно́ grain

зима́ winter; **зимо́й** in the winter

зи́мний winter('s)

зло evil

злой evil, wicked, malicious

знак sign, symbol

знако́мый acquaintance

знать to know

зна́чить to mean, to signify

зо́лото gold

золото́й golden

зо́нтик umbrella, sunshade

зри́тель (*m.*) spectator, viewer

зуб tooth

и and, also, too
и... и... both . . . and
игла́ needle
иго́лка needle
игра́ game
игра́ть to play
иде́я idea
идти́ *det.*, ходи́ть *indet.* to go on foot
из (+ *gen.*) out of, from
изве́стка lime
извиня́ть, извини́ть to pardon, to forgive
издева́ться (над + *instr.*) to scoff at, to make fun of
изменя́ться, измени́ться to change
изобрета́ть, изобрести́ to invent
изуча́ть to study
икра́ caviar
и́ли or
иль = и́ли
имени́ны name-day
и́менно just
иму́щество property
и́мя (*gen.* и́мени) name
ина́че otherwise
И́ндия India
индю́к turkey
иногда́ sometimes
ино́й other, one, (in *pl.*) some
иностра́нец (*gen.* -нца) foreigner
иностра́нный foreign
инсти́нкт instinct
интере́сный interesting
ирла́ндец (*gen.* ирла́ндца) Irishman
Ирла́ндия Ireland
ирла́ндка Irishwoman
ирла́ндский Irish
иска́ть (ищу́, и́щешь) to seek, to look for
и́скра spark
и́скренно sincerely
иску́сно skilfully
испа́нец (*gen.* -нца) Spaniard
Испа́ния Spain
испа́нка Spanish woman
испа́нский Spanish
исправля́ть, испра́вить to mend, to correct
испуга́ть *pfv.*, пуга́ть *impfv.* to frighten
иссо́хнуть *pfv.*, со́хнуть *impfv.* to dry up
истребля́ть, истреби́ть to exterminate
исчеза́ть, исче́знуть to vanish, to disappear
ита́к (and) so
и так да́лее and so on, etc.
Ита́лия Italy
италья́нец (*gen.* -нца) Italian (man)

италья́нка Italian woman
италья́нский Italian
итти́ see идти́
их their
ию́ль July
ию́нь June

к (ко) (+ *dat.*) to, towards
каба́к pub
каби́на cabin
кабине́т study
Кавка́з Caucasus
ка́дка tub, vat
ка́ждый each, every
каза́ться to seem
как as, how; ∼ раз just; ∼ бы as if, 'sort of'; ∼ то́лько as soon as
како́й what kind of
како́й-то some . . . or other, some sort of
ка́к-то somehow
ка́ктус cactus
кали́тка gate
ка́мера chamber, cell
ками́н fire-place
кана́ва ditch
Кана́да Canada
кана́л canal
канаре́йка canary
кана́т rope
кани́кулы holidays
капита́л capital
капу́ста cabbage
каранда́ш pencil
карау́л guard, help!
каре́та carriage
карма́н pocket
ка́рта card, map, игра́ть в к-ы to play cards
карте́чь (*f.*) buck-shot, grape-shot
карти́на picture
карто́фель (*m.*) potatoes
ка́рточка (ration-)card, visiting-card
каса́ться, косну́ться (+ *gen.*) to touch
ка́сса (savings) bank, cash-desk, pay-box, box-office
касси́р cashier
ката́ть to roll
ката́ться to go for a ride
като́к (*gen.* катка́) skating rink
кату́шка reel
кача́ть, качну́ть to rock
кача́ться to swing
каю́та cabin
кварти́ра apartment
квас kvass (a drink)
кг (килогра́мм) kilogram
кида́ть, ки́нуть throw

килогра́мм kilogram
киломе́тр kilometre
кино́ cinema
кио́ск kiosk
кирпи́чный brick
кит whale
кита́ец (*gen.* кита́йца) Chinese (man)
Кита́й China
кита́йский Chinese
китая́нка Chinese woman
класс class
класть (кладу́, -ёшь), положи́ть to
　put, to place
клева́ть, клю́нуть to bite
клён maple
кле́тка cage
кло́ун clown
клуб club
кля́кса blot
кни́га book
кни́жка book(let)
ковёр carpet
когда́ when
колбаса́ sausage
колеба́ться (колеблю́сь, колеб-
　лешься) to hesitate, to waver
колле́га colleague
кольцо́ ring
колю́чий prickly, piercing
ком lump, clod
команди́р commander
кома́р mosquito
коме́та comet
ко́мик comedian
ко́мната room
комо́к small lump, bundle
компози́тор composer
конве́рт envelope
конво́й convoy
конду́ктор conductor
коне́ц end, в конце́ концо́в at last,
　finally
коне́чно of course
консе́рвы preserves, jams
конта́кт contact
конто́ра office
контраба́нда contraband
конфе́ты sweets
конце́рт concert
конча́ть, ко́нчить to finish
ко́нчиться *pfv.*, конча́ться *impfv.* to
　end
конь (*m.*) horse, steed
коню́шня stables
копа́ть to dig
ко́пия copy
кора́бль (*m.*) ship
корзи́нка basket
коридо́р corridor

корми́ть to feed
коро́бка box; спи́чечная ~ match-box
коро́бочка little box
коро́ва cow
короле́ва queen
коро́ль king
коро́ткий short
коры́то trough
коси́ться to squint
косми́ческий cosmic, space (*adj.*)
косну́ться *pfv.*, каса́ться *impfv.*
　(+ *gen.*) to touch
кость (*f.*) bone
костю́м suit
кот tom-cat
котёнок (*gen.* —нка) kitten
котле́та chop
кото́рый which, what
ко́фе coffee
кочерга́ poker
ко́шка cat (female)
кра́деный stolen
край region, land, edge
краса́вица a beauty
краси́вый beautiful
кра́сить, покра́сить to paint
кра́ска paint
красне́ть, покрасне́ть to blush
кра́сный red
кре́пкий strong
кре́сло armchair
крест cross
крестья́нин (*nom. pl.* крестья́не)
　peasant
криво́й crooked
кривоно́гий bandy-legged
крик a cry
кри́кет, игра́ в кри́кет cricket, a game
　of cricket
кри́кнуть *pfv.*, крича́ть *impfv.* to cry
　out
крова́ть (*f.*) bed
крокоди́л crocodile
кро́ме except, besides
крот mole
кро́шка crumb
круг circle
кругово́й circular
круго́м round, all round
кру́пный large
крути́ть to twist
круто́й, кру́то steep (*adj.* and *adv.*)
крыло́ (*nom. pl.* кры́лья) wing
Крым Crimea
крыть, покры́ть to cover
кры́ша roof
крючо́к (*gen.* крючка́) hook
кто who; кто́-то someone
кто... кто... some . . . others

кубок (*gen.* кубка) presentation cup
кувшин jug
кувырком upside down
куда whither, where (motion)
кулак fist
кулинар, кулинарка culinary expert
купить *pfv.*, покупать *impfv.* to buy
купленный *p.p.p.* bought
купон coupon
курить, по- to smoke
курица hen, chicken
курс course
кусать to bite, to sting
кусок (*gen.* куска) lump
куст bush
кухарка cook
кухня kitchen
куча heap
кушак belt

лабиринт labyrinth
лавка stall, shop
лавочник shop-keeper
лагерь (*m.*) camp
лад manner
ладно all right, O.K.
ладонь (*f.*) palm (of hand)
лампа lamp
лампада (ikon-)lamp
ласточка swallow
лёгкий easy, light
легко easily
легковая машина car
лёгкое lung
лёд (*gen.* льда) ice
лежать, по- to lie
лекарство medicine
Лёля, Лёна, Лёночка, Лёнушка
  Helen (diminutive forms)
лентяй lazy person
лепить to stick to, to get stuck to; to
  model
лес wood, forest
леска (fishing) line
лесник forester
лесной forest (*adj.*)
лесок (*gen.* леска) copse
лестница staircase
летний summer('s)
лето summer
лётчик, лётчица pilot, airman/air-
  woman
ли whether, 'interrogative particle'
лидер (оппозиции) leader (of the
  opposition)
лимон lemon
лист (*nom. pl.* листья) leaf
листок (*gen.* листка) leaflet
литература literature

лить, на- to pour
личинка larva
лично personally
лов, ловля catching, catch
ловить, поймать to catch
ловко agilely, cleverly
лодка boat
ложка spoon
локомотив engine
ломать, с- to break
лохань (*f.*) (wash)tub
лошадь (*f.*) horse
луг meadow
лук onions
луна moon
лунка hole
луч ray
лучше better
лучший better, best
лыжи skis
любимый favourite
любитель (*m.*) amateur
любить to like, to love
любоваться (+ *dat.*) to admire, to
  look with admiration at
люди people
лягушка frog

мазать (мажу, мажешь), по- to
  smear, to grease
май May
майор Major
мак poppy
макароны macaroni
малейший slightest
мало little, few
малый, маленький small
мальчик boy
мальчишка little boy
мама Mummy
мамин Mummy's
Маня Manya (diminutive form of
  Мария)
Мария Mary
марка stamp
март March
Марфа Martha
маска mask
масса mass
математика mathematics
матерой or матёрый big, strong,
  mature
матрас mattress
матрос sailor
мать (*gen.* матери) mother
машина machine, car; пишущая ~
  typewriter
машинист enginedriver, mechanic
машинистка typist

мая́к lighthouse
маха́ть (машу́, ма́шешь), по- + *instr.* to wave
МГУ Moscow State University
ме́бель (*f.*) furniture
медвежо́нок (*gen.* –нка, *nom. pl.* медвежа́та) bear-cub
ме́дленный slow
ме́дный copper
ме́жду (+ *instr.*) between
ме́лкий fine, small, shallow, petty
ме́лочь (*f.*) trifle
ме́ра measure
ме́рить, из- or по- to measure
мёрзнуть, за- to freeze, to be cold
месте́чко place, spot, small town
ме́стный local
ме́сто place
ме́сяц month
мете́ль (*f.*) snowstorm
ме́ткий accurate; ме́тко to the point, accurately
метр metre
метро́ Underground
меха́ник mechanic
мечта́ dream
меша́ть, по- (+ *dat.*) to hinder, to annoy
мешо́к (*gen.* мешка́) sack
микро́б microbe
миллио́н million
миллионе́р, миллионе́рша millionaire, millionairess
ми́мо (+ *gen.*) past, by
мини́стр Minister
мину́та minute
мину́точка minute, moment
мир world
мир peace
ми́тинг meeting
Михаи́л Michael
Ми́ша short for Michael
младе́нец (*gen.* –нца) baby
мла́дший youngest, younger
мне́ние opinion
мно́го much, many
многоуважа́емый Dear (beginning of letters)
могу́щий able
мо́дный stylish, fashionable, modern
мо́жет быть perhaps
мо́жно it is permissible, one may
мо́йка washing; also the name of a river
мо́кнуть, про- to be soaked
мо́крый wet, damp
молниено́сный as in с м–ой быстрото́й with lightning speed
молодо́й young
мо́лодость (*f.*) youth
молоко́ milk

молото́к (*gen.* –тка́) hammer; бить –тко́м to hammer
моло́чный milky, of milk
молча́ть, по- to be silent
моме́нт moment
момента́льно in a moment, immediately
моне́та coin
моро́з frost
моро́зный frosty
Москва́ Moscow
москви́ч Muscovite, person from Moscow
моско́вский Moscow, of Moscow
мост (*loc.* мосту́) bridge
мото́р motor
мотоpо́ллер motor-scooter
мотоци́кл motorcycle
мотоцикли́ст motorcyclist
моты́ль (*m.*) (*gen.* –ля́) maggot
моча́лка face-cloth, flannel
мочь (могу́, мо́жешь… мо́гут), смочь to be able
мрак gloom
муж (*nom. pl.* мужья́, *gen. pl.* муже́й) husband
мужчи́на man
музе́й museum
му́зыка music
му́ка torment
мука́ flour
му́скул muscle
мы we
мы́ло soap
мы́лить to soap
мы́слить to think
мыть, по- or вы́- to wash
мы́ться to wash oneself
мыча́ть to moo, to low, to moan
мышь (*f.*) mouse; мышо́нок (*gen.* –нка) baby mouse
мя́гкий soft
мясна́я butcher's (shop)
мясни́к butcher
мя́со meat
мя́та mint
мяч ball

на (+ *acc.*) on to, into; for (in expression of time); (+ *prep.*) on, in
на! take it! (вот тебе́ и на! Well, there you are!)
на́бережная embankment
наби́т битко́м stuffed, full, chock full
наве́рно probably, certainly
нависа́ть to hang over, to hang down
на́волочка pillow-case
навстре́чу to meet, towards, from the opposite direction

нагружа́ть, нагрузи́ть to load
надева́ть, наде́ть to put on
на́до it is necessary, one must (+ *dat*.)
нае́зженный well-trodden, trampled
наём (*gen*. на́йма) hire, hiring
наёмник hireling
наза́д backwards, (тому́) н– ago
на́званный called
назва́ть *pfv*., называ́ть *impfv*. to name
называ́ться, назва́ться to be called
найти́ *pfv*., находи́ть *impfv*. to find
наклоня́ть, наклони́ть to incline, to bend
наконе́ц finally
накорми́ть *pfv*., корми́ть *impfv*. to feed
нале́во to the left, on the left
нали́ть *pfv*., лить *impfv*. to pour
нало́г tax
нанима́ть, наня́ть to hire
наоборо́т on the contrary
напада́ть, напа́сть на (+ *acc*.) to attack
напе́в melody
напи́ток (*gen*. напи́тка) drink
напи́ться (+ *gen*.) to have a good drink (of)
напомина́ть, напо́мнить to remind
направле́ние direction
направля́ться, напра́виться to be directed, to make one's way to
напра́во to the right, on the right
нараста́ть, нарасти́ to grow, to increase
наро́д people, a crowd
наро́чно deliberately
насеко́мое insect
наст frozen snow-crust
настоя́щее the present
настоя́щий real, present
настрое́ние frame of mind, mood
наступа́ть, наступи́ть to approach
натяну́ть *pfv*., натя́гивать *impfv*. to pull on
науга́д at random
нау́ка science
научи́ться *pfv*., учи́ться *impfv*. to learn
находи́ть, найти́ to find
находи́ться to be situated
национализова́ть to nationalize
нача́ло beginning, principle
нача́льник boss, chief, director
нача́льство the heads, command
нача́ть *pfv*., начина́ть *impfv*. to begin
начина́ться, нача́ться to begin, to commence
наш, -а, -е, -и our

нащу́пывать, нащу́пать to feel for, to grope
не not
неаккура́тный untidy, unpunctual
небе́сный heavenly
не́бо sky
небольшо́й small
неве́рно, неве́рный wrong, false, untrue
невнима́ние inattention
невозмо́жно impossible (*adv*.)
невозмо́жный impossible
не́где there is nowhere
неглубо́кий shallow
негр negro
недалеко́ not far off
неде́ля week
нездоро́вый unhealthy, unwell
незнако́мый stronger
неизве́стно it is not known, unknown
неинтере́сный uninteresting
неи́стовый furious, violent
нейло́новый of nylon
не́кого there is no-one /nobody
не́который some
некру́пный small, medium-sized
не́куда there is nowhere
нельзя́ it is impossible, one cannot, one may not
неме́дленно without delay, at once
не́мец (*gen*. не́мца), не́мка German man, woman
неме́цкий German
немно́го a few, a little
немно́жко a little
необходи́мый necessary, essential
неожи́данный unexpected
нео́пытный inexperienced
непоня́тный unintelligible
непра́вда lie, falsehood
непра́вый unjust, wrong
непреры́вный unbroken, continuous
неразу́мно unwisely
не́сколько several, some
нести́ *det*., носи́ть *indet*. to carry
нести́сь to be carried, to travel, to sweep (along)
нет no, there is /are not
нетерпе́ние impatience
неуве́ренный uncertain, hesitant
неудо́бно uncomfortable, inconvenient
неуже́ли really
неуклю́жий clumsy
неумы́тый unwashed
нехорошо́ bad
не́чего there is nothing
ни as in; ни оди́н not a single; ни... ни... neither . . . nor . . .
ни ни! No, no! Don't you dare!

нидерла́ндец (*gen.* –дца) Dutchman
Нидерла́нды Netherlands
нидерла́ндка Dutchwoman
нидерла́ндский Dutch
ни́зкий low
ни́зко low
ни́зший lower, inferior, lowest
никако́й not of any kind, not any
никто́ nobody
никуда́ nowhere
ни́тка thread
ничего́ nothing, all right, it doesn't matter, not bad
ничто́ nothing
но but
нововведе́ние innovation
но́вости news
но́вость piece /item of news
нога́ foot, leg
но́готь (*gen.* но́гтя) (finger-)nail
ноздря́ nostril
нож knife
но́жка leg of furniture, small foot /leg
но́мер (*nom. pl.* -а́) number, room (in a hotel); position, place
Норве́гия Norway
норве́жец (*gen.* –жца), норве́жка Norwegian man, woman
норве́жский Norwegian
нос nose
носи́ть to wear
носово́й плато́к handkerchief
носо́к (*gen.* носка́) sock
но́ты music (score)
ночева́ть, пере- to pass the night
ночно́й night('s)
ночь (*f.*) night; но́чью at night
ноя́брь (*m.*) November
нра́виться, по- (+ *dat.*) to please
ну well, now; ну́-ка! well then! ну как? well, how are things?
ну́жный necessary
ныть (но́ю, но́ешь) whimper, mope, ache
ня́ня nanny, nurse

о, об(о) (+ *prep.*) about, concerning; (+ *acc.*) against
обвиня́ть, обвини́ть to accuse
обе́д dinner, lunch
обе́дать, по- to dine, to lunch
обеспоко́иться *pfv.*, беспоко́иться *impfv.* to be disturbed, to worry
обеща́ть to promise
обжига́ть, обже́чь to scorch
оби́деть *pfv.*, обижа́ть *impfv.* to offend
оби́дно, оби́дный offensive; ему́ оби́дно he feels hurt

о́блако cloud
о́бласть (*f.*) *oblast*, province
обледене́лый covered in ice
обледене́ть to become covered in ice
обня́ть *pfv.*, обнима́ть *impfv.* to embrace
обогну́ть *pfv.*, огиба́ть *impfv.* to bend round
оборо́на defence
оборо́тный reverse
образова́ться to be formed
обрати́ть *pfv.*, обраща́ть *impfv.* to turn; ~ внима́ние на (+ *acc.* to pay attention to)
обра́тно return, back
обши́рный vast
объединя́ть, объедини́ть to unite
объясне́ние explanation
объясня́ть, объясни́ть to explain
обыкнове́нно usually, commonly
обы́чно usually, traditionally
ове́с (*gen.* овса́) oats
овца́ sheep
овчи́нный sheep('s)
огло́хнуть *pfv.*, гло́хнуть *impfv.* to go deaf
огля́дываться, огляну́ться to look around
огонёк (*gen.* огонька́) (small) light
ого́нь (*m.*) (*gen.* огня́) fire, light
огра́да bulwark, wall
огро́мный huge, vast
огу́рчик cucumber, gherkin
оде́тый dressed
оде́ться *pfv.*, одева́ться *impfv.* to dress
одея́ло blanket
одино́кий lonely
одино́чество solitude
одна́жды once
оживлённо animatedly
о́зеро lake
оказа́ть, ока́зывать to render, to exert as in ~ по́мощь to render help
оказа́ться *pfv.*, ока́зываться *impfv.* to turn out to be
океа́н ocean
окно́ window
о́ко (*nom. pl.* о́чи) eye (archaic, poetic)
око́шко window
окружа́ть, окружи́ть to surround
окуна́ть, окуну́ть to dip
о́кунь (*m.*) perch (fish)
он, она́, оно́, они́ he, she, it, they
опа́сный dangerous
опозда́ние delay
опозда́ть *pfv.*, опа́здывать *impfv.* to be late
оппози́ция opposition

опря́тно neatly
опуска́ть, опусти́ть to lower
опуска́ться, опусти́ться to be lowered, to descend
опу́шка edge (of a wood)
о́пытный experienced
опя́ть again
организова́ть to organize
оса́ wasp
осёл (*gen.* осла́) donkey, ass
осе́нний autumn('s)
о́сень (*f.*) autumn; о́сенью in the autumn
ослепи́тельный blinding, dazzling
осле́пнуть *pfv.*, сле́пнуть *impfv.* to go blind
осложне́ние complication
осо́бенно especially
осо́бый special
остава́ться, оста́ться to remain
оставля́ть, оста́вить to leave (trans.)
остально́й remaining
остана́вливать, останови́ть to stop (trans.)
остана́вливаться, останови́ться to stop
остано́вка stop (bus etc.)
острие́ point
остри́чь *pfv.*, острига́ть *impfv.* to cut (hair)
осуди́ть *pfv.*, осужда́ть *impfv.* to condemn
от (+ *gen.*) from
отве́рстие opening, aperture
отве́сный sheer
отве́т answer
отводи́ть, отвести́ to lead away, to take away
отдалённый distant
отда́ть *pfv.*, отдава́ть *impfv.* to give back
отделе́ние department
отделя́ть, отдели́ть to divide, to separate
о́тдых rest
отдыха́ть, отдохну́ть to rest
оте́ц (*gen.* отца́) father
оте́чество fatherland
отказа́ть *pfv.*, отка́зывать *impfv.* to refuse
отказа́ться *pfv.*, отка́зываться *impfv.* to renounce, to give up
открыва́ть, откры́ть to open, to discover
откры́тка postcard
отложи́ть *pfv.*, откла́дывать *impfv.* to postpone
отнима́ть, отня́ть to take away, to deprive

относи́ть, отнести́ to carry away
отогре́ться *pfv.*, отогрева́ться *impfv.* to get warm
отопле́ние heating
отправля́ть, отпра́вить to send off
отправля́ться, отпра́виться to set off
о́тпуск leave
отре́зать *pfv.*, отре́зывать *impfv.* to cut off
отры́вок (*gen.* отры́вка) extract, fragment
отста́ивать, отстоя́ть to defend
отста́лость (*f.*) backwardness
оттого́ that is why, for that reason
отту́да from there
отходи́ть, отойти́ to move away
отце́пленный unhitched, uncoupled
отчего́ why
отчёт report, account
отъе́зд departure; быть в отъе́зде to be away
отъезжа́ть, отъе́хать to drive away, to set off
оты́скивать, отыска́ть to search for / out
офице́р officer
официа́нт waiter
ох! oh!
охо́та hunt, hunting
охо́титься to hunt
охо́тник hunter
оце́нивать, оцени́ть to evaluate
о́чень very
о́чередь (*f.*) turn; queue; в пе́рвую о́чередь in the first instance
очища́ть, очи́стить to clean
ошиба́ться, ошиби́ться to make a mistake

Па́вел (*gen.* Па́вла) Paul
па́дать, упа́сть to fall
паке́т parcel
па́лка stick
па́лец (*gen.* па́льца) finger
па́лочка small stick
пальто́ (*indecl.*) (over)coat
па́мять (*f.*) memory
па́па Papa
пар steam, vapour
па́ра pair
пара́граф paragraph
Пари́ж Paris
парикма́херша (woman-)hairdresser
парла́мент parliament
парохо́д steamer
па́ртия party game
па́спорт passport
па́спортный of passport
пассажи́р passenger

пассажи́рский passenger('s)
пау́к, *dim.* паучо́к (*gen.* **-чка́**) spider
па́хнуть to smell
па́чка bundle, (cigarette) packet
пейза́ж landscape
пенс penny
перебра́ть *pfv.*, перебира́ть *impfv.* sort out
перевёртывать, переверну́ть to turn over
перево́д translation
переводи́ть, перевести́ to translate
перевора́чивать, see перевёртывать
перегиба́ть, перегну́ть to bend
пе́ред (+ *instr.*) in front of, before
пе́реданный transferred, handed over
передвиже́ние movement
пере́дняя anteroom, hall
перее́зд removal
пережива́ть, пережи́ть to experience, to live through
пережида́ть, пережда́ть to wait till something is over
перекрёсток (*gen.* перекрёстка) cross-roads
перекрыва́ть, перекры́ть to cover
переле́зть *pfv.*, перелеза́ть *impfv.* to crawl /climb across
перепи́ска correspondence
перепры́гивать, перепры́гнуть to jump over
перепу́тать *pfv.*, перепу́тывать *impfv.* to mix up
переры́в interval, pause, break
переса́дка change (of trains)
переса́живать, пересади́ть to transplant
переса́живаться, пересе́сть to change (trains, seats)
переставать, переста́ть to stop, to cease
переставля́ть, переста́вить to shift, to transpose
пересыла́ть, пересла́ть to send across
переходи́ть, перейти́ to go /come across
пе́рец (*gen.* пе́рца and пе́рцу) pepper
пери́од period
перо́ (*nom. pl.* пе́рья) pen, feather
перро́н platform
перча́тка glove
пе́сня song
пёстрый variegated, brightly coloured
пе́тля bow, loop
петь (пою́, поёшь), с- to sing
пече́нье pastry
пе́чка stove
пешко́м on foot

пешня́ or пе́шня crowbar, implement for breaking ice (see Lesson 39, § 5)
пивна́я pub
пиджа́к jacket
пиро́г pie
пиро́жное cake, tart
письмо́ letter
пить, вы́пить to drink
пи́ща food
пища́ть (*2nd conj.*) to squeal, to cry
пла́вать *indet.*, плыть *det.* to swim, to sail
плавни́к fin
пла́кать (пла́чу, пла́чешь), по- to weep
план plan
плати́ть, заплати́ть to pay
платфо́рма platform
плащ cloak, raincoat
племя́нник nephew
племя́нница niece
плоти́на dam
пло́тный solid
пло́хо bad(ly)
плохо́й bad
пло́щадь (*f.*) square
пляса́ть to dance
по (+ *dat.*) according to, along, on, by; (+ *acc.*) for; (+ *prep.*) after
по-англи́йски in English
побежа́ть *pfv.* to run, to set off running
поби́ть *pfv.* to beat, to defeat
побоя́ться *pfv.* to be slightly afraid
побри́ть *pfv.*, брить *impfv.* to shave
побри́ться *pfv.*, бри́ться *impfv.* to have a shave
по-ва́шему in your opinion
повезти́ *pfv.* to transport
пове́рить *pfv.*, ве́рить *impfv.* to believe (+ *dat.*); to believe in (в + *acc.*)
поверну́ть *pfv.*, повора́чивать *impfv.* to turn (something) round
повести́ *pfv.* to lead
пови́дло thick jam
повиса́ть to hang
поворча́ть *pfv.* to grumble (a little)
повторя́ть, повтори́ть to repeat
пога́снуть *pfv.*, га́снуть and погаса́ть *impfv.* to dim, to be extinguished
поги́бнуть *pfv.*, ги́бнуть *impfv.* to perish, to be lost
поговори́ть *pfv.* to talk (for a while)
пого́да weather
под below, under (+ *acc.* motion, + *instr.* location)
подбега́ть, подбежа́ть to run up

432

подборо́док (*gen.* **-дка**) chin
подвози́ть, подвезти́ to bring up
подержа́ть *pfv.* to hold
подзыва́ть, подозва́ть to call up
подлёдный under the ice
поднима́ть, подня́ть to raise, to lift
подно́с tray
подожда́ть *pfv.*, ждать and поджида́ть *impfv.* to wait
подрасти́ *pfv.* to grow bigger
подро́бность (*f.*) detail
подро́бный detailed
подрожа́ть *pfv.* to tremble a little
подру́га friend
подсека́ть, подсе́чь to hook (a fish), to gaff
подскочи́ть *pfv.* to come leaping up
подта́лкивать, подтолкну́ть to shove, to push under
поду́мать *pfv.* to think (a while)
поду́ть *pfv.* to start to blow
поду́шка pillow, cushion
подходи́ть, подойти́ to walk up to, to come up to
подъе́зд approach, drive, porch, main entrance
подъезжа́ть, подъе́хать to drive up to
подыма́ть, подня́ть to lift, to raise
по́езд train
пое́хать *pfv.* to set off
пожале́ть *pfv.*, жале́ть *impfv.* to be sorry
пожа́луйста please
пожа́р fire (a building on fire)
пожива́ть as in **как вы пожива́ете?** how do you do?
поза́втракать *pfv.*, за́втракать *impfv.* to have breakfast /lunch
позавчера́ the day before yesterday
позапро́шлый the one before the last
позва́ть *pfv.*, звать *impfv.* (зову́, зовёшь) to call
позволя́ть, позво́лить to allow
позвони́ть *pfv.*, звони́ть *impfv.* to ring, phone (+ *dat.*)
по́здно late, too late
поздравля́ть, поздра́вить to congratulate
по́зже later
познако́мить *pfv.*, знако́мить *impfv.* to introduce
поигра́ть *pfv.* to play (a little)
пойма́ть *pfv.*, лови́ть *impfv.* to catch
пойти́ *pfv.* to set off, to go
пока́ while, for the time being; **пока́ не** until
пока́зывать, показа́ть (покажу́, пока́жешь) to show

пока́зываться, показа́ться to appear
покра́сить *pfv.*, кра́сить *impfv.* to paint
покрасне́ть *pfv.*, красне́ть *impfv.* to blush
покрича́ть *pfv.* to shout a little
покро́в cover
покрыва́ться, покры́ться to be covered, to cover oneself
покупа́ть, купи́ть to buy
поку́пка purchase; **идти́ за —ами** to go shopping
покури́ть *pfv.* to smoke (a little)
пол (*loc.* **полу́**) floor
пол half
по́ле field
полежа́ть *pfv.* to lie (for a while)
поле́но log
полете́ть *pfv.* to start, to fly, to fly off
полите́хникум polytechnic
поли́ть *pfv.* to pour (a little)
полк regiment
по́лка shelf
полко́вник colonel
полме́тра half a metre
по́лно enough
по́лный full
полови́на half
положе́ние position
положи́ть *pfv.*, класть *impfv.* to put
полома́ть *pfv.* to break
полоса́ strip, stripe
полоте́нце towel
полуста́нок (*gen.* **-нка**) halt
получа́ется the result is, the impression produced is
получа́ть, получи́ть to receive
полфу́нта half a pound
полчаса́ half an hour
по́льзоваться (+ *instr.*) to use, to have, to enjoy
по́лька Polish woman
по́льский Polish
По́льша Poland
полюби́ть *pfv.* to come to like /love
полюбова́ться *pfv.* to gaze admiringly
поля́к Pole
поля́нка glade
помидо́р tomato
по́мнить, вспо́мнить to remember
помога́ть, помо́чь (+ *dat.*) to help
по-мо́ему in my opinion
помолча́ть *pfv.* to be silent (a while)
по́мощь (*f.*), оказа́ть по́мощь help, to render help
помча́ться *pfv.*, мча́ться *impfv.* to dart, to rush
помы́ть *pfv.* to wash (a little)
помы́ться *pfv.* to wash (oneself)

по-нашему in our opinion
понедельник Monday
понести *pfv.* to carry, to start to carry
пони pony
понимать, понять (пойму, поймёшь) to understand
понуря голову with bowed head
пообедать *pfv.*, обедать *impfv.* to have dinner /lunch
попасть *pfv.*, попадать *impfv.* to get to, to find oneself in
попевать, попеть to hum, to sing a little
поплавок (*gen.* –вка) float
поплакать *pfv.* to cry a little
попозже a little later
попросить *pfv.*, просить *impfv.* to ask
популярность (*f.*) popularity
пора time, it is time; с тех пор (как) since
поработать *pfv.* to work (a little)
порог threshold
порода type, breed
поросёнок (*gen.* –нка, *nom. pl.* поросята) piglet
порох powder, gunpowder
порошок (*gen.* –шка) powder, tooth-powder
портной tailor
портрет portrait
португалец (*gen.* –льца) Portuguese man
Португалия Portugal
португалка Portuguese woman
португальский Portuguese
портфель (*m.*) briefcase
порядок (*gen.* порядка) order
посадить *pfv.*, сажать and садить *impfv.* to put, to seat
посеять *pfv.*, сеять *impfv.* to sow
посидеть *pfv.* to sit for a while
посланный sent
послать *pfv.*, посылать *impfv.* to send
послевоенный post-war
последний last (ultimate)
послушать *pfv.* to listen (a while)
посмотреть *pfv.*, смотреть *impfv.* to glance, to look
посольство embassy
поспать *pfv.* to sleep a while
посредине, посередине in the middle
поставить *pfv.*, ставить *impfv.* to put, to stand
постоять *pfv.* to stand (a while)
постричь *pfv.*, стричь *impfv.* (стригу, стрижёшь, стригут) to cut (hair)

постричься *pfv.*, стричься *impfv.* to have a haircut
построить *pfv.*, строить *impfv.* to build
постучать *pfv.* to bang, to thump (a little)
посчитать *pfv.* to count
посылать, послать to send
посылка parcel (post)
потащить to drag
потерять *pfv.*, терять *impfv.* to lose
потом then (after that)
потому that is why
потому что because
потонуть *pfv.*, тонуть *impfv.* to sink, to drown
потребовать *pfv.*, требовать *impfv.* (+ *gen.*) to demand
потряхивать to shake
потушить *pfv.*, тушить *impfv.* to put out, to extinguish
потянуться *pfv.*, потягиваться *impfv.* to stretch oneself
поужинать *pfv.*, ужинать *impfv.* to have supper
похожий (на + *acc.*) similar (to)
похрустывать to crunch
почва soil
почём how much, at what price
почитать *pfv.* to read (a little)
почта post
почуять *pfv.*, чуять *impfv.* to scent, to sense
пошутить *pfv.*, шутить *impfv.* to joke
поэт poet
поэтому so, therefore
появиться, появиться to appear
правда truth, that's right; неправда ли? isn't it? etc.
правило rule
правильно correct(ly)
правительство government
править (+ *instr.*) to guide
право right
правый right
праздник festival
практика practice
практиковать to practise
предложение proposal; sentence
предместье suburb
представить *pfv.*, представлять *impfv.* to present, introduce
предшествовать (+ *dat.*) to precede
прежний former
президент president
прекрасно very well, excellently
прекрасный beautiful, fine

прекраще́ние cessation
пре́мия reward
премье́р-мини́стр Prime Minister
пре́сса the press
при (+ *prep.*) at, by, in, during, while
прибега́ть, прибежа́ть to come running, to run up
прибира́ть, прибра́ть to tidy
приближа́ться, прибли́зиться to approach
приблизи́тельный approximate
приве́т greeting(s), regard(s)
приводи́ть, привести́ to bring, to lead to
привози́ть, привезти́ to bring, to cart to
привыка́ть, привы́кнуть к (+ *dat.*) to grow accustomed to
привы́чка habit
привя́зывать, привяза́ть to attach, to tie to
приговори́ть *pfv.*, приговаривать *impf.* to sentence
приго́дный suitable
приго́товить *pfv.*, гото́вить and пригота́вливать *impfv.* to prepare, to cook
приготовля́ться, приго́товиться to prepare oneself
при́данный added
приде́лывать, приде́лать to attach
прие́зд arrival
приезжа́ть, прие́хать to arrive
при́званный called up, invoked
признава́ть, призна́ть to admit, to recognize
призыва́ть, призва́ть to call up
прийти́ *pfv.*, приходи́ть *impfv.* to come
прика́зчик shop-assistant
прикаса́ться, прикосну́ться к + *dat.* to touch
прикла́дывать, приложи́ть to apply
прикоснове́ние touch, contact
прикрыва́ть, прикры́ть to cover
прила́вок (*gen.* прила́вка) counter (in shop)
прилета́ть, прилете́ть to arrive (by plane), to fly up
прима́нка bait, lure
примеча́ние note (textual)
принести́ *pfv.*, приноси́ть *impfv.* to bring
принима́ть, приня́ть to accept, to receive
принима́ться, приня́ться (за + *acc.*) to set about
припа́янный soldered

прислу́га servants, maid-servant
прислу́шиваться (к + *dat.*) to listen (to)
притя́гивать, притяну́ть to attract, to draw
причи́на reason
прия́тель (*m.*) friend
прия́тно pleasant(ly)
прия́тный pleasant
про (+ *acc.*) about, concerning
пробива́ть, проби́ть to pierce, to knock through
пробура́вливаться, пробура́виться to be bored through, to be pierced
прова́ливаться to fall through (into)
провожа́ть, проводи́ть to accompany
про́волочка wire
прогла́тывать, проглоти́ть to swallow
програ́мма programme
прогре́сс progress
прогу́ливаться to walk up and down
прогу́лка walk
продава́ться to be for sale, to be sold
продвиже́ние advance, progress
продолжа́ть, продо́лжить to continue
продолже́ние continuation
продолжи́тельный lengthy, prolonged, long
проду́кт product
проду́кты provisions
проезжа́ть, прое́хать to travel through
прожива́ть, прожи́ть to live through, to experience
про́житый or прожи́тый spent, lived through
прозра́чный transparent
производи́ть, произвести́ to produce
происходи́ть, произойти́ to occur, to take place
прока́лывать, проколо́ть to pierce
прокла́дывать, проложи́ть to lay down
пролета́ть, пролете́ть to pass, to fly by /over /through
промахну́ться *pfv.*, прома́хиваться *impfv.* to miss
промелькну́ть *pfv.* to flash
промёрзнуть *pfv.* to become frozen through
промо́кнуть *pfv.*, мо́кнуть *impfv.* to get soaked through
промы́шленность (*f.*) industry
промы́шленный industrial
прони́зывать, прониза́ть to pierce, to penetrate
пропага́нда propaganda

пропага́ндный *adj.* of propaganda
пропа́сть *pfv.*, пропада́ть *impfv.* to be lost
просёлочный as in просёлочная доро́га country lane, side road
проси́ть, попроси́ть to ask
прослу́шать *pfv.* to listen to
прослужи́ть *pfv.*, служи́ть *impfv.* to serve
прости́ть *pfv.*, проща́ть *impfv.* to forgive
про́сто simply, just
просто́й simple, ordinary
просто́р space
просту́да cold
простыня́ sheet
просу́нуть *pfv.*, просо́вывать *impfv.* to push through
про́тив (+ *gen.*) opposite, against
противополо́жный opposite
профессиона́льный professional
профе́ссор professor
проха́живаться to walk up and down
прохо́д passage
проходи́ть, пройти́ to go through /past
прочёсть *pfv.* = прочита́ть
прочита́ть *pfv.*, чита́ть *impfv.* to read
про́чный strong, durable
про́шлый last (past)
проща́ние farewell
проща́ть, прости́ть to forgive
проща́ться, прости́ться to say goodbye
пружи́на spring
прут (*nom. pl.* пру́тья) rod, twig
пры́гать to jump, to hop
прыжо́к (*gen.* прыжка́) spring, jump
прямо́й straight, *adv.* пря́мо
пти́ца bird
пу́блика audience, public
публикова́ть, опубликова́ть to publish
пуга́ть, испуга́ть to frighten
пуза́тый paunchy
пурга́ blizzard
пуска́ть, пусти́ть to let, to allow
пуска́ться, пусти́ться to set off, to rush
пусто́й empty
пусты́нный desert, barren
пустя́к trifle, rubbish
пу́тать, спу́тать to confuse, to muddle
пу́таться, спу́таться to be confused
путеше́ствовать to travel
пу́тник traveller, wayfarer
путь (*m., gen.* пути́) way
пуши́стый downy
пыта́ться, попыта́ться to try
пье́са play

пья́ный drunk
пя́тка heel
пятна́дцать fifteen
пя́тница Friday
пя́тый fifth
пять five
пятьдеся́т fifty
пятьсо́т five hundred

рабо́та work
рабо́тать to work
рабо́тник, рабо́тница worker
рабо́чий worker
равни́на plain
равно́ as in ему́ всё равно́ he doesn't care, it's all one to him
равня́ться (+ *dat.*) to be equal to
ра́дий radium
ра́дио radio
ра́довать, об- to gladden
ра́достный joyful
ра́дость (*f.*) joy
раз time, once
разбежа́ться *pfv.*, разбега́ться *impfv.* to run in different directions
разби́ть *pfv.*, разбива́ть *impfv.* to break, to shatter
разбо́йник brigand
разбра́сывать to throw about, to scatter
ра́зве really, surely
разверну́ть *pfv.*, развёртывать *impfv.* to unwrap
разверну́ться *pfv.* to turn round
разве́шивать, разве́сить to hang out
разви́тие development
развяза́ть *pfv.*, развя́зывать *impfv.* to untie, to undo
разгова́ривать to converse
разгово́р conversation
разгоня́ть, разогна́ть to scatter
раздава́ться, разда́ться to resound, to be heard
разда́ть *pfv.*, раздава́ть *impfv.* to distribute
разде́ть *pfv.*, раздева́ть *impfv.* to undress
разде́ться *pfv.*, раздева́ться *impfv.* to undress (oneself)
разжа́ть *pfv.*, разжима́ть *impfv.* to release pressure, to relax the grip
разлета́ться, разлете́ться to fly off
разли́чный varied, different
разложи́ть *pfv.*, раскла́дывать *impfv.* to lay out
разлюби́ть *pfv.* to stop loving
разма́тываться, размота́ться to be unwound, to unwind, to unreel
разме́р dimension

разнести́ pfv., разноси́ть impfv. to deliver, distribute, to carry to different places

разнести́сь pfv., разноси́ться impfv. to be carried about; to resound

ра́зный various, different

разобра́ть pfv., разбира́ть impfv. to sort out, to disentangle, to decipher

разогна́ть pfv., разгоня́ть impfv. to drive away, to drive apart

разоде́ться pfv., разодева́ться impfv. to dress up

разойти́сь pfv., расходи́ться impfv. to go in various directions (on foot)

разорва́ть pfv., разрыва́ть impfv. to tear to pieces

разосла́ть pfv., рассыла́ть impfv. to send out, to distribute

разре́зать pfv., разре́зывать impfv. to cut up

разруби́ть pfv., разруба́ть impfv. to chop up

разры́ть pfv., разрыва́ть impfv. to dig up, to unearth

ра́зум reason

разу́мный reasonable, sensible

разучи́ться pfv., разу́чиваться impfv. to forget (what one has learnt)

разъезжа́ть to ride around

разъе́хаться pfv., разъезжа́ться impfv. to part, to go one's ways

райо́н region

рак crayfish; cancer

ра́ма frame

ра́нить pfv. and impfv. to wound

ра́но (too) early

ра́ньше earlier

раскопа́ть pfv., раска́пывать impfv. to dig out, to excavate

раско́пки excavation

раскра́ска colouring

раскрича́ться pfv. to begin shouting, to burst out shouting

раскры́ть pfv., раскрыва́ть impfv. to uncover, to open up

распла́каться pfv. to dissolve into tears

располага́ться, расположи́ться to take up one's position

расположенный situated, distributed

распределя́ться, распредели́ться to distribute oneselves, to take up one's positions

рассве́т dawn

расска́з tale

рассказа́ть pfv. (расскажу́, расска́жешь), расска́зывать impfv. to tell, to narrate

рассмея́ться pfv. to dissolve into laughter

рассова́ть pfv., рассо́вывать impfv. to shove about, to put into different places

расставля́ть, расста́вить to place, to put out

расстоя́ние distance

расстро́енный disconcerted, put out, upset

раста́птывать, растопта́ть to stamp on, to crush

растворя́ть, раствори́ть to dissolve

расти́ to grow

растяну́ться pfv., растя́гиваться impfv. to stretch, to go sprawling

расчи́стка clearing, cleaning-up

рвать, рва́ться to tear

рва́ться to rush

ребёнок (gen. ребёнка) child

ребя́та chaps, lads, fellows

ревни́вый jealous

ревнова́ть to be jealous

револю́ция revolution

ре́дко rarely

ре́зать (ре́жу, ре́жешь) to cut

рези́на rubber; рези́новый (adj.)

ре́зко sharply, abruptly

ре́зкий sharp, abrupt

река́ river

ремо́нт repairs, redecorating

респу́блика republic

рестора́н restaurant

ре́чка stream

реша́ть, реши́ть to decide

Рим Rome

рис rice

риско́ванно risky

рискова́ть, рискну́ть (+ instr.) to risk

ритми́чно rhythmically

ро́бкий timid

ро́бко timidly

ро́вно exactly

ро́дина native land

роди́тель (m.) parent

родно́й native, home, dear

ро́дственник relative

рожде́ние birth

ро́за rose

ро́зданный distributed

роль (f.) rôle

ром rum

рома́н novel

Росси́я Russia

рост growth

ро́стбиф roast beef

рот (gen. рта) mouth

ро́ща grove, thicket

роя́ль (*m.*) grand piano
руба́шка shirt
руби́ть to hack, to chop
рубль (*m.*) ruble
ружьё gun
рука́ hand, arm
рукоплеска́ние clapping, applause
румя́нить to flush, to redden
ру́сский Russian
ру́чка handle
ры́ба fish
рыба́к angler
рыба́цкий fisherman's
ры́бка little fish
рыболо́в fisherman
рыболо́вный магази́н fishing-tackle suppliers
ры́нок (*gen.* **ры́нка**) market
рысь (*f.*) lynx
рыть (**ро́ю, ро́ешь**) to dig, to delve
рыча́ть (*2nd conj.*) to growl, to snarl
рю́мка (wine-)glass
ряд row
ря́дом along-side, beside (**с** + *instr.*)

с (+ *gen.*) from, off; (+ *instr.*) with; (+ *acc.*) about, approximately
сад garden
сади́ться, сесть to sit down
сала́т salad, lettuce
салфе́тка napkin
сам, сама́, само́, са́ми self (*emphatic pronoun*)
са́мка female
самова́р samovar
самолёт aeroplane
са́мый the most, the very
са́ни sledge
са́нки sledge
сантиме́тр centimetre
сапо́г (*gen. pl.* **сапо́г**) boot, shoe
сбега́ться, сбежа́ться to run together
сбережённый (*p.p.p.*) saved
сбере́чь *pfv.*, **сберега́ть** *impfv.* to save
сбива́ть, сбить to knock down
сби́ться *pfv.*, **сбива́ться** *impfv.* **с доро́ги** to lose one's way
сбра́сывать, сбро́сить to throw down, to throw together, to pile up
сва́дьба wedding
сведе́ние information
сверка́ть to glitter
сверну́ть *pfv.*, **свора́чивать** *impfv.* to turn, to change direction
све́рху above, from above
свет light, world
свети́ть to shine

светло́ bright(ly), light
све́тлый bright
све́чка candle
свида́ние meeting, rendezvous; **до свида́ния** goodbye
свини́на pork
свино́й of pork
свисте́ть to whistle
своеобра́зный peculiar
свой, своя́, своё, свои́ (one's) own
связа́ть *pfv.*, **свя́зывать** *impfv.* to tie together, to link
свято́й holy, Saint
сгуща́ться, сгусти́ться to thicken
сде́лать *pfv.*, **де́лать** *impfv.* to do, to make
сде́латься *pfv.*, **де́латься** *impfv.* to become, to be made
себя́ self (*reflexive pronoun*)
се́вер north; **на ~** to the north; **на –е** in the north
се́верный northern
сего́дня today
сего́дняшний today's
сейча́с now, at once
секрета́рша secretary
секу́нда second
селе́ние, селе́нье settlement
село́ village
семна́дцать seventeen
семь seven
се́мьдесят seventy
семья́ (*gen. pl.* **семе́й**) family
се́мя (*gen.* **се́мени**) seed
сентя́брь (*m.*) September
серди́то angrily
серди́тый angry
серди́ться, рас- to be/get angry
се́рдце heart
серебро́ silver
середи́на, среди́на middle
се́рый grey
серьёзный serious; **–но** seriously
сестра́ sister
сесть (**ся́ду, ся́дешь**) *pfv.*, **сади́ться** *impfv.* to sit down
сеть (*f.*) net
се́ять to sow
сжать *pfv.*, **сжима́ть** *impfv.* to press together, to tense
сза́ди behind (as preposition, takes *gen.*)
сигаре́та cigarette
сигна́л signal
сиде́ть, по- to be sitting
си́ла strength, power, force
симфо́ния symphony
си́ний blue
системати́ческий systematic

ска́зка (fairy-)tale
сканда́л scandal, row
ска́терть (*f.*) table-cloth
скачо́к (*gen.* скачка́) leap
скла́дываться, сложи́ться to be put together
склоне́ние declension
сковорода́ frying-pan
ско́лько how many, how much
ско́ро soon, quickly
ско́рость (*f.*) speed
ско́рый fast, swift, express (train)
скро́мно modestly
скрыва́ться, скры́ться to be hidden
ску́чный boring, tedious
сла́бый weak, feeble
сла́ва fame, glory
сла́дости sweetmeats
слать (шлю, шлёшь), по- to send
сле́ва from the left, on the left
слегка́ a little, (s)lightly
след track, trace
следи́ть, по- (за + *instr.*) to watch, to keep an eye on
сле́довать to follow
сле́довать impersonal verb + *dat.* as in ему́ сле́дует he ought
сле́дующий following
сле́пнуть, о- to go blind
слепо́й blind
слета́ться, слете́ться to fly together
сли́шком too (much)
сло́вно as if
сло́во word
сложи́ть *pfv.*, скла́дывать *impfv.* to fold up, to put together
сло́жный complicated
слой layer
слон elephant
слу́жащий official, white collar worker
слу́жба service, work
служи́ть to serve
слух rumour
случай incident, case; в тако́м слу́чае in that case, in that event
случа́ться, случи́ться to happen
слу́шать to listen (to)
слы́шать (*2nd conj.*) to hear
слы́шаться to be heard
слы́шно one can hear
слы́шный audible
сме́лый bold
сменя́ть, смени́ть to change, to replace
сменя́ться, смени́ться to be replaced, to take turns
смерть (*f.*) death
сметь to dare
смех laughter

смеша́ться *pfv.*, сме́шиваться *impfv.* to be mixed up
смея́ться to laugh
смотре́ть, по- to look, to watch
смочь *pfv.*, мочь *impfv.* to be able
смысл sense
снача́ла at first, in the beginning
снег snow
снегопа́д snowfall
сне́жный show(y)
снима́ть, снять to remove, to take (off)
снима́ть, снять to take (a photograph)
сни́мок (*gen.* сни́мка) photograph
сно́ва (over) again
соба́ка dog
соба́чий dog's
собо́й *instr.* of себя́ (q.v.)
собо́р cathedral
собра́ние meeting, collection
собра́ть *pfv.*, собира́ть *impfv.* to gather
со́бственно properly, as a matter of fact
сове́товать, по- (+ *dat.*) to advise
сове́тский soviet
совсе́м quite, entirely; не совсе́м not quite; совсе́м не not at all
согна́ть *pfv.*, сгоня́ть *impfv.* to drive together, to herd
согну́ть *pfv.*, сгиба́ть *impfv.* to bend, to fold
сожале́ние regret, pity; к сожале́нию unfortunately
со́званный convoked
созва́ть *pfv.*, созыва́ть *impfv.* to convoke
сойти́сь *pfv.*, сходи́ться *impfv.* to meet
соли́стка soloist (woman)
со́лнце sun
соль (*f.*) salt
сон (*gen.* сна) sleep, dream
сообще́ние report, communication
сопровожда́ть, сопроводи́ть to accompany
сопровожда́ться to be accompanied
со́рок forty
сорокале́тний forty-year old
сорт quality
сосе́д (*nom. pl.* сосе́ди) neighbour
сосе́дний neighbouring
соси́ска sausage
сосна́ pine (tree)
составля́ть, соста́вить to compile, to make up
состоя́ться *pfv.* to take place
сосу́д vessel, bowl, jar
со́ус sauce
со́хнуть, вы́-, за- to get dry

сочине́ние work (of literature)
спа́льня bedroom
спаси́бо thank you; **большо́е спаси́бо** thank you very much
спасти́ *pfv.*, **спаса́ть** *impfv.* to save
спать to sleep
сперва́ at first
спеть *pfv.*, **петь** *impfv.* to sing
специа́льный special
спе́шно quickly, hurriedly
спе́шный urgent
спина́ back
спи́сок (*gen.* **спи́ска**) list
спи́чечный match (*adj.*)
спи́чка match
спозара́нок very early
споко́йный peaceful, calm
спорт sport
спорти́вный sports'
спо́соб means
спотыка́ться, **споткну́ться** to stumble
спра́ва from the right, on the right
спра́шивать, **спроси́ть** to ask
спря́тать *pfv.*, **пря́тать** *impfv.* (**пря́чу пря́чешь**) to hide
спу́тать *pfv.*, **пу́тать** *impfv.* to confuse
спя́щий sleeping
сравне́ние comparison; **по сравне́нию** (**с** + *instr.*) in comparison (with)
сра́зу at once
среда́ Wednesday
среди́ (+ *gen.*) among, in
сре́дний middle, average
срок period, time
ссо́риться, **по-** to quarrel
СССР U.S.S.R.
ста́вить, **по-** to put, to place
стадио́н stadium
стака́н glass
стально́й steel
станови́ться, **стать** to become, to take up one's position
стари́к old man
старичо́к (*gen.* **—чка́**) (little) old man
ста́рость (*f.*) old age
стару́ха old woman
ста́рший eldest, elder
ста́рый old
стать *pfv.* to start (doing something); to stop, to come to a standstill (no *impfv.* in these meanings)
статья́ article
ста́я pack
ствол trunk
стека́ние flowing, running down or together
стека́ть, **стечь** to flow, run down

стека́ться, **сте́чься** to flow, run together, to meet
стекло́ glass
стенографи́стка shorthand-typist
стере́ть (**сотру́**, **сотрёшь**; **стёр**, **стёрла**) *pfv.*, **стира́ть** *impfv.* to rub off
сте́рлинг sterling
сти́рка wash
стихи́ verses, poems
сто hundred
сто́йка counter (bar)
стол table
столб pillar
столи́ца capital
столо́вая dining-room
сто́лько so much, so many
сторона́ side; **с одно́й/друго́й с—ы** on the one /other hand
стоя́ть, **по-** to stand
страна́ country
стра́нный strange
стра́стный passionate
страх fear
стрело́к (*gen.* **стрелка́**) rifleman
стреля́ть, **вы́стрелить** to shoot
стро́гий severe, strict
стро́ить, **по-** to build
стро́иться, **по-** to be built
строй order, formation
стро́йный shapely, graceful
струя́ jet, stream, current
стря́хивать, **стряхну́ть** to shake off
студе́нт, **студе́нтка** student (male and female)
студе́нческий student('s)
стук knock, banging
сту́кнуть *pfv.*, **стуча́ть** *impfv.* (*2nd conjug.*) to knock, to bang
стул (*nom. pl.* **сту́лья**) chair
ступа́ть to step
ступе́нька step
суббо́та Saturday
суд court (of justice)
суди́ть to judge
су́дно (*nom. pl.* **суда́**) ship, vessel
сук (*nom. pl.* **су́чья**) bough
сукно́ cloth
су́мерки dusk
суме́ть *pfv.*, **уме́ть** *impfv.* to know how, to be able
су́мка handbag
су́мрак gloom, twilight
сунду́к trunk
суп soup
су́тки twenty-four hours, a day (and a night)
сухо́й dry
сучо́к (*gen.* **сучка́**) twig

существи́тельное noun
существо́ being, person, creature
существова́ть to exist
схвати́ть *pfv.*, хвата́ть *impfv.* to seize
сходи́ть *pfv.* to go (and come back almost at once)
сходи́ть, сойти́ to come off, to come / go down
схорони́ться *pfv.*, хорони́ться *impfv.* to hide oneself
счастли́вый happy, lucky
сча́стье happiness, luck
счетово́д accountant
счита́ть, счесть to count, to consider
сшить *pfv.*, шить *impfv.* to sew
съезжа́ться, съе́хаться to come together
съесть *pfv.*, есть *impfv.* to eat
сын (*nom. pl.* сыновья́) son
сыр cheese
сы́ро, сыро́й damp, raw
сы́тный full, satisfying
сюрпри́з surprise
сяк as in и так и сяк this way and that

таба́к tobacco
таз basin
та́йна secret
так so, thus; не так ли? isn't it? etc.
так как since, for, because
таки́м о́бразом thus, so
тако́в, -а́, -о́, -ы́ such
тако́й such, this kind of
такси́ taxi
там there
танки́ст soldier in the tank corps
танцева́ть to dance
таре́лка plate
та́чка barrow
тащи́ть to pull
та́ять, рас- to melt
тве́рдый firm, hard
творе́нье, творе́ние creation, creature
твори́ть, со- to create
т.е. – то́_есть i.e.
теа́тр theatre
телеви́дение television
телеви́зор television set
телегра́мма telegram
телеграфи́ровать, про- to telegraph, to 'wire'
телеско́п-рефле́ктор reflector-telescope
телефони́ровать, про- to telephone
телефо́нный telephone (*adj.*)
те́ло body
теля́тина veal

темне́ть, с- to grow dark, to darken, to show dark
темнота́ darkness
тёмный dark
те́ннис tennis
тео́рия theory
тепе́рь now
тепло́ warm(ly); (as noun), heat
тёплый warm
тере́ть (тру, трёшь; тёр, тёрла) to rub
террито́рия territory
тетра́дь (*f.*) exercise-book
тётя aunt
тече́нье, тече́ние course, current (river etc.)
тип type
типи́чный typical
ти́хий quiet, ти́хо quiet(ly)
тишина́ quiet, silence
тишь (*f.*) stillness
тиф typhus, typhoid
то then; то́_есть that is, i.e.
това́р goods
това́рищ comrade, friend, companion
тогда́ then (at that time)
ток current (electric)
токова́ть to utter mating calls (of certain birds)
толпа́ crowd
толсте́ть to grow fat
то́лько only
том tome, volume
тома́т tomato
тому́ наза́д ago
тон tone, hue
то́нкий fine, subtle
тону́ть, по- to sink, to drown
то́пать (нога́ми) to stamp
торгова́ть to trade, to carry on one's business
торго́вец (*gen.* –вца) trader, dealer, shopman
торопи́ться, по- to be in a hurry
торт flan
торча́ть to stick up or out
тоска́ longing, yearning, melancholy
тот, та, то, те that, those
то́т же the same
то́чка point, dot, full-stop
то́чно exactly, as if
то́чный exact
тра́ктор tractor
тра́нспорт transport
тре́бовать (+ *gen.*) to demand
трево́га alarm
тре́тий third
треща́ть to crack, to crackle

трещётка rattle
три three
тридцать thirty
тринадцать thirteen
триста three hundred
трогать, тронуть to touch
тройка troika, team of three
тропинка path
тротуар pavement
труба chimney
трубка pipe, tube
трубочист chimney-sweep
труд work, labour
трудный difficult, hard
трястись to shake, to quiver
туда there, thither
тулуп fur-coat
туман mist, fog
турецкий Turkish
турист tourist
турок (gen. sing. турка; gen. pl. турок) Turk
Турция Turkey
турчанка Turkish woman
тут here
туфля shoe, slipper
туча (big, dark) cloud
тушить, по- to put out, to extinguish
ты thou, you
тыл (loc. тылу) rear (military)
тысяча thousand
тюрьма prison
тяжёлый heavy
тянуть, по- to pull, to draw; его тянет he wishes, he longs for

у (+ gen.) at, in, by, have (see Lesson 5, § 10)
убегать, убежать to run away
убеждать, убедить to convince
убитый killed, slain
убор attire
уборная lavatory
уважаемый respected, dear (at beginning of letters)
уважать to respect
уверенно confidently
увидать pfv. to see, to catch sight of
увидеть pfv., видеть impfv. to see, to catch sight of
увозить, увезти to take /cart away
уволить pfv., увольнять impfv. to dismiss, to sack
увязать pfv., увязывать impfv. to stick, to get stuck
угадывать, угадать to guess
уговорить pfv., уговаривать impfv. to persuade

угодно as in что вам угодно 'What do you wish?' 'What can I do for you?'
угождать, угодить (+ dat.) to please, to oblige
угол (gen. угла) corner, angle
уголь (gen. угля) coal
угрожать (+ dat.) to threaten
удар blow
удача success
удивляться, удивиться to be surprised
удобный comfortable, convenient
удовольствие pleasure
удочка fishing-rod
уезжать, уехать to drive away
ужас horror
ужасный horrid, horrible
уже, уж already, now
ужинать, по- to have supper
узел (gen. узла) bundle, knot
узкий narrow
узнавать, узнать to recognize
уйти pfv., уходить impfv. to go away
указать pfv., указывать impfv. to point out
укорять, укорить to rebuke
украденный (p.p.p.) stolen
украсть (украду, украдёшь) pfv., красть impfv. to steal
улетать, улететь to depart (by plane), to fly away
улов catch
улыбаться, улыбнуться to smile
умереть (умру, умрёшь; умер, умерла) pfv., умирать impfv. to die
уметь to know how, to be able
умно cleverly
умный clever
умолкать, умолкнуть to fall silent
умывальник wash-stand
унести pfv., уносить impfv. to carry away
университет university
униматься, уняться to decrease
уничтожать, уничтожить to destroy
уносить, унести to take away, to carry away
упаковка packing
упасть pfv., падать impfv. to fall
Урал Ural
уральский Ural (adj.)
урожай harvest
урок lesson
ус and усы (pl.) moustache
усиливать, усилить to intensify
ускакивать, ускакать to hop or gallop away
условие condition

услы́шать *pfv.* to hear
успева́ть, успе́ть to succeed
успе́х success
успе́шный successful
успока́ивать, успоко́ить to soothe, to calm
уста́лый tired
устана́вливаться, установи́ться to be placed, to take up a position
устремля́ться, устреми́ться to rush, to aim for
ута́птывать, утопта́ть to trample down
утёнок (*gen.* утёнка, *nom. pl.* утя́та) duckling
у́тка duck
утону́ть *pfv.*, тону́ть *impfv.* to sink
у́тренний morning('s)
у́тро morning; у́тром in the morning
утю́г (flat) iron
у́хо (*nom. pl.* у́ши) ear
уходи́ть, уйти́ to go away
учени́к pupil
учёный learned; *as noun* scholar, scientist
учи́тель (*m.*) teacher
учи́ть, на- to teach
учи́ться, на-, вы- to study, to learn
уша́т tub
ую́тный comfortable, cosy

фа́брика factory
факт fact
факти́чески in effect, in fact
фа́ктор factor
фами́лия surname
фарфо́ровый china
фасо́ль (*f.*) haricot beans
февра́ль (*m.*) February
федерати́вный federal
Фёдор Theodore
фе́рма farm
фе́рмер farmer
фиа́лка violet
фи́зика physics
финля́ндец (*gen.* финля́ндца), финля́ндка Finn (man and woman)
Финля́ндия Finland
финля́ндский Finnish
флаг flag
флажо́к (*gen.* -жка́) pennant
флот fleet
фон background
фона́рь (*m.*) street-lamp, lantern
фонта́н fountain
фо́рма form
формуля́р list
фото́граф photographer
фотогра́фия photograph

фра́за phrase
Фра́нция France
францу́женка Frenchwoman
францу́з Frenchman
францу́зский French
фунт pound
фут foot
футбо́л football

хала́т dressing-gown, smock, overall
хао́с chaos
ха́та hut
хвали́ть, похвали́ть to praise
хвата́ть, хвати́ть to be enough; to snatch
хвост tail, queue
хлеб bread
хлоп bang
хло́пать to bang, to slam
хму́риться to lower, to glower
ход course, march, motion, move; на ходу́ while walking, while in motion
ходи́ть *indet.*, идти́ *det.* to go, to come, to walk
хо́лод cold
хо́лодно, холо́дный cold
холостя́к bachelor
хор chorus
хорони́ть, по- to bury
хорошо́ good, all right, O.K.
хоте́ть, захоте́ть to want (see Lesson 9, § 3)
хотя́ although
храни́ть to keep, to preserve
храпе́ть (*2nd conj.*) to snore
Христо́с (*gen.* Христа́) Christ
хрома́ть to limp
хромо́й lame
хру́пкий brittle
хруст crunch
худо́жник artist
худо́й bad, thin
ху́дший worst, worse

царе́вич tsarevich
цари́ца tsaritsa, czarina
ца́рство kingdom, empire
царь (*m.*) tsar
цветна́я капу́ста cauliflower
цветно́й coloured
цвето́к (*gen.* цветка́, *nom. pl.* цветы́) flower
цвето́чпый горшо́к flowerpot
целова́ть, по- to kiss
цена́ price
центр centre
цех workshop, shop (in factory)
цинк zinc
цирк circus

цифра figure, number
цыга́н gypsy
цыплёнок (*gen.* цыплёнка, *nom. pl.*
  цыпля́та) chicken

чай tea
ча́йник teapot, tea kettle
час hour, one o'clock
ча́сто often
часы́ watch, clock
ча́шка cup
челове́к man, human being
челове́чество humanity
чем than
чемода́н suitcase
чепуха́ rubbish
червячо́к (*gen.* –чка́) maggot
черда́к attic
че́рез (+ *acc.*) across, in (in expressions
  of time)
чересчу́р excessively, too
черне́ть, почерне́ть to be black, to
  turn black
черни́ла (*neut. pl.*) ink
чёрный black; *as noun* negro
чёрт (*nom. pl.* че́рти) devil
черта́ trait, feature
чертёж draught, sketch, plan
чеса́ть (чешу́, че́шешь), при- to
  comb; чеса́ть, по- to scratch
честь (*f.*) honour
четве́рг Thursday
че́тверть (*f.*) quarter
четы́ре four
четы́реста four hundred
чех, че́шка Czech (man and woman)
Чехослова́кия Czechoslovakia
че́шский Czech (*adj.*)
чино́вник civil-servant
чи́стить, по-, вы́- to clean
чи́стка cleaning
чи́сто clean(ly)
чи́стый clean
чита́ть, прочита́ть and проче́сть to
  read
член member, limb
что what, that, why; что вы? What do
  you mean? How can you? что за
  what a, what sort of; что тако́е?
  What is (it)?
что́бы in order to, in order that
что́-то something, somewhat, rather
чте́ние reading
чу́вствовать, почу́вствовать to feel
чугу́нный (of) cast-iron
чуда́к crank, eccentric
чу́дный wonderful, marvellous
чу́до marvel

чужо́й other's, someone else's
чула́н closet, lumber-room
чуло́к stocking
чу́ткий sharp of hearing, sensitive
чу́ять, по- to scent, to sense

шаг step, pace
шага́ть, шагну́ть to stride, to step
ша́пка cap
ша́хматы chess
шахтёр miner
швед, шве́дка Swede (man and woman)
шве́дский Swedish
Шве́ция Sweden
швейца́р door-keeper, janitor
швейца́рец (*gen.* швейца́рца) Swiss
  (man)
Швейца́рия Switzerland
швейца́рка Swiss (woman)
швейца́рский Swiss
шесть six
шестьдеся́т sixty
ше́я neck
ши́ллинг shilling
ши́на tyre
шипе́ть (*2nd conj.*) to hiss
широ́кий broad, wide
шить (шью, шьёшь), сшить to sew
шкаф cupboard
шко́ла school
шля́па hat
шокола́д chocolate
шоссе́йный trunk, arterial
шотла́ндец (*gen.* шотла́ндца)
  Scot(s)man
Шотла́ндия Scotland
шотла́ндка Scotswoman
шотла́ндский Scottish
шофёр driver
штормово́й gale-force
шу́ба fur-coat
шум noise
шуме́ть (*2nd conj.*) to make a noise
шу́мный noisy
шу́тка joke

ще́пка chip
щети́на bristle
щётка brush
щи (*gen.* щей) cabbage soup
щу́ка pike

Эдинбу́рг Edinburgh
экра́н screen
элега́нтный elegant
электри́ческий electric
электри́чество electricity
эне́ргия energy

444

этáж floor, storey
э́тот, э́та, э́то, э́ти this, that; these, those
э́хо echo

ю́бка skirt
юг south; на юг to the south; на ю́ге in the south
юли́ть to bustle, to fuss
ю́мор humour

я I
я́блоко apple
я́года berry, berries

ядрó nucleus, kernel
язы́к tongue, language
яйцó egg
я́корь (m.) anchor
я́ма pit, hole
янвáрь (m.) January
ярд yard
я́ркий bright, vivid
я́рмарка fair
я́сно clear(ly)
я́сный clear
я́щик drawer, box
я́щичек work-box

ENGLISH - RUSSIAN

able, to be мочь (могý, мóжешь... мóгут; мог, моглá), смочь
about о (об, обо) + prep.
abroad за грани́цу (motion); за грани́цей (location)
accompany, to провожáть, проводи́ть; (escort) сопровождáть
ache, to болéть (боли́т, боля́т), за-
across чéрез + acc.
actress актри́са
address áдрес (nom. pl. адресá)
administrative администрати́вный
advise, to совéтовать, по- (+ dat.)
afraid, to be – of боя́ться (+ gen.)
after lunch послеобéденный
again снóва, опя́ть
ago томý назáд
agreement соглашéние; to reach an ~ приходи́ть, прийти́ к соглашéнию
airport аэропóрт
all весь, вся, всё, все
along по + dat.
already ужé
also тóже
although хотя́
always всегдá, всё
a.m. утрá
among мéжду (+ instr.) among ourselves мéжду собóй
and и, а
angry, to get/become серди́ться, рас-
another другóй; one another, each other друг дрýга (See Lesson 28, § 7)
answer отвéт (на + acc.); to ~ отвечáть, отвéтить (на + acc.)
anything чтó-нибудь, чтó-либо; (with negative) ничегó + не

approach, to подходи́ть, подойти́
armchair крéсло
arrive, to (in an aeroplane) прилетáть, прилетéть
ask, to проси́ть, попроси́ть
assemble, to собирáться, собрáться; сходи́ться, сойти́сь
at на (+ prep.), в (+ prep.), у (+ gen.)
at once срáзу же
aunt тётя
autumn óсень (f.)
awful ужáсный; adv. ужáсно

bachelor холостя́к
bad дурнóй, нехорóший, плохóй; he feels bad емý дýрно
Baltic Балти́йское мóре
bang, to стучáть (2nd conj.), по-
bank (of river) бéрег; on the ~ на берегý
banker банки́р
barrow тáчка
be, to быть (fut. бýду, бýдешь)
bear, to терпéть (2nd conj.)
because потомý что
because of из-за (+ gen.), благодаря́ (thanks to) + dat.
bed, to go to ложи́ться, лечь спать
before пéред (+ instr.), до (+ gen.), прéжде чем (+ infin.)
beginning началó
behind за (+ acc. motion; + instr. location)
believe, to вéрить, по- (+ dat.); to believe in вéрить, по- в (+ acc.)
bell кóлокол (nom. pl. колоколá)
beside ря́дом с (+ instr.)
bicycle велосипéд

445

big большо́й
birthday день рожде́ния
blow, to дуть, по-
board (ship) борт; **on board** на борту́
bon voyage счастли́вого пути́
book кни́га
born, to be роди́ться
boss нача́льник, хозя́ин, шеф
boy ма́льчик
break, to лома́ть, с-
breakfast, to за́втракать, по-
bridge мост; **on the bridge** на мосту́
bring, to приноси́ть, принести́; води́ть (*indet.*), вести́ (*det.*); приводи́ть, привести́; привози́ть, привезти́; **to bring out** выводи́ть, вы́вести
brother брат (*nom. pl.* бра́тья)
build, to стро́ить, по-
building зда́ние, дом (*nom. pl.* дома́)
bundle свя́зка
burn, to горе́ть, с- (*intrans.*): жечь, с- (*trans.*); **burnt** сожжённый
burst into tears, to запла́кать, распла́каться
bus авто́бус
but но, а
buy, to покупа́ть, купи́ть
by (place) у (+ *gen.*), о́коло (+ *gen.*), при (+ *prep.*)

call, to звать (зову́, зовёшь...), позва́ть
call in, to заходи́ть, зайти́; заезжа́ть, зае́хать (*at*, в + *acc.*); **to call on** *same verb with* к + *dat.*
called на́званный
can, *see* **able, to be**
car автомоби́ль (*m.*), (авто)маши́на
card ка́рта, **to play cards** игра́ть в ка́рты
carry, to носи́ть (*indet.*), нести́ (*det.*)
carry out, to выноси́ть, вы́нести
cast, to отлива́ть, отли́ть
cathedral собо́р
century век, столе́тие
chair стул (*nom. pl.* сту́лья)
change, to меня́ться; изменя́ться, измени́ться
chemist апте́карь (*m.*); ~'s shop апте́ка
children де́ти
cigarette папиро́са, сигаре́т(к)а
city го́род (*nom. pl.* города́)
close, to закрыва́ть, закры́ть
clothes оде́жда
coat пальто́ (*indecl.*)
coffee ко́фе (*m.*)
coincidence совпаде́ние
cold холо́дный
colleague колле́га (*m.*)

collect, to собира́ть, собра́ть (соберу́, соберёшь)
come, to ходи́ть (*indet.*), идти́ (*det.*); е́здить (*indet.*), е́хать (*det.*); приходи́ть, прийти́; приезжа́ть, прие́хать
come home, to возвраща́ться, верну́ться домо́й
come out, to (*on foot*) выходи́ть, вы́йти
come to, to приходи́ть, прийти́ (к + *dat.*)
comfortable удо́бный
concert конце́рт (**to a concert** на + *acc.*; **at a concert** на + *prep.*)
conclude, to заключа́ть, заключи́ть
confuse, to пу́тать, спу́тать
contract контра́кт
conversation разгово́р
corner у́гол (*gen.* угла́; *loc.* углу́); *dim.* уголо́к (*gen.* уголка́)
cosy ую́тный
council сове́т
counter сто́йка (**bar-counter**); прила́вок (**shop-counter**)
country дере́вня; страна́
course, of коне́чно
crackle, to треща́ть (*2nd conj.*), по-
customs office тамо́жня
cut, to разреза́ть, разре́зать

damp сыро́й
dangerous опа́сный
day день (*gen.* дня); **by day** днём; **day before** *see* **eve**; **on the following day** на друго́й день
deaf глухо́й
deaf, to go гло́хнуть, о-
decide, to реша́ть, реши́ть; **to come to a decision** реша́ться, реши́ться
decipher, to разбира́ть, разобра́ть
deck па́луба
deep глубо́кий
delegate делега́т
deliver, to разноси́ть, разнести́ (*on foot*); развози́ть, развезти́ (*in a vehicle*)
depart, to уходи́ть, уйти́; отходи́ть, отойти́; уезжа́ть, уе́хать; отъезжа́ть, отъе́хать; улета́ть, улете́ть; отлета́ть, отлете́ть
desk пи́сьменный стол
die, to умира́ть, умере́ть (умру́, умрёшь; у́мер, умерла́)
differently ина́че
difficult тру́дный
dine, to обе́дать, пообе́дать
director дире́ктор
distant далёкий, да́льний
disturb, to меша́ть (+ *dat.*)

doctor до́ктор (*nom. pl.* доктора́)
dog соба́ка
door дверь (*f.*)
dress, to одева́ть, оде́ть; (oneself) одева́ться, оде́ться
drink, to пить, вы́-
drive, to е́здить (*indet.*), е́хать (*det.*)
drive in, to въезжа́ть, въе́хать
drop in on, to заходи́ть, зайти́ к (+ *dat.*); заезжа́ть, зае́хать к (+ *dat.*)
dry сухо́й

earlier ра́ньше, ра́нее
early ра́но; *adj.* ра́нний
east восто́к; восто́чный
eat, to есть (see Lessons 3, § 3; 9, § 5)
Edinburgh Эдинбу́рг
eighteen восемна́дцать; **-th** восемна́дцатый
eldest ста́рший
eleven оди́ннадцать
empty пусто́й
engage, to нанима́ть, наня́ть
engine парово́з
engine-driver машини́ст
engineer инжене́р
English англи́йский; **in English** по-англи́йски
envy, to зави́довать (+ *dat.*)
eve кану́н; **on the eve** накану́не
evening ве́чер; **in the evening** ве́чером
every ка́ждый; **every hour** ежеча́сно
everything всё
exactly то́чно, ро́вно
exercise-book тетра́дь (*f.*)
exhibition вы́ставка
expect, to ожида́ть

face лицо́
fact, in на са́мом де́ле
factory заво́д; **to the factory** на + *acc.*; **at the factory** на + *prep.*
fall off, to па́дать, упа́сть с (+ *gen.*)
fall silent, to умолка́ть, умо́лкнуть; замолка́ть, замо́лкнуть
family семья́
far away далеко́
father оте́ц (*gen.* отца́)
Father Christmas Дед-Моро́з
fear, to боя́ться (+ *gen.*)
few ма́ло (+ *gen. pl.*); **a few** немно́го, не́сколько (+ *gen. pl.*)
field по́ле
fifty пятьдеся́т
finally наконе́ц
find, to находи́ть, найти́
fine хоро́ший
finish, to конча́ть, ко́нчить

fire ого́нь (*gen.* огня́), пожа́р (**building on fire**)
fire(-place) ками́н
firm фи́рма
first пе́рвый; **at first** снача́ла
five пять
flat кварти́ра
fly, to лета́ть (*indet.*), лете́ть (*det.*)
fly away, to; scatter, to разлета́ться, разлете́ться
fly in, to прилета́ть, прилете́ть
fly out/away, to улета́ть, улете́ть
following day, on the на друго́й день
food еда́, пи́ща
foot нога́; **on foot** пешко́м
for для (+ *gen.*); за (+ *instr.*)
foreign иностра́нный
forget, to забыва́ть, забы́ть
forget something learnt, to разучи́ваться, разучи́ться
forgive, to проща́ть, прости́ть
former пре́жний
forty со́рок
found, to осно́вывать, основа́ть
four четы́ре
France Фра́нция
free свобо́дный
freely свобо́дно
freeze, to мёрзнуть (мёрз, мёрзла), за-
friend друг (*nom. pl.* друзья́)
friendly дру́жеский
frost моро́з
furniture ме́бель (*f.*)
further да́льше

gallery галлере́я
garage гара́ж
garden сад (*loc.* саду́)
gate воро́та (*nom. pl.*)
get up, to встава́ть, встать
get use to, to привыка́ть, привы́кнуть (к + *dat.*)
give, to дава́ть, дать
give up a habit, to отвыка́ть, отвы́кнуть (от + *gen.*)
glad рад, -а, -ы
glance, to посмотре́ть (*pfv.*); взгляну́ть (*pfv.*)
glass стака́н
glove перча́тка
go, to (**travel**) е́хать (*det.*), е́здить (*indet.*); пое́хать (*pfv.*)
golden золото́й
goodbye до свида́ния
go off, go one's ways, to разъезжа́ться, разъе́хаться
go quiet, to утиха́ть, ути́хнуть
go round, to *see* **to drop in**
go to bed, to ложи́ться, лечь спать

447

gradually ма́ло-пома́лу
grand-daughter вну́чка
grateful благода́рный
great большо́й
green зелёный
greet, to приве́тствовать; to greet one
  another здоро́ваться, по-
group гру́ппа

habit привы́чка
hair во́лосы; a hair во́лос
half an hour полчаса́
hall зал
hand рука́; on the one/other hand с
  одно́й/друго́й стороны́
handbag су́мка
handwriting по́черк
hang (up), to ве́шать, пове́сить (p.p.p.
  пове́шенный)
happy счастли́вый
hard тру́дный
harmoniously дру́жно
harvest урожа́й
he он
hear, to слы́шать
heat жара́
help, to помога́ть, помо́чь (+ dat.)
her('s) её
here тут, здесь
hill гора́
hold, to держа́ть (2nd conj.)
home дом; at home до́ма; home
  (-wards) домо́й
hope, to наде́яться
hop in, to влеза́ть, влезть
horse ло́шадь (f.)
hospital больни́ца, го́спиталь (m.)
host хозя́ин (nom. pl. хозя́ева); хозя́йка
  (f.)
hot жа́ркий
house дом (nom. pl. дома́)
house, to помеща́ть, помести́ть (p.p.p.
  помещённый)
how как
however всё-таки
hurry, to спеши́ть, поспеши́ть; торо-
  пи́ться, поторопи́ться
hurt, to вреди́ть, повреди́ть (+ dat.)
husband муж (nom. pl. мужья́, gen. pl.
  муже́й)
hut до́мик

I я
if е́сли
in в, на, у, при
insist, to наста́ивать, настоя́ть (on на
  + prep.)
interesting интере́сный

interpreter перево́дчик (m.), пере-
  во́дчица (f.)
it он, она́, оно́

jacket пиджа́к
joy ра́дость (f.)
July ию́ль (m.)
just про́сто, то́лько

keep on, to продолжа́ть
knock, to стуча́ть (2nd conj.), по-
Kremlin Кремль (m.)

lady да́ма
lamp ла́мпа
last про́шлый (past); после́дний (ultimate)
last, to продолжа́ться
later по́зже, поздне́е
lead, to води́ть (indet.), вести́ (det.)
learn, to учи́ться, вы́-, на-
leave, to уезжа́ть, уе́хать; отъезжа́ть,
  отъе́хать; уходи́ть, уйти́; отходи́ть,
  отойти́
leave by plane, to вылета́ть, вы́лететь
  (из + gen.)
Leningrad Ленингра́д
less ме́ньше, ме́нее
lesson уро́к
let (us) дава́й(-те), (him, them) пу-
  ска́й, пусть
let in, to впуска́ть, впусти́ть
letter письмо́
lie down, to ложи́ться, лечь
lift up, to поднима́ть, подня́ть
like, to нра́виться, по-; he likes ему́
  нра́вится (impersonal verb)
listen, to слу́шать, по-
little ма́ло; a little немно́го
live, to жить, про-
load, to грузи́ть; нагружа́ть, нагрузи́ть
lock away, to заключа́ть, заключи́ть
lock up, to запира́ть, запере́ть
London Ло́ндон
long дли́нный
long (of time) до́лгий
Long-Arm Долгору́кий
look, to смотре́ть, посмотре́ть
look after, to ходи́ть за (+ instr.)
lorry грузови́к
lose, to теря́ть, по- (something);
  заблужда́ться, заблуди́ться (one's
  way); прои́грывать, проигра́ть (a
  game)
lot, a мно́го (+ gen. sing. and pl.)
loud гро́мкий
lucky счастли́вый
luggage бага́ж

448

lunch, have lunch, to за́втракать, по-; обе́дать, по-

make into, to де́лать, сде́лать (+ *instr.*)
man челове́к (*person*), мужчи́на (*male person*)
manager управля́ющий (+ *instr.*)
many мно́го (+ *gen. pl.*); мно́гие
marriage заму́жество (**of women**)
marry, to жени́ться на (+ *prep.*) (of men)
me меня́
meal еда́
meet, to встреча́ть, встре́тить (**somebody**); сходи́ться, сойти́сь (**to come together**); собира́ться, собра́ться (**to assemble**)
merrily ве́село
middle середи́на
middle (*adj.*) сре́дний
milk молоко́
milkman моло́чник
minister мини́стр
ministry министе́рство
mist тума́н
Monday понеде́льник
more бо́льше, бо́лее
morning у́тро; **in the morning** у́тром
Moscow Москва́
most, the са́мый
mother мать (*gen.* ма́тери)
much (+ *comparative*) гора́здо, мно́го
music му́зыка; но́ты (**score**); аккомпанеме́нт (**accompaniment**)
must прихо́дится, приходи́лось, пришло́сь, придётся + *dat.*; до́лжен, должна́, должны́; на́до + *dat.*
my мой

narrow у́зкий
native родно́й
nearly почти́
negotiations перегово́ры
neither … nor … ни… ни…
never никогда́
new но́вый
news но́вости, изве́стия; (**piece of**) news но́вость (*f.*)
newspaper газе́та
next door (to) ря́дом (с + *instr.*)
nickname, to прозыва́ть, прозва́ть
night ночь; **at night,** но́чью
nineteen девятна́дцать
no нет
nobody никто́
noise шум; **to make a noise** шуме́ть (*2nd conj.*)
noisy шу́мный

no, none (whatever) никако́й
not не
not at all не́ за что, ничего́
note, to запи́сывать, записа́ть
note-book записна́я кни́жка
not far away недалеко́
nothing ничего́, ничто́
now тепе́рь
nowhere, not anywhere нигде́ (*location*); никуда́ (*motion*)
number но́мер, число́

occupy, to занима́ть, заня́ть
o'clock час, часа́, часо́в (see Lesson 31, § 1)
off-chance, on the на аво́сь
offend, to обижа́ть, оби́деть
office конто́ра, бюро́
official слу́жащий
often ча́сто
old ста́рый
old age ста́рость (*f.*)
old man стари́к
old woman стару́ха
on на, в
once раз; **at once** сейча́с, сра́зу же
one оди́н; **one day** одна́жды
one and a half полтора́
oneself сам, сама́, само́, са́ми
open, to открыва́ть, откры́ть
or и́ли
organize, to организова́ть
other друго́й; **each other** друг дру́га, *etc.* (see Lesson 28, § 7)
otherwise а то; ина́че
our наш, на́ша, на́ше, на́ши
out of из (+ *gen.*)
outside на дворе́

package паке́т
packet па́чка
papa па́па
paper бума́га
parcel паке́т
park парк
pass, to проезжа́ть, прое́хать
pass through, to проходи́ть, пройти́
passenger пассажи́р
pen перо́ (*nom. pl.* пе́рья)
people лю́ди
perhaps мо́жет быть
Peter the Great Пётр Вели́кий
pipe (smoker's) тру́бка; (**for water** труба́
pity, it's a жаль, беда́
place ме́сто
plan план
plane самолёт
play, to игра́ть, поигра́ть

pleasure удово́льствие
plenty мно́го
p.m. дня, ве́чера
porter носи́льщик
postman почтальо́н
present настоя́щее; **at present** в на-
стоя́щее вре́мя
present пода́рок (*gen.* пода́рка)
press пре́сса
pretend, to де́лать вид
pretty краси́вый
prince князь (*nom. pl.* князья́, *gen. pl.*
князе́й)
probability вероя́тность (*f.*)
probably вероя́тно
problem пробле́ма
pub каба́к
public пу́блика
put, to класть, положи́ть; сади́ть, по-
сади́ть; ста́вить, поста́вить; дева́ть,
деть (see Lessons 35, §§ 1, 2, 3; 36, § 1)
put out, to (**fire**) туши́ть, потуши́ть

quiet ти́хий
quieten (**down**), **to** утиха́ть, ути́хнуть
quieter ти́ше
quite совсе́м

radio ра́дио (*indecl.*)
rattle стук
reach, to доходи́ть, дойти́ (до + *gen.*);
доезжа́ть, дое́хать (до + *gen.*)
recently неда́вно
recognize, to узнава́ть, узна́ть
relative ро́дственник
remember, to по́мнить, вспо́мнить
rename, to переименова́ть (в + *acc.*)
rest, to отдыха́ть, отдохну́ть
return, to возвраща́ться, верну́ться
rich бога́тый
ride, to (**on horseback**) е́здить, е́хать
верхо́м
right пра́вый
river река́
road доро́га
room ко́мната
round and round (всё) круго́м
Russian ру́сский; **in Russian** по-ру́с-
ски

sack, to разоря́ть, разори́ть
sailor моря́к
same тот/та/то/те же; тако́й же
say, to говори́ть, сказа́ть
school шко́ла
scissors но́жницы
score но́ты
sea мо́ре; **by sea** мо́рем
secretary (**woman**) секрета́рша

see, to ви́деть
see off, to *see* **to accompany**
sell, to продава́ть, прода́ть
Senate Сена́т
set off, to пойти́ (*pfv.*); пое́хать (*pfv.*);
уходи́ть, уйти́; уезжа́ть, уе́хать; от-
правля́ться, отпра́виться; полете́ть
(*pfv.*)
settle, to реша́ть, реши́ть
sew, to шить, сшить
shallow ме́лкий
she она́
ship су́дно (*nom. pl.* суда́), парохо́д
shirt руба́шка
shop магази́н
shopping поку́пки; **to go shopping**
идти́, пойти́ за поку́пками
short коро́ткий
shout, to крича́ть, по-
silence тишина́
sight достопримеча́тельность (*f.*)
sing, to петь, с-
sister сестра́
sit, to сиде́ть, по-
sit down, to сади́ться, сесть
sixteen шестна́дцать
sleep, to спать (*2nd conj.*)
small ма́ленький
smell, to па́хнуть (of + *instr.*)
smoke дым
smoke, to кури́ть; **to smoke all ...** вы́-
курить все...
snow снег; **it is snowing** снег идёт
so так; поэ́тому; ита́к
soap мы́ло
solicitor адвока́т
some не́сколько (+ *gen. pl.*)
son сын (*nom. pl.* сыновья́, *gen. pl.*
сынове́й)
south юг; **to the south** на юг; **in the
south** на ю́ге
souvenir сувени́р
Soviet (**council**) сове́т
Soviet Union Сове́тский Сою́з
spectator зри́тель (*m.*)
spend, to (**time**) проводи́ть, провести́
stand, to стоя́ть, постоя́ть; ста́вить, по-
ста́вить
start, to начина́ть, нача́ть
State Stores ГУМ
station вокза́л
stay пребыва́ние
steamer парохо́д
still всё-таки, всё же
stop, to перестава́ть, переста́ть
street у́лица
strict стро́гий
string верёвка
such тако́й

suitcase чемода́н
summer ле́то; **in summer** ле́том
supper обе́д, у́жин; **to have supper** обе́дать, пообе́дать; у́жинать, поу́жинать
suppose, to предполага́ть, предположи́ть

table стол
take, to брать (*impfv.*) (беру́, берёшь), взять (*pfv.*) (возьму́, возьмёшь); **to take away** отвози́ть, отвезти́ (*in a vehicle*)
tale расска́з, по́весть (*f.*)
talk, to говори́ть, по-
tall высо́кий
tasty вку́сный
telephone телефо́н
television телеви́дение; ～ **set** телеви́зор
tell, to говори́ть, сказа́ть (**somebody something**); расска́зывать, рассказа́ть (**a story**); сказа́ться (**of something making itself felt**)
thanks, thank you спаси́бо
that (*conj.*) что
that (*pron.*) тот, та, то, те; э́тот, э́та, э́то, э́ти
theatre теа́тр
then тогда́ (**at that time**), пото́м (**after that**)
there там (*location*), туда́ (*motion*)
there is/are вот
they они́
thing вещь (*f.*)
think, to ду́мать, поду́мать
thirteen трина́дцать
this э́тот, э́то, э́та, э́ти
though хотя́
three три
throw, to броса́ть, бро́сить
throw out, to выбра́сывать, вы́бросить
ticket биле́т
tie together, to свя́зывать, связа́ть
time вре́мя (*gen.* вре́мени); **in time** во́время; **by this time** уже́
to в, на, к
to (in order to) что́бы
tobacco таба́к
today сего́дня
together вме́сте
tom-cat кот
tomorrow за́втра
too и, то́же, та́кже (**also**); сли́шком (*as in* **too much**)
tourist тури́ст
towards к (+ *dat.*)
towel полоте́нце

town го́род (*nom. pl.* города́)
train по́езд
travel, to путеше́ствовать
tree де́рево (*nom. pl.* дере́вья)
trip пое́здка
trunk сунду́к
truth пра́вда
tsar царь
turn о́чередь (*f.*); **in turn** по о́череди
twelve двена́дцать
two два/две
type, to писа́ть на маши́нке
typewriter (пи́шущая) маши́нка
typist машини́стка

umbrella зо́нтик
uncle дя́дя
under под (+ *acc. motion;* + *instr. location*)
undo, to развя́зывать, развяза́ть
unhealthy нездоро́вый
union сою́з
unpack, to раскла́дывать, разложи́ть
untrue непра́вда, непра́вильный (*adj.*)
untruth непра́вда, ложь (*f.*)
us нас
U.S.S.R. СССР
usually обы́чно

van маши́на, фурго́н
very о́чень
view вид
village дере́вня
visible ви́димый; **is/are visible** ви́дно (+ *acc.*)
visit, to посеща́ть, посети́ть
vodka во́дка
voice го́лос (*nom. pl.* голоса́)

wait, to ждать; поджида́ть, подожда́ть
waiter официа́нт
wall стена́
want, to хоте́ть (see Lesson 9, § 3)
war война́
warm тёплый
warm, to греть, отогре́ть
wash, to мыть (мо́ю, мо́ешь), помы́ть *and* вы́мыть
watch, to смотре́ть, посмотре́ть
water вода́
way путь (*m.*); **on the way** по пути́; **by the way** кста́ти
we мы
week неде́ля
well хорошо́; ну
what (sort of) како́й
what что
when когда́
where где (*location*); куда́ (*motion*)

451

which который
while в то время как; время (*as in a little while*)
white бе́лый
who кто; кото́рый
whole весь, це́лый
wife жена́
wind ве́тер (*gen.* ве́тра)
window окно́
wine вино́
wish, to жела́ть, пожела́ть
with с (+ *instr. or instr. alone*)
without без (+ *gen.*)
woman же́нщина
wood лес (**forest**); дрова́ (*nom. pl.* **firewood**)
word сло́во
work, to рабо́тать, порабо́тать

world (*adj.*) мирово́й
worry, to меша́ть (+ *dat.* **to worry somebody**); беспоко́иться, обеспо-ко́иться (**to be worried**)
write, to писа́ть (пишу́, пи́шешь), написа́ть
writer писа́тель (*m.*)
wrong не тот/та́ *etc.*, непра́вильный; **wrong one** не тот

yard двор
yes да
yesterday вчера́
yet ещё; уже́
you вы (*acc.* вас)
young молодо́й
youngest мла́дший
youth мо́лодость (*f.*)

Index

References to Part I are given thus: 4.10, meaning Lesson 4, § 10. Raised numbers refer to notes in the section indicated, thus: 7.6¹, meaning Lesson 7, § 6, note 1. Where sections have been broken up into paragraphs with notes after each paragraph, which happens in the later lessons, the reference goes: 34.4, para. 3¹, meaning note 1 of the third paragraph in Lesson 34, § 4. Some sections have been sub-divided into a, b, c etc. These sub-divisions are also given, as for instance 18.4e. References to Part II, Grammar, are *page* references. Thus 331 means 'page 331'. Ample multiple references are provided.

INDEX:RUSSIAN